# JAPAN'S LOVE-HATE RELATIONSHIP WITH THE WEST

# Japan's Love–Hate Relationship with the West

Sukehiro Hirakawa

GLOBAL
ORIENTAL

JAPAN'S LOVE–HATE RELATIONSHIP WITH THE WEST

by Sukehiro Hirakawa

First published 2005 by
GLOBAL ORIENTAL LTD
P.O. Box 219
Folkestone
Kent CT20 2WP
UK

www.globaloriental.co.uk

ISBN 978-1-901903-81-2

**British Library Cataloguing in Publication Data**
A CIP catalogue entry for this book is available
from the British Library

---

The Publishers wish to thank Otemae University for their
generous support in the making of this book

---

Set in Garamond 11 on 12 pt by Mark Heslington, Scarborough, North Yorkshire
Printed and bound in England by CPI Antony Rowe, Chippenham, Wilts.

To the greatest of Japan interpreters:
George Sansom
and
Arthur Waley

The length of coats and the width of hats in the last thirty years
Time and again have chopped and changed in a quite senseless way.
Happily for me I have always stuck to the same old style
And, looking about me, I find I am dressed in the very latest fashion.
                    (*Yuan Mei, Eighteenth-century Chinese Poet*)

# CONTENTS

## Part IV: From War to Peace

## Part V: Attempt at Cross-Cultural Elucidation

## Part VI: Japanese Writers between East and West

# PREFACE

---□---

*Japan's Love-Hate Relationship with the West* is a collection of essays that deal mainly with Japan's intercultural relations with the Western world. In order to clarify the problems, I have tried to look at them from both sides, using literary materials of various languages. My *explication de texte* approach is essentially humanistic, and I have generally focused my attention on their psychological aspects, while analysing the texts.

I am a made-in-Japan professor of comparative cultural history, and my academic base of half a century has always been Tokyo University. However, I have spent thirteen years of my university life outside Japan, and have had many opportunities to give talks in English at various universities in America, Europe and Asia. I feel immensely grateful for those stimulating occasions. While discussing the same topics both in Japanese and English, I have felt, however, a great discrepancy between Japanese views and Western views, not only among the general public, but also among academics of both sides. I feel that the differences still remain very wide even among scholars specializing in international and intercultural relations between Japan and the Western world. Publishing this book is my effort to bridge some of the gaps, breaking linguistic and cultural barriers.

To some extent *Japan's Love-Hate Relationship with the West* corresponds to one of my earlier books written in Japanese, *Wakon yōsai no keifu* (Japanese Spirit, Western Learning. Tokyo: Kawade Shobō publishers, 1971). The book consists of studies on the psychological state of the Japanese, trying to catch up with the West in the

Meiji and Taishō periods (1868–1926). As the author wishes to
explain Japanese reactions to an advanced civilization, there are
many common inherent factors in both books. However, there is a
difference. In the case of *Wakon-yōsai no keifu*, there is the central
figure of Mori Ōgai (1862–1922). Since Ōgai studied in Leipzig,
Munich and Berlin between 1884 and 1888, my interest in that book
tends to be German-oriented, while in this book the main topics are
concerned mostly with Japan's responses to Anglo-Saxon challenges.

Nevertheless, the underlying theme of my *Wakon-yōsai* book was
already clear, namely Japan's love-hate relationship with the West.
Incidentally, '*wakon-yōsai*' (Japanese spirit, Western learning), which
was the slogan for modernization in late nineteenth century Japan,
is a variation of the earlier '*wakon-kansai*' (Japanese spirit, Chinese
learning) of Heian Japan of a thousand years ago.

Thus, in this book, the reader moves inevitably from 'Japan's
Love-Hate Relationship with China' (Part I) to 'Japan's Love-Hate
Relationship with the West' by passing through such historical
phases as 'Japan's Turn to the West' (Part II) and 'Return to the
East' (Part III). I have almost doubled the contents of chapters
dealing with 'First Translations from Western Literature',
'Europeanization Fever', 'Reaction against Slavish Westernization'
and 'Yearning for the West and Return to the East' which I wrote at
first in Japanese a quarter century ago for the *Cambridge History of
Japan*, vol. 5 (ed. Marius Jansen, Cambridge U.P. 1989) and which
was later reprinted in paperback, *Modern Japanese Thought* (ed. Bob
Wakabayashi, Cambridge U.P. 1998). World War II and Japan's
ensuing resurgence as an American ally were extreme phases of that
love-hate relationship. I have taken up some significant episodes
hitherto little known to Western readers in the ensuing period of
'From War to Peace' (Part IV). I have also included in Part V, six of
my attempts at cross-cultural elucidation, using well-known
Western literary classics such as Aesop's *Fables* and Dante's *Divine
Comedy*. I have tried to illuminate certain aspects of them from a
Japanese perspective of my own, or indeed vice versa. For example,
I have tried to explain certain aspects of Japanese *Nō* plays, using
Dante's *Purgatory*. Though not all chapters in Part V may be directly
related to the emotional confrontations of love-hate relationship
between the Western world and Japan in historical or political
terms, all of them are concerned with the psychological aspects of
intercultural confrontations. Finally, I have dealt with modern,

renowned Japanese authors' psychologies oscillating between East and West (Part VI), and the book ends with the chapter 'Changing Appreciations of Japanese Literature: Basil Hall Chamberlain versus Arthur Waley', as they symbolically reflect the underlying *Hassliebe* towards Japan of the Western side.

As there have been and are so many persons involved in Japan's love-hate relationship with the West, it is natural that there should be no single central figure in this book. Readers, however, will perceive a unifying similar pattern of bi-cultural approach repeatedly appearing through almost all the chapters. I have witnessed anti-West mass hysteria not only on the eve of and during the World War II years but also later in the 1960s in Japan and elsewhere in East Asia. There is a latent leitmotif of the author: to explain Japanese intellectuals' ambivalence *vis-à-vis* the West. It is this deep-rooted motivation, that has impelled me to write these papers. There are indeed many 'touchy' subjects which are worthy of some attention for their interest as a study of the morbid anatomy of cultural intercourse. My bifocal views may hopefully be of some interest to readers inside and outside Japan. I have tried to update the contents as far as possible, while editing this book.

About Lafcadio Hearn, who may be considered a conspicuously controversial literary figure in our ambivalent relationship between the West and Japan, I have dealt rather briefly in this book. I will collect my papers on Hearn written in English for another volume dedicated to that writer, *Lafcadio Hearn in International Perspectives,* which will complement the previously published volume (Hirakawa ed., *Rediscovering Lafcadio Hearn*, Global Oriental, 1997).

I am grateful for the help of many people. I would like to thank my family for their unfailing support over many years in various countries of the world: we have learnt many languages together. I would like to thank my daughter Setsuko Adachi for her help in editing this book, and also my student Masayuki Hamada for his efficient technical help. I also owe special thanks to Eileen Kato, a long-time friend, who read these essays and made valuable comments. Last but not least, I thank the staff of Otemae University's Center for Intercultural Relations for their support in many ways.

Sᴜᴋᴇʜɪʀᴏ HIRAKAWA
Professor Emeritus, Tokyo University
Honorary Member, MLA
Tokyo, 6 March, 2005

A NOTE ON NAMES

Personal names of Japanese and other East Asians appear in the East Asian order, surname first and given name second. However, two great Japanese authors are generally referred to simply by their pen-names, e.g., Ōgai and Sōseki, instead of Mori Ōgai (Mori Rintarō) and Natsume Sōseki (Natsume Kinnosuke). Their complete works, too, are called *Ōgai zenshū* and *Sōseki zenshū*. It has been customary for Japanese to call some poets by their given names. The poet-sculptor Takamura Kōtarō is generally referred to by his given name Kōtarō. Other Japanese names appear in the normal Japanese order. The Nobel prize-winner Kawabata Yasunari is referred to by his surname Kawabata.

Chinese names are transcribed in principle according to the pinyin spelling, except when translators already wrote them according to the Wade spelling, as is the case with Arthur Waley's translation of Chinese poems.

However, most East Asians, who work in the English-speaking world, conform themselves to the English usage: given name first and surname second. It is mostly the same with East Asians who write in Western languages. In the case of the author of the present volume Sukehiro is, therefore, the given name and Hirakawa is the surname. This is a question of language and not of nationality. So long as he wrote in English, Lafcadio Hearn kept this name and name order, although he acquired Japanese citizenship in 1896 under the Japanese name of Koizumi Yakumo.

In the case of some major Italian poets, they are referred to by their given names only, as is the custom with Dante, whose surname is Alighieri. It would be difficult to unilaterally impose a 'global standard'.

# PART I

# JAPAN'S LOVE–HATE RELATIONSHIP WITH CHINA

# CHINESE CULTURE AND JAPANESE IDENTITY: TRACES OF BAI JU-YI IN A PERIPHERAL COUNTRY

The word 'nationalism', with its various Japanese equivalents, has been associated in many Japanese minds, as well as in foreigners' minds, with nationalistic wars which Japan fought within the time-span of fifty-one years: from 1894 to 1945. Japan fought against China in 1894–95, against Russia in 1904–05, entered World War I in a secondary role, and played an important 'villain's' role in World War II. The Americans and the British talk a great deal about the Japanese ultra-nationalism of the war years; their knowledge of Japan seems almost exclusively drawn from the World War II experience, so much so that other aspects of the East Asian tradition are often overshadowed.

I would first like to mention, therefore, earlier expressions of nationalism which were largely in reaction to a Japanese sense of inferiority to China. Discussions about nationalism depend heavily on its definition. But perhaps it would be better for me to avoid theoretical assumptions and confine myself to a straightforward narrative since readers are not always familiar with this part of the globe.[1]

In the last quarter of the twentieth century, Japan was considered an economic power; however, Japan has always been conscious of its small size geographically: a peripheral poor archipelago lying along the Asian continent. Diplomatic relations between Japan and China have not necessarily been equal because the Chinese perception of the world order was hierarchical, while the Japanese were not always satisfied with that world view. Shōtoku Taishi, Prince Regent of Japan towards the end of the sixth century, sent the following letter to the Emperor of China:

> The Son of Heaven in the land where the sun rises addresses a letter to the Son of Heaven in the land where the sun sets. We hope you are in good health.

Yang-di, the Emperor of Sui China, was not pleased with this letter and said: 'This is an impolite letter from the barbarians. Such a letter should not again be brought to our attention.' (This is found in the *Sui History's* chapter on East Barbarians.) The Chinese were accustomed to a Sino-centric view of the world order and conceived of themselves as being on a higher plane than other peoples.

So far as the cultural relationship is concerned, in Japan's history, the first era of assimilating Chinese culture was in the sixth, seventh and eighth centuries when envoys and students were sent to Tang China. The second was around the fourteenth century when ships were sent to Ming China. The third era was from the seventeenth century to the opening of the country in 1868. At that time, Confucianism became the ideological underpinning of the shogunal government in Japan. The fourth surge in Sino-Japanese cultural relationships went in the opposite direction, with China sending several thousand students a year to Japan after Japan's victory over Russia in 1905, at a time when the decadent Qing dynasty abolished the examination system for governmental officials. This is the general background of Sino-Japanese relations.

All through those years of contact with Chinese culture, the foreign book most widely read and studied in Japan was the *Analects* of Confucius. Indeed, there was a time when the Chinese *Analects* were far easier for many Japanese to understand than the Japanese *Tale of Genji*. Today, there are still quite a number of Japanese men whose names derive from the Chinese sacred book, which is one indication of how deep its influence has been in Japan. As Confucian influence in East Asia was so immense, there is little point in discussing it. It is analogous to Westerners' speaking about the influence of the Bible in the Western world. Instead, I have chosen a literary figure, Bai Ju-yi, more commonly known in the West by the Wade spelling of Po Chü-i, a Chinese poet of the eighth century (AD 772–846) as an example, in order to consider the relationship between Chinese and Japanese literature, as well as to examine some expressions of Japanese cultural nationalism.

Accordingly, my essay consists of two parts: the first part concerns Bai Ju-yi's influence; the second part details Japanese reaction.

On the life and times of this poet, there is an excellent biography written by Arthur Waley.[2] However, Waley did not deal at any length with the question of the poet's reputation after his death down to the present day. I traced his influence in Japan in one of my books[3] written in Japanese, and I shall try to communicate some of its contents. First, I shall introduce readers to some examples of Po's poetry translated by Waley, who used the Wade system of Romanization of the Chinese. I, too, use it hereafter in this chapter:

> In Ch'ang-an the year draws to its close;
> A great snow fills the Royal Domain.
> And through the storm, on their way back from Court,
> In reds and purples the dukes and barons ride.
> They can enjoy the beauty of wind and snow;
> To the rich they do not mean hunger and cold.
> At a grand entry coaches and riders press;
> Candles are lit in the Tower of Dance and Song.
> Delighted guests pack knee to knee;
> Heated with wine they throw off their double furs.
> The host is high in the Board of Punishments;
> The chief guest comes from the Ministry of Justice.
> It was broad daylight when the drinking and music began;
> Midnight has come, and still the feast goes on.
> What do they care that at Wên-hsiang to-night
> In the town gaol prisoners are freezing to death?

In this poem, the poet is obviously criticizing the bureaucracy. In fact, in 809, Po wrote a memorial which dealt with the case of some prisoners, saying:

> In some cases, owing to their long incarceration, their wives have taken fresh husbands; in others, when a father has died in prison, his son has been brought to gaol to take his place ...

Po Chü-i did not confine himself to writing just this memorial. He also tried to arouse popular interest in the prison question by making it the subject of a ballad. This was the Tang equivalent of a letter to *The Washington Post*.

As a bureaucrat, Po was often sent to remote, unhealthy places. He wrote:

> The sun has risen in the sky, but I idly lie in bed;
> In my small tower-room the layers of quilts protect me from the cold;
> Leaning on my pillow, I wait to hear I-ai's temple bell,
> Pushing aside the blind, I gaze upon the snow of Hsiang-lu peak...[4]

The bureaucrat in a remote province obviously has little to do. He consoles himself by writing poems.

Now let us review the influence of the Chinese poet in the imagery of a Japanese scholar-statesman, Sugawara no Michizane, who was born in 845, one year before Po's death. Michizane was sent into exile in Kyushu, where he wrote many poems in Chinese. (It is important to note at this point that despite the proximity of the two empires, the Japanese and Chinese languages had little in common. Therefore, speaking in Japanese and writing in Chinese was a great strain. Yet the knowledge of written Chinese was indispensible to scholars and government officials in Japan.)

*Hearing Wild Geese*

I am a banished man and you guests;
We are both lonely wayfarers.
Leaning on my pillow, I wonder when I shall be allowed to go back;
But you, wild geese, can no doubt go back home next spring.

*Not Going Out of the Gate*

Since I was banished and put in this poor hut,
I have always been in horror of death.
I only gaze upon the colour of Tofurō's roof
And listen to Kwannon's temple bell.

As the place of Michizane's exile was Dazai-fu in Kyushu, the temple in the poem was changed from the Chinese I-ai to the Japanese Kwannon, and the snow of Hsiang-lu peak to the colour of Tofurō's roof. (Tofurō was a government building whose roof is said to have been built with Chinese tiles.) Michizane in this way still wrote poems imitating Po Chü-i. He was a banished man who was 'always in horror of death', and actually did die in exile.

Michizane lived during the Heian period, so named because the capital of Japan was at Heian, present-day Kyoto. This period, from 794 to 1184, was also called the Fujiwara period because Japan was dominated by the Fujiwara family. Institutionally, Japan and China were quite different. Japan was governed by an aristocracy while China was governed by a bureaucracy, and Chinese bureaucrats were selected by state examination. This examination system was imported for the sake of formality, but it did not fit the Japanese reality. Michizane at first was promoted to a high rank in Court for his scholarly merit, but later he was banished by the Fujiwara family and died in exile. Michizane must have been popular, though, among the people who did not owe loyalty to the Fujiwara family. After Michizane's death, many natural disasters and calamities occurred. People saw them as an expression of divine wrath. In order to placate the spirit of Michizane, he was deified and a Shinto shrine erected in his memory. Michizane was considered to be the symbol of those who by their own scholarly merits attain a very high rank. His Tenjin shrine in Kyoto still has many devotees, notably mothers who, by buying amulets, pray for their children's success in university entrance examinations.

Now let us consider the depth of the penetration of Chinese culture into Japanese courtly life. Sei Shōnagon was a lady-in-waiting who, around the year 1000, which was more than a century after Michizane's time, wrote in Japanese *The Pillow Book*. Po Chü-i was known to the Japanese during his lifetime, and by the year 1000 his *Literary Collection* was widely read among the Japanese. Sei Shōnagon herself put the book at the head of her list of important works to read. The *Pillow Book* contains the following episode:

> One day, when the snow lay thick on the ground and it was so cold that the lattices had all been closed, I and the other ladies were sitting with Her Majesty, chatting and poking the embers in the brazier.
> 'Tell me, Shōnagon,' said the Empress, 'how is the snow on Hsiang-lu peak?'
> I told the maid to raise one of the lattices and then rolled up the blind all the way. Her Majesty smiled . . .[5]

It was because Shōnagon, as well as the Empress, had remembered the phrase in Po's poem quoted above that she instantly took the hint. If a princess in Japan today refers to a phrase from Shakespeare at Court, I do not think any lady-in-waiting would catch the allusion. It is not a question of quality of the ladies-in-waiting; I wish merely to suggest that even a representative of English literature like Shakespeare cannot have as much influence today as Po Chü-i had one thousand years ago. I also doubt whether even at the English Court a princess would convey her thought to a lady-in-waiting in a phrase from Shakespeare, as if they had a code between them.

In Japan of the tenth century, however, people who memorized famous phrases of Po, like Empress Sadako and Sei Shōnagon, were not necessarily exceptions. Lady Murasaki, a contemporary of Shōnagon's, wrote in her *Tale of Genji* as follows:

> Once when all day long he (Kaoru) had sat watching the snow whirling through the dark sky, at dusk the clouds suddenly cleared, and raising the blinds and leaning on his pillow, he looked out on such moonlight as only

the glittering nights of late winter can show. Far off the faint chiming of the temple-bell whispered that another day had passed.[6]

Needless to say, it is that this image also came from the poem by Po quoted earlier, although the passage from the *Tale of Genji* has aesthetically a different mood from Po's poem, in which the poet idly lay in bed in the late morning. There is also an episode in which Lady Murasaki teaches Po's *Literary Collection* to Empress Akiko, to whom she was a lady-in-waiting. Murasaki wrote in her diary that, despite the prejudice against women studying Chinese (which was thought to be uniquely a gentleman's occupation),

> ... since the summer before last, very secretly, in odd moments when there happened to be no one about, I have been reading with Her Majesty the two books of ballads (by Po) ...[7]

It is well known, too, that the authoress made many references to Po's poems, and especially to 'The Everlasting Remorse' in the first chapter of the *Tale of Genji*.

In addition, we have material which statistically shows how widely Po Chü-i was read in Japan in that era. The *Tale of Genji* was written about AD 1000, and in about 1018 a Sino-Japanese anthology called *Wakan-Rōei-shū* was compiled by Fujiwara no Kintō. This Sino-Japanese anthology served as a standard textbook in Japan for more than five hundred years. When the Jesuits came to Japan towards the end of the sixteenth century, an edition was published by the Christian printing press in Nagasaki as a Japanese-language text. The contents of the anthology are classified as follows:

*Wakan-Rōei-shū* (Sino-Japanese Anthology) compiled in 1018

Total 804 poems:
   588 Chinese poems, of which
      234 by Chinese poets (138 by Po Chü-i),
      354 by Japanese poets (44 by Sugawara no Fumitoki, and 38 by
      Sugawara no Michizane)
   216 Japanese poems (of which
      26 by Ki no Tsurayuki)

The anthology indicates something of the tastes of the Japanese in that era, and it continued to influence them. Even the *Nō* plays written four centuries later in the Muromachi era contain many references to Po's verses collected in this anthology.

Po Chü-i knew that his poems were read in Japan, for he said in 845 that copies of his works had been taken to Japan and Korea. As for the relationship between Po and Japan, there is the following episode in *The Life and Times of Po Chü-i*. Po Lo-t'ien (Haku Rakuten in Japanese) is the pseudonym of Po Chü-i:

A curious story, connected with Po's cult of the Future Buddha Maitreya, is told in a collection of anecdotes called *I Shih,* which dates from the second half of the ninth century: In the first year of Hui Ch'ang (841), when Li Shih-lêng was Inspector General of Ch'ê-tung (the region just south of the Yangtze delta) a merchant met with a hurricane which blew his ship far out off its course. At last, after more than a month, he came to a great mountain, upon which the clouds, the trees, the white cranes were all of strange and magical form unlike any that he had ever seen in the World of Men. Presently, someone came down from the mountain-side and having asked how he had got there and heard the merchant's story, told him to tie up his boat and come on shore. 'You must present yourself to the Heavenly Master,' he said. He then led the merchant to a vast building that looked like a Buddhist or Taoist monastery. After his name had been sent in, the merchant was brought into the presence of a venerable Taoist whose hair and eyebrows were completely white. He was seated at the upper end of a large hall, with some twenty or thirty attendants mounting guard over him. 'Being a man of the Middle Kingdom,' the aged Taoist said, 'it must be by some special ordinance of Fate that you succeeded in reaching this place. For this, I would have you know, is the fairy mountain P'êng-lai. But as you are here, I expect you would like to have a look round.' And he told one of the attendants to take the merchant round the Palace precincts and show him the sights. He was led on, past jade terraces and trees of halcyon brightness that dazzled him as he passed. They went through courtyard after courtyard, each with its own name, till they came at last to one the gate of which was very tightly locked and barred. But he was allowed to peep in, and saw borders full of every kind of flower. In a hall that opened on to the garden was a cushioned couch, and on the steps that led up to the hall incense was burning. The merchant asked what courtyard it was. 'This,' said his guide, 'is the courtyard of Po Lo-t'ien. But he is still in the Middle Kingdom and has not yet come to take possession of it.' The merchant made note of what he had heard, and when after a voyage of some weeks he arrived back at Yüeh-chou, he told the whole story to Li Shih-lêng, who in turn sent a full report to Po Chü-i. Po had always striven for rebirth in the Paradise of Maitreya, and he replied by sending to Li two poems:

> A traveller came from across the seas
> Telling of strange sights.
> 'In a deep fold of the sea-hills
> I saw a terrace and tower.
> In the midst there stood a Fairy Temple
> With one niche empty.
> They all told me this was waiting
> For Lo-t'ien to come.'

Traveller, I have studied the Empty Gate;[8]
I am no disciple of Fairies.
The story you have just told
Is nothing but an idle tale.
The hills of ocean shall never be
Lo-t'ien's home.
When I leave the earth it will be to go
To the Heaven of Bliss Fulfilled.[9]

Arthur Waley imagines the circumstances in which the two poems were written: according to Waley there is not very much doubt as to what actually happened. Po's immense popularity in Japan had already begun, and some Chinese merchant visiting Japan was asked whether Po was still alive and was told that if the poet ever came to Japan a wonderful reception awaited him, or words to that effect. Hearing of this, Li Shih-lêng wrote a story somewhat on the lines of the one just quoted, transposing the merchant's report into a typical Taoist tale in which Japan figures as one of the Islands of the Blest (as it often was in poetic language). Li Shih-lêng's story was an elegant trifle meant to flatter and amuse Po, of whose illness Li had no doubt heard.

I happened on the following anecdote in a Japanese book entitled *Kokon chomon jū*. It reveals the psychology of the Japanese who were waiting for Po to come. The title of the anecdote is 'Ōe no Tomotsuna converses with Po Lo-t'ien in his dream.' It says:

On the eighteenth of the tenth month of the sixth year of Tenryaku (952), Po Lo-t'ien appeared in Councillor Tomotsuna's dream. Tomotsuna was enchanted to see Po, who was dressed in white and a dark ruddy face. Four men in blue followed him. When Tomotsuna asked him, 'Have you come from the Heaven of Bliss Fulfilled?' the poet replied, 'Yes.' Although Po said he had come to say something to Tomotsuna, he awoke just then from his dream and felt very sorry.[10]

Tomotsuna must have known the two poems of Po quoted above, so he could ask him if he had come from 'the Heaven of Bliss Fulfilled,' the Paradise of Maitreya.

Po Chü-i was a Buddhist devotee, but in Japan he was once deified in a Shinto shrine near Kyoto. The deification is understandable since Sugawara no Michizane, who was regarded as Po's Japanese counterpart, was deified in the shrine of Kitano Tenjin, it would seem appropriate that Po be worshipped as an incarnation of wisdom and poetry.

If one tries to find a parallel in the West for the relationship between Chinese culture and the surrounding East Asian countries, the relationship between classical Latin culture and the European countries will correspond. As written Chinese had been the cultural language and lingua franca of the East Asian countries for more than 1,200 years, so was Latin for European countries. An example of the correlation is the image of the teacher of Chinese classics who often appeared in Japanese novels and who resembles the teachers of Latin in Western novels. He is conservative and severe, wears a moustache and makes his pupils memorize passages. The pupils do not like this old-fashioned manner of teaching, but later they remember the classes with nostalgia. James Hilton's *Goodbye Mr. Chips* has its counterparts in Japanese literature.

Nevertheless, there are some aspects of the relationship between Chinese culture and the peripheral East Asian countries which differ from the relationship between classical Latin culture and the European countries. First, many European languages belong to the same linguistic family as Latin, whereas Japanese and Korean do not belong to the same family as Chinese. The origins are different. Second, some Europeans may regard themselves as the inheritors of classical Latin culture, but it is impossible for the Japanese to think that they are the direct inheritors of Chinese culture. There are more than a billion Chinese living on the Chinese continent. Even if the present-day Chinese of the mainland are rather ignorant of their own past and if perhaps some Chinese classics are more studied in Japan than they are in China, still the direct inheritors of the Chinese culture are those who speak Chinese in their daily life. Finally, Latin culture now (unlike in the days of the Roman Empire) threatens nobody, while China, with its great population, can still be a threatening presence for the surrounding countries.

What I have said in the first half of my paper may appear to have nothing to do with Japanese nationalism. It was a rough sketch of Chinese literary influence on Japan, and particularly of Po Chü-i's immense popularity among educated Japanese. But I should not say too much about the cultural borrowings of the Japanese because it confirms the stereotype of Japan as a nation of borrowers. Literary historians look for Po Chü-i's influence in the *Tale of Genji,* but what is most important is the fact that the literary genre of the psychological novel was a Japanese invention. Chinese began to write novels of a certain length only in the fourteenth century.

Now I come to the second, and main, part of my discussion of Japanese nationalism. Among Japanese literary genres I very much appreciate Nō plays. In one of them, written probably by Zeami, I think we can recognize early expressions of Japanese cultural nationalism. The title of the Nō play in question is *Haku Rakuten,* which is the Japanese pronunciation of the Chinese poet Po Lo-t'ien (Po Chü-i). As I said earlier, in the ninth century the composition of Chinese verse became fashionable at the Japanese Court. Japanese men like Sugawara no Michizane wrote in Chinese, as Europeans of the Middle Ages tended to write in Latin instead of the vernacular languages. But fortunately, in Japan, thanks to sexual discrimination, women were supposed to be uncultured and therefore continued to write in Japanese. That was one reason why the masterpieces of Japanese literature of that time were written by ladies-in-waiting.

Native forms of poetry disappeared almost completely in Korea, where the Chinese influence was overwhelming. In Japan, too, under the strong foreign influences, Japanese had a sort of identity crisis, though fortunately native literature survived thanks mostly to women writers. The Nō play *Haku Rakuten* deals with this literary peril. It was written at the end of the fourteenth century, a time when Japanese art and literature were for the second time becoming subject to strong Chinese influence.

Historically, Po Chü-i (Haku Rakuten) never came to Japan. In Zeami's play, however, Haku Rakuten is sent by the Emperor of China to subdue Japan with his art. On arriving at the coast of Kyushu, he meets two Japanese fishermen. One of them is in reality the god of Japanese poetry, Sumiyoshi no Kami. In the second act the god's identity is revealed. He summons other gods, and a great dancing scene ensues. Finally, the wind from their dancing sleeves blows the Chinese poet's ship back to his own country. As a drama it is almost nonsensical, but it is interesting because it sheds light on the ambivalent attitude of the Japanese towards Chinese culture.

The play's author, Zeami (1363–1443), lived about six hundred years after Po Chü-i. As Zeami felt the strong, all-pervasive influence of Chinese culture around him, the name of Po, Haku Rakuten, occurred to him as the representative Chinese poet. I imagine Zeami must have had the same state of mind as Dante when Dante let Virgil appear in the *Divine Comedy* as the representative Latin poet. Po Chü-i was, as it were, the symbol of Chinese culture. The Nō play begins with Po Chü-i's self-introduction:[11]

I am Haku Rakuten, a courtier of the Prince of China. There is a land in the East called Japan. Now at my master's bidding, I am sent to that land to make proof of the wisdom of its people. I must travel over the paths of the sea.

(Bertolt Brecht, incidentally, who was very interested in Nō plays, adopted this style of self-introduction in many of his plays.) Following Po Chü-i's introduction, two Chinese verses are used to describe the voyage across the sea. On arriving, the poet finds two Japanese fishermen, the elder of whom speaks to him:

OLD FISHERMAN.
... I am an old fisher of Nihon. And your Honour, I think, is Haku Rakuten of China.

HAKU.
How strange! No sooner am I come to this land than they call me by my name! How can this be?

Then follows a conversation between the two:

HAKU.
Answer me one question. Bring your boat closer and tell me, Fisherman, what is your pastime now in Nippon?

FISHERMAN.
And in the land of China, pray how do your Honours disport yourselves?

HAKU.
In China we play at making poetry.

FISHERMAN.
And in Nihon, may it please you, we feast our hearts on making *uta*-poetry.

When Haku talks about Japan, he calls it Nippon, while the fisherman pronounces it Nihon. This is a theatrical device to emphasize that Haku is a foreigner. *Uta* is a native form of Japanese poetry composed of thirty-one syllables.

It might be because of their different social positions that Haku Rakuten omits the honorific terms of speech while the fisherman speaks deferentially. Haku even composes a Chinese poem about the scene before him, which the fisherman instantly puts into *uta* form, to Haku's surprise:

HAKU.
How strange that a poor fisherman should put my verse into a sweet native measure! Who can he be?

FISHERMAN.
A poor man and unknown. But as for the making of *uta*, it is not only men that make them. 'For among things that live there is none that has not the gift of song.'

The old fisherman who thus preaches the virtues of Japanese poetry is in reality Sumiyoshi no Kami, the chief of the three gods of *uta*-poetry, and in the second act his identity is revealed. The poetry contest ends in a great dancing scene:

> CHORUS
> The God of Sumiyoshi whose strength is such
> That he will not let you subdue us, O Rakuten!
> So we bid you return to your home,
> Swiftly over the waves of the shore!
> First the God of Sumiyoshi came.
> Now other gods have come –
> ......
>
> As they hovered over the void of the sea,
> Moved in the dance, the sleeves of their dancing dress
> Stirred up a wind, a magic wind
> That blew on the Chinese boat
> And filled its sails
> And sent it back again to the land of Han.
> Truly, the God is wondrous;
> The God is wondrous, and thou, our Prince,
> Mayest thou rule for many, many years
> Our Land Inviolate!

In Japan in the latter half of the twentieth century there are about two million people who take lessons in Nō chanting or dance. Very few of them are interested in the libretto of *Haku Rakuten* because the dramatic quality of the play is not very high. To professional actors, the play is interesting mainly for its dancing scenes. But to cultural historians who are interested in the love-hate relationship between China and Japan, the play is in many ways extremely revealing.

The problem of Chinese culture and Japanese identity is closely related to the problem of the Japanese language. In East Asia, almost all the peripheral countries that came under the Chinese influence adopted the Chinese writing system. The Vietnamese spoke Vietnamese but wrote in Chinese, the Koreans spoke in Korean but wrote in Chinese. Neither country developed its own writing system for more than ten centuries. It was rather natural for them to write their histories in Chinese, just as the first histories of many European countries were written first in Latin. In Japan, however, something different happened. At the beginning of the eighth century, the Japanese compiled their first histories. One is called *Kojiki* or the *Records of Ancient Matters*, and the other is called *Nihon shoki (Nihongi)*. The compiler of the *Kojiki* wrote some parts of what a professional reciter of old legends dictated to him in Japanese. At that time the Japanese syllabary had not yet been invented, so the compiler took great pains to devise a method for representing Japanese sounds using Chinese characters phonetically. This must have been much harder for him than simply writing the whole book in classical Chinese. Yet he must have wanted to be true to his conviction that some parts of the national records should not or could not be translated into Chinese. These parts are Japanese poems.

*Manyoshū*, the first anthology of Japanese poems, was compiled around the year 760. In 905, the second anthology of *uta* poems was compiled. This anthology, *Kokinshū*, has a preface in Japanese which begins by insisting on the virtues of Japanese poetry: 'Everyone can make a *uta* poem, rich or poor, known or unknown, not only human beings but also warblers on plum trees; even frogs in ponds can express their poetic emotions ...'

In order to write poems in Chinese you must be reasonably well read; on the other hand, it is much easier to produce poems in the 31-syllable *uta* form. Indeed, the first anthology of the eighth century contained poems composed by people of all walks of life – from emperors and empresses down to soldiers, beggars and prostitutes. In the Nō play *Haku Rakuten*, the Chinese poet was surprised when a poor Japanese fisherman put his Chinese verse into a *uta* poem. Po Chü-i asked 'Who can he be?' and the Fisherman replied:

> A poor man and unknown. But so far as the making of *uta*, it is not only men that make them. 'For among things that live there is none that has not the gift of song.'

The quotation is precisely from the preface in Japanese of the second national anthology *Kokinshū*, and this needs some more explanation. In the first national anthology there were verses composed by people from all walks of life. In *uta* poetry there was very little discrimination by education.[12] Everyone knows it is not easy for all to be equal in the use of a language, as a distinction can be made on the basis of the abundance or poverty of one's vocabulary. As far as verbal richness is concerned, an uneducated person cannot be a match for a learned man, but in the case of *uta* poems, these verses are supposed to consist of exclusively native Japanese words; the use of words of foreign origin is discouraged. Adoption of such words would give rise to a 'discrimination by education'. As long as the vocabulary permissible for use in Japanese *uta* poems remains restricted to native Japanese words, there is little danger of verbal discrimination. Ki no Tsurayuki may have exaggerated, but, rich or poor, educated or uneducated, Japanese are equal before *uta* poems.

From this discussion, one definition of what a Japanese is becomes easy. A person can be identified as a Japanese if he writes a *uta* poem. This sense still somewhat remains within the Japanese. In 1974, there was an American-born Japanese lady living in Oregon and in 2004 a Brazilian gentleman whose *uta* poem was chosen for the traditional New Year's *uta* contest held annually before the Emperor. We saw them as Japanese regardless of their citizenship. In fact, they were invited to meet the Emperor. Also among those whose poems were selected was a blind person, and there is no discrimination by sex or wealth.

In the Nō play *Haku Rakuten*, the *uta*'s superiority is supposed to be proved when the wind from the dancing sleeves of the native gods blows the Chinese ship back to China. The Chorus sings a song in praise of the Emperor which might show that the Emperor and *uta* were the conditions for the self-identification of the Japanese. I quote the final phrase:

> The god is wondrous, and thou, our Prince (emperor),
> Mayest thou rule for many, many years Our Land Inviolate!

This song, as well as the phrase 'And the land of Reeds and Rushes/ Ten thousand years our land inviolate!' which the god recites when he begins to dance, is quite similar to the verse of the Japanese national anthem, *Kimi ga yo*. Although the national anthem was selected in the middle of the nineteenth century from the tenth-century *uta* anthology of *Kokinshū*, the person who chose it intuitively discerned the age-old aspirations of the Japanese nation.

Reading the Nō play *Haku Rakuten* after having seen a series of episodes that show how the Japanese wished Po Chü-i to come, one is tempted to smile wryly, for the play shows so plainly the contradictory psychology of the Japanese intellectual confronting an advanced, great nation – China.

As I have already mentioned, Po himself knew of the existence of Japan and that his poems were read there, but he cannot have had any intention to go abroad. The Japanese, however, desired so earnestly that Po would visit Japan that they even dreamed of it. However, when the influence of Chinese culture became overwhelming and the Japanese began to feel uneasy about their cultural independence, they made Po visit Japan, held a contest with him to triumph over him, and eventually drove him back to China with the divine wind – all in their imagination. It is like a weak child who fights with himself and thinks he has won; yet, in spite of such childishness, this play is interesting, for it shows the psychological effects of cultural conflict.

The French Canadians who do not like to use English, the Flemish Belgians who revolt against the French imperialism of the Walloons, and the Gaels of Ireland and Scotland, as well as the many people of Southeast Asia who are obliged to speak the language of their former colonial masters, all must have experienced the same sort of feeling. When we look back at the history of Western Europe, we find many similar examples. The early expression of Italian national self-identi-fication is found in Dante's use of vernacular language; the French began to talk about *l'esprit gaulois* in the sixteenth century when Joachim du Bellay wrote the defence and illustration of the French language. This was a nationalist movement more than two centuries before the French Revolution. What is interesting about Dante, Joachim du Bellay and Ki no Tsurayuki is that they were all poets. Scientists, philosophers and diplomats could express themselves in written Latin or written Chinese, but to express the innermost poetic feeling, the most convenient vehicle is the mother tongue. This is a well-known fact. We are not always aware, however, of the following phenomenon – in cases of mixed languages such as Japanese, English or German, some poets tend to use words of native origin. For example, Nietzsche, when he wrote *Thus Spake Zarathustra*, used words of exclusively Germanic origin. That is why the language in *Zarathustra* is as powerful as an orchestra's performance. The first stanza of John Masefield's poem *Sea Fever* – a most fascinating theme for the British – contains only one word of Latin origin: face. Although originally borrowed, 'face' has been so perfectly assimi-lated into English that few will doubt its being 'native'.

This instinctive inclination of the British to use Anglo-Saxon words in expressing sentiments while relying on borrowings of Latin-Romance origin when it comes to descriptions of intellectual matters is an exact parallel to the Japanese situation.

The difference is that in Japan there are millions of people who write poetry in *uta* form. I am not very sure of the number, but at least 20,000 poems are sent to the Imperial poetry contest every year. Professional poets select them, but poems written by housewives, businessmen, farmers and others are often far superior to those composed by the professional poets themselves or by the members of the Imperial family. In the art of *uta* or *haiku* poetry, Japanese are very democratic people. Every newspaper has its page of *uta* and *haiku* poetry, even the Communist Party paper.

Now if we look back at the Nō play *Haku Rakuten*, we see some other expressions which are associated with Japanese nationalism. In the play Japan is protected by Shinto gods and by the divine wind. This is a mythological adaptation of the historical events surrounding abortive Mongol attempts to invade Japan in the thirteenth century. The Japanese withstood the attacks with the fortuitous help of typhoons. Hence the expression 'divine wind' – *kamikaze* in Japanese. These Mongol invasions were the only serious foreign incursions the Japanese experienced before the twentieth century. As is well known, when the situation in World War II became unfavourable in late 1944, the Japanese called on the same imagery when deploying thousands of *kamikaze* attack planes.

The other day our Polish colleague Andrzej Walicki talked about the notion of the historic nation. Japan is a historic nation, but it is also very important to take into account the fact that Japan is a geographic nation. Among the world's greater nations, Japan was one of the most isolated and a latecomer in the society of nations. The physical isolation of the Japanese archipelago from its nearest Asian neighbours is a decidedly important factor in the shaping of the Japanese nation. Japan was ideally semi-detached in the sense that it was able to introduce the products of Chinese civilization without being politically dominated. Great Britain's contact with the Eurasian continent has been much more complicated. The Japanese could remain outside power struggles among continental empires, and Japanese governments never tried to divide and rule the continental Chinese, at least not before the twentieth century. Dover strait, which is only 34 kilometres wide, is easy to cross, but Tsushima strait is more than 100 kilometres wide and impossible for anyone to swim across. It was quite understandable that many Japanese intellectuals were pro-Chinese in past centuries because the Japanese were practically never threatened by expansions of the Chinese Empire. This pro-China sentiment is still very powerful among the Japanese, and Zhou En-lai utilized it remarkably well when he tried to normalize Sino-Japanese relations.

What should not be overlooked, though, is the fact that the

Japanese, like many other peoples, have borrowed foreign ideas when it made sense to do so. Moreover, from time to time Japan became less eager to introduce foreign ideas. There were even nationalistic reactions, as we have seen in the case of the Nō play *Haku Rakuten*. In the eighteenth century the self-conscious cultural nationalistic movement occurred in Japan. At that time, Confucianism was the official ideology of the shogunal government, and Chinese studies prospered in isolated Japan. At the same time, though, Japanese scholars began to study Japanese mythology and early anthologies of *uta* poems, as well as the *Tale of Genji*. Among the so-called National Scholars, Motoori Norinaga (1730–1801) was the greatest of the philologists. He wrote commentaries on the *Kojiki* compiled one thousand years earlier. Webster's definition of 'nationalism' fits Motoori well:

> ... loyalty and devotion to a nation, especially an attitude, feeling or belief characterized by a sense of national consciousness, an exaltation of one nation above others, and an emphasis on loyalty to and the promotion of culture and interests of one nation.[13]

I should say something about Chinese nationalism. Nationalism was lacking in China. The reason is very simple: China was a world in itself. The Chinese for many centuries did not take very seriously the 'barbarians' who were living outside the sphere of Chinese influence. China was a self-sustained world economically, politically and culturally. There was no psychological reason for the Chinese of pre-modern times to be nationalists, except under Mongol domination.

However, Chinese students became nationalists when they came to Japan around the turn of the twentieth century. Thousands of Chinese students who came to Japan wanted to rebuild their country, wanted to modernize China. But the Meiji Japan which they considered as the model of modernized nations turned out to be an imperialistic power. It must have been a very painful experience for the Chinese students in Japan to be despised by the Japanese whom they had considered Eastern barbarians. Japan became a hotbed of Chinese revolutionaries; Zhou En-lai was one of those students who came to study in Japan.

Finally, I would like to relate an episode which deals with the end of Japan's nationalistic venture in World War II. The episode is also about the suggestive power of Po Chü-i's verse.

The Japanese Admiralty building had been burnt down in an air raid in May, 1945. Later, Navy Minister Yonai Mitsumasa was on

duty in a big air raid shelter at the site of the office. At the beginning of June, Admiral Yamanashi Katsunoshin visited the Navy
Minister. Yamanashi was senior to Yonai; he had served as the Vice-
Minister of the Navy at the time of the London conference of
1930. (For his efforts to conclude the disarmament treaty, he was
later expelled from the Navy.) During the war, the retired admiral
was the principal of the Peers College. When the old Yamanashi
said he was anxious about the Navy Minister's high blood pressure,
Navy Minister Yonai said: 'Well, I can't take care of myself, now that
even the Admiralty office is burnt down!' Then Yamanashi suddenly changed the topic: 'Have you ever read Po Chü-i's poems? I'm
now studying him, and have found a nice poem:

> The prairie fires never burn it up;
> The spring wind blows it into life again.

No matter how much you worry, you can do nothing at the
moment. The grass in the burnt fields will grow again when the
spring wind blows. Yonai, didn't Po say a wonderful thing?' And
Yamanashi went off.[14]

Admiral Yamanashi was giving a hint: 'Don't hesitate to make
peace now. Japan in defeat surely looks like burnt fields, but the grass
will grow in the fields.' That was Yamanashi's suggestion – which
Yonai followed.

> Thick, thick the grass grows in the fields;
> Every year it withers, and springs anew.
> The prairie fires never burn it up;
> The spring wind blows it into life again.[15]

When I recite this poem by Po Chü-i, I clearly remember the vast
burnt fields of Tokyo in 1945. After the fiasco of militaristic adventures of the ultra-nationalistic Japanese Empire of the 1940s,
Japanese efforts were shifted to the field of economic recovery. On
those Japanese who saw the burnt fields of Tokyo or of Hiroshima,
this verse of Po Chü-i still makes a strong impression.

*Notes*

[1] This paper was given, May 1978, at the Woodrow Wilson International
Center for Scholars, which was located in the castle-like Smithsonian
building, Washington, D.C. On the door of the elevators in the building,
the motto of the Smithsonian Institution is inscribed: 'For the Increase
and Diffusion of Knowledge Among Men.' Behind the inscription there

are two hemispheres; however, both are Western hemispheres. Japan and China are lacking – non-existent. If they exist, they exist only in clichés.

[2] Arthur Waley: *The Life and Times of Po Chü-i* (London: George Allen & Unwin Ltd., 1949). See especially pp. 62–63.

[3] Hirakawa: *Yōkyoku no shi to seiyō no shi* (Tokyo: Asahi shimbunsha, 1975).

[4] Translation by Ivan Morris in *The Pillow Book of Sei Shōnagon* (Penguin Classics, 1971), p. 368.

[5] Translation by Ivan Morris, in *op. cit.* p. 241.

[6] Translation by Arthur Waley in *The Tale of Genji* (London: George Allen & Unwin, 1957), p. 889. As the phrase 'leaning on his pillow' is lacking in Waley's translation, I added it in the quotation.

[7] *Murasaki Shikibu Nikki,* (Tokyo: Iwanami shoten, Nihon koten bungaku taikei), p. 501. The English translation is mine as are all the following cases where names of translators are not mentioned.

[8] 'The Empty Gate' means Buddhism.

[9] The episode and the two poems are translated by Arthur Waley, *op. cit.* pp. 197–198.

[10] *Kokon chomon jū,* vol. 4, story 108 (Tokyo: Iwanami shoten, Nihon koten bungaku taikei), pp. 123–24.

[11] The following excerpts of *Haku Rakuten* are from Arthur Waley's *Nō Plays of Japan* (London: George Allen & Unwin, 1921), pp. 248–57. I made a slight modification: instead of 'we venture on the sport of making *uta,*' I inserted the line 'we feast our hearts on making *uta* poetry,' as this is an important difference in attitude towards poetry.

[12] I owe this argument to Professor Watanabe Shōichi's article 'On the Japanese Language.' The English translation of Watanabe's article appeared in *Japan Echo,* vol. 1, No. 2, 1974.

[13] In 1977 a book was written on Motoori Norinaga by a Japanese critic, Kobayashi Hideo, which got many favourable book reviews and was almost unanimously chosen as the best book of the year. It is symbolic that the book *Motoori Norinaga* (Tokyo: Shinchōsha) that earned such high credits is about the National Scholar Motoori. Japanese in the 1970s were again becoming more and more confident in their traditional values and in their native systems of behaviour. After the 'second opening of Japan' following World War II, Japan was entering the phase of using imported ideas in a more 'Japanese' way, incorporating them into the existing culture.

[14] One of the Navy officers who were present witnessing the conversation between Yamanashi and Yonai was rear admiral Takagi Sōkichi (1893–1979). I cannot find the magazine in which Takagi wrote the episode concerning Po Chü-i's poem. Takagi used the *on*-pronunciation of *yaka* for 'prairie fires'. I guess, however, that Yamanashi used more familiar *kun*-pronunciation of *nobi.*

[15] Translation by Arthur Waley in *The Life and Times of Po Chü-i,* p. 13.

# NATIONAL POETICS AND
# NATIONAL IDENTITY

———————□———————

Hearing the title of the symposium, 'Japanese Cultural Nationalism', an Australian friend advised me before my departure from Tokyo that, if an inexperienced scholar like myself travels to the Southern Hemisphere, he could easily become an ideal target for academic Japan-bashers.[1] They attack violently anyone defending or explaining Japanese nationalism in positive terms. It would be extremely difficult for a Japanese scholar to defend himself, using English, a foreign tongue.

My Australian friend's explanation as to the hostile irritability of some of his compatriots is as follows: So long as the destiny of the countries in the Oceania region depends too much on Japan's gigantic economy, people cannot be at ease. It is true that some of them admire Japan and some of them hate Japan, and some have completely mixed feelings. Is this not a love-hate relationship, in reverse direction, between English-speaking countries and Japan? In the Pacific Rim region, the interest in Japan is rapidly growing, and, accordingly, Japanese studies have made remarkable progress. Australians and New Zealanders now teach Japanese to high school students; Japanese, replacing French, Spanish or German, is becoming the first foreign language for many of them. This is all the more surprising as the Japanese themselves are rather indifferent towards this southern part of the globe. As asymmetry in attention, however, is one of the salient characteristics of a love-hate relationship, this imbalance in inter-cultural relations surely poses a rather delicate psychological problem.

I was embarrassed to hear that caution, as I belong to the generation of Japanese who were raised during the period of Japanese ultra-nationalism and who fortunately outlived not only the war years but also the more miserable post-war years – by eating whale meat (so I am, therefore, the more unpardonable). Japan's once strong economy, however, has become weaker and has been stagnant for the last decade of the twentieth century, and fortunately or unfortunately, the vocal Japan-bashers also seem to have become much calmer and quieter.

In the meantime I will try to do my best, using a language that is not my native tongue, to give you a talk in defence of the use of mother tongue. This contradictory situation seems to me one of the fundamental roots of Japanese nationalism and national identity in the coming age of globalization, which, in many respects, is 'Americanization' in disguise. Non-English speaking peoples feel more and more strongly that they are obliged to live under the hegemonic use of English.

Before discussing the linguistic background of nationalism, by way of precaution, I should say a few words concerning some preconceived ideas about nationalism. There is a widespread notion in the West that the origin of nationalism has something to do with the French Revolution and Napoleonic wars. One of the characters of Aldous Huxley's novel *After Many a Summer* (1939) says as follows on the eve of WWII (part one, chapter nine):

> Napoleon came out of the French Revolution... German nationalism came out of Napoleon. The war of 1870 came out of German nationalism. The war of 1914 came out of the war of 1870. Hitler came out of the war of 1914...

This seems to be a kind of explanation shared by many Europeans. Are there, then, any similar chain reactions in the case of Japanese nationalism and wars that Japan waged between 1894 and 1945? Or should we try to look at other less well known aspects of Japanese history to find out the origin of Japanese nationalism, especially when we are asked to discuss the problems of Japanese cultural nationalism together with the problems of Japanese identity?

Here I have to tell you something about Euro-centric views of history. Events in Japanese history have often been explained through Western parallel experiences. It is true that analogical approach is sometimes very effective and understandable. It has frequently been applied to Japanese cases both by Western and Japanese scholars and intellectuals, firstly as it was difficult for historians to be familiar with histories of more than one country; and secondly, many scholars believed in laws of universal historical development, valid for all nations. Indeed, that was the case with most theoretical historians who believed in the linear evolutional development of mankind. Their belief in progress in history was all too clear – for example, Fukuzawa Yukichi (1835–1901) divided human progress into three stages: uncivilized barbarous peoples (such as the aborigines of South Africa or Australia), semi-civilized nations (such as Turkey and Japan) and civilized nations (such as Great Britain and France). Throughout the nineteenth century, progress was optimistically welcomed, and civilization and enlightenment were considered the goals of all mankind. Fukuzawa's 'civilizational' view of history (*bunmei-shikan*) was not properly his own creation. It was the dominant view of history preached by many leading historians of the Western world whom Fukuzawa read in English books and with whom he generally agreed. Buckle, Guizot and Spencer were popular among the Japanese of the Meiji period (1868–1912). Even Lafcadio Hearn, who did not always like the Westernization of Japan, believed in the law of progress, and imagined that the religious development of Japan in the nineteenth century was following belatedly the course of religious development in the Mediterranean city states as depicted by Fustel de Coulanges in *la Cité Antique*. Marxist historians, of course, believed in the idea of progress. Believers in so-called scientific socialism were believers in laws of ineluctable historical development. In the middle of the twentieth century, one of the hot issues among Japanese historians was how to define the Meiji Revolution of 1868: was it a bourgeois revolution or not? They tried to situate the history of Japan on the assumption that every nation follows the same single track course of progress. Some scholars discussed the nature and stage of Japanese capitalism, comparing it with preceding West European examples. Some other scholars insisted on the premodern characteristics of Japanese capitalism, emphasizing the remnants of feudalism in the Japanese society. Most of them tended to deduce their conclusions from pre-established 'scientific' laws, and very few ventured to abstract laws by gathering and analysing historical facts.

Similar kinds of scholastic discussions based on Western analogies have been repeated since World War II. The case of Japanese nationalism, especially the case of the militaristic ultra-nationalism of the war years, has been understood as a Far Eastern version of Fascism.[2]

Probably readers will laugh at these simplistic ideological

approaches through easy analogies, but there has been a curious alliance between Japanese leftists and some Western Marxist historians. Moreover, there are people who like to categorically condemn Japan and the Japanese, using whatever standard they like, every time Japan becomes a conspicuous presence. These are my preliminary remarks before entering the main topic of Japanese cultural nationalism, about which I would like to attempt a linguistic consideration in wider comparative perspectives.

In this age of globalization when hegemonic power of the English language expands rapidly, what will be the future of the mother tongues of peoples who are not originally English-speaking? Before answering this disquieting question, I would like to sketch the relationship between classical written Chinese and Japanese language of Yamato, *yamato-kotoba* – that is, Japanese of Japanese archipelago origin – the relationship between classical Latin and Italian (so-called vulgar language or *volgare*) and finally the relationship between classical written Chinese (*wenyanti*) and spoken Chinese (*baihuati*) of modern times. All these relationships – together with the self-assertion of native tongues – are closely interrelated to the aspiration of every one of us to express ourselves in our mother tongue, and especially with the fundamental desire to write poetry in our own language. These linguistic urges are born, when we are obliged to use other languages than our own. As these aspirations are closely connected with the birth of nationalism, let us consider the issues of nationalism and national identity from a linguistic perspective. In this present age of globalization, we are witnessing the English language become the world's master language. The acceleration of the process is surprising. However, have there never been similar monopolizations of the world language before? And at that time, what sort of nationalistic reactions were born in the end? Were those aspirations of minorities just reactionary or were they sound and healthy?

Let us take a look at our past in East Asia. There was once in that part of the world, a cultural phenomenon that may be called Sinicization of the cultural sphere where Chinese civilizing influence was more or less felt. It was a kind of partial 'globalization'. For that experience of the past being practically terminated,[3] we may consider it as a model for the coming global Anglicization and possible nationalistic reactions against it.

Since the time of Tang dynasty, or even before, classical Chinese became the hegemonic language of East Asia, where Chinese ideograms were used as an indispensable writing system. In that cultural sphere, which included China, Korea, Vietnam, Japan and other neighbouring countries, the lingua franca par excellence was Chinese. Early histories of these countries were first recorded mostly in Chinese, and official communications between the peoples belonging to various linguistic groups were often conducted in written Chinese. For Europeans it is easy to understand this linguistic situation, because in Western Europe, Latin occupied a position comparable to that occupied by Chinese in East Asia. The first history of England was written not in English but in Latin by the Venerable Bede (673?–735), just as one of the first histories of Japan, *Nihongi* (720) was compiled in Chinese by Prince Toneri. It was the same with the first history of France, written in Latin by Gregory of Tours towards the end of the sixth century.

In Japan, the awakening of the national, linguistic and poetical consciousness was late. The first declaration of Japanese *art poétique* was made by Ki no Tsurayuki (868?–945) at the beginning of the tenth century. It was a conscious effort to counterbalance the overwhelming Chinese influence. National poetical awakening, however, took place much later in many countries of Western Europe. Although there have been time lags, poets everywhere have claimed their own national poetics based on their mother tongue. As this claiming or *revendication* in matters of national poetics, which is generally of the same nature, has not yet sufficiently drawn the attention of those who study issues of nationalism and national identity, I would like to describe briefly the cases of France, Japan, Korea and Italy before giving my tentative explanation concerning the case of modern China.

What I am going to present here is a comparative historical perspective, a bird's-eye view of intercultural relations between a central civilization and a peripheral civilization. There have been psychologically parallel phenomena that would allow us to foresee the future destiny of our mother tongue in the coming global society. My deduction is that there is a psychological law, that is, there is a common attitude shared by members of minorities to wish to express themselves in their own mother tongue and that need of expression is an important driving force of nationalism.

Let us examine, first, a well-known historical example: *La Défense et Illustration de la Langue Française* and, later, its East Asian counterparts. For the French, *La Défense et Illustration de la Langue Française* (1549) by Joachim Du Bellay (1522–60) is the first work of literary criticism of exceptional importance in the history of French literature. Du Bellay insists on the meaning of writing poetry not in Latin but in French. The literary historian Gustave Lanson (1857–1934) defines the cultural and linguistic position of the Pléiade poetical group, of which Du Bellay was the spokesman, as follows:

> Du Bellay and Ronsard had to fight against two sorts of enemies, the ignorant and the humanists. Against the humanists, they upheld the opinion that one cannot compete with the ancient in their languages ... Against the ignorant, they insisted on the need for study. Nature herself alone cannot produce a masterpiece; only the Greeks and Romans teach us how to make masterpieces ...[4]

A parallel example is found in the history of Japanese literature. The linguistic and poetic self-assertion of the mother tongue was made in 905, when Ki no Tsurayuki wrote the Japanese preface for the poetical anthology *Kokinshū* (Collection of Ancient and Modern Poems), in which the poet defended Japanese *uta* poetry against the encroachment of Chinese poetry. The name of Yamato[5] for Japan is just like the name of Gaul for France. When insisting on their own cultural identity, the Japanese talked about *yamato damashii* or the Japanese spirit, just as French poets such as Ronsard and Du Bellay talked about *esprit gaulois*. The following is the beginning of the Japanese (*kana*) preface to *Kokinshū* by the poet Ki no Tsurayuki:

> The seeds of Japanese poetry of Yamato lie in the human heart and grow into leaves of ten thousand words. Many things happen to the people of this world, and all that they think and feel is given expression in the description of things they see and hear. When we hear the warbling of the mountain thrush in the blossom or the voice of the frog in the water, we know every being has its song.
>
> It is poetry which, without effort, moves heaven and earth, stirs the feelings of the invisible gods and spirits, smooths the relations of men and women, and calms the hearts of fierce warriors.
>
> Such songs came into being when heaven and earth first appeared ...[6]

In his defence of Yamato-*uta*, Japanese poetry, the national Japanese poetry was implicitly opposed to Kara-*uta*, Chinese poetry, which was in fashion at the Imperial Court of Kyoto. Persons of culture of the time were supposed to compose poems in classical Chinese. That psychology reminds us of the attitude of the French humanists for whom to write poetry meant to compose poems in Latin. Tsurayuki, however, defended national poetry of mother tongue, because, according to him, it alone is natural and divine. Georges Bonneau, the French translator of the preface, was struck by the similarity between Tsurayuki's claim on behalf of his mother tongue and Du Bellay's *Défense et Illustration de la Langue Française*.[7]

*Kokinshū* has two prefaces: apart from the famous Japanese *kana* preface by Ki no Tsurayuki, there is also a Chinese (*mana*) preface. The Japanese passion for things Chinese was very intense through the early Heian period. The appellations of *mana* (true letter) for Chinese characters and *kana* (temporary or borrowed letter) for Japanese syllabary reflected the high prestige that Chinese written culture enjoyed in Heian Japan. At that time there was no scholarly writing that was not composed in classical Chinese. Nowadays, it is English that plays a similar role, when an academic publication in Japan, as in many other countries, has a summary written in that language. The *Kokinshū* compilers, therefore, asked a learned person named Ki no Yoshimochi to draft a preface in Chinese for the anthology of Japanese *uta*-poems, a preface that would defend Japanese poetry against the encroachment of Chinese poetry. The fact that the anti-Chinese argument in matters of poetics was written in Chinese became a laughing stock of posterity. Bonneau remarked the contradiction, ridiculing: 'la chose est piquante'. However, such defences of the mother tongue quite often are written in the academic language of the time. The well known example is the defence of Italian by Dante (1265–1321), which was written in Latin: *De Vulgari Eloquentia* (1305?), a treatise on the vernacular, that is, the Italian tongue. We should add, moreover, that the *Défense de la Langue Française* is, in fact, an adaptation or, in actual fact, a plagiary of the defence of the Italian language by Sperone Speroni(1500–81) and that Ki no Yoshimochi's defence of Japanese poetics against the encroachment of Chinese poetics is no other than an adaptation of Chinese poetics with many Chinese quotations.

If we take a broader view of things, we will know that it is a common practice to defend a mother tongue by borrowing the poetics of a central civilization.

Let us take a look at a Korean case. The following passage from Kim Manjung's (1637–92) *Sop'o manp'il* (or *Xipu manbi*, for it was originally composed in Chinese) shows the awakening of Korean poetical consciousness. Kim insisted on the importance for Korean poets of expressing themselves in their mother tongue, that is, in Korean. Kim, however, wrote his argument not in *han-gul* but in Chinese. In this essay, the Korean scholar made references to the words of Kumarajiva (344–413), a great Buddhist translator, who complained that he could convey only the meanings of the Sanskrit texts, and that he was unable to transmit the poetical beauty of the original in Chinese translation. Here is Kim Manjung's argument:

We understand Kumarajiva's difficulty: it is indeed not easy to convey the stylistic beauty of the Indian language. Language is what we let express our heart through our mouth. Poetry is a well cadenced expression of our language. Although languages of the world are different, those who excel in language are those who express themselves in their own proper language. In this sense, the qualities of all languages are everywhere the same. That which is well expressed, in whatever language, is capable of moving heaven and earth and stirring the feelings of demons. In this regard the language of the Middle Kingdom has no privileged monopoly. Now in our country Korean men of letters give up the use of our own language and study uniquely the language of another country. Although their Chinese looks like the language of the Chinese, what they are speaking is in reality the language of a parrot.[8]

It is interesting to note that Ki no Tsurayuki, Ki no Yoshimochi and Kim Manjung used the same expression 'to move heaven and earth and to stir the feelings of demons', an expression that derives from the Great Preface to the Chinese classic *Shijing*. In order to fight against the encroachment of Chinese poetry, not only the Japanese but also the Korean scholar-poet turned to Chinese poetics.

The next questions I would like to ask are: What was Japanese poetical consciousness and what was the distribution of masculine and feminine linguistic roles? Historically speaking, to compose *uta*-poems means to write them in the mother tongue of Yamato. *Uta* is also called *waka*, and *wa* is the *on*-pronunciation of the second of the two Chinese characters composing the word Yamato. It means exactly that *uta* or *waka* should be written, using the Japanese *hiragana* syllabary. The propagation of these phonetic signs during the Heian period established the tradition. Moreover, it was understood that *uta* or poems in thirty-one syllables should be written, using words of Japanese origin exclusively. Thus in composing *uta*-poems one should refrain from using not only Chinese characters but also Japanese words of Chinese origin. It is requested not to use *on* (Chinese-style) pronunciation in these Japanese poems. Those who write *uta*-poems still respect almost unconsciously this distinction between the two kinds of Japanese words of different origins. I do not know whether among British poets today there are those who explicitly avoid the use of words of Latin origin.

The reason why the self-assertion of national linguistic consciousness took place rather early in Japan, compared with Korea or Vietnam, is very simple. The Japanese archipelago being separated by sea and situated further away from the Asiatic continent than other neighbouring countries of China, it was much easier for the Japanese to cut the cultural bonds of the Chinese Empire. In the countries connected with China by land like Korea, where the examination system for the selection of bureaucrats was introduced, the prestige of written Chinese was, inevitably, extremely high, since the results of the examination were determined by the knowledge of Confucian classics. It was, therefore, very difficult for Koreans, being proud of their classical Chinese culture, to use their maternal Korean language for official use. It was in 1443 that the system of the Korean phonetic signs was invented. This system, *han-gul*, however, was considered for a long time as a writing system for women. In short, the Korean language transcribed in *han-gul* was considered a vulgar tongue.

In the case of Japan, around the year 1000 it was ladies of the Heian Court who wrote masterpieces of Japanese literature. *The Tale of Genji* and *the Pillow-Book of Sei Shōnagon* are the best known works among them. As they belonged to the fair sex, the authoresses were supposed to know little of Chinese characters. In a sense it is ironic, but it was thanks to this sexual discrimination that the feminine speech developed as literary expression, and romances like *Genji monogatari* (*The Tale of Genji*) were transcribed in the phonetic signs of *hiragana*. There was, so to speak, a distribution of roles in the Japanese language: official and public matters were recorded in the masculine style of *kanbun* or *kanbun-kundoku-tai*, a mixed Sino-Japanese style, while private and personal matters were written in feminine-style Japanese or *wabun-tai*, which is, in my opinion, the Japanese equivalent of *dolce stil novo*. Sweet and feminine sentiment was expressed much better and in a more natural way in the mother tongue than in a tongue taught at school. If the feminine *wabun-tai* is less rational, it is rich in emotion. One could talk much more freely in one's mother tongue of private matters as well as of feminine feelings. The old French expression, *enromancier*, means to talk in vulgar languages – that is, talk not in Latin but in Romance languages. *Enromancier* and the similar Japanese word, *monogataru*, were defined in contrast with the official and masculine expressions of Latin in Europe and classical Chinese in Japan. As ladies-in-waiting of the European Middle Age told romances, Japanese ladies at the Heian court told *monogatari*, using the vocabulary of almost exclusively Japanese origin, except official titles and other technical terms concerning the religious rites of Buddhism.

Now, starting from these examples, let us try a more audacious comparison: Dante's discovery of a new linguistic vehicle: Florentine, and Lu Xun's discovery of a new linguistic vehicle: colloquial Chinese. The poets of regions far away from mainland China, such as Japan, tended early on to express themselves in their mother tongue. The grip of central culture was less rigid in these peripheral countries. It was the same with European peripheral regions. In the time of Dante (1265–1321), outside the Italian peninsula poets had already begun to write in their own tongues: for example, Bertran de Born (1140–1215) in one of the languages of *oc* in the Perigord, Arnaut Daniel (1150–?) in Provençal in Provence, and some others in Sicilian in Sicily. Dante, having travelled widely through Europe, was very sensitive to poetical values of languages other than Latin. He appreciated poems written or chanted in their native tongues so much that he quoted eight lines of Arnaut Daniel directly in Provençal in Canto XXVI of *Purgatory*. The poet Dante must have recognized very early how advantageous it was, even for a highly qualified Latinist like him to express his inner sentiments in his Florentine mother tongue. He had acknowledged the merits, when he wrote *Vita Nova*, using it. However, Latin had so high a prestige in Central Italy, where classical Roman traditions were deeply entrenched, that no other Florentine scholars dared write in their native tongue, except some clerics. It was the genius of Dante that first broke the old Latin conventions. It was something quite extraordinary that Dante wrote his major work in his mother tongue; other Florentines like Boccaccio then followed him in writing prose works in Florentine.

A linguistic situation comparable to what I have just mentioned was found in East Asia: classical Chinese was respected not only by Chinese literati but also by the Confucian élite of other East Asian countries for more than fifteen hundred years. As Latin was surrounded by a glow of authority, classical Chinese too had an aura of prestige among men of learning. These Confucian scholars were naturally not in favour of vulgar Chinese for their literary expression. There was a kind of inhibition for Chinese literati to write in other Chinese than in classical literary Chinese, called *wenyan-ti*. Confucian orthodoxy, embodied in sacred books written in classical Chinese, was so much respected that popular novels, written in vernacular Chinese, often by those who had failed the state examination, were not held in high esteem. Compared with countries like France, the social position of novelists has not been very high in China. Until the Sino-Japanese War of 1894–95, a small number of Chinese literati, coming to Japan, could communicate with Japanese of Confucian leanings through writing. They did not feel the need for studying Japanese. The cultural situation, however, changed. Young Chinese students like Lu Xun (1881–1936), having been to Japan at the beginning of the twentieth century, found that classical Chinese in that part of East Asia was in decline. With Japan's turn to the West, the level of classical Chinese culture among Japanese intellectuals was beginning to lower, and Japanese began to write poetry using their mother tongue. Until the generation of Mori Ōgai (1862–1922) and Natsume Sōseki (1867–1916) the word *shi* meant Chinese poetry, and both Ōgai and Sōseki could compose poems in classical Chinese. However, to Japanese contemporaries of Lu Xun and his brother Zhou Zuoren *shi* meant Japanese poetry of a new style.

In terms of psychological process, there were many similarities – between Dante's discovery of the poetical value of the vernacular tongue (*volgare*) following his travels through peripheral regions of the former Roman Empire, and Lu Xun's discovery of the poetical value of the vernacular tongue (*baihua*) following his travel to Japan, a peripheral region of the ancient sphere of Chinese cultural influence. There were, of course, other circumstances favourable for a new literature movement in China. It was already accelerated by the abolition of the *keju* examination system, which called into question the authority of Confucian classics. Hu Shi (1891–1962) wrote in his diary entry of 5 April 1916 that all first-class literatures had been written in a native tongue. He named as examples, the cases of Dante for Italian literature, Chaucer for English literature and Martin Luther for German literature. Although the West-oriented Hu Shi did not mention it, the case of Japan seems to have exercised a decisive influence on Chinese writers like Lu Xun and Zhou Zuoren, who adopted Chinese vernacular or *baihua* as a new vehicle for their literary expression. With the adoption of the vernacular as the national language, Chinese nationalism was also born.

Globalization will be accelerated inevitably in this twenty-first century with the rapid development of the means of communication. The role English plays as the world language will be extending also rapidly in many fields. In scientific or technological fields, in commercial or financial affairs, it will be relatively easy for anyone to use a language other than their own. There will be a kind of linguistic colonization or assimilation all over the world. Except for the original English-speaking regions, bilingualism will become the general tendency. Linguistic immigrants into English will also increase in many parts of the globe.

However, those who wish to express thoroughly what they feel in the depth of their heart will continue to write in their mother tongue. This will be the destiny and mission of poets. This kind of poetical consciousness will be felt more keenly than ever among many peoples. Already in the time of the Renaissance the French poet Ronsard raised his voice in a poem:

> Le Grec vanteur, la Grece vantera,
> Et l'Espaignol, l'Espaigne chantera,
> L'Italien, les Itales fertiles,
> Mais moy Françoys, la France aux belles villes
> Et son sainct nom, dont le crieur nous sommes,
> Ferons voler par les bouches des hommes.[9]

It will be the same with Asiatic poets singing and vaunting in their own tongues. Some of them may one day become *poètes maudits*, for having raised their voices and for having incited the people to rebellion in coming linguistic wars.[10]

In the course of this new century when globalization and Americanization are going to be synonymous, we shall have to fight against two kinds of enemies: first, narrow-minded linguistic nationalists, and second, globalists without any root of national or local identity.

Against the cosmopolitan globalists who are self-centred and are contented with the privileged use of English, those who were not born to be English-speaking will have to say that to compete fairly with English-speaking people in their language is not possible, and that as non-English-speaking people they will remain in a disadvantageous position so long as they are obliged to use English. This sense of unfair treatment in language in the coming global society will be the soil in which antagonistic nationalism thrives.

Scholars already foresee the extinction of quite a few languages used by minorities in the actual process of globalization.[11] If we miss the extinction of rare birds, rare insects, fish or whales, why don't we miss rare languages and their cultures? Why do we not try to preserve them as they are?

To conclude, let me make two recommendations: first with nationalists of the classical type who always accuse other nations of responsibility for past wars and who always refer to the grudges of long ago, I believe we had better advise them to recall the wise words of Mustafa Kemal Ataturk who said of the Anzac casualties at Gallipoli:

Therefore rest in peace. There is no difference between the Johnnies and the Mehmets to us where they lie side by side here in this country of ours. You, the mothers, who sent their sons from far away countries, wipe away your tears; your sons are now lying in our bosom and are at peace. After having lost their lives on this land they have become our sons as well.

I very much admire Ataturk for the magnanimity of these words written in 1934, less than twenty years after the tragic event.

Second, with nationalists of the new type, who are now being born from the linguistic situations unfavourable for those who do not speak English, we have to insist on the meaning of intercultural understanding from both sides. The unilateral linguistic dominance of English was already a fact in the nineteenth century, accomplished through the spread of the British Empire around the world. Rudyard Kipling, who was born in India, was surprised on finding that the Japanese, despite all their efforts at Westernization, did not speak English at all. He, therefore, mocked the Japanese for wearing Western clothes but being incapable of speaking English. This was in 1889. His Japanese letters[12] testify to the mentality of those who believed in Anglo-Saxon superiority. The dominance of a single language, English, in the coming global society is probably inevitable. It is an advantage for English-speaking peoples, as the values firmly entrenched in the language itself will tend to become universal values. However, I am very much afraid that nationalistic, linguistic and cultural reactions will be aroused by the hegemonic monopoly of English as the lingua franca of the twenty-first century.

What should we do? We have to break the bottlenecks of narrow-minded nationalism. Without knowing how to communicate with other peoples in languages other than one's own, one cannot live peacefully in the coming age of global society. After the fall of Singapore in February 1942 the once glorified idea of 'White Man's Burden' was broken down. However, this time non-English speaking peoples, have to take up instead another extremely heavy burden: the burden of the English language.

*Notes*

[1] This paper was given at the symposium 'Japanese Cultural Nationalism' which was held at Otago University, Dunedin, New Zealand, 21 August, 2002.

[2] The reason why the studies by political scientist Maruyama Masao became so popular in and out of Japan derives probably because of his parallel approach, which is more understandable than straightforward nar-

ratives of small historical details of an Asian country. In the year following Japan's defeat Maruyama made his debut with an article comparing Japanese war criminals with German war criminals, condemning especially the former for the evasion of their responsibility. Maruyama's arbitrary use of documents, however, has been revealed by Ushimura Kei, *Beyond 'the Judgment of Civilization'* (Tokyo: International House, 2003) pp.17–34. Maruyama's intellectual integrity is seriously put in doubt.

The Allied accusations and judgements given at the international military tribunals at Nuremberg and Tokyo reinforced parallel interpretations of history. In short, the Allied war propaganda against Japan has been perpetuated not only during the American occupation of Japan but also through the post-war period under scholarly disguise. David Bergamini and the like went so far as to accuse the wartime Emperor Hirohito by a forced analogy with Hitler with their conspiracy theory. We should remember that already in the 1930s Soviet historians had compared the Japanese Imperial system with Russian czarism. There are history books read even before you open them, since they belong to the category of books read before being written.

[3] Let me tell you briefly some episodes indicative of the vicissitudes of the hegemonic language in East Asia in modern times. When the European powers were beginning to exercise their pressure upon Asian countries with gunboats, the Asiatics perceived the necessity to learn the languages of aggressors, whose technological superiority was evident. The names successively given to the Japanese school of Western studies show the ambivalent attitudes of the Japanese *vis-à-vis* Europeans, the first name given in 1856 was *bansho shirabesho*, that is the bureau of investigations of barbarous books. It becomes the bureau of investigations of European books, *yōsho shirabesho* in 1862, and the school of instruction *kaiseisho* in 1863, and finally, in 1877, is called the University of Tokyo. More curious is the name given to the first school of foreign languages opened in China in 1860. It was called *Tongwenguan*, that is, the school of the same letters. It was opened with foreign professors for the teaching of foreign languages, or more precisely for the formation of interpreters. The school, however was called the school of the same letters, and the name seems to contradict the purpose of the founding of the school. However, there was no contradiction in this seemingly ridiculous name. For the strongly Sinocentric Chinese, to learn foreign languages did not mean to learn a culture other than their own. It was in order to make their culture known to others that they began to study foreign languages. It was in order to convert barbarians to the virtuous way of the Middle Kingdom. That is the traditional meaning of *tongwen tonggui* 'with the same letters, the same way'. The symbolical turning point was in 1876, when the Japanese minister Mori Arinori and the Governor General Li Hongzhang met in Beijing. The Japanese minister, a radical Westernizer, spoke English to Li. It was for the first time that official discussions between the representative of an Asian

country and the representative of the Chinese Empire were conducted through English interpretation. The proceedings of the discussions, recorded in English, are extremely interesting. See Takeyama Michio's use of the discussions in Part IV Chapter 4.

[4] This is my abridged translation of Gustave Lanson: *Histoire de la Littérature Française,* (Paris: Hachette, 1960) pp. 278–279.

[5] By the way Italian Japanese studies have often been called *yamatologia.*

[6] Laurel Rasphea Rodd et al. tr. *Kokinshū* (University of Tokyo Press, Princeton University Press, 1984). I modified the English translation slightly.

[7] Georges Bonneau's doctoral thesis together with the French translation of the preface of *Kokinshū* was presented to the Imperial University of Kyoto in 1933. Ki no Tsurayuki: *Préface au Kokinshū* ('*Deffence et Illustration*' *de la poésie japonaise*), édition critique par Georges Bonneau (Paris: Paul Geuthner, 1933), p. 16.

[8] Kim Manjung: *Sop'o manp'il* (Seoul: Tongwen-guan, photographic edition, 1971). The English translation is mine.

[9] 'L'Hymne de France' *Œuvres de Ronsard,* éd. Laumonier (Paris: Hachette), t. I, p. 25.

[10] In some regions of the world, such as Basque and Flanders conflicts called 'linguistic wars' are already taking place. Their terrorisms are often as violent as religious conflicts.

[11] See, for example, Claude Hagège: *Halte à la mort des langues* (Paris: Editions Odile Jacob, 2000), chapitre 8.

[12] See, for example, the 11th letter, from Tokyo, of the year 1889, in *Kipling's Japan* (The Athlone Press, 1988).

# THE AWAKENING OF ASIA

———————☐———————

'The Meiji Restoration in Japan was the first step that leads to our revolution in China.' This famous pronouncement made by Sun Yat-sen (Sun Wen, 1866–1925) summarizes the impact of that event upon other neighbouring Asian countries.[1] Asia was obliged to 'awaken' because of the sense of crisis Asians felt at the onslaught of Western colonizing powers. They felt more or less the necessity to cope with the antagonizing situations that shattered their traditional agricultural societies. However, this Asiatic consciousness of crisis was born not only from the impact of the West upon one's own country, but also from the events that befell in other parts of Asia. We may say, therefore, putting Sun's words in another way: 'The Opium War in China of 1840–42 was the first shock that leads to the awakening of Asia.'

*Haiguo tuzhi*, compiled first in 1842 by the Chinese scholar-bureaucrat Wei Yuan (1794–1857) who worked under the Governor Lin Ze-xu (1785–1850), was read not only by the Chinese but also by Japanese political ideologues. Wei's book of world geography was written for the purpose of 'Know thy enemy'. Intellectual interactions among East Asians were quite considerable. One of the most conspicuous examples of stimulating influence, however, was, as remarked by the leading Chinese revolutionary, that of Japan's modernization. Regarding this contagious example, Marius Jansen writes as follows:

> The (Meiji) Restoration led to a unified national state which struggled to achieve international equality and leadership in Asia. The success of the Japanese leaders had an effect on neighboring Asian societies as stimulating as was that of revolutionary France on Europe. Sun Yat-sen, K'ang Yu-wei, Kim Ok-kiun, Emilio Aguinaldo, Subhas Chandra Bose, and many others dreamed of creating in their own countries something of the drive and

unity that had first established in Japan the equality of Asian with European strength and ability.[2]

Against this general historical background, we are going to check how ideas were transmitted from one country to another, or from one person to another, as the analysis of linguistic media is the starting point of any East Asian intercultural studies. Literary relations between Asian countries themselves were no less important than those between Western countries and Asian countries. Let us revise the West-centred view of history, by looking from Asian angles. For example, by the term 'students abroad of the Meiji period' (Meiji-ki ryūgakusei, Mingzhi-qi liuxuesheng) what sort of students do we imagine? The word generally reminds the Japanese of Japanese students sent abroad, who, on their return home, had contributed so much to build up the Meiji nation-state. However, although it is still little known, compared with the relatively limited number of Japanese students sent abroad during the Meiji period (1868–1912),[3] a greater number of Asian students were sent from China, Korea, Vietnam and other countries to Japan. After Japan's victory over Russia and after the abolition of the examination system in Qing China in 1905, the number increased sharply. In the year 1906, Chinese students in Japanese schools were said to total 8000.[4] It was inevitable that those students of the Meiji period who went abroad should become transmitters of ideas.

Then, what were the main intermediaries of cultural transactions among East Asians? We will focus our attention on the three linguistic media, through which practically all the movements of ideas were successively conducted. The languages used were: first classical Chinese, second English and third Japanese.

In East Asia, traditionally the lingua franca was Chinese. Written Chinese was used as the language of communication not only between the Chinese and the non-Chinese but also among the Chinese of various provinces, whose pronunciations of the same Chinese characters were as different as French and English words of the same Latin origin. Classical Chinese was studied by all the intellectuals of the neighbouring countries and regions which were under Chinese cultural influence: Japan, Korea, Mongolia, Manchuria, Taiwan, Tibet, Uighur, Vietnam.

*Haiguo tuzhi* was reprinted in Japan to be studied, first, because the Japanese, as a nation in a geographically and culturally peripheral position, had always been curious about what was going on outside their country and, second, their literacy in classical Chinese was relatively high. The Sino-centric Chinese literati in the capital of the Qing Empire were probably less crisis-conscious than the contemporary Japanese samurai, even though the Opium War was fought in the southern part of their own Guangdong province. Samurai, although having become scholar-bureaucrats towards the end of the peaceful Tokugawa period, were originally men-at-arms, and compared with the past-oriented Confucian men of letters, they were more practical-minded in matters of national defence. No Chinese or Korean Confucian literati volunteered to go to the West in the two decades following the Opium War, Japanese samurai-scholars were more willing to go to study abroad.

Throughout the Meiji period intellectuals in Japan were those who were trained in Chinese classics. Even the father of English Studies in Japan, Fukuzawa Yukichi (1835–1901), who ridiculed Confucian scholars as 'rice-consuming dictionaries', had penetrated deeply into the Chinese classics and history, when he was young. It was, therefore, easy for Chinese diplomats, men of letters and revolutionaries to communicate with Japanese in the 1880s and 1890s. Among those Chinese who enjoyed the intellectual companionship of the leading Japanese Confucian scholar Nakamura Masanao (1832–91) was Huang Zun-xian (1848–1905), a diplomat and China's first Japanologist. Nakamura explained him by writing in classical Chinese Japan's experiences in the Meiji Restoration. Their relation was friendly and Huang wrote in his poems about the kindergarten and girls' normal school of which Nakamura was the first principal. Huang collected the poems and published *Riben zashi-shi* in 1879, describing Japan's little known aspects both traditional and modern. In 1887, Huang went one step further: he compiled the first comprehensive study of Japan *Riben guozhi*, which influenced Kang You-wei (1858–1927), the theoretical leader of the unsuccessful Wu-Xu Bianfa coup of 1898, and other East Asian modernizers. If we check carefully Kang's *Riben shumuzhi* we can recognize Nakamura's view reflected in his phrases. Both Nakamura and Kang say that the strength of the West does not derive from the armed forces alone, and Nakamura argues that it derives rather from people's having the rights of self-determination (taisei no tsuyoki-wa jinmin-ni jishu-no ken aru ni yoru) while Kang insists on the meaning of studying the *new law* (er zai qi shiren zhi xue xinfa zhi shu). The communication was easy between the scholars, as Nakamura had written in classical Chinese his explanations of Smiles's *Self-Help*, which will become the best guidebook for Japan's industrialization, as we shall see in the chapter dealing with first translations from Western literature.

His knowledge of Chinese and English was what enabled the Japanese romantic Miyazaki Tōten (1871–1922) to join Asian revolutionary movements. His autobiography, *My Thirty-three Years' Dream*, tells us eloquently that he conversed in writing classical Chinese not only with Chinese revolutionaries such as Sun Wen and Kang You-wei but also with the Korean leader Kim Ok-kiun. It is a pity that all the conversation records were burnt to ensure secrecy.[5]

With the passing of Miyazaki's generation, the Japanese ability in classical Chinese dropped sharply. Intellectual exchanges between East Asians began to depend on other linguistic mediums than written Chinese. Sun Wen himself, being educated in Hawaii, depended very much on Legge's English translation even for the understanding of Confucius' *Lun yu*. In 1896, when he was abducted by Chinese officials in the capital of Great Britain and miraculously saved from the Chinese legation, Sun Wen immediately wrote a pamphlet, *Kidnapped in London*, to make an appeal to the international audience, condemning the disregard for human rights of the Qing regime. That was one of the first successful attempts by East Asians to use English for their anti-governmental self-assertion. *Kidnapped in London* was translated into Japanese by Miyazaki. Towards the end of the nineteenth century Japan succeeded in establishing equality with European countries by abolishing extraterritorial rights. However, in other parts of Asia imperialistic advances or aggression were most conspicuous. Miyazaki, by sending arms, tried to help Aguinaldo, who proclaimed independence for the Philippines.

Two events that greatly affected Asian consciousness were the Meiji Restoration of 1868 and Japan's victory over Russia in 1905. Japan fought against the Russian Empire with the backing of the Anglo-Japanese Alliance, yet the victory was perceived by the Japanese and Asians alike as the breakdown of the myth of the White Man's invincibilty. Of course, revolutionaries such as Lenin and Sun Wen wished Japan's victory; furthermore, at that time many Asians wished it too.It was particularly true of Chinese students residing in Japan at the time.[6] The impact of Japan's victory was recounted by Nehru (1889–1964) in his *Autobiography:*

> … Japanese victories stirred up my enthusiasm and I waited eagerly for the papers for fresh news daily. I invested in a large number of books on Japan and tried to read some of them. I felt rather lost in Japanese history, but I liked the knightly tales of old Japan and the pleasant prose of Lafcadio Hearn.

Nationalistic ideas filled my mind. I mused of Indian freedom and Asiatic freedom from the thraldom of Europe.

The Awakening of Asia was now spreading through the linguistic medium of English beyond the cultural sphere of Chinese characters. The Japanese art historian Okakura Tenshin (known also as Okakura Kakuzō, 1862–1913) began to advocate Asian cultural solidarity, by using English. His famous slogan 'Asia is One', however, contained one basic contradiction, namely, that Pan-Asianistic idea could be understood by other Asians only through the language of their colonial masters: English. Okakura wrote most of his works in English for Western readership, and the one which was not published during his lifetime had the title, *Awakening of Asia*. However, thanks to his exceptional mastery of English, not only many colonized peoples of Asia but also some Irish people could sympathize with the ideologue Okakura in their common cause:[7] they were one in their opposition against Anglo-Saxon domination. Already in Shiba Shirō's (1852–1922) political novel, *Kajin no kigū*, written in 1885, an Irish girl called Kōren appears. This must be the phonetic transcription of Colleen. The destiny of political underdogs in the era of imperialism must have appealed to the Chinese revolutionary Liang Qi-chao (1873–1929). After the failure of Wu-Xu Bian-fa, he sought refuge in Japan and translated the novel into Chinese. It was serialized in the journal, *Qingyibao* which he edited in Yokohama.

It was a healthy reaction to the overzealous Westernization fever that Okakura together with Ernest Fenollosa (1853–1908) tried to rehabilitate Japanese traditional arts in the 1890s. It was precisely the time when some Western writers such as Lafcadio Hearn (1850–1904), not always satisfied with Occidental civilization, began to be actively interested in the folklore and folk arts of traditions other than their own. Hearn, who married Koizumi Setsuko, daughter of an impoverished samurai family, 'went native'. He took Japanese citizenship under the Japanese name of Koizumi Yakumo and rewrote in English many ghost stories based on Japanese folk materials. Yanagi Muneyoshi (1889–1961), who had rediscovered Japan through Hearn's books, began to be interested in the nameless arts of common Asian people. He wished to become another Hearn in Korea and discovered beauty in objects of everyday use. Of course, there are many errors in what Hearn and Yanagi wrote about Japan and Korea. It is nonetheless undeniable that reappraisal of artistic traditions in Asia came not only from within but also from outside. The cultural awakening of Asia was a complex phenomenon. Bernard Leach (1887–1979) had read Hearn and on his arrival in Japan in 1909 became a member of the artistic magazine *Shirakaba* and joined Yanagi's *Mingei* (folk art) movement. On his return in 1920, Leach with his Japanese friend Hamada Shōji (1894–1978) built a kiln at St Ives, Cornwall. Although Leach's *A Potter's Book* (1940) is now a sacred book for Western potters, it is little known that its East Asian origin was connected with friendships formed during the Taishō-democracy period. Leach counted among his Japanese friends the poet sculptor Takamura Kōtarō, the writer Shiga Naoya and other artists gathered around the monthly *Shirakaba*.

Some Asians, overexposed to Western culture, tried to reaffirm their own Asian identity. There was, of course, a psychological reaction in this kind of quest. One of the most conspicuous examples was the Chinese scholar Ku Hung Ming (Gu Hong-ming, 1854–1928) who in 1915 wrote in English *Spirit of the Chinese People* in defence of Old China, about whom I will discuss more in Part III Chapter 1.

The case of the Japanese poet Yone Noguchi (Noguchi Yonejirō, 1875–1947) showed also this kind of reactionary return to the East. He began his career as a poet in the United States, by writing poetry in English and ended it by writing anti-American propagandistic poetry in Japanese during World War II. It was Noguchi who defended Japanese ways in the name of the awakening of Asia when the Indian poet Rabindranath Tagore (1861–1941) came to Japan and criticized the Japanese militaristic tendency.[8]

The theme of awakening of Asia is, therefore, ambivalent and lends itself to many interpretations. In the field of juvenile literature, the work that captivated the Japanese youth in pre-World War II years was *Ajia no akebono* (1931–32) which means 'the Dawn of Asia' by Yamanaka Minetarō (1885–1966). Yamanaka was a classmate of Tōjō Hideki in the military academy and was a brilliant graduate of the War College. However, because of his friendship with Chinese classmates then studying in Japan, he went with them to China to devote himself to the cause of the Xin-Hai revolution. His military career thus abandoned, Yamanaka was obliged to live by his pen. The main theme of his children's literature may be summarized as 'the Anglo-American imperialism is the common enemy of Asians'.

The characteristic of East Asian great powers was that, as late starters in modernization, they thought themselves to be oppressed by Western powers. While advocating anti-imperialism, they themselves behaved like imperialistic powers, trying to expand their influences. It is known that in exchange for Japan's acquiescence to the American occupation of the Philippines, the United States gave its acquiescence to Japan's annexation of Korea. Japan, accusing Great Britain of colonialism, behaved itself as the Great Britain of the East. Japan's efforts to build an empire in the East might be called anti-imperialistic imperialism.

Ironically, the languages of imperial powers tended to become the lingua franca in the transactions of ideas: after Chinese and English, Japanese played the role of intermediary. Lu Xun's awakening to national consciousness while studying in Sendai, Japan, is all too well known. Ch'oe Nam-son (1890–1957) came to Japan in 1906, and after two years of study went back to Seoul to publish a journal, in which he serialized his Korean translation from Japanese of Smiles's *Self-Help*. Considering the importance the book had played in Japan in the pursuit of its nation-building, the young intellectual leader tried to encourage the Korean youth by that publication. Incidentally, it was the Shūeisha printing company that had published the Japanese translation of *Self-Help, Saikoku risshi hen*, in Tokyo that helped Ch'oe's printing enterprise in Seoul. What Smiles advocated and what Nakamura stressed was individual self-help as well as national self-help. It was quite natural that Ch'oe Nam-son, imbued with that idea, drafted the *Declaration of Independence* in 1919, when the Wilsonian idea of self-determination was widely spread. It was a failure on the part of Japan not to be able to respond adequately to aspirations of neighbouring nations.

In the 1920s, the Japanese language was used as the medium through which the dream of red internationalism was being propagated over East Asia. As to the merits and demerits of the introduction of Marxism via Japan, there seems to be a wide divergence in critical judgements. However, the statistical fact, that more than two-thirds of Chinese words concerning social science were coined in Japan, suggests the role Japan played as the intermediary of ideas.

It is true that by learning languages other than their own people discover their own language. It is also true that people, by being exposed to cultures other than their own, become conscious of their own cultural identity. There is, therefore, an awakening. Through such processes, there emerge persons who refuse 'contamination' and return to the roots of their own culture. Sometimes nationalists become prisoners of their nationality as well as of their identity.[9]

## Notes

[1] Sun Wen made this famous pronouncement in 1924 in his speech in Kobe and on many other occasions.

[2] Marius Jansen: *Sakamoto Ryōma and the Meiji Restoration* (Princeton University Press, 1961) p. ix.

[3] See the study by Watanabe Minoru: *Kindai Nippon kaigai ryūgakusei shi* (Tokyo: Kōdansha, 1978). According to the list attached to the book, Japanese students sent to study abroad on a scholarship given by the Ministry of Education between the 8th year of Meiji (1875) and the 45th year (1912) totalled 683. This number, however, does not include students sent abroad by the Ministry of Foreign Affairs, the Navy and the Army. The exact number of the students who went abroad at their own expense during the Meiji period is not known.

[4] Sanetō Keishū, *Chūgokujin Nihon ryūgakushi* (Tokyo: Kuroshio shuppan, 1960) p. 58.

[5] Miyazaki Tōten's autobiography was translated by Etō Shinkichi and Marius Jansen as *My Thirty-Three Years' Dream* (Princeton University Press, 1982).

[6] Zhou Zuo-ren's recollection of it is recorded in Hō Kisei (Fang Ji-sheng) ed.: *Shūsakujin sensei no koto,* (Tokyo: Kōfūkan, 1944) pp. 224–232.

[7] Okakura counted among his lady friends who helped him during his stay in India, Nivedita (Margaret Elizabeth Noble, 1867–1911) and Josephine McLeod (1859–1949).

[8] Yone Noguchi's son, by his American wife, Isamu Noguchi, showed more complicated and more interesting reactions. The sculptor's case is astutely analysed by Ian Buruma in his *The New York Review* article, 4 March 1999.

[9] This paper was written as a chapter for *Comparative History of East Asian Literature* originally prepared by Asian executive members of International Association of Comparative Literature for its 2003 congress in Hong Kong.

# PART II

# JAPAN'S TURN TO THE WEST

# THE MEANING OF DUTCH STUDIES IN TOKUGAWA JAPAN

———————□———————

## *A Preliminary Overview: A German Jurist's Observation about Japan's Constitution*

Before discussing specific problems concerning Japan's turn to the West, let us examine macroscopically what the reality of Japan's national isolation was in terms of its inter-cultural relations.[1]

Although Japan was never a 'closed country' in the sense that *sakoku* literally implies, it did awaken from two hundred years of substantial 'national isolation' in the last half of the nineteenth century to devote all its energy towards the realization of one goal – the establishment of a modern nation-state. This effort alone is better evidence than anything else of Japan's turn to the West, for the concept of a modern nation-state had yet to manifest itself in any non-Western country. In economic terms, a modern nation-state is a state that has experienced an industrial revolution; in social terms, it is a state with a centralized political system under which popular participation is structured through the parliamentary institutions of a constitutional order. By any measure, such characteristics of a state are thoroughly Western in nature and origin.

These distinguishing characteristics were not to be found in the Tokugawa *bakuhan* state. It was composed of the shogunal 'monarchy' known as *bakufu* and of more than two hundred feudal domains known as *han*. Nineteenth-century Japanese society was pre-industrial, and its economy was based on forms of production that depended on animate rather than mechanical sources of power. A large bourgeoisie did exist to carry on commercial and financial enterprise, but it was excluded from participating in political decisions. The Tokugawa political structure was composed of a bureaucracy, representing feudally privileged classes that operated within a system that reconciled theoretically incompatible elements of feudalism and absolute shogunal 'monarchy'. Despite Japan's high level of cultural homogeneity – or perhaps because of it – the concept of a people as a 'nation' that participated actively in the affairs of a 'state' was unknown.

Confronted by an apparently superior 'civilization' represented by the states of Europe and America, the Japanese had to set themselves goals for achieving modernity – making themselves into a 'nation' and a 'state' – following the opening of their country (*kaikoku*). To that end, they had to create a central government, train bureaucrats to run the state, establish an army and a navy based on universal conscription, organize a legal system, foster capitalism, abolish feudal privilege, implement the 'equality of the four status groups', consolidate a system of education, and reform their customs.

The individual who was perhaps most responsible for formulating these goals and was central to their execution in early Meiji years was Ōkubo Toshimichi (1830–78), a Satsuma leader who held real political power during the first decade of Meiji rule. Compared with his Chōshū colleague Kido Takayoshi (Kōin, 1833–77), Ōkubo was more conservative and less willing to sacrifice tradition in the quest for modernization. Let me epitomize his state of mind by quoting one of his *uta*-poems. At the seashore near Osaka one day, Ōkubo gazed despondently at a clump of tree stumps – all that remained of a pine grove famous for its beauty – that had been levelled as a consequence of the policy of 'foster industry and promote enterprise' (*shokusan kōgyō*), of which he himself was the leading proponent. Feeling the need to admonish the prefectural governor responsible for this insensitive act, Ōkubo composed the following poem:

> The pines at Takashi beach
> in spite of their renown,
> could not escape the ravage of
> historic tidal waves.[2]

Even for Ōkubo, however, the policy of 'civilization and enlightenment' (*bummei kaika*) that Japan had adopted remained synonymous with Westernization. In an apparent belief that the

Western powers were pure and simple embodiments of civilization, he wrote that 'at present all the countries in the world are directing all their efforts towards propagating teachings of "civilization and enlightenment", and they lack for nothing. Hence we must imitate them in these respects.'[3]

A revealing anecdote about the process by which the Meiji constitution was formulated points by extension to the larger question of preconditions within Japanese society that affected, assisted and channelled the process of appropriating the Western example. In 1883, Itō Hirobumi (1841–1909), the chief architect of the future constitution, led a delegation to Europe to study its various national constitutions. Because the Meiji government had already more or less decided to model its new constitution on that of Prussia, Itō and his delegates first visited the jurist Rudolf von Gneist (1816–95) in Berlin to seek his advice. Gneist's advice was cool and discouraging. He told them that several years earlier Bulgaria, one of newly independent and semi-independent countries that developed in the Balkans after the Russo-Turkish War of 1877–78, had asked for assistance in framing a constitution. Though all of Gneist's colleagues were hampered by a lack of knowledge about conditions in that country, one legal scholar had volunteered to go there to produce a constitution within six months' – an offer that brought scornful amusement. True to his word, however, the man made good his boast. But upon his return to Berlin, he had provoked loud laughter among his colleagues with the quip: 'After all, how long does it take to gloss over a bronze vessel with gold paint?'

Gneist went on to advise his Japanese guests as follows:

> I am most grateful that you have chosen to come all the way to Germany on your mission. Unfortunately, I know nothing of Japan, and have never studied it. Let me first ask you about Japan, about the relationship between ruler and ruled, its manners and customs, about the sentiments of its people, and about its history, etc. Clarify all these things for me first, and then I will think about them and provide you with an answer that might be of some assistance to you.[4]

In short, Gneist began by bluntly admonishing Itō that only those nations possessing a minimum degree of latent potential, that is, a certain level of cultural advancement, were capable of creating a truly meaningful constitution. To undertake such a task before acquiring the requisite capacity would merely result in an elaborately embellished piece of paper. Gneist then insinuated that in Japan's case the drafting of a constitution might very well be meaningless.

This brusque reply was thoroughly disheartening to Itō, the representative of a small, backward, East Asian country who stood face to face with a European civilization that was at the zenith of its power and glory and that was convinced of its own superiority as none other in recorded history had been. How could the words of a famous Berlin jurist fail to ring true in both East Asian and European ears?

Yet if as Gneist asserted, a constitution, the framework of a modern nation-state, 'is more a legal document', if indeed it is 'the manifestation of a people's spirit and the measure of a nation's capacities', then the fact that a modern nation-state did emerge in nineteenth-century Japan indicates that something in the 'relationship between ruler and ruled', the 'manners and customs', the 'sentiments of its people', and its 'history, etc.' facilitated the creation of a new form of state based on the Meiji Constitution. To put it differently, this process, and indeed the rapidity of Japan's Westernization, indicates that the gap between Japan and the West at that time was entirely bridgeable.

Japan's turn to the West had to be carried out in two separate dimensions: (1) the importation and assimilation of modern ideas and institutions on a technical, formal level, such as Gneist's constitutional 'legal document'; and (2) the adaptation of an indigenous, traditional culture and institutions to bring out their latent potential, in Gneist's terms, 'the national spirit and capacities.'

### *The Meaning of Dutch Studies in Tokugawa Japan*

Tokugawa society was culturally creative and produced much of what we now consider 'traditionally Japanese', but Japan was not by any means intellectually secluded during its period of national isolation. Intellectual activity during the Edo period can be broadly classified into three categories: (1) Confucianism, which had a distinguished pedigree and possessed great prestige; (2) Japanese learning (*kokugaku*), which arose in mid-Tokugawa times as a reaction to the Sino-centrism that then prevailed in scholarly circles; and (3) Dutch studies (*rangaku*), whose emergence was signalled by the translation into Japanese of a Dutch translation of a German work on anatomy by Kulmus called *Ontleedkundige tafelen,* and also referred to as *Tafel Anatomia,* which was completed in 1774 by Sugita Gempaku (1733–1817) and his colleagues. Dutch studies sprang up as an adjunct to medicine and gradually spread to other areas, such as language study, astronomy, geography, physics, chemistry and military science. Although they appeared on the academic scene relatively late, Dutch studies had wide currency by late Tokugawa times, and the awareness of some Dutch studies specialists of the need to reconsider the system of national seclusion played an important role in bridging the intellectual gap between the West and Japan in the nineteenth century.

It is significant that two of these three principal fields of Tokugawa learning derived from China and the West and were alien in origin. Japan remained in contact with China and Holland, the cultural homelands of Confucianism and Dutch studies, throughout the Edo period, although to be sure the degrees of contact differed greatly. Nevertheless, conventional generalizations about the period of 'national isolation' prepare one poorly for understanding the amount and quality of information about the outside world that was accessible to Tokugawa thinkers. Chinese books, including Chinese translations of Western works, were imported every year from Qing China. The Dutch East India Company maintained a Nagasaki outpost whose superintendent was required to submit reports on foreign affairs (*Oranda fūsetsugaki*) to the shogunal government via the Nagasaki magistrate whenever Dutch ships made visits to that port. The same superintendent was obliged to travel to Edo at regular intervals for a formal shogunal audience, at first annually, then every other year, and finally every four years. On these trips, he and his associates were able to convey information to doctors and astronomers there who were thirsting for knowledge about the West. There was, therefore, direct though limited, contact with representatives of European civilization. Just as Tokugawa Confucians reaped the benefits of Qing philological and historical scholarship, Japanese students of Dutch studies profited from many of the modern scientific advances in contemporary Europe. Consequently, despite the restrictions imposed by national isolation, there was a considerable degree of openness and receptivity to East and West in the intellectual milieu of Tokugawa Japan.

Even so, one cannot fail to be struck by the extraordinary speed with which Dutch studies spread. That speed reflects both the intense curiosity of those Japanese who pledged themselves to this new exotic discipline and the enthusiasm with which they pursued it. Moreover, the seemingly unsystematic activities of the Dutch studies specialists belie a certain underlying regularity. All these elements – speed of diffusion, curiosity, enthusiasm, and selective approach – anticipate Japan's more ambitious, post-Restoration attempts to assimilate modern Western civilization.

In 1815, Sugita Gempaku published *Rangaku kotohajime* (The beginnings of Dutch studies), in which he recalled the circumstances under which he, Maeno Ryōtaku, and their associates had begun the formidable task of translating a volume of anatomical tables, *Tafel Anatomia (Ontleedkundige Tafelen)*, forty-three years earlier in 1771. It can be said that with that endeavour they initiated modern Japan's independent and eclectic assimilation of advanced Western civilization through the medium of books. Sugita decribed the speed with which Dutch studies subsequently spread and the strength of will displayed by its early proponents:

> At present, Dutch studies are in great fashion throughout Japan. Those who have decided to pursue them do so avidly, although the ignorant among the populace praise and admire these studies in greatly exaggerated terms.
>
> Reflecting upon the beginnings of Dutch studies, I realize that in those days, two or three friends and I decided to take them up almost on the spur of the moment. Yet close to fifty years have since elapsed, and how strange it is! When we began, I never in my wildest dreams thought that Dutch studies would achieve the popularity they enjoy today.
>
> It was only natural for Chinese studies to develop and prosper gradually here in Japan. After all, in ancient times the government dispatched scholarly missions to China; later, learned clerics were also sent to the continent where they studied under Chinese masters. In either case, after their return to Japan, such persons were placed in positions to teach high and low, nobility and commoners, alike. But that was not the case with Dutch studies ...[5]

Sugita, probably like other Japanese intellectuals with a similar historical consciousness, saw his own efforts at assimilating Western culture as sharply at variance with Japan's established methods of assimilating Chinese culture, which had been followed for over a millennium. He posited three principal methods through which a foreign civilization could be assimilated: (1) experience, observation, and study abroad; (2) instruction by foreign or Japanese teachers; and (3) books. Between AD 607 and 894, the Japanese court had sponsored over a dozen scholarly missions to China for the direct observation of and instruction in Sui and Tang culture. The contrast between these subsidized enterprises and Sugita's own humble efforts loomed large in his mind, for the sole medium of cultural assimilation accessible to him and his colleagues was books written in a language they could not read.

Despite these handicaps – the lack of official support and awesome linguistic difficulties – towards the end of his life, Sugita remarked that Dutch studies had developed like 'a drop of oil, which, when cast upon a wide pond, disperses to cover its entire surface,' a process that 'brings me nothing but jubilation'. The advances made by Dutch studies had now reached a point at which, as Sugita noted in 1815, 'every year new translations appear'.[6] With historical hindsight, we can add that the tide of translations from the Dutch in early nineteenth-century Japan may have been roughly comparable to the amount of translation from Japanese into Western languages a century-and-a-half later.

Sugita's jubilation was well founded: unlike the days when Japan had imported Chinese civilization, study in the West was out of the question, and devotees of Dutch studies could not even get instruction from fellow Japanese, much less from foreign teachers, except for the bits and pieces of information they could cull from Japanese interpreters who accompanied the Dutch East India Company representatives during their stays in Edo. Deprived of even the most elementary language training, Sugita and his associates had to begin their translation of *Tafel Anatomia* by substituting Japanese equivalents of foreign names for parts of the body that appeared on anatomical diagrams:

> For example, we spent a long spring day puzzling over such simple lines as 'An "eyebrow" is hair growing above the eye.' We sometimes stared at each other blankly from morning to dusk, unable to decipher a single line from a one-to two-inch passage of text.[7]

Nevertheless, they gradually overcame these difficulties by application and enthusiasm:

> Yet we believed that 'Man proposes, Heaven disposes' and persevered. We would meet six or seven times a month and devoted ourselves body and soul to the project. No one ever begged off on the scheduled meeting days; we all assembled without being prevailed upon to do so, and we would read and discuss the text together. 'Perseverance will prevail', we would reassure ourselves and pressed on.
>
> After a year or so, our command of vocabulary gradually increased, and we naturally discovered a great deal about conditions in Holland. Later on, we became capable of reading as much as ten or more lines of text per day if the particular passage was not too difficult.[8]

Sugita's satisfaction in recollecting these experiences lay in the fact that the cultural legacy of Dutch studies to subsequent generations of Japanese owed its existence to the determination and zeal displayed by this small group of pioneers.

In the 1860s, Dutch studies and the Dutch language were abandoned in favour of English, which soon became the primary Western language for Japanese intellectuals. This transition from Dutch studies to Western learning was depicted by Fukuzawa Yukichi in his autobiography in which he described his experiences in the foreign sector of Yokohama after the ports had been opened in 1859. Fukuzawa tried to speak Dutch with foreigners only to find to his dismay that communication was impossible. Undaunted, he made up his mind to 'devote himself to English'. Fukuzawa was a pioneer in the study of English and became an Enlightenment thinker who explained the development of Japanese history in Western terms. By emphasizing the importance of fundamental changes needed in Meiji Japan, he tended to slight Tokugawa achievements. Yet even Fukuzawa expressed his indebtedness to men like Sugita in the Dutch studies tradition. Having obtained a copy of Sugita's *Rangaku kotahajime,* Fukuzawa and Mitsukuri Shūhei (1825–86) sat opposite to each other and read and reread it. When they reached the passage that compared the way that those pioneers had set out on the translation of *Tafel Anatomia* to sailors 'drifting about in a boat without rudder or oar, helpless and baffled on a vast expanse of ocean', he wrote that they 'sobbed wordlessly until they came to the end'. Fukuzawa wrote: 'Each time we read this book we realize how great their toil must have been; we are amazed at their courage; we feel their singleness of purpose; and it is difficult for us to hold back the tears.'[9] Fukuzawa republished Sugita's book at his own expense in 1868, and in the foreword he related his feelings after having first read the work: 'It was like encountering an old friend, someone I thought was dead, reborn and well.' He wrote that the source of energy propelling Meiji Japan towards modernization could be traced to forerunners like Sugita and argued that 'the beginnings of knowledge of Western civilization existed' a century before his time among scholars on this small island in East Asia, that 'today's progress ... is not a product of blind chance.'[10]

The deciphering of *Tafel Anatomia* by Sugita and his associates illustrates Japan's positive response towards Western civilization. There are two explanations for this enthusiastic response. First, it reveals the Japanese intellectuals' unusually strong curiosity towards the outside world, and it shows that the value system to which they were committed did not emphasize intellectual self-sufficiency: to a large extent, alien doctrines and learning could be absorbed and accommodated. Second, the personal motivation that sustained the pioneers demonstrates both their intellectual curiosity and their pragmatism. Maeno Ryōtaku 'desired to make Dutch studies his life's work, to learn all there is to know about that language and thus to find out all there is to know about conditions in the West and to read numerous books',[11] whereas Nakagawa Jun'an 'had long been interested in what things were made of and wanted by this means to learn about Western products ...'[12] On the one hand, we discover an orientation of almost purely intellectual curiosity, and on the other, one of practicability, both driving people towards Dutch studies. In Sugita's own case, the motivation for translating *Tafel Anatomia* lay in his professional consciousness of being a physician. As he put it:

> First and foremost, I wanted to make manifest the fact that actual dissections performed on human bodies confirmed the accuracy of Dutch anatomical diagrams and disproved Chinese and Japanese theories. Then I wanted to apply the Dutch theories in clinical treatment and to make these available to other physicians in order to encourage the development of new techniques.[13]

Sugita's sense of mission had first been sparked by witnessing an autopsy performed at Kotsugahara in Edo in 1771. On the way home, he wrote, he discussed its results with Maeno and Nakagawa:

> What a revelation that day's demonstration had been! We were truly embarrassed to discover our ignorance. Each of us, who was responsible for serving our lord as a physician, proved to be totally ignorant of the basic anatomical structure of man, which is fundamental to medical science. It was a disgrace that we had been carrying on our duties all along in this state of ignorance.[14]

Some writers have tended to associate Dutch studies with a critical attitude towards feudal authority, but here we find one of its most devoted proponents troubled by the sense of 'disgrace' stemming from his unworthiness to 'serve his lord' properly. Such an ethos, emphasizing as Sugita did with the responsibilities of a physician's hereditary status, easily transforms itself into an occupational ethic. The intensity of this spirit – related also to *bushidō* – and the ease with which it could be transformed into an occupational ethic can be considered two key factors that made Japan's turn to the West possible at an early stage, thereby distinguishing the Japanese experience from that of other non-Western countries. We can trace the results of Japanese Dutch scholars' efforts in Tokugawa lexicography. Let us have a look at its significance in comparative perspective.

In the initial phase of contact between Western and non-Western peoples, most lexicography was a product of the burgeoning, expansive West. This is seen, for instance, in the *Vocabulario da Lingoa de Iapam* containing over thirty thousand entries compiled by the Jesuit João Rodriguez Tcuzzu in 1603. Later, however, non-Western peoples who perceived Europe to be 'advanced' and strove to 'catch up' with Western civilization seized this lexicographic initiative. The Japanese provide a good example. The growth of Dutch studies in Japan was ensured after 1796, when Inamura Sampaku (1758–1811) published a Dutch-Japanese dictionary, the *Edo Halma.* This was an adaptation of François Halma's eighty-thousand-word Dutch-French dictionary in which Inamura substituted Japanese translations for the French equivalents. In the era of early encounters with English-speaking peoples that followed, Dutch-English conversation books, English-Dutch dictionaries, and then English-language dictionaries were used. Webster's dictionary first reached Japan via the Perry squadron; and later, in 1860, Fukuzawa Yukichi and Nakahama Manjirō (1827–98) each brought back a copy from San Francisco. The first English-Japanese dictionary, the six-thousand-word *Angeria gorin taisei,* was compiled at the *bakufu*'s direction by the Nagasaki Dutch interpreter, Motoki Shōzaemon, in 1814; but Hori Tatsunosuke's *Ei-wa taiyaku shūchin jisho,*[15] containing over thirty thousand entries and published in 1862, received far greater use. Hori used entries and sample phrases and sentences from the English-Dutch portion of H. Picard's A *New Pocket Dictionary of the English-Dutch and Dutch-English Languages,* eliminated the Dutch definitions, and supplied Japanese equivalents from the *Nagasaki Halma,* a Nagasaki version of the *Edo Halma* that had more colloquial expressions. Thus the study of English developed from that of Dutch, and knowledge accumulated rapidly. Among the dictionaries compiled by Americans in Japan is the *Wa-ei gorin shūsei,* a work containing over twenty thousand words, published in 1867 by James Hepburn (1815–1911), a Presbyterian medical missionary who came to Japan in 1859. However, thereafter, almost all the best dictionaries, whether English-Japanese, Japanese-English, German-Japanese, Japanese-German, French-Japanese, Japanese-French, or Russian-Japanese, were compiled by Japanese.[16]

A nineteenth-century figure who perceived the significance of Tokugawa lexicography was Sakuma Shōzan (1811–64), a scholar of both Confucian and Western learning. Sakuma planned to publish a revised and enlarged edition of the *Edo Halma*, and to cover the expenses he borrowed twelve hundred *ryō* from his domain by pledging his own stipend of one hundred *koku* rice as collateral. Although this plan came to naught because the *bakufu* refused to grant permission, Sakuma's petition shows his perception of the importance and meaning of the enterprise he proposed:

> If only you would see this project as a way of laying the foundation for access to and mastery of proficiency in the arts and sciences, as a step toward adopting the strong points of countries on every continent in order to create a Japan forever able to maintain its autonomy in the world, then whatever criticism it might draw would be as inconsequential as the flapping of a mosquito's wings.[17]

The 'science' referred to in Sakuma's famous slogan, 'Eastern morality, Western science' is often taken to mean only 'technology', but in fact, his term has broader implications, including the arts and sciences that form the basis of that technology. This can be seen in comments he made to a correspondent:

> At present the learning of China and Japan is not sufficient; it must be supplemented and made complete by inclusion of the learning of the entire world. Columbus discovered a new world by 'investigating principle'; Copernicus worked out the theory of heliocentricity; and Newton recognized the truth of gravitational laws. Since these three great discoveries were made, all arts and sciences have been based on them – each is true, not one is false.[18]

Sakuma believed that Confucianism was fully compatible with Western military technology and hence that Chinese and Western doctrines were ultimately identical. To him, dictionary compilation was an indispensable means to acquire this fundamentally identical knowledge. In the petition cited earlier, he also stated:

> Nothing is more important to the conduct of war, nor is there anything more pressing in present-day coastal defense, than Sunzi's adage 'Know the enemy'. Hence, I would like to see all persons in the realm thoroughly familiar with the enemy's conditions, something that can best be achieved by allowing them to read barbarian books as they read their own language. There is no better way to enable them to do this than publishing this dictionary.

The compilation and publication of this dictionary thus symbolized Sakuma's desire to understand foreign civilization in a fundamental and comprehensive manner. He was also eager to disseminate such understanding among his countrymen. The assimilation of Western culture through such a process of enlightenment was pursued on a national scale by the Meiji government a few years later, but to Sakuma, it still seemed as though the task hinged entirely on the *bakufu*'s approval for publishing his laboriously brush-copied dictionary manuscript. Such was this Tokugawa intellectual's intensity on the eve of the Meiji Restoration.

What was then the cultural milieu that allowed development of Dutch studies? What were the specific trends of eighteenth-century intellectual life in Japan? Some Tokugawa intellectuals were aware of their ancestors' ability to adopt and adapt Chinese civilization; a millennium earlier, the Japanese had also thought of their land as existing on the outer fringes of a world cultural sphere. In a sense, nineteenth-century Japanese intellectuals needed only to transfer that centre from China to the West. In this regard, the Japanese consciousness and problems differed strikingly from those of China, and consequently Japanese thinkers were probably better equipped psychologically for assimilating Western culture than were their Chinese counterparts. Just as they had earlier studied Chinese civilization under the slogan 'Japanese spirit, Chinese learning', now they spoke of 'Japanese spirit, Western learning'.

The eighteenth-century pioneers in Dutch studies were fully aware of this parallel. Sugita Gempaku concluded his recollections of the growth of Dutch studies by asking: 'Was it not because our minds had already been trained through Chinese learning that Dutch studies were able to develop this rapidly?'[19] Moreover, the 'training' he had in mind had linguistic as well as attitudinal aspects. Unlike other East Asian peoples on the fringe of the Chinese cultural sphere, the Japanese early developed a method for adapting texts in classical Chinese to the syntactical rules of their own language, instead of reading classical Chinese as a foreign language. The result, known as *kambun* reading, was a complex and cumbersome procedure, but it involved rigorous intellectual training in translation that had as one consequence the nationalization of a foreign language.

Partly because of this and partly because of its relative isolation, Japan was never overwhelmed by Chinese – or Western – learning but retained a substantial cultural autonomy from which assimilation could be managed. Just enough could be learned about the outside world to whet the curiosity of men seeking knowledge and instil in them admiration for the West without totally absorbing them into the 'superior' culture. Given the physical isolation in which Tokugawa scholars of Dutch studies laboured, there was never any possibility of their identifying themselves completely with the alien culture; their admiration for the West was fated to be pursued along purely intellectual lines. This geographical limitation contributed to the emphasis on retaining and strengthening the 'Japanese spirit' while pursuing 'Western skills'. Hashimoto Sanai (1831–59), a leader of the Restoration movement, wrote that Japan should 'adopt mechanical devices and techniques from the West but retain the benevolence, righteousness, loyalty, and filial piety of Japan.'[20] Yokoi Shōnan (1809–69) agreed and urged his countrymen to 'make manifest the Way of Yao, Shun, and Confucius and to obtain a thorough knowledge of mechanical techniques from the West.'[21] Sakuma Shōzan also spoke of 'Eastern morality and Western techniques'. The future Meiji government accepted these goals under the slogan, 'Adopt what is best in the culture of Europe to compensate for shortcomings in that of Japan'.

One of the eighteenth-century intellectual trends that helped give rise to Dutch studies in Japan was empiricism. For the most part, the era was characterized by it, a development that arose also within Cheng-Zhu Confucianism. It was a grand system of speculative philosophy that provided the principal current of orthodox learning during the Edo period. I will limit the discussion only to the development of empirical trends in relation to Tokugawa medicine, the womb from which Dutch studies emerged. Japan first encountered Western civilization in the late sixteenth century, before the national isolation of Tokugawa times. In that warring era, survival of the fittest was the rule, and political leaders were keenly aware of the need to appropriate any new device that would increase their chances of achieving victory. They were utterly indifferent as to whether cultural accretions like firearms or surgery were of foreign or native origin. At that time, the Japanese learned early Western-style surgery through direct observation of Iberian practice rather than through written accounts, and a distinct school of 'southern barbarian' surgery developed. This school of surgery was dominant until it was superseded by techniques developed by students of Dutch studies, but it contributed almost nothing to the latter's emergence. The impetus behind Dutch studies lay elsewhere, in Tokugawa Confucianism.

Towards the end of the seventeenth century, a number of private scholars challenged the Cheng-Zhu Confucian school that then dominated the Tokugawa scholarly world. One of the foremost was Itō Jinsai (1627–1705) of Kyoto, who propounded the so-called

Ancient Learning (also known as the School of Ancient Meanings), which rejected medieval commentaries and sought the 'Way of the sages' by going directly back to the *Analects,* the *Mencius,* and other Confucian classics. Thus Jinsai's school may be considered a form of antiquarian revivalism. Slightly later, Ogyū Sorai (1666–1728), also an advocate of Ancient Learning, had an even greater impact on the contemporary intellectual scene. The influence of these teachings was felt beyond the field of Confucian scholarship. For example, Japanese learning (*kokugaku*) held that the pristine, 'true Japanese heart' could be discovered only by rejecting the 'spirit of China' that had come to muddy it in later ages and that this could best be done through studying the *Kojiki,* the *Manyōshū,* and other ancient Japanese classics.

Until the middle of the Edo period, Tokugawa medical thought was dominated by the Li-Zhu school of Chinese medicine that had developed under Li Dong-yuan and Zhu Dan-xi during the Jin and Yuan periods. It was a form of speculative philosophy that discussed human pathology in terms of *yin-yang,* the Five Elements, the Five Circulations, and the Six *qi.* However, under the influence of mid-Tokugawa Ancient Learning, a movement arose among non-government scholar-physicians to reject such speculative ideas as latter-day inventions and to return to the 'Way' that medicine had supposedly been practised in ancient China, as depicted in works such as *Shanghan lun.*[22] This movement was related to the School of Ancient Learning in its emphasis on the empirical. Gotō Konzan (1659–1733), who was an admirer of Itō Jinsai, sent one of his own disciples, Kagawa Shūan (1683–1755), to study at Jinsai's private academy. Under Kagawa, there evolved a form of Confucian medical thought that viewed Confucius' 'Way of the sages' as being basically identical with a 'Way of medicine'. According to Kagawa, the sages and worthies of antiquity were staunch in their reverence for empirical fact, and latter-day speculative philosophers had obfuscated that emphasis. The School of Ancient Method, as it came to be known, repudiated such latter-day accretions in favour of a return to the direct study of ancient Chinese medical texts.

The critical basis for this antiquarian revivalism was a positivism that insisted that hypotheses be verified. In time, this emphasis made its proponents sceptical of the validity of ancient as well as medieval medical texts. For example, one scholar, Nagatomi Dokushōan (1734–66), related the story of a Tang palace painter, Han Gan, who, when ordered by the emperor to paint a horse, was offered pictures done by former palace artists for reference. He replied: 'I have no desire to look at such pictures, for the horses kept in Your Majesty's stables will provide far better reference.' The physician, too, Nagatomi concluded, must work in this manner. The mere reading of texts was insufficient; the physician had to be free of preconceived notions, tend a real patient, conduct a close and direct examination, and use his own ingenuity to devise a cure. This process was known as *shinshi jikken* (personal examination and actual experience). Yoshimasu Tōdō (1702–73), who stressed this method of *shinshi jikken,* devoted himself to what is now called the 'symptomatic treatment' of diseases. In his book *Medical Diagnoses,* he wrote that 'principles' (*li*), or a priori speculative theories, are subjective, vary with the people who hold them, and lack established standards by which they can be confirmed or disproved. Diseases, on the other hand, have specific symptoms. In short, a doctor should not employ subjective theories without careful and accurate diagnoses of the diseases. Yamawaki Tōyō (1705–62) was long skeptical of the traditional anatomical diagrams used by Tokugawa specialists of Chinese medicine. With encouragement from his teacher, Gotō Konzan, he dissected an otter. Next, in 1754, after obtaining official permission, he performed an autopsy on an executed criminal and recorded his observations in a work entitled *Zōshi* (*Account of An Autopsy*). This work shocked the Tokugawa medical world. Yamawaki became the object of much censure and attack, but he steadfastly maintained his views. In his *Account,* he wrote:

> Theories [*li*] may be overturned, but how can real material things deceive? When theories are esteemed over reality, even a man of great wisdom cannot fail to err. When material things are investigated and theories are based on that, even a man of common intelligence can perform well.

Yamawaki and his colleagues brought to the autopsy a Dutch translation of a textbook on anatomy written by Johann Vesling, a German-born professor at Padua University. They were astonished to discover how closely the book's diagrams matched the corpse's organs. Yamawaki had originally viewed Vesling's diagrams with some disbelief because of their great discrepancy with prevailing Chinese medical theories, but when he compared these Western diagrams with actual human anatomy and verified their accuracy, he realized how outlandish the Chinese versions were. As he put it in his *Account*: 'He who treads the Way of fact reaches the same end though living ten thousand miles away. How can I suppress my admiration?' This reveals the idea that differences of nation or race are irrelevant to the quest for objective fact and the realization that the road to truth, which had been obscured in China since medieval times, paradoxically existed among those very Westerners normally considered 'barbarians'.

There was thus a clear relationship between the textual rigour of the School of Ancient Learning and the practical and empirical emphases of Dutch studies. The connection can also be traced in personal as well as intellectual terms. Kosugi Genteki, a student of Yamawaki Tōyō who witnessed the autopsy, was a domain physician in Obama and thus a colleague of Sugita Gempaku. Another Yamawaki disciple, Kuriyama Kōan, himself performed two autopsies in Hagi, the castle town of Chōshū, and Sugita, in 1771, managed to arrange and be present at an autopsy in Edo, which he described as the starting point of his dedication to truth through experiment. The accuracy of the anatomical tables of the Kulmus volume he had with him that day so impressed him that he and his colleagues resolved to translate the entire work.

Sugita's memoirs no doubt risk exaggerating the role of this event in a tradition already being transformed, but it should at the least be considered symbolic if not pivotal. There is a sense, moreover, in which Sugita and his contemporaries followed Ancient Learning to go a step beyond the promising beginning made earlier by Yamawaki. Despite the rhetoric of practicality and observation found in Yamawaki and his contemporaries, they tended in practice to restrict themselves to the wisdom of antiquity and refrained from pushing their ideas to their logical conclusions.[23] Sugita, however, in his *Nocturnal Dialogues with My Silhouette*, described how his reading of Ogyū Sorai's treatise on military science, *Kenroku gaisho*, motivated him to try to formulate a systematic study of medicine based on empirical methods:

> Sorai writes that true warfare is very different from what so-called masters of the art of war teach us. Topography may be hilly or flat, and armies may be strong or weak. One cannot make identical cut-and-dried preparations that will be right for all times and all places; one cannot discourse on victory and defeat in unvarying, stereotyped fashion prior to the commencement of an engagement ... Victory or defeat are determined on a case-by-case basis by constant study of strategic principles and by the capacities of great generals.[24]

In this way, military strategy discussed by the leading proponent of Ancient Learning was transferred to the realm of medicine, combined with systematic observation *(shinshi jikken),* and applied to the appropriation and utilization of Dutch medical and scientific lore by the pioneers of Dutch studies in late eighteenth-century Japan. A half-century later, the crisis in foreign relations found the emphasis shifting back to military concerns; ultimately it flowered in the Meiji government's policies of selective Westernization. These developments were, thus, of momentous significance for Japanese thought and Japan's assimilation of Western culture.

*Notes*

[1] The first five Chapters of Part II 'Japan's Turn to the West' were originally written in Japanese by the author. They were translated by Bob Wakabayashi and then revised by myself for Marius Jansen, ed.: *Cambridge History of Japan,* vol. 5 (Cambridge University Press, 1988). This time I have revised Part II and doubly enlarged Chapters 'First Translations from Western Literature', 'Reaction against Slavish Westernization' and 'Yearning for the West and Return to the East', and I have added two new Chapters: 'Rokumeikan: The Europeanization Fever in Comparative Perspective' and 'Benjamin Franklin and Fukuzawa Yukichi – Two Autographies Compared.' I have also changed some chapter titles. Except those of which sources are mentioned in notes, all quotations translated from Japanese in the first five chapters of Part II were originally Bob Wakabashi's. I wish to renew my thanks to Professor Wakabayashi for his kind help. I thank also the Cambridge University Press for permission to use these chapters.

[2] Nihon shiseki kyōkai, ed. *Ōkubo Toshimichi monjo,* vol. 9 *(Nihon shiseki kyōkai sōsho,* vol. 36) (Tokyo: Tokyo daigaku shuppankai, 1969), p. 347.

[3] Ōkubo Toshimichi, 'Seifu no teisai ni kansuru kengensho,' in *Ōkubo Toshimichi monjo,* vol. 3, p. 11.

[4] Yoshida Masaharu, 'Kempō happu made', in Oka Yoshitake, ed.: *Kindai Nihon seiji-shi* (Tokyo, Sōbunsha, 1962), vol. I, pp. 286–7.

[5] Odaka Toshio and Matsumura Akira, eds.: *Nihon koten bungaku taikei,* vol. 95: *Taionki, Oritakushiba no ki, Rantō kotohajime* (or *Rangaku kotohajime*) (Tokyo: Iwanami shoten, 1964), p. 473.

[6] Ibid. p. 515.

[7] Ibid. p. 493.

[8] Ibid. p. 495.

[9] Quoted in 'Rangaku kotohajime saihan no jo', in *Fukuzawa Yukichi zenshū* (Tokyo: Iwanami shoten, 1962), vol. 19, p. 770.

[10] Ibid.

[11] *Nihon koten bungaku taikei,* vol. 95, p. 498.

[12] Ibid. p. 499.

[13] Ibid.

[14] Ibid. p. 491–2.

[15] Hori changed the 'pocket' of Picard's pocket dictionary to a kimono sleeve; hence the character *shū*, as in *sode*.

[16] Professor N. I. Konrad's *Japanese-Russian Dictionary*, a possible exception, remains unsurpassed by Japanese efforts, a fact that probably indicates Japanese priorities in foreign-language study. What has been said about Western-language dictionaries applies equally to Chinese. Morohashi Tetsuji's dictionary of classical Chinese, *Dai kan-wa jiten*, published in 1960 by a publishing house that had to set the work a second time after its plant was destroyed in 1945, is recognized as standard in all countries where Chinese characters serve as the written medium. Like the Western-language dictionaries, this work represents an attempt to assimilate a superior foreign culture by a less developed civilization, but it nevertheless surpasses all similar lexicographical achievements in China itself.

[17] 'Haruma wo hangyō nite kaihan sen koto wo chinzu', in *Shōzan zenshū* (Tokyo: Shōbunkan, 1913), vol. 1, p. 128.

[18] 'Letter to Yanagawa Seigan,' dated 3/6/Ansei 5 (1858), in ibid. vol. 2, pp. 845–6.

[19] *Nihon koten bungaku taikei*, vol. 95, p. 505.

[20] 'Letter to Murata Ujihisa', dated 10/21/Ansei 4, in Nihon shiseki kyōkai, ed. *Hashimoto Keigaku zenshū*, vol. 2 *(Nihon shiseki kyōkai sōsho*, vol. 47) (Tokyo: Tokyo daigaku shuppankai, 1977), pp. 471–2.

[21] 'Letter to Nephews Studying in the West', in Nihon shiseki kyōkai, ed., *Yokoi Shōnan kankei shiryō*, vol. 2 *(Zoku Nihon shiseki kyōkai sōsho*, vol. 40) (Tokyo: Tokyo daigaku shuppankai, 1977), p. 726.

[22] *Shanghan lun* is a medical text written by Zhang Zhong-jing of the later Han dynasty. The oldest extent edition was compiled by Wang Shu-he of the Western Jin. Centuries later Lin Yi published a new edition.

[23] For developments in medicine and thought on the eve of the rise of *rangaku*, see Fujikawa Hideo, 'Kohōka to rangaku,' in Fujikawa Hideo, *Saitō shiwa* (Tokyo: Tamagawa daigaku shuppanbu, 1974), pp. 9–20.

[24] Sugita Gempaku, 'Keiei yawa,' (Nocturnal Dialogues with My Silhouette) in Fujikawa Yū et al. ed, *Kyōrin sōsho* (Kyoto: Shibunkaku reprint, 1971), vol. 1, p. 106.

# JAPANESE EXPERIENCE ABROAD

────────────□────────────

One of the striking phenomena of mid-nineteenth-century Japan is the strong desire of educated Japanese to see the outside world. With an eighty-year history of Dutch studies behind them, many Japanese grew dissatisfied with relying solely on books to learn about the West. Presented with the evidence of Perry's 'Black Ships' that Japan had fallen behind during its two-century absence from the stage of world history, many young men resolved to meet the challenge posed by technological superiority of the West by investigating Western civilization at its source. Yamaji Aizan described the late Tokugawa *zeitgeist* as a 'desire to speed to foreign shores and take up the great task of observing far-off lands.'[1] Miyake Setsurei, in his *History of Our Times,* wrote:

> Only the ignorant and indolent among the samurai were surprised upon learning of [Yoshida] Shōin's plan to visit America, for not a few like-minded men were making similar preparations. Ultimately his plan was implemented in the form of sending a *bakufu* warship to San Francisco in 1860.'[2]

Thus, the steam engines of Perry's Black Ships, considered symbolic of the West's superior technology, convinced Japanese of their country's inferiority; their 'consciousness of crisis' dictated that 'there is no more pressing need in our defence against the barbarians at present than "knowing the enemy".'[3] This realistic, empirical outlook made it a prime task to 'investigate enemy conditions,' a goal mirrored in the title of Fukuzawa Yukichi's best-seller, *Conditions in the West* (Seiyō jijō, 1866–69).

That this determination was shared by different sorts of men can be shown by comparing the cases of Yoshida Shōin and Niijima Jō.

At first glance, they seem an unlikely pair. Yoshida Shōin (1830–59) is known to history as a fiery nationalist and exponent of unquestioning loyalty to the Emperor. His fury at the bakufu's agreement to sign the humiliating unequal treaties led him into teaching and plotting so extreme that he was executed in the Ansei purge carried out by Ii Naosuke. His unwavering espousal of the imperial cause as the highest duty made him a rallying point and martyr for later nationalism and nationalists. As early as 1867, the Chōshū loyalist Takasugi Shinsaku, and as recently as 1970 the novelist Mishima Yukio, invoked his words in justifying ritual suicide in the national cause. Niijima Jō (1843–90), on the other hand, is known to his countrymen as an ardent Christian and Westernizer, a runaway from feudal jurisdiction who found protection, kindness and Christianity in America. He was educated at Amherst College and Andover Seminary, and returned to Japan to found its first Christian university (Dōshisha) in Kyoto, the ancient capital and heartland of Japanese Buddhism. Nevertheless, Yoshida and Niijima shared a basic receptivity and curiosity regarding the West as well as a great desire to learn in the hope of preparing themselves and their country to accept the challenge posed by the West.

Yoshida Shōin's encounter with the West came at the dawn of Japan's forced opening by the squadron of American Black Ships. Commodore Perry arrived in 1853, left President Millard Fillmore's letter requesting formal diplomatic relations, and sailed away with a warning that he would return for a reply in the spring of 1854. In the interim, Sakuma Shōzan counselled his young student Shōin that it would be worthwhile to try to leave Japan with the squadron when it returned in order to equip himself with direct knowledge of the West.

While Perry's ships were inspecting the harbour of Shimoda in April 1854, J. W. Spaulding, captain's clerk of the *Mississippi*, was ashore for a stroll one afternoon when two young men dressed as samurai approached him, ostensibly to examine his watch chain. Once within reach, one of them thrust a letter into the vest of the startled clerk. Flawlessly written in classical Chinese, which S. W. Williams, the American interpreter, could read, it stated: 'We have ... read in books, and learned a little by hearsay, what the customs and education in Europe and America are, and we have been for many years desirous of going over the "five great continents".' The exaggerated metaphors of the *kambun* document reveal the intensity of Shōin's desire to learn about the world outside Japan:

When a lame man sees others walking, he wishes to walk too; but how shall the pedestrian gratify his desires when he sees another one riding? We have all our lives been going hither to you, unable to get more than thirty degrees east and west, or twenty-five degrees north and south; but now when we see how you sail on the tempests and cleave the huge billows, going at lightning speed thousands and myriads of miles, scurrying along the five great continents, can it not be likened to the lame finding a plan for walking, and the pedestrian seeking a mode by which he can ride?[4]

The abortive effort of the two young men to secure passage on the *Mississippi* in the dead of night, before an answer could be given to this document, is well known. Perry felt it poor policy to help them break the laws of their government against travel overseas so soon after securing the treaty he had come to negotiate, and he reluctantly denied their request after discussing it with them through the interpreter on board. What should be noted, however, is the recklessness of the attempt and the intensity and, no doubt, naïveté of their behaviour. This disregard for personal danger and single-mindedness of purpose earned the warmhearted understanding of S. Wells Williams, the interpreter, which can be inferred from Shōin's *Account of a Spring Night,* Spaulding's *Japan Expedition,* and F. L. Hawks's *Narrative.*

Spaulding's account described the consequences for the two:

A few days afterward, some of our officers in their strolls ashore ascertained that there were two Japanese confined in a cage at a little barrack back of the town, and on going there they were found to be the persons who had paid the midnight visit to our ships, and they also proved to be my unfortunate friends of the letter. They did not appear greatly down-cast by their situation, and one of them wrote in his native character on a piece of board, and passed [it] through the bars of his cage, to one of our surgeons present...[5]

The officers of the American fleet discussed the possibility of intervening to save the men's lives, but the next time they went ashore, the two were nowhere to be seen. Rumour had it that they had been transferred to an Edo prison, and when an official they questioned gestured ominously with hand to throat, the Americans realized that the two had or would soon be executed. Spaulding, recalling that the writing on the letter that had been thrust into his vest appeared 'neat and sharply defined', concluded that the writer was surely 'a man of intelligence and taste,' and Hawks's *Narrative* account of the initial encounter concurs that

... the Japanese were observed to be men of position and rank, as each wore the two swords characteristic of distinction, and were dressed in the

wide but short trousers of rich silk brocade. Their manners showed the
usual courtly refinement of the better classes ...[6]

Clearly, the Americans were impressed by the courageous sense
of purpose shown by Shōin, convinced of his qualities, and sympathetic towards his fate. The affair no doubt served to convince them
all the more strongly of the justness of their mission to open Japan.

The message written on a small piece of wood that Shōin was
able to hand to the American naval surgeon who happened to pass
by his cage was described by Hawks as a 'remarkable specimen of
philosophical resignation under circumstances which would have
tried the stoicism of Cato'. It read in part:

> When a hero fails in his purpose, his acts are then regarded as those of a
> villain and robber ... while yet we have nothing wherewith to reproach our-
> selves, it must now be seen whether a hero will prove himself to be one
> indeed. Regarding the liberty of going through the sixty States [Japanese
> provinces] as not enough for our desires, we wished to make the circuit of
> the five great continents. This was our hearts' wish for a long time.
> Suddenly, our plans are defeated ... Weeping, we seem as fools; laughing,
> as rogues. Alas! for us; silent we can only be.[7]

Shōin lived another five years, during which he inspired a generation of Chōshū disciples in the academy that the domain
authorities permitted him to direct during his confinement. As he
explained to one such student, Shinagawa Yajirō:

> If one is loath to die at seventeen or eighteen, he will be equally reluctant
> at thirty, and will no doubt find a life of eighty or ninety too short. Insects
> of the field and stream live but half a year, yet do not regard this as short.
> The pine and oak live hundreds of years, yet do not regard this as long.
> Compared to the eternity of Heaven and Earth, both are ephemeral
> insects. Man's life-span is fifty years; to live seventy is a rarity. Unless one
> performs some deed that brings a sense of gratification before dying, his
> soul will never rest in peace.[8]

This was not to be; further plotting brought Shōin's extradition
to Edo and his execution in 1859. Shōin described himself as one
'who fails in every enterprise undertaken, who bungles every chance
for power and fortune'. All the schemes he concocted, not only his
trip to America, seemed to go awry. Yet his determination to know
the West and his fervent loyalism lived on in his students and caught
the eye of a sympathetic writer as early as 1882. Robert Louis
Stevenson learned of Yoshida Shōin through a student of his
Chōshū school, Masaki Taizō, who was studying at Edinburgh, and

the stories that Masaki told about his teacher became a chapter in Stevenson's *Familiar Studies of Men and Books*. Stevenson quoted Thoreau to the effect that 'if you can "make your failure tragical by courage, it will not differ from success"' and concluded that 'this is as much the story of a heroic people as that of a heroic man'.[9] Stevenson's other heroes in this volume possessed characteristics similar to those with which Japanese admirers have associated Yoshida Shōin: bravery, self-reliance, tenacity of will, a high sense of honour and fervent aspiration. They were qualities required by Japanese who resolved to travel to the West in late Tokugawa days, and they were surprisingly common.

Yoshida Shōin and Niijima Jō were part of the same late Tokugawa phenomenon, an urge to experience the West directly. Shōin's attempt was abortive partly because it was made too early, in 1854, and partly because he chose the official channels of Perry's fleet on its initial diplomatic mission. By contrast, Niijima's attempt came a decade later, in 1864, and through the private auspices of an American merchant ship. Moreover, during the ten intervening years, there had been much exchange and travel. The Tokugawa warship, *Kanrin maru* had sailed to the California coast to accompany the shogunal mission to Washington in 1860, the first of a series of ever-larger and evermore observant official missions to the West as treaty relations intensified. In 1862, the shogunate had sent Nishi Amane, Enomoto Takeaki and Tsuda Mamichi to Holland to study. In 1863, the domain of Chōshū violated shogunal law by sending Itō Hirobumi and Inoue Kaoru, students of Yoshida Shōin's, to study in England; and the southern domain of Satsuma was preparing a large mission of fourteen students to go to England in 1865. Knowledge of such travel usually spread to, at least, the families of those involved. When the Chōshū samurai (and later foreign minister) Aoki Shūzō visited the castle town of Nakatsu in Kyushu while Fukuzawa Yukichi was abroad as interpreter for one such official mission, Fukuzawa's mother was able to show him letters and photographs – the first Aoki had ever seen – from her distant son.

Nevertheless, individual travel was still quite different, and very dangerous. Niijima later described in English, still far from perfect, his eagerness to travel: 'Some day I went to the seaside of Yedo, hoping to see the view of the sea. I saw largest man-of-war of Dutch lying there, and it seemed to me a castle or a battery, and I thought too she would be strong to fight with enemy.'[10] The excitement felt by this late Tokugawa youth is apparent. Niijima was acutely aware of Japan's need to create a navy and of the important benefits to be had from seaborne trade.

Niijima was chosen by his domain of Annaka to study Dutch, and he learned to read books on natural science. ('I read through the book of nature at home, taking a dictionary of Japan and Holland.') He had studied at the *bakufu*'s Naval Training Institute for a time but found this inadequate and unsatisfying and decided that he must go overseas himself. Niijima was motivated by precisely the same simple-minded directness that Shōin had shown, and as in Shōin's case, Americans – the captain of the *Berlin,* who smuggled him out of Hakodate against instructions, and the captain of the *Wild Rover,* to which Niijima transferred in Shanghai and who accepted responsibility for him during the year-long voyage to Boston – found themselves drawn to him by the intensity of his passion. In Boston, the Alpheus Hardys, owners of the *Wild Rover,* after reading Niijima's poorly composed English explanation for coming to America, generously paid his school fees and supported him through his undergraduate education at Amherst College and his theological training at Andover Seminary.

When Niijima discovered that the captain of the *Berlin,* who had taken him on board, had been dismissed for having helped him leave Hakodate, he made the following diary entry:

> Ah, I feel torn with guilt for having caused that good man such grief. But what is done is done, and cannot be undone. In the future, when my schooling is finished, I will do all I can to repay each and every one of his kindnesses to me. Maybe then I can make up for a small part of my wrong-doing against him.[11]

Westerners could no longer be considered 'barbarians' by a man of such gratitude and conviction.

Individual Westerners, of course, could still provoke strong reactions. Niijima served as the captain's valet, 'cleaning his cabin, waiting on him, washing his cups and saucers, and caring for his dog' – duties that he could stoop to perform only because there were no other Japanese to watch him. Having been trained in etiquette in Annaka, Niijima was well equipped to minister to the captain's needs, and we may imagine that he did so splendidly; but his samurai pride was often gravely injured. On one occasion, he was reprimanded for not obeying directions given in English by a passenger whose services he had requested as a language teacher. An expert swordsman, Niijima raced back to his cabin, took his sword and prepared to cut down the passenger when he remembered his mission and stopped. No doubt such endurance and self-restraint were required more than once during the voyage.

After transferring to the *Wild Rover* at Shanghai, Niijima asked its captain to take him to America and presented him with the longer of his two samurai swords as a token of his gratitude. He also had the captain sell the shorter sword for $8.00 so that he might purchase a translation of the New Testament in classical Chinese. This captain, whom Niijima admired greatly, was unable to pronounce Niijima's Japanese name. He called the Japanese boy 'Joe'. In 1876, Niijima formally adopted 'Jō' as his first name. He later wrote his name 'Joseph Hardy Neesima' in English, using 'Hardy' to express his gratitude to the Boston shipowner couple who had cared for him and for whom he 'felt a greater sense of gratitude than for his own parents'. Niijima, the eldest son of his family, justified his violation of filial piety and his illegal departure from Japan in terms of serving his 'Father who art in Heaven'. He became a Christian, found a new father and mother in the Hardys and pursued his studies in America with total peace of mind.

In time, official Japanese policy turned to support what had been the goals of Niijima's decisions for disobedience and flight. When the Iwakura mission came to the United States in 1871, Niijima was still studying in the United States. He was asked to serve as official interpreter for his country's highest officials, and upon his return to Japan in 1874, Niijima was able to win the confidence and help of high officials like Kido Takayoshi (a member of the Iwakura mission) in gaining permission to found his Christian college in Kyoto. By then, Japan's policy of 'civilization and enlightenment' seemed virtually indistinguishable from Niijima's personal mission to convert his fellow Japanese to Christianity. At that time, Niijima clearly had a linear view of progress, and he saw Westernization, civilization and Christianization as a single goal to be sought. As he put it in an appeal for support for his college in 1884:

> It is the spirit of liberty, the development of science and the Christian morality that have given birth to European civilization ... We cannot therefore believe that Japan can secure this civilization until education rests upon the same basis. With this foundation the State is built upon a rock ...[12]

Two points emerge from these two dramatically different careers. The first is that Yoshida Shōin, no less than Niijima Jō, began his study of the West with a warm, optimistic view of it, whose strengths he proposed to appropriate for his backward but beloved country. The second is that Niijima Jō, just like Yoshida Shōin, broke the national law forbidding travel abroad in the same conviction that he was contributing to the 'foundation of the state', though he committed himself to the West totally in terms of personal relations and spiritual beliefs.[13]

Yoshida Shōin and Niijima Jō were not the only Japanese longing to experience the West directly; high-ranking officials in the very *bakufu* that prohibited travel to foreign lands strongly desired to see the West with their own eyes and create a navy equal to those of Western nations. As early as 6 February, 1858, Japanese representatives negotiating the Treaty of Amity and Commerce between the United States and Japan were reported by the American consul, Townsend Harris,

> [to have] proposed, if I [Harris] was willing, to send an ambassador in their steamer to Washington via California for that purpose! I told them nothing could possibly give me greater pleasure. That, as the United States was the first power that Japan ever made a treaty with, I should be much pleased that the first Japanese Ambassador should be sent to the United States.[14]

Japanese documents record this incident as follows: 'Your nation has sent a total of three missions (including this one) to obtain this treaty. Now that it has been concluded, would it be possible for us to send a mission of our own to Washington for purposes of exchanging the documents?'[15]

Iwase Tadanari, who made this statement, probably did so in the hope of being sent himself, but two years of political upheaval, which included the Ansei purge, elapsed before the project was realized. Finally, in 1860, Shimmi Masaoki was selected as chief ambassador ('due to my father's achievements', as he put it); Muragaki Norimasa was deputy ambassador; and Oguri Tadamasa was superintendent and inspector (*metsuke*). Muragaki, a man of gentle disposition, left the detailed *Kōkai nikki* (Voyage diary) in which he described his feelings when he was summoned to Edo Castle and informed of his appointment:

> Although we did dispatch 'official envoys' to Tang China in ancient times, that neighboring land was only a strip of water away; but America lies a myriad miles beyond our Divine Land, and when it is daytime there, it is nighttime here.
>
> I humored [my daughters, boasting,] 'a man could achieve no greater honor than to assume this heavy, unprecedented responsibility and thereby attain renown throughout the five continents.' But on second thought I realized, 'a foolish man like myself accepting this first of all missions to a

foreign land? Should I fail to execute the shogunal decree, our Divine Land will suffer humiliations untold.' Just then, the moon was shining so clear and bright that I felt moved to a toast in solemn thanks for shogunal confidence:

> Henceforth foreigners as well
> will gaze
> upon the moon
> of our Japan.[16]

The tension in this poem contrasts with the following, which Muragaki composed upon his arrival in San Francisco:

> Foreign lands as well,
> lie beneath the same sky.
> Gaze upward and behold
> the mist-veiled spring moon.

Clearly, the sense of self-importance enabling Muragaki to carry out his duties had weakened. Finally, the following poem expressed his sentiments when he parted with the captain and crew of the *Powhatan* in Panama:

> Though a glance reveals
> that they are foreigners,
> the sincerity of heart they display
> differs not from our own.[17]

Thus Muragaki expressed his appreciation to the American crew. After travelling with them, he had discovered the universality of human nature.

After 'the Tycoon's envoys' ratified the Treaty of Amity and Commerce between the two nations in Washington with Louis Cass, President James Buchanan's secretary of state, they made their way to New York. In his diary, Muragaki described in detail their welcome there on 28 April, 1860. Walt Whitman (1819–92) also described the festivities in his 'A Broadway Pageant'. The poem describes not only Broadway, which on that day 'was entirely given up to foot-passengers and foot-standers', but also the joy of seeing the union of East and West and the oneness of the universe.

The welcome received by the members of the mission became known throughout Japan after their return home, and the mistaken image of Westerners as barbarians was modified, albeit gradually and among a limited number of intellectuals. In Yokoi Shōnan (1809–69)'s remote Kumamoto country school, lectures on the *Analects* were revised. Shōnan's gloss on the first entry reads:

[*Analects*]: 'Is it not a joy to have friends come from afar?'
[Shōnan's gloss]: The phrase 'have friends' means that when we appreciate learning and are eager to study, if we voluntarily approach, become intimate with, and speak to a man of virtuous repute whether he lives near or far away, that person will as a matter of course confide in us and become intimate with us in return. This is what is meant by the principle of 'feeling and response' (*kannō*). The term *friends* is not limited to scholar-friends. When we study to adopt the good points of any person, all men in the world are our friends.[18]

Then this scholar-statesman cited recent historical developments and advocated revising Japan's international relations on the basis of universal brotherhood:

> Viewed from a wider perspective, this principle of 'feeling and response' may be witnessed in the warm reception extended by the Americans to the recent bakufu embassy sent to their land. Their cordiality was deep indeed. By extending this meaning [of friends] to all people in the world, and not just to those in Japan, they are all our friends.

Because sentiments of xenophobia shouting 'Expel the Barbarians' were intense in Kumamoto domain, a feigned champion of righteousness could have cut an imposing figure by dancing to this tune of the times. But in Shōnan's lecture notes, we see a different figure, that of a Japanese thinker responding in kind to the hand of friendship offered by Whitman and other Americans. Until after the Russo-Japanese War, when American attitudes towards Japan began to change, the Japanese people felt a friendliness towards Americans that differed from their feelings towards other Western powers.

Some people in the first *bakufu* embassy played a significant role upon their return. Oguri Tadamasa refined his knowledge while in the United States. After returning to Japan, he served as commissioner for foreign affairs (*gaikoku bugyō*), and then naval commissioner (*kaigun bugyō*), exercised his capabilities in finance, sought assistance from France and built the Yokosuka foundry and shipyard. After the *bakufu*'s defeat at Toba-Fushimi in 1868, Oguri opposed concessions by the shogun, was captured and executed.

However, retrospectively, the most famous member of this embassy was on an auxiliary vessel, the *Kanrin maru,* which was the first Japanese ship to cross the Pacific. Fukuzawa Yukichi (1835–1901), then a young student of Dutch, requested and received permission to escort Kimura Yoshitake on this trip to San Francisco. The chapter of his *Autobiography* entitled, 'I Join the First Mission to

America', contains many interesting episodes, but perhaps the most surprising of these is that his reading of Dutch books and scientific training at the Ogata school in Osaka had given him enough of a background in natural science to facilitate his understanding of the explanations of the latest inventions made in America. By contrast, 'things social, political and economic proved most inexplicable'. For example, when he asked 'where the descendents of George Washington might be,' an American replied, 'I think there is a woman who is directly descended from Washington. I don't know where she is now.' The answer was 'so casual as to shock' this Japanese, who had more or less equated the social positions of Tokugawa Ieyasu and George Washington, both of whom had founded the political systems then existing in Japan and the United States.[19]

Katsu Kaishū (1823–99), the captain of the *Kanrin maru,* was originally a low-ranking Tokugawa official, but he rose to the highest positions of authority within the *bakufu* and ultimately became the person responsible for surrendering Edo Castle to the Restoration forces. Immediately after returning to Japan from this mission, Katsu earned the rancour of his colleagues by asserting that unlike the situation in Japan, all men in positions of leadership in America possessed leadership capacity. In the late Tokugawa era, knowledge of the West gradually proved effective in criticizing the existing order for its inability to deal satisfactorily with the crises confronting Japan.

After this first mission abroad, the bakufu sent large and small embassies abroad each year or every other year until its demise in 1868. The second embassy, led by Takeuchi Yasunori in 1862, toured the states of Europe to seek approval for postponing the opening of four additional treaty ports. The third mission, to France, was led by Ikeda Naganobu in a futile effort to secure the closing of Yokohama as a port. Shibata Takenaka led the fourth mission, which went to France and England in 1865 to negotiate conditions for constructing the Yokosuka foundry and shipyard. The fifth toured Europe and headed for Russia in 1866 when its chief ambassador, Koide Hidezane, conducted negotiations to establish the boundary between Japan and Russia on Sakhalin (Karafuto). The sixth mission, headed by the shogun Tokugawa Keiki's personal representative, Tokugawa Akitake, attended the Paris World's Fair in 1867. This last embassy was entrusted with the secret mission of persuading France to increase its aid to the *bakufu,* and it was still in Europe when the *bakufu* collapsed in 1868.[20]

Although these 'envoys of the Tycoon' had specific diplomatic assignments for dealing with the domestic situation or foreign relations at the time of their appointment, intentionally or not, they also made important contributions to Japan's study and assimilation of Western civilization. In addition, when we consider the students sent to Europe by the *bakufu* and (illegally) by the domains of Chōshū, Satsuma, or Hizen, we realize that the movement to study 'in barbarian lands', launched by Yoshida Shōin in 1854, had expanded and developed to the *bakufu* or national level. If we include the crew of the *Kanrin maru* on the first *bakufu* mission abroad, over three hundred Japanese travelled to foreign shores before the Meiji period.

Each of these missions investigated the institutions and civilization of the nations to which it was dispatched, but the second led by Takeuchi Yasunori was the most thorough and systematic, having been instructed 'to pay particular attention to politics, school administration and military systems'. Fukuzawa Yukichi, Matsuki Kōan (Terashima Munenori), Mitsukuri Shūhei, and other students of Western learning recorded their observations in pamphlets, entitled 'An Investigation of England', 'An Investigation of France', and 'An Investigation of Russia'. On the Takeuchi mission, Fukuzawa, who had already been to America two years earlier, did more than gaze at Europe with the bedazzled eyes of a tourist; he had discerned the inevitability of the sociopolitical transformation that would soon take place in Japan and began to see himself as an enthusiastic 'engineer of civilization'. Thus the beginning of Fukuzawa's enlightenment activities in Meiji times can be gleaned from his travel in Tokugawa service.

Fukuzawa's *Account of My Voyage to the West* and *Notes on My Voyage to the West* are full of memos scribbled in a hotchpotch of Japanese, Dutch, English and French. A glance at these works shows Fukuzawa to be a virtual walking antenna, eager to absorb any and all information in these foreign lands. Whereas other Japanese became caught up in the small facets of Western civilization, Fukuzawa sought to integrate these facets and observe the overall organization that made this civilization function. For example, his colleagues might admire the size of a locomotive, note how fast the train ran, or measure the width and height of its rails. But Fukuzawa went well past such concerns; his interests led him to investigate the composition of railway companies, their banking activities, or the joint control enjoyed by England and France over Egypt's railways.

In short, he tried to grasp not only the technology but also the social aspects of Western civilization. In his *Autobiography,* he wrote:

> I did not care to study scientific or technical subjects while on this journey, because I could study them as well from books after I returned home. But I felt that I had to learn the more common matters of daily life directly from the people, because Europeans would not describe them in books as being too obvious. Yet to us those common matters were the most difficult to comprehend.

So while in Europe, 'whenever I met a person whom I thought to be of some consequence, I would ask him questions and would put down all he said in a notebook ...'[21] After returning home, Fukuzawa organized the notes he had taken during these question-and-answer sessions, checked them against information found in books that he had bought abroad, and published them from 1866 to 1869 under the title *Conditions in the West* (Seiyō jijō).

Fukuzawa wrote the following account of one of these investigations in his *Autobiography:*

> A perplexing institution was representative government. When I asked a gentleman what the 'election law' was and what kind of a bureau the Parliament really was, he simply replied with a smile, meaning I suppose that no intelligent person was expected to ask such a question. But these were the things most difficult of all for me to understand. In this connection, I learned that there were bands of men called political parties – the Liberals and the Conservatives – who were always fighting against each other in the government.
>
> For some time it was beyond my comprehension to understand what they were fighting for, and what was meant, anyway, by 'fighting' in peacetime. 'This man and that man are enemies in the house,' they would tell me. But these 'enemies' were to be seen at the same table, eating and drinking with each other. I felt as if I could not make much out of this. It took me a long time, with some tedious thinking, before I could gather a general notion of these separate mysterious facts. In some of the more complicated matters, I might achieve an understanding five or ten days after they were explained to me. But all in all, I learned much from this initial tour of Europe.[22]

*Conditions in the West,* the fruit of such labours, was the first systematic account of the structure of Western civilization written by a Japanese, and it was phrased in language that anyone could understand. In one sense, it was designed to heighten Japan's appreciation of the West, but in another, it provided a vision of the future Meiji state as envisioned through Fukuzawa's reformism. Thus, the *bakufu* missions abroad greatly contributed to the building of Meiji

Japan by teaching numerous Japanese about the West and producing popular best-sellers such as Fukuzawa's *Conditions in the West*
and Nakamura Masanao's translation of Samuel Smiles's *Self-Help*.
The Meiji Restoration altered Japan's political leadership totally and
strengthened Japan's resolve to learn from the West that was already
forming by 1868. The greatest of all the official missions followed
the Restoration. On 23 December 1871, the new Meiji government
dispatched Ambassador-Plenipotentiary Iwakura Tomomi to the
United States and Europe as the head of a forty-eight-member delegation that took with it fifty-nine students of the ex-samurai class,
five of whom were women.

At this point, we should mention the subsequent course of anti-
foreign sentiment told by Fukuzawa at the end of the chapter 'I Join
the First Mission to America'. On his way back to Japan in 1860,
Katsu Kaishū playfully displayed on board the *Kanrin maru* the
Western umbrella he had bought overseas. When he asked, 'What
would happen if I tried to use this in Japan?' other members of the
delegation cautioned him not to invite assassination. In 1862, when
Fukuzawa returned from his second trip, cry for 'Expel the barbarians' had become more intense. As a student of Western learning,
Fukuzawa lived in constant fear of being cut down by xenophobic
extremists, and for ten years he refused to go out after dark,
choosing instead to concentrate on translations and his own
writing.[23] But by 1871, this sentiment had spent its force. The
appearance among the members of the Iwakura mission of seven-
year-old Tsuda Umeko, carrying a doll, symbolized the return of
peace. The idea of a girl studying overseas would have been
unimaginable before the Restoration. After her long sojourn in the
US, Tsuda returned to Japan and founded what later became
Tsudajuku College for Women, an institution that along with
Fukuzawa's Keiō University and Niijima's Dōshisha made important contributions to private higher education in modern Japan.

We can only marvel at the new Meiji government's stability,
which allowed it to send the Iwakura mission to America and
Europe for such a long period of time, even allowing for the fact
that civil war had ended and peace had been restored. Only four
years after its access to power, the new government abolished the
old domains and provinces of Tokugawa Japan and forced through
the establishment of a modern prefectural system. Then only four
months after that, leaders such as Iwakura Tomomi, Kido
Takayoshi, Ōkubo Toshimichi, and Itō Hirobumi went abroad and,

extending the originally planned length of their overseas stay by almost a full year, returned to Japan on 13 September 1873, after a tour that had lasted 631 days. The Iwakura mission's ostensible objective was to revise the unequal treaties ratified and exchanged in Washington by the first Tokugawa mission to America in 1860, but its members' real intention was to discover conditions in the West and adapt these to Japan in order to create a new Meiji state. The Meiji leaders realized that to revise the unequal treaties, they would have to restructure Japan and put it on a par with Western states, which meant reforms of domestic laws and institutions to bring them into line with those of the Western powers. The Iwakura mission was larger than the ones sent by the bakufu, but its purpose and task were essentially the same: to study and learn from the West. One piece of evidence for this continuity of purpose can be found in the embassy's membership. Although this time its leaders were court nobles and prominent power-holders from the domains that had emerged victorious in the Restoration wars, the secretarial staff supporting these leaders, however, included many veteran diplomats, such as Tanabe Taichi, who had served under the *bakufu* and were knowledgeable about or had actually travelled to the West.

The mission looked at chambers of commerce, schools for the deaf and dumb, museums, shipyards, biscuit factories, girls' schools, prisons, telegraph offices, army maneuvers – all at a whirlwind pace. Kume Kunitake, a student of Chinese learning, went as scribe and published *A True Account of the Observations of the Ambassadorial Mission to America and Europe,* which describes the embassy's brisk day-to-day routine:

No sooner had our train arrived and we had unloaded our baggage at the hotel than our tour began. During the daytime we rushed about from place to place, viewing machines that peeled and locomotives that roared. We stood amidst the acrid smell of steel with smoke billowing around us and became covered with soot and dirt. Returning to our hotel at dusk, we barely had time to brush off our dirty clothes before the hour of our banquet approached. At the banquet we had to maintain a dignified manner; if invited to the theatre, we had to strain eyes and ears to follow what took place on stage, and all of this led to exhaustion. No sooner had we retired at night, than morning greeted us with an escort sent to guide us around a factory. In this way, strange sights and sounds filled our eyes and ears; our spirits sagged and our bodies were exhausted by all the invitations we received to this and that event. Though we might have wished to drink a cup of water or stretch out and nap with bent elbow for a pillow, we could not, for any personal slovenliness on our part would constitute a lack of propriety in negotiations between Japan and foreign nations.[24]

The daily schedule of Ōkubo Toshimichi, who concentrated his investigations on industry and economic systems, no doubt resembled this. He questioned factory foremen, sought advice from legal scholars, exchanged speeches with city mayors and discussed issues with the foreign ministers of various governments. In London, he experienced a blackout caused by striking electrical workers seeking higher wages and thus discovered the serious effects that labour disputes might have. He toured the East End after sunset to see the misery and wretchedness lurking beneath the surface of modern Western 'civilization'. Ōkubo concluded that 'the prosperity of English cities occurred after the invention of the steam engine', and Kume noted that 'the contemporary phenomenon of wealth and population in European states presented itself after 1800 and has become pronounced only in the last forty years'. On the one hand, the members of the mission marvelled at the cumulative nature of civilization in Europe, saying that 'the light of civilization shines because knowledge has been accumulated through the ages', but at the same time, they braced themselves and stirred their often-flagging spirits by realizing that the gap between Japan and the West, which had just experienced the Industrial Revolution, could be bridged. Thus, they resolved to overtake the West.

Like Fukuzawa's *Conditions in the West,* Kume's *True Account* was organized according to individual countries. Japanese thinkers ranked Western nations according to their relative 'superiority' or 'inferiority'. The scholars of Dutch learning had already discovered that Dutch medical texts were mostly translations from German. As a matter of fact, their first translation into Japanese of a Western medical science, *Tafel Anatomia,* was already a Dutch translation of work on anatomy by the German doctor Kulmus. Japanese were able to discern and learned of Germany's superiority in the field. In similar fashion, the Japanese, through their study of books, through travelling abroad, and through advice obtained from foreign teachers, chose to assimilate the best that each particular Western nation had to offer. Fukuzawa challenged his countrymen to turn away from scholars of Chinese learning, arguing that they were so oblivious to world developments as to be 'little more than rice-consuming dictionaries,' and to adopt Western culture, which was based on practicality. By the same token, he himself abandoned Dutch for English in 1859, after acknowledging the superior material civilization of the Anglo-Saxon nations. The Japanese modeled themselves after England for industrial and naval development; Prussia, which defeated France in 1871, provided a model for military organization; France offered the model of its centralized police system and educational and legal structures; and the United States of America stimulated agricultural development in the northernmost island of Hokkaido. The Iwakura mission found in Prussia a model of a late-developing modernizer that seemed particularly appropriate to emulate. With regard to Prussia, which then was exporting agricultural products to obtain the capital necessary to develop its mining and industry, Kume wrote:

> In terms of the determining features of national policy, it (Prussia) actually bears a close resemblance to Japan, and there is more to be gained from studying the policies and customs of this country than conditions in Britain and France.[25]

It was only natural for the Meiji Japanese to turn to North America and Western Europe rather than to Asian countries in formulating plans to modernize their nation rapidly, and they were wise to select the strong points of each Western nation to further this process. Their selectiveness, based on considerations of efficacy, seems totally different from the traditional Confucian view of a world order centred on China.

Japan's knowledge of and experience with the West may seem to have progressed further during the Taishō and Shōwa eras than during the Meiji. But on closer examination, we find that at least with regard to Japan's leaders, their knowledge of foreign countries did not improve qualitatively and quantitatively. The 'elder statesmen of the Restoration', as they later were called, were on the one hand raised in accordance with traditional Tokugawa values, but at the same time, they also knew a great deal about the West. The Restoration activists exercised a shrewd sensibility in their contact with foreigners. For the Meiji government leaders, the Iwakura mission provided first-hand contact with the Western world. For most of them, it was their first trip, although Ito had gone to England as a young Chōshū student. What mattered was that the experience shared by Iwakura, Ōkubo, Kido, and Itō produced a consensus on Japan's future course. These men were convinced of the need for domestic reforms first of all, and upon returning home in 1873, they canceled the plans for putting pressure on Korea that had been prepared by the 'caretaker' government in their absence. This was the first case of a split in views on national policy engendered by the experience or lack of experience of the outside world and the knowledge or ignorance of foreign affairs.

## Notes

[1] Yamaji Aizan: 'Niijima Jō ron', in Yamaji Aizan: *Kirisutokyō hyōron, Nihon jimminshi* (Tokyo: Iwanami shoten, 1966), p.44.

[2] Miyake Setsurei: *Dōjidaishi* (Tokyo: Iwanami shoten, 1949), vol. 1, pp.2–3.

[3] Ibid.

[4] Yamaguchi-ken kyōikukai, ed.: *Yoshida Shōin zenshū* (Tokyo: Iwanami shoten, 1936), vol. 10, p. 876. Also in Francis L. Hawks: *Narrative of the Expedition of an American Squadron to the China Seas and Japan: Performed in the Years 1852, 1853, and 1854, Under the Command of Commodore M. C. Perry, United States Navy, the Official Account* (Washington, D.C.: Beverley Tucker, Senate Printer, 1856), p.420.

[5] Hawks: *Narrative*, pp. 884–5.

[6] Ibid.

[7] *Yoshida Shōin zenshū*, vol. 10, pp. 874–5; and Hawks: *Narrative*, pp. 422–3.

[8] 'Letter to Shinagawa Yajirō', dated circa 4/Ansei 6, in *Yoshida Shōin zenshū*, vol. 6, p. 318.

[9] Robert Louis Stevenson: *Familiar Studies of Men and Books* (London: Heinemann) p. 114. The article appeared in the March 1880 issue of *Cornhill Magazine*.

[10] A. S. Hardy: *Life and Letters of Joseph Hardy Neesima* (Boston: Houghton Mifflin, 1892), p. 6.

[11] Diary entry, 9/13/Meiji 1, in *Niijima Jō sensei shokan shū zokuhen* (Kyoto: Dōshisha kōyūkai, 1960), p. 239.

[12] 'Meiji Semmon Gakkō setsuritsu shushi,' in *Niijima sensei shokanshū* (Kyoto: Dōshisha kōyūkai, 1942), pp. 1158–9.

[13] As for the attitudes towards America of other mid-nineteenth-century Japanese travelers, see Part III Chapter 2 'Uchimura Kanzō and America'.

[14] M. E. Cosenza, ed.: *The Complete Journal of Townsend Harris* (Rutland, Vt: Tuttle, 1959) p. 531.

[15] Dated t 2/23/Ansei 4, in *Dainihon komonjo: Bakumatsu gaikoku kankei monjo* (Tokyo: Tokyo teikoku daigaku, 1925), vol. 18.

[16] Muragaki (Awaji no Kami) Norimasa, *Kōkai nikki* (Tokyo: Jiji shinsho, 1959). This work was translated by Helen Uno as *Kōkai Nikki: The Diary of the First Japanese Embassy to the United States of America* (Tokyo: Foreign Affairs Association of Japan, 1958). That translation has been modified here.

[17] Uno: *Kōkai Nikki*, pp. 38, 51.

[18] Yokoi Tokio, ed.: *Shōnan ikō* (Tokyo: Min'yūsha, 1889), pp. 447–8.

[19] 'Seiyō jijō', in *Fukuzawa Yukichi zenshū* (Tokyo: Iwanami shoten, 1959), vol. 7, p. 95. Also Eiichi Kiyooka, trans.: *The Autobiography of Fukuzawa Yukichi* (Tokyo: Hokuseido Press, 1948), p. 125.

[20] Haga Tōru discusses these embassies in *Taikun no shisetsu* (Tokyo: Chūōkōronsha, 1968).

[21] *Fukuzawa Yukichi zenshū*, vol. 7, p. 107; *The Autobiography*, pp. 142–3.

[22] *Fukuzawa Yukichi zenshū*, vol. 7, pp. 107–8; *The Autobiography*, p. 144.

[23] Ibid, in the chapter entitled 'Ansatsu no shinpai' (In fear of assassination).

[24] Kume Kunitake ed.: *Bei-ō kairan jikki* (Tokyo: Iwanami shoten, 1977), vol.1 p. 12. The English translation here quoted is by Bob Wakabayashi. Kume Kunitake: *Bei-ō kairan jikki*, was translated into English by Martin Collcutt et al: Kume: *The Iwakura Embassy: A true account of the Ambassador Extraordinary & Plenipotentiary's Journey of Observation Through the United States of America and Europe* (Tokyo: The Japan Documents 5 vols. 2002. See the same passage, vol. 1. p. 6.) For detailed information on the Iwakura mission, see Tanaka Akira, *Iwakura shistetsu dan* (Tokyo: Kōdansha, 1977); and Haga Tōru, *Meiji ishin to Nihonjin* (Tokyo: Kōdansha gakujutsu bunko, 1980), pp. 219–43. For the Iwakura mission, see Marlene Mayo, 'The Western Education of Kume Kunitake 1871–1876' *Monumenta Nipponica* 28 (1973). The daily experiences and observations of Kido Takayoshi can be followed in Sidney D. Brown and Akiko Hirota, trans.: *The Diary of Kido Takayoshi*, vol. 2: 1871–1874 (Tokyo: University of Tokyo Press, 1985).

[25] Kume: *Bei-ō kairan jikki*, vol. 3, p. 298; Kume: *The Iwakura Embassy: A true account of the Ambassador Extraordinary & Plenipotentiary's Journey of Observation Through the United States of America and Europe*, vol. 3, pp. 291–2.

# TEACHERS OF 'ARTS AND SCIENCES': FOREIGNERS IN MEIJI GOVERNMENT EMPLOY

———————□———————

J apan's use of foreign employees in the late Tokugawa and early Meiji periods presents an interesting and useful perspective on the larger turn to the West, and it was also in some sense prophetic of the role of foreign advisers in the reconstruction of Japanese institutions after World War II. The relative success with which the American Occupation of Japan completed its work contrasts with the problem of American counsellors in their efforts to channel reform in other developing countries in the late 1940s and 1950s. But when considered with regard to Japan's use of foreign advisers in the nineteenth century, it suggests that much of that 'success' was actually Japan's. The Meiji government and society, like those of developing states in the twentieth century, were intensely nationalistic, but the country's skill in using and then replacing outside foreign employees is too often forgotten.

The rush with which Japan adopted foreign institutions and customs following the Meiji Restoration sometimes gave Westerners (and not a few conservative Japanese) the impression that Japan was scrapping its entire traditional civilization to appropriate all the material and spiritual attributes of modern Western states. Of course, much of this programme was tactical. Britain's defeat of China, followed by the extension of unequal treaties to Japan in the wake of Commodore Matthew Perry and Townsend Harris, filled Japan's leaders with apprehension. Japanese felt themselves exposed to a military threat and concluded that if they were to enter the arena known as the family of nations, they, too, must equip themselves with the weaponry possessed by the Western Powers. They also realized that the basis of Western power was not limited to weaponry; to the extent that such power was based on a civil society that had undergone the economic and social transformations of the Industrial Revolution, Japan's quest for power also entailed the building of political and social institutions based on the Western model.

Although the overthrow of the Tokugawa *bakufu* was conducted under the slogan 'revere the Emperor, expel the barbarians!' (*sonnō jōi*) the Meiji regime that followed immediately implemented a policy of 'open the country, establish friendly relations' (*kaikoku washin*). After the policy of 'expulsion' of the 'barbarians' was rejected in light of the recognition of the international situation, the same nationalism that produced the slogan was transformed into a quest for 'civilization and enlightenment'. It was likewise for 'reverence' for the sovereign: The overthrow of the *bakufu* resulted not in a restoration of direct imperial rule as it had existed in antiquity, but in a new form of monarchy.

In pursuing its goals of remaking the Japanese state on a European model and of achieving equality with the West, the Meiji government created slogans for all aspects of its endeavours – 'enrich the country, strengthen the army' (*fukoku kyōhei*), 'civilization and enlightenment' (*bummei kaika*), and 'revise the (unequal) treaties' (*jōyaku kaisei*). The government obtained the assistance of foreign teachers and technicians to achieve these goals. In their efforts to overtake the West, the Japanese, who had progressed from book-learning to direct experience of the West, now adopted a state policy of inviting large numbers of foreign teachers.

The countries of their origins and their numbers are as follows. Immediately after the opening of the country, the foreigners under whom the Japanese studied were mainly Dutch in the late 1850s and early 1860s. The first systematic instructor in Western arts and sciences, however, was a German, P. F. von Siebold (1796–1866), who arrived in Nagasaki as a physician with the Dutch trading post in 1823. While studying Japan's language, history, geography, animals and plants, he practised and taught medicine to Japanese students in a private academy set up for him, the Narutakijuku. The language Siebold used was mainly Dutch. In the Tokugawa years, Japanese curiosity began with Western medicine and astronomy, but by late Tokugawa times, their concerns had shifted to Western arms and military methods, reflecting the gravity of the international situation. In 1855, the bakufu set up a naval training institute in Nagasaki to which it invited a team of Dutch instructors to provide training in navigation. Thus Japan's first 'foreign employees' were Pels Rijcken and a group of twenty-two instructors, who arrived in 1855, and Huyssen van Kattendycke and a team of thirty-seven, who came slightly later.

In 1858, parallel treaties were concluded with the United States, Holland, England, France and Russia. Once Holland was no longer the sole avenue for studying Western civilization, Dutch prestige suffered precipitously, and as the Japanese discovered that England, France, Germany and America were the leading Western powers, they discarded the Dutch language and began studying English, French and German. Thereafter, selected few Japanese were dispatched to England, America, France, and (in Meiji times) Germany to study.

Initially, few foreigners were employed, and most of them were from France and Britain. In its final conflicts with Satsuma and Chōshū, the *bakufu* sought closer relations with France, whereas Satsuma and Chōshū looked to England. In 1862, the *bakufu*, with help from France, built a shipyard in Yokosuka and began a foundry in Yokohama as well as establishing a French-language school there. Oguri Tadamasa, a leading official in these final *bakufu* reforms, remarked to a colleague: 'The Tokugawa may have to transfer this old house [the *bakufu*] to someone else, but it will look a lot better with a new storehouse on the premises.'[1] In fact, the Meiji government did take the decrepit bakufu structure off the hands of the Tokugawa a few years later and received the new Yokosuka arsenal 'storehouse' as a bonus. Moreover, it is important to note that not only the plant itself but also the foreign employees operating it were taken over by the new regime. The Meiji government acquired new facilities, and furthermore precious human talent. They were the Japanese who had been sent abroad by the *bakufu* in the late Tokugawa period.

In the early Meiji period, there was a rapid increase in the number of foreign employees serving in government and private capacities. The number of foreign government employees peaked in 1875 with approximately 520 persons employed, but by 1894 and after, the annual totals were fewer than 100. In contrast, the number of foreigners in private employ was small at first but reached a high of approximately 760 in 1897. By occupation in government, engineers and educators in the ministries of Industry and Education were most numerous, and in the private sector, the number of educators increased as time went on. Classified by nationality, among government employees, the British were most numerous as educators and engineers, followed by the Germans; in the private sector, American educators predominated. With regard to the relative influence of the different nationalities, it is interesting to note the changes in numbers of foreigners employed in the various government bureaux. In 1872 out of a total of 213 government-employed foreigners, 119 were from the United Kingdom, of whom 104 were engineers in the Ministry of Industry, and 49 were French, of whom 24 were shipbuilding technicians. By 1881, however, the statistics show 96 English, 32 Germans, 12 Americans and 10 French. Areas in which certain nationalities were particularly influential included the English in the ministries of Industry, Navy and Communications; and the Americans in the development of Hokkaido.[2]

Budget figures are revealing: at some points, foreigners' salaries accounted for one-third of the Ministry of Industry's regular budget and one-third of the budget allocations for Tokyo Imperial University, the first modern university to be established in Japan. The foreigners' salaries clearly placed great strains on the budgets of all government ministries and bureaux, to say nothing of the costs of studying abroad. Yet perhaps it was precisely because of these great costs that the Japanese studied so assiduously under their expensive foreign teachers. These costs were heavy when the foreigners were conscientious and of good character, but when they assumed an attitude of superiority towards their Japanese employers, the costs must have seemed heavier still – all the more reason, no doubt, for the diligence with which the Japanese strove to master the new teachings.

What did the Japanese desire when they employed foreign teachers? In November 1873, Itō Hirobumi, minister of Industry, delivered a directive to mark the opening of the government's new Kōgakuryō, which later evolved into the Department of Engineering of Tokyo Imperial University. Itō pointed out that the new enterprises that Japan was developing should be considered the foundation of future greatness. To create a 'great civilization' meant educating 'high and low alike', and it had to be done quickly so that 'Japan could take its rightful place among the nations of the world' in wealth and power. Because only a few Japanese had mastered the skills required up to that point, the country had 'no choice but to employ many foreigners to assist us at the outset'. But it was not enough to rely on the skills of others; to do so might bring temporary gains but not the 'wealth and strength that will endure through myriads of generations'. Consequently, Itō concluded:

> It is imperative that we seize this opportunity to train and educate ourselves fully. On this solemn occasion, I urge all ambitious youths to enrol in this school, to study assiduously, to perfect their talents and to serve in their various posts with dedication. If this is done, then as a matter of course, we will be able to do without foreigners. We ourselves will fill the realm with railways and other technological wonders that will form the basis for further developments to continue for a myriad generations. The glory of our Imperial Land will shine forth to radiate upon foreign shores, while at home, high and low will share in the benefits of a great civilization. Therefore, let all ambitious youths throughout the land proceed vigorously with their studies.[3]

It is clear that the Meiji leaders intended foreign employees to play only a subsidiary and temporary role in Japan's development and wanted Japanese nationals to be trained to replace them as soon as possible. The Japanese realized that in order to 'lay the foundations for national wealth and strength that will last a myriad generations', they would have to 'train and educate' themselves and that they had no choice but to develop and increase their own capabilities. It was also Japan's good fortune that even in the West, scientific and technological development had a history of only a few decades. And so although it was almost fully dependent on foreign teachers and technicians at the beginning, Japan succeeded in transplanting Western industrial techniques and in producing enough talented men to become surprisingly self-sufficient in the relatively short span of fifteen to twenty years. Tokyo Imperial University's engineering department had a total of 411 graduates between 1879 and 1885. This number of trained technological leaders was not far below the number of foreigners employed by the Ministry of Industry since the beginning of the Meiji period.

Tokugawa Japanese had gained a fair understanding of Western science, a fact that can be discerned in the observations made by Fukuzawa Yukichi during his 1860 visit to San Francisco. He was not in the least surprised by the modern phenomena of the telegraph, metalworking, or sugar-refining. As is generally true for backward nations, however, Japan began its own development by availing itself of advanced Western science and technology.

In connection with the introduction of new technology, there was also the entry of new Western modes of life. The numerous foreigners employed by the Meiji government facilitated Japan's turn to the West. They served first of all as teachers, but they did more in the broader sense of introducing new life-styles. For example, at one time during the first half of the 1870s, there were as many as twenty foreigners (most of them English) employed at the government mint, where it is reported that as early as 1870–1 Western clothing, the solar calendar and Sunday holidays were adopted. Western clothing became compulsory for government officials in November 1872, when a directive established Western clothing as the official ceremonial dress. In 1876, frock coats were decreed standard business attire.[4]

Calendar reform took place in November 1872, when the government decreed that the third day of the twelfth month of the lunar calendar would become January of the following year.[5] This was how the solar calendar was introduced to Japan.[6] The rationale behind calendar reform deserves a slight digression. The solar calendar was not unknown during the Tokugawa period, through Dutch studies. As early as 1795, Ōtsuki Gentaku and his *rangaku* friends had celebrated the eleventh day of the eleventh lunar month as 'Dutch New Year's Day'. The actual use of the solar calendar after its adoption in 1872, however, was not particularly rapid or widespread. The traditional lunar-solar 'Tempo calendar', intricately connected with the pulse of agricultural seasons, suited the Japanese life patterns well. For a time, the new Meiji calendar was dubbed the 'Imperial Court calendar', as opposed to the 'Tokugawa calendar', to which the people were accustomed. Not until 1911 were the lunar listings of days removed from the calendars, and even today many Japanese feel a certain nostalgia for the old lunar calendar.

One reason that the new regime pushed through calendar reform so early probably stemmed from budgetary considerations. Because there was one intercalary month to be added to the lunar calendar every three years, changing to the solar calendar meant saving the intercalary month's expenditures. When the new government converted to the solar calendar in 1872 and 'erased' two days, it withheld salaries for those days, not only for Japanese but also for foreign employees whose salaries were drawn on a monthly rather than a yearly basis. The government mint, which took the lead in adopting Western dress and the solar calendar, also pioneered in Western accounting methods, reserve funds for work injuries, medical clinics and other matters hitherto unknown in Japan. In addition, it quickly introduced gas lights and telegraph lines, which became symbols of 'civilization and enlightenment' in Japan, even though none of these innovations was directly concerned with minting techniques. In addition, many of the customs inherent in 'civilization and enlightenment', or capitalist enterprise, were introduced by foreign employees of the Meiji government. Christmas, for instance, which became a holiday, came with the foreign residents. Many aspects of Western life were taught by the foreigners through daily affairs rather than through formal instruction.

Individual foreign teachers often had astonishing influence through the strength of their personal example and assumed almost oracular importance for young students who were only partly rooted in traditional values and eager to learn the inner strength of 'civilization'. For instance, the artillery Captain L. L. Janes in Kumamoto and the agronomist William Clark in Hokkaido proved to be more successful religious teachers than were the numerous missionaries who were sent to Japan after the government rescinded the prohibitions against Christianity in 1873, and major groupings of the small but influential Protestant church derived from the 'Kumamoto Band' and 'Hokkaido Group'.[7]

Christianity provides one example of Japan's 'Japanization' of the Western thought and institutions. When Western value systems came into contact with Japanese values, there were three possible outcomes: (1) The two could conflict; (2) the values might be adopted totally; or (3) they might be altered in the process of being accepted. Just as it had been the case with Buddhism, it was the last outcome that Japanese Christianity took. The problem, however, is delicate, as believers in a religion generally believe that they embrace its values totally. Another example can be found in Japan's civil code, which was drafted under the guidance of the French jurist G. E. Boissonade. By examining this draft, we may discover Japan's reaction to 'teachers of arts and sciences' who attempted to introduce Western morality as well.

Social order was well maintained in Tokugawa Japan, but not because the Japanese of that era were bound by written laws. The unequal treaties concluded by the *bakufu* in 1858 posed a new problem and need in this regard. They were inequitable and humiliating; Japan was forced to relinquish tariff autonomy and concede extraterritoriality to Westerners. To obtain equal status with the West, the early Meiji government would first have to prove that

Japan was a 'civilized' country, deserving equal status and treatment, and part of that process involved compiling legal codes similar to those possessed by the European states. Thus, the adoption of a Western-style legal system was not simply a domestic matter; it was also essential to the resolution of an external problem that demanded an urgent solution.

When the French legal system first came to the attention of the Japanese in late Tokugawa, they greeted it with enthusiasm. The Tokugawa official Kurimoto Joun, who travelled to France in 1867, noted in his memoirs:

> 'Deciding a lawsuit with half a word' is something that requires the wisdom of Zi-lu and is beyond the capability of men of only average abilities and intelligence. How much more impossible for a man without human feelings. The complete elimination of argumentation in court would have been impossible even for the sage Confucius. That, at any rate, was what I thought until I learned of this Napoleonic code … I was overwhelmed with admiration and envy.[8]

The reason for Kurimoto's praise was that two Japanese merchants who had accompanied his party had been arraigned and brought to court, where he saw the French judge 'base his decision and pronounce sentence in accordance with Article X, Provision Y of the Napoleonic code'.

In 1869, the Meiji government ordered Mitsukuri Rinshō to translate all five French law codes. At that time, Etō Shimpei (1834–74) suggested that they 'merely translate the French civil code verbatim, call it the "Japanese Civil Code", and promulgate it immediately'.[9] His aim was to revise the unequal treaties: the laws need not be perfect, and it would be sufficient if they were part of a new judicial system. This would convince the West that Japan was indeed a 'civilized' nation.

A group under Etō's direction began compiling a civil code based on Mitsukuri's translation. In 1872, the French lawyer Georges Bousquet was hired to assist them, and the next year Gustave Emile Boissonade de Fontarabie (1825–1910)[10] followed; the latter worked in Japan until 1895. In addition to their work of compilation, these men served as instructors in Western legal concepts at the Ministry of Justice. Before this, Inoue Kowashi (1854–95), who deserves much credit for his work to implement Western institutions, had been sent to France by the Ministry of Justice, where he had studied under Boissonade, who was then a professor of law at the Sorbonne. In Japan, Boissonade cooperated with Inoue on many projects. In public law, he strove to establish concepts like the principle of legality and the principle of evidence and to abolish torture. He also drew up criminal and penal codes, which were Japan's first modern law codes. In private law, he worked on the civil code, drawing up sections on property, securities and evidence. In addition, he was influential in determining what was to go into the sections on personal and family relations and property acquisitions. Boissonade's drafts passed final review in the Privy Council and were scheduled to go into effect in 1890. A noteworthy aspect of his draft was the ideal of equality between individuals in the inheritance of property. However, these provisions drew sharp criticism from those who held that they would threaten the primacy of the house (*ie*), and as a result, implementation of the code was held up just before it was to become law. Boissonade's provisions were rejected and replaced by requirements that the household head inherit all property. In sum, the Meiji government placed more emphasis on maintaining the 'house' (*ie*) as a structural unit than on respecting the individual's right to inheritance.[11] This 'civil code issue' raged for several years.

The controversy over the new code had many facets, but in general terms, it can be viewed as a conflict between the universalistic, theoretical legal thought espoused by French jurists of natural law and a more particularistic and empirical set of ideas advanced by proponents of historicist legal thought who drew their arguments from English and especially German traditions. The latter group argued that the concept of 'house' (*ie*) and the sentiments it engendered were an intrinsic part of particularistic and traditional Japanese society and values. Hozumi Yatsuka (1860–1912), a spokesman for the latter group, became famous for his catchphrase: 'Loyalty and filial piety will perish with the enactment of the civil code.' He wrote:

> With the spread of Christianity in Europe, a self-righteous 'Father who art in Heaven' has come to monopolize the love and respect of all men. Perhaps for that reason, Westerners neglect the worship of ancestors and the Way of filial piety. With the spread of doctrines like equality and humanity, they slight the importance of ethnic customs and blood-ties. Perhaps that is why no 'house' system exists among them anymore; instead they create a society of equal individuals and try to uphold it by means of laws centred on the individuals.
>
> Japan has never forgotten the teaching of ancestor reverence because of the coming of foreign religions. However, the spirit in which this civil code is drafted will bring repudiation of the national religion and destruction of

our 'house' system. The words *house* and *household head* do appear briefly, but the draft obscures the true principles of law, and thus, is worse than if it were a dead letter. Alas, these men are trying to enact a civil code centred on extreme individualism, ignoring three thousand years of indigenous beliefs![12]

Hozumi explained why the proposed civil code would lead to 'the loss of Japan's individuality': (1) the section on property, by idealizing unlimited freedom of contract for individuals, might raise society's productive capacities, but at the cost of widening the gap between rich and poor, thereby producing conflicts between owners and workers, 'contradictions inherent in capitalism'; and (2) the section on personal and domestic relations, based as it was on an imitation of Western individualism, had been drafted with the idea that husbands and wives, and elder and younger brothers were separate individuals. Consequently, there was danger that the code would break up Japanese society, which had always been upheld by teachings of reverence for ancestors, who continued to be central to the house.[13] Instead, Hozumi advocated the enactment of a civil code that would emphasize 'a spirit suited to the nation' and 'the familial relations of the "house system".'

As a result of this civil code issue, the Diet (parliament) voted to postpone until 1896 the enactment of the civil code due to go into effect the following year. It was still in limbo when Boissonade, who had poured heart and soul into the code during a residence of over twenty years in Japan, returned to France in 1895. Inoue Kowashi composed a commemorative poem in classical Chinese for Boissonade from his sick-bed and died soon after. New forces came into play.

The code was, in effect, recompiled by a new commission headed by Itō Hirobumi and Saionji Kimmochi, and was finally enacted in 1898. Their two guiding principles, which together defined the Meiji civil code, are of great interest: (1) Indigenous Japanese institutions and practices should be taken fully into account; and (2) the strong points of legislative theories from all Western nations should be adopted, and not just those of France and Italy, as had been the case previously.

The section on property was left virtually unchanged. It incorporated principles of legal equality between the sexes and the former social-status groups as well as the principles of individual choice, personal ownership of property and liability arising from negligence, all based on the spirit of individualism. It also contained a system of real and obligatory rights based on the idea of equal rights and duties. However, the section on social relationships was greatly revised to establish the power of the household head by means of special provisions for family heads, parents and fathers. As a result, individuals were constrained by being placed within a status hierarchy of family relationships. According to Western historical concepts, Japan's civil code was thus based on a dual structure, whose two layers were logically inconsistent: the return of the individual to a _gemeinschaft_-type of 'house' unit in personal relationships versus the recognition of that person's status as an individual in capitalistic society. A modern society is presumably made up of individuals, but the Japanese people were continually forced to adjust themselves to a 'house system' in which each individual was rooted.

That the enactment of Japan's civil code went through these vicissitudes and that the end product came about by such contradictory compromises are hardly surprising. Quite the contrary: the civil code epitomizes the basic pattern taken by Japan's turn to the West. Etō Shimpei, who, as mentioned earlier, once suggested that Japan enact a word-for-word translation of the French civil code, is said to have given the following instructions to Inoue Kowashi when the Ministry of Justice sent him to France:

> The most vital task for all of you who are being sent to Europe is to inspect various European countries and institutions and then adopt their strong points while discarding their weaknesses. You are not being sent to study about the conditions in each country and to import Western ways wholesale into Japan. Hence, you should no longer think in terms of learning from Westerners, but instead, observe them in a spirit of critical inquiry. As Japan proceeds along the path of civilization, it is vital to adopt Western institutions and ways to improve our governmental processes. Nevertheless, we must not become so infatuated with the West that we fail to discern its defects. If that is the case, the institutions and ways we adopt with so much toil and trouble will not be fit for our use.[14]

In his memoirs, Inoue stressed that the Meiji constitution and all other areas of reform in which he had had a hand in implementing show the spiritual characteistics of Japan. In contrast, Saionji Kimmochi (1849–1940), who spent ten years of his youth in France and who placed his faith in the universality of civilization, criticized such particularism as follows: 'Usually, what is termed "particular to" a certain nation or race is a shortcoming or idiosyncrasy... Most traits that present-day educators in Japan babble about as being distinctively Japanese would distress men of learning ...'[15]

Hozumi Yatsuka, who overemphasized the importance of the 'house system' and the 'teaching of ancestor reverence', was derided by the intellectuals of his day. Yet, it must be noted here that when the sections on family relations and inheritance in Japan's civil code were drastically revised during the American Occupation in 1947, the concept of 'house' was thoroughly repudiated. Many Japanese still opposed such 'morality' imposed from abroad. They feared that Western-style individualism would weaken family ties and create new problems in caring for the elderly, and the fear was realized. It had become a problem of great concern by the 1980s. Hence, the opposition to some aspects of Western 'morality' represented more than a conservative, emotional reaction, for it was reinforced by a desire to make Japan achieve 'modernity' while avoiding the alienation and atomization of human relationships inherent in capitalistic society.

*Notes*

[1] Fukuchi Gen'ichirō: *Bakumatsu seijika* (Tokyo: Min'yūsha, 1900), p. 266.

[2] Umetani Noboru: *Oyatoi gaikokujin: Meiji Nihon no wakiyakutachi* (Tokyo: Nihon keizai shimbunsha, 1965), pp. 209–23. In English, see Hazel Jones, *Live Machines: Hired Foreigners in Meiji Japan* (Vancouver: University of British Columbia Press, 1980).

[3] Umetani Noboru: *Oyatoi gaikokujin* (Tokyo: Kajima kenkyūsho shuppan, 1968), p. 210.

[4] Tsuji Zennosuke: *Nihon bunkashi* (Tokyo: Shunjūsha, 1950), vol. 7, p. 18.

[5] Satō Masatsugu: *Nihon rekigakushi* (Tokyo: Surugadai shuppansha, 1968), p. 479.

[6] The Julian method of intercalation was used at this time, but the Gregorian method was adopted in 1900.

[7] John F. Howes, 'Japanese Christians and American Missionaries', in Marius B. Jansen, ed.: *Changing Japanese Attitudes Toward Modernization* (Princeton, N.J.: Princeton University Press, 1965), pp. 337–68. For Janes, see F. G. Notehelfer: *American Samurai: Captain L. L. Janes and Japan* (Princeton, N.J.: Princeton University Press, 1985).

[8] This opening phrase is a quotation from *The Analects* of Confucius. Kurimoto Joun, 'Gyōsō tsuiroku', in Nihon shiseki kyōkai, ed.: *Hōan ikō* (*Zoku Nihon shiseki sōsho*, vol. 4) (Tokyo: Tokyo daigaku shuppankai, 1975), p. 24.

[9] Etō Shimpei, 'Furansu mimpō wo motte Nihon mimpō to nasan to su', in Hozumi Nobushige: *Hōsō yawa* (Tokyo: Iwanami shoten, 1980), pp. 210–13.

[10] See Ōkubo Yasuo: *Nihon kindaihō no chichi, Bowasonādo* (Tokyo: Iwanami shoten, 1977) for a discussion of this legal consultant.

[11] On the compilation of the civil code and the 'civil code issue', in addition to Ōkubo: *Nihon kindaihō no chichi*, see Ishii Ryōsuke, ed.: *Meiji bunkashi: Hōsei-hen* (Tokyo: Genyōsha, 1954), p. 515. This work is vol. 2 of the Centennial Cultural Committee Series, *Meiji bunkashi,* and was translated by William Chambliss as *Japanese Legislation in the Meiji Era* (Tokyo: Pan-Pacific Press, 1958).

[12] Hozumi Yatsuka, 'Mimpō idete, chūkō horobu', *Hōgaku shimpō,* vol. 5 (August 1891).

[13] On Hozumi's theory of state, see Richard Minear: *Japanese Tradition and Western Law: Emperor, State, and Law in the Thought of Hozumi Yatsuka* (Cambridge, Mass.: Harvard University Press, 1970).

[14] Matono Hansuke, *Etō Nampaku* (Tokyo: Hara shobō reprint, 1968) vol. 2, p. 107.

[15] Miyazawa Toshiyoshi, 'Meiji kempō no seiritsu to sono kokusai seijiteki haikei' in Miyazawa Toshiyoshi: *Nihon kenseishi no kenkyū* (Tokyo: Iwanami shoten, 1968) pp. 134–5.

# FIRST TRANSLATIONS FROM WESTERN LITERATURE

———————————□———————————

*Robinson Crusoe*

A striking indication of Japan's turn to the West can be found in the great number of translations from Western literature made during the Meiji period and after. During the early decades, however, translators were concerned more with causes than with literature. From the last days of Tokugawa rule through the first decades of Meiji, numerous translations were really practical tracts of agitation, often known as 'political novels', that reflected the conditions of the time. More often than not, they were translated to suit the convenience of those who supported a cause or political position. Regardless of their literary value or lack thereof, however, these translations are interesting for what they reveal about the way that Japanese in that era reacted to the foreign intercourse that followed the breakdown of national isolation.

After their return home, Japanese castaways were often interrogated by *bakufu* officials. Their accounts of conditions overseas were transcribed, and Japanese intellectuals began reading them towards the end of the Edo period. Against that background, two translations of *Robinson Crusoe* appeared before the Meiji Restoration. The first was a partial translation from a Dutch version, entitled *The Account of a Castaway* by Kuroda Kōgen, a student of Dutch studies, which was completed before Perry's arrival in 1853. The following preface to the Dutch edition was also included in Kuroda's translation:

Robinson Crusoe of England was a man with a desire to traverse the four quarters. He set out to sea and lost his ship in a tropical storm. He managed to stay alive but was cast adrift in a lifeboat, captured by pirates, and finally sold to a fisherman. Later, he escaped from that fishing boat and, while fleeing from pursuers, was unexpectedly rescued by a Portuguese merchant vessel. He grew sweet potatoes and became very wealthy, but his misfortunes at sea did not deter him from returning to it in a great vessel he constructed. He ran into many storms, was shipwrecked, and then marooned on a desert island. He used all his wits to survive on this island for twenty-eight years before an English ship chanced to come and take him home.

Any reader of these accounts cannot help but be overwhelmed with admiration. When it was published in England, readers devoured it and rushed to buy it in droves; at one point its publication reached forty thousand copies. Its Dutch translation is being read more avidly than was the English original. Moreover, this book supplements gaps in our knowledge of geography. Although there are numerous other accounts of sea voyages, these merely describe stormy seas or the contours of lands discovered; none reports anything like the miraculous nature of Crusoe's achievements. Readers who learn of his countless hardships and his resourcefulness in overcoming these cannot but develop their own mental faculties.

I personally feel that although life is full of vicissitudes, no one has experienced as many as Crusoe. Each account of his experiences on that deserted island has great relevance to our own understanding of affairs in society. You should never forget the sufferings Crusoe experienced and become conceited and self-indulgent.

Moreover, Crusoe was adept solely in navigation, not in any other technical skills. Yet the mind of man is indeed a marvellous thing! Once he landed on the deserted island, he sewed his own clothes, gathered his own food, built his own house, constructed his own ship, made his own pottery, grew his own vegetables – succeeded in meeting all his personal needs by himself ...[1]

This translator was apparently unaware that *Robinson Crusoe* was a fictional product of Daniel Defoe's pen and instead believed that it was a true account. Furthermore, *Robinson Crusoe* was not considered a children's story by the Japanese of that era. Rather it was read by adults as a true account of a castaway.

Translations of this type suggest Japan's initial orientation towards the sea, as well as their yearning for information about foreign affairs. In the case of Niijima Jō, about whom we have discussed in the Chapter entitled 'Japanese Experience Abroad', his desire to find out about conditions of the outside world was accelerated by reading a translation of *Robinson Crusoe* lent to him by his teacher of Dutch studies. He then smuggled himself out of Japan.

After spending well over a year at sea, he found himself in the United States of America in 1865, engaged in manual labour with no idea of what the future held in store for him: 'Exhausted after each day's labour, I would fall asleep as soon as my head hit the pillow. When I awoke each morning, my entire body ached so badly that I could hardly move.'[2] This continued for weeks. Then he bought a copy of *Robinson Crusoe* in the original English. This book, along with a Dutch book about Christ and a Bible translated into classical Chinese, was what induced him to become a Christian. Niijima, too, believed that Crusoe was a real person and seems to have compared his own experiences with those of that solitary castaway. When he was stranded in Boston, he was insulted by burly sailors and found out about the grim living conditions caused by post-Civil War inflation. In that black hour, he is said to have gained the strength to carry on by repeating Crusoe's prayer.

This is a most interesting account of the circumstances surrounding the conversion of one Japanese to Protestantism. Today we are used to reading editions of *Robinson Crusoe* rewritten for children and forget the emphasis on Divine Providence in Defoe's original. The author's intention, scholars tell us, was to edify readers and impress them with the importance of moral behaviour. *Robinson Crusoe* was a parable of the role of Providence in human affairs, and accordingly, Niijima's interpretation was probably truer to the original than is that of most modern readers.

Protestantism enlarged upon this idea of diligence and work based on the individualism of a God-fearing person, and for that reason, it is often associated with the flowering of capitalism. What Defoe depicted in *Robinson Crusoe* was an individual in relation to an absolute God, and that relationship made for an autonomous individual. Niijima perceived in Crusoe such a religious man, but he also saw the prototype of those who would later develop capitalism.

After returning to Japan, Niijima established the Dōshisha English School in Kyoto in 1875. His goal was to foster 'talented men of conscience', a phrase that suggests Max Weber's 'spirit of this-worldly asceticism'. One might even suggest that with the abolition of feudal society, Niijima and his associates set out to reconstruct and transform the ethics of the samurai, who had been taught to 'do everything humanly possible and trust in Heaven's fate' in Meiji society through the medium of Protestantism.

Except for a period in the 1880s when the number of converts to Protestantism seemed to be growing rapidly – a phenomenon not unrelated to the exigencies of treaty reform – the young Meiji church probably did not enroll more than about thirty thousand converts. They were a strategic and able group of educated and usually ex-samurai youths. Prejudice in Kumamoto brought L. L. Janes's 'Kumamoto Band' to Niijima's Dōshisha, and the association of Protestantism with Western dynamism by adventurous and able youth made the influence of Protestantism much larger than the modest number of its adherents would suggest. Yet its significance can also be exaggerated, for adherents to the new faith came as often from a commitment to this-worldly values as they did to other-worldly, transcendent beliefs.

## *Samuel Smiles's* Self-Help

During the 'civilization and enlightenment' of early Meiji, the first Western ideas to enter Japan were generally those associated with English and American thinkers like Mill, Bentham, Spencer, de Tocqueville and Buckle – utilitarianism, civil liberties, natural rights and rational positivism. Slightly later, French republicanism associated with Rousseau arrived and spread. Together, these ideas destroyed the hierarchical status system of Tokugawa times and ushered in an ethos of 'achieving success and rising in the world' (*risshin shusse*). This ethos was powerfully stated in the phrases of Fukuzawa Yukichi's *Gakumon no susume* (An encouragement of learning) in 1872: 'People are not born exalted or base, rich or poor. It is simply that those who work hard at their studies and learn much become exalted and rich, while those who are ignorant become base and poor.'[3] This later became the Meiji government's ideology.

Japan's traditional work ethic was instilled anew in early Meiji youths in the form of this demand for a modern education. As a result, an enthusiasm for 'personal cultivation' (*shūyō*) spread. Under slogans such as 'hard work and application' (*kokku benrei*) or 'thrift, diligence and effort' (*kinken doryoku*) Meiji youths prepared to carry out their future duties and to acquire knowledge from the West in various capacities – as pupils in the newly-created school system, as apprentices in traditional crafts, as live-in disciples in the homes of famous scholars and as students studying in universities abroad.

In 1883, a new translation of *Robinson Crusoe* by Inoue Tsutomu appeared as *An Extraordinary Adventure: An Account of Robinson Crusoe, the Castaway*. In his preface, Inoue treated Crusoe as a fictional character, not as an actual person, but he also asserted that the novel was no mere adventure story and that it served to teach young Englishmen to overcome hardship. Inoue interpreted *Robinson Crusoe* in the following terms: 'This book should not be thought of as trivial, for if men read it carefully they will see that it shows how an island can be developed by stubborn determination.'[4] It is clear that what Inoue had in his mind, while translating *Robinsoe Crusoe*: it was the development of an island-state called Japan.

But it is the enthusiastic reception given to *Self-Help* that best illustrates Japanese general concern for the industrial development of their country. Nakamura Masanao's translation of Samuel Smiles's book testifies, moreover, the fusion of two work ethics, Protestant and Confucian. Its enduring success through Meiji times suggests the transformation of Asiatic agricultural work ethic under the impact of Western habits of industrial society. This best-selling guidebook for Meiji Japan's industrialization, therefore, is worth attention. Japanese responses to the translation shows the dominant hold maintained by the traditional work ethic vested in new forms in Meiji Japan.

During the 1870s after Fukuzawa Yukichi, Nakamura Masanao was the most influential exponent of the Enlightenment movement. Half of Nakamura's influence stemmed from his translation of John Stuart Mill's *On Liberty*; the other half from Samuel Smiles's *Self-Help*. Precisely because his major works consisted of translations, Nakamura is not considered an original thinker and attracts far less attention than Fukuzawa. This academic indifference towards the great translator is a mistake, if we are to pay attention to problems of intercultural relations.

Nakamura Masanao[5] alias Keiu (1832–91) was born to a low-ranking samurai family but was admitted to the most authoritative Shōheikō academy on the basis of his scholarly promise. As a China scholar he belonged to Wang Yangming school of thought[6]. In the final years of the Tokugawa shogunate he held the most prestigious professorship in Japan of *o-jusha* at his alma mater. He was, however, one of the first Japanese samurai-scholars sent to the capital of England in 1866. The accomplished Confucian scholar of his own will accompanied twelve young students to London nominally as their supervisor. The fact is, he had secretly been drawn to Western studies. In London, Japanese students were impressed with material aspects of the Western civilization. Nakamura paid attention to moral elements of English life as well. To the Confucian scholar, the discovery of the Protestant work ethic was a kind of culture shock, and Nakamura became the first Japanese to point out that if important elements of Western civilization were to be borrowed, the ethical background of which they were an outgrowth must not be neglected.

The book in which Nakamura thought to have found the secret of the industrial greatness of Victorian England was *Self-Help* written by Samuel Smiles (1812–1904) in 1859. While he was studying abroad, the shogunal government that had dispatched Nakamura's group to London was collapsing, and upon his return Nakamura was obliged to retire, together with other ex-retainers loyal to the deposed Shogun, to the countryside of Shizuoka, where he translated *Self-Help*. His translation was published in the fourth year of Meiji, in 1871, and that was the first English book ever translated in its entirety into Japanese. It became eventually the most influential single Western book translated into Japanese. The sale of *Self-Help* was unbelievably good: more than one million copies of Nakamura's translation had sold by the end of the Meiji era of 1912.[7] The original was a best-seller in England, too, and a quarter of a million copies had sold by 1905.[8] That enthusiastic reception of *Saikoku risshi hen,* which is the Japanese title of *Self-Help,* indicates an important aspect of Japanese response to the demands of industrial society. Many interesting traces of influence are left by his Japanese translation among people of different professions, from writers like Kōda Rohan, Kunikida Doppo to the great inventor Toyoda Sakichi. As was seen in the Chapter entitled 'Awakening of Asia', its influence was also clear in the Korean case of Ch'oe Nam-son.[9]

First, the problems of transfer (or readjustment) of work ethic need be clarified, that is, how diligence of people working in an agricultural society transformed itself into diligence and inventiveness fit for an industrial society, and how the impact of a foreign book could open new perspectives.

In the life of a nation as well as in the life of an individual, the impression left by the first foreign book often remains deep in the heart. In the case of China it was Thomas Huxley's *Evolution and Ethics* published in 1894 and translated into Chinese in 1898 by Yan Fu under the title of *Tianyan-lun* which left a decisive impression on Chinese intellectuals. Towards the end of the nineteenth century Qing China was at the mercy of imperialistic powers. The social Darwinian idea of the survival of the fittest seemed to explain the harsh international realities surrounding China, in which the stronger nations preyed upon the weaker nations. Huxley's book helped Chinese intellectuals to understand the destiny of the weak who were becoming the victim of the strong.

Compared with China, Japan was lucky, for it had opened the country much earlier in 1868 and the first English book translated was more optimistic in its nature: *Self-Help*. The book enabled the Japanese to help themselves. Unlike Huxley's book, Smiles's book served positively as a guidebook for the industrialization of Japan. Incidentally, the second English book which Nakamura translated into Japanese in 1872 and which Yan Fu translated into Chinese in 1903 is the same: John Stuart Mill's *On Liberty*. However, Yan Fu will be remembered only as the Chinese translator of *Evolution and Ethics*. Compared with the enthusiastic welcome[10] that Nakamura's Japanese translation of *On Liberty* had got, Yan Fu's Chinese translation received little attention. While the word *jiyū*, which is the Nakamura's translation for the English word *liberty* took root in Japan with the Popular Rights movement, the word *ziyou*, which is Yan Fu's translation with his use of a difficult ideogram, did not take root in China.

Every time a Japanese historian is invited by Chinese universities to give a talk about Japan's turn to the West, he always receives the same questions, which are as follows. Why was it possible for a Confucian scholar like Nakamura to go to London and to study English? Why was it possible for a defeated Tokugawa official to publish the translation of *Self-Help* and eventually to become one of the most influential intellectual leaders of Meiji Japan? In the case of Yan Fu he did not wish to study abroad. However, as his family was not rich enough, after the death of his father Yan Fu gave up the hope to become a government official by taking examinations, and he reluctantly chose to go to England in 1877 with a scholarship.

Nakamura was drawn to Western studies, although, as has been stated, his education was fundamentally Confucian. Under the influence of Sakuma Shōzan and especially with the keen sense of an imminent national crisis, the Confucian scholar secretly learnt Dutch and later English. This sort of deviation was not imaginable for Sino-centric Chinese men of letters but was possible for a Japanese samurai-scholar, because what was important for him was to find the best way to defend his country. After the coming of Perry's squadron in 1853, Tokugawa Confucian élite, too, wished to know the reality of Western countries. Moreover,

Japanese intellectuals have always thought, consciously or unconsciously, that the centre of the civilization is situated not within Japan itself but somewhere beyond the sea. It should be noted here that Confucian studies had slightly different meanings to Chinese officials and to Japanese samurai-scholars. Confucian studies, being genuinely Chinese, could not be discarded by Chinese scholar-statesmen without provoking their identity crisis, while in Japan Confucian studies, although orthodox under the Tokugawa regime were more or less regarded as something of foreign origin. The National scholars or *kokugakusha* in fact argued for studies originating in Japan, and the Dutch scholars or *rangakusha* turned their focus away from Confucian studies while studying physical sciences. Compared with China or Korea of the mid-nineteenth century, Japan enjoyed a relatively wider breadth of freedom of thought, the co-existence of these various schools of thought other than that of Confucius being a clear point of difference. The appearance in Japan of scholars like Nakamura was not a mere coincidence.

In the midst of life, Nakamura experienced two shocks: in London he was overwhelmed by the greatness of Western civilization. That culture shock was the reason why the leading *kangakusha* or scholar of Chinese classics of the Shōheikō academy became belatedly a *yōgakusha* or Western scholar. To be more precise, Nakamura became a scholar with two legs grounded in both East and West. From the ancient China of the sages Nakamura made a turn to the West. He showed a new model for Japan to follow, by going abroad and by translating *Self-Help*. He discovered in the person of Smiles a new sage who preached the gospel of work for Japan's coming capitalistic society.

Nakamura was not only favourably impressed by what he saw and heard in London, but also found the Chinese account of the Countries Overseas, *Haiguo tuzhi*, compiled by Wei Yuan after the Opium War, rather misleading. In the capital of Great Britain, Nakamura discovered what democracy is and became the first Oriental to illustrate what a constitutional monarchy is, by describing the daily life of Queen Victoria and her relationship with Parliament. Furthermore, by translating Smiles's *Self-Help* into Japanese, Nakamura became the first Japanese to open the eyes of his compatriots: the Japanese understood for the first time the moral principles by which Westerners were guided: self-help, industry, perseverance, scientific pursuits, integrity and honesty, courage and gentleness. The lives and deeds of Westerners described by Smiles tend to be idealized, but the moralistic tone with which the book was written, although displeasing to readers of later generations both in England and in Japan, suited well the taste of Japanese readers brought up according to Confucian ethical traditions. Through the hands of Nakamura, Smiles became a sort of Victorian Confucian, which partly explains the exceptional success of Nakamura's translation.

The second shock was the collapse of the Tokugawa shogunate. Upon his return home, Nakamura, ex-retainer of the Tokugawa shogun, who had distinguished himself under the old regime, had no prospect for the future, and initially it was to encourage young men in similar distressful situations that Nakamura began to translate *Self-Help*. He spent four years as a political exile in the countryside of Shizuoka. Fortunately, the translation of the English book by the most accomplished Confucian scholar of the time made a strong appeal to the Japanese on both sides, Imperial as well as shogunal. When their country was widely opened in 1868, the Japanese were shocked and bewildered by the industrial civilization of the West. Compared with Western intruders, they seemed to know nothing about how to get along in the world. Recognizing their backwardness, and becoming anxious to catch up with the developed nations, they turned their eyes to the West. The Japanese were thirsting for knowledge of the West and were eager to know the secret of its industrial greatness. It was the same thirst which made the overseas returnee Fukuzawa Yukichi's book *Seiyō-jijō* (Conditions in the West) the best-seller of the day. While Fukuzawa explained physical conditions in Europe and America, Nakamura, respected Confucian scholar recently returned from the West, made moral sides of the Westerners known to the Japanese. *Self-Help* was welcomed as the first book that gave information in such respects. Smiles's book, written for young people, is composed largely of biographical sketches of eminent Westerners: numerous examples are cited in it of what famous statesmen, engineers and inventors had done to help themselves reach higher planes of achievement. Ambitious youths in Japan, in the same way as ambitious youths in England or America, enjoyed reading the book's stories of struggles and achievements of others. Smiles was a son of the industrial revolution, and took a special interest in the lives of inventors and engineers. The first sentences both in the English original and in Nakamura's *kanbun-kundoku-tai* Japanese are sonorous:

'Heaven helps those who help themselves' is a well-tried maxim, embodying in a small compass the results of vast human experience. The spirit of self-help is the root of all genuine growth in the individual; and, exhibited in the lives of many, it constitutes the true source of national vigour and strength. Help from without is often enfeebling in its effects, but help from within invariably invigorates.[11]

'Ten wa mizukara tasukurumono wo tasuku' to ieru kotowaza wa, kakuzen keiken shitaru kakugen nari. Wazukani ikku no naka ni amaneku jinji seibai no jikken o hōzo seri. Mizukara tasuku to iukotowa yoku jishu-jiryū shite, tanin no chikara ni yorazarukotonari. Mizukara tasukuru no seishin wa, oyoso hito tarumonono saichi no yotte shōzurutokoro no kongen nari. Oshite kore o ieba, mizukara tasukuru jinmin ōkereba, sono hōgoku kanarazu genki jūjitsushi, seishin kyōsei narukoto nari. Tanin yori tasuke o ukete jōjuseru mono wa, sononochi kanarazu otorouru koto ari. Shikaruni uchi mizukara tasukete nasu tokoro no koto wa, kanarazu seichō shite fusegu bekarazaru no ikioi ari.[12]

Nakamura's Japanese may seem rather complicated at first sight for Western Japan scholars. However, it is not. The book's easy, flowing style was an element of what made it popular. Nakamura achieved a style that still strikes a respondent chord in many people. Nakamura, moreover, was cautious enough to ask Koga Kin'ichirō, a senior Confucian scholar, and Sanda Kanemitsu, an open-minded National scholar, to write introductions recommending *Self-Help* to Japanese readers. Nakamura himself wrote in vigorous Chinese personal comments which were most convincing. Nakamura's introductory note written in lucid Chinese to Chapter II 'Leaders of Industry – Inventors and Producers' is indeed a hymn to the achievements brought by the Industrial Revolution to the peoples of the West.

The Meiji government was tolerant towards ex-retainers of the Tokugawa shogunate. Together with Fukuzawa's Keiō gijuku, Nakamura's private school Dōjinsha opened in Edogawa, Tokyo, enjoyed an immense popularity. Both Fukuzawa and Nakamura could hire Westerners as teachers because both of them earned large amounts in royalties from their books. The two books, which many members of the Iwakura mission read before and during their two-year trip (1871–73) to America and Europe were without doubt Fukuzawa's travel guidebook, *Seiyō tabiannai,* and Nakamura's translation of *Self-Help.* Smiles's book must have suggested to the members what they should see in the West, especially in British factories. The weaving machine that the Iwakura mission saw in Manchester on 3 September 1872, was minutely recorded by Kume

Kunitake, official scribe of the mission. That record is a sort of continuation of the description of weaving machines written by Smiles. There in a factory at Manchester, an interesting conversation took place between Kido Takayoshi (Kōin) and an English engineer. The Japanese vice-minister asked about the possibility of outsiders imitating the machine. The possibility of a Japanese imitation of the machine never crossed the English engineer's mind, and he replied: 'Germans have tried hard to advance in this field. However, as they are clumsy, it is impossible for them to overtake the British.'[13]

However, the translation of Smiles's book provided an incentive to a provincial Japanese youth: Toyoda Sakichi[14] went on to more than 'imitate' – he invented. Sakichi was born as the son of a carpenter in a village near the lake Hamana-ko in 1867[15] while Nakamura was still studying in London. Even though Sakichi's schooling was limited to four years he became a very productive inventor of weaving machines. In East Asia, Japan is comparatively rich in inventors, and the statistics concerning inventors and inventions are generally estimated by the number of patent-holders. In short, the very notion of patent, the system of royalty, licence to use a patented invention and the existence of industrialists who welcome practical applications of scientific principles are the prerequisites, without which it would be difficult for any industrializing country to have an inventor.

In Japan it was Smiles's account of the life of a British inventor Heathcoat,[16] which propagated the notion of patent. A very interesting story is told about Heathcoat's trial, when Sir John Copley (afterwards Lord Lyndhurst) was retained for the defence in the interest of Heathcoat. When Heathcoat's rights as a patentee were disputed and his claims as an inventor called into question, Copley learnt to work the bobbinet-machine in order that he might master the details of the invention. The gist of the story is as follows: On reading over his brief, Copley immediately offered to go down into the country and he did not leave the lace-loom until Copley himself could make a piece of bobbin-net with his own hands, and thoroughly understood the principle as well as the details of the machine. When the case came up for trial, Copley was able to work the model on the table with such ease and skill, and explain the precise nature of the invention with such clarity, that everyone present was astonished – judge, jury and spectators. Hence the reason why Heathcoat's patent right was publicly recognized.

This anecdote, which became common knowledge among Japanese readers of *Self-Help,* highlighted the importance of the patent system; consequently, the patent act, drafted by Takahashi Korekiyo, was promulgated in Japan on 18 April 1885. The timing was very good. From around the year 1887, Toyoda Sakichi began his career as inventor, and his man-powered, made of wood weaving-machine was first patented in 1891. Between then and the year of his death in 1930, Toyoda Sakichi obtained 84 Japanese patents and 13 foreign patents for his inventions.

They were of course his own inventions but sadly, the popular biographies of Toyoda Sakichi were embarassing and not very fair. I have discovered that practically all of them are retold stories of the life of John Heathcoat. Of course they are written using Japanese names. The reason for this literary imitation is as follows: when Toyoda Sakichi died in 1930, Yora Matsusaburō, a Nagoya journalist, asked ghost-writers to write Sakichi's biography. As they knew the legend that the young Sakichi was enthusiastic about inventing new machines and that he was very much encouraged by the lives of inventors told by Smiles in his *Self-Help,* Yora and his ghost-writers used Smiles's book freely, and in 1931 wrote the fictitious life of Toyoda Sakichi modelled on that of John Heathcoat.

In juvenile literature, Japanese authors do not pay much attention to historical facts or exactitude; writers hired by rival publishing companies copied, varied, amplified or digested the Yora version of the life of Toyoda Sakichi. It is really deplorable that there exist so many kinds of biographical writings about Toyoda Sakichi which, although very similar to each other, are full of myths either imagined or anecdotes copied from *Self-Help.* In these biographies for children, authors insist on the meaning of originality, on the importance of invention, on the civilized practices of patent and intellectual property rights, while those authors themselves are writing the life of the inventor Toyoda Sakichi by plagiarizing works written by others, which are in their turn products of literary thefts. Toyoda museums are full of these Toyoda Sakichi biographies written for children.

In the official biography published by the Toyoda Corporation in 1933 and reprinted in 1955, there is no plagiarism, and no mention of Sakichi's having read Smiles's *Self-Help* either. Instead, in the official biography written during the years of Japanese nationalism, the agricultural reformer Ninomiya Sontoku's influence on the young Sakichi is much stressed. What is interesting, however, is the historical fact that Smiles's utilitarian morality and teaching of self-help could be readjusted in Japanese soil without much opposition because they could be grafted onto traditional Japanese ideas of the work ethic almost naturally. This process may be attested by the following episode.

In a story entitled *Tetsu-santan* which Kōda Rohan wrote in 1890 to instil the work ethic into young people, the book that its hero is to read is Ninomiya Sontoku's *Hōtoku-ki* (Account of Recompensing Virtue) written in 1856.[17] Ninomiya Sontoku is an agricultural reformer. When Smiles's book became popular, Rohan changed the title of his hero's inspiration to Nakamura's translation of *Self-Help*. Yet the admonition of the author to the hero: 'The fruits of your labours will derive from Heaven's boundless abundance'[18] is the same. Rohan's exclamations, 'This book made me what I am', fits either source of inspiration equally well.[19]

The process of the transfer of the work ethic from that of an agricultural reformist to that of an industrial inventor is minutely told by Suzuki Tōsaburō (1855–1913), born and brought up in the same region of Hamana-ko. Suzuki was older than Toyoda Sakichi by twelve years: Suzuki's autobiographical writing[20] is an eloquent illustration of how people working diligently in an agricultural society under the influence of Ninomiya Sontoku (1787–1856) could become inventive workers and diligent engineers in a newborn industrial society. Okada Ryōichirō (1839–1915), disciple of Ninomiya Sontoku, was the most well known agricultural reformer of that region in the final years of the Tokugawa shogunate; he later became a leading figure in the local industrialization movement in the early years of Meiji. It was Okada who imported British-made weaving machines in 1884 in order to open the Enshū spinning company. Toyoda Sakichi, who was living nearby, must have had the opportunity to examine them, before proceeding to invent his own automatic looms.

The novelist Kunikida Doppo (1871–1908), in a short story entitled *Hibon-naru bonjin* (An Uncommon Common Man) written in 1903, portrays Katsura Shōsaku, a youth fully imbued with the spirit of *Self-Help*. Katsura, a boy brought up in a village, idealizes Watt, Edison and Stephenson, saves his money, and goes to Tokyo to work his way through school. Though poor, he exhibits none of the heedlessness towards life's necessities that has often been depicted as a quality in the traditional swashbucking hero-gallant of East Asia. Instead, Katsura supports himself and his brother while going on to become an electrical engineer who is earnestly 'absorbed in the work he is daily performing'.[21] He walks around and around some equipment, checking to discover the cause of its malfunction and then repairs it. It would be difficult to find such an uncommon common man who has set his mind to do something with his own hands in other East Asian countries in the first years of the twentieth century, since his behaviour is contrary to the Confucian ideal of a gentleman who is not an implement (*junzi buqi*). Katsura, however, fits Smiles's description of a man devoted to his trade. In his preface to the translation of *Self-Help* Nakamura hailed in exclamations: 'Ah, how happy Western peoples are today!' The reason that Japan could follow examples of Western peoples rather quickly and could enjoy the benefits of electrical lighting in rural villages so early is that the majority of Japanese shared Doppo's sympathy with Katsura: there was a large reservoir of uncommon common men toiling diligently in the Meiji era. The most familiar figure of Meiji literature is undoubtedly Botchan, hero of Natsume Sōseki's novel written in 1906. Although readers do not pay much attention to its ending, the hero, having given up his teaching position in Matsuyama, became, like Katsura of Doppo's novel, an electrical engineer with the monthly pay of twenty-five yen. It is quite symbolical that the most popular hero of modern Japanese literature ends his career this way.

The lessons preached by Smiles were quickly transplanted into Japanese soil and became the foundation for 'overcoming adversity' and for 'earnest application' in Meiji youths. The philosophy implied in these slogans – that possibilities were unlimited for the individual with ability and that everything depended on personal application – fit the realities of early Meiji society. This philosophy was also expressed in common parlance. However, one should also keep in mind the less glamorous reasons when explaining why this transplantation took place so smoothly. One reason is that at least superficially, the lessons contained in *Self-Help* are arbitrarily and conclusively stated. In both the original and the translation, the doctrines are asserted with categorical authority. This arbitrary though edifying style, which is rather at odds with the work's purpose, was probably congenial to men born and raised in a feudal, authoritarian value system. As George B. Sansom wrote:

> It was unfortunate that, when at last the Japanese had time to consider the nobler efforts of the Western mind, it was the dreary ratiocinations of Herbert Spencer or the homiletic of men like Benjamin Franklin and Samuel Smiles which seemed best to stay their intellectual pangs.[22]

A Japanese raised within the Tokugawa Confucian tradition could accept the injunctions of Smiles and Franklin precisely because he was accustomed to their style of homily.

In 1878, the Meiji empress translated Benjamin Franklin's 'Twelve Virtues' into traditional Japanese *uta*-poems. Regarding industry, Franklin had written in his *Autobiography*: 'Industry: Lose no time; be always employed in something useful; cut off all unnecessary actions.' The young empress, who had learned Franklin's 'Virtues' from her Confucian imperial tutor Motoda Eifu as part of her education, transcribed this into traditional poetic form and 'bestowed it upon the Tokyo Women's Normal School,' whose students had previously accompanied her procession at the school's opening ceremonies presided by the principal Nakamura Masanao. The poem,[23] adapted to music composed by Oku Yoshiisa, soon gained popularity and was sung in every part of the country:

> A diamond left unpolished
> Will give out no jewel light;
> Only after earnest learning
> Is one's true worth seen to shine.
>
> If we know to prize the sunlight
> Doing our best the whole day
> Like the clock's hands never idle,
> There's no work that can't be done.

The tendency to modernize from above is discernible in all late modernizing countries, but in the Meiji era, when the need to 'foster industry and promote enterprise' was felt especially keenly, the royal poetess saw in Franklin's 'Virtues' a new morality for civil society and took the initiative of Japanizing and introducing it to the people through the medium of traditional poetry.

Of course, the virtues of diligence and application were not new to the Japanese people in the Meiji period. The school song composed by the empress was, to be sure, Franklin's injunction in one sense, but in other respects, it was fully Japanese. In Tokugawa times, there was a saying that 'hardships polish one into a jewel'. The thirteenth-century Zen monk Dōgen wrote:

> The jewel becomes a jewel through polishing. Man becomes really human through training. No jewel shines in its natural state. No novice is characterized by keenness from the very beginning. They must be polished and trained.[24]

If we go back even further, we will find virtually the same injunction in the *Book of Rites*: 'Unless the jewel is polished, it does not become a jewel; unless men study, they do not learn the Way.'[25] Precisely because this idea of character-building had a long tradition in Buddhism and Confucianism in East Asia, the Japanese were able to educate themselves so diligently and in such a sustained fashion during the Meiji 'Civilization and Enlightenment' period. Indeed, Ninomiya Sontoku's *Account of Recompensing Virtue* (*Hōtoku-ki*) was reevaluated after the Russo-Japanese War. Ninomiya's asceticism of self-restraint and moral cultivation was an ethos that dominated the rural villages until the end of World War II and much later.

Every age, however, has its fashions. For example, 'becoming a success and rising in the world' sounds old-fashioned and pretentious, but when rephrased as 'self-realization', the same aspiration becomes modern and chic. Similarly, in early Meiji times, when everything traditionally Japanese or Asian seemed anachronistic, young hearts were not inspired by quotations from Dōgen or the *Book of Rites*.

The ratiocinations of Spencer and the homiletics of men like Franklin and Smiles are surely dreary. After *Self-Help* had outlived its early popularity, the book was regarded as a joke[26] in Japan also,[27] but principally by young people who had not read it. The comment given to *Self-Help* in *Kenkyusha's New English-Japanese Dictionary* (4th edition, 1960) defined it curtly as the book that teaches honesty and diligence are the elements of success in life. In the 5th edition (1980) the name of *Self-Help* itself disappeared.

Nonetheless, there was something touching in the following episodes: Masaoka Shiki, a great Meiji reformer of Japanese poetry, – he had used Spencer to justify his poetical innovation – read Franklin's *Autobiography* on his death-bed when ill with tuberculosis and was deeply impressed by it. Shimazaki Tōson, later a naturalist writer of great renown, used Franklin's *Autobiography* as a text at a country school when he was a young teacher of English. These curious combinations were possible in the Meiji era, and these details illustrate what the Japanese were concerned about during the period of their nation's rise to statehood.

Finally, we must consider that just as the activities of citizens in Western societies, many of them Protestants, later supported nationalism, the 'diligence and application' of Meiji youths also became linked with nationalism in Japan. Self-cultivation did not stop at the personal level for Meiji youths but became associated with preserving Japan's independence in the face of Western encroachment. Morality and application came together in service to the larger community. As Fukuzawa Yukichi put it, again in *An Encouragement of Learning*:

> When we compare Oriental Confucianism with Western civilization, we discover that what is possessed by the latter and is lacking in the former is (1) mathematics in the realm of the tangible and (2) the spirit of independence in the realm of the intangible.[28]

Fukuzawa advocated cultivating the individual's spirit of independence. Based on Mill's view that 'the worth of a State, in the long run, is the worth of the individuals composing it', Fukuzawa proposed that every Japanese 'achieve his own independence, and then Japan would be independent'. It is interesting to note that the Confucian spirit repudiated by Fukuzawa functioned quite smoothly in this process, as Confucianism held that 'personal cultivation and regulation of family affairs' was requisite to 'ordering the realm and bringing peace to all under Heaven'. Each citizen's 'self-culture' in the form of 'self-help' led directly to 'ordering the realm' in the sense of 'national wealth and power' (or its synonym, 'national independence').[29] Thus it was fortunate for Japan that 'overcoming hardship through diligence' and 'becoming a success and rising in the world' in private life were in complete harmony with Japan's fortunes as a state. In this sense, self-help was by no means at odds with traditional Japanese values; it was reinforced by them.

It is said that the Protestant work ethic, which Smiles so much extolled, has corroded in Protestant countries. In Japan, too, alas, the names of Smiles and of Nakamura Masanao have begun to be forgotten. In the latter half of the twentieth century, for example, the word 'welfare' enjoys greater popularity than 'self-help'. People tend to rely more on public sectors' help and to neglect self-reliance. However, I for one, still believe that self-help is the best help and that our philosphy of development assistance to other countries as well as to other individuals should be: 'Help others to help themselves'.

*Notes*

[1] Kokusho kankōkai, ed.:*Bummei genryū sōsho* (Tokyo: Kokusho kankōkai, 1913), vol. 1 p. 136.

[2] 'Hakodate yori no ryakki' in Morinaka Akimitsu ed.: *Niijima sensei shokanshū* (Kyoto: Dōshisha kōyūkai, 1942–1960), p. 1137.

³ 'Gakumon no susume (shohen)' in *Fukuzawa Yukichi zenshū*, vol. 3, p. 30. This work has been translated into English by David Dilworth and Umeyo Hirano as *An Encouragement to Learning* (Tokyo: Sophia University Press, 1969).

⁴ Inoue Tsutomu's translation was published in Tokyo by Hakubunsha in 1883. See also George B. Sansom: *The Western World and Japan* (New York: Knopf, 1950), p. 419.

⁵ As for Samuel Smiles and his Japanese translator Nakamura, there are short but sharp observations made by G. B. Sansom: *The Western World and Japan* (London: Cresset, 1950) p. 484, and also by Sansom: *Japan, A Short Cultural History* (London: Cresset, 1932) p. 504. Marius B. Jansen made an interesting remark in Marius B Jansen ed.: *Changing Japanese Attitudes Toward Modernization* (Princeton University Press, 1965), p. 67. I wrote a serialized study on Nakamura Masanao and *Self-Help* entitled 'Ten wa mizukara tasukurumono wo tasuku' in the monthly *Gakutō* (April, 2001–December, 2003 issue).

⁶ Nakamura's translation of *Self-Help* is entitled *Saikoku risshi hen*, Wang Yangming school had put an emphasis on *risshi* (*lizhi* in Chinese). That is the reason why Nakamura, a Yangming scholar, put the word in its Japanese title. To retranslate it into such English titles as *The Establishment of Will Power in the West* (Haru Reischauer: *Samurai and Silk*, Belknap Harvard, 1986, p.181) is a mistake; *Collection of Stories about Success in the West* (Kinmonth: *The Self-Made Man in Meiji Japanese Thought*, University of California Press, 1981) is also misleading. *Shi* (*zhi* in Chinese, or *kokorozashi* in *kun* reading in Japanese) means *will* as an ambitious student has it. *Shi* in *risshi* has a connotation nobler than a common will to succeed. This will be seen from the English translation given by Jansen to *shishi*, Restoration activists, as *men of high purpose* (Marius Jansen: *Sakamoto Ryōma and the Meiji Restoration*, Princeton U.P. 1961). We should not overlook this nuance of *high purpose* in the word *shi*.

⁷ *Saikoku risshi hen* is reprinted and still available (Tokyo: Kōdansha gakujutsubunko, 1981)

⁸ See A. Briggs: *Victorian People* (Penguin Books, 1990), p.124.

⁹ One of the first texts of moral education widely used in Japanese elementary and middle schools in the 1870s was no other than Nakamura's translation of *Self-Help*, and the book's influence is recognizable in later texts of moral education. I myself was brought up during WWII, but as a schoolboy I learnt the story of the British physician Jenner in my textbook when Japan was at war with the British Empire. That story of the discoverer of vaccination was taken almost word for word from Smiles's book.

¹⁰ Nakamura's translation of *On Liberty* became a fountainhead of liberalism during the Meiji Enlightenment. As an ex-retainer of the defeated Tokugawa shogunate, Nakamura must have tried to check the establishment of a new arbitrary government by the victorious Imperial powers: that must be one important reason why he introduced J. S. Mill's arguments on his return home. Nakamura's clear Japanese translation is far better than Yan Fu's Chinese translation.

[11] Samuel Smiles: *Self-Help* (London: John Murray, one shilling edition, 1913) p. 1.

[12] Nakamura Masanao: *Saikoku risshi hen* (Tokyo: Fuzanbō, 1938) pp. 2–3. This Fuzanbō edition edited by Yanagida Izumi is most reliable among many editions of *Saikoku risshi hen*.

[13] The anecdote is recorded in Kume Kunitake: *Kyūjūnen kaikoroku* (Tokyo: Waseda daigaku shuppanbu, 1934). The English translation is mine.

[14] In order to distinguish the public aspect from the private, Toyoda Sakichi used Toyota for his weaving machine companies while he retained Toyoda for his family use. By the way, Sakichi's grandson, Toyoda Shōichirō, chairman of the Toyota Motor Corporation, was the chairman of *Keidanren* (the Japan Federation of Economic Organizations) in the 1990s.

[15] Incidentally, the writer Kōda Rohan, who in the 1890s became the leading proponent of the ideas of *Self-Help*, was also born in that year 1867.

[16] Samuel Smiles: *Self-Help* (London: John Murray, one shilling edition, 1913) pp. 56–65.

[17] *Tetsu-santan* was first published in the monthly *Shōnen-en* of January issue, 1890. See *Rohan zenshū* (Tokyo: Iwanami shoten, 1953) vol. 10, pp. 229–233.

[18] *Rohan zenshū*, vol. 10, p. 233.

[19] In answer to an *enquête* by the monthly *Seikō*, April, 1904, Kōda Rohan counts among books that inspired him Ninomiya Sontoku's *Hōtokuki* and Nakamura's *Saikoku risshi hen*. Other books mentioned are *Lun yu, Mencius,* Wang Yangming's *Zhuanxilu* and the *New Testament*.

[20] Suzuki Tōzaburō, 'Kōchi kaihatsu shugi' in Tomeoka Kōsuke ed.: *Hōtoku no shinzui* (Tokyo: Keiseisha, 1908).

[21] Kunikida Doppo, 'Hibon-naru bonjin' in *Kunikida Doppo shū* (Tokyo: Kaizōsha, 1927) p. 162.

[22] George B. Sansom: *Japan, a Short Cultural History* (London: Cresset, 1932) p. 504. See also Earl H. Kinmonth: *The Self-Made Man in Meiji Japanese Thought: From Samurai to Salary Man* (Berkeley and Los Angeles: University of California Press, 1981)

[23] For the original poem, see Inoue Takeshi, ed.: *Nihon shōkashū* (Tokyo: Iwanami shoten, 1958), pp.48–9. The translation is Eileen Kato's.

[24] Nihon koten bungaku taikei, vol. 81: *Shōbōgenzō, Shōbōgenzō zuimonki* (Tokyo: Iwanami shoten, 1965), p. 397.

[25] See the chapter 'Music' in *The Book of Rites*. For further details see *Raiki; Kokuyaku kambun taisei*, vol. 24 (Tokyo: Kokumin bunko kankōkai, 1921) p. 351.

[26] The observation was made by Robertson Davies, *A Voice from the Attic* (Penguin Book, 1990) p. 39. It should be noted that Davies adds after the phrase, 'It was no joke.'

[27] One of the first Japanese who mocked at the idea of success as illustrated by Smiles and his Japanese followers is Sōsuke, protagonist of

Natsume Sōseki's novel *Mon* (1910). Sōsuke coolly discards the monthly *Seikō*. See *Sōseki zenshū* (Tokyo: Iwanami shoten, 1956) vol. 9, p. 54.

[28] 'Kyōiku no hōshin wa sūri to dokuritsu', in *Fukuzawa Yukichi zenshū*, vol. 3, p. 198.

[29] The quotations are from the Confucian *Great Learning*. Words prior to Chapter I. Nakamura as the first principal of Tokyo Women's Normal School explained the objective of the new education not only in terms of the Civilization and Enlightenment movement but also in these traditional terms at the opening ceremony speech of the school in 1875. The school, first higher institution for women in East Asia, is today called Ochanomizu joshi daigaku.

# REACTION AGAINST 'SLAVISH' WESTERNIZATION

———————□———————

I n Japan, during the first two decades of the Meiji era, it seemed
as if the entire nation was determined to Westernize itself completely, but in the late 1880s, a reaction set in. Nevertheless, this
'return to Japan' or 'return to being Japanese' was not a reversion to
the blind xenophobia of late Tokugawa times. It was a kind of reaction against 'slavish' Westernization.

In 1887, Foreign Minister Inoue Kaoru was pursuing a policy of
Westernization symbolized by balls and garden parties in the
Rokumeikan that were designed as an aid to procuring treaty revi-
sions from the Western powers.[1] Inoue spoke of the 'recovery of
judicial authority' for Japan, but in reality he was willing to accept
the Westerners' treaty demands that foreign judges continue to pre-
side in all cases involving foreign nationals. When an opposition
faction headed by Inoue Kowashi learned of this, it leaked certain
secret documents, thereby inciting fierce anti-government agitation.
Among those documents was a criticism by Boissonade of the government's frivolous Westernization policy. The French jurist, one of
the most respected hired foreigners in Meiji Japan, pointed out that
at that time in all areas – the armed services, administration, finance,
education – in which foreigners served as employees or advisers,
they were not permitted to obtain government posts or to wield
actual government authority. Any system under which judicial
authority was delegated to foreigners, he stressed, would be inju-
rious to Japan's national interests and would open the door to
foreign intervention in domestic affairs.[2]

It is noteworthy that foreign employees like Boissonade were critical of Japan's craze for Westernization. Nevertheless, the 'return to Japan' was not triggered solely by the advice of such well-intentioned foreigners. What is more important is that some Japanese began to criticize Westerners in terms of the universal principles of 'civilization' they had learned from the West. One example was the *Normanton* incident.

In 1886, the *Normanton,* an English ship, sank off the Wakayama coast. Its English captain and foreign crew scrambled to safety in lifeboats, leaving all the Japanese passengers to drown. Despite widespread public indignation, a consular court in Kobe exonerated the captain and crew of charges of criminal negligence. The reaction was predictable: 'The news spread like lightning throughout the four quarters, and all people, whether in or out of government, were overwhelmed with grief and righteous indignation. Newspapers were filled with editorials and articles treating the incident in a tragic or righteously indignant light.'[3] This sense of outrage played its part in bringing to a close the craze for Westernization symbolized by Inoue Kaoru's balls at the Rokumeikan.

What provoked Japanese ire about the shipwreck and the court's verdict, in addition to the realization of racial prejudice, was the fact that the English captain and court had not lived up to the West's self-avowed standards. They had been furnished to the Japanese through Nakamura's Japanese translation of Smiles's *Self-Help*. Many Japanese originally were inspired by *Saikoku risshi hen*, because of its anecdotes of those who give their life in order to achieve Goodness. For example, one story proclaims that when the British ship *Birkenhead* sank off the coast of Africa, the English army officers and soldiers turned over the lifeboats to women and children. The 37th story of Chapter XIII reads:

> There was no boat remaining, and no hope of safety; but not a heart quailed; no one flinched from his duty in that trying moment. 'There was not a murmur nor a cry amongst them,' said Captain Wright, a survivor, 'until the vessel made her final plunge.' Down went the ship, and down went the heroic band, firing a *feu de joie* as they sank beneath the waves.

The hearts of Meiji readers were struck by 'this memorable illustration of the chivalrous spirit of common men'. East Asians were proud of their Confucian ethics. The Japanese ruling class, being warriors, held in high respect the following teaching of the *Analects*: 'The true gentleman sacrifices his life to preserve his virtue.'[4] The samurai had learnt by heart the sage's maxim: 'Neither the knight who has truly the heart of a knight nor the man of good stock who has the qualities that belong to good stock will ever seek life at the expense of Goodness.'[5] However, actually East Asians had not heard such commendable stories of nautical chivalry.

The rule of the British Navy that 'a captain goes down with his ship' was followed again and again until the end of World War II, not only in the Japanese Imperial Navy but also in Japan's merchant marine. Japanese youths had devoted themselves to creating a modern Japan based on Western models precisely because the injunctions and exemplars contained in *Self-Help* seemed to conform to their own ethical ideals. When these overly idealized images were betrayed and exposed as false by the actual deeds of living Englishmen, the Japanese reaction was to explode with anger and indignation.

This incident itself, to be sure, should not be interpreted as ending Japan's turn to the West. The 'return to Japan' claimed more and more vocally by some Japanese intellectuals was not a wholesale rejection of the West in favour of a total return to ancient foundations so much as a genuine appropriation of the best in Japanese tradition. It was a practical and realistic reaction.

Education reflects the change, and what can be called the 'Japanization' of education took place.

Upon his arrival in Japan in 1873, Basil Hall Chamberlain (1850–1935), who later became the dean of foreign Japanologists residing in Japan, worked as an instructor of English in the then fledgling Imperial Japanese Navy. He taught English, using Southey's *Life of Nelson*. About the young Japanese naval officers, successors of the Tokugawa samurai, whom he taught, Chamberlain wrote that they were 'fairly fluent in English, and dressed in a serviceable suit of dittos, might almost be a European, save for a certain obliqueness of the eyes and scantiness of beard'.[6] Education was conducted totally in English by British naval instructors. At that time even the national anthem was also sung in English, as was the anthem *God save the Queen*!

Chamberlain noted the fluency in English of the first generation of Meiji naval officers. This held true beyond the students in Japan's naval academy, for the generation born around 1860 produced an élite better able to communicate in foreign languages than could its successors. Men like Okakura Kakuzō (alias Tenshin, b. 1862), Uchimura Kanzō (b. 1861), and Nitobe Inazō (b. 1862) all wrote books in English; and Mori Ōgai (b. 1862) probably did more than anyone else to introduce Western literature to Japan.

Natsume Sōseki (1867–1916), who was born a few years later, graduated from Tokyo Imperial University in 1893, took over Lafcadio Hearn's post as the first Japanese lecturer in English literature in 1903, and then in late Meiji left academic life to concentrate on his writing. His remarks about the capabilities of Japanese students in English over time provide a revealing insight into the Japanization of Meiji higher education. The students' command of English was declining, he noted, because of the proper and predictable progress achieved by Japanese education:

> In my generation, all instruction at regular schools was done in English. In all courses – geography, history, mathematics, botany and biology – we used foreign-language textbooks. Most students who came a little before us even wrote their answers in English; and by my generation, there were some Japanese instructors who taught mathematics in English.[7]

In that era, he went on, English was only one aspect of an excessive subordination to foreign culture: 'Men would show off by dangling gold watches, wearing Western dress, growing beards, and interjecting English phrases when speaking ordinary Japanese.'[8] Not only was English fashionable, but modern knowledge was as yet inaccessible in Japanese:

> Because we had so much English training outside regular English classes, our ability to read, write and speak developed naturally. But we all are Japanese in mind, and considering our independence as a nation, such an educational system is, in a sense, a disgrace. It invokes in us the feeling that we are no different from India, that we are subjects of England. We all agree on the importance of Japan's nationality; it is not something to be exchanged for a mere knowledge of English. Hence, as the foundations for our state's survival are solidified, the aforementioned educational system ought naturally to fall into disuse; and in fact, this is precisely what is taking place.[9]

Not enough had been translated yet, and the use of many foreign textbooks was still unavoidable. But scholarship was universal, and once there were adequate materials and competent Japanese teachers, Japanese students were increasingly taught in their own language.

> From the standpoint of widely diffusing scholarship in society, it would be best to teach in Japanese, the language in which our students have been brought up and which they use naturally ... The declining use of English is natural and to be expected.[10]

But government policy also came into play and might even have proved more important than these cultural aspects. As Sōseki saw it:

The biggest cause for declining English abilities in Japan was man-made, in the form of a policy adopted, I believe, when the late Inoue Kowashi was minister of education [1892–6]. The decision was to teach all subjects except English in Japanese as much as possible. While emphasizing the importance of the Japanese language in teaching, Inoue sought to revive Japanese literary and classical Chinese studies as well ... This man-made decision to suppress the use of foreign languages [in education] is an overwhelmingly important factor behind the present decline in language abilities.[11]

In early Meiji years, the modernization of Japanese institutions and ways was construed as 'Westernization'. However, the desire to modernize was generated by an external crisis. To achieve independence for the Japanese people and nation became a categorical imperative. It was, therefore, inevitable that Japanese students studying abroad would, upon their return home, appropriate the positions temporarily held by foreign employees in and out of government.

Inoue Kowashi, too, advocated modernization with less Westernization. Like many other Meiji leaders, his objective was not 'the importation of things Western' but, rather, 'Western-style production' in Japan. After the 'political crisis of 1881', he submitted a political programme to the government in which he outlined the educational policies that he thought the state should adopt. Two clauses in his programme read:

*The Promotion of Chinese Studies:*
Since the Restoration, English and French studies have had high priority, and this has caused the sprouts of revolutionary thought to appear in our country for the first time. However, for teaching the Way of loyalty to ruler, love of country and allegiance – values in danger of disappearing at present – nothing equals Chinese studies. We must revive these values and thereby maintain a balance.[12]

*Encouraging the Study of German:*
Under our present educational system, the only students who study the German language are found in medicine. Students studying law and related subjects all learn English and French. It is only natural that those who study English admire English ways, and that those who study French envy French government. But of all nations in present-day Europe, only Prussia is similar to us with regard to the circumstances of its unification ... If we want to make men throughout the land more conservative minded, we should encourage the study of German and thereby allow it, several years hence, to overcome the dominance now enjoyed by English and French.[13]

It was Inoue who, with Motoda Eifu, drafted the Imperial Rescript on Education promulgated in 1890. In the preceding passage, we can see that as early as 1881 Inoue wanted to return to East Asian traditions and to uphold national unity by means of a philosophy stressing virtues such as loyalty to ruler, love of nation and allegiance to superiors.

This turn of its course on education had, however, a significant side-effect. Among the generation that studied directly under foreign teachers in Japan, there was a clarity of understanding regarding international affairs that proved lacking in later days. Naval officers are a case in point. Officers in the Russo-Japanese War for the most part fought on warships made in Britain. Unlike the officers in World War II, who fought on ships and flew in planes manufactured in Japan, they went to Britain or other foreign countries, observed how ships were built, and delivered the finished products to Japan themselves. At times, they might witness British labourers staging strikes, for example, and this broad range of experience made navy men international-minded. After that generation retired in the 1920s, the naval officers, like the ships they commanded, were 'made in Japan'. This was true also for the leaders in all other areas of government. In the 1930s, the entire nation was seized by a very narrow nationalism. That nationalism was partly due to conditions external to Japan, but it was able to gain ground in part because of the parochialism of Japanese education in that era.

An overview from the Charter Oath proclaimed in the first year of Meiji to the Imperial Rescript on Education further exemplifies the point, and suggests other areas of concern. The Charter Oath issued in 1868 and the Imperial Rescript on Education promulgated in 1890 may be considered official proclamations that mark the beginning and end of an era. With regard to the West, the Charter Oath states:

> All absurd usages of the past shall be broken through, and everything shall be based upon just and equitable principles of Nature.
> Wisdom and knowledge shall be sought throughout the world and thus the foundations of the Empire shall be strengthened.[14]

These two articles were declared by the victorious loyalists (*sonnō-ha*) to be the cultural and political policies to be undertaken by a unified new Japan. It is interesting to note that once the anti-foreign loyalists had toppled the *bakufu* and seized power themselves, they immediately proclaimed a policy of peace and opened the country to foreign trade and diplomatic intercourse. This fact exposed the slogan 'revere the Emperor, expel the barbarians' for what it had really been – a catchphrase devoid of meaningful content that was used to unite and mobilize the energies of dissident samurai activists.

Yet the new Meiji government's declaration that 'wisdom and knowledge shall be sought throughout the world' should not be interpreted as a simple by-product of its policy to establish peace and open the country. Yoshida Shōin, who defied *bakufu* law, had also 'sought knowledge throughout the world', and his purpose, too, was 'to strengthen the foundations of the Empire'. The commitment to abandon 'all the absurd usages of the past' was clearly indicative of the realization that Japan in 1868 was as yet unequipped to be a modern nation-state and showed a singular desire to learn from the West.

As opposed to the Charter Oath, which sought models to adopt in foreign nations, perceived to possess cultural superiority, the Imperial Rescript on Education issued twenty-two years later in 1890, sought these models, at least rhetorically, in a transcendent Japanese historical character. The Rescript reads:

> Be filial to your parents, affectionate to your brothers and sisters; as husbands and wives be harmonious, as friends true; bear yourselves in modesty and moderation; extend your benevolence to all; pursue learning and cultivate arts, and thereby develop intellectual faculties and perfect moral powers; furthermore, advance public good and promote common interests; always respect the Constitution and observe the laws; should emergency arise, offer yourselves courageously to the State; and thus guard and maintain the prosperity of Our Imperial Throne coeval with heaven and earth.[15]

These virtues appealed deeply to feelings traditionally held by the Japanese people. Moreover, the Rescript asserts that 'ever united', the nation 'has from generation to generation illustrated the beauty' of those virtues, thus pushing national unity and the source of national morality far back to the historical origins of the Japanese people. Conversely, such historicism posits the continued existence of national unity and morality throughout all periods of Japanese history, thereby giving birth to the concept of a historically transcendent 'national character' (*kokutai*).[16]

The Rescript was not anti-Western in thrust. The exhortations to 'pursue learning and cultivate arts, and thereby develop intellectual faculties and perfect moral powers; furthermore, advance public good and promote common interests' are almost identical to those put forth by Smiles in *Self-Help*. Thus, although it is often characterized as a simple piece of Confucian reaction, elements meeting the demands of a new age are to be found in this document. The

Rescript did not assert that Japanese traditions were universal principles; rather, it proclaimed that values then regarded as universal in nature really conformed to traditional Japanese ways.

Yet, it is also evident that foreign nations disappeared from view in the Rescript. One distinguishing characteristic of the history of Japan after Perry's arrival in 1853 is that, unlike the period of national isolation, an inescapable influence was exerted on Japan by Western powers. In the Charter Oath of 1868, we find a declaration that for Japan, a latecomer to international society, in order to preserve national independence, the Japanese people must learn from foreign countries and progress along the road to civilization and enlightenment. By contrast, the only reference to Japan's relations with foreign countries mentioned in the Imperial Rescript on Education of 1890 is 'should emergency arise, offer yourselves courageously to the State; and thus guard and maintain the prosperity of Our Imperial Throne coeval with heaven the earth', which posits a hypothetical state of war.

The Imperial Rescript on Education, which ignored the existence of foreign civilizations and extolled the virtues of Japan's 'national character', was by no means indicative of recovered national self-confidence. The omission of foreign nations actually suggests a Japan filled with doubt and anxiety, a Japan unable to reject foreign influences completely and, therefore, driven to rely all the more on indigenous values. Such doubt and anxiety are revealed in the fact that, as opposed to the Charter Oath, the Rescript depicts foreign nations in a negative, almost menacing, light. The Rescript's aim is to create internal solidarity among the people by maintaining a common national morality, and a consciousness of that morality as stemming from shared origins in Japan's past. This aim is manifested from the beginning – 'Our Imperial Ancestors [stemming from the sun goddess, Amaterasu] have founded Our Empire on a basis broad and everlasting, and have deeply and firmly implanted virtue; Our subjects ever united in loyalty and filial piety ...' – to the end: 'It is Our wish to lay it to heart in all reverence, in common with you, Our subjects, that we may all attain to the same virtue.'[17]

Thus, the Imperial Rescript on Education clearly decreed the end of a fervent turn to the West, whose start was symbolized by the Charter Oath. Whereas the Charter Oath posited 'just and equitable principles of Nature', values assumed to be hitherto lacking in Japan, as a goal to be attained, the Rescript asserted that a 'national essence', whose values were already manifested in Japan's feudal past, should be the foundation for future action.

The Charter Oath can be compared to a small child just beginning to understand what is going on around him who seeks to
absorb things from his environment; in short, it shows the desire to
identify with the world. Conversely, towards the end of the 1880s,
after deciding that its turn to the West had been too sudden and
extreme, Japan sought an identity of its own, and part of this
straining to confirm an identity can be seen in the Imperial Rescript
on Education of 1890.

Japan, a non-Western nation, adopted from the West a tremendous amount of what was fundamental and essential to
modernization during these twenty-two years. Without those ideas
and institutions, the establishment of a national identity would have
been impossible, and the existence of an independent Japan, within
a society of nations dominated and ordered by the West, could not
have been maintained. At the same time, however, because of this
wholesale borrowing from the West, the basic establishment of a
'self', which had to be attained and upheld by the Japanese themselves, became a process filled with anxiety and uncertainty. In
short, the assimilation of Western culture was dictated by reasons
of state, yet such efforts were fraught with an uneasiness that
Japan's cultural self-identity might be violated. Because this psychological problem – a sense of pride easily injured – lay constantly at
the bottom of Japan's modernization process, the Japanese displayed what might be called a strange fanaticism in every
subsequent foreign crisis involving the West. The fact that the
slogan 'defend the national character' (*kokutai goji*)[18] had such a
powerful hold over Japanese hearts is undoubtedly also closely
related to this psychological problem.

*Notes*

[1] See Donald H. Shively: 'The Japanization of Middle Meiji', in Donald H.
Shively, ed.: *Tradition and Modernization in Japanese Culture* (Princeton N.J.:
Princeton University Press, 1971), pp. 77–119.
[2] See 'Bowasonaado gaikō iken', in *Meiji bunka zenshū*, vol. 6: *Gaikō-hen*
(Tokyo: Nihon hyōpronsha, 1928), pp. 451–2.
[3] For journalism on the Normanton Incident, see *Shimbun shūsei Meiji hen-
nenshi*, vol. 6 (Tokyo: Rinsensha, 1936), pp. 350, 356–7, 361, 365. See also
Richard T. Chang, *The Justice of the Western Consular Courts in Nineteenth
Century Japan* (Westport, Conn.: Greenwood Press, 1984).
[4] The translation is by James Legge. Confucius: *Confucian Analects, The
Great Learning & The Doctrine of the Mean* (New York: Dover, 1971) p. 297.

The Chinese original of the *Analects* (Book XV, 8) reads: 'Sha shen cheng ren.' It reads in Japanese: 'Mi o koroshite jin o nasu.'

[5] Arthur Waley: *The Analects of Confucius* (London: Unwin Hyman, 1988) p. 195.

[6] Basil Hall Chamberlin: *Things Japanese* (Rutland, Vt.: Tuttle, 1971), p. 1.

[7] 'Gogaku yōseihō', in *Sōseki zenshū* (Tokyo: Iwanami shoten, shinshoban, 1957), vol. 34, p. 233.

[8] Ibid. p. 233.

[9] Ibid. p. 233–4.

[10] Ibid. p. 234.

[11] Ibid. p. 234.

[12] 'Kangaku o susumu', in Inoue Kowashi denki-hensan iinkai, ed.: *Inoue Kowashi-den, shiryō* (Tokyo: Kokugakuin daigaku toshokan, 1966), vol. I, p. 250.

[13] 'Doitsugaku o okosu', in *Inoue Kowashi-den, shiryō*, pp. 250–1.

[14] This is my translation. There are many translations of the *gokajō no go-seimon*. As for a different official translation of the Charter Oath made on 1 January 1946, see Chapter 'R. H. Blyth and Hirohito's Denial of the "Divine" Character of the Japanese Emperor'.

[15] See R. Tsunoda and W. T. de Bary, eds.: *Sources of Japanese Tradition* (New York: Columbia University Press, 1958), pp. 646–7. This is the Japanese official translation of the Rescript. For the genesis of the Rescript, see also D. H. Shively, 'Motoda Eifu: Confucian Lecturer to the Meiji Emperor,' in D. S. Nivison and A. F. Wright, ed.: *Confucianism in Action* (Stanford University Press, 1959), pp. 302–3.

[16] *Kokutai* is a word, which may be translated 'national essence' in this context. It is more often translated as 'national polity' or 'national structure'.

[17] Quoted here is also the official translation. See George Sansom: *The Western World and Japan* (London: Cresset, 1950) p. 490. A better translation, originally published in the Tokyo educational magazine *The Museum*, is found, for example, in Lafcadio Hearn, 'The Diary of an English Teacher' in *The Writings of Lafcadio Hearn* (Boston and New York: Houghton Mifflin Company, 1922), vol. VI, pp. 119–120.

[18] The slogan '*kokutai goji*' was strongly claimed by many Japanese at the time of Japan's surrender 15 August 1945, although they could not define exactly what *kokutai* is. In this case 'national structure' would be a more suitable translation than 'national essence'. One thing is certain that when many Japanese claimed '*kokutai* goji', they wished that the Emperor's status after surrender would not be changed.

# ROKUMEIKAN: THE EUROPEANIZATION FEVER IN COMPARATIVE PERSPECTIVE[1]

If we look at the history of Russia and the history of Japan in terms of their relations with the West, we can find many parallel phenomena. Indeed, there is a book entitled *The Modernization of Japan and Russia* edited by Cyril E. Black and Marius B. Jansen.[2] In this comparative study the problems are mostly dealt with in abstract terms by distinguished social scientists. To the dissatisfaction of humanists like the present writer there are practically no references to the psychology of modernization and no mention at all of works of literature.[3] I found the study somewhat off-balance, and in this chapter I shall rely on some literary materials and try to analyse the ambivalent attitudes of the Japanese towards Westernization by referring to some corresponding Russian examples. This is a parallel comparison of Japan's and Russia's love-hate relationship with the West.

The symbolic event of the 'Europeanization fever' (*ōka-netsu*) in Japan, which I am going to deal with in this chapter, is the balls held at the Rokumeikan. The Rokumeikan was, according to the description given by the dictionary *Kōjien*,[4] 'the international social club built in the sixteenth year of Meiji (1883) in Kōjimachi, Tokyo (the vicinity of the Imperial Palace), for the exclusive use of the Japanese upper class and foreign dignitaries, and in that Western-style building, many evening parties, balls, fancy balls, masquerades, and charity gatherings were held. The place was the centre of the imitation of Western manners and customs. The name selected for the club (Deer Cry Pavilion) was taken from a banquet poem (#183) in the *Book of Songs.*' *Rokumei no en,* according to the same *Kojien,* is a synonym for a banquet for distinguished guests.

There are several literary works which deal with this international club. Akutagawa Ryūnosuke (1892–27) wrote 'Butōkai' (the Ball) in 1919. Mishima Yukio (1925–1970), who very much liked Akutagawa's short story, wrote a play 'Rokumeikan' in 1956. Etō Jun (1932–99) popularized again the international club in his serialized television drama 'Meiji no gunzō – Umi ni karin o' (Let's go abroad on a paddle-wheeler – portraits of Meiji people) in 1976. Beautiful ball scenes of by-gone days were a tremendous success on television. The Japanese audience apparently looked back upon the modernization efforts of the Meiji period with a sense of satisfaction. The Japanese of the 1970s seemed to feel that the prosperity of late-twentieth-century Japan owes much to the efforts of the modernizing élite of the late-nineteenth century. Moreover, they are increasingly aware of the distinction that modernization does not always mean Westernization; that must be one of the reasons that the viewers of Etō's television drama could enjoy the ball scenes of the Rokumeikan with a sense of detachment. The balls seemed quaint and exotic not only to Western guests of the 1880s but also to present-day Japanese. The scenes have qualities of the *ukiyo-e* prints of Kobayashi Kiyochika. Pierre Loti, who was invited to a Rokumeikan ball, recorded in his 'Un Bal à Yeddo' that Japanese ladies and girls in Parisian dress dance very correctly, but one feels that it is something *learnt* ('Elles dansent assez correctement, mes Nipponnes en robe parisienne. Mais on sent que c'est une chose *apprise.*'[5] There was something that was not natural in their dances. Indeed, Japanese had learned in a hurry how to dance. The teacher who had given intensive lessons in the waltz, mazurka and quadrille to Japanese was a German called Janson, hired by the Japanese government. In 1976, it was a Japanese teacher, hired by NHK, the producing television network, who gave lessons to Western extra actors in how to do classical European dances of bygone centuries. In the television drama Etō seems to have embellished the Meiji people's efforts to modernize the country. He seems to be a little narcissistic in his evocation of the past; moreover, there seems to be an infatuation on the part of the Japanese audience in general. A question arises in one's mind: were the Rokumeikan balls really so beautiful? Or was it merely the ridiculous centre of the Europeanization fever? To begin with, how and when did the

Japanese become acquainted with Western balls? When and by whom were Western balls discovered?

For the sake of comparison I would like to quote here two records of the encounter at balls, first, between the West and Russia and second, between the West and Japan.

Peter the Great (1672–1725) had made a stop in Germany and danced with German princesses. This was while he was returning home from Holland where he had spent some time as a ship's carpenter. His study abroad is said to be the beginning of the modernization movement in Russia. According to the letters written in French by two of the German princesses who attended the ball,[6] Peter took the steel bones of their corset for real bones and told his gracious partner with a naïve air of surprise: 'You German girls have terribly hard bones indeed!' The tsar was a physically attractive nobleman who knew well how to dance, but he still seemed very vulgar to European princesses. One of them asked him if he liked hunting. Peter's answer was: 'My father liked it. But as for me I preferred from my younger days shipbuilding and fireworks. I build ships myself,'[7] and the tsar made her touch the corns of his rough hands. The palms of the Russian Imperial shipwright were callused. The calluses seemed to her to be symbolic of his character.

Callused or not, social contacts thus began at dancing parties between Russian aristocrats and West Europeans. Their contacts had a much longer history than Japanese contacts with the West. By the time the Japanese opened their country to Westerners, upper-class Russians seemed to have adopted Western manners and customs so thoroughly that some Russians began to consider themselves Westerners. For their part, the Japanese had little trouble considering Russia a part of the Christian West. (Consequently it has been difficult for many Japanese to understand the Western terminology of East and West during the period of the Cold War.) The image of Russia formed by great books and films of Russian authors – for example, the famous ball scenes in Tolstoy's *War and Peace* with the main characters' dazzling conversation in French – convinced the Japanese of Russia's strong Western tradition.

Compared with the Russians, the Japanese were slow to discover Western balls. It was more than a century-and-a-half after Peter the Great that the Japanese came passively to the West. Under foreign pressure, the shogunal government sent a diplomatic mission to

Washington in 1860, and there they discovered the curious Western habit of dancing. The Japanese delegation was amazed at the promiscuous nature of American great balls. Muragaki Awajinokami Norimasa, deputy-ambassador, described in his diary the evening party offered by Secretary of State Lewis Cass in honour of the Japanese delegation:

> As it was the invitation given by the Secretary of State, we thought that it would be very ceremonious. Contrary to our expectation the hall was fully crowded from the entrance through corridors with hundreds of men and women. A number of gas lamps were hung from ceilings; glasses decorated with gold and silver were shining before mirrors as if it were daytime. Amazed by the strangeness of the scene, we entered a hall thrusting our way through the crowd. Cass welcomed us, saluting us with cordiality. His children and grandchildren came to salute us, by taking our hands. Although I took a seat, so many men and women came, hustling and jostling, to see me. Each of the Americans took my hand and greeted me; but as I was already out of reach of the interpreter, I could not understand their words at all, and there was more and more confusion ... I was then guided into another hall where the floor was beautifully polished. At one side of the hall there was a band playing music with violins and other Western instruments. There were men with epaulettes wearing a sword, and women with naked shoulders. The latter were clothed in white, thin garments, wearing around the waist an expanded skirt. Men and women formed pairs, and making steps they went round the hall to the sound of music. The scene reminded me of mice turning round in a cage. There was neither grace nor art. Many pairs were turning, and the skirts of the ladies swelled more and more with the wind. This was the so-called 'dance' which roughly corresponds to the Japanese 'odori'. It is said that not only high officials but also old women like to take part in it. Hundreds of men and women, after having been to the buffet and after having helped themselves to wine and meat, came back to the floor and danced all through the night, changing partners from time to time. I really did not understand if it was reality or dream. I was just amazed and was struck dumb.[8]

This was the first Japanese impression of a Western ball at the very beginning of the contacts between Japan and the West. We see in Muragaki's observation his Confucian criticisms of the manners and customs of Western society.

Then, what was the first Western impression of a 'Western' ball in Japan. The Europeanization fever was seen through the eyes of Pierre Loti (1850–1923) in 1889 and was novelized thirty years later in 1919 by Akutagawa Ryūnosuke (1892–1927).

The modernizing elite of Meiji Japan (who had replaced the shogunal officials in the revolutionary year 1868) were, however, extremely flexible in their efforts to catch up with the Western powers. A quarter of a century after the return of the shogunal mission headed by Muragaki and others, the new government opened the Rokumeikan in 1886. The display of Western customs in the capital of Japan – which was now called Tokyo instead of the older name of Yedo, Yeddo or Edo – was calculated to impress Westerners with the degree of Westernization that had taken place in Japan. Foreign Minister Inoue Kaoru, host of the Rokumeikan ball, said in a speech that it would be necessary to make of Japan 'a newly Westernized country among the nations of Asia'. His main concern was to gain more favourable terms in revising the unequal treaties and in curtailing extraterritoriality, which had been inherited from the last days of the Tokugawa regime.

To many contemporary Japanese, however, the Rokumeikan was the symbol of a rotten high society. To Japanese intellectuals of later generations, it was the ridiculous centre of the pseudo-Westernization movement of their fathers and grandfathers. It is difficult to imagine that the sophisticated novelist, Akutagawa Ryūnosuke[9] liked the indiscriminate imitation of Western manners and customs symbolized by the Rokumeikan. Still, the young writer took to the theme and wrote 'The Ball'. The reason that Akutagawa took to it is simple and obvious: he read Pierre Loti's description of a Rokumeikan ball.[10] It must have been very refreshing for Akutagawa to be able to look at early Meiji days through the eyes of a French writer. More than a quarter of a century had already passed, since the opening of the Rokumeikan and even after the decline of the Europeanization fever. Nevertheless, in 1919 Akutagawa was still trying to recreate the Watteauesque ball scene of the time when Japanese leaders had tried hard to swallow the West. The Rokumeikan seen through Loti's eyes seems to have opened some new perspectives. Before analysing the psychology of the writers of latecomers to modernization and their selective use of French sources for the description of their own past, I would like to quote Akutagawa's 'The Ball' in full, as the story is very short:[11]

THE BALL

I

It was the night of the third day of the eleventh month of the nineteenth year of Meiji (1886). Akiko, the seventeen-year-old daughter of the distinguished family of—, accompanied by her bald-headed father, climbed the stairs of the Rokumeikan, where the ball that night was to be held. Great chrysanthemum blossoms, which seemed almost to be artificial, formed threefold hedges up the sides of the broad, brightly gas-lit stairs. The petals of the chrysanthemums, those at the back pink, those in the middle deep yellow and those in front pure white, were all tousled like flag tassels. And near where the banks of chrysanthemums came to an end, already floated out incessantly from the ball-room at the top of the stairs lively orchestra music like an irrepressible sigh of happiness.

Akiko had early been taught to speak French and dance. But to-night she was going to attend a formal ball for the first time in her life. Wherefore in the carriage, when her father spoke to her from time to time, she returned only absent-minded answers. Thus deeply had an unsettled feeling that may well be defined as a glad uneasiness taken root in her breast. Till the carriage finally came to a stop in front of the Rokumeikan, time and again she lifted impatient eyes and gazed out of the window at the scanty lights of the Tokyo streets drifting by outside.

But immediately she entered the Rokumeikan, she experienced that which made her forget her uneasiness. When half way up the stairs, she and her father overtook some Chinese officials ascending just ahead of them. And as the officials separated in their fatness to let them go ahead, they cast surprised glances at Akiko. In good truth, with her simple rose-coloured ball gown, a light blue ribbon around her well-formed neck and a single rose exhaling perfume from her dark hair, Akiko that night was fully possessed of the beauty of the girls of enlightened Japan, a beauty that might well startle the eyes of these Chinese officials with their long pigtails hanging down their backs. And just as she noticed this, a young Japanese in swallow-tails came hurrying down the steps and, as he passed them, turned his head in a slight reflex action and likewise gave a glance of surprise after Akiko as she went on. Then for some reason, as if suddenly having an idea, he put his hand up to his white bow-tie and went on hurriedly down through the chrysanthemums toward the entrance.

When they got to the top of the stairs, at the door of the ball-room on the second floor they found a count with grey whiskers, who was the host of the evening, with his chest covered with decorations, and the countess, older than himself, dressed to the last degree of perfection in a Louis XV gown, extending a dignified welcome to the guests of the evening. Akiko did not fail to see the momentary look of naïve admiration that appeared and faded away somewhere in the crafty old face even of this count when he saw her. Her good-natured father, with a happy smile, introduced her briefly to the count and countess. She experienced a succession of the feelings of shame and pride. But meanwhile she had just time to notice that there was a touch of vulgarity in the haughty features of the countess.

In the ball-room, too, chrysanthemums blossomed in beautiful profusion everywhere. And everywhere the lace and flowers and ivory fans of the ladies waiting for their partners moved like soundless waves in the refreshing sweetness of perfume. Akiko soon separated from her father and joined one of the groups of gorgeous women. They were all girls of about the same age dressed in similar light blue and rose-coloured ball gowns. When they turned to welcome her, they chirped softly like birds and spoke with admiration of her beauty that night.

But no sooner had she joined the group than a French naval officer she had never seen before walked quietly up to her. And with his two arms hanging down to his knees, he politely made her a Japanese bow. Akiko was faintly conscious of the blood mounting to her cheeks. But the meaning of that bow was clear without any asking. So she looked round at the girl standing beside her in a light blue gown to get her to hold her fan. As she turned, to her surprise, the French naval officer, with a smile flitting across his cheek, said distinctly to her in Japanese with a strange accent,

'Won't you dance with me?'

In a moment Akiko was dancing the Blue Danube Waltz with the French Naval officer. He had tanned cheeks, clear-cut features and a heavy moustache. She was too short to reach up and put her long-gloved hand on the left shoulder of his uniform. But the experienced officer handled her deftly and danced her lightly through the crowd. And at times he even whispered amiable flatteries into her ear in French.

Repaying his gentle words with a bashful smile, she looked from time to time about the ball-room in which they danced. She could see between the sea of people flashes of curtains of purple silk crape with the Imperial crest dyed into them, and the gay silver or sober gold of the chrysanthemums in the vases under Chinese flags on which blue claw-spread dragons writhed. And the sea of people, stirred up by the wind of gay melody from the German orchestra that came bubbling over it like champagne, never stopped for a moment its dizzy commotion. When she and one of her friends, also dancing, saw each other, they nodded happily as they went busily by. But at that moment, another dancer, whirling like a big moth, appeared between them from nowhere in particular.

But meanwhile, she realized that the naval officer was watching her every movement. This simply showed how much interest this foreigner, unaccustomed to Japan, took in her vivacious dancing. Did this beautiful young lady, too, live like a doll in a house of paper and bamboo? And with slender metal chopsticks did she pick up grains of rice out of a tea-cup as big as the palm of your hand with a blue flower painted on it and eat them? Such doubts, together with an affectionate smile, seemed ever and anon to come and go in his eyes. If this was amusing to Akiko, it was at the same time gratifying. So every time his surprised gaze fell to her feet, her slender little rose-coloured dancing pumps went sliding the more lightly over the slippery floor.

But finally the officer seemed to notice that this kitten-like young lady showed signs of fatigue, and peering into her face with kindly eyes, he asked,

'Shall we go on dancing?'

'*Non, merci,*' said Akiko in excitement, this time clearly. Then the French naval officer, continuing the steps of the waltz, wove his way through the waves of lace and flowers moving back and forth and right and left, and guided her leisurely up to the chrysanthemums in vases by the wall. And after the last revolution, he seated her neatly in a chair there and, having once thrown out his chest in his military uniform, again respectfully made her a deep Japanese bow.

Then after dancing a polka and a mazurka, Akiko took the arm of this French naval officer and went down the stairs between the walls of white and yellow and pink chrysanthemums to a large hall.

Here in the midst of swallow-tails and white shoulders moving to and fro unceasingly, many tables loaded with silver and glass utensils were piled high with meat and truffles, or pinnacled with towers of sandwiches and ice-cream, or built up into pyramids of pomegranates and figs. Especially beautiful was a gilt lattice with skilfully-made artificial grape vines twining their green leaves through it on the wall at one side of the room above the piled-up chrysanthemums. And among the leaves, bunches of grapes like wasps' nests hung in purple abundance. In front of this gilt lattice, Akiko found her bald-headed father, with another gentleman of the same age, smoking a cigar. When he saw her, he nodded slightly with evident satisfaction, and without taking further notice of her, turned to his companion and went on smoking.

The French naval officer went to one of the tables with Akiko, and they began to eat ice-cream. As they ate, she noticed that ever and anon his eyes were drawn to her hands or her hair or her neck with the light blue ribbon round it. This did not, of course, make her unhappy. But at one moment a womanly doubt could not but flash forth in her. Then, as two young women who looked like Germans went by with red camelias on their black velvet breasts, in order to hint at this doubt, she exclaimed,

'Really how beautiful Western women are!'

When the naval officer heard this, contrary to her expectation, he shook his head seriously.

'Japanese women are beautiful, too. Especially you—'

'I'm no such thing.'

'No, I'm not flattering. You could appear at a Parisian ball just as you are. If you did, everybody would be surprised. For you're like the princess in Watteau's picture.'

Akiko did not know who Watteau was. So the beautiful vision of the past called up for the naval officer by his words – the vision of a fountain in a dusky grove and a fading rose – could only disappear without a trace and be lost. But this girl of unusual sensibility, as she plied her ice-cream spoon, did not forget to stick to just one more thing she wanted to speak of.

'I should like to go to a Parisian ball and see what they're like.'

'No, a Parisian ball is exactly the same as this.'

As he said this, the naval officer looked round at the sea of people and the chrysanthemums surrounding the table where they stood; then suddenly, as a cynical smile seemed to move like a little wave in the depths of his eyes, he put down his ice-cream spoon and added as if half to himself,

'Not only Paris. Balls are just the same everywhere.'

An hour later, Akiko and the French naval officer stood arm in arm on a balcony off the ball-room under the starlight with many other Japanese and foreigners.

Out beyond the balcony railing the pines that covered the extensive garden stood hushed with their branches interwoven, and here and there among their twigs shone the lights of little red paper lanterns.

In the bottom of the chilly air the fragrance of the moss and fallen leaves rising from the garden below seemed to set adrift faintly the breath of lonely autumn. And in the ball-room behind them, that same sea of lace and flowers went on ceaselessly moving under the curtains of purple silk crape with the sixteen petalled chrysanthemums dyed into them. And still up over the sea of people, the whirlwind of high-pitched orchestra music mercilessly goaded them on.

Of course from the balcony, too, lively talk and laughter stirred the night air ceaselessly. More, when beautiful fireworks shot up into the sky over the pines, a sound almost like a shout came from the throats of the people on the balcony. Standing in their midst, Akiko had been exchanging light chit-chat with some young lady friends of hers near them. But she finally bethought herself, and turning to the French naval officer, found him with his arm still supporting hers, gazing silently into the starry sky up over the garden. It seemed to her somehow that he was experiencing a touch of homesickness. So looking furtively up into his face, she said half teasingly, 'You're thinking of your own country, aren't you?'

Then the naval officer, with a smile in his eyes as always, looked round at her quietly. And instead of saying '*Non*', he shook his head like a child.

'But you seem to be musing on something.'

'Guess what.'

Just then among the people on the veranda arose again for a time a noise like a wind. As if by agreement, Akiko and the naval officer stopped talking and looked up into the night sky that pressed down heavily on the pines of the garden. There a red and blue firework, throwing its spider legs out against the darkness, was just on the verge of dying away. To Akiko, for some reason or other, that firework was so beautiful that it almost made her sad.

'I was thinking of the fireworks. The fireworks, like our lives,' said the French naval officer, looking gently down into Akiko's face and speaking as if teaching her.

## II

It was autumn in the seventh year of Taisho (1918). The Akiko of that time, on her way back to her villa at Kamakura, met by chance on the train a young novelist with whom she was slightly acquainted. The young man put a bunch of chrysanthemums which he was taking to a friend in Kamakura up into the rack. Then Akiko, who was now the elderly Madame H—, told him that there was a story of which she was always reminded whenever she saw chrysanthemums and recounted to him in detail her reminiscences of the ball at the Rokumeikan. He could not but feel a deep interest when he heard such reminiscences from the mouth of the woman herself.

When the story was over, he casually asked,

'Madame, do you not know the name of that French naval officer?'

Then old Madame H— gave him an unexpected answer.

'Of course I do. His name was Julian Viaud.'

'Then it was Loti, wasn't it? It was Pierre Loti, who wrote *Madame Chrysanthème*, wasn't it?'

The young man felt an agreeable excitement. But old Madame H— simply looked into his face wonderingly and murmured over and over,

'No, his name wasn't Loti. It was Julian Viaud.'

If one reads Loti, it is evident that Akutagawa used many passages from his 'Un Bal à Yeddo', which is included in *Japoneries d'Automne*. For example, Akutagawa owes to Loti the descriptions of great chrysanthemum blossoms, the Japanese countess dressed to the last degree of perfection in a Louis XV gown, and the *Blue Danube* waltz of the German orchestra. Akutagawa borrowed not only these external decorative elements but also the inner feeling of the French naval officer towards a Japanese young lady. As usual Akutagawa tried to hide his source. He gave readers the impression that the ball was actually seen through the eyes of Akiko. 'The Ball' is composed of two parts, and the second part is added to suggest that the story was told by Akiko, now the elderly Madame H—, to Akutagawa, a young novelist with whom she was supposed to be slightly acquainted. The second part serves therefore as the frame to the story. Yet like so many of Akutagawa's stories, this one, too, has a bookish source. Take a look at a passage from 'Un Bal à Yeddo':

> La plus gentille de mes danseuses est une petite personne en rose éteint avec bouquets pompadour – quinze ans au plus – encore très bébé, et sautant de tout son cœur, fort distinguée dans son enfantillage, elle serait vraiment jolie si elle était mieux ajustée, s'il ne manquait à sa toilette le je ne sais quoi indéfinissable …
>
> Tout à l'heure pourtant, en rentrant chez elle, dans quelque maison à chassis de papier, elle va, comme toutes les autres femmes, quitter son corset en pointe, prendre une robe bordée de cigognes ou d'autres oiseaux quelconques, s'accroupir par terre, dire une prière shintoiste ou boudhiste, et souper avec du riz dans des bols, à l'aide de baguettes … Nous sommes devenus très camarades, cette brave petite demoiselle et moi. Comme la valse est longue – une valse de Marcailhou – et qu'il fait chaud, nous imaginons d'ouvrir une porte-fenêtre et de sortir par là, afin de prendre l'air sur la terrasse.[12]

It is easy to enumerate Akutagawa's many borrowings from Loti. However, what I intend to analyse in this chapter is not the details of the debt Akutagawa owes to the French writer. There have already been many articles on the topic in Japanese academic journals.[13] Here I am more interested in the psychology of the intelligentsia in societies modernizing late, especially in their use of Western materials in dealing with their own national problems.

Like so many writers of his generation, Akutagawa embraced Western notions of the 'modern' and measured Japan against them. The attitude is typical of the second generation of modernizers, and we can say that the attitude was to a certain extent shared by certain Russian writers. Akutagawa was born thirty years later than Mori Ōgai (1862–1922), the first modernizer of Japanese literature, and belongs to the second generation; Akutagawa is the representative writer of the Taishō period (1912–26). My comparison here with Russian writers, especially with Pushkin, does not mean that there were any factual relations between Alexandr Pushkin (1799–1837) and Akutagawa Ryūnosuke (1892–1927). However, in order to situate Akutagawa in his relations to the West and in his relations to the first Japanese modernizers of the Meiji period (1868–1912), I would like to draw some parallels between Pushkin's 'Roslavlev' and Akutagawa's 'The Ball'. Both works are composed on the basis of French observations of their writers' own societies: the Muscovite society of 1812 by Madame de Staël and the Tokyo society of 1886 by Pierre Loti.

The intelligentsia – the word was originally coined to indicate the Russian intellectuals – suggests by its etymology[14] from 'intelligere', the value orientation of the educated class of Imperial Russia. The Russian intelligentsia were first of all those who understood the knowledge of the West and conveyed that Western learning to their own underdeveloped country. They were a sort of secular missionaries in their task of civilizing the Russian nation. The Russian élite tried, therefore, to educate themselves and identify themselves with West-European intellectuals. They learned and spoke West-European languages: French, German, English, or Italian. While Akiko, the Japanese heroine of Akutagawa's 'The Ball', 'had early been taught to speak French and dance,' Polina, the Russian heroine of Pushkin's 'Roslavlev', is totally immersed in French culture. Her degree of Westernization is described as follows:

> Polina was a great reader of every kind of book. She had the key to her father's library. This consisted mainly works of eighteenth-century writers. She was well acquainted with French literature, from Montesquieu to the novels of Crébillon. Rousseau she knew by heart. There was not a single

Russian book in the library … she probably read nothing in Russian, not even the verses dedicated to her by Moscow versifiers.[15]

In 'Roslavlev' the young heroine of the story attends the banquet offered in honour of Madame de Staël, who came to Moscow in the summer of 1812. This famous Swiss-French woman writer, who had clashed with Napoleon, exiled herself in Russia shortly before the French invasion of the country. As Akutagawa's 'The Ball' has a French source by Loti, so the materials on which Pushkin drew are, in my opinion, Madame de Staël's *Dix Annees d'Exil* (Ten years of exile), published in 1821. In the book the French writer is sometimes critical of the Russians: their level of culture was low; there were no interesting conversations, although their welcome was very obliging. She found their conversation devoid of substance:

> L'accueil des Russes est si obligeant, qu'on se croirait, dès le premier jour, lié avec eux, et peut-être au bout de dix ans ne le serait-on pas. Le silence russe est tout à fait extraordinaire: ce silence porte uniquement sur ce qui leur inspire un vif intérêt. Du reste, ils parlent tant qu'on veut: mais leur conversation ne vous apprend rien que leur politesse; elle ne trahit ni leurs sentiments, ni leurs opinions. On les a souvent comparés à des Français; et cette comparaison me semble la plus fausse du monde.[16]

Some Russian critics and book reviewers were angry about the book. A well-known journalist of the time named Mukhanov accused Mme de Staël of not having praised Russia and the Russians enough in her *Dix Années d'Exil*. Pushkin, however, sided with Mme de Staël in the critical appraisal of the Russians, and he very much regretted that Mukhanov had attacked the French woman writer:

> I am sorry Mukhanov wrote about Staël. He is my friend, and I would not touch him. But all the same he is at fault: Mme de Staël is ours – don't touch her.[17]

Pushkin was of the opinion that, among all works written by Mme de Staël, *Les Dix Années d'Exil* was one of those which ought to draw the attention of the Russians: 'The penetration of her views, the freshness and the variety of her remarks, the gentleness which guides the writer's pen – all in the book testifies abundantly to the quality of the spirit and the sentiment of that extraordinary woman … The Russians should be grateful to Mme de Staël …' This was Pushkin's opinion expressed in the *Muscovite Telegraph* in 1825.[18] Pushkin of course knew that her criticisms of the Russians were harsh; take another example, which seems to have been significant to Pushkin. This remark by Mme de Staël later became one of the central themes of his story. Russian society does not consist of a circle of intelligent men and women who are pleased to talk together. The Russians are different from the French in this point:

> La societé ne consiste pas chez eux (les Russes), comme chez nous, dans un cercle d'hommes et de femmes d'esprit, qui se plaisent à causer ensemble.[19]

Instead, said Mme de Staël, the Russians came to social gatherings in order to eat rare products of Asia and Europe. Pushkin fully agreed with her remarks, and in his 'Roslavlev' Russian wits are described as 'far more pleased with the fish-soup than with the talk of Madame de Staël', and 'these (Russian) wits and ladies only rarely broke the silence, convinced of the insignificance of their thoughts and feeling intimidated by the presence (of Mme de Staël)'. Apparently, Pushkin as a francophile Russian intellectual shared Mme de Staël's views of the Russians. In 'Roslavlev' he criticizes his fellow countrymen in the light of Western notions of 'society'. We can imagine the following psychological process: while reading Mme de Staël's *Dix Années d'Exil*, Pushkin must have felt as if he himself sat on thorns, and he must have transposed his embarrassed feeling to Polina in 'Roslavlev'. In the story, throughout the entire dinner the Russian heroine 'sat as if on pins and needles'. His compatriots described in Mme de Staël's records were despairingly uncivilized in their behaviour towards the West-European celebrity. Pushkin cried with indignation in a letter addressed to Vyazemsky in June, 1826: 'In our relations with foreigners, we have neither pride nor decency.' Five years later, in his 'Roslavlev', Pushkin made his Russian heroine cry out with a sense of shame. Polina bursts out in indignation:

> 'Oh my dear, I am in despair! How worthless our great society must seem to that unusual woman! She has been used to being surrounded by people who understand her, on whom a brilliant remark, a strong beat of the heart, an inspired word is never lost; she has been used to absorbing and highly cultured conversation. And here ... my God! Not a single thought, not a single remarkable word in the course of three hours! Dull faces, dull pomposity – that's all! How bored she was! How tired she seemed! She realized what they wanted, what those apes of enlightenment could understand, and she threw them a pun. And they threw themselves at it! I burned with shame and was on the verge of tears ... But let—' Polina continued warmly – 'let her take away an opinion of our society – rabble such as they deserve.'

The feeling of self-abasement ascribed to the heroine must be the feeling of Pushkin himself, who was almost excessively aware that his fellow countrymen were of a lower nature or state of development than those of more advanced nations.

Akutagawa Ryūnosuke is also known for the sense of self-abasement peculiar to late-comers to Westernization. As a writer well versed in Western literatures, he was critically aware that his nation was in need of Westernization. In a short story entitled 'The General' (*Shōgun*), Akutagawa made a mockery of General Nogi. Nogi Maresuke, the hero of Port Arthur, who committed ritual suicide following the death of Emperor Meiji, was considered to be the incarnation of the Bushido spirit. Westernizing intellectuals of the second generation, however, revolted against the traditional values exemplified by the old general. Nogi as an educator – he was principal of the Peers College towards the end of his life – was a failure. Writers of the now rising *Shirakaba* group, such as Shiga Naoya and Mushanokōji Saneatsu, who had suffered as students at the Peers College under the heavily moralistic strictures of the aged principal, were unanimous in denouncing the old, traditionalist style of education. Akutagawa gladly joined them in criticizing and satirizing the general. For example, in 'The General,' an episode is told by an old man as a proof of Nogi's humanizing influence upon his students: one summer day while Nogi and his students were in the Nasu plain, where the vast field lies open to the horizon, young peers competed to find a convenient place for Nogi's wife to go to the toilet. A young man in the story, who apparently stands proxy for Akutagawa, mutters to himself: 'It is an innocent anecdote indeed; but I hope that it will not reach the ears of *Westerners.*'

Just as Pushkin was embarrassed by the rude manners of his fellow countrymen in the presence of Mme de Staël, Akutagawa too was exceedingly sensitive to reactions of Westerners. He was a stylist not only in literary matters. He cared very much how his compatriots looked to foreigners, whether they were presentable or not.[20]

Like Pushkin Akutagawa was prone to feel that his countrymen were less worthy or able than individual Westerners. In 'The Ball', the author begins the story by referring to the 'scanty lights of the Tokyo streets'. The remark already shows Akutagawa's deep sense of inferiority of the material conditions of the Japanese capital at the time. The expression (especially in its original Japanese) 'Akiko's balded father' hints at the 'parvenu' nature of the 'distinguished families'. It is on purpose that Akutagawa repeats that expression. The small but interesting difference between Loti and Akutagawa is that the French writer confesses frankly: that despite her low origin, the Japanese countess, an ex-geisha, is above his expectation:

> J'attendais donc une créature bizarre, portant toilette à la chien savant ... et je m'arrête surpris devant une personne au visage distingué et fin, gantéee jusqu'à l'épaule, irréprochablement coiffée en femme comme il faut.[21]

Akutagawa, unable to believe Loti's description that the Japanese countess is impeccable, adds to it sarcastic remarks in his Japanese version of the story. He could not resist denigrating the Meiji greats and their spouses:

> She (Akiko) had just time to notice that there was a touch of *vulgarity* in the *haughty* features of the countess. (italics mine)

Like Polina in Pushkin's story, Akutagawa must have thought and felt that the Japanese dignitaries of his father's generation were 'apes of enlightenment'.

Polina's case may be extreme, even in the Russia of the 1810s or 1820s. However, many intellectuals of peripheral countries try to adopt values of a central civilization, and in course of that, they admire, learn and copy the foreign models. If we use Pushkin's own words, the intelligentsia 'took from their childhood the habit of thinking in a foreign language, because all their knowledge and all their ideas came from foreign books'. Their degree of Westernization was different, but the West-oriented writers like Pushkin and Akutagawa could identify themselves with French writers, when they used de Staël's or Loti's writings for their own purposes. They could look down upon their fellow countrymen as if they themselves belonged to a privileged class. When they criticized the vulgar, ludicrous 'society rabble', seeing with French writers' eyes, and when they thought with French writers' thoughts, they could enjoy a certain superior attitude (the superiority complex of intelligentsia who have one foot in the central civilization), but at the same time they felt as if they sat 'on pins and needles' when the French writers made remarks about the underdeveloped nature of their society (the inferiority complex of intelligentsia who have another foot in the peripheral civilization of their own). Both Pushkin and Akutagawa showed the same syndrome. Pushkin wrote about the contradictory feeling in his letter to Vyazemsky, June 1826:

> I despise my country. But it is insupportable if foreigners too share this feeling.

The intelligentsia of peripheral regions was burdened with a common dilemma. Intellectuals of peripheral nations tend to criticize their fellow countrymen by applying measures of comparison based on the values of a central civilization. Yet, even a francophile Pushkin confessed that as a Russian he could not endure the contemptuous attitude of foreigners. The dilemma of the intelligentsia of Tokugawa Japan was well illustrated by a hypothetical question put by a nationalistic Confucian scholar, Yamazaki Ansai (1618–82). He asked his disciples: 'If China attacks our country with several tens of thousands of soldiers headed by a commander called Confucius and a vice-commander called Mencius, what shall we do, we students of the Way expounded by Confucius and Mencius?' Many of his disciples evaded the question by answering that there would be no such eventuality.

However, to the Russian intellectuals of 1812, it was not a hypothetical question. The French Grand Army of Napoleon was approaching Russian frontiers. In the latter half of 'Roslavlev', changes in Russian attitudes towards the French language and civilization are described with a caustic tone. Here is the first phase:

> Everyone was talking about the coming war, and, so far I can remember, quite lightheartedly. It was fashionable to imitate the French tone of the time of Louis XV. Love of one's fatherland seemed pedantic. The intellectuals of the period exalted Napoleon with fanatical servility and joked about our misfortunes. Unhappily, the people who spoke up in defence of their country were a little simple-minded; they were derided – quite amusingly – and had no influence. Their patriotism was limited to a cruel censure of the use of the French language in society ... The young people spoke with contempt and indifference about everything Russian.

As the great war with Russia was already over in Taishō-period Japan, it was fashionable for Akutagawa and writers of the *Shirakaba* group to imitate cosmopolitanism. Love of one's fatherland seemed pedantic, and the people who continued to speak up in defence of Japan were a little simple-minded and out-of-date. The majority of the Japanese were in favour of the Washington treaty, which put a stop to the arms-race. The late general Nogi and other conservatives were derided. The young people spoke with contempt and indifference about everything Japanese. Akutagawa could jokingly write caricatures of Japanese military leaders loaded with decorations. 'Only children and generals like decorations' was his remark in a story. Akutagawa, who died in 1927, had never faced the problem of a foreign invasion. He was the most popular literary figure of the Taishō democracy.

A more interesting psychological situation arose when suddenly the Muscovites were surprised by the news of the invasion. The cynics grew quiet, and the persecutors of the French language took a decisive lead in society; 'the drawing-rooms became filled with patriots'. The observation inevitably reminds us of the Japanese persecutors of the English language who took a lead on the eve of the Pacific War. Pushkin's caustic comment also reminds us of Mushanokōji, Takamura Kōtarō and others becoming all of sudden patriots with the news of Pearl Harbor. The Taishō writers' conception of cosmopolitanism was decidedly a shallow one.

Pushkin (or at least his heroine in 'Roslavlev') could fortunately remain faithful to Mme de Staël. Polina was consistent in her praise of French civilization throughout the invasion period. She felt no need to change her mind, because Mme de Staël was a dissident and fought against Napoleon. In the very name of 'liberté, égalité, fraternité', the Russian heroine could fight against the invading French army, and symbolically her fiancé was killed at the battle of Borodino. The story – though it is said to be unfinished – ends with the news of the burning of Moscow, which means the ruin of the entire French army.

Japanese reactions to the psychological invasion – the 'Europeanization fever' symbolized by the Rokumeikan – could be put into several patterns. Some pro-governmental newspapers were eager to applaud the success of Rokumeikan parties. As the display of Western customs was calculated to impress foreign dignitaries with the degree of Westernization that had taken place in Japan, the self-laudatory phrases were foregone conclusions. After the great ball held on 3 November 1885, the birthday of Emperor Meiji, the *Nihon Shimbun* of the day said:

> We cannot help paying respect to these Japanese ladies who have made such wonderful progress in dancing, in greeting and in conversing with acquaintances ... They are really worthy ladies of a civilized nation. (*Appare bunmeikoku no fujin nari.*)[22]

The governmental self-praise was curiously taken for truth by the violent anti-government groups. The more vehemently they criticized the luxury and extravagance of upper-class people, the more gorgeous the Rokumeikan looked in the popular imagination. The simple-minded nationalists were outraged by their leaders intoxication with the West. The poor people were dissatisfied with the rotten high society. First, the Rokumeikan and later the Imperial Hotel balls became the symbol of the spiritual pollution of the

Sacred Land. It was not a laughing matter. One evening in the late 1930s, a Japanese ultra-nationalist broke into a ballroom of the Imperial Hotel and, drawing a Japanese sword, gave a demonstration of *kenbu* (traditional sword dance), to the great consternation of foreign and Japanese guests, and the silent but eloquently menacing performance put an end to all dancing parties à *l'européenne* in pre-war Japan. The incident might be called an extreme case of nativistic reaction.

There were other Japanese who, less simple-minded than the extreme right-wingers, knew what the reality of the celebrated Rokumeikan was. Some conservatives were very worried. As D. H. Shively points out, for them Westernization in its worst sense came in the mid-1880s with the opening of the Rokumeikan. Concerning the developments of these years, Nishimura Shigeki recalled [23]:

> ... the new administration of the Itō Cabinet imitated Europe and America in every detail in the legal system, customs and ceremonial, and decked itself completely with foreign civilization. It gave special hospitality to foreigners, presenting such foreign amusements as balls, masquerades, tableaux vivants, assiduously sought to win their favour, and seemed to disregard and abandon the spirit of loyalty, filial piety, honour, duty, valour and shame which had been the traditional foundation of our country since ancient times. The officials who were appointed were largely men of cleverness and flattery, and those who were simple and sturdy were always rejected... After one year, the customs and manners of the people became increasingly rash and flippant and frivolous.[24]

There were others who tended to be cynical about the ludicrous nature of the pseudo-Westernization movement. Japanese dignitaries in masquerades were such good targets for mockery, as many caricatures of ball scenes made by contemporary Japanese and foreign cartoonists such as the Frenchman Georges Bigot amply testify.

Although born after the heyday of the Europeanization fever, Akutagawa knew that the Rokumeikan was in reality not that magnificent even as a piece of architecture. He read Loti's description of it: 'Bâti à l'européene, tout frais, tout blanc, tout neuf, il ressemble, mon Dieu, au casino d'une de nos villes de bains quelconque ...' Akutagawa was a cynic, and it must have been very easy for him to make a caricature of 'the apes of enlightenment'. The Rokumeikan Pavilion, according to the cynical French writer, looked like a casino in a French provincial spa town. However, in 'The Ball', the Japanese author did not adopt the mocking tone of Pierre Loti. Akutagawa did not find the blasé Frenchman sympathetic. Five years later, in 1923, when he heard the death of Loti, he wrote: 'Loti was not a great writer. The Japan described by Loti is less accurate and less truthful than the Japan described by Hearn. But we cannot deny that there are many good 'tableaux' among his descriptions. We are thankful to him for that.'[25] Perhaps as a Japanese, Akutagawa could not accept Loti's raillery: Loti found Japan 'encore très bébé (still very babyish)'.[26]

Akutagawa's covert reaction to the Rokumeikan is hinted at towards the end of 'The Ball'. Like Loti, he was aware that the Rokumeikan was shabby in many respects. But still the Japanese writer made the French naval officer of the story answer the inquiring Japanese demoiselle. Akiko says: 'I should like to go to a Parisian ball and see what they're like.' He answers: 'A Parisian ball is exactly the same as this,' and he adds: '—Not only Paris. Balls are just the same everywhere.' If the Rokumeikan is vain, all other balls also are vain. In this generalization, we can recognize the nihilistic smile of Akutagwa. (This conversation between the French naval officer and Akiko is entirely Akutagawa's invention.) Akutagawa does not admit any contrast between a Rokumeikan ball and a Parisian one. He sees in dancing figures everywhere the shadows of the condemned Paolo and Francesca, who are obliged to dance eternally blown by the whirlwind of Hell. Akutagawa's final description – 'And still up over the sea of people, the whirlwind of high-pitched orchestra music mercilessly goaded them on' – comes from Canto V of Dante's *Inferno*.

Before bringing the story to an end, Akutagawa suggests again the transient nature of all human activities. The French naval officer mutters at the finale of the evening:

'I was thinking of the fireworks. The fireworks, like our lives.'

Nine years later, in 1927, Akutagawa commited suicide at the age of thirty-five. His life was really like a display of fireworks. I do not like the nihilistic reaction which underlies Akutagawa's final remarks. By pointing out the vainglorious nature of the Rokumeikan, Akutagawa became, without knowing it, a forerunner of the *'kindai no chōkoku'* (overcoming modernity) movement in the early 1940s. The modernization was practically a necessity imposed from outside in that century of imperialism. The late-starters were not always in a favourable position in this kind of international game. The first generation responded to the challenge, however comical they might look. Some intellectuals of the second generation, perhaps because of their weakness of character, did not want to participate in a game in which they knew they were handicapped from the beginning.

Alienated intellectuals could step down from the game. It was easy for them to laugh at the clumsy pseudo-Westernization of their fathers. Yet in the last century for the responsible government leaders to bring to Japan all of the trappings of the diplomatic social life of a European capital was a very serious matter. It is true that, as Marius Jansen points out,[27] the Rokumeikan was described by Ōkura Kihachirō[28] (who later built the Imperial Hotel) as being a part of tactics as carefully worked out as those of Ōishi Kuranosuke and his forty-seven *rōnin* in Genroku times. But the reference to Ōishi Kuranosuke should be understood to include his legendary debauchery at geisha houses in Kyoto. Ōishi Kuranosuke indulged in dissipation in order to put his enemies off guard. As the Meiji leaders were accused of leading dissolute lives because of the extravagance of the Rokumeikan, Ōkura defended their behaviour from moralistic accusations by referring to Ōishi Kuranosuke's well-known story dramatized on the Kabuki stage. The Rokumeikan seemed to be frivolous, but it had its political objectives to achieve.

Loti was aware that he was witnessing a very interesting phase in the evolution of this rapidly changing country. He writes at the end of his 'Un Bal à Yeddo' that one day Japanese themselves will be amused, reading that stage of their history recorded by his pen:

> Dans ce pays qui se transforme si prodigieusement vite, cela amusera peut-être aussi des Japonais eux-mêmes, quand quelques années auront passé, de retrouver écrite ici cette étape de leur évolution; de lire ce que fut un bal décoré de chrysanthèmes et donné au Rokou-Meïkan pour l'anniversaire de la naissance de S.M. l'empereur Muts-Hito, en l'an de grâce 1886.[29]

It is indeed amusing to recall here one of his remarks. Loti said: 'Si par hasard la mesure est perdue, il faut les arrêter et les faire repartir.'[30] Some Japanese were lost, not knowing how to step in the middle of a dance. However, the leading Meiji men were not afraid of being laughed at. Among sneering fault-finders they seemed to reply to Loti's remark by making a bold step. They seem to tell us still today:

'In dealing with foreigners, if we make a false step, let's stop and let's try again from the beginning.'

*Notes*

[1] This is a modified English version of the article 'Seiōka no shakōkai: Pushikin no "Rosurāburefu" to Akutagawa no "Butōkai,"' in *Roshiya, Seiō, Nippon* [Russia, Western Europe and Japan, *Kimura Shōichi Kanreki Kinen Ronbun-shū*] (Tokyo: Asahi Shuppan-sha, 1977)

[2] Cyril Black and Marius Jansen eds.: *The Modernization of Japan and Russia* (Free Press, 1975)

[3] The only reference to a literary writer in *The Modernization of Japan and Russia* is Shakespeare (p. 8). With the characteristically American tendency to emphasize the meaning of modernity, the authors write: 'All the non-modernized have more in common with one another than with their modernized descendants ... Only a very few greats like Shakespeare speak across all the gaps.' I am of the opinion, however, that some mythological stories in the *Kojiki* as well as some poems of the *Manyōshū* speak across twelve centuries to many modernized Japanese more eloquently than a number of modernized authors, Japanese or foreign. All comparisons, of course, depend on the measures of comparison that we choose.

[4] Shinmura Izuru ed,: *Kōjien* (Tokyo: Iwanami shoten, 1975).

[5] Pierre Loti: *Japoneries d'Automne* (Paris: Kalash, 2000) p. 53. The English translation is mine.

[6] These letters are quoted by Prosper Merimée in his *Histoire du Règne de Pierre le Grand,* ed. Lambert, p. 101. The English translation is mine.

[7] The first Japanese student sent to Europe to learn shipbuilding was Akamatsu Daizaburō Noriyoshi. He arrived in Holland after a voyage of more than three hundred days in 1863. Akamatsu later became vice-minister of the Navy, and was Mori Ōgai's first father-in-law.

[8] Muragaki (Awajinokami) Norimasa: *Kōkai Nikki* (Tokyo: Jiji shinsho, 1959) p. 158. Translation was by Helen Uno. Some slight modifications have been added.

[9] Akutagawa was a highly talented man of letters who could appreciate Chinese poems together with their French translations by Judith Gautier. He could discern subtle nuances in different interpretations. See his essay 'Pasuteru no ryū'.

[10] Akutagawa read Loti: *Japoneries d'Automne* probably in Takase Toshio's Japanese translation, Piēru Roti: *Nihon inshōki,* published in 1914.

[11] Akutagawa, Ryūnosuke: *Tales Grotesque and Curious,* tr. Glenn W. Shaw, (Tokyo: Hokuseido Press, 1930), pp. 99–107. For the original, 'Butōkai', *Akutagawa Ryūnosuke zenshū* (Tokyo: Iwanami shoten, 1996) vol. 5, pp. 248–257.

[12] Pierre Loti: *Japoneries d'Automne.* pp. 54, 57.

[13] Ōnishi Tadao, 'Akutagawa Ryūnosuke saku 'Butōkai' kōshō' in *Tenri Daigaku Gakuhō,* No. 10.

[14] The Latin verb 'intelligere' means 'to understand'. The Russian word 'intelligentsiya,' is the origin of the English word 'intelligentsia' or 'intelli-

gentzia'. It means 'the class consisting of the educated portion of the population and regarded as capable of forming public opinion'(*The Shorter Oxford English Dictionary*). For Russians intelligentsia were those who were capable of understanding modern Western thought.

[15] All quotations from 'Roslavlev' are taken from Alexandr Pushkin:*The Complete Prose Tales of Alexandr Pushkin*, tr. G.R. Aitken (New York: W.W. Norton, 1966).

[16] Madame de Staël, *Dix Années d'Exil*, ed. Paul Gautier (Paris: Plon, 1904) p. 297.

[17] Alexander Pushkin: *The Letters of Alexander Pushkin*, tr. J.Thomas Shaw (Madison: University of Wisconsin Press) p. 255.

[18] This opinion of Pushkin's is reproduced in the note attached to the letter quoted above.

[19] Madame de Staël: *Dix Années d'Exil*, p. 298.

[20] I would like here to make one distinction. The awkward feeling of the kind particular to late-comers to modernization should not be confused with the bashful self-abasement based on the so-called shame culture. The embarrassment felt by rustics for the behaviour of their fellows is a more universal phenomenon. For example, some Europe-oriented American intellectuals despaired over the behaviour of their fellow Yankees in the presence of Europeans, as is so well described in Henry James's novels.

[21] Pierre Loti: *Japoneries d'Automne*, p. 48.

[22] Quoted in Haga Tōru: *Meiji hyakunen no jomaku* (Tokyo: Bungeishunjū, 1969), p. 343.

[23] As for Nishimura Shigeki's view, see Donald H. Shively, 'Nishimura Shigeki: A Confucian View of Modernization' in Marius Jansen, ed.: *Changing Japanese Attitudes toward Modernization*, (Princeton, N.J.: Princeton University Press, 1965) pp. 193–241.

[24] Nishimura Shigeki: *Ōjiroku*, pp. 193–194. tr. Shively, ibid. p. 213.

[25] 'Piēru Roti no shi,' *Akutagawa Ryūnosuke zenshū*, (Tokyo: Iwanami shoten, 1996) vol. 10, p. 87–89. The English translation is mine.

[26] Akutagawa used himself the French words. Ibid. p. 88.

[27] *Changing Japanese Attitudes toward Modernization*, p. 69.

[28] Ōkura Kihachirō, 'Rokumeikan jidai no kaiko' (Remembrances of the days of the Rokumeikan) in *Gendai Nihon Kiroku Zenshū*, vol. 4, Chikuma Shobō. Incidentally Ōkura (1837–1928) belonged to the generation inspired by Smiles. Ōkura's appreciation can be seen in the fact that he later sent a gift of thanks to Nakamura Masanao for his translation of *Self-Help*.

[29] Pierre Loti: *Japoneries d'Automne*, p. 59.

[30] Ibid. p. 53.

# BENJAMIN FRANKLIN AND FUKUZAWA YUKICHI: TWO AUTOBIOGRAPHIES COMPARED[1]

---

Benjamin Franklin is a great man for Americans; Fukuzawa Yukichi is a great man for Japanese. The question I am going to raise in this chapter is not at all theoretical but quite simple: who is greater, Franklin or Fukuzawa? – Some readers may have misgivings about the feasibility of a comparison which may tend to be prejudiced by national pride. However, so long as we are interested in literary relations West and East, and so long as we are aware of the importance of the historical positions respectively occupied by the United States and Japan, we may be allowed to make this kind of comparison.[2]

I am almost certain that most readers believe that Franklin, the 'greatest' man of the 'greatest' country in the world, is of course greater than Fukuzawa Yukichi. I, too, am practically of this opinion. However, I would like to offer you a humorous comparison as a starter for this argument: what we should examine in this kind of academic research is by how much Franklin may be greater than Fukuzawa? I can give you an answer in numerical terms. For a long time Franklin was more valuable than Fukuzawa by three point six times, however, since the mid-1980s Franklin is in monetary terms of more worth than Fukuzawa by one point four times, although there is some fluctuation everyday. American and Japanese readers, of course, understand what these numerical comparisons mean: Franklin is featured on the American one hundred dollar bill, while Fukuzawa is featured on the Japanese ten thousand yen bank-note. We know the rapidly changing exchange rate, and we see how rapidly Fukuzawa's value has increased and is approaching that of Franklin. One day Fukuzawa may overtake Franklin, or one day Fukuzawa may be shelved, as there are too many people who try to forge false banknotes of ten thousand yen: there are so many things unpredictable in the world of finance.

My remark may be seen as a joke, but it is not without a point. Great men in history were not always great men. Many of them owe their place in history to all sorts of extrinsic causes. They owe their place, first to the greatness of the country to which they belong. It is the same with masterpieces in literature. 'Masterpieces' were not always masterpieces and may at any moment cease to be so. Think of what has happened to the so-called masterpieces of Nobel prize-winners. It may be the same with some autobiographies. We know quite well how difficult it is for us to make meaningful comparisons of great men who belong to different countries of different cultures, as we students of the humanities may not always be free from pre-conceived ideas and feelings. There is no doubt, however, that for almost all Americans, Benjamin Franklin is greater than Fukuzawa Yukichi, simply because, while they know the name of Franklin, they do not know the name of Fukuzawa. It is natural that great men of other countries whom they do not know do not exist in their con-sciousness; therefore, such 'non-existent' persons are generally less great than great men they know. Moreover, great men of great coun-tries tend to go on becoming greater.

However, from time to time, strange things happen in the aca-demic world: while teaching at Princeton University, I discovered to my great surprise that American graduate students of Japanese studies had not read the *Autobiography of Benjamin Franklin,* one of the founding fathers of the United States, while they had all read the *Autobiography of Fukuzawa Yukichi,* one of the founding fathers of modern Japan. How could this happen? The answer is simple: Fukuzawa's *Autobiography,* which is available in English translation,[3] was to be found at the top of the reading list of the graduate course in Japanese studies that year. It is almost the same with Japanese American experts. They are required to read Franklin's *Autobiography* very carefully, as the book is always found at the top of the reading list for Japanese students specializing in American studies. Not only that, Franklin has been read in English as well as in Japanese transla-tion by Japanese general readers for more than a hundred years: for example, Franklin's *Letters* were translated and published in 1942, when Japan was at war with the United States. After WWII, some Japanese scholars of American studies seem to have unconsciously accepted the American evaluation that Franklin's *Autobiography* is the best autobiography ever written. The problem with some Japanese American specialists is that they tend to accept this kind of evaluation made in America, without having ever carefully checked Fukuzawa's *Autobiography*. They tend to be more American in their positive appreciation of things American; so much so that I cannot accept their statements at face value, especially when they talk about Japan, as these Japanese American specialists inevitably tend to depreciate Japanese values by way of contrast. It is my apprehension that some area specialists, both Japanese and American, are not always well balanced in their judgements. That is the reason I prefer a comparative approach.

The comparison that I am going to make is about Franklin's and Fukuzawa's lives seen through their autobiographies. For those of you who have read them, my choice justifies itself: Franklin's *Memoirs* generally known as his *Autobiography* is very interesting, probably the most interesting autobiography ever written in English, while Fukuzawa's autobiography, *Fukuojiden,* is in my opinion the most fascinating autobiographical writing ever written in Japanese. Moreover, these two books have many strikingly common characteristics; and when two autobiographies resemble each other, it means that the lives of the two authors have many features in common. I would like, therefore, to make a literary comparison of the two autobiographies, and by so doing, I would like to add a few observations about the relationship between the samurai ethic and the rise of Japanese capitalism.

I am of course aware that Franklin and Fukuzawa are different persons who lived in different countries in different centuries. However, instead of emphasizing the many differences that exist between the two great men, I would like to point out meaningful similarities that the American and the Japanese have in common.

First, Franklin's and Fukuzawa's short biographical notices:

Benjamin Franklin was older than Fukuzawa Yukichi by one hundred and twenty-nine years. He was born in Boston in 1706 of Protestant parents. At the age of twelve he was apprenticed to his brother James as a printer. Benjamin went to Philadelphia in 1723 and pursued his trade of printer. He went to England, and on his return, he began to write extensively. *Poor Richard's Almanack* was a spectacular success. Franklin was also engaged in scientific ventures. At the time of the American Revolution he was active as a statesman and a diplomat. He went to Europe many times. As Franklin never became President of the United States, he is remembered more as an educator and a philosopher of enlightenment ideas than as a politician. His *Autobiography* is full of interesting anecdotes and humour. Franklin died in 1790, satisfied with what he had accomplished in his long and useful life. When Franklin was born, America was a British colony; when he died, the United States was emerging as a modern nation.

Fukuzawa Yukichi was born in Osaka in 1835 of a samurai family of low rank. After his father died the following year, his family moved to Nakatsu in Kyushu. At the age of fourteen or fifteen he began to attend a school of Chinese classics; in 1854, Fukuzawa went to study Dutch at Nagasaki. The previous year Commodore Perry's American squadron had entered Edo Bay and even the remote Nakatsu domain felt the necessity to study gunnery through Dutch books. In 1855, Fukuzawa went to the Ogata Dutch school in Osaka. In 1858, he came to Edo, present-day Tokyo, and soon discovered the necessity of learning English instead of Dutch. Fukuzawa became one of the first Japanese to learn English; in 1860, he had the opportunity to visit San Francisco on board the first Japanese ship to sail to America. In 1862, he visited European countries as an interpreter attached to a shogunal mission. From 1866 onwards, Fukuzawa published *Seiyō jijō* (Conditions in the West), which became the best-seller of the day. After resigning from a low governmental post, Fukuzawa directed a private school of Western studies, which was later to become the prestigious Keiō University. After the Meiji Restoration of 1868, he was active as an educator and also as a journalist he founded the influential newspaper *Jiji-shimpō*. As Fukuzawa had never been in the Meiji government, he, too, is remembered more as an educator and a philosopher of enlightenment ideas. His *Autobiography* is full of interesting anecdotes and humour. Fukuzawa died in 1901, satisfied with what he and his nation had accomplished in his lifetime. When Fukuzawa was born, Japan was under a feudal regime and the country was threatened by Western powers; when he died, Japan was emerging as a modern state. As an ally of Western powers, Japan was successfully crushing the Boxer Rebellion in North China.

Let us take a quick glance at the similarities between Franklin and

Fukuzawa. Both are great men in their respective countries. They lived before and after the greatest revolution their nation experienced in modern times: Franklin was active before and after the American Revolution of 1776, while Fukuzawa was active before and after the Meiji Restoration of 1868. However, Franklin was not Washington; Franklin was active as a philosopher, an educator and a diplomat. He is considered the father of American capitalism. Fukuzawa parallels him. He was neither Ōkubo nor Itō. Although Fukuzawa's influence was immense in many fields, it was exercised mainly through his writings. Fukuzawa was active as a philosopher and an educator. Together with Shibusawa Eiichi, Fukuzawa is considered the father of Japanese capitalism.

Although people still continue to call them philosophers, Franklin's and Fukuzawa's names are rarely mentioned in academic histories of philosophy: they were essentially propagandists of ideas, political and social reformers; like the so-called *philosophes,* French encyclopaedists of the eighteenth century, both Franklin and Fukuzawa worked for universal enlightenment and for social reform. If Franklin was the champion of the mass education drive in America, Fukuzawa was the unquestionable leader of the mass education campaign in Japan. Thanks to the immense influence of their ideas in their respective countries, both succeeded in setting national examples that many of their countrymen followed. 'The wisest American' is also called 'the father of all Yankees' (Carlyle). 'The sage of Mita'[4] is also called 'the intellectual father of more than half the men who now direct the affairs of the country'.[5] The evaluation was made by the British scholar Basil Hall Chamberlain in his *Things Japanese.* These are the overviews of the lives of Franklin and Fukuzawa; however, what is fascinating about their lives lies in the minute details of their life stories. Literary studies start when we examine and compare some significant events and experiences of Franklin and Fukuzawa, by juxtaposing corresponding passages of their *Autobiographies.*

First, let us start with their family background. Son of a lower-ranking samurai, Fukuzawa was educated in a Confucian school. But since his family was poor, Fukuzawa did many things usually done by artisans. Fukuzawa writes:

> Besides these studies at school, I was very clever at doing little things with my hands, and I loved to try inventing and devising things. When something fell in the well, I contrived some means to fish it out. When the lock of a drawer failed to open, I bent a nail in many ways, and poking into the mechanism, somehow opened it. These were my proud moments.[6]

Later, I began to earn money by making wooden clogs and fitting out swords. I never learned to polish the blade, but I could lacquer the sheath, wind the cords around the handle, and somehow put on the metal fittings. I still have a short sword which I fitted out myself, though of course it is of poor workmanship as I look at it now. I learned these arts from various acquaintances among the samurai who were practising them to add to their living.[7]

Fukuzawa later developed a very matter-of-fact, utilitarian outlook upon life. He was very different from the abstract-minded, speculative-minded Confucian thinkers of the day. As he was very much interested in concrete details, he kept clear memories of them throughout his life. Fukuzawa writes:

For any work in metals it is very necessary to have a good file; I had a difficult time in making one for myself. I knew how to make an ordinary file from a steel bar, after a fashion, but the fine file for sharpening saws was beyond my art. Years later, when I first came to Edo, I was surprised at the sight of a boy, an apprentice to a blacksmith, making a saw-file. I still remember the place. It was at Tamachi on the right-hand side of the street as I entered the city. The boy had the file on a piece of leather on an anvil, and was chiseling away at very fine notches as if he never realized there was any wonder in it. I stopped and watched him, thinking what a great city of industry this must be where even a youngster could make a saw-file such as I myself had never dreamed of making. This was the first shock I received on coming to the city.[8]

In this way ever since his childhood in the provincial town of Nakatsu in Kyushu, besides his love of books, Fukuzawa was accustomed to working with his hands for practical needs, although he did not understand good taste. According to a long established convention among the samurai class, it was shameful to handle planes and chisels. It was even more shameful for them to be seen handling money. In the castle-town of Nakatsu, it was customary for samurai to wrap their faces with handtowels and go out after dark whenever they had an errand to do. But the child, Yukichi, was very unconventional in his behaviour. He writes:

I hated having a towel on my face and have never worn one. I even used to go out on errands in broad daylight, swinging a wine bottle in one hand, with two swords at my side as I became a man of samurai rank.

'This is my own money,' I would say to myself. – 'I did not steal it. What is wrong with buying things with my own money?' Thus, I believe, it was with a boyish pride and conceit that I made light of the mock gentility of my neighbours.[9]

There is a reason for Fukuzawa's unconventional behaviour. Before coming back to their hometown of Nakatsu, the Fukuzawa family had lived in Osaka for a long period of time, since Yukichi's father was the overseer of the treasury of the Nakatsu domain at Osaka, the commercial centre of Japan during the closing years of the Tokugawa period. The Fukuzawa children continued to speak the highly accented, rapid Osaka dialect even after their return home to Kyushu. The Fukuzawa children never mixed with other children of Nakatsu. Brought up in this manner, Fukuzawa could not fit into the stiff restrictions of a class-ridden society. The young boy revolted against the feudalistic milieu. Here is a passage describing his conversation with his older brother who was the head of the Fukuzawa family after their father's premature death in 1837:

> One day I had an amusing conversation with him.
> 'Yukichi, what do you intend to be in the future?' he asked me.
> 'Well, Sir, I would like to be the richest man in Japan,' I answered, 'and spend all the money I want to.'
> He made a wry face and gave me a piece of his mind. So I asked him in return: 'What do you want to be?'
> He answered gravely in stilted Chinese phrasing: 'I will be dutiful to my parents, faithful to my brethren and loyal to my master until death.'
> 'H'm!' I exclaimed. And there the conversation ended.
> That was my brother.[10]

Fukuzawa Yukichi was the youngest of five children. Benjamin Franklin was the youngest son of seventeen children. Benjamin's father came to New England in about 1685. Benjamin helped his father in his business of tallow-chandler and soap-boiler. Benjamin liked handicraft work as did the young Fukuzawa. Franklin writes:

> It has ever since been a pleasure to me to see good workmen handle their tools; and it has been useful to me to have learned so much by it as to be able to do little jobs myself in my house, when a workman could not readily be got, and to construct little machines for my experiments when the intention of making these was warm in my mind.[11]

Although school education was lacking, Franklin was 'passionately fond of reading', and all the little money that came into his hands was laid out in the purchasing of books: Bunyan, Burton, Plutarch, Defoe, Cotton Mather, etc. Franklin recalls:

> This bookish inclination at length determined my father to make me a printer, though he had already one son (James) of that profession. In 1717 my brother, James, returned from England with a press and letters to set up his business in Boston. I liked it much better than that of my father, but still had a hankering for the sea. To prevent the apprehended effect of such an inclination, my father was impatient to have me bound to my brother. I stood out some time, but at last was persuaded and signed the indenture,

when I was yet but twelve years old. I was to serve as apprentice till I was twenty-one years of age, only I was to be allowed journeyman's wages during the last year. In a little time I made a great progress in the business and became a useful hand to my brother. I now had access to better books.[12]

As Yukichi revolted against his narrow and hierarchical surroundings, Benjamin revolted against the stiffness of his domineering older brother. He writes:

Though a brother, he considered himself as my master and me as his apprentice, and accordingly expected the same services from me as he would from another; while I thought he demeaned me too much in some he required of me, who from a brother expected more indulgence. Our disputes were often brought before our father, and I fancy I was either generally in the right or else a better pleader, because the judgement was generally in my favour. But my brother was passionate and had often beaten me, which I took extremely amiss, I fancy his harsh and tyrannical treatment of me might be a means of impressing me with that aversion to arbitrary power that has stuck to me through my whole life (33).[13]

Both Fukuzawa and Franklin wanted to get away from their hometown. Fukuzawa made his first trip to Nagasaki on the clan's order to study Dutch in 1854. Even a provincial clan in Kyushu was conscious of a national crisis, and Nagasaki was the only port town where the Japanese of that period could gather information of Western lands. After a year when he was about to be recalled to his hometown because of his superior's jealousy, Fukuzawa deserted his home domain and went on his own initiative to Osaka to continue his study of Dutch, the only Western language then known to very few Japanese. Here are some adventures during his travel from Nagasaki to Osaka, of which the distance of 700 kilometres is a little longer than that between Boston and Philadelphia

In crossing the strait from Kokura we had something of a narrow escape. As we were about in the middle of the channel, the wind blew up and the sea became choppy. The sailors seemed much alarmed and called on me to help them. I did join in, pulling the ropes and carrying things around, and enjoyed the excitement.

But when I told the hostess in (the inn) Sembaya what had happened, and showed her how my clothes were wet with spray, she looked much concerned and said: 'That was dangerous! If those men were real sailors, it would have been all right. But they are really farmers. In this idle time, some of them take to ferrying for side-work. But the farmers don't know the sea. They often have sad mishaps even in a little wind. You are lucky to have come through safely.'[14]

Fukuzawa felt a belated scare. In the Inland Sea there are many famous spots worth visiting, and tourism was very much in vogue during that civilized and peaceful Tokugawa period. However, as Fukuzawa had no money to spare, he stayed on board ship throughout. Naturally, the captain did not feel very kindly towards the young samurai, and he stared at Fukuzawa as he was eating the ship's fare. Other passengers turned up the next morning, every one of them drunk and happy. At Akashi, Fukuzawa thought he had put up with the company long enough, and walked from there to Osaka thirty-eight miles in a single stretch. He writes:

> When I was approaching Osaka, I was ferried across many rivers. These are somewhat recognizable to me now, for as we travel by train today, we pass over many bridges on the western side of the city. Fortunately a samurai was exempt from toll. But soon the day was over, and in the dark, moon-less night passers-by were few. I hardly dared inquire the way anyhow, for if a man passed in a lonely spot, I was more afraid of him than eager to find out which road to take. I did feel helpless, for though the short sword I wore was a fine one by the swordsmith Sukesada, the long sword was thin and light, not of much use in an actual fight.
>
> But then, as I learned, Osaka was not especially noted for murders, and I had no great cause to be afraid. However, a lone traveller on a dark, strange road cannot well help feeling some chills run up and down his spine, and looking with a certain security to the sharp objects on his side. But as I think back over it, it seems to me that I was really the one to be feared rather than the one to be afraid.[15]

Fukuzawa is very frank, confessing that he was afraid; one should say that Fukuzawa had the courage to describe his true feelings. Several years later, on the eve of the Meiji Restoration, Fukuzawa became a target of assassination, as he was an advocate of pro-moting intercourse with Western nations. He was so afraid of being attacked by an assassin that he even made a secret hole dug in the floor for escape. Fukuzawa recalls another scary experience. It hap-pened in Edo, capital of the tycoon, of the mid-1860s. The time had already turned an hour past midnight – a cold and clear winter night with the moon shining brightly overhead. Its silent, white beams made him feel unusually chilly for no good reason. In those revolutionary days, strolling ruffians had been appearing every night, cutting down unfortunate victims at dark corners. Fukuzawa tucked up the wide ends of his skirt-trousers in order to be ready to run at the first signal. Fukuzawa's art of story telling reminds us of a *kōdanshi,* professional story-teller of Edo tradition:

> As I was passing Gensuke-chō, or thereabouts, I saw a man coming towards me. He looked gigantic in the moonlight though now I would not swear to his stature at all. On came the giant. Nowadays, there are

policemen to depend upon, or we can run into someone's house for protection, but at that time no such help was to be expected. People would
only bar their doors more heavily and would never think of coming out to
assist a stranger calling for help.

'Now, here is a pretty pass,' I thought. 'I cannot run back, for the rascal
would only take advantage of my weakness and chase me more surely.
Perhaps I had better go ahead. And if I go ahead, I must pretend not to be
afraid. I must even threaten him.'

I moved out diagonally to the middle of the street from the left side
where I had been walking. Then the other fellow moved out too. This gave
me a shock, but now there was no retreating an inch. If he were to draw, I
must draw too. As I had practised the art of *iai* (swordplay), I knew how to
handle my sword.

'How shall I kill him? Well, I shall give a thrust from below.'

I was absolutely determined that I was going to fight and felt ready if he
showed the slightest challenge. He drew nearer.

I really hated the idea of injuring a man – I could not stand seeing a man
hurt, much less inflicting the injury myself. But now there seemed no alternative. If the stranger were to show any offence, I must kill him. At that
time there was no such thing as police or a criminal court. If I were to kill
an unknown man, I would simply run home, and that would be the end of
it. We were about to meet.

Every step brought us nearer, and finally we were at a striking distance.
He did not draw. Of course I did not draw either. And we passed each
other. With this as a cue, I ran. I don't remember how fast I ran. After going
a little distance, I turned to look back as I flew. The other man was running
too, in his direction. I drew a breath of relief and saw the funny side of the
whole incident. A coward had met a coward as in a farce. Neither had the
least intention of killing the other; each had put up a show of boldness in
fear of the other. And both ran at the same moment.[16]

You see the humorous quality of Fukuzawa's story-telling. If you
are vainglorious, you cannot recall such incidents. Fukuzawa was
apparently a Japanese not bound by the chivalrous code of the
samurai. Neither was he the modest man of olden times who
refused to talk about his own life. In this regard, too, Fukuzawa was
totally free from traditional inhibitions. In his *Autobiography*,
Fukuzawa did not try to aggrandize himself, nor did he make efforts
to look smaller than he really was. Benjamin Franklin too was very
frank in his *Autobiography* so much so that he admits the usefulness
of human vanity. At the beginning of the book, in a passage
addressed to his son, Franklin explains his motives in writing about
his own life: vanity is one of them. He says:

And lastly (I may as well confess it, as the denial of it would be believed by
nobody) I shall perhaps not a little gratify my own vanity. Indeed, I never

heard or saw the introductory words, 'Without Vanity I may say,' etc., but some vain thing immediately followed. Most people dislike vanity in others whatever share they have of it themselves, but I give it fair quarter wherever I meet with it, being persuaded that it is often productive of good to the possessor and to others who are within his sphere of action.[17]

This frank recognition of the part played by vanity in our life seems to me to be preferable to a hypocritical negation of it. Franklin was an anti-British Yankee in his affirmative attitude towards the positive effect of vanity.

Fukuzawa was consciously anti-traditional with regard to swords, which had long been considered the soul of the samurai. Fukuzawa says that even several years before the Meiji Restoration, which introduced the abolition of the custom for warrior-class members to wear two swords, he had already sold all the swords in his possession except for a short one, which appeared like a long one, and a kitchen knife set in a sheath. For ten years before and after the Restoration of 1868, Fukuzawa did not go out after dark. He stayed at home writing pamphlets, translating all sorts of Western books, and in the daytime he taught at his private academy of Western learning. The Fukuzawa school opened in the third year of Keiō, 1867, and is today known as Keiō University, whose motto is 'the pen is mightier than the sword'.

Let us examine here the quality of Fukuzawa's pen. His style is exceptionally lucid. In the introduction to his collected works Fukuzawa tells us that his constant endeavour had been to write so clearly that 'not only every uneducated tradesman or peasant should understand him perfectly, but that even a servant-girl fresh from the country, chancing to hear a passage read aloud by some one on the other side of a screen, should carry away a good general notion of the sense'. Fukuzawa adds that he had been in the habit of submitting his writings to the test of comprehension by reading his work to a poor neighbour woman and her children, simplifying every expression on which they stumbled. Fukuzawa's practice reminds us of the popular Chinese poet Bai Ju-yi (Po Chü-i), who did the same thing more than one thousand years before. Little wonder that an author so truly democratic should have achieved an unequalled popularity.

Among all his writings I most appreciate *Fukuō-jiden,* Fukuzawa's *Autobiography.* The same could be said about Franklin's writings. I like Franklin's *Autobiography* more than any other of his well-known works such as *Poor Richard's Almanack,* which is more didactic and less poetic than the *Analects* of Confucius. Fukuzawa's *Autobiography* is one of the masterpieces of Japanese literature, although it is seldom mentioned in histories of Japanese literature. Hitherto Japanese literary historians have neglected some of the most important works of Japanese literature for the simple reason that they are non-fictional in nature. Arai Hakuseki's autobiography or Fukuzawa Yukichi's autobiography have been ignored by many narrow-minded literary critics. It is true that Fukuzawa was not a novelist, but it is nonetheless true that Fukuzawa's *Autobiography,* published in 1899, is one of the most remarkable works of Japanese literature. The book is very interesting even in the English translation made by Professor Kiyooka, a grandson of Fukuzawa Yukichi. I recommend this book. In order to form your own opinion of things Japanese, it is advisable to read books written by Japanese before you read books on Japan written by Western scholars. It is often more agreeable and more refreshing to drink fresh water directly from fountainheads. It is better to try to gain direct access to primary sources rather than be satisfied with secondary commentaries. As for Fukuzawa's *Autobiography,* it would of course be better if you could read *Fukuō jiden* in the original Japanese than to read its English translation. At the beginning of the twentieth century the British Japanologist Basil Hall Chamberlain made the following remark in his *Things Japanese*:[18] 'The fact that [Fukuzawa's *Autobiography*] is written in colloquial [Japanese] should facilitate its perusal by foreign students.' He added that in his opinion it is one of the most interesting books in the Japanese language.

As for his writing style, Franklin, too, is a very democratic person. The printer and publisher Franklin was well aware that in order to sell a book you must write with clarity. Franklin's ideal in this regard is very similar to Fukuzawa's: he says his writing should be understood by his chambermaid. Both Franklin and Fukuzawa were great popularizers of ideas. The 'philosophy' of Franklin as well as that of Fukuzawa was perhaps not very original, and 'amounted at best to little more than an amiable optimism of a utilitarian cast'.[19] Such as they were, the leading minds of America and Japan adopted their ideas, and that had much to do with their lucid writing style. Franklin tells us in his *Autobiography*, how he mastered his style by imitating the *Spectator*. After having read the British journal, Franklin laid it by a few days and then without looking at it he tried to reproduce the content of the paper again. As for the style of their autobiographies another similarity could be pointed out. In Fukuzawa's narrative there is a mixture of narration and dialogue, as his *Autobiography* was first dictated and then revised by Fukuzawa himself. The stylistic quality of Franklin's *Autobiography* is almost the same; the author himself tells us that he had learnt to mix narration and dialogue from John Bunyan's *Pilgrim's Progress*. Franklin says:

> Honest John was the first that I know of who mixes narration and dialogue, a method of writing very engaging to the reader, who in the most interesting parts finds himself, as it were, admitted into the company and present at the conversation.[20]

Let us examine here, though a bit belatedly, Benjamin Franklin's revolt against traditional guild customs and his consequent flight from Boston. Franklin got away on board a ship whose sails were torn to pieces by a squall. He was wet and without food or drink save a bottle of poor-quality rum. Benjamin walked from Burlington and took a boat bound for Philadelphia:

> As there was no wind, we rowed all the way; and about midnight, not having yet seen the city, some of the company were confident we must have passed it and would row no farther; the others knew not where we were, so we put towards the shore, got into a creek, landed near an old fence, with the rails of which we made a fire, the night being cold in October, and there we remained till daylight. Then one of the company knew the place to be Cooper's Creek, a little above Philadelphia, which we saw as soon as we got out of the creek, and arrived there about eight or nine o'clock, on the Sunday morning and landed at the Market Street wharf.
>
> I have been the more particular in this description of my journey, and shall be so of my first entry into that city, that you may in your mind compare such unlikely beginnings with the figure I have since made there.
>
> I was in my working dress, my best clothes being to come round by sea. I was dirty from my journey; my pockets were stuffed out with shirts and stockings; I knew no soul, nor where to look for lodging. Fatigued with walking, rowing, and want of sleep, I was very hungry, and my whole stock of cash consisted of a Dutch dollar and about a shilling in copper coin, which I gave to the boatman for my passage. At first they refused it on account of my having rowed, but I insisted on their taking it. A man is sometimes more generous when he has little money than when he has plenty, perhaps through fear of being thought to have but little. I walked towards the top of the street, gazing about till near Market Street, where I met a boy with bread. I have often made a meal of dry bread, and inquiring where he had bought it, I went immediately to the baker's he directed me to. I asked for biscuit, meaning such as we had in Boston, but that sort, it seems, was not made in Philadelphia. I then asked for a threepenny loaf and was told they had none such. Not knowing the different prices nor the names of the different sorts of bread, I told him to give me three penny-

worth of any sort. He gave me accordingly three great puffy rolls. I was surprised at the quantity but took it, and having no room in my pockets, walked off with a roll under each arm and eating the other.[21]

Mankind has always been divided into two groups: those who have experienced hunger and those who have not. I am convinced that those who know what hunger means by their own experience appreciate the more the humorous quality of the young Benjamin walking off with a great roll under each arm and another at his mouth. Franklin once said that while studying in Boston, he saved half what his brother paid for his board; his meals consisted of no more than a biscuit or a slice of bread, a handful of raisins or a tart from the pastry cook's, and a glass of water: 'I made the greater progress from that greater clearness of head and quicker apprehension which generally attend temperance in eating and drinking.' Do you think that there are young men around you who console themselves by reading this passage? In North America maybe there aren't any. However, in the late 1940s some Japanese students, I for one, encouraged themselves with this passage. Nothing is more real than hunger; once experienced, the bitterness of under-nourishment remains in one's memory throughout life. As one belonging to the generation that grew up in Japan towards the end of the Pacific War, I cannot help feeling a sense of guilt when I throw away an unfinished meal. Do we not have an ominous presentiment that today's consumer societies will not and cannot go on forever and that we will sooner or later be punished? Post-industrial affluent societies seem to me to be incompatible with Franklin's cardinal virtues of frugality and temperance. The more I admire Franklin's way of life, the more difficult it becomes for me to admire the societies in which consumption is considered a virtue. As for Franklin's thirteen virtues, I have discussed them already in relation to the modernization movement of Meiji Japan in Part II Chapter 4.

Franklin's success as a writer had much to do with his profession as a printer. He could have easy access to journalism and was able to publish many of his writings thanks to this trade. In Fukuzawa's case, it was just the opposite: it was his success as a writer that made him instal a printing-house for his personal use in his own school compound. Japan is a country where the publishing business has flourished for more than a century-and-a-half. Several million copies of Fukuzawa's writings were sold during his lifetime. Many pirated editions continued to appear. It was mainly to defend his own interests that Fukuzawa had a printing-house established, which was later to become Keiō University Press. Fukuzawa's financial contribution helped that private institution to be independent. It is only a recent phenomenon that Keiō University receives public financial subsidies. Fukuzawa preached the importance of money: financial independence is a prerequisite of spiritual independence, a lesson he knew from his own experience and an attitude he learnt from Anglo-Saxons.

Franklin established himself as a printer in Philadelphia within months after his arrival. Having succeeded in this, the financially independent Benjamin went back to Boston for a brief period of time. His unexpected appearance surprised his family. Here is the reaction of his brother James, whom he went to see at his printing-house:

> I was better dressed than ever while in his service, having a genteel new suit from head to foot, a watch, and my pockets lined with near five pounds sterling in silver. He received me not very frankly, looked me all over, and turned to his work again. The journeymen were inquisitive where I had been, what sort of a country it was, and how I liked it. I praised it much and the happy life I led in it, expressing strongly my intention of returning to it; and one of them asking what kind of money we had there, I produced a handful of silver and spread it before them, which was a kind of rare show they had not been used to, paper being the money of Boston. Then I took an opportunity of letting them see my watch, and lastly (my brother still glum and sullen) I gave them a piece of eight to drink and took my leave. This visit of mine offended him extremely. For when my mother sometime after spoke to him of a reconciliation, and of her wish to see us on good terms together, and that we might live for the future as brothers, he said I had insulted him in such a manner before his people that he could never forget or forgive it. In this, however, he was mistaken.[22]

Compared with Benjamin's attitude towards his older brother, there was much more self-restraint in Yukichi's behaviour towards *his* older brother. In February of 1855, Fukuzawa Yukichi was obliged to leave Nagasaki, having received an order to come back to his old castle town of Nakatsu. The order was given by a jealous superior of the Okudaira Clan. Yukichi then made up his mind to desert the domain and wanted to pursue his study of Dutch at the capital, Edo. As we have already seen, he made a stop at Osaka on his way. The storage office of the Nakatsu Domain was there where his late father had served as overseer of the treasury. At that time, his older brother was serving in the office, and persuaded Yukichi to stay in Osaka. At their first meeting, his brother asked him why he had returned so suddenly. Yukichi told his big brother exactly what had happened. The brother then assumed his guardian's right and objected to Yukichi's plan to go to Edo to study. He said:

> I cannot let you go on your proposed career to Edo, because though Nakatsu is nearly on a line from Nagasaki to Osaka, I see you avoided the town in your journey. If I were not here, your going on to Edo without taking leave of mother might be excusable. But as I am here and I have met you, I cannot think of allowing myself to be a partner in disrespect. She herself might not think much about it, but I cannot permit myself. Therefore, stay in Osaka. I am sure there will be just as good a teacher here as in Edo.[23]

So Yukichi obediently stayed in Osaka and entered a private school of Dutch studies, which turned out to be the best school of its kind in Japan, Ogata Kōan's Teki-juku school. It was in many ways very fortunate for Yukichi. The level of the school was so high that three years later when he came up to Edo, it was not to learn but to teach Edo students. Moreover Fukuzawa Yukichi was at home in Osaka. He saw there many older people who still remembered him. Among them was the wife of a workman, his wet-nurse, and on old man named Buhachi, who had served his father before, and was now serving his older brother. Here is Yukichi's remembrance of bygone days:

> The day after I arrived I was walking with him in Dōjima Street. 'Well, Sir, I remember the night you were born. It happened in the night, and I went for the midwife. The old dame midwife still lives over there in that street. When you were big enough, I used to carry you around in my arms, and I took you sometimes over to the wrestling ring to watch the practice.'
>
> He pointed out to me the house of the midwife and the wrestlers' practice-arena. It all came back to me as we walked along and I could not keep back the tears that were prompted by dear memories. I could not think I was on a trip; it was just as if I had come home after a long absence.[24]

Let us examine Fukuzawa's and Franklin's respective formative years, their attitudes towards eating, drinking and clothing, their study habits, their methods of learning foreign languages, their scientific experiments, and moral principles as self-made men. Both Fukuzawa and Franklin talk considerably about their eating habits: the Oriental Fukuzawa was one of the first Japanese who challenged the taboo against eating animal meat, while the Occidental Franklin was a one-time vegetarian. Franklin writes:

> I had stuck to my resolution to eat nothing that had had life; and on this occasion I considered ... the taking [of] every fish as a kind of unprovoked murder, since none of them had or even could do us any injury that might justify this massacre. All this seemed very reasonable. But I had formerly

been a great lover of fish, and when this came hot out of the frying pan, it smelled admirably well. I balanced some time between principle and inclination till I recollected that when the fish were opened, I saw smaller fish taken out of their stomachs. 'Then,' thought I, 'if you eat one another, I don't see why we mayn't eat you.'[25]

Thus Franklin dined upon cod very heartily and ever after ate as other people.

In Japan, a Buddhist nation, to eat something that has life was not recommended; although fish were eaten, to kill an animal that has four legs was considered a sin. However, young students of Ogata's school were very daring; they were probably under the influence of Western eating habits which they knew. Fukuzawa recalls his student days:

> When we felt rich – which meant we had as much as one or two *shu* to spend – we would go to a restaurant for a carouse. That was a great luxury which did not happen often. More frequently we went to the chicken-restaurants. Still oftener we went to the cheapest place – the beef-stand.
>
> There were only two places in Osaka where they served beef; one was near Naniwa Bridge, and the other near the prostitute quarters of Shinmachi – the lowest sort of eating places. No ordinary man ever entered them. All their customers were city bullies, who exhibited their fully tattooed torsos, and the students of Ogata's school. Where the meat came from and whether it was of a cow that was killed or that had died, we did not care. They served plenty of boiled beef with wine and rice for a hundred and fifty *mon*. Certainly this meat was often tough and smelled strong.[26]

After the Meiji Restoration eating beef was curiously identified with the Civilization and Enlightenment movement, and a popular catchword was created: *Gyūniku kuwaneba hirakenu.* ('Those who do not eat beef are not enlightened.') Fukuzawa was the first to write an advertisement[27] for a steak house in 1871. The taboo against its eating was, however, very strong in the 1850s. Here is another anecdote of these Ogata school pioneers:

> One day, the proprietor of our favourite beef-shop bought a pig, but the man, being a soft-hearted fellow, could not force himself to kill it. So he came to us.
>
> 'All right,' said our spokesman. 'But what will you give us if we do it?'
> 'Well, Sir, er –'
> 'Will you give us the head?' 'Yes, Sir.'
> So the crowd set out. Being medical students, they knew that the easiest way of securing death was by suffocation. They tied the pig's four legs together and threw it into the river nearby. And for their reward, they did bring back the decapitated head, and borrowing an axe, cut the head up

into sections. Then the would-be medical men had a fine time studying the brain, eyes and so forth. After the scientific investigation was over, they cooked up the pieces and ate them. No wonder the beef-shop keeper and others thought we were like *eta*.[28]

Slaughterers of cattle and dealers in leather were segregated in the Tokugawa society as the lowest stratum of the social order. *Eta* were outcasts from Japanese society, and the use of the expression itself may trigger a strong reaction today.

As for drinking, Franklin was probably by nature free from the habit. He recalls his experience in London where he worked in Watts' Printing-house:

I drank only water; the other workmen, near fifty in number, were great guzzlers of beer. On occasion I carried up and down stairs a large form of types in each hand, when others carried but one in both hands. They wondered to see from this and several instances that the 'Water-American,' as they called me, was *stronger* than themselves who drank *strong* beer. We had an ale-house boy who attended always in the house to supply the workmen. My companion at the press drank every day a pint before breakfast, a pint at breakfast with his bread and cheese, a pint between breakfast and dinner, a pint at dinner, a pint in the afternoon about six o'clock, and another when he had done his day's work. I thought it a detestable custom; but it was necessary, he supposed, to drink *strong* beer that he might be *strong* to labour. I endeavoured to convince him that the bodily strength afforded by beer could only be in proportion to the grain or flour of the barley dissolved in the water of which it was made, that there was more flour in a pennyworth of bread, and therefore if he would eat that with a pint of water, it would give him more strength than a quart of beer. He drank on, however, and had four of five shillings to pay out of his wages every Saturday night for that muddling liquor, an expense I was free from.[29]

Franklin's explanation based on calculations of calories even before the notion of calorie was clearly defined is in a sense very scientific and rational; however, rational explanations generally do not satisfy the question of appetites.

Fukuzawa was, on the contrary, extremely fond of drinking. He says: 'To begin with the shortcomings, my greatest weakness lay in drinking.'

My use of the rice-wine was not a formed habit; I was born with it. Though very faintly. I still remember how I used to cry whenever my mother shaved my head, because it hurt when she scraped the top of my head. Then she would say: 'I will give you a little sip of the wine, so let me scrape you a little more.' Then I kept still and let her go on. Thus began my early taste for wine.[30]

Fukuzawa would do anything to have a taste of saké, rice-wine. He said himself: 'I have no excuse to make even if I should be called a coward on this point.' Still, he made up his mind not to drink while studying at Nagasaki. For a whole year he was a man dead to all indulgence. When he left Nagasaki the next year, however, Fukuzawa stopped at the first town on the way and drank till his one year's thirst was satisfied. He tells us the following anecdote:

> My Nagasaki master, Yamamoto, had, of course, believed that I was a tee-totaller. Some years later, on my way to Europe, when our ship called at Nagasaki, I visited my old master in that harbour city. After expressing my gratitude for his kindness to me as a young student, and telling him about my new venture abroad, I confessed that my being a teetotaller was a lie. Then I showed him my true self, for we drank together, and I heroically, till he and his good wife were thoroughly surprised.[31]

Fukuzawa's *Autobiography* is extremely interesting, because it describes in detail the student life at the Ogata school of Dutch medical learning. Here is what the dormitory was like:

> Although the majority of the students were samurai who could have worn the two swords of their rank, most of them, about fifty or sixty students, had pawned their swords so that there were perhaps only two or three pairs in the whole dormitory. Among these were my own, because I had not then, nor have I since, pawned any of my property. Yet we had no difficulty, for the few pairs of swords were like our common property, and anyone wore them who wished to appear in formal dress. On ordinary days we went around with only one sword so as not to lose entirely the dignity belonging to samurai.[32]

In the early eighteenth-century autobiography of Arai Hakuseki there are conspicuous traces of sword fetishism, while there is none in Fukuzawa's *Autobiography;* the contrast is striking.[33] During the summer Ogata students lived without wearing proper clothes, and their nakedness brings many adventures and blunders:

> One evening five or six of us had obtained a generous amount of wine. One of the group suggested that we take it out on the roof-porch, the open porch on the housetop used for drying laundry. But just as we were climbing out, we discovered our teacher's maids already there enjoying the evening breeze. If we drank while they were there, certainly talk about us would be reported to the teacher later on. Then Matsuoka Yuki, bolder than others, declared that he would get those women off the porch. He climbed up, without one stitch of clothes on.
> 'A warm evening, isn't it?'
> With these words he stretched himself out on the floor. This was too much for the maids. A bit confused, they scurried away. As soon as they

went out of sight, Matsuoka called down to us in Dutch that all was well. 'Come on up, old chaps, and take care of that wine.'

There is another incident ... One evening I heard a woman's voice calling my name from the lower floor. 'What could the maid want at this ungodly hour?' I thought, for I had just lain down after a hearty bout. But if I was called, I could not very well lie quietly. I jumped up, and without stopping to put any clothes on, I strode downstairs and stood before the woman. 'What do you want?' I shouted.

Before I could get the words out of my mouth, I froze to the spot. It was not the maid, but our teacher's wife! I could not run, nor could I kneel or bow before her, naked as I was. I was helpless. Madame Ogata then perhaps felt sorry for my plight. She walked away without saying anything. I could not bring myself to call on her the next morning to say how sorry I was for my misdeed the night before. So the incident passed without an apology, but I have never forgotten it. A few years ago when I had occasion to be in Osaka again, I visited the old Ogata house, and recalling what had once happened at the foot of that same staircase, I felt again the shame of forty years before.[34]

Among the three East Asian countries, China, Korea and Japan, the people who have most strictly conformed themselves to Confucian norms are the Koreans. Korea may even be said to have suffered from a Confucian malady, since in later centuries its growth seems to have been arrested by excessive devotion to Confucian norms. But the Japanese were saved by some happy strain in their temperament which resisted its moral strictness and allowed them, while respecting Confucian tradition, to adapt the sage's teaching to their needs. When we compare the modernization of Japan and that of Korea in the nineteenth century, the cultural significance of the harbour city of Nagasaki becomes clear, as there existed no corresponding door to Western civilization in Korea. The part played by Nagasaki in the development of Japan during two centuries-and-a-half of national isolation was immeasurable. Although many scholars have hitherto emphasized the exceptional character of Japan's isolation from the rest of the world during the Tokugawa period, the closing of an Asian country to Westerners was not peculiar to Japan. It was a part of the general pattern of reaction shown by all the East Asian countries. If there was any significant difference between Korea's and Japan's response to the Western impact, it was that Japan allowed Hollanders to come to the port of Nagasaki. Through that tiny channel, Dutch studies developed in Japan, first in Nagasaki, and then in Edo, Osaka and other places. However, even if Western studies had developed in Korea at that time, I cannot imagine that there could have been

Korean students of Dutch living without clothes in a dormitory. Some people would argue that the warm monsoon climate of the Japanese summer must have been the cause of the nudity of students of the Ogata school, but as students of Osaka universities today are properly clothed even in the warm and humid season, that habit must have something to do with their anti-conventional attitude. That taste for barbarism became after the Meiji Restoration a tradition in Japanese higher school dormitories, and lasted until after WWII.

There was indeed a surprising contradiction in the daily habits of those medical students: in that dormitory, sanitation was all but disregarded. Lice, along with students, were permanent residents of the dormitory. Whenever a man took off his clothes, he could easily catch five or ten of them. Fukuzawa was scientifically minded and he once tried a new method of killing the pests. In the case of the pig it was death by suffocation, this time it is different:

> I said that the method the laundresses used often – that of pouring boiling water on the clothes – was too trite; I would show how to kill them off with one single operation. So I took my underwear to the roof-porch one frosty winter night, and let both the creatures and the eggs freeze to death in the cold. But I could not claim the invention; someone had suggested this to me.[35]

All these anecdotes give us the impression that they led a pretty rough and lawless life as students, but according to Fukuzawa they were very friendly and genuine among themselves. Fukuzawa enjoyed trying his wits on some interesting topics. He explains:

> If the theme of the *Forty-Seven Rōnin* came up, I would challenge my comrades: 'I will take whichever side you are against. If you say the *Forty-Seven Rōnin* were loyal, I will prove they were disloyal. Or if you want to prove the contrary, I will take the opposite side, for I can make them loyal men or disloyal men at the twist of my tongue.'[36]

From the age of twenty to twenty-three Fukuzawa studied at the Ogata's school. Compared with Franklin, he was lucky having all these experiences of a student. Generally speaking, students can play more pranks than farmers or artisans of the same age. However, many similarities can be found in Franklin's life. For example, he describes his art of debating:

> Keimer and I lived on a pretty good familiar footing and agreed tolerably well ... He retained a great deal of his old enthusiasm and loved argumentation. We therefore had many disputations. I used to work him so with my

Socratic method and had trapanned him so often by questions apparently so distant from any point we had in hand, and yet by degrees leading to the point and bringing him into difficulties and contradictions, that at last he grew ridiculously cautious and would hardly answer the most common question without asking first: 'What do you intend to infer from that?'[37]

Franklin once played a prank on Keimer. He says:

Keimer wore his beard at full length, because somewhere in the Mosaic Law it is said, 'Thou shalt not mar the corners of thy beard.' He likewise kept the seventh day Sabbath, and these two points were essentials with him. I disliked both but agreed to admit them upon condition of his adopting the doctrine of not using animal food. 'I doubt,' says he, 'my constitution will bear it.' I assured him it would and that he would be the better for it. He was usually a great glutton, and I wished to give myself some diversion in half-starving him. He consented to try the practice if I would keep him company; I did so, and we held it for three months. Our provisions were purchased, cooked, and brought to us regularly by a woman in the neighborhood who had from me a list of forty dishes to be prepared for us at different times, in which there entered neither fish, flesh, not fowl. This whim suited me better at this time from the cheapness of it, not costing us above eighteen pence sterling each per week ... I went on pleasantly, but poor Keimer suffered grievously, tired of the project, longed for the flesh-pots of Egypt, and ordered a roast pig. He invited me and two women friends to dine with him, but it being brought too soon upon table, he could not resist the temptation and ate it all up before we came.[38]

Franklin and Fukuzawa share the same humorous quality in their descriptions of appetite. There are of course differences between the two. In the Ogata school what mattered was intellectual achievement. Students did not care at all about their clothing. Franklin was a tradesman, and as such he was obliged to pay more attention to appearances. We have already seen how well he was dressed on his first return home, having a genteel new suit from head to foot, having a watch and his pockets lined with five pounds sterling in silver. Franklin recalls his rise in the world:

I began now gradually to pay off the debt I was under for the printing house. In order to secure my credit and character as a tradesman, I took care not only to be in *reality* industrious and frugal, but to avoid all *appearance* of the contrary. I dressed plain and was seen at no places of idle diversion. I never went out a fishing or shooting; a book, indeed, sometimes debauched me from my work, but that was seldom, snug, and gave no scandal; ... Thus being esteemed an industrious, thriving, young man, and paying duly for what I bought, the merchants who imported stationery solicited my custom; others proposed supplying me with books, and I went on swimmingly.[39]

Probably this stage of Franklin's career should be compared with the later stage of Fukuzawa's activities, when he successfully administered his Keiō school and his newspaper, the *Jiji-shimpō;* Fukuzawa too went on swimmingly. As Franklin felt a strong necessity to dress plainly, so in religious matters too he tried to avoid bad appearances. He explains his state of mind with regard to the moral principles that influenced the later events of his life. Though his parents had early given him religious education, when he was scarcely fifteen, he began to doubt revelation itself. Franklin confesses:

> Some books against deism fell into my hands; ... It happened that they wrought an effect on me quite contrary to what was intended by them; for the arguments of the deists which were quoted to be refuted appeared to me much stronger than the refutations. In short, I soon became a thorough deist.[40]

Revelation as such bore no weight with Franklin. However, he says he grew convinced by experience that truth, sincerity and integrity in dealings between man and man were of the utmost importance to the felicity of life, and concludes:

> I entertained an opinion that tho' certain actions might not be bad *because* they were forbidden by it [revelation], or good *because* it commanded them, yet probably those actions might be forbidden *because* they were bad for us or commanded because they were beneficial to us, in their own natures, all the circumstances of things considered.[41]

Franklin's position is surprisingly similar to many of the Japanese of the post-Tokugawa period. They did not believe in religion, still they followed ethical norms derived from them.

In Japan secularization is considered to have taken place during the Tokugawa period. Fukuzawa's attitude towards religion and superstition, which were practically synonymous for him, is vividly described in the following anecdotes:

> One day when I was twelve or thirteen years old, I ran through the room in one of my mischievous moments and stepped on some papers which my brother was arranging on the floor. Suddenly he broke out in disgust:
> 'Stop, you dunce!'
> Then he began to speak solemnly. 'Do you not see what is written here?' he said. 'Is this not Okudaira Taizen-no Tayū – your lord's name?'
> 'I did not know it,' I hastily apologized. 'I am sorry.' 'You say you did not know,' he replied indignantly. 'But if you have eyes, you should see. What do you think of trampling your lord's name under foot? The sacred code of lord and vassal is ...'

> Here my brother was beginning to recite the samurai rules of duty.
> There was nothing for me to do but bow my head to the floor and plead:
> 'I was very careless, please forgive me.'
>
> But in my heart there was no apology. All the time I was thinking: 'Why
> scold about it? Did I step on my lord's head? What is wrong with stepping
> on a piece of paper?'
>
> Then I went on, reasoning in my childish mind that if it was so wicked
> to step on a man's name, it would be very much more wicked to step on a
> god's name; and I determined to test the truth.[42]

So Fukuzawa stole one of the temple charms, bearing sacred
names, and trampled on it. As no heavenly vengeance followed, he
went a step further and took the charm to the lavatory and put it in
the excrement. He was a little afraid, but nothing happened. He
later became more reckless, and conceived the idea of finding out
what the Shinto god of Inari shrine really was. He opened the
shrine and found only a stone. He threw it away and put in another
stone which he picked up on the road. In another shrine the token
of the god was a wooden tablet; he threw it away and waited for
what might happen. When the season of the Inari festival came,
many people gathered to put up flags, beat drums and make offer-
ings of the sacred rice-wine. During all the round of festival
services, the young Fukuzawa was chuckling to himself, saying,
'There they are – worshipping my stones, the fools!'[43]

Franklin's as well as Fukuzawa's mind did not run in theological
channels. It must be for this reason that their 'philosophies' have
often been slighted by self-important scholars. However, it is fortunate that the precisionism of the Puritan heritage was alien to
Franklin's own broad secular spirit. He thought of New England's
brand of Calvinism as 'dry doctrine'. Franklin had, however, no
more enthusiasm for disagreement with religion than for devotion
to it. Franklin's beliefs were supported by social necessity.

Fukuzawa, too, was very secular-minded. He was not at all devo-
tional, but this does not mean that he was not ethical in his conduct,
as it is often said, devotion and ethics, theology and conduct, are
separate things. He explains his opinion concerning religion in his
mature years:

> It goes without saying that the maintenance of peace and security in society
> requires a religion. For this purpose any religion will do. I lack a religious
> nature, and have never believed in any religion. I am thus open to the
> charge that I am advising others to be religious, when I am not so. Yet my
> conscience does not permit me to clothe myself with religion, when I have
> it not at heart ... Of religions, there are several kinds – Buddhism,

Christianity and what not. Yet, from my standpoint, there is no more difference between these than between green tea and black tea. It makes little
difference whether you drink one or the other. The point is to let those
who have never drunk tea partake of it and know its taste. Just so with religion. Religionists are like tea-merchants. They are busy selling their own
kind of religion. As for the method of procedure in this matter, it is not
good policy for one to disparage the stock of others in order to praise his
own. What he ought to do is to see that his stock is well selected and his
prices cheap, etc., etc.[44]

Fukuzawa is almost Voltairian in his humorous comments on
religion which he regarded as a social constraint.

Franklin, too, was not a religious man, but he did author the substance of religious creed:

That there is one God who made all things.
That he governs the world by his providence.
That he ought to be worshipped by adoration, prayer, and thanksgiving.
But that the most acceptable service to God is doing good to man.
That the soul is immortal.
And that God will certainly reward virtue and punish vice, either here or
hereafter.[45]

It was a great surprise for Japanese parents that in many states in
the United States, where freedom of religion is guaranteed and state
and religion are separate, their children were requested to pledge
allegiance in public schools in the name of one God and of one
nation. I was surprised to see on television the newly-elected
President pledge himself by putting his hand on the Bible. It was
then that I understood why Franklin Roosevelt evoked the name of
God when he declared war against Japan. When I saw on American
coins the motto, 'In God we trust', I was not at ease and asked one
of my American friends if there really exists a free space in this
country where agnostics can openly express their opinions. He
answered no, and said that the God mentioned on US coins is
Mammon, God of the almighty dollar. If you do not have trust in
it, you cannot live in this country. His joke may be partly true, but I
also understand this sort of joke must be painful to many decent
people. Nevertheless, the fact that monotheism is taken for granted
in the present-day US made me uneasy as I come from a polythe-
istic background, the Shinto of Japan. I realized this attitude could
be already in Franklin's above-mentioned creed.

Fukuzawa, who made experiments with the sacred charm, putting it into the excrement or changing the sacred stone with an
ordinary one, was in a sense scientifically-minded. They were

childish but, nonetheless, scientific experiments. He later made dis-
sections of a pig's head. His method of killing lice and their eggs on
a cold winter night was also of scientific inspiration. Fukuzawa and
his classmates tried every new scientific technique. He writes:

> Of course, at that time there were no examples of industrial machinery. A
> steam engine could not be seen anywhere in the whole of Japan. Nor was
> there any kind of apparatus for chemical experiments. However, learning
> something of the theories of chemistry and machinery in our books, we of
> the Ogata household spent much effort in trying out what we had learned,
> or trying to make a thing that was illustrated in the books.[46]

Fukuzawa's description of how ammonium chloride was produced by the students is unforgettable: the first requisite for the
experiment was bone, and they bought horse's hooves which were
used as fertilizer:

> We took a large quantity of the hoofs and covered it in an earthenware jar
> with a layer of clay; then placed it on a charcoal fire in a large bowl. As we
> fanned the fire vigorously, a smelly vapour came out; this we condensed in
> an earthenware pipe.
>     Our experiment was going very well, and the condensed vapour was
> dripping freely from the pipe, but the disadvantage proved to be the awful
> stench of the vapour. It can easily be imagined what the result of heating
> bones and horse-hoofs would be, especially in the small back yard of the
> dormitory. Our clothing became so saturated with the gas that when we
> went to the bath-house in the evening, the street dogs howled at us. Then
> we tried the experiment naked... The young men were so keen on their
> experiment that they stood the smelly ordeal without complaint. But all the
> neighbours objected and the servants in the Ogata household wailed that
> they could not eat their meals on account of the sickening gas.
>     After all our hardships and the complaints and apologies, a strange pow-
> dery thing was the result.[47]

It was not the correct crystals of ammonium chloride, and the
students continued the experiment, hiring a boat on the Yodo River,
placing their brazier on board. Still the vapour penetrated the
nearby shores, and the people would come out and yell to them to
go away. Then the young students had the boat rowed upstream,
continuing with the experiment until they were urged to return
downstream. This was Japan's first chemical pollution and the first
battle of environmentalists.

In 1860, Fukuzawa contrived to be taken on a voyage to America.
At San Francisco, the American hosts were very considerate to the
first Japanese delegation to their country, and showed them examples of modern industry. Fukuzawa's remark on this point is very
important and suggestive:

There was as yet no railway laid to the city (of San Francisco), nor was there any electric light in use. But the telegraph system and also Galvani's electroplating were already in use. Then we were taken to a sugar refinery and had the principle of the operation explained to us quite minutely. I am sure that our hosts thought they were showing us something entirely new, naturally looking for our surprise at each new device of modern engineering. But on the contrary, there was really nothing new, at least to me. I knew the principle of the telegraphy even if I had not seen the actual machine before; I knew that sugar was bleached by straining the solution with boneblack, and that in boiling down the solution, the vacuum was used to better effect than heat.[48]

Natural science is universal in character, so it was rather easy for Japanese to understand such scientific principles and mechanisms at the very beginning of their actual contact with the West. Fukuzawa's remark was without doubt unexpected on the part of Americans; it is still so on the part of today's readers of his *Autobiography*.

Franklin was of course a great inventor and scientist. His 'Philadelphia Experiments' were well known. I learnt about them, especially his experiment in electricity with a kite, in my English textbook for eighth-graders, at which time Japan was at war with the United States. While undergoing indiscriminate American bombings Japanese boys including myself felt keenly that Japan was lagging behind in science and technology. That technological gap seemed to be so immense, especially in the decade following Japan's defeat, that I could not have imagined that one day I would drive a Japanese car in North America. Since this was so unimaginable even to me, it is understandable that some Americans resent Japan's export offensive. Some knowledgeable Westerners criticize the Japanese, arguing that all they can do is to improve technology originally imported or borrowed from the West. These American critics, however, have forgotten that the same criticism was once directed against the Americans, when the United States, a comparatively late-starting nation, began to export mechanical products to Western Europe in the first half of the twentieth century. Yet even at that time European critics recognized that in the United States there was a great inventor, Thomas Edison, and before Edison, Benjamin Franklin.

As Franklin's experiments are too well known, I prefer to show you here an example of his scientific observation. While in London, Franklin met a certain Mr Whitfield, who had a loud and clear voice. When he preached from the top of the courthouse steps, which are in the middle of Market Street, he could be heard from a great distance. Franklin was curious to learn how far he could be heard. So he retired backwards down the street towards the river, and found his voice distinct till he came near Front Street, when some noise in that street obscured it. Imagining then a semi-circle, of which his distance should be the radius, and that it were filled with an audience, to each of member of which Franklin allowed two square feet, he calculated that the preacher might well be heard by more than thirty thousand. That calculation reconciled Franklin to the newspaper accounts of Mr Whitfield's having preached to thirty-five thousand people in the fields. In Goethe's *Italienische Reise*, there is a similar description.[49] The scientific-minded German author measured the distance reached by a voice alongside the shore of Venice.

However, what is important about both Franklin and Fukuzawa is that, by applying that scientific spirit to social and political matters, they could bring about many new reforms.

As we have already seen, contrary to the expectations of many people, Fukuzawa and other Dutch students understood fairly well the material aspects of Occidental civilization. Fukuzawa said in San Francisco: 'As for scientific inventions and industrial machinery, there was no great novelty in them for me. It was rather in matters of life and social custom and ways of thinking that I found at a loss in America.'[50] About the difficulty of understanding a foreign society, Fukuzawa says that 'things social, political and economic proved most inexplicable.'[51] As has already been referred to in the chapter dealing with Japanese experience abroad, Fukuzawa was shocked, finding that his American interlocuter did not know the whereabouts of George Washington's descendants. Although Fukuzawa knew that America was a republic with a new president every four years, he still could not help feeling that the family of the founder of the United States would be revered above all other families just like the Tokugawa family of the Shoguns.

Fukuzawa, however, was inquisitive about almost every aspect of Western civilization. Fukuzawa's greatness lies in his efforts to understand and explain things political and economic of Western civilization to the Japanese people. He took notes of what he saw and heard, and on his return home, he published books which gave first-hand knowledge of things Western to the Japanese public for the first time.[52]

I would like to discuss here, Franklin's and Fukuzawa's mastery of foreign languages. Franklin later became a diplomat in European capitals; Fukuzawa went three times abroad before the official opening of Japan of 1868, as an interpreter attached to diplomatic missions. Without having acquired a considerable knowledge of foreign languages, it would not have been possible for them to get these posts, which in turn enlarged their intellectual horizons. One of the most moving passages in Fukuzawa's *Autobiography* concerns the diligence of Ogata students. If by chance you are under the impression that these students of Dutch led a happy-go-lucky life, you are mistaken. Their manner of study was arduous:

> In the beginning, each new student was given two books of grammar. These were texts that had been printed in Edo, one called *Grammatica* and the other *Syntaxis*. The new student began with *Grammatica*, and was taught to read it aloud by the help of some explanatory lectures. When he had studied this through, he was likewise given *Syntaxis*. And that was the end of his instruction in Ogata academy. Whatever in addition to this he might accomplish was through his own independent study.[53]

They then copied Dutch texts, and with the help of a Dutch-Japanese dictionary they tried to understand the contents. A class was composed of ten to fifteen students of the same level with a monitor. When a student could not construe his translation, the next one would take up the passage, and so on through the class until the entire text was rendered. Whoever made a perfect translation without a hitch for three months in succession would be promoted to a higher class. That seminar-competition was held on the days of the month containing ones and sixes or threes and eights. It was really like having examinations six times a month. Fukuzawa describes the competition:

> Though we were all really good friends – the older ones helping the new students in every way – this assistance did not extend to the preparation for the seminar-competition.[54] Then it was a point of honour never to expect or receive any help; each student had to depend on his own ability with the grammars and the one big dictionary the school possessed.[55]

As the beginners could not use a Dutch-Dutch dictionary, they consulted a Dutch-Japanese dictionary compiled by Dr Doeff, captain of the Dutch factory at Nagasaki, in collaboration with Japanese interpreters. Fukuzawa recalls the assiduity of the students:

> So on the day before our seminar-contests, there was always a big crowd in the 'Doeff room' silently taking turns in looking up words. It was a precious aid, and there were no idle students on that evening, nor was there scarcely a one who took a nap through the night.[56]

One day, on a visit to Yokohama in 1859, the year after he reached Edo, Fukuzawa tried to speak with Western merchants in Dutch and found that they did not understand him. A German could somehow understand his Dutch when he put it in writing. To say the least he was greatly disappointed. However, on discovering that English was the language of the future, he set about learning it at once. After a while he came to see that English was a language not so entirely foreign to him, since he had already studied Dutch. He had feared that all the labour expended to learn this language had been in vain. Fortunately, his knowledge of Dutch applied directly to his learning of English.

Then how about Franklin's learning of foreign languages? He began to study rather late, when he was twenty-seven years old, in 1733. He says:

> I soon made myself so much a master of the French as to be able to read the books with ease. I then undertook the Italian. An acquaintance who was also learning it used often to tempt me to play chess with him. Finding this took up too much of the time I had to spare for study, I at length refused to play any more unless on this condition-that the victor in every game should have a right to impose a task, either in parts of the grammar to be got by heart, or in translation, etc., which tasks the vanquished was to perform upon honour before our next meeting. As we played pretty equally, we thus beat one another into that language. I afterwards with a little painstaking acquired as much of Spanish as to read their books also. I have already mentioned that I had only one year's instruction in a Latin school, and that when very young, after which I neglected that language entirely. But when I had attained an acquaintance with the French, Italian, and Spanish, I was surprised to find, on looking over a Latin Testament, that I understood so much more of that language than I had imagined – which encouraged me to apply myself again to the study of it; and I met with the more success, as those preceding languages had greatly smoothed my way. From these circumstances I have thought that there is some inconsistency in our common mode of teaching languages. We are told that it is proper to begin first with the Latin, and having acquired that, it will be more easy to attain those modern languages which are derived from it; and yet we do not begin with the Greek in order more easily to acquire the Latin. It is true that if you can clamber and get to the top of a staircase without using steps, you will more easily gain them in descending; but certainly if you begin with the lowest, you will with more ease ascend to the top.[57]

Those who have studied Romance languages have, I believe, shared the same experience with Franklin. He wisely recommends us to start with French rather than with Latin.

Fukuzawa, with his knowledge of Dutch and especially of

English, accompanied shogunal missions abroad three times before the official opening of Japan in 1868. It is true that Fukuzawa's spoken English was not very impressive. His cross-cultural experiences, however, are probably more interesting than Franklin's voyages to England and to France, as Franklin's experiences are essentially limited to Western civilization. Fukuzawa's travels abroad were eye-openers for him and for the Japanese public. Thanks to those learning missions, he took many notes of what he saw, heard and experienced in many countries of Europe and America. He complemented his keen observations with knowledge drawn from books, and wrote *Seiyō jijō* (Conditions in the West), in which he explained to his countrymen many mechanisms and ideas that lie behind the dazzling evidence of Western civilization. *Seiyō jijō* was the book that made Fukuzawa's reputation. It was a straightforward account of Atlantic civilization, describing the political and military systems of the principal states, national debts, taxation, joint-stock companies, post offices, banks, libraries, museums, the highly developed sense of the rights of the citizen and similar features of the national life of modern Western countries. The Japanese people were not entirely ignorant of these things, but Fukuzawa's book responded to, and even created, a demand for fuller information. The literacy of the Japanese was very high towards the end of the Tokugawa period, and *Seiyō jijō* was widely read, and its influence was immense. Of the first edition 150,000 copies were sold at once, and pirated editions followed. We are reminded here of the success of Franklin who published from his own printing-house *Poor Richard's Almanack* from 1732 on. 10,000 copies every year was a tremendous success in North America of the first half of the eighteenth century. In the 1757 preface to *Poor Richard's Almanack,* which came to be known as *The Way to Wealth,* Franklin said he had met many people quoting not only his maxims but also adding 'As Poor Richard says'. Franklin's writings were very popular. Fukuzawa's books were also very popular. As the champion of the Westernization movement of early Meiji, he wrote extensively. Fukuzawa was the most widely read author from 1867 through 1887. He was a prolific writer, and his name became so familiar as an authority on Western matters that in the early years of Meiji all books dealing with foreign matters were popularly called *Fukuzawa bon* or 'Fukuzawa books'. To show our readers the range of his writing, I will list some titles of his books and pamphlets. They will also suggest what kinds of information were lacking at that time:

1867      *A Guide to Foreign Travel*
          *Western Ways of Living*
1868      *An Illustrated Account of Natural Sciences*
1869      *The English Parliament*
1872      *Lessons for Children*
1872–76  *Encouragement of Learning*

*Encouragement of Learning (Gakumon no susume)* is famous for its beginning, 'Heaven never created a man above another nor a man below another', it is almost Jeffersonian, although the connotation of the word 'Heaven' (*ten*) sounds more Confucian or Shinto than Christian in Japanese.

1873      *Book-keeping*
          *Procedure at Meetings*
1875      *Outline of Civilization*
1876      *The Division of Powers*
1877      *Popular Economics*
1878      *Popular Discourse on People's Rights*
          *Popular Discourse on National Rights*
1879      *Reform of National Sentiment*

Is it possible to summarize all his writings under a single title? I have a suggestion. In 1979, Ezra Vogel published a book entitled *Japan as Number One – Lessons for America.* I would say what Fukuzawa wrote, in his whole-hearted belief in Western civilization, was *West as Number One – Lessons for Japan.* The difference between Vogel's book and Fukuzawa's work is that while Fukuzawa's books were read by his intended readers, the Japanese people, Vogel's book was not much read by his intended readers, the American people. Still Vogel's book was a million-seller, as its Japanese translation was a tremendous success in Japan.

Fukuzawa thus became the champion of Western studies in modernizing Japan. He devoted himself to educational reform, arguing that schools and colleges must prepare young people for practical life. The private academy Fukuzawa founded in 1863 later developed into Keiō University where the curriculum was devoted mainly to practical subjects of economy and much stress was laid on the study of English books. Keiō University is today well known for having produced many distinguished businessmen. At this point we are reminded of Franklin's founding an academy that later grew into the University of Pennsylvania. From the titles of Fukuzawa's books you could gather that Fukuzawa was very instrumental in spreading knowledge about Western political systems. Sir George

Sansom mentions Fukuzawa as one of the three Japanese whose influence was so far-reaching that the history of political thought between 1860 and 1880 might well be written in the form of the biographies of Fukuzawa, Katō Hiroyuki and Itagaki Taisuke. Sansom writes in his *Western World and Japan*:

> Of these Fukuzawa deserves special attention as a pioneer of Western learning in many fields. This remarkable man may be taken as an epitome in his own person of those qualities of mind and heart which characterized the active leaders of reform in the crucial period just before and after the Restoration.[58]

Fukuzawa was in a sense extremely anti-traditional. He was not by any means blind to the importance of good behaviour, but he was impatient with the traditional standards of Japanese culture, which in his view paid far too much deference to useless knowledge. He expressed his frank opinions in his *Gakumon no susume* (Encouragement of Learning). His attack on classical Chinese studies, the equivalent of the classical humanities in Europe, is interesting. Fukuzawa was very skillful in attacking. I quote the passages translated by Sansom:

> The only purpose of education is to show that Man was created by Heaven to gain the knowledge required for the satisfaction of his needs for food, shelter and clothing, and for living harmoniously with his fellows. To be able to read difficult old books or to compose poetry is all very nice and pleasant but it is not really worth the praise given to great scholars of Chinese and Japanese in the past.
>
> How many Chinese scholars have been good at managing their domestic affairs? No wonder that a wise parent, a shopkeeper, or a farmer is alarmed when his son displays a taste for study! ... What is really wanted is learning that is close to the needs of a man's daily life.
>
> A man who can recite the *Chronicles* but does not know the price of food, a man who has penetrated deeply into the classics and history but cannot carry out a simple business transaction such people as these are nothing but rice-consuming dictionaries, of no use to their country but only a hindrance to its economy. Managing your household is learning, understanding the trend of the times is learning, but why should reading old books be called learning?[59]

According to Fukuzawa, education in the West was needed only to turn out men who would be useful, to fit them for the practical business of life. I doubt if Fukuzawa's interpretation was entirely correct; but he wanted to put more emphasis on practical aspects of learning.

However practical both Franklin and Fukuzawa seemed to be,

they still had occasion to make reflections upon the meaning of life. One of the most striking coincidences between Franklin and Fukuzawa is that both of them compared human life with the life of an ephemera.[60] While staying in Paris as the American representative, an aging Franklin sent an essay of his called 'bagatelle' to his lady friend, Madame Brion, saying that human life is as brief as that of an ephemera, so let us spend the rest of our life *joyeusement,* if I may use this French adverb to summarize Franklin's rather hedonistic attitude towards women. An aging Fukuzawa also says in his *Fukuō hyakuwa* (Hundred Essays) that life is ephemeral. However, instead of sending gallant words to ladies, Fukuzawa tells us his resolution as a man. Let me summarize his philosophical argument: 'Even though we are creatures similar to maggots and ephemeras, still we very well know what we human beings should do in this short span of our life.'[61] Fukuzawa seems to suggest that to work diligently is in itself a source of joy. This affirmative attitude towards work, shared unconsciously by so many Japanese, seems to differ considerably from the Christian notion of work, as work has often been considered to be a sort of punishment, as is expressed in *Genesis* 3:19: 'In the sweat of thy face shalt thou eat bread, till thou return unto the ground.' There is, however, a lot more in the Scriptures about work, and Christianity has often described work as the highest form of prayer.

At the beginning of this chapter I, jokingly, referred to the monetary values of Franklin and Fukuzawa: both of them are symbolically featured on the most valuable banknotes of their respective country. That choice is most reasonable: Franklin is considered the father of American capitalism. As Franklin was mistaken for a worshipper of the Almighty Dollar, so Fukuzawa, too, was mistakenly called the founder of Japanese mammonism. Franklin left many proverbs recommending diligence, thrift, and honesty. It was Fukuzawa who adopted into colloquial Japanese many of Franklin's, or more precisely Poor Richard's, sayings. For the last two decades of the twentieth century, we have seen in many cities in continental China slogans such as 'Time is money' *(shijian jiushi jinqian).* In Japan, it was Fukuzawa who made popular that idea *(toki wa kane nari)* more than one hundred and twenty years ago.

In this world where economic progress by technological means has become the most powerful ideology, it is understandable that Franklin attracted the attention of many economic historians. In 1905, when economically flourishing regions were almost all

Protestant countries with the exceptions of France and Northern Italy, Max Weber's book *The Protestant Ethic and the Spirit of Capitalism* was published and has been widely read ever since. The German sociologist dwells a great deal on Franklin's autobiographical writings when he explains the influence upon economic life of Protestantism in general and Puritanism in particular. Eighty years after the publication of Weber's work, people around the world have become more and more interested in the Japanese work ethic. If Weber's theories are really correct, there should be some relationship between Japanese ethical beliefs and the Japanese economic development. Recently, some hasty people have been trying to find the secret of the Japanese success story in Morita Akio's autobiography. The life story of the outspoken chairman of the Sony Corporation is written in English and is entitled *Made in Japan.*[62]

However, in order to understand the entrenched cultural values behind the modernization movement of Japan, Fukuzawa's *Autobiography* is far more suggestive, because Fukuzawa had lived in the pre-modern Japan of Tokugawa era as well as in the modernizing Japan of the Meiji era. His life-span of sixty-six years is divided into two equal parts: born in 1835, he had lived thirty-three years before the Meiji Restoration of 1868 and another thirty-three years in the new era and died in the thirty-fourth year of Meiji, that is, 1901. As he himself tells us, Fukuzawa had lived two lives in a single life. He knew the feudal age as well as the capitalistic society. He knew in detail the traditional society as well as its modern transformation. Culturally speaking, Fukuzawa was one of the first Japanese with two legs, one grounded in the East and the other grounded in the West; this we may say, Fukuzawa was a man soundly grounded on both sides of the Pacific Ocean which he had crossed four times before the Meiji Restoration. By the way, Fukuzawa was one of the first Japanese to visit Hawaii. If we call Franklin one of the finest products of the Atlantic civilization, then we may call Fukuzawa the great pioneer of the new era of the Pacific civilization.

Some of you who have not yet read the two autobiographies in question might have some misgivings about my having stressed the similarities of the two great men. However, it is not my arbitrary opinion. As early as 1903, the poet Kunikida Doppo wrote about the similarities of the two characters. The critic Saeki Shōichi, too, insists on the strikingly common features of the two autobiographies in his *Nihonjin no jiden* (Kōdansha, 1974). Among Westerners, Basil Hall Chamberlain writes in his *Things Japanese:*

The democracy which Fukuzawa had found in America, the simple family life, and also, it must be owned, the commonsense empiricism, the 'Franklinism' (if one may so style it) of America exactly suited Fukuzawa's keen, practical, but somewhat pedestrian intellect.[63]

Fukuzawa, then, is a Franklinist, if one may so call him. As I noted earlier, Fukuzawa was the first Japanese to introduce Franklin's sayings into common usage in Japan. Had Fukuzawa read Franklin's *Autobiography* before he himself began to write his own? – This is a very intriguing question, and I am sure that Fukuzawa's Keio students were well aware of Franklin's *Autobiography* when they asked Fukuzawa to write his autobiography. Fukuzawa himself mentioned Franklin's name many times in his writings, but not his *Autobiography.* Thus, I do not think Fukuzawa had in mind Franklin's precedent while writing *Fukuō jiden.* Besides, all passages of Fukuzawa I have quoted deal with his younger days, that is the time when Fukuzawa did not even know the name of Franklin. So the similarities in subject matter should be considered fortuitous.

According to Basil Hall Chamberlain, Fukuzawa's self-imposed task was 'enlightening his countrymen, detaching them from Orientalism, Europeanizing them, or it might be better said, Americanizing them, – for America was ever his cynosure among Western lands'.[64] Chamberlain was the most respected dean of Western Japanologists at the beginning of the twentieth century. For him as well as for Fukuzawa, modernization was synonymous with Westernization.[65] As I have written in the chapters dealing with 'Japan's Turn to the West', Japanese attention had long been directed to the Asian continent. Fukuzawa was the most vocal ideologue who succeeded in switching Japanese attention from China to the West. What Chamberlain said by the phrase 'detaching the Japanese from Orientalism' means this cultural re-orientation, Japan's turn to the West. Accordingly, as I said before, Fukuzawa's voluminous writings may be summarized under a single title such as *America as Number One, Lessons for the Japanese.* I am sure Americans would enjoy reading Fukuzawa's *Autobiography.*

However, what is often overlooked by Western readers, including the very British Chamberlain, is the importance of the pre-modern background of the Japanese society which made possible the 'Civilization and Enlightenment' movement in the latter half of the nineteenth century. Sir George Sansom's observation is more penetrating in this regard. He picks up Fukuzawa as a Japanese pioneer of Western learning in many fields, yet he still includes the following comment:

> He owed a great deal of his success to the early training that he received in the modest samurai family from which he came. Though unorthodox and anti-traditional, he was nonetheless a typical exponent of those virtues which were the most admirable features of the feudal code of behaviour – a high sense of duty coupled with self-control and a certain contempt for worldly goods.[66]

I think Fukuzawa's *Autobiography* is interesting not simply because he tells us about his work as the champion of the Westernization movement in Japan but also because he tells us in concrete details many aspects of the so-called pre-modern background which produced such a personality.

I would like to continue the parallel observations on Franklin and Fukuzawa. However, I am afraid I have to stop here. Apart from the problem of space, I have a reason for stopping them in the middle of their careers. The reason is that although Fukuzawa's *Autobiography* covers practically his entire life – the book appeared in 1899 two years before his death – Franklin's *Autobiography* brings the consecutive story of his life only up to July 1757. I am therefore obliged to stop the comparison of their lives midway, referring neither to Franklin's activities in the new-born country nor to Fukuzawa's career after the Meiji Restoration.

Now let me put the final question: Which of the two autobiographies is more interesting? I give you my answer. If you read Franklin's and Fukuzawa's autobiographies in English, Franklin is more interesting; but if you read them in Japanese, *Fukuō jiden* is far more interesting than *Furankurin jiden*.

*Notes*

[1] This paper was given as the closing address at the conference on *Literary Relations East and West* organized by Ryūkoku University and University of Hawaii in June 1989 in Kyoto and printed in *Literary Relations East and West: Selected Essays,* edited by Jean Toyama and Nobuko Ochner, published by College of Languages, Linguistics and Literature, University of Hawaii at Manoa and the East West Center, 1991.

[2] Hirakawa published a book in Japanese dealing with Franklin and Fukuzawa Yukichi, S. Hirakawa: *Shinpo ga mada kibō de atta koro* (Tokyo: Shinchō-sha, 1984).

[3] Y. Fukuzawa: *The Autobiography,* tr. Eiichi Kiyooka (New York: Columbia University Press, 1966). When this English translation was first published

by Hokuseido Press, Tokyo, in 1934, one of the first Western readers to recognize immediately the value of the book was Professor Sinclair of the University of Hawaii.

[4] Mita is the district of Tokyo in which Fukuzawa resided. It is also the location of Keiō University.

[5] Basil Hall Chamberlain: *Things Japanese,* now published under the title *Japanese Things* (Rutland, Vermont: Tuttle, 1971) p. 367.

[6] Y. Fukuzawa: *The Autobiography,* p. 9.

[7] Y. Fukuzawa: *The Autobiography,* p. 10.

[8] Y. Fukuzawa: *The Autobiography,* p. 10.

[9] Y. Fukuzawa: *The Autobiography,* p. 11.

[10] Y. Fukuzawa: *The Autobiography,* p13.

[11] Benjamin Franklin: *The Autobiography and Other Writings* (New York: New American Library, 1961) p. 26. Hereafter cited in the text.

[12] Franklin: *The Autobiography,* pp. 26–57.

[13] Franklin: *The Autobiography,* p. 33.

[14] Y. Fukuzawa: *The Autobiography,* pp. 30–31.

[15] Y. Fukuzawa: *The Autobiography,* p. 66.

[16] Y. Fukuzawa: *The Autobiography,* pp. 230–237.

[17] Franklin: *The Autobiography,* p. 17.

[18] Chamberlain: *Things Japanese,* p. 293.

[19] Chamberlain: *Things Japanese,* p. 367.

[20] Franklin: *The Autobiography,* p. 36.

[21] Franklin: *The Autobiography,* pp. 38–39.

[22] Franklin: *The Autobiography,* pp. 43–44.

[23] Y. Fukuzawa: *The Autobiography,* p. 35.

[24] Y. Fukuzawa: *The Autobiography,* p. 34.

[25] Franklin: *The Autobiography,* pp. 48–49.

[26] Y. Fukuzawa: *The Autobiography,* pp. 58–59.

[27] Hirakawa: *Shinpo ga* pp. 47–48.

[28] Y. Fukuzawa: *The Autobiography,* pp. 62–63.

[29] Franklin: *The Autobiography,* pp. 58–59.

[30] Y. Fukuzawa: *The Autobiography,* p. 52.

[31] Y. Fukuzawa: *The Autobiography,* p. 53.

[32] Y. Fukuzawa: *The Autobiography,* p. 59.

[33] Refer to S. Hirakawa's article, 'Hakuseki to Yukichi' in. Saeki Shōichi ed.: *Jiden bungaku no sekai* (Tokyo: Asahi-shuppansha, 1983) pp. 47–61.

[34] Y.Fukuzawa: *The Autobiography,* pp. 60–61.

[35] Y. Fukuzawa: *The Autobiography,* p. 62.

[36] Y. Fukuzawa: *The Autobiography,* p. 78.

[37] Franklin: *The Autobiography,* p. 49.

[38] Franklin: *The Autobiography,* pp. 49–50.

[39] Franklin: *The Autobiography,* pp. 78–79.

[40] Franklin: *The Autobiography,* p. 70.

[41] Franklin: *The Autobiography,* p. 70.

42  Y. Fukuzawa: *The Autobiography*, p. 16.

43  Y. Fukuzawa: *The Autobiography*, p. 17.

44  'Shūkyō wa cha no gotoshi' *Fukuzawa Yukichi zenshū* (Tokyo: Iwanami shoten,1961) vol. 16, pp. 91–93.The English translation of Fukuzawa's *Jiji-shimpo* article appeared in *Japan Herald*, 9 September 1897. See Chamberlain: *Things Japanese*, p. 408.

45  Franklin: *The Autobiography*, p. 106.

46  Y. Fukuzawa: *The Autobiography*, p. 84.

47  Y. Fukuzawa: *The Autobiography*, pp. 85–86.

48  Y. Fukuzawa: *The Autobiography*, p. 119.

49  Goethe: *Italienische Reise* (Hamburg: Christian Wegner Verlag, 1954) p. 85. The entry is either 6 or 7 October 1786.

50  Y. Fukuzawa: *The Autobiography*, p. 110.

51  Y. Fukuzawa: *The Autobiography*, p. 116.

52  Haga Tōru: *Taikun no shisetsu* (Tokyo: Chūōkōron-sha, 1968) pp. 38–40.

53  Y. Fukuzawa: *The Autobiography*, p. 80.

54  A remnant of this kind of seminar-competition existed in 1948, when I was a student at the Komaba campus of Tokyo University when it was still an integral part of the First Higher School (Dai ichi kōtō gakkō).

55  Y. Fukuzawa: *The Autobiography*, pp. 81–82.

56  Y. Fukuzawa: *The Autobiography*, p. 82.

57  Franklin: *The Autobiography*, p. 111.

58  George B. Sansom: *The Western World and Japan* (London: Cresset Press, 1950) p. 451.

59  Sansom: *The Western World and Japan*, p. 480.

60  Fukuzawa Yukichi, 'Ningen no anshin' in *Fukuō hyakuwa, Fukuzawa Yukichi senshū*, (Tokyo: Iwanami shoten, 1981) vol. 11, pp. 31–32. For a more detailed study, see Hirakawa: *Shinpo ga*, p. 156–166.

61  Fukuzawa Yukichi, 'Ningen no kokoro wa kōdai muhen nari' in *Fukuō hyakuwa, Fukuzawa Yukichi senshū*, (Tokyo: Iwanami shoten, 1981) vol. 11, p. 35.

62  Akio Morita: *Made in Japan* (New York: Dutton, 1986)

63  Chamberlain: *Things Japanese*, p. 366.

64  Ibid.

65  No less interesting than the comparison between Franklin's and Fukuzawa's autobiographies would be a comparison between Fukuzawa's and Yung Wing's autobiographies. Fukuzawa and Yung Wing (Rong Hong) were the first Westernizers in their respective countries. China had had some talented boys educated in the West earlier than Japan through the good offices of Western missionaries, who recruited them by paying money to their parents. It was Samuel R. Brown who gave lessons of English to Yung Wing (1827 near Macao-1912 Hartford) in Hong Kong and later Amenomori Nobushige in Yokohama. Amenomori was the model for Hearn's 'A Conservative', about whose pilgrimage to the West and return to Japan I will discuss in Part III Chapter 1. Yung Wing became

the first Asian graduate of an American university (Yale, 1853). A remarkable thing about this American educated Chinese is that, convinced of the superiority of Western civilization, Yung Wing tried hard to modernize China by sending more than hundred Chinese youths to the United States in the 1870s. As a Westernizer Yung had many common features with Fukuzawa. If we compare Fukuzawa's autobiography (1899) with Yung Wing's *My Life in China and America* (1909), we will see all the more clearly the different courses that followed the two East Asian nations in the latter half of the nineteenth century: Meiji Japan was quick in responding to Western challenges, while Qing China, bound by historical forces, was slow to change. The two autobiographies show not only the individual difference in personal fortunes but also the national difference of reception waiting for oversea returnees: they could hold key positions in Westernizing Japan, while in Sino-centric China, Chinese overseas returnees could not hold more than secondary positions. Unable to expect a sympathetic understanding from his Chinese compatriots for what he had done in China and America, Yung wrote his autobiography in English for his American wife and American readers towards the end of his life in 1909. He died in the United States as an American citizen.

[66] Sansom: *The Western World and Japan*, p. 451.

# PART III

# RETURN TO THE EAST

# YEARNING FOR THE WEST AND RETURN TO THE EAST: PATTERNS OF JAPANESE AND CHINESE INTELLECTUALS

———————□———————

In many Western countries, I, a Japanese, have often been mistaken for a Chinese; in many Asian countries Westerners, too, must have experienced something similar. It is indeed difficult for peoples living in a Far Eastern or a Far Western country to distinguish peoples belonging to other national, racial or ethnic groups than one's own, especially when they are living on the other side of the world. Those Westerners who have been to Japan must have been called 'Amerika-jin' by innocent children, for Westerners of any nationality have generally been identified as Americans by ordinary Japanese citizens since the time of the American occupation of Japan (1945–52).

Therefore, allow me to begin by examining Westerners' indiscriminate notions about Japan and China before proceeding to discuss some psychological tendencies distinctively peculiar to the two East Asians, which I believe were decisive in the conduct of many Japanese samurai-scholars and Chinese literati, when they were exposed to Western challenges. Apart from the problem of the past, I have another concern for the future, which is the following: why quite a few of them, even if pro-Western in their youth, became different in later life? And in that seemingly regressive process are there any distinctive patterns of Japanese and Chinese intellectuals?

My preliminary question about the Western notion of Japan and

China is very simple. Is Japan situated in the East? Almost all
Westerners will doubtlessly answer yes and the Japanese also agree
about this rudimentary geographical fact. Euphemistically speaking,
Japan is the country of the Rising Sun, while Europeans are living,
if I use a German expression, in the *Abendland*, in the Occident.
Then how about China? Most Westerners would say that China,
too, is situated in the East, and the Japanese, too, agree that China
is a part of the East, which is called in Japanese *Tōyō* and in Chinese
*Dongyang*: though the pronunciations are different, the two Chinese
characters used here for the East are the same. A problem, however,
arises from this fundamental geographical notion, for most Chinese
did not think that China is located in *Dongyang*, or in the East. To
them Japan is located in the East. In the minds of many Chinese,
China was, and subconsciously still is, located in the centre of the
universe. The Chinese call their country *Zhongguo*; *zhong* means
centre, *guo* means country. The expressions *the Middle Kingdom, das
Reich der Mitte* or *le royaume du milieu* precisely derive from the
Chinese word *Zhongguo*. (By the way, the Chinese insist on the use of
these two Chinese characters even to the Japanese, under the pretext that the Japanese term *Shina*, which originally derives from the
Italian *Cina*, is a pejorative, reminiscent of Japan's imperialistic
aggression.) That hierarchical notion putting China at the top-
centre among the countries of the world is deeply rooted in the
Chinese mind.

In the chapter dealing with problems of Japanese identity vis-à-
vis Chinese culture, I have already referred to the letter the Japanese
Prince Shōtoku sent to the Emperor of China towards the end of
the sixth century. It says:

> The Son of Heaven in the land where the sun rises addresses a letter to the
> Son of Heaven in the land where the sun sets. We hope you are in good
> health.

Yang-di, the Emperor of the Sui dynasty was not pleased with
this letter that insists on the equality of the two countries. This psychological imbalance between the two countries is not a thing of
the past. When diplomatic relations between Japan and the People's
Republic of China were established in 1972, the Chinese ambassador in Tokyo was received in audience by Japanese Emperor
Hirohito, while the Japanese ambassador to China, Ogawa
Heishirō, was not granted an audience by Chairman Mao during the
four years of his ambassadorship in Beijing. The Japanese and the

Chinese have evidently different notions about their respective geo-cultural positions in the world.

There are also differences between Japanese and Chinese intellectuals' attitudes towards the West, which have something to do with these historically established self-definitions of the positions of Japan and of China. I would like first analyze the case of Japan and then China.

Even before the Japanese knew the existence of Europe, they had already experienced a desire for the cultural products of a distant western empire – in that case, China. Throughout much of Japan's history, the inhabitants of the peripheral country have selectively borrowed many things from abroad. Japanese envoys and students were sent to Tang China, and then to Ming China. From the seventeenth century to the Meiji Restoration of 1868, the official ideology of the governing Tokugawa shogunate was Confucianism. The Meiji Restoration was, politically speaking, the emergence of Japan as a modern state: Japan opened its doors to the West, and from that time on the West replaced China as the 'Other' for the Japanese. The fourth surge in the Sino-Japanese cultural relationship went in the opposite direction, with the coming of several thousand Chinese students a year to Japan after Japan's victory over Russia in 1905, at a time when the decadent Qing dynasty abolished the examination system for the selection of governmental officials. After Mao Zedong's death, we entered the fifth stage: students from the People's Republic of China are coming again in large numbers to Japan. (The number of Chinese students in Japan is second only to the number in the United States during the last two decades of the twentieth century.) The Chinese students' attitudes towards Japan are more or less ambivalent. On the one hand, Japan is seen as an imperialistic power that committed acts of aggression against China. On the other hand, Japan is a nation that succeeded in transforming itself from a feudalistic agricultural society into a modern industrial one in a comparatively short span of time, first after the Meiji Restoration of 1868 and second after the defeat of 1945. Why was it possible for Japan to adopt a system of constitutional government and to modernize rapidly, while China lagged behind would be a question that some students might well have.

It would be very difficult to find a definitive answer. As I have some misgivings about the effectiveness of theoretical approaches to history, either Marxist or Maoist, let us look at concrete facts and examples. In the Part II entitled 'Japan's Turn to the West', I have examined two intellectual leaders of Japan's 'civilization and enlightenment' movement: Fukuzawa Yukichi (1835–1901) and Nakamura Masanao (1832–91). Fukuzawa's *Autobiography* is extremely interesting and revealing. He recommended the Japanese not to read any more Chinese classics; he encouraged them to read books written in English. In Fukuzawa's words, Japanese scholars of Chinese classics were 'rice-consuming dictionaries', who were of little practical use in solving the problems of the day. Fukuzawa was a sort of iconoclast, while another scholar, Nakamura, who had held the highest position in the Tokugawa Confucian academy of Shōheikō, was considered in the 1860s the best Japanese scholar in classical Chinese studies. Nakamura, however, volunteered to study in London, as I have mentioned before. He was very much impressed with the results of the Industrial Revolution. The Confucian scholar paid special attention to the Protestant work ethic. Nakamura translated Samuel Smiles's *Self-Help* in 1870 on his return home, and the book taught the Japanese how to build an industrial nation comparable to England.

The Japanese turned to the West and had that Westernization fever as early as the 1870s and 80s, while other Asian countries were much slower in their modernization efforts. In the case of colonized parts of Asia it is understandable that peoples under Western rule were left behind and became late starters in the modernization race. Then how about China? There are many explanations, political, economic and historical, for the belated awakening of that empire which was once called 'a sleeping lion'? The official Marxist interpretations tend to attribute all faults to foreign aggressors, reactionary Manchu and Chinese bureaucrats of the old regime and corrupt merchants. However, young Chinese scholars themselves do not believe any more in such simplistic ideological explanations. An interpretation I am going to attempt in this chapter is a psychological one, as that aspect of the problem is often overlooked by believers in historical materialism. I would like to stress some psychological tendencies to explain the ambivalent nature of the problem of longing for the West and return to the East.

Before analyzing the two cases of East Asian intellectuals, one Japanese and the other Chinese, the attraction of force of vision needs to be remembered: longing or nostalgia moves people in a certain cultural direction. In Jacob Burckhardt's *Civilization of the Renaissance in Italy*, the influence that Graeco-Roman culture exercised over Italian men of letters of the *trecento* and *quattrocento* is vividly described.[1] Western humanists had a strong longing or nostalgia for the idealized past of classical antiquity. Longing or *Sehnsucht* sometimes serves as a driving force in history. The difference between Chinese intellectuals and Japanese intellectuals of the mid-nineteenth century lay precisely in the directions of their longing or nostalgia. It is true that Chinese intellectuals, too, had their nostalgia. China was the cradle of a great civilization and had remained its centre for several thousand years. During that time-span Chinese civilization was almost self-sufficient. The problem with China was that until its encounter with the West it had no 'Other' to cope with. It is true that China was conquered by Mongols in the thirteenth century and by Manchus in the seventeenth century. However, in both cases, the conquerors were in the end culturally assimilated by the conquered. If Confucian scholar officials had nostalgia, it was for their own idealized past, governed by the legendary sages. Even in the later years of the nineteenth century, the classical culture of ancient China continued to attract Chinese literati. For them, Westerners were red-haired barbarians, bestial beings to be shunned. To the chauvinistic samurai of Japan, Westerners were devils, too. However, as warriors, the Japanese samurai at least recognized the superiority of Western military technology.

Let us compare Japanese and Chinese slogans of modernization. One of the most influential Japanese samurai-ideologues of the mid-nineteenth century was Sakuma Shōzan (1811–64), who was the teacher of Yoshida Shōin and Nakamura Masanao whom I have already referred to. When China was defeated by the British in the Opium War, Sakuma coined the phrase '*tōyō dōtoku, seiyō geijutsu*', meaning 'Eastern Ethics, Western Technology'. Sakuma advocated that slogan in order to introduce the products of Western science. A motto more commonly used by Japanese modernizers was '*wakon yōsai*', meaning 'Japanese Spirit, Western Learning'. True or not, it was necessary for the Japanese to insist on their spiritual superiority. Sakuma genuinely believed in Japanese samurai ethics. In China similar eclectic ideas were expressed by reform-minded people, when Qing China was defeated by Japan in 1895. The Chinese also began, belatedly, to feel the need for modernization and coined their slogan '*zhongti xiyong*' which may be translated as 'Chinese substance, Western application', or 'Chinese learning for the essential, Western learning for the application', insisting on Chinese spiritual initiative in using Western material techniques.

Compared with the rapid and widespread acceptance of that eclectic idea in Japan, the Chinese were slow in changing their cultural direction: there was a time lag of more than forty years, which suggests how psychological resistance was deeply rooted in the Sinocentric mentality. An explanation I offer of the difference between Chinese mentality and Japanese mentality regarding the cultural direction is as follows. For the Japanese, it was not so difficult to adopt the slogan 'Japanese Spirit, Western Learning', as it was a variation of a much older phrase 'Japanese Spirit, Chinese Learning'. Indeed, an expression similar to 'Japanese Spirit, Chinese Learning' appeared in the *Tale of Genji*. The contrast between '*yamato-damashii*' (Japanese spirit) and '*kara-zae*' (Chinese learning) was first mentioned in the *Otome* (the Maiden) chapter of the *Tale of Genji* written around the year 1000 AD and a pertinent remark was made by Arthur Waley, the first translator of Lady Murasaki, in his article 'The Japanese Spirit'.[2] Japanese intellectuals were obliged to be ambivalent, first, vis-à-vis Imperial China, and then, vis-à-vis the West.

In short, to abandon classics written in Chinese and to begin reading books written in Western languages was less difficult for the Japanese samurai than for the Chinese literati. Confucian values have something to do with the pride of the Chinese élite and with their own cultural identity. It was easier for the Japanese to get rid of Chinese classics than it was for the Chinese literati to get rid of their own 'sacred' teachings.

As I have discussed in the chapter 'National Poetics and National Identity', the position held by classical Chinese in East Asia roughly corresponded to the position held by Latin in medieval Europe. How was it possible then for Europeans to free themselves from Latin-dominated culture? To learn Latin is a good thing; however, to be dominated by Latin at the expense of one's mother tongue is another thing. It is the same with classical Chinese. A macroscopic comparison suggests that it was generally peoples living in peripheral regions of a great civilization that began to express their inner feelings in their own vernacular tongues, while in the centres of old cultural traditions, such as in Central Italy or the central regions around Beijing, the prestige of classical Latin or classical Chinese was so deeply rooted that it was very difficult to change. It was only with the emergence of the genius of Dante that Latin finally gave way to vernacular Italian.

The first modern Chinese author Lu Xun (1881–1936), who came to study medical science in Japan after the Chinese defeat in the Sino-Japanese War, found that the use of classical Chinese was already in decline in the peripheral regions of Asia at the beginning of the twentieth century. Like Dante, who had travelled widely in the peripheral regions of Southern Europe and had become familiar with their native poetry in vernacular tongues, Lu Xun felt that true inner sentiment could only be expressed through one's own vernacular language. When Lu Xun studied in Japan, Japanese authors were producing works of literature in vernacular Japanese, instead of composing in classical Chinese, as they used to do in the Tokugawa period. Witnessing this literary renaissance in an Asian country, Lu Xun on his return home became, in 1918, the first modern Chinese author to use *baihua*, or vernacular Chinese to write works of literature. In brief, in the process of modernization of East Asia, although it had an aspect of Westernization, the movement contained an element of cultural nationalism and return to native traditions as well.

This is the general background of the time when Japan turned to the West, looking for an alternative to the cultural model of classical China. That is also the time when Japanese longing for Europe began. Let me insert here a curious example of that longing for a faraway country, *Sehnsucht nach jenseitigem Land*. It is significant that one of the most popular German poems ever translated into Japanese is the following by Carl Busse (1872–1918):

> Über den Bergen, weit zu wandern,
> Sagen die Leute, wohnt das Glück.
> Ach, und ich ging im Schwarme der andern,
> Kam mit verweinten Augen zurück.
> Über den Bergen, weit, weit drüben,
> Sagen die Leute, wohnt das Glück ...[3]

> Yama no anata no sora tōku
> Saiwai sumu to hito no yū
> Ā ware hito-to tomeyukite
> Namida sashigumi kaerikinu
> Yama no anata ni nao tōku
> Saiwai sumu to hito no yū

Ueda Bin's translation known as '*Yama no anata no sora tōku*' appeared in 1903, and this poem by a little known German Volksdichter became immensely popular among the Japanese. Why? Apart from the artistic reason that the poem was most skilfully translated, there is another factor. Busse sings the psychology of a young person who longs for a faraway land beyond the mountains where, people say, 'happiness lives' (*wohnt das Glück*). 'I' went there together with others and came back, weeping. People say that happiness lives in a still faraway land beyond the mountains.

My prose translation conveys only clumsily the meaning of the original German poem. Psychoanalytically speaking, however, there is a strong element of *Sehnsucht*, or longing for a far away paradise beyond the mountains in Ueda Bin's translation, because in form as well as in content the Japanese translation is a modern variation of earlier Japanese poems in praise of the Budda's Western Paradise called *wasan*. This must be a reason why the poem '*Yama no anata no sora tōku*' appeals to traditional Japanese sentiment.

After the Meiji Restoration of 1868 the unapproachable distant paradise, which had existed either in a fabulous India or in the western part of the vast Chinese empire, seems to exist, this time, somewhere in Western Europe. The more inaccessible the new paradise was, the more attractive it seemed to young Japanese wishing to go abroad for study. Even after the opening of the country only a very few people were given the chance to go to the Western world. Though the Japanese themselves were not very conscious, however, there was continuity in Japanese longing for the Western land faraway beyond the sea. This longing for the Western paradise, however, seems to have lost its intensity, in the last quarter of the twentieth century, once it became possible for any Japanese to travel freely overseas.

In the chapter 'Japanese Experience Abroad' the strong desire of educated Japanese to see the outside world was explained, and in the chapter 'Reaction against "Slavish" Westernization' the problem of 'return to Japan' was discussed, rather briefly. Modern Japanese intellectuals' longing for the West, that is, Europe and America, and their subsequent return to the mother country, requires, therefore, further study in detail.

The phenomenon of the Westernized intellectual returning to native traditions is by no means restricted to Japan but is also found in thinkers and leaders in Russia, in many Asian countries and also in Islamic countries. This is, indeed, a very important problem in the coming age of globalization. In *The Western World and Japan,* George Sansom, while discussing the case of a Meiji liberal Baba Tatsui, wrote as follows about the Japanese who re-embraced their native land:

> An interesting chapter of modern Japanese history could be written by
> tracing the careers of clever young men educated in liberal surroundings in

England or America who returned to Japan flushed with democratic enthusiasms and in course of time lapsed into a bitter nationalism accompanied by a strong dislike of the West, which had nourished their youthful ardours. Not long ago an able and experienced member of this class observed to me that most of his contemporaries, products of Western education, had turned against the Western democracies feeling that their liberalism was a sham.[4]

In fact, Sansom is referring not only to the attitude of the Japanese of the Meiji period but also of the Japanese intellectuals during WWII.[5]

To describe the typical experience of a Japanese intellectual of the Meiji period, I will borrow from the writer Lafcadio Hearn (1850–1904) an account of a pilgrimage to the idealized West and the return home. The story is entitled 'A Conservative', which is included in Hearn's third book on Japan *Kokoro,* published in 1896.[6] The gist of the story is as follows.

Hearn's protagonist was a high-ranking samurai born around the year 1858 and raised in a domain castle town. Trained in the martial arts and schooled in Confucian and other traditional values, he was disciplined to honour the spirits of his forebears and to scorn death. This warrior witnessed the coming of the American Black Ships; soon 'barbarians' were employed as teachers of military science within his castle town, as that was the policy of 'Japanese Spirit, Western Learning'. After the Meiji Restoration of 1868, the protagonist left home to learn English in the open port city of Yokohama under a foreign missionary. At first, he believed that love of country required him to learn about enemy conditions in a detached, cool manner, in keeping with the dictum 'Know thy enemy'. But before long he was deeply impressed by the overwhelming superiority of Western civilization and decided that because the basis of its power lay in Christianity, he was duty bound as a Japanese patriot to accept this higher religion and encourage all his countrymen to convert. So intense was his conviction that he became a Christian despite his parents' opposition. To discard the faith of his ancestors was cause for more than a moment's distress: he was disowned by his family, scorned by his friends, deprived of all the benefits accompanying his noble status and reduced to destitution. Still, the samurai discipline of his youth enabled him to persevere with fortitude despite all the hardships to which he fell victim. As a true patriot and seeker of the truth, he ascertained where his convictions lay and pursued these without fear or regret.

However, Hearn's protagonist was soon disturbed to discover

that the knowledge derived from modern science, which had
enabled his missionary-teachers to demonstrate the absurdity of
Japan's ancient beliefs, could also be used to demonstrate absurdi-
ties in the Christian faith. The Western missionaries were often
surprised and shocked to discover that the more intelligent their
Japanese students were, the sooner they tended to leave the church.
So it was with this youth, who became an agnostic in religious matters and a liberal in political affairs.

Forced to leave Japan because of his political stand, he went to
Korea and then to China, where he earned his living as a teacher for
a time before making his way to Europe. There he lived for many
years, observing and obtaining a knowledge of Western civilization
matched by few Japanese. He lived in many European cities and
engaged in various types of work. The West appeared to him a land
of giants, far greater than he had ever imagined. On both the material and the intellectual fronts, Hearn's hero gained two articles of
faith. Japan was being forced by necessity to learn Western science
and to adopt much from the material culture of its enemies; nevertheless there was no compelling reason to discard completely the
concepts of duty and honour and ideas of right and wrong that had
been inherited from the past. The prodigality inherent in Western
life taught him to value the strength found in his country's honourable poverty. He would do his utmost to preserve and protect
the best in Japan's traditions.

What was of value and beauty in Japanese civilization – things
that could be comprehended and appreciated only after coming
into contact with foreign culture – now seemed clear to him. Thus,
he had become a man longing to be allowed to go back home, and
on the day that he set out for his return to Yokohama, he did so not
as a blind xenophobe of the final years of the Tokugawa times but
as 'a conservative' who was 'returning to Japan'.

Though Hearn's character portrait was modelled on his friend
Amenomori Nobushige,[7] it can perhaps be considered a composite
of the samurai-intellectuals who came to grips with Western civilization in the early-Meiji era. It was so with many of the early
Dōshisha student Christians, not a few of whom came as 'band'
members from Kumamoto. Even Uchimura Kanzō, the leading
member of the early Hokkaido Christian group, wrote of a
moment in the United States when his homeland began to appear
'supremely beautiful' to him. Another example can be found in the
physician-writer Mori Ōgai, who, like Hearn's conservative,

received a samurai education in a domain castle town. As a child, Ōgai was often warned by his parents in no uncertain terms: 'You are the son of a samurai, so you must have enough courage to cut open your belly.' Others, like Nakamura Masanao or Uchimura Kanzō, studied under missionaries and accepted Christianity probably out of a sense of patriotic duty. Many converts, however, subsequently repudiated Christianity. In fact, although this is a little-studied area in modern Japanese thought, the great majority of Japanese thinkers seem to have 'returned' to Japan in some sense. 'China activists' like Miyazaki Tōten and journalists such as Tokutomi Sohō were both Christians at one time.[8] Baba Tatsui was a liberal who took refuge abroad, and Shiga Shigetaka and other members of the periodical *Nihon oyobi Nihonjin* (Japan and the Japanese) bring to mind the intellectual who returned to Japan bent on discovering its true 'national essence'.

Hearn's piece, in that it foreshadows a floodtide of *weltschmerz* stemming from an observation of the darker aspects of Western civilization, has something in common with Natsume Sōseki's later critique of modern civilization. Hearn's short story contains many aspects of thought and action that match those of later Japanese intellectuals. Stated conversely, later Japanese intellectuals, for all the surface brilliance and diversity of their variegated philosophical spectrum, have much in common with Hearn's hero on a deeper level of feeling. In these respects, 'A Conservative' is a precursor of many modern Japanese intellectuals.[9] The piece is also worth noting for the subsequent appeal it has had to young Japanese.

How should we evaluate this return to Japan? Is it simply a reaction to the earlier enthusiasm? According to the comment written casually by William Griffis, who had taught our protagonist Amenomori Nobushige at the castle town of Fukui in 1871, Amenomori 'visited Europe and came home more intensely Japanese than ever.[10] (He) quaffed Occidental civilization and rejected it.' I do not believe, however, that our protagonist's rejection of Occidental civilization was that total.

For Westerners like the missionary-teacher William Elliot Griffis, the Westernization movement in Asian nations was unquestionably good. The more Westernized, the better. Many Westerners and quite a few Japanese insisted in the 1870s and 80s that Japan should Westernize wholeheartedly. There was a man such as Mori Arinori, who argued that the Japanese should adopt English as their national language, wishing to make a clean break with Japan's feudal past and to make Japan a wholly Western, liberal, democratic, industrial society. Incidentally, that same man later became the Japanese Minister for Education, however, by that time he had already made a return to nationalism. It is easy to see how unrealistic and even comical the idea of total Westernization is. The Japanese Westernizers' motto, 'Western Spirit, Western Learning' could not be accepted, since, apart from the inherent impracticability of the idea, it left no room for a Japanese identity.

What about the cultural politics of 'Japanese Spirit, Western Learning', which some conservatives proclaimed to be the guideline of the Japanese nation from the time of Sakuma Shōzan in the 1850s? The problem now was that the young generation, imbued with knowledge coming from the West, did not embrace traditional values in their entirety. The model for Hearn's story insisted on the preservation of the national essence (*kokusui*). He, however, did not try to defend Confucian ethics in terms of their universal validity or to legitimize Confucianism in terms of the new rationalist thought. In short, he did not have a nostalgia for the idealized mythological past of China or of Japan. He did not long for an archaic Confucian or Shinto Utopia. Instead, he gave traditional values a nationalist justification. On his return home, that is in the early 1890s, Amenomori argued that the preservation of traditional morals and customs was psychologically necessary to the nation because they provided the binding, integrative basis on which Japan's cultural identity and nationalism could be built. Amenomori and the group Meiji-kai, for which he worked as editor-in-chief of its monthly journal, sought piecemeal change and argued for selective borrowing from the West to improve Japanese society. Amenomori, therefore, criticized Japanese Westernizers of the civilization and enlightenment movement symbolized by the Rokumeikan.

Amenomori adopted the historicist and holist arguments characteristic of conservative theorists in Europe. Interestingly, he translated, in 1890–91 for the Meiji-kai journal, *Allgemeines Staatsrecht* written by Johann Kaspar Bluntschili. The Swiss jurist and political scientist expounded in it the organic theory of the state, carrying the theory to a complete equation of the life of a state and the life of a person. According to Amenomori, those who believed in the universal values of Western civilization failed to grasp the historic organic relationship between the nation and the individual. One of his contemporaries, the journalist Kuga Katsunan expressed similar views; Kuga argued that a Japanese acted not as a member of a bloodless humanity governed by universal values; he acted rather as a member of his own vibrant people, inspired by Japan's own national spirit.

The problem with Amenomori's 'preservation of the national essence' movement, however, is that it was used by reactionaries, who made a xenophobic defence of traditional culture. In my opinion, so long as there is self-abasement on the one hand, that kind of reaction seems to be inevitable on the other. Some Japanese dislikes were extended not merely to political subjugation by Western political powers but also to cultural subservience to Western intellectual fashions.

The Westernization movement continues these days under the form of globalization, and the 'Return to Japan' movement continues under the form of return to local values. Which way should we go? This fundamental issue is not yet fully resolved even today. Mori Ōgai (1862–1922), the greatest cultural leader towards the turn-of-the-century Japan, wrote about his own psychological state, when he returned home from four years' study in Germany. He knew that the metaphysical aspects and the physical aspects of a civilization are not always separable. Mori Ōgai, therefore, did not advocate the slogan, 'Japanese Spirit, Western Learning' which was used by narrow-minded nationalistic reactionaries as their defensive pretext. Instead, he preferred to state what sort of a man would be needed in the twentieth century. According to Ōgai, the ideal man for the future of Japan would have two legs, one soundly grounded in his own culture and the other in Western culture, and he would be neither slavishly enamoured of the West nor anxious to reject its value and importance. The metaphor does not work well, as two human legs cannot be both grounded in two distant places at one time physically. How to surmount that difficulty is the metaphysical implication of Ōgai's metaphor.

Finally, I would like to consider the case of a Chinese intellectual who travelled to the West and then returned to China. This is, in fact, an attempt at a triangulation approach. In the twenty-first century a person with only two compasses will not be competent enough to make a balanced judgement: that means two compasses, even though soundly grounded in Japan and in the West, are not enough to open up a more wanted three-dimensional perspective.

The person in question was the first Chinese Professor of English at the University of Peking, called Ku Hung-Ming (or according to the pinyin system Gu Hongming, 1854–1928); his pen-name, Dongxi Nanbei, means East-West-South-North. His career is most curious. Ku was born in the South, on the Malaysian island of Penang as an overseas Chinese of Fujian ancestry. He went to the West at the age of twelve, together with a Scottish missionary returning home. He studied in Edinburgh and other European countries until the age of twenty-three, mastering many languages. He married a Japanese woman called Yoshida Sadako, and served for two decades under the Chinese reformer Zhang Zhidong (1837–1909), Governor of Hunan Province, who propagated the idea of *zhongti xiyong* (Chinese substance, Western application) through his book *Quanxue-pian* (Encouragement of Learning, 1898). Ku later resided in the North, in Beijing, as the first Chinese professor of English at Peking University after the Revolution of 1911. We understand from this background why he called himself East-West-South-North.

Ku obtained a knowledge of Western civilization matched by few Chinese of his generation. However, his return to native traditions was more than remarkable. He used his knowledge of English not for the Westernization of China but for the propagation abroad of Chinese civilization: Ku translated the *Analects* and other works of Confucius into English and most of his works were written in English. He tried hard to defend the traditional ways of the Chinese. His defensiveness probably came from his having been too much exposed to all sorts of contempt from Europeans, as he was obliged to negotiate with high-handed foreigners as Governor Zhang's secretary for seventeen years. That experience must have had something to do with his excessive self-esteem as a Chinese scholar. He defended Old China, and wrote in English, among other works the *Spirit of the Chinese People* (1915), which was translated into many languages.

When, after the Xinhai Revolution of 1911, Ku came to Peking University to chair the department of English, he was not at all sympathetic towards the young Chinese students enthusiastic for reforms. Ku definitely became a reactionary. He did not cut his pigtail hair. His old hair-style became his trademark. He was well known among Japanese writers of the Taishō period. 'If you go to Peking, you may skip a visit to the old Imperial Palace, Zijincheng, but you must not miss a chance to see Ku Hung-Ming.' The Japanese writer Akutagawa Ryūnosuke was so told before going to China in March 1921. When Akutagawa met him, Ku complimented Akutagawa on his China dress, and said jokingly that it was a pity that Akutagawa's hair was not plaited in a pig-tail. Ku constantly spoke English, while ceaselessly writing Chinese characters on straw papers.[11] He swore loyalty towards the demolished Manchu dynasty, and criticized republicanism and things Western in general. Students called him 'crazy' and Ku became very unpopular among the new generation of Chinese intellectuals. When he came to Japan in 1924, he met the young Chinese writer Tian Han in a Western suit. Ku shook his own pig-tail, saying in English, 'This is my tie'. As a guest scholar, Ku gave a series of lectures in English, which, however, were welcomed by Japanese conservative intellectuals, faithful to Confucian traditions. Ku declared that the essence of Eastern culture was now preserved better in Japan than in China, as the Confucian cardinal virtues of loyalty to the sovereign and filial piety to parents were better preserved in monarchical Japan. Japanese Confucianists were pleased. Ku's lectures were translated into Japanese (*Ko Kōmei ronshū*, tr. Satsuma Yūji, Tokyo: Daitōbunka kyōkai, 1925; rpt. Kōkoku seinen kyōiku kyōkai, 1941) and his *The Spirit of the Chinese People* (tr. Ogaeri Yoshio, Tokyo: Meguro-shoten, 1940). The irony of the situation is that in the case of Ku Hung-Ming as well as that of Okakura Kakuzō discussed in the Chapter entitled 'The Awakening of Asia', their Pan-Asian idea could be better understood by other East Asians through English.

After the defeat of Japan in 1945 and the Communist take-over of mainland China in 1949, Ku Hung-Ming's name was completely forgotten. However, to my great surprise, Ku has recently been rehabilitated. In April 1998, Peking University celebrated its centenary, and Ku Hung-Ming was counted among the famous professors of the past. His selected writings had been translated from English into Chinese and were published in two volumes in 1996. This resurrection seems to reflect the psychological state of some Chinese intellectuals in recent times. Twenty years have passed since the reopening of China under the strong initiative of Deng Xiaoping. At first the Chinese were dazzled, finding that the capitalistic society of the outside world was flourishing, contrary to what they had been taught. Fortunately, every year, the living standard in China has risen, and the Chinese are beginning to regain confidence in their future. A book entitled *China that can say no* has sold well. They do not want to be dictated to by outsiders. They would like to be self-assertive. In this psychological context, persons like Ku Hung-Ming, who argued in foreign languages in defence of Chinese culture, are favourably remembered as patriots.

To have a longing for a foreign country and for its advanced culture is a common phenomenon. Many students wish to study abroad. And it is natural that when they return home, they are happy to be back in their own culture. It also happens that some people harbour mixed feelings about the object of their longing, as was the case with Gottfried Keller.[12]

Some people would say, after having seen these examples, that to long for a far away country when one is young and then to come back to one's own native country to mature is a general process of human formation. It is indeed a course generally followed by the heroes of *Bildungsroman*.

However, what is interesting is that there is a remarkable difference in the patterns of Japanese intellectuals and Chinese intellectuals. Japanese intellectuals are more at ease depending on foreign authorities, while Chinese intellectuals tend to be Sino-centric. That difference in attitude made the Japanese more receptive to Western civilization in the mid-nineteenth century. Psychological tendencies built into a nation's psyche can sometimes play a decisive role at a turning point of history.[13]

We know that it is not possible for Japanese to return to Japan of pre-Meiji times, to its childhood to enjoy peace within their own walls of *pax Tokugawa*. Japan was obliged to open the country in 1868. The Japanese archipelago had enjoyed two centuries-and-a-half of continual peace under the Tokugawa shoguns. Japan seemed to be forced to re-open a second time after its defeat in WWII.

However, there was a decisive difference in the second opening. Since the time of the American occupation, Japan has been militarily dependent on the US. There has been a psychological regression of the Japanese people within the invisible walls of *pax Americana*. This situation has exacerbated the Japanese tendency to be passively dependent in its relations with the outside world. Many Japanese took for granted that Japan should be protected and taken care of by its American ally. The psycho-analytical concept of *amae* concerning the anatomy of dependence has so far been applied to human relations, but it may also be applicable to international relations. Dr Takeo Doi's insight concerning the ambivalence of *amae* will also be instrumental in interpreting Japan's love-hate relationship with the West. Is it not true that psychological dependence or *amae* was conspicuous when Japan, as a student-country, was learning something from teacher-countries? However, an economic power like Japan cannot eternally remain in the passive position of a receptive student. How to mature in the society of nations is the problem of the Japanese in their dealings with others. Instead of indefinitely staying in the introvert stage of one-sided dependency, what the Japanese now must learn is how to build up effective networks of interdependence.

*Notes*

[1] See Jacob Burckhardt: *The Civilization of the Renaissance in Italy* (tr. S.G.C. Middlemore, New York: Harper, 1958) Part III 'The Revival of Antiquity', especially chapter IV 'Humanism in the Fourteenth Century', pp. 211–17.

[2] Arthur Waley, 'The Japanese Spirit', *The New Statesman*, Oct.16, 1943, p. 247.

[3] Ueda Bin translated the poem '*Über den Bergen*' which Ueda found included in Ludwig Jacobowski: *Neue Lieder der besten neueren Dichter für's Volk* (Berlin: M.Lieman, 1899).

[4] G. B. Sansom, *The Western World and Japan*, (London, Cresset, 1950), p. 442.

[5] Sansom's remark seems to have been written after he had met Ishibashi Tanzan, liberal journalist and the future Prime Minister and Ayuzawa Iwao, former ILO official, in Tokyo on 25 January 1946. See Katharine Sansom: *Sir George Sansom and Japan* (Tallahassee: The Diplomatic Press, 1972) p. 152.

[6] I am afraid that there are many Western readers who have not heard of Lafcadio Hearn or of the story 'A Conservative'. Fortunately, it comes very highly recommended by no less an authority than Hugo von Hofmannsthal. On hearing of the death of Hearn in 1904, the eminent literary critic wrote an essay (Hugo von Hofmannsthal: *Prosa II*. Frankfurt am Main: S.Fischer Verlag, 1959, pp. 104–7) in which he evaluates the story as follows:

> … und das liebe Buch *Kokoro*, vielleicht das schönste von allen. Die Blätter, aus denen sich dieser Band zusammensetzt, handeln mehr von dem inneren als dem ausseren Leben Japans – dies ist der Grund, weshalb sie unter Titel 'Kokoro' ('Herz') verbunden wurden.

Then comes Hofmannsthal's extremely high evaluation of the story 'A Conservative':

> Und daneben das Kapitel 'Ein Konservativer.' Das ist keineswegs eine Novelle: das ist eine Einsicht, eine politische Einsicht, zusammengedrängt wie ein Kunstwerk, vorgetragen wie eine Anekdote: ich denke, es ist kurzwege ein Produkt des Journalismus, des höhstkultivierten, des fruchtbarsten und ernsthaftesten, den es geben kann.

[7] 'A Conservative', in *Kokoro*, vol. 7 of *The Writings of Lafcadio Hearn* (New

York: Houghton Mifflin, 1922), pp. 393–422. For a detailed analysis of 'A Conservative' and of the model Amenomori Nobushige, see 'Nihon kaiki no kiseki – uzumoreta shisōka, Amaenomori Nobushige', in Hirakawa Sukehiro: *Yaburareta Yūjō* (Tokyo: Shinchō-sha, 1987) pp. 145–300.

[8] Miyazaki's autobiography was translated by Etō Shinkichi and Marius B. Jansen as *My Thirty-three Years' Dream: The Autobiography of Miyazaki Tōten* (Princeton, N.J.: Princeton University Press, 1982).

[9] To the question why it was possible for Hearn to understand so clearly the psychology of the Japanese hero coming back to Japan lies in Hearn's own state of mind. It has often been said in Hearn's biography that his experience in Japan was a curve, veering from early infatuation to disillusioned realism. I think that Hearn's curve is almost identical with the curves of the experience in the West of many Japanese writers and painters, identical in nature but different in direction. Incidentally 'return to the West' is recognizable in many of Western Japan specialists.

[10] The converse is true of many Europeans. The repudiation of youthful enthusiasms is not restricted to Japanese. It is universally attested. The problem here treated, however, is some peculiar patterns of Japanese intellectuals' and Chinese intellectuals' 'return to their native traditions'.

[11] Akutagawa Ryūnosuke: 'Pekin nikki shō' (formerly 'Shina yūki') in *Akutagawa Ryūnosuke zenshū,* (Tokyo: Iwanami shoten, 1996) vol. 12, p. 209.

[12] This paper was given at Universität Zurich, 7 April 1999 as the opening lecture in the series 'Interdisziplinäre Ringvorlesung Ostasien, Thema: Kulturkontakt'. That was the reason I used, in the original lecture, as an example the local writer Gottfried Keller. Keller was not satisfied to stay for ever in Zurich and went to study in Munich. However, according to his French biographer Baldensperger, Keller had ambivalent feelings towards Munich. I quote in this note what Baldensperger said about Keller in his doctoral thesis (*Gottfried Keller, sa vie et ses œuvres/ Thèse présentée à la Faculté des Lettres de Paris,* 1899): 'Plus tard, quand la Terre promise se fut transformée pour Keller en une lande stérile, il eut un jour dans un accès de rancune retrospective, des paroles de colère contre la capitale bavaroise.' Keller spoke ill of the capital of Bavaria, scribbling rude words that I refrain from reproducing.

[13] We should add, however, that this Japanese longing for foreign authority, be it Chinese or Western, has not always been sound. It is true that intellectuals of peripheral regions tend to become opinion leaders within their own countries, because of their roles as intellectual intermediaries. By depending on foreign authorities, native agents of ideas can become sometimes authoritative within their national borders: they can criticize the backwardness of their compatriots. Generally speaking, these left-wing intellectuals look smarter than simple-minded right-wing nationalists who blindly boast of the uniqueness of their nation. However, the Japanese intelligentsia, too, are like Russian intelligentsia depicted by Pushkin in 'Roslavlev'. So long as their ideological fatherlands are friendly,

there arise no problems. Once there is a deterioration in friendly relations, some intellectuals feel betrayed and become emphatically nationalistic, as was the case with the Japanese Christian Uchimura Kanzō or the poet-sculptor Takamura Kōtarō.

# UCHIMURA KANZŌ AND AMERICA: REFLECTIONS ON THE PSYCHOLOGICAL STRUCTURE OF ANTI-AMERICANISM[1]

Just as a man like Mori Ōgai (1862–1922), the great innovator of modern Japanese literature, cannot be omitted from discussions of Japanese-European relations, so Uchimura Kanzō (1861–1930) is one figure not to be neglected when relations between Japan and America are discussed. While Mori Ōgai did not exhibit any extreme reaction towards Japan's relationship with the West, Uchimura Kanzō's response was so strong that in 1924 he was referred to as a 'champion of the "hate-America" movement'.[2] To a great extent, Uchimura's attitude was an outgrowth of his own problematic personality. But that it also owed something to his being a Christian should not be discounted. His value system had roots outside Japan, and America held a large part of his heart; when he asserted himself as a Japanese, it seems he could not help becoming emphatically anti-American. Throughout his life, he continued to have ambivalent and seemingly contradictory feelings towards the United States.

The eldest son of a samurai household of the Takasaki domain, Uchimura Kanzō was a patriotic man of the Meiji Era, with memories of being exposed to the menacing power of Western nations. At the same time, he was a Christian convert, a man who during his early adulthood spent nearly four years in the United States. He thus could be very sensitive to problems in Japanese-American relations.

Uchimura expressed his sentiments quite vividly in *How I Became a Christian*,[3] a work he wrote in English for American readers. I would like to examine its sixth chapter, 'The First Impressions of Christendom', as it clearly shows his love-hate feelings towards the United States.

Right after his divorce from his first wife in 1884 he set out almost compulsively for America. Uchimura tells of his first impression of America, his 'Holy Land', as follows:

> At the day-break of Nov. 24, 1884, my enraptured eyes first caught the faint views of Christendom. Once more I descended to my steerage-cabin, and there I was upon my knees; – the moment was too serious for me to join with the popular excitement of the hour. As the low Coast Range came clearer to my views, the sense of my dreams being now realized overwhelmed me with gratitude, and tears trickled rapidly down my cheeks. Soon the Golden Gate was passed, and all the chimneys and mast-tops now presented to my vision appeared like so many church-spires pointing toward the sky ... As my previous acquaintance with the Caucasian race had been mostly with missionaries, the idea stuck close to my mind; and so all the people whom I met in the street appeared to me like so many ministers fraught with high Christian purpose, and I could not but imagine myself as walking among the congregation of the First-born.[4]

Twenty-three years old at the time, he had 'learnt all that was noble, useful, and uplifting through the vehicle of the English language', starting with the Bible and biblical commentaries. Then too, the 'great men' he had learned about, George Washington and the like, were for the most part Americans or Englishmen. He writes of these ideals in a rather poetic vein:

> My idea of Christian America was lofty, religious, Puritanic. I dreamed of its templed hills, and rocks that rang with hymns and praises. Hebraisms, I thought, to be the prevailing speech of the American commonality, and cherub and cherubim, hallelujahs and amens, the common language of its streets.[5]

As Uchimura entered into conversation with people he encountered on the streets, this sort of vision quickly melted away. Living in straitened circumstances, confronted by the difference of customs, and above all disillusioned in his expectations, he ceased to shed those warm tears of joy which had flowed on first reaching the land of his dreams.

This chilling of the white heat of enthusiasm is nothing unusual. But Uchimura, interestingly, used Christian principles to fasten a moral critique on his experience of disillusionment. With his personal 'American Dream' in tatters, he describes the cold

American reality and his own painful feelings in somewhat exaggerated terms:

> The report that money was the almighty power in America was corrobo-
> rated by many of our actual experiences. Immediately after our arrival at
> San Francisco, our faith in 'Christian civilization' was severely tested by a
> disaster that befell one of our numbers. He was pickpocketed of a purse
> that contained a five-dollar-gold piece! 'Pick-pocket-ing in Christendom as
> in Pagandom', we cautioned to each other.[6]

Uchimura was also shocked that a black 'church deacon' who
kindly helped him with his luggage demanded a tip in return. Since
the bell was loudly clanging the train's departure, those in the group
could do nothing but give the man fifty cents each to get their bags
back. The Japanese looked at each other in amazement and said,
'Even charity is bartered here'.

A year later, he boarded a pleasure ship in Massachusetts and
there had his new silk umbrella stolen. Uchimura, struggling to get
through school, was enraged:

> Here upon Christian waters, in a floating palace, under the spell of the
> music of Handel and Mendelssohn, things were as unsafe as in a den of
> robbers.[7]

The urge to revile 'Christian' America, by reflex caused him to
praise the Orient of his birth. Moreover, while writing *How I Became
a Christian*, he was envisioning an audience of American readers
who knew little of East Asia. Thus, Uchimura mingled fact and
fancy, making some rather strange statements. 'Even the Chinese
civilization of forty centuries ago could boast of a state of society
where nobody picked up things dropped on the street.' Mixing
wrath over his stolen umbrella with pride in his own country, he
asserts:

> We in our heathen homes have but very little recourse to keys. Our houses,
> most of them, are open to everybody. Cats come in and out at their own
> sweet pleasures, and men go to siesta in their beds with zephyrs blowing
> over their faces ... But things are quite otherwise in Christendom. Not only
> are safes and trunks locked, but doors and windows of all descriptions,
> chests, drawers, ice-boxes, sugar-vases, all ... A bachelor coming home in
> the evening has first to thrust his hand into his pocket to draw out a cluster
> of some twenty or thirty keys to find out one which will open to him his
> lonely cell.[8]

A closer look at Uchimura's preoccupation with the use of locks
in America reveals an aspect of cultural comparison and also which

psychological difference in attitude Uchimura failed to see with due balance. If one lives in a closely knit community where everyone knows one another, locks might not be necessary, but certainly locks and keys are necessary to anyone who is on the road. Also, in today's large cities where there is a possibility of unlocked cars being used for crimes, it might even be said that forgetting to lock up is an anti-social act.

However, even while realizing that the use of lock and key is only natural, it was an odd feeling for me to see a lock on the telephone in the house where I boarded while in Europe. It was as though right from the start the landlady suspected I might make long-distance calls without permission. Even more, when, visiting a Western missionary's home in Asia, they see a lock on the refrigerator, most Japanese – not only men like Uchimura – feel rather strange. In *The Japanese and the Jews* Isaiah Ben Dasan explains why Japanese are liable to misinterpret the use of locks and keys.[9] Ben Dasan notes that Christians operate from the assumption that man is basically sinful and easily subject to temptation. Thus, creating an environment where people can easily yield to temptation – say, a refrigerator one can easily steal from – is considered wrong. Uchimura loudly criticized Westerners' use of locks only to keep men honest. A Japanese businessman who has worked in the United States notes, however, that in America salesmen sell cash registers saying, 'This is a machine that keeps people honest'. He adds that in Japan this type of advertisement does not work. A Japanese shopkeeper would say, 'I use a cash register so that there'll be no chance of suspecting a person unjustly and thus hurting his feelings'. In a Japanese hotel if a young man is admonished not to tempt, he'll get angry, because it means that he is suspected of seeking to seduce a chambermaid, while in an American hotel, 'Don't tempt' means not to leave valuables in a room, as servants can easily yield to temptation, while the guest is out; therefore lock the safe with a key.

When one notes the differences among cultural spheres, the differences in the ways of thinking become obvious, but this problem does not always have a direct bearing on moral superiority or inferiority. The anthropologist, Ishida Eiichirō notes the differences between 'Lock-and-Key Culture and *Fusuma* (sliding door) Culture'.[10] He points out that most of Asia, including China, belongs to the lock-and-key cultural sphere, while Japan is unique in this regard. Locks were already evident in the writings of China's

Zhou and Han periods, and the one who held the keys was the one who wielded the real power in the household. Nakane Chie elaborates on 'Japan, the lockless culture'[11] in *Tekiō no jōken*. Professor Nakane discusses the experience of a Japanese girl who went to teach at a kindergarten in an Indian farming village:

> This girl noted that at the kindergarten boxes for books and other articles were always locked up, and thought it deplorable that even at such a young age things would disappear if not under lock and key. 'We must teach children not to take things even when not locked up.' She saw this as her mission. For that whole year she did everything she could to persuade the children that even without a lock things would not be stolen. At last, however, her efforts were fruitless and she desparingly returned to Japan.
>
> Ignorance of the cultural system of the land she was in resulted in a great loss of energy for her and the imposition of a foreign system on her pupils. In India, locking things up does not necessarily imply fear that someone will steal them, that others are wicked. A person puts on a lock when he wants to indicate, 'It'll be inconvenient if someone borrows this without my knowledge. I'd like this left as it is'. Even in a large household where only intimate family members and trusted servants may be living, the locking of closets and drawers containing personal belongings is the usual thing.[12]

Though I agree with Professor Nakane's opinion, I would like to point out in passing that even among people of 'lock-and-key' cultures the use of locks may be accompanied by a sense of wrong. For example, in the masterpiece of French juvenile literature, *Sans Famille* (Nobody's Boy), the child Remi arrives in Paris and enters the Garofoli household. During Mr Garofoli's absence, one of the children was looking after the house. A large pot was left hanging in the fireplace, and the soup in it was aboil, but there was a lock on the lid, so that the child would not take any of the soup. It is a scene which evokes much pity from the reader, because although Mr Garofoli has not returned home yet, the lock is a presentiment of his cold personality and of children crying from hunger. Thus, needless to say, it is not only a Japanese who can feel this way about locks.

Be that as it may, did Uchimura really have good cause to assert that:

> (an American household) is a miniature feudal castle modified to meet the prevailing cupidity of the age. Whether a civilization which requires cemented cellars and stone-cut vaults, watched over by bulldogs and battalions of policemen, could be called Christian is seriously doubted by honest heathens.[13]

There are certainly people both among Americans and among Japanese who would seriously doubt whether Uchimura's criticism of Christian civilization is really a valid one. However, regardless of whether or not *How I Became a Christian* has objective relevance, when read as a glimpse into one man's psyche, it is a most interesting document. Taking a glance at Uchimura's subjective world, we might ask ourselves how to account for the drastic change in the image he had of America.

Less than one year after he arrived in America, he wrote to his father Uchimura Nobuyuki: 'I have to say that no matter what our Japan is awful, awful, awful.'[14] When he returned to Japan four years later, did he completely forget this sentiment and the other criticisms he wrote of Japan in comparison to America?

Since American society itself did not change so drastically at the time, what so greatly swayed Uchimura's judgement was not so much an objective image of American society as it really was, but rather his own subjectively projected image of America – and of Japan. Japan enters our consideration at this point, because as his image of America declined his image of Japan and Asia rose accordingly. By going to the United States, he was forced to become conscious of his being a member of 'the yellow race', a Japanese. The word 'race' is used quite often in *How I Became a Christian*. At times he uses 'race' seemingly interchangeably with words like 'nation' and 'people'. Resentment, rooted in the heart of race-conscious Uchimura, was not much exacerbated by the black racial problem in America, but as a member of the yellow race he was enraged by the exclusion of Chinese from the flow of immigrants to America. Always of an easily inflamed nature, Uchimura gave vent to his wrath in the face of the problem:

> But strong and unchristian as their feeling is against the Indians and the Africans, the prejudice, the aversion, the repugnance, which they entertain against the children of Sina are something which we in heathendom have never seen the like. The land which sends over missionaries to China, to convert her sons and daughters to Christianity from the nonsense of Confucius and the superstitions of Buddha, – the very same land abhors even the shadow of a Chinaman cast upon its soil. There never was seen such an anomaly upon the face of this earth. Is Christian mission a child's play, a chivalry more puerile than that engaged the wit of Cervantes, that it should be sent to a people so much disliked by the people who sent it?[15]

In Uchimura's criticism, a cry of opposition to Western religious imperialism can be heard. Uchimura offers three reasons[16] why Chinese were hated in America:

1. The Chinese carry all their savings to their home, and thus impoverish the land.

Standing in the position of the Americans at that time, one sees that the fact they and their forebears came from Europe with the intention of living and dying on American soil made them fundamentally different from any Chinese laborers. It is easy to see then how salaries and savings could become an emotional issue.

2. The Chinese with their stubborn adherence to their national ways and customs, bring indecencies upon the Christian community.

Uchimura counters with another point of view:

True, pigtails and flowing pantaloons are not very decent things to be seen in the streets of Boston or New York. But do you think corsets and compressed abdomens are fine things to see in the streets of Peking or Hankow?

Lastly, the third reason Uchimura refers to is the friction between immigrant and native labour.

3. The Chinese by their low wages do injury to the American labourer.

This is an argument which is still repeated today. Because of low wages in China cheap products made in the People's Republic invade markets of other countries, and some Americans advocate a 'protection policy'. This is not a friction directly between immigrant and native labour, but it might be seen as related to an economic problem of the same nature.

The history of Chinese exclusionism in America, from the California Gold Rush to the massacre of Chinese at Rock Spring, Wyoming, on 2 September 1885, is sketched succinctly in Wakatsuki Yasuo: *Hainichi no rekishi*.[17] The Governor of Wyoming reported to the federal government that at the Rock Spring Massacre, sixteen Chinese were beaten to death, up to sixty corpses recovered from the burnt buildings and innumerable bodies unrecoverable. Since enraged mobs were still rampaging, he requested the help of troops. After this incident, a number of suspects were arrested but all were released by a court for lack of evidence.

These events took place a year after Uchimura arrived in America in 1884. Two years before he arrived, the Chinese Exclusion Act went into effect for a term of ten years. Then in 1892, just before he wrote *How I Became a Christian*, this act was renewed. As a member of the 'yellow race' Uchimura could not consider this problem as having no relation to himself. Burning with righteous indignation, he offers some proposals:

Go to some more lordly occupations befitting your Teutonic or Celtic origin. Let them (the Chinese) wash all your cuffs and collars and shirts for you; and they will serve you with lamblike meekness, and for half the price your own Caucasian laundrymen charge you with … 'Strike' is yet unknown among the poor heathens, unless some of you teach them how to do it. A class of laborers so meek, so uncomplaining, so industrious, and so cheap, you cannot find anywhere else under the sun.[18]

Uchimura was hoping for an America where not just those of Anglo-Saxon descent, but also Irish and Chinese could live and prosper together. And he believed that this hope would be consistent with his own view of Christianity.

America and Japan, Japan and China, China and America – in the sphere of international politics, since 1945 Japan has been bound in an 'American-Japanese' relationship. Earlier, during the 1930s and the Second World War, American sympathies were drawn towards China, as the popularity at the time of Pearl Buck's *The Good Earth* illustrates. The 'American-Chinese' bond was quite strong. This sort of grouping is possible on a more personal level as well.

We have seen already Uchimura's yearning for America, 'the Holy Land'. Because this bond had a religious basis, it was in some ways stronger and deeper than the ties of other Japanese students overseas. However, a revision of his value judgements took place, because of the 'culture shock' and his growing self-awareness as an Asian. He became eager to revive the ancient bonds between Japan and China and to push anti-Americanism into the foreground of his attitude towards his 'second homeland'.

In 1902, the entry of Chinese immigrants into America was completely forbidden, but after the Russo-Japanese War (1904–05), the entry of Japanese immigrants, too, became in various ways a critical issue between Japan and America. Infuriated by laws forbidding land purchases by Japanese in California (1913) and limiting Japanese immigration (1924), Uchimura wrote a number of fiery articles in Japanese newspapers at the time. If we select from his writings certain statements and combine them with a collection of the trends of those times, it might not be too difficult to construct an image of 'Uchimura Kanzō, the Anti-Americanist'.

Right after Congress passed the Immigration Act of 1924 containing the anti-Japanese provisions, he renewed his relationship with Tokutomi Sohō – later to become a chief ideologue of the 'Greater East Asia War' – and sent a letter to the newspaper *Kokumin Shinbun*, of which Tokutomi was editor.

I completely agree with your opinions regarding the difficulties with America, Mr. Tokutomi. I am happy to be reading the *Kokumin Shinbun* again as I did thirty years ago ... There is no reason at all to fear America ...[19]

But for all his ranting about America's attitude towards the Chinese, it is of great interest to note that he felt insulted when mistaken for a Chinese in the United States. In *How I Became a Christian*, he writes:

I am never ashamed of my racial relationship to that most ancient of nations, – that nation that gave Mencius and Confucius to the world, and invented the mariner's compass and printing machines centuries before the Europeans even dreamed of them.[20]

It nevertheless infuriated him when he himself was identified with the 'coolies from Canton'. He gives example after example of the slights he received – or thought he received. He recalls ironically the 'polite language' of an Irish coachman in Chicago who called out something about 'Chinamen' when picking up Uchimura and his group of fellow Japanese travellers. A well-dressed man sitting next to him in a coach asked to borrow his comb, and instead of thanking him after combing his 'grizzly beard', he asked, 'Well, John, where do you keep your laundry shop?' At another time, an intelligent-looking gentleman asked him and his group when they cut their queues. When they told him that they had never had any queues he replied, 'Why, I thought all Chinamen have queues'. To Uchimura, each exchange seemed to be a sign of unbearable contempt and whenever he heard such comments he became terribly annoyed. Many Japanese of the time had this sort of pride and he notes the following anecdote with great relish:

A group of young Japanese engineers went to examine the Brooklyn Bridge. When under the pier, the structure and tension of each of the suspending ropes were being discussed upon, a silkhatted, spectacled, and decently dressed American gentleman approached them. 'Well John,' he intruded upon the Japanese scientists, 'these things must look awful strange to you from China, ey!' One among the Japanese retorted the insulting question, and said, 'So they must be to you from Ireland'. The gentleman got angry and said, 'No, indeed not. I am not an Irish.' 'And so we are not Chinese,' was the gentle rejoinder. It was a good blow, and the silk-hatted sulked away.[21]

This episode recalls a similar one involving Okakura Tenshin (Kakuzō). Possibly because he had heard the question many times before, when once asked, 'Are you a Chinese, Javanese or Japanese?'

he promptly replied, 'Are you a donkey, monkey or Yankee?'
Though this type of ready repartee scores admirably, both in
Okakura's case and in Uchimura's, did the one who asked the question really do so with such ill will? The very replies to these
questions seem somewhat ill-natured. To demand that Westerners
recognize the difference between Japanese and Chinese is rather
unreasonable. In Japan today, all Westerners are usually taken for
Americans, but this, too, is no cause for them to get angry, either.

The sight of a man who had sided with the Chinese because of
the Exclusion Act, now suddenly disdaining to be associated with
them creates a strange impression. That he felt displeasure at being
mistaken for a Chinese while in America is a fact which appears
even in letters to his father:

> Everywhere I go I'm taken for a Chinaman, and it really annoys me. (21
> December 1884)[22]

> Everywhere I am looked on as a Chinaman, and no matter where I go I'm
> jeered at. I can't tell you how painful it is. (9 August 1885)[23]

While this is apparently indicative of racial discrimination, Ōta
Yūzō notes in his study of Uchimura that this might not be entirely
so.[24] We should recall, he explains, that Uchimura's feelings were
due also to the humiliation he felt at being identified with manual
labourers, while he was in reality a holder of an official position
with the Japanese government.

This sort of inconsistency between what he said and how he felt
might be a characteristic peculiar to Uchimura. His indignation was
the result of a strong tendency towards self-justification, but what
kept it from becoming obnoxious was the echo of an almost comical rhetorical overstatement in the background. In the exaggerated
manner of expression, a bit of Anglo-Saxon humour can be felt,
due in part, perhaps, to the influence of the satiric tradition in
English literature. There was something about him, which enabled
him to speak more frankly and freely when speaking in English to
Americans than when speaking in Japanese. This might have been
because his emotional life was to a large extent cultivated through
the medium of the English language. Moreover, speaking in a high-
flown tone enabled him to parade his anger and hurt feelings and
pout before his American friends. No doubt this was because he
thought, 'If they're friends, they're *supposed* to understand why I'm
angry'.

Many young Japanese who read this book might say in indignation, 'America is a shameful place, a land of racial prejudice'. But perhaps most human beings have a little of the Uchimura Kanzō within them. When it suited him, he supported the Chinese, but when his own pride became involved, he, too, was willing to discriminate. The righteous indignation of a man with a strong sense of self-justification is somehow laughable, and most adults will see through his contentions. A man who cries, 'We don't have racial prejudice like Americans', is himself guilty of prejudice – a prejudice called 'anti-Americanism'. The psychological background for Uchimura's critique of America was somewhat similar to that which provided the dynamics for Japanese anti-Americanism after the Second World War.

In the sixth and seventh chapters of *How I Became a Christian*, Uchimura explained his yearning for America before he arrived there and the feeling of a need to return to things Japanese which was born during his stay in America:

> That I looked upon Christendom and English-speaking peoples with peculiar reverence was not an altogether inexcusable weakness on my part. It was the same weakness that made the Great Frederick of Prussia a slavish adorer of everything that was French. I learnt all that was noble, useful, and uplifting through the vehicle of the English language.[25]

Uchimura had studied German language and literature while in America, and knew something about the cultural history of Germany in the eighteeenth century; he knew enough to try to excuse his past infatuation with Western culture by making reference to Frederick's adoration of French culture. However, what is more important to us in connection with Uchimura's study of German culture is that he must have learned not only about the period of slavish imitation of French culture at the time of Frederick but also about the blossoming of German culture at the time of Goethe and Schiller, which was a direct result of discovery of the values of their own culture and subsequent cultural self-assertion of the German people. By knowing this precedent in German cultural history, Uchimura must have been helped to gain a greater confidence in his own culture. In this, I believe it is possible to catch a glimpse of the psychology behind Uchimura Kanzō's return to Japan.

Interestingly enough, Mori Ōgai referred to the same example during the time of his studies in Germany. A year younger than Uchimura, he travelled to the West in the same year 1884, and emphasized his identity as a Japanese in his notes, *Eindrücke*, written during his stay in Germany. Here are Ōgai's 'impressions:

Preservation of nationality. Opposed to 'substituting English for Japanese, *Yomiuri Shinbun'*. German culture. Frederick the Great's disdain for the German language and worship of the French, a perversion. The flowering of the German spirit after Goethe and Schiller. 'There is a beautiful literature in Japan. We must avoid replacing Japanese with another language.' Civilization stands on historical foundation. Even if you bring ready-made Western ideals to Japan, it is an impossibility to realize them there in the same way.[26]

The beginning of the second decade of the Meiji period saw the cooling off in Japan's Europeanization fever. In the seventh chapter of *How I Became a Christian*, Uchimura explains the loss of his wholehearted devotion to Western civilization and his rediscovery of Japan as follows:

It was well said by a Chinese sage that 'he who stays in a mountain knows not the mountain.'... So with one's own country. As long as he lives *in* it, he really knows it not. That he may understand its true situation, it as part of the great whole, its goodness and badness, its strength and weakness, he must stand *away* from it.[27]

The reference to the Chinese sage and proverb long familiar in Japan seems almost emblematic of his 'back to the East' sentiments. Uchimura continues:

'Send your darling son to travel', is a saying common among my countrymen. Nothing *dis*enchants a man so much as traveling. My views about my native land were extremely one-sided while I stayed in it. While yet a heathen, my country was to me the centre of the universe, the envy of the world ... But how opposite when I was 'converted'! I was told of 'happy lands far, far away'; of America, with four-hundred colleges and universities; of England, the Puritan's home; of Germany, Luther's Fatherland; of Switzerland, Zwingli's pride; of Knox's Scotland and Adolphus's Sweden. Soon an idea caught my mind that my country was really 'good-for-nothing.'... Speaking of any of its moral or social defects, we were constantly told that it was not so in America or Europe. Whether it could ever be a Massachusetts or an England, I sincerely doubted.[28]

What Uchimura says might seem a bit strange to a person unfamiliar with or unsympathetic to the deep cultural inferiority felt towards the West by many Japanese intellectuals of the time. The following reflections might appear rather commonplace, but they are indicative of Uchimura's feelings towards his overseas experience:

Under no other circumstances are we driven more into ourselves than when we live in a strange land. Paradoxical though it may seem, we go into the world that we may learn more about ourselves. Self is revealed to us nowhere more clearly than where we come in contact with other peoples and other countries. Introspection begins when another world is presented to our view.[29]

He noted how he who had once thought his country 'good-for-nothing' once again took pride in it by being forced to behave as its representative.

> One is more than an individual when he steps out of his country. He carries in himself his nation and his race. His words and actions are judged not simply as his, but as his race's and his nation's as well. Thus in a sense, every sojourner in a strange land is a minister plenipotentiary of his country. He represents his land and his people. The world reads his nation through him. We know that nothing steadies a man so much as the sense of high responsibility.[30]

Although his utterances show how violently his state of mind changed, this change was born not only of his recognition of Japan's value and based not only in self-confidence. It was also based on the sense of betrayal and disappointment derived from the dashing of his great expectations, a feeling that his love was cruelly unrequited. Just as a man rejected by a woman often starts acidly criticizing her whom he once loved, so Uchimura rages against industrialized American society:

> Peace is the last thing we can find in Christendom. Turmoils, complexities, insane asylums, penitentiaries, poor-houses![31]

Some American thinkers, too, were already making similar criticisms of American civilization. But we might note that at the time this book was written in 1893, there were no social welfare institutions in Japan at all, with the exception of Shibusawa Eiichi's poor-house. Full of pride as a Japanese, Uchimura sang of the beauties of agricultural Japan:

> O for the rest of the Morning Land, the quietude of the Lotus Pond! Not the steam-whistle that alarms us from our disturbed sleep, but the carol of the Bird of Paradise that wakens us from our delicious slumber; not the dust and jar of an elevated railroad, but a palanquin borne by a lowing cow; not marble-mansions built with the price of blood earned in the Wall Street battle-market, but thatched roofs with sweet contentment in Nature's bounties.[32]

When they visited the old European continent, Americans like Mark Twain used to boast of the still-uncontaminated pure soul of 'American innocence', in contrast to the decay and decadence of European civilization. William Dean Howells once wrote in a letter to one of his friends that 'no one knows how much better than the whole world America is until he tries some other part of the world. Our people are manlier and purer than any in Europe.'[33] Words similar to these were directed at America by Uchimura. We might call these sentiments about unspoiled Japan an expression of 'Japanese innocence'. However, it leaves room for doubt whether the Japan he thus enthusiastically refers to was as 'innocent' as he thought.

A reading of the thatched roofs and lotus ponds in this section of *How I Became a Christian* might suggest to us an 'environmental hymn', flowing with anti-industrial romanticism, which anticipates the movement by eighty years. Even so, this is not the type of work one should accept at face value. Addressed to American readers, it was a work of self-assertion, denying the values of industrialized society. Because he presupposed American Christians as readers, Uchimura introduced the lotus pond, a symbol of Buddhism, to make American 'Christian' society appear to suffer by comparison. Uchimura brags to his Western readers, 'Not the steam-whistle that alarms us from our disturbed sleep', but he knew very well that the call of the steam-whistle was indeed sounding throughout Meiji Japan too. He also knew that this was a beautifully happy sound to the Japanese. When the people of the Meiji era, adults and children alike, sang the popular song about hearing the whistle as the train chugged out of Shinbashi Station, they were expressing not only joy at setting out on a trip; but also joy at Japan's journey from an agricultural society to an industrialized one. In that *Song of the Railroad*[34] can be felt the almost childlike exuberance of the flowering of a new age of Japanese civilization. Uchimura directed one line of boasting towards Westerners, but as an individual Japanese among his own countrymen he would have welcomed that call of the train whistle with all his heart.

In *Chijin-ron*, a treatise on geography written in Japanese shortly after *How I Became a Christian*, he celebrated the fact that in Japan, too, rails had been laid; and expressed pride in being Japanese – drawing China, it should be noted, into an unfavourable comparison. He writes in the ninth chapter of *Chijin-ron*:

America sought our acquaintance, we welcomed it and shook its hand. Its culture quickly seeped into us. Japan, already having studied China and India to the fullest, with her innate powers of assimilation began to inhale the West ... When our neighbor to the West still had not one yard of railroad, a culture of miles and miles of steel road stretching to the remotest of places had already been imported here. In thirty years, Japan has become un-Oriental.[35]

At the time of the Sino-Japanese War in 1894, the railway already reached from Shinbashi in Tokyo to Hiroshima. It was that which made it possible for the General Headquarters of the Imperial Army to move to Hiroshima. The state of mind which caused Uchimura to celebrate Japan's turning away from Asia and towards the West in contrast to China, was, no doubt, related to the nationalistic exaltation prevalent around the time of the Sino-Japanese War.

As has been seen, a love-hate relationship was at work in Uchimura's way of looking at things. He has affirmed his unity with the yellow peoples at one time, and at other times denying this identity by affirming his own nationality according to the needs presented by each situation. Considering how violent Uchimura's emotional states were, it can be easily recognized why such fierce anti-American feelings arose at the time the anti-Japanese immigration laws were passed in 1924. In articles he wrote for such influential newspapers as the *Kokumin Shinbun* and the *Yomiuri Shinbun*, there are such statements as:

> What America has is money. If you exclude money, America has almost nothing. It has neither philosophy nor art worth the name. The noble gentlemen who once were have now for the most part disappeared without a trace. It is no exaggeration to say that as a civilization, America minus money equals zero.[36]

Statements like this recurred, on the eve of the Greater East Asia War in 1941, by many Imperial Army officers addressing the troops.

Unlike other students who went to America in search of merely practical knowledge, Uchimura Kanzō looked at America within the framework of Christianity as a standard for value judgement. When he attempted to measure American society with this idealistic, ethical standard, he found various facts far removed from this standard. From this shock came his anti-American rhetoric. Despite his disappointment in America, he could not completely turn his back on it and break off all ties. While he could reject American industrial culture – at least on the surface – he could not cast Christianity away and return to his former self. On this point, Uchimura was different from 'A Conservative' whom Lafcadio Hearn describes in *Kokoro* and whose peregrinations we have seen in the chapter 'Yearning for the West and Return to the East'. Towards the end of the sixth chapter of *How I Became a Christian*, confronted with cold reality and fondly reminiscing about his departed grandmother, Uchimura exclaims:

O heaven, I am undone! I was deceived! I gave up what was really Peace for that which is no Peace! To go back to my old faith I am now too over-grown; to acquiesce in my new faith is impossible. O for blessed Ignorance that might have kept me from the knowledge of faith other than that which satisfied my good grandma! It made her industrious, patient, true; and not a compunction clouded her face as she drew her last breath. Hers was peace and mine is doubt; and woe is me that I called her an idolater, and pitied her superstition, and prayed for her soul, when I myself had launched upon an unfathomable abyss, tossed with fear and sin and doubt. One thing I shall never do in the future: I shall never defend Christianity upon its being the religion of Europe and America.[37]

While revolt against Christian society in the West was expressed in terms of yearning for the old Japanese faith, it did not amount to a farewell to Christianity itself. The Christian faith had penetrated Uchimura too deeply for that. Kamei Shunsuke notes that this excerpt praising the 'Blessed Ignorance' of Uchimura's grand-mother resembles a verse in the fifteenth chapter of *Jeremiah*, a verse also quoted in Uchimura's *Gaikokugo no kenkyū*.[38] Regarding the influence of the Biblical style on Uchimura's English writings, Kamei suggests that 'we should not look on this resemblance as a direct imitation. What is more important is the Bible's overall influ-ence, which when it surfaces produces this type of similarity.'

With such depth of commitment to the scriptures, that Uchimura was unable to return to his old beliefs is of no surprise. He did indeed return to Japan, but he could not accept his old Japan in its entirety. He remained, however, strong in his resolve 'never to defend Christianity upon its being the religion of Europe and America'. This resolve was connected with his dislike of Western missionaries and concealed in the ethical and psychological neces-sity he felt for starting the 'Non-church Christianity' movement.

In this way, Uchimura emphasized his being a Japanese. Sometimes he also emphasized 'Asia', a geographical term originally used by Romans only as another word for 'non-Western', and in reality having neither the religious nor cultural uniformity Uchimura seemed to suppose. Uchimura repeated that Christianity is a world religion. Or rather, following Uchimura's own convenient geog-raphy, Christianity started in Asia, and is most suited to Asia.[39]

He emphasized that there is no mistake greater than calling Christianity a Western religion. According to Uchimura, the West did not make Christianity, but rather Christianity made the West, and Christianity in Japan has already born fruit different from that of the West. The Christianity which has appeared through the

Japanese is what Uchimura calls *Nihonteki kirisutokyō* – a real Japanese Christianity.[40]

It was to Japan, the land of his birth and place where he could labour tirelessly, that his love belonged. For Uchimura all was 'for Japan', and all was 'for Jesus'. When he composed the inscription for his tombstone in both English and Japanese, the first line read: 'I love two J's and no third; one is Jesus, and the other is Japan.'

One is left to wonder if he really had banished America completely from his heart. If so, one might ask with a slightly ironic smile: 'Then why did Uchimura Kanzō have his grave inscription written not only in Japanese, but in English too? Who did he want to read it?'

## Notes

[1] This chapter was originally written in Japanese and was published in Hirakawa Sukehiro: *Seiō no shōgeki to Nippon* (Western Impact and Japan)(Tokyo: Kōdansha, 1974), pp. 161–199. The English translation of this chapter is John Boccellari's.

[2] For the strong reaction of Uchimura to the Immigration Act of 1924, see Ōta Yūzō: *Uchimura Kanzō: sono sekaishugi to nihonshugi o megutte* (Tokyo: Kenkyūsha, 1977), pp. 227–257.

[3] Uchimura Kanzō: *How I Became a Christian, Uchimura Kanzō zenshū* (Tokyo: Iwanami shoten, 1933) vol. 15. pp. 1–171.

[4] Uchimura Kanzō: *How I Became a Christian*, p. 81

[5] Uchimura Kanzō: *How I Became a Christian*, p. 80.

[6] Uchimura Kanzō: *How I Became a Christian*, p. 82.

[7] Uchimura Kanzō: *How I Became a Christian*, p. 84.

[8] Uchimura Kanzō: *How I Became a Christian*, p. 84.

[9] Isaiah Ben Dasan: *Nipponjin to Yudayajin* (Tokyo: Bungei shunjū, 1997) p. 22.

[10] Ishida Eiichirō: *Ningen to bunka no tankyū* (Tokyo: Bungei shunjū, 1970), pp. 106–9.

[11] Of course this is no longer true. The change from 'Japan, the lockless culture' to 'Japan, the lock-and-key culture' has taken place because of the urbanization and internationalization of Japanese society.

[12] Nakane Chie: *Tekiō no jōken* (The Condition of Adaptation), (Tokyo: Kōdansha, 1972), pp. 32–33.

[13] Uchimura Kanzō: *How I Became a Christian*, p. 85.

[14] 'Letter to Uchimura Yoshiyuki', dated 8/9/1885 in *Uchimura Kanzō nikki-shokan zenshū* (Tokyo: Kyōbunkan, 1964–65) vol. 5, p. 163.

[15] Uchimura Kanzō: *How I Became a Christian*, p. 86.

[16] Uchimura Kanzō: *How I Became a Christian*, pp. 86–88.

[17] Wakatsuki Yasuo: *Hainichi no rekishi* (The Anti-Japanese Movement in the US) (Tokyo: Chūōkōronsha, 1972).

[18] Uchimura Kanzō: *How I Became a Christian*, pp. 88–89.

[19] *Uchimura Kanzō nikki-shokan zenshū*, vol. 8, pp. 133–134. See also Uchimura's letter to Tokutomi Roka, younger brother of Tokutomi Sohō, 16 August 1924, ibid. p. 146.

[20] Uchimura Kanzō: *How I Became a Christian*, p. 89.

[21] Uchimura Kanzō: *How I Became a Christian*, p. 90.

[22] *Uchimura Kanzō Nikki-shokan zenshū* (Tokyo: Kyōbunkan, 1964) vol. 5, p. 107.

[23] Ibid., p. 164.

[24] Ōta Yūzō: *Uchimura Kanzō*, p. 36.

[25] Uchimura Kanzō: *How I Became a Christian*, p. 80.

[26] Mori Ōgai: *Ōgai zenshū* (Tokyo: Iwanami shoten, 1975) vol. 38, p. 88. 'Ōgai's 'Eindrücke' (impressions) were originally written in German mixed with phrases in Chinese. Translation mine.

[27] Uchimura Kanzō: *How I Became a Christian*, p. 92.

[28] Uchimura Kanzō: *How I Became a Christian*, p. 93.

[29] Uchimura Kanzō: *How I Became a Christian*, p. 94.

[30] Uchimura Kanzō: *How I Became a Christian*, p. 95.

[31] Uchimura Kanzō: *How I Became a Christian*, p. 91.

[32] Uchimura Kanzō: *How I Became a Christian*, p. 91.

[33] *Life in Letters of William Dean Howells* (New York: Russel and Russel), vol. 1, p. 90.

[34] 'The Song of the Railroad' begins with the famous phrase 'Kiteki issei Shinbashi o haya waga kisha wa hanaretari' (with a toot of the steam-whistle our train has already started from Shinbashi Station.)

[35] *Uchimura Kanzō zenshū* (Tokyo: Iwanami shoten, 1932–33), vol 1, p. 642. Translation is Mr Boccellari's.

[36] *Uchimura Kanzō chosakushū* (Tokyo: Iwanami shoten, 1953–55), vol. 4, p. 372. Translation is Mr Boccellari's.

[37] Uchimura Kanzō: *How I Became a Christian*, pp. 91–91.

[38] Kamei Shunsuke, 'Uchimura Kanzō to eigo' (Uchimura Kanzō and English) in *Kokugo tsūshin* (Tokyo: Chikuma shobō, 1973), no. 143.

[39] Asia Minor shares nothing particularly common with East Asia except the name. Uchimura's statements are not always scientifically grounded.

[40] Uchimura wrote on many occasions on 'Japanese Christianity' or 'Nihon teki kirisutokyō.' As an example, it is better to quote an article written directly in English by Uchimura Kanzō. The article 'Japanese Christianity' appeared in *Seisho no kenkyū*, 10 December 1920 (*Uchimura Kanzō zenshū* (Tokyo: Iwanami shoten, 1981, vol. 25, p. 592):

> Japanese Christianity is not a Christianity peculiar to Japanese. It is Christianity received by Japanese directly from God wihtout any foreign intermediary; no more, no less. In this sense, there is German Christianity, English Christianity, Scotch

Christianity, American Christianity, etc.; and in this sense, there will be, and already is, Japanese Christianity. 'There is a spirit in man: and the inspiration of the Almighty given him understanding.' The spirit of Japan inspired by the Almighty is Japanese Christianity. It is free, independent, original and productive, as true Christianity always is.

No man was ever saved by other men's faith, and no nation will ever be saved by other nations' religion. Neither American Christianity nor Anglican faith, be it the best of the kind, will ever save Japan. Only Japanese Christianity will save Japan and the Japanese.

CHAPTER 3:3

# THE YELLOW PERIL AND
# THE WHITE PERIL:
# THE VIEWS OF
# ANATOLE FRANCE[1]

---□---

Les hommes imaginent des races au gré de leur orgueil,
de leur haine ou de leur avidité.

*Sur la Pierre Blanche*

In January 1947, the editors of *Tenbō*, a Japanese monthly periodical, asked Yanagita Kunio[2] which foreign author had exerted the most profound influence on him. Yanagita readily replied that it was Anatole France. He continued:

> I have been extremely influenced by him. When I was in France, I read his works very often in order to learn French. Anatole France is probably the only author whose novels and other writings I have read over and over. In fact, I have read some of his books three or four times. For instance, *Sur la Pierre Blanche,* I read it in English translation, then in French, and then again in a Japanese translation.

Yanagita Kunio's interest in *Sur la Pierre Blanche* was based mainly on its treatment of the 'yellow peril' and the 'white peril'. In this novel, France expounds upon the historical significance for the world of Japan's victory in the Russo-Japanese War, the victory of a nation belonging to the 'yellow' race. However, under the American Occupation, anyone in Japan who attempted to grapple directly with the significance of the Russo-Japanese War would no doubt have been dismissed as an out-and-out reactionary. At that time all wars that Japan had waged since its opening in 1868 were categorically condemned as wars of aggression. Therefore, perhaps it was for this reason that Yanagita mentioned *Sur la Pierre Blanche* in his conversation with Nakano Shigeharu. In other words, Yanagita Kunio may have mentioned the works of Anatole France in order to encourage the Japanese of the early post-war period to view more objectively, through the eyes of a third person, the history of Meiji Japan. Thus, Yanagita may have been striving to combat the negative evaluation of Meiji Japan which, then, seemed to be prevalent among the intellectual circles of post-war Japan.

This conversation between Yanagita and Nakano was published in *Tenbō* as 'Literature, Learning and Politics'. It was later included in a collection of Yanagita's conversations entitled *Yanagita Kunio Taidanshū.*[3] In this chapter, I shall attempt to analyse the views of Anatole France concerning the 'yellow peril'.

Anatole France (1844–1924), who was known for his acute *esprit de contradiction*, represented a minority opinion running counter to the prevailing Western view regarding the 'yellow peril'. This no doubt was a further reason why his ideas appealed so strongly to Yanagita Kunio and other Japanese intellectuals who were, after all, members of the 'yellow' race. Despite Anatole France's declining prestige as a writer in contemporary France and the lack of interest in this writer of pre-World War I vintage among the younger generation in present-day Japan, France's remarks about the 'yellow peril' and the 'white peril' continue to contain a great deal worthy of our attention.

This racial issue first arose when the Europeans began to assert their rule over Asia, and was further complicated when the 'anti-Western backlash' began to occur, in other words, when Asian nations began to move towards independence and modernization. In this world there have been many racial problems. For the Japanese, however, inter-racial problems between the White and the Yellow races became their main concern.

The 'yellow peril' was a racist political idea first propounded in April 1895 by Kaiser Wilhelm II as an ideological justification for the tripartite intervention of Russia, Germany and France into Sino-Japanese negotiations following Japan's victory in the Sino-Japanese War. Although the idea first appeared at this time in letters written by Wilhelm II to Tsar Nicholas II of Russia, the theory of the 'yellow peril' had spread throughout the entire Western world by the time of the Boxer Rebellion in 1900. The massacre of the German minister and other foreigners was compared to the massacres of Europeans by the Huns or Mongols of the Middle Ages and the liberation of Peking by allied armies was made reminiscent of the liberation of the holy places in Jerusalem by the Crusaders. In 1904–5, the victory of 'yellow' Japan over 'white' Russia in the Russo-Japanese War stunned many in Europe and America, bringing to reality the fear of the 'yellow peril'. Indeed, this victory was partially responsible for the ensuing movement in the United States to exclude Japanese immigration, thus providing some of the underlying psychological animosity which surfaced during World War II.

Anatole France's *Sur la Pierre Blanche* was published in February 1905 between the fall of Port Arthur on 1 January and the battle of Mukden on 10 March. According to the bibliographical data in the 1927, Calmann-Lévy edition of the *Œuvres Complètes* of Anatole France, the book had actually been completed in 1903. This fact is confirmed also by French students of the works of Anatole France as well as by Professor Gonmori, who did the Japanese translation.[4] However, Chapter IV of the book, which deals with the question of the 'yellow peril', mentions the Russo-Japanese War and it must be assumed that at least this portion of the book was written in 1904. Moreover, on 25 November 1904, Anatole France spoke at the congress of the French Socialist Party,[5] and the speech also contained his views about the significance of the Russo-Japanese War and about the 'yellow peril'. This section of the speech has been inserted almost verbatim into the novel *Sur la Pierre Blanche*. Nicole Langelier, one of the novel's characters expressed nearly identical ideas. Since Nicole Langelier is identified as the scion of the 'old Parisian family of the Langeliers, printers and humanists', one may safely assume that this character represents, in somewhat idealized form, Anatole France himself, for the writer was born into a family of Parisian publishers.

Anatole France begins with a broad panoramic sketch of the history of East-West contacts, a sketch which anticipates the history of interaction between Eastern and Western cultures depicted half a century later with such a wealth of detail by the British diplomat and historian G. B. Sansom in *The Western World and Japan*. Anatole France mentions the silk trade between the Roman Empire in the West and the Han Empire in the East, contacts during the late Ming and early Qing dynasties (when Matteo Ricci and other Jesuits rounded the Cape of Good Hope and reached Beijing via Guangzhou), and the period of China's partition by the imperialist powers of the nineteenth century. When he comes to a description of the attitudes of the white race towards the yellow race and the policies of the European powers towards Qing China, his narrative is enlivened by the irony in which France excelled. France's remarks embrace such historical events as the Opium War (1840–42), the occupation of Beijing by the British and French armies in 1860, the Sino-French War of 1884–85, and the Boxer Rebellion of 1900–1. His views are consistently anti-clerical and anti-imperialist and stand in opposition to the policies of acquiring colonies espoused by successive French governments. Incidentally, it is interesting to recall that the opposition parties in the French parliament in those days were strong enough to overthrow the cabinet of Jules Ferry when the French expeditionary forces were defeated by the armies of Qing China in North Vietnam (1885). Anatole France writes:

> In our own times, the Christians acquired the habit of sending jointly or separately into the vast Empire, whenever order was disturbed, soldiers who restored it by means of theft, rape, pillage, murder and incendiarism, and of proceeding at short intervals with the pacific penetration of the country with rifles and guns. The poorly armed Chinese either defend themselves badly or not at all, and so they are massacred with delightful facility. They are polite and ceremonious, but are reproached with cherishing feeble sentiments of affection for Europeans. The grievances we have against them are greatly of the order of those which Mr Du Chaillu[6] cherished towards his gorilla.[7]

Thus, Anatole France accuses the Christian nations of reducing China to the state of a semi-colony under the guise of protecting peace and order. France continues his account as follows:

> Mr Du Chaillu, while in a forest, brought down with his rifle the mother of a gorilla. In its death, the brute was still pressing its young to its bosom. He tore it from this embrace, and dragged it with him in a cage across Africa, for the purpose of selling it in Europe. Now, the young animal gave him just cause for complaint. It was unsociable and actually starved itself to death. 'I was powerless,' says M. Du Chaillu, 'to correct its evil nature.' We complain of the Chinese with as great a show of reason as Mr Du Chaillu of his gorilla.[8]

In 1898, Germany leased Jiaozhou Bay, Russia leased Port Arthur and Dalian, and Britain leased Weihaiwei and the Kowloon Peninsula. In 1899, France leased Guangzhou Bay. Characterizing the actions of these Western powers, Anatole France said that they signed 'innumerable treaties by which they guaranteed the integrity of China, whose provinces they divided up amongst themselves'. Port Arthur on the Liaodong Peninsula, which Japan had been forced to give up in 1895 as a result of the tripartite intervention, was leased from China by the Russians in 1898 and then fortified. When Russia's appetites extended to Korea, the Russo-Japanese War broke out. Anatole France commented:

> Since the immense bear stretched out its snout indolently over the Japanese bee-hive, the yellow bees, with all of their wings and stingers armed to the utmost, riddled him with flaming stings.

In this analysis of the Russo-Japanese War, Anatole France argued that it was an event of decisive importance in world history.

A high Russian official had said that the Russo-Japanese War was a 'colonial war'. However, the fundamental principle of every colonial war was that the Europeans should emerge victorious over the peoples they were fighting against. The Europeans must attack with artillery, and the Asians or Africans must defend themselves with such primitive weapons as bows and arrows, clubs, or tomahawks. Even the Chinese, who equipped their arsenals with porcelain shells, were still abiding by the rules of colonial warfare. However, the Japanese departed from the time-honoured rule. As Anatole France writes:

> They wage war in accordance with the principles taught in France by General Bonnal.[9] They greatly outweighed their adversaries in knowledge and intelligence. While fighting better than the Europeans, they show no respect for the consecrated usages, and act to a certain degree in a fashion contrary to the law of nations.[10]

When he said that the Japanese were acting 'contrary to the law of nations', he meant that, by defeating an army of white men, the Japanese by this very action were showing disregard for the usages of the past, were turning against the commonly accepted ideas of international behaviour, and in this sense were breaking the 'law of nations'. He did not mean such infractions of international law in the technical sense, such as the cruel treatment of prisoners of war in defiance of international conventions, or the like. Anatole France was using such ironical expressions to reveal the arbitrariness and injustice of the white man and his 'Law'.

The concept of the 'yellow peril' also reflected the white man's fear that the modernization of the colonized world and the utilization of its cheap labour would disturb markets in the advanced countries. In Europe, warnings against the so-called 'economic yellow peril' constantly appeared, especially in the writings of economic protectionists in France. Anatole France is also careful to introduce the theory of economist Edmond Théry, who argued that the Japanese ought to have been defeated by the Russians in terms of European economic interests. Théry was the editor of the review *l'Économiste Européen*, and in 1901 published a book called *Le Péril Jaune* (yellow peril), in which he stressed the economic implications of the yellow peril. He concluded that, if China, modelling itself after Japan, were ever to succeed in industrializing itself, these two Asiatic nations would present a mortal threat to Europe as economic competitors. However, Anatole France pointed out that, if there were a 'yellow peril' coming from the industrialization of Asia, then there ought also to be an 'American peril' following the industrialization of North America. Both perils were historically inevitable, and it was stupid to make such a subjective judgement of the economic realities. Suppose that America or Japan or China should indeed appear as a new competitor and place cheap commodities on the market, thereby disturbing the European economy, he argued. Rather than being the fault of America, or Japan, or China, Anatole France wrote that this disturbance of the European economy is due to the fact that 'we have taught the Japanese both the capitalistic *régime* and war. They are a cause of alarm because they are becoming like ourselves.'[11]

One result of the vulgarization of Darwinism at the end of the nineteenth century was the birth of racist theories advocating the superiority of the white race, often corroborated by the so-called anthropological evidence. Nearly forty years after publication in 1855, Gobineau's *Essai sur l'Inégalité des Races Humaines* (the inequality of human races) attained remarkable popularity in Germany around the turn of the century. The composer Richard Wagner was among those who played a prominent role in popularizing the ideas of Gobineau. Both Wilhelm II and Hitler were also influenced by Gobineau's *Essai*.[12]

While the theory of evolution was being misinterpreted and, thereby the groundwork for racism being laid, its humorous aspects also provided writers with a perfect target for exercising their satirical gift. At one speech, Anatole France introduces the physiologist Charles Richet, with a skeleton in his hand. Professor Richet argues that the Japanese, who are a prognathic race, could not possibly oppose the Russians, who are brachycephalic. The following 'well-meaning' advice to the Japanese is attributed to the learned professor:

Bear in mind that you (Japanese) are links between monkey and man, as a consequence of which, if you should defeat the Russians or the Finno-Letto-Ugro-Slavs, it would be exactly as if monkeys were to beat you. Is it not plain to you?[13]

This theory, which viewed the Japanese as intermediaries between monkey and man, was proposed by Charles Richet (1850–1935), a noted professor of physiology, who was awarded the Nobel Prize in 1913.

After poking fun in this way at the learned gentleman's topsy-turvy pseudo-science, which would be most unconvincing to any Oriental, Anatole France resumes his serious tone and points out the evils of Western colonialism:

At the present moment, the Russians are paying the penalty, in the waters of Japan and in the gorges of Manchuria, not only of their grasping and brutal policy in the East, but of the colonial policy of all Europe. They are now expiating, not merely their own crimes, but those of the whole military and commercial Christianity.[14]

Here Anatole France uses the expression 'the whole military and commercial Christendom' (toute la chrétienté militaire et commerciale). Those in France who advocated colonialism maintained that it was necessary for the sake of the noble cause of spreading Christianity and promoting civilization. This was all the more reason for Anatole France, who since the Dreyfus case had sided with socialism and taken an anti-clerical stand, to rebel against colonialism. Moreover, France's colonial policies appear to have been carried out largely for the sake of national prestige. In negotiations with the Qing dynasty, France demanded assurances concerning the activities of the Catholic Church but attached little importance to the commercial treaty (the diplomatic agreements of 1844). It would appear that French colonial politics were not explicable simply in terms of the Marxists' theories of imperialist expansion for the sake of securing markets for monopoly capital. Policies centering on considerations of national prestige are often closely tied to the personal ambitions of politicians and military leaders, so the psychological interpretations offered by writers like Anatole France may also be convincing in many ways.

Anatole France, who took a vehement stand against the government following the Dreyfus affair in 1898, had a strong sense of empathy for and psychological understanding of the oppressed underdog. This certainly enabled him to see things from a non-Western viewpoint and made his arguments much more concrete than, for example, the abstract considerations offered by Paul Valéry in his 'Yalou', which was written under the impact of the Sino-Japanese War.[15] France's arguments, furthermore, are even more remarkable, because they transcend European ethnocentrism. Even today, almost a century later, most Western writers and critics are unable to project themselves beyond the Western cultural traditions, in which they have been formed. Nevertheless, at this early date, Anatole France attained considerable cultural detachment. Concerning the 'yellow peril', he made the following observations:

> The Japanese cross the Yalu and defeat the Russians in good form [in Manchuria]. Their sailors annihilate artistically a European fleet. Immediately do we discern that a danger threatens us. If it indeed exists, who created it? ... For many long years have Asiatics been familiar with the White Peril. The looting of the Summer Palace, the massacres of Peking, the drownings of Blagoveshchensk, the dismemberment of China, were these not enough to alarm the Chinese? And could the Japanese feel secure under the guns of Port Arthur? We created the White Peril. The White Peril has engendered the Yellow Peril.[16]

In Japan during this period, the massacre of thousands of Chinese at Blagoveshchensk became the subject of a popular song sung at the First Higher School. The song relates how 'Amur River ran with blood' (Amūrugawa no ryūketsu ya). The incident was also recorded in the autobiographical novel, *Kōya no hana* by Ishimitsu Makiyo.[17] During the Sino-Soviet dispute of the 1960s, the incident was rehashed once more. The idea that the Yellow Peril was created by the White Peril brings to mind the assertion of the Blacks of today who insist that the White-Black problem should not be called the Black problem since it is really a White problem.

Examining more closely the economic bases of the Yellow Peril and the idea that cheap commodities produced by cheap labour in the Orient would invade the markets of Europe, Anatole France stood on unbiased ground, remarking nonchalantly that 'It does not, however, appear at first sight that the Yellow Peril, of which European economists are terrified is to be compared to the White Peril suspended over Asia.'[18] Subjecting the question to a re-examination from the Eastern point of view, he reconsiders the Boxer Rebellion in the following manner:

> The Chinese do not send to Paris, Berlin, and St. Petersburg missionaries to teach Christians the Fung-chui, and sow disorder in European affairs. A Chinese expeditionary force did not land in Quiberon Bay to demand of the Government of the [French] Republic *extra-territoriality, i.e.,* the right of trying by a tribunal of mandarins cases pending between Chinese and

Europeans. Admiral Togo did not come and bombard the Brest roads with a dozen battleships, for the purpose of improving Japanese trade in France. The flower of French nationalism, the *élite* of our Trublions, did not besiege in their mansions in the Avenues Hoche and Marceau the Legations of China and of Japan, and Marshal Oyama did not, for the same reason, lead the combined armies of the Far East to the Boulevard de la Madeleine to demand the punishment of the foreigner-hating Trublions. He did not burn Versailles in the name of a higher civilization. The armies of the Great Asiatic Powers did not carry away to Tokio and Peking the Louvre paintings and the silver service of the Elysée.[19]

The final sentence alludes not to the Boxer Rebellion, but rather to the occupation of Peking by the English and French armies in 1860 and their destruction of the Yuan-ming-yuan gardens.

Anatole France's interpretations of political affairs were not always accurate, but he made a noteworthy prediction concerning the outcome of the Russo-Japanese War. On 25 November 1904 – at a time when the Japanese army had already defeated the Russian army at the battle of Liaoyang but well before Port Arthur had fallen – Anatole France pointed out that the Russian weakness was due to 'the stupidity of the government and the ineptness of the military command', whereas Japan's weakness was its limited financial resources. Unlike Russia, Japan would have to rely on difficult and onerous loans. Nevertheless, he continued, 'the English and the Americans intend to assist Japan in order to weaken Russia, but not in order to make Japan powerful and formidable'. He also observed that Japan's victory would bring in its wake a deterioration of relations between Japan and the Anglo-Saxons. The view was not an original insight into the state of affairs, but was far superior to the emotional judgements of the Japanese themselves. He also commented: 'But if Japan [by defeating Russia] makes the yellow men respected by the white men, it will have greatly served the cause of humanity.'[20] Thus, Anatole France felt that Japan was contributing to the liberation of the yellow races as a whole without its own knowledge or perhaps even in contradiction to its own wishes.

In the 1960s, certain right-wing intellectuals in Japan began to suggest that Japan's role in World War II ought to be assessed more positively.[21] According to them, since the nations of Southeast Asia were able to escape from their colonial state and attain independence as a result of World War II, Japan's role in the war ought to be at least partially justified. However, the independence of the countries of Southeast Asia resulted from the power vacuum following the expulsion of the British, American, Dutch and French forces from the area by the Japanese armies and the subsequent defeat of Japan itself. The independence which they attained was not the same kind of independence for Asia which had been envisioned by the wartime leaders in Japan. The actual results were far from their anticipations. Indeed, if we are to justify in retrospect Japan's role in World War II, arguing backwards through time from the actual results, then we ought also to justify the domination of the Western powers over Asia in the sense that it evoked the nationalistic consciousness in the peoples of Southeast Asia which has contributed directly to their independence movement and subsequent interest in industrialization. From perhaps not a dissimilar viewpoint, the historical significance that Anatole France attributed to the Russo-Japanese War was also based upon the unexpected consequences, which completely surpassed all the conscious intentions of its participants, including the rulers of Japan. The destruction of the myth of the invincibility of the white races restored self-confidence to the peoples of Asia. At the same time, however, this spiritual awakening transformed China into a nationalistic entity with aims and goals that were in conflict with those held by the near-sighted rulers of Japan.

At the beginning of the twentieth century there were still many who believed in the progress of mankind. Anatole France believed that history surpasses expectations of all ruling authorities and leads mankind to a better future. Consequently, he concludes with the optimistic vision of an idealist. France declares that it is to the advantage of humanity as a whole that peoples of all races and all colours be powerful, free, and rich:

> The great human asset is man himself. In order to rate the terrestrial globe, it is necessary to begin by rating men. To exploit the soil, the mines, the waters, all the substances and all the forces of our planet, it needs man, the whole of man: humanity, the whole humanity. The complete exploitation of the terrestrial globe demands the united labour of white, yellow and black men. By reducing, diminishing and weakening, or, to sum it up in one word, by colonizing a portion of humanity, we are working against ourselves. It is to our advantage that yellow and black men should be powerful, free, and wealthy.[22]

Statements of this sort are often adopted with unanimity and acclaimed in declarations on human rights. Nevertheless, our problem today is that, despite the affirmation given to such principles, in actual fact racial problems have sometimes grown even more intense, and we do not have in sight any prospects for totally solving them. To merely uphold Rousseauan ideals of how things ideally ought to be does not necessarily serve to bring about a solution of the problem.

These ideals of Anatole France – his firm belief in progress, his emphasis on serving all humanity, rather than one part of humanity, and his readiness to denounce the evils of his own fatherland for this sake identify him as being a lineal descendant of the philosophers of the eighteenth century, particularly Voltaire (1694–1778). A century and a half before Anatole France, Voltaire had also written about relations with China in 1764:

> But why have we for such a long time sought permission to go among them [the Orientals], while not a single Japanese has ever desired even to make a voyage among us? We have gone to Meaco [Kyoto], to the land of Yesso [Hokkaido], to California … Ever since the Europeans overcame the Cape of Good Hope, the Propaganda has inflated itself in the hope of subjugating all peoples living on the Eastern oceans and converting them. Trading in Asia is done only with the sword in one hand, and each of our Western countries has begun to dispatch one after another groups of merchants, soldiers, and priests.[23]

Voltaire's objective account of the expansion of European religious and commercial imperialism into the East perhaps served as the model for Anatole France, who vividly described the expansion of military and commercial Christendom into China. Adopting a standpoint of relativism, Voltaire preached tolerance to his fellow Europeans, quoting to them the words of Emperor Yung-cheng (Yongzheng) of the Qing dynasty:

> Let us inscribe in our troubled brains these memorable words of emperor Yung-cheng, spoken when he expelled from his empire all the Jesuit and other missionaries. Let them be written over the gates of all of our monasteries: 'What would you say if we went, under the pretext of trading in your countries, to tell your peoples that your religion was worthless and that it was absolutely essential to embrace ours!'

Voltaire had already quoted these words of emperor Yongzheng, – the French author spelled Yontching – the fifth emperor of the Qing dynasty, in his work *Siècle de Louis XIV* (1751),[24] in which he drew upon the reports sent from Peking by the Jesuits Parrenin and Bouvet. Upon reading these passages, we notice immediately that Anatole France's arguments are only the twentieth-century version of Voltaire's original.

When we consider this spiritual lineage, it will be readily agreed that topics such as the 'yellow peril' and 'white peril', however non-

literary they may appear, are really important themes in the history
of ideas in the broadest sense. In contemporary literature, we can
easily see the anti-colonialist views set forth by Jean-Paul Sartre in
his *Situations V.* Indeed, the traditional views of Voltaire and
Anatole France have continued to live. In a preface for a collection
of photographs by Henri Cartier-Bresson entitled *D'une Chine à
l'Autre*, Sartre wrote the following in 1954. Although the style is
Sartrean, the content offers little that is new; the Voltairean argument remains intact:

> At the point of origin of the picturesque, we find war and the refusal to
> understand the enemy. Indeed, our information about Asia came to us first
> from disgruntled missionaries and from soldiers. Later, there arrived the
> travellers – the businessmen and tourists – who are military men grown
> cold. The pillage is called 'shopping', and rape is practised onerously in spe-
> cialized shops. But the basic attitude has not changed. The natives are killed
> less often, but they are despised in a lump, which is the civilized form of
> the massacre.[25]

Turning our eyes eastward from France, let us now look at
Russia. 14 January 1905, Lenin wrote an article 'The Fall of Port
Arthur', which begins with the following statement:

> *Port Arthur has surrendered.*
> This event is one of the greatest events in modern history. These four
> words, flashed yesterday to all parts of the civilized world, create a crushing
> impression, the impression of an overwhelming appalling catastrophe, a
> disaster that beggars description.[26]

Writing about the historical significance of the fall of Port
Arthur, Lenin continued:

> The main objective of the Japanese in this war has been attained.
> Advancing, progressive Asia has dealt backward and reactionary Europe an
> irreparable blow. Ten years ago this reactionary Europe, with Russia in the
> lead, was perturbed by the defeat of China at the hands of young Japan,
> and it united to rob Japan of the best fruits of her victory.[27] Europe was
> protecting the established relations and privileges of the old world, its pre-
> rogative to exploit the Asian peoples – a prerogative held from time
> immemorial and sanctified by the usage of centuries ... Russia held Port
> Arthur for six years and spent hundreds of millions of rubles on the
> building of strategic railways, harbours, and new towns, on fortifying a
> stronghold which the entire mass of European newspapers, bribed by
> Russia and fawning on Russia, declared to be impregnable. Military com-
> mentators write that Port Arthur was as strong as six Sevastopols. And
> behold, little Japan, hitherto despised by all, captures this stronghold in
> eight months, when it took England and France together a whole year to
> capture Sevastopol. The military blow was irreparable.[28]

'The recovery of Port Arthur by Japan is a blow struck at the whole of reactionary Europe.'[29]

This evaluation by Lenin reminds us of Anatole France's statement quoted above that 'the Russians are paying the penalty, in the waters of Japan and in the gorges of Manchuria, not only of their grasping and brutal policy in the East, but of the colonial policy of all Europe.' In reality, it is no coincidence that the views of Lenin and Anatole France, two men of completely antithetical natures, should have coincided so closely. Anatole France expressed his views at a congress of the French Socialist Party while Lenin's article was written in opposition to the arguments of the *Revolutsionnaya Rossiya* (Revolutionary Russia), the official newspaper of the Russian Social Revolutionary Party (SR). Rather, Lenin sought to support the French socialist Jules Guesde's evaluation of the Russo-Japanese War:

> The class-conscious proletariat, an implacable enemy of war, cannot shut its eyes to the revolutionary task which the Japanese bourgeoisie, by its crushing defeat of the Russian autocracy, is carrying out. The proletariat is hostile to the bourgeoisie and to all manifestations of the bourgeois system, but this hostility does not relieve it of the duty of distinguishing between the historically progressive and the reactionary representatives of the bourgeoisie. It is quite understandable, therefore, that the most consistent and staunch representatives of revolutionary international Social-Democracy, such as Jules Guesde in France and Hyndman in England, unequivocally expressed their sympathy with Japan, which is routing the Russian autocracy. Here in Russia, of course, some socialists were found to have muddled ideas on this question, too. *Revolutsionnaya Rossiya* rebuked Guesde and Hyndman, saying that a socialist could only be in favour of a workers' Japan, a people's Japan, and not of a bourgeois Japan ... Guesde and Hyndman did not defend the Japanese bourgeoisie or Japanese imperialism; they correctly noted in this conflict between two bourgeois countries the historically progressive role of one of them.[30]

In this context, one can understand how natural it was for Lenin's viewpoint supporting Guesde to overlap with the viewpoint of Anatole France. Jules Guesde was born in 1844, the same year as Anatole France. He had collaborated with Marx in working out a programme for class struggle, and served as the editor of the newspaper *Egalité* and as a parliamentarian. Guesde played an extremely active role as a spectacular orator in the congresses of the French Socialist Party during the early years of the twentieth century. Generally speaking, the pronouncements of Anatole France on political questions were extremely subjective judgements unworthy

of serious consideration, but his observations in this seem to have
been rather astute. It may be added here that for those acquainted
with the views of Anatole France and Lenin, Stalin's speech immediately after Russia's declaration of war on Japan on 9 August 1945
must have seemed most bizarre. Appealing to nationalistic sentiments, Stalin justified Soviet Russia's entrance into the war against
Japan and its occupation of Manchuria in terms of revenge for the
humiliating defeat of the Russo-Japanese War. Stalin (or his ghost-
writer) had obviously quite forgotten about Lenin's short article on
the fall of Port Arthur. When Lenin, then far from the seat of
power, wrote his article on the fall of Port Arthur, he was interested
in an objective analysis of the international situation. Generalissimo
Stalin was appealing to nationalistic feelings in a 'Great Patriotic
War'. The latter was relying more on an emotional appeal based
on domestic issues rather than on scientific analysis or historical
evaluation.

In the discussion of the yellow peril and the white peril, so far the
French intellectual world showed itself able to uncover the evils
within their own nation. Neither Voltaire nor Anatole France was
well informed about the actual state of affairs in China, but both
attempted to divorce their thinking from the narrow standpoint of
the Frenchman. However, it must be recognized that, even in
France, only a minority of the intellectuals were capable of this
detachment. After World War II, when the former colonies were
gaining their independence, France was unable to acquit itself as
gallantly as Britain and sacrificed much blood in a futile attempt to
reestablish its colonial empire. The ending of the Algerian crisis
owed much more to the personal abilities of the dictatorial general
de Gaulle than to the efforts of Sartre or other luminaries of the
intellectual world.

De Gaulle, for all his acute political penetration and ability to act
decisively, nevertheless made no effort to conceal his French or
rather European patriotism. 'From the Atlantic to the Urals' was his
declaration for a Greater Europe and his concept of 'America, the
daughter of Europe' was also a slogan emphasizing the superiority
of Western European culture. On 24 August 1958, de Gaulle made
a speech in Brazzaville, advocating that the local population join in
the formation of a Franco-African Community:

> The formation of a Franco-African Community is indispensable for us
> French and African to become strong politically, for us to develop together
> economically, for us to develop culturally, and also, if necessary, for us to

defend ourselves. There is no one who does not know that there are immense dangers lurking in today's world and that these dangers are suspended over our heads, especially over Africa. In Asia, immense human masses are about to expand beyond their borders, since they lack sufficient means of livelihood within their own borders alone. Naturally, this expansion is carried out under the mask of ideology, as is always the case. However, behind this ideology, there is always present the imperialism of interests, which attempts to secure political bridgeheads in foreign territories. This is a clear fact.[31]

This de Gaullean grand vision may be called a racist view of politics in the broad sense. It is true that all who hold dear the tradition of individualism cannot help feeling a certain anxiety deep in their hearts, towards Asians working under the Communist regime in the People's Republic of China. The immense human masses were called 'several hundred millions of ants' by *le Monde* correspondent, Robert Guillain. The expression is distasteful; but this anxiety, which is widely shared by Westerners, sometimes manifests itself overtly, while at other times it tends to be utilized as a reason justifying the support of definite international policies.[32]

Even after WWII or even after the fall of Dien Bien Phu in 1954, most French politicians were speaking of the *mission civilisatrice* and of the *œuvre de chrétienté*. The cause of developing and maintaining colonies was understood as the mission of propagating civilization and spreading Christianity. The clear implication was that this glorious task must be carried on and that it was necessary to oppose any policy of abandoning the colonies. Looking at the other side of the yellow peril, we find deeply engraved the idea of the superiority of Western civilization among those who refer to yellow peril. Wilhelm II, who originated the idea of the 'yellow peril', also had a clearly defined crusading spirit when he spoke of 'defending our sacred wealth' and 'protecting the Cross and Christian European culture from Mongolian and Buddhist incursions'.[33]

This sense of mission served as the spiritual justification for suppressing movements for independence among those in the non-Western world. This is not to say that all Western cultural, political or economic activities abroad are necessarily to be termed evil. Some of the achievements stood quite apart from religious and cultural imperialism. One only need mention the abundance of educational and social work, the education of women in mission schools in pre-war Japan being a prime example. Indeed, large numbers of Westerners crossed the five continents, labouring as missionaries, teachers, and social workers. Even the modernization of China benefited from the educational activities of the missionaries, as a glance at the background of Sun Yat-sen will indicate.

Nevertheless, it must not be overlooked that this sense of cultural mission is also fraught with the danger of being linked with a crusading spirit and the possibility of degenerating into a 'holy' or ideological war. To convince oneself of this, it suffices to recall the concept of *hakkō-ichiu* ('the eight corners of the world under one roof') which was popular in Japan during World War II. This line of reasoning (it is questionable whether it was sufficiently concrete or developed to be called a bona fide ideology) certainly symbolized for many Japanese, Japan's mission of radiating her Imperial light into all directions. In nations with strong traditions of cultural ethnocentrism, one frequently notes that blind confidence in the national culture often degenerates into a self-righteous egoism and xenophobia. During the age of Rivarol in the eighteenth century, it was quite possible for Frenchmen to belittle the existence of other cultures and to advocate the supremacy of a French Europe. However, in today's world, one would like to think that such ideas, however attractive to some Francophiles, are rejected by the general population.

Concerning issues of this type, rather than discussing the attitudes of others, one ought to pay closer attention to the responses of one's own compatriots. For example, the focus should be on how the Japanese have responded in the past to assertions of such cultural egocentrism in other countries. Now, it is time to take a macroscopic glance at the Japanese attitudes towards foreign cultures.

The Confucian scholars, who tended to dominate the Japanese intellectual scene during the Tokugawa period (1603–1867), had a pronounced tendency to idealize China as the land of the sages, although they themselves were completely lacking in any actual experience of Qing China itself. Attracted by the centripetal force peculiar to the ethnocentric way of thinking of the Central Flowery Kingdom, the Japanese Confucians completely subordinated themselves to the Chinese, and even an independent-minded great thinker like Ogyū Sorai (1666–1718) did not hesitate to accept a nickname meaning 'eastern barbarian'. However, by the middle of the Tokugawa period, the *Kokugakusha*, those scholars of the 'national school' which specialized in the Japanese classics, began to attack the 'Chinese minded' Confucians. In a collection of essays, *Anzai zuihitsu*, Ise Sadatake (1717–84) wrote indignantly:

The Japanese Confucians have assumed a most unfavourable disposition – one which leads them to know only of the land to the west while being ignorant of things in our own country. Their manner of deriding, jeering, and scorning the things of our country is woeful. Such perfidious Confucians constantly honour the Western land, which they call the Central Flowery Kingdom, while they despise our country, calling it Vulgar Japan. This is breach of all propriety.[34]

The same argument was expanded in an even more masterful manner by Motoori Norinaga (1730–1801) in *Tama-katsuma* and other writings. However, the awareness on the part of the Japanese that they were not located in the centre of civilization continued until long after the Meiji Restoration. Thus, the Japanese attitude towards foreign cultures did not change much before or after the Meiji Restoration of 1868. Indeed, many Japanese intellectuals during and after the Meiji period wholeheartedly came to accept the major tenets of Europe's ethno-centric thinking in place of that of China.

Furthermore, this impairment often resulted, not from a backwardness in foreign studies, but rather from an extremely advanced state of narrow specialization in foreign studies, indeed, a kind of 'going native' in reverse. In many cases specialization meant getting absorbed in the foreign culture and thereby magnify the subject of their specific observation out of all proportion. For this reason, Japanese scholars studying the West did not always fit together in a well-balanced fashion the culture assimilated from abroad and the culture of their own native country. Writing in 1912, the last year of Meiji, Mori Ōgai already had a premonition that the tendency towards uncompromising worship of everything Western in Japanese intellectual circles would be followed some day by a reaction in the opposite direction: that is, a tendency towards an exclusive emphasis on the Orient. Mori wrote that 'the age demands scholars with two feet' but lamented that 'such persons are exceedingly difficult to come by'.[35] Largely on account of these circumstances, many of the most talented Japanese scholars in the field of the humanities and the social sciences were irresistibly attracted by European ethnocentrism. After becoming faithful adherents of such thought-patterns, they spent their whole lives as unoriginal exponents of this or that Western theory. Referring to this psychological peculiarity among the Japanese intelligentsia, Watsuji Tetsurō wrote the following in 1952:

Towards the end of the Meiji period, we young people customarily looked down upon things Japanese ... The youth of those days felt that, generally speaking, Western things were good but Japanese things were not. The person who taught these young people that Japan was a great country after all was not a Japanese; for me, it was Anatole France ... At that time, I was quite surprised by what I read, since I had thought that the Russo-Japanese War, being something done arbitrarily by the military men, was of no importance. But I changed my mind after being made to see it in terms of world history. Thus, I came to realize that it was a remarkable event, an event which had put an end to a certain trend in world history.[36]

It was Yanagita Kunio who recommended *Sur la Pierre Blanche* to Watsuji. When exposed to these frank and honest recollections of Watsuji, even those who are not very favourably impressed by Anatole France's pedestrian style and his rather fickle political statements may be forced to recognize at least the indirect importance of Anatole France in having opened the eyes of such outstanding Japanese intellectuals as Yanagita and Watsuji, making them aware of Japan's role in world history. While seeking a cultural identity, they met with Anatole France, and both of them discovered anew their native country, and finally both Yanagita and Watsuji became leading figures in Japanese studies. That was an unexpected effect of France's *Sur la Pierre Blanche*.

*Notes*

[1] This article, originally written in French under the title 'Le Péril Jaune et le Péril Blanc-Le point de vue d'Anatole France', appeared in *Études de Langue et Littérature Françaises*, (Tokyo: Hakusisha, 1969) No. 14, pp. 49–62.
[2] Yanagita Kunio was born in 1875 in Hyōgo Prefecture. He joined the literary circle *Bungakukai* and wrote poetry when he was a student in the First Higher School. After graduating from the University of Tokyo, he entered the Ministry of Agriculture. As a leading folklorist, he made many studies of Japanese customs. He died in 1962.
[3] *Yanagita Kunio Taidanshū*, (Tokyo: Chikuma Shobō, 1965)
[4] Anatōru Furansu: *Shiroki ishi no ue nite*, tr. Gonmori (Tokyo: Hakusuisha, 1950). The first Japanese translation of *Sur la Pierre Blanche* by Hirabayashi Hatsunosuke was published in 1924. The English translation by Charles E. Roche, entitled *The White Stone* was published by London: The Bodley Head, 1909.
[5] The text of this speech is reprinted in *Vers les Temps Meilleurs*, (Paris: Calmann-Lévy, 1906); it is famous as France's profession of his faith in socialism.
[6] Du Chaillu was a French-American famous for his explorations in Africa.
[7] Anatole France: *The White Stone*, p. 158, and *Sur la Pierre Blanche, Œuvres* (Paris: Gallimard, 1991), vol. 3 p. 1084.

[8] Anatole France: *The White Stone,* p. 158, and *Sur la Pierre Blanche,* pp. 1084–1085.

[9] General Bonnal (1844–1917) was the director of the French military academy, École supérieure de guerre. He wrote a book called *l'Esprit de la Guerre Moderne.*

[10] Anatole France: *The White Stone,* p. 160, and *Sur la Pierre Blanche,* p. 1085.

[11] Anatole France: *The White Stone,* p. 165, and *Sur la Pierre Blanche,* p. 1088.

[12] It is well known that Gobineau's classification of the mankind in three categories was taken up by Hitler in the 11 chapter of *Mein Kampf* as Kulturbegründer, Kulturträger and Kulturzerstörer. The Aryan race alone was counted as race capable of creating culture by both Gobineau and Hitler.

[13] Anatole France: *The White Stone,* p. 161, and *Sur la Pierre Blanche,* p. 1086.

[14] Anatole France: *The White Stone,* p. 161–162, and *Sur la Pierre Blanche,* p. 1086.

[15] Paul Valéry's wrote 'Yalou' in 1895, after having read Lafcadio Hearn's 'The Japanese Smile'.

[16] Anatole France: *The White Stone,* p. 162, and *Sur la Pierre Blanche,* pp. 1086–1087.

[17] Ishimitsu Makiyo: *Kōya no hana* (Tokyo: Chuōkōronsha, 1978) pp. 27–48.

[18] Anatole France: *The White Stone,* p. 163, and *Sur la Pierre Blanche,* p. 1087.

[19] Anatole France: *The White Stone,* pp. 163–164, and *Sur la Pierre Blanche,* p. 1087.

[20] Anatole France: *The White Stone,* p. 166, and *Sur la Pierre Blanche,* p. 1089.

[21] Hayashi Fusao's *Daitōa sensō kōtei ron* published by Chūōkōron, Tokyo, in 1964, is an attempt at revaluation of the part played by Japan in the process of the liberation of South-East Asia from Western colonizing powers.

[22] Anatole France: *The White Stone,* p. 175, and *Sur la Pierre Blanche,* p. 1094.

[23] Voltaire: *Dictionnaire Philosophique,* 1764. Translation mine.

[24] See Chapter XXXIX, Voltaire: *Le Siècle de Louis XIV* (Paris: Garnier, 1930), vol. 2, pp. 240–250.

[25] Jean-Paul Sartre: *Situations V* (Paris: Gallimard, 1964). Translation mine.

[26] Lenin: *Collected Works* (Moscow: Foreign Languages Publishing House, 1962), vol. 8. p. 47.

[27] Lenin was referring here to the tripartite intervention in 1895.

[28] Lenin: *Collected Works,* vol. 8, pp. 48–49.

[29] Lenin: *Collected Works,* vol. 8, p. 48.

[30] Lenin: *Collected Works,* vol. 8, p. 52.

[31] See *Le Monde,* August 25, 1958. p. 1. Translation mine.

[32] There is always a danger that this anxiety may again become overt. In mid-October 1967, James Reston of the *New York Times* crossed swords with Secretary of State Dean Rusk about the 'yellow peril' issue and the incident was reported in newspapers all over the world. In the 1980s

Americans were aware of the phrase 'economic yellow peril'. Japan-bashing might have been an expression of the vague feeling of anxiety.

[33] See, for example, Kaiser Wilhelm II's letter dated 10 July 1895 in Herman Bernstein ed.: *The Willy-Nicky Correspondence* (Letters exchanged between Wilhelm II of Germany and Nicholas II, last czar of Russia) (New York: A. Knopf, 1918).

[34] Ise Sadatake: *Ansai zuihitsu* (Tokyo: Meiji tosho shuppan, 1993) chapter 7, essay entitled 'Fugiju' pp. 174–175. Translation mine.

[35] Mori Ōgai, 'Teiken sensei' in *Ōgai zenshū* (Tokyo: Iwanami shoten, 1951), vol. 23, pp. 423–26.

[36] Watsuji Tetsurō, *Kaizō*, July 1952, p. 207.

CHAPTER 3:4

# NATSUME SŌSEKI AND HIS TEACHER JAMES MURDOCH: THEIR OPPOSITE VIEWS ON THE MODERNIZATION OF JAPAN[1]

————————□————————

Evaluations of modern Japanese writers differ considerably in Japan and in the West. In Japanese histories of Japanese literature, Mori Ōgai (1862–1922) and Natsume Sōseki (1867–1916) have always been considered the two greats in the field of modern Japanese literature, while in the Western world the names of Kawabata Yasunari (1899–1972) and Tanizaki Junichirō (1886–1965) are better known. There is a good reason for this difference of estimation. As I see it, Ōgai and Sōseki are important figures especially from the viewpoint of the intellectual history of modern Japan, while Kawabata and Tanizaki are great in the more restricted sense of literary history. For example, we can discuss the views on the modernization of Japan held by Ōgai or Sōseki; but it is rather difficult to treat problems of this kind with Kawabata or Tanizaki.

Natsume Sōseki was the first Japanese to teach English literature at the Imperial University of Tokyo at the beginning of the twentieth century, and he later turned to a writing career. Together with Ōgai, Sōseki was the representative Japanese intellectual of the time, and I do not think there is any disagreement on this point. In this chapter, I would like to throw light on Sōseki's relations with his teacher James Murdoch (1856–1921) and other foreigners, and in so doing I would like to discuss Sōseki's views on the modernization of Japan.

Natsume Sōseki and James Murdoch were in contact during two distinct periods of their lives: the first was 1889–1890 when Sōseki was Murdoch's student in Tokyo; Sōseki was his best student at the First Higher School (dai-ichi kōtō-gakkō). Contact was reestablished twenty-two years later in 1911, when Murdoch sent Volume I of his *A History of Japan* to the already well-known writer Sōseki. As a response to Murdoch's views concerning the modernization of Japan and its future, which were very optimistic, Sōseki very frankly expressed a view that was extremely pessimistic. Since contrasts of views similar to the difference in the opinions held by Murdoch and Sōseki continue to appear from time to time among those who are interested in the history of modern Japan, I believe it worthwhile to examine in some detail their relationship and their opposite views on the modernization of Japan.

As is generally recognized, the problems of the modernization of non-Western countries were closely associated with the problems of their relations with Western civilization. Consequently, these problems should be discussed in an inter-cultural perspective. This kind of viewpoint is important not only when we deal with Japan's emergence as a modern state, but also when we examine the intelligentsia of modernizing Japan or of any other non-Western countries. Although most of Sōseki's major works have been translated into English, Sōseki's relations with foreigners have not yet been the focus of attention of Japan specialists in the West. However, as some of the foreigners with whom Sōseki was more or less closely related were great pioneers in Japanese studies, Sōseki's relations with them might be of interest to readers.

Natsume Sōseki was born in 1867, one year before the Meiji Restoration. He died half a century later in 1916. The three people whose relations with Sōseki I wish to discuss are foreigners who came to Japan. The first and the most important figure is British, more precisely a Scotsman, James Murdoch by name, one of the greatest pioneers in Japanese studies. He wrote a monumental *History of Japan* in three volumes. Murdoch, born in 1856 in a village near Aberdeen, was eleven years older than Sōseki. He was Sōseki's teacher of English and history at the First Higher School.

The second foreigner is a Russian who later took French citizenship, a name familiar to all Western Japan specialists, Serge Elisseeff (1889–1975), one of the founders of Japanese studies in North

America and in France. In 1908, Elisseeff distinguished himself by becoming the first Western student ever admitted to Tokyo Imperial University. Sōseki had already resigned from the university in 1907 to devote himself entirely to writing. However, the Japanese friends, with whom Elisseeff studied and also spent much of his leisure even frequenting the gay quarters together, were former students of Sōseki, and Elisseeff quite often visited Sōseki's house which was a sort of literary salon. There is even a *haiku* improvised by Sōseki; '*Samidare ya momodachi takaku kitaru hito*'. It describes the long-legged Western student, Elisseeff dressed a little awkwardly in *hakama,* the traditional double skirt, visiting Sōseki on a rainy day in June: a picturesque sketch of his first impression.

The third figure is a Chinese, Lu Xun (Rojin, in Japanese pronunciation; 1881–1936), the greatest Chinese writer of the first half of the twentieth century, at least in the estimation of Chairman Mao and his followers. Lu Xun rented together with two friends a house in which Sōseki had lived. In his opinion Sōseki was Japan's best writer. Lu Xun admired Sōseki but had no chance to converse with him, as Sōseki had already moved out before Lu Xun's arrival. However, he was the first translator of Sōseki's works into Chinese. Unlike his younger brother who later became a professor of Japanese literature at Peking University, Lu Xun himself was not a Japanologist in the strict sense of the term, but he was a sort of 'Japan expert', as he had spent seven years of his youth in Tokyo and Sendai. For this reason although he had no direct association with Sōseki in person, I am putting Lu Xun's name after Murdoch and Elisseeff in the list of foreign Japanologists related to Sōseki.

The general questions which I would like to raise here are what did these foreign Japanologists mean to Sōseki and what did Sōseki mean to them, and more specifically what was Sōseki's response to Murdoch's views concerning the modernization of Japan.

First, let us take a brief look at Sōseki's schooldays. As a middle school student, Sōseki chose a regular school, *seisoku gakkō*. The courses were entirely given in Japanese and much emphasis was put on studies of Chinese classics. The young Sōseki was very fond of them. However, as a Meiji youth, Sōseki began to feel uneasy about his future. After the opening of Japan in 1868, a knowledge of English became indispensable, and intensive courses in English were offered mainly in irregular schools, *hensoku gakkō*. In those irregular schools almost all courses were taught by the direct method in English with English textbooks. Sōseki felt that he was lagging behind the times; in that transition period of the 1880s the so-called irregular schools were the royal road that led to the Imperial University of Tokyo. Sōseki belatedly switched from a regular school to an irregular school so that he could be accepted as a student at the University. The reason why Sōseki was two or three years older than other students when he was admitted to the First Higher School, which was the preparatory course for the University, derives from his having gone by that roundabout way. Sōseki thought he had lost precious years by taking wrong steps, but throughout his life his knowledge and love of the Chinese classics proved to be of great value. In 1903, Sōseki became a lecturer at the University of Tokyo, and his lectures on eighteenth-century English literature are still worth reading, as his occasional comparisons, remarks and references to Oriental literatures make the lectures very interesting. Sōseki was a comparative literature professor *avant la lettre*. As a writer and especially as a poet, his knowledge of the Chinese classics played a still more important role.

With this background, then, let us examine his relationship with Murdoch. When Murdoch came to Tokyo in 1889, Sōseki was the best student in his class. Sōseki the late-comer was eager to learn English, and according to his own recollections[2] he not only attended Murdoch's classes in English and in history five or six times a week but also went to his home to listen to him talk. Such was his eagerness that he visited his teacher's home even very early in the morning. Once Murdoch let Sōseki sit at his table and asked if Sōseki had already finished his breakfast; while posing questions Murdoch continued to eat his meal. There was a fried egg on a plate. Sōseki had never seen a fried egg before. According to Sōseki's recollections, he was surprised to see that a Westerner's breakfast consists of such a thing. He did not even know the English term 'a fried egg' at that time. One may smile at the naïveté of the twenty-two-year-old Sōseki. Yet it is virtually the same with Western tourists coming to Japan. When they stay in a Japanese inn, they find an egg served at their breakfast table. Thinking that this is a boiled egg, they break it only to find, to their amazement, that it is raw. Neither can we laugh at Sōseki's ignorance of the term 'a fried egg'. Japanese tourists today are puzzled at their first breakfast in North America when they are asked by a waitress if they want their eggs sunny side up. All these 'eggs-periences' that seem very strange and alien to us until they have been actually faced and easily coped with are a sort of Columbus's egg of our times.

Let me describe here briefly Murdoch's life, using some materials which have hitherto not been easily accessible to readers. Murdoch's life is described at the beginning of Volume III of his *History of Japan,* published in 1926 by Kegan Paul, Trench, Trubner, five years after the death of the author. The ten-page biography, which was unsigned, was written not by the editors of the book, Joseph Longford or L.M.C. Hall, as is generally believed, but by Robert Young, editor of the *Kobe Chronicle,* who wrote the piece as an obituary for his paper at the time of Murdoch's death in Sydney in 1921.[3]

According to the article, James Murdoch, son of a poor shopkeeper, did not get sent to the village grammar school until the age of eleven. That school had a bursary for Aberdeen University and the poor diligent boy won it. Alexander Bain, one of the professors of the university, took a great interest in the student, whose origins were not unlike his own. Murdoch lived on his meagre scholarship, his father not being able to supplement it. One pound was all the money that his father ever gave him.[4]

As for Bain's great interest in Murdoch, there is a passage in Sōseki's recollections which corroborates it: Murdoch lent Bain's book to his Japanese student. Sōseki wanted to read Bain's philosophical writings, but as he was busy with his other studies, he could not finish the book so soon. After a while Murdoch told Sōseki that Bain was his teacher and he wanted to keep the book as a precious memento. It had been read many times by Murdoch and the covers were half gone, but it was evident that Murdoch still set great value by the book.[5]

After graduating from Aberdeen University, Murdoch went to Oxford, Göttingen and Paris. At the age of twenty-four Murdoch became assistant professor of Greek at Aberdeen. However, he resigned the post the following year and went to Queensland, Australia to become headmaster of a grammar school. It was probably a financial consideration that made Murdoch leave Scotland for Australia. Over a period of eight years, he worked at two different grammar schools. He received a thousand pounds a year. Robert Young comments that a thousand pounds a year was 'a fortune to a boy brought up as Murdoch was'.[6] Murdoch's English wife, however, committed suicide.[7] Her maiden name was Lucy Parkes: they were married while Murdoch was at Oxford.[8]

He gave up his position as second-master of Brisbane grammar school and went into journalism. At that time, the Labour Movement in Australia was greatly agitated by the question of Chinese immigration. The 'White Australia' prejudice was beginning to take shape. Murdoch received a commission from a leading newspaper, probably the *Telegraph* of Sydney, to investigate the subject and took passage for China. In order to see how the Chinese lived on board the steamers, Murdoch travelled in steerage from Sydney to Port Darwin. He protested against the bad conditions of steerage, but his protests of course went unheard. At Port Darwin, as there were no other white passengers left in steerage, Murdoch switched to first class. The captain, not knowing that he had changed his status, was greatly offended by his presence in the salon. These experiences are humorously recounted in a book entitled *From Australia and Japan*, published in London in 1892 by Walter Scott Ltd. Although Murdoch's name does not appear at all, the initials of the author A.M. are without doubt the pseudonym for James Murdoch.

After completing his investigations in Hong Kong and Canton and sending the results of his inquiries on the Australian coolie traffic to his newspaper, Murdoch on his way back to Sydney stopped over in Japan. Here he found a university classmate working as a teacher in a school at Nakatsu in Kyushu, a private school founded by the former daimyō Okudaira on the advice of his former retainer Fukuzawa Yukichi. He travelled through many parts of Japan, hitherto untrodden by Westerners, with Sasaki Yūtarō[9] as his guide. The life in Japan attracted Murdoch. He returned to Australia, settled his affairs, and came back to Japan with his son Kenneth. He received the position of teacher of English and history at the First Higher School on 11 September 1889. According to the official documents preserved at the Komaba campus of Tokyo University, his pay, which was two hundred yen per month, was ten times as high as that of his Japanese colleague Hanawa Toratarō, who recommended Murdoch for that post. The twenty-two-year-old Natsume Sōseki was to get a loan scholarship of seven yen per month. Financially, Murdoch and foreign employees in general were very generously treated by the Japanese government.

Murdoch had a strong Scottish accent and it was difficult even for Sōseki who always sat near the teacher to understand what he was saying. Robert Young wrote as follows in the ten-page biography:

> He (Murdoch) described his accent, himself, as a strong Doric, and to the last Englishmen had sometimes a difficulty in following his rapid and strongly accented speech. This was scarcely a good foundation either for

teaching Japanese students English or for teaching English students Japanese. Yet he was remarkably successful as a teacher because of the intellectual quality he put into his work.[10]

According to Sōseki's recollections, many of his classmates were puzzled by the teacher's strong accent. Still, they respected Murdoch and no one complained about his teaching.[11] Some eager students went to see him at his house, and Murdoch welcomed them. Murdoch even helped some poor students financially. Yamagata Isoh was one of them. It seems that his teaching was not always very methodical. Sometimes he digressed, and he went so far as to read aloud a poem in Greek. It was of course impossible for Sōseki to understand it, but as Murdoch's pronunciation was always very difficult to follow, Sōseki asked if this was also English. Murdoch, who was conscious of his own special accent, began to laugh at Sōseki's unexpected question.[12] It is beyond my power to translate into English all the fine details of Sōseki's description of the somewhat bohemian gentleman, but Sōseki's recollection 'Hakushi mondai to Mādokku sensei to yo' (The question of the doctorate and Mr Murdoch and myself) touches its readers with Sōseki's very warm and genuine affection.

Sōseki was a man who stayed free of the bonds of the conventional master-disciple relationship. There remains very little recollection of his Japanese teachers; philosophy professor Inoue Tetsujirō was slightly mocked both in Sōseki's haiku and in his novel *Sanshirō*. Sōseki talked very much about his friends of university days. The poet Masaoka Shiki, who initiated Sōseki into the world of *haiku*, was a sort of big brother, and biographers of Sōseki such as Komiya Toyotaka and Etō Jun talk extensively of their friendship. A number of articles have been written on their friendship, yet little research has so far been done on Sōseki's teachers. In the formative years of the early Meiji twenties – that is, in the late 1880s and early 1890s – there were perhaps no distinguished professors. At the Faculty of letters of Tokyo University, to which Sōseki moved in September 1890, the chair of English literature was occupied by another Scotsman named James Dickson. He later became a professor of English at Washington University, St Louis, Missouri. Sōseki's evaluation of Dickson was, however, not very high. Sōseki wrote about professor Dickson in the following terms:

> ... At that time Dickson was teaching. He let me read English poems and prose before him and corrected my pronunciation. When I presented English compositions, he often scolded me for my misuse of articles. At examinations the questions he put were: 'When was Wordsworth born?'

'How many folios of Shakespeare are still extant?' 'Write the titles of
Walter Scott's works in chronological order' and so on. Imagine if this kind
of lecture could really be called a lecture on English literature. One cannot
understand what literature is, so long as one is taught in this way.[13]

Apparently, Dickson's lecture style did not have any appeal for
the intelligent student that Sōseki was. His disappointment with
Dickson was probably all the greater for his having had at the First
Higher School a teacher of the calibre of James Murdoch.

Murdoch's attitude towards Japan and the Japanese was at first
frivolous. In his early years in Japan Murdoch's attitude was similar
to that of the French writer Pierre Loti. As Loti wrote about a
Nagasaki geisha and published *Madame Chrysanthème* in 1887, so
Murdoch wrote a romance about a Misaki girl and published *Ayame
san,* Madame Iris, in 1892. Murdoch in his first four-year-stay in
Japan had not yet found his true vocation as a historian. He published books such as *Don Juan's Grandson in Japan* (Tokyo:
Hakubunkan, 1890). As the title suggests, its content is not very
serious. According to Young's article, Murdoch was 'from his university days an agnostic, the religion in which he had been brought
up, being slipped away from him'. In the poem *Don Juan's Grandson
in Japan* Murdoch made fun of conditions in the local foreign community and of the reputations of some very serious and solemn
persons, Christian missionaries included. It does not mean, however, that Murdoch himself led a life of debauchery; still, he could
describe very well some foreign professors' dissipated lives in
Tokyo. The Christian writer Uchimura Kanzō was a teacher of
English at the same First Higher School when Murdoch was there.
Uchimura wrote several years later an article in English for the
newspaper *Yorozu Chōhō* (27 February 1897), accusing 'Licentious
Foreigners'. Uchimura took seriously the misconduct of Don Juan's
grandchildren in Japan.

In the early years of his stay in Tokyo, Murdoch's views on the
modernization of Japan seemed to be the same as shared by the
majority of Westerners residing in Japan at that time. In one of a
series of books, which were more like travel guides, entitled *the
Tokaido* (1892) and beautifully illustrated with photographs taken by
Ogawa Kazumasa, Murdoch complained of the present state of the
capital of Japan. In the preceding Edo period, Japan had a style of
its own, as the eighteenth century German traveller Kaempfer had
amply described it. Japan of the 1890s that tried hard to imitate the
West looked rather ludicrous to Western observers. The

Westernization seemed superficial and clumsy. By borrowing a remark attributed to a French diplomat, Murdoch epitomized his views on the results of Westernization efforts of Meiji Japan: *'une traduction mal faite'*, a poor translation of Western civilization. Murdoch quoted this on the first page of Ogawa's book. However, what is interesting about Murdoch is that his attitude towards Japan changed considerably over time.

James Murdoch, son of a poor village shopkeeper in Scotland, was a fervent socialist at that time. He preached socialism to his Japanese students. One of them, Yamagata Isoh, who later became the best collaborator of Uchimura Kanzō and editor of the English edition of the daily journal *Yorozu Chōhō*, embraced socialism under his influence. Uchimura and Yamagata preached pacifism during the Russo-Japanese War. Although interesting, this group of Christian pacifists is outside the scope of my discussion.

In the year 1893, Murdoch took part in a curious adventure. After four years' service at the First Higher School, the Scotsman went to Paraguay. He was already attracted to socialism while he was in Australia. The Fabian Society was established in 1884 and he referred to the movement in one of his travel books. A friend of his named William Lane, who was both a visionary and a practical man of affairs, organized a communist colony in Paraguay, where he had obtained a grant of some 25,000 acres of land from the Paraguayan government. To this land of promise William Lane brought a group of families and single men from Australia in order to form a community called New Australia.[14]

At that time there were many like-minded movements. For example, Elisabeth Förster, sister of the philosopher Friedrich Nietzsche, went to Paraguay with her husband some ten years earlier to form an ideal community. Murdoch, who knew Lane in his Australian days and had formed a very high opinion of him, resolved to join the community to which he offered his services as schoolmaster. Murdoch's letter sent to the principal of the First Higher School is preserved in translation in the archives of Tokyo University's Komaba campus.[15] It stated that the four years he had spent at the First Higher School were really very pleasant and he had no complaint whatsoever, but as he had important and urgent business in Paraguay he requested that his engagement be brought to an end. Murdoch went to South America. When he finally arrived at the colony, he found the people already dispirited by their earlier experiences of a way of life for which many were quite unfit. There were constant bickerings and dissensions, leading to disputes in which there were threats of the use of arms. Here is a passage from the article by Young, who must have heard the story from Murdoch himself:

> 'My experience of the practical working of socialism,' he once said, 'was the serving out of meat to a community almost starving, with envy and jealousy so strong that the butcher weighed the meat with one hand while he kept a revolver in the other.' Lane had developed from the gentle and thoughtful leader of equalitarians unto an autocrat. The strain developed a curious fanaticism and mysticism in a man hitherto known for his equable temperament and total absence of religious credulity. One morning he rode up to the place where Murdoch was lying on the grass prior to the assembling of the school and remarked that he had been consulting with God about the affairs of the community. Saying this he eyed Murdoch sharply. 'Maybe,' said Murdoch gravely, finding that an answer was required. Eyeing Murdoch again, but getting nothing further, he rode away. 'But that incident decided me,' said Murdoch, 'when the leader professed to be ordering his movements and policy by the instructions of a supernatural being, New Australia was no longer any place for James Murdoch.'[16]

Disillusioned, Murdoch left the community. He fell gravely ill at Rio de Janeiro, and for some weeks was in a very critical condition. While recovering from his illness, Murdoch must have reflected deeply on his past and on his future. He was then thirty-seven years of age. He had published several books, but they were all of dubious value. When he graduated from Aberdeen University, Murdoch came out first in no less than five subjects. As for classical languages, he went up for examinations thirty-two times in the four universities of Aberdeen, Oxford, Göttingen and Paris, and he came out first in thirty examinations, an achievement unprecedented in the entire history of Aberdeen University graduates. He must now devote himself to a lifework which would be worthy of a James Murdoch. While waiting for a ship to get away from South America, he must have made up his mind. The project he proposed to himself was the writing of a history of Japan during the century of early foreign intercourse.

His failure to build a socialistic paradise in Paraguay seems to have been a turning point in his life; even his style of English itself changed. It became more sober. Murdoch began to keep his feet on the ground. He first went to Britain, but it was not to go back to his native village. He stayed in London and made an extensive study of the materials by early Western travellers to Japan in the British Museum. As he could read Portuguese, Spanish, Italian, Latin and

Dutch, not to mention English, French and German, Murdoch could gain a very good historical knowledge and an excellent perspective, especially of the Western side. Murdoch was a gifted linguist, but still he preferred to be called a historian, and his interest in Japanese history had already begun in the early stage of his stay in Japan. For example, in 1890, the second year of his teaching at the First Higher School, Murdoch gave as the subject of a term essay 'Japan and England in the Sixteenth Century'. Natsume Sōseki's and Masaoka Shiki's essays together with one by a certain Nakayama were printed in a student magazine called the *Museum*.[17] I wonder if they satisfied the examiner as history essays. Sōseki's essay is, however, quite good as an English composition, and we know also that Murdoch was conscientious in his work, providing proper corrections and good comments.

As Murdoch already had a reputation for being a teacher respected by his students, when he came back from Paraguay to Japan via Britain and North America in 1894, his Japanese friends found him a post at the Higher School at Kanazawa. After several years he left Kanazawa and came to Tokyo to teach at the Higher Commercial School, the present Hitotsubashi University. His friend Hanawa Toratarō introduced him to Okada Takeko, daughter of an ex-retainer of the *bakufu*. In 1899, Murdoch married her. Every time Murdoch met Hanawa, he would express his gratitude for having received such a real helpmate who sacrificed all to make him happy and enabled him to engage in his lifework, the writing of a history of Japan. He repeated: '*Nihon no onna wa sekai-ichi.*' (A Japanese wife is the best in the world.) As Murdoch had a health problem since his Paraguayan adventure, he preferred to go to the south and found a job at the Higher School at Kagoshima in 1901. Yamagata Isoh, who was his student at the First Higher School, later wrote articles about Murdoch both in Japanese and in English. In the 5 October 1926 issue of *The Japan Christian Intelligencer*, an English language monthly edited by Uchimura Kanzō, Yamagata writes:

> At first it had been his intention to write a history of Japan during the century of early foreign intercourse with Japan from the year 1542, when some Portuguese adventurers came to Japan for the first time, down to the year 1639, when the Tokugawa Government drove out all foreigners from the country. When he came up to Tokyo from Kanazawa, he asked me to assist him in his intended work by supplying materials from the Japanese sources. Remembering the many favours he had extended to me while I was a student, I could not refuse, though I had not much time to spare for such

work, as I was then engaged in daily journalism. I decided to accede to his request, with the result that I never worked harder than I did during the following few years.[18]

Robert Young, the editor of the *Japan Chronicle* and the first publisher of Murdoch's first history book – at the time of that publication in 1903 the newspaper was still called the *Kobe Chronicle* – also recognized the excellent relationship between Murdoch and his former students. In the obituary Young writes:

> As a teacher Murdoch acquired an extraordinary control and influence over his pupils. His teaching was quite different from the conventional method ... Many of the students who received instruction from him now hold important positions in Japan, and it is to their honour that they never forgot their old teacher and were always ready to do him any service on his account.[19]

Yamagata Isoh, in his recollection of Murdoch the historian written in Japanese and appearing in the November 1926 issue of the monthly journal *Taiyō,* recounted that he helped Murdoch without any remuneration. He helped because he wanted to repay Murdoch for his kindness. Yamagata once visited him at Kagoshima while Murdoch was engaged in the writing of his history:

> I ... found him engaged in his work by candle-light in a cave, which he had caused to be excavated in a hill-side behind his house. He explained to me that he did so for the purpose of insuring from possible fire the safety of those valuable materials his two friends (Basil Hall Chamberlain and Ernest Satow) had so kindly lent him.[20]

The time was long before the invention of the xerox machine, and the eccentric Murdoch wrote his history in a cave. Yamagata continues his *Japan Christian Intelligencer* article:

> I assisted him on the production of Vol. II. Besides collecting materials from Japanese sources I translated them into English. It was a hard work, the hardest I have ever undertaken. After the day's work at the newspaper office was over, I set myself to it and week after week sent to Kagoshima what I had managed to finish during the week. Like Oliver Twist, Murdoch always wanted more and I was sorely pressed. Almost every night I worked until the clock struck twelve and often out of sheer exhaustion I fell asleep over the desk. Had I been an employee or been paid for my work, I would have soon given it up. But it was a labour of love and I was determined to see it through. When it was finished after I had turned out thousands of pages in the course of three years or so, I felt as if a heavy burden had been lifted from my shoulders.[21]

Yamagata was not a historian. He asked Murakawa Kengo, a Tokyo University graduate, to select historical documents from

Japanese sources. Murakawa, who later became a professor of Greek history at his alma mater, was very competent in the selection. As Yamagata himself acknowledged in his *Japan Christian Intelligencer* article, what Yamagata did was no more than assisting Murdoch as a translator. Murdoch, however, insisted on putting on the title page Yamagata's name as collaborator. Thanks to this assistance and to the fact that Murdoch was at home with European personages and European documents, this book, in which he deals with foreign intercourse and which later became Volume II of his *History of Japan,* is considered the best by far of the three volumes.[22]

What is admirable about Murdoch is that after the completion of this volume, he conceived the idea of writing the whole history of Japan from its beginnings to the present day and that he began to learn Japanese when he was approaching fifty years of age. At that time, the myth still prevailed that the Japanese language is impossible for Westerners to master, and someone tried to dissuade Murdoch from taking it up. He replied: 'Cato began his study of Greek at eighty. I am not too old.' With his wife Takeko as his teacher Murdoch studied Japanese and, 'by dint of his indomitable will', persisted until in time he could read not only the Japanese language of the twentieth century but also texts such as *Kojiki* and *Manyōshū* of the eighth century.[23] He learned how to read Chinese classics as well. Yamagata once told Natsume Sōseki that Murdoch's handwriting of Chinese characters could not be called beautiful or good but it was correct. Without the assistance of Yamagata, Volume I of *a History of Japan* was finished and published by the Asiatic Society of Japan in 1910. Volume I covers the long period from prehistoric ages down to the arrival of the Portuguese in 1542; the date is triply significant as it was the year when Tokugawa Ieyasu was born in Japan, and Queen Mary in Scotland. To Volume I Murdoch added a very interesting introductory chapter in which the historian discussed the emergence of modern Japan against its Tokugawa background.

In March 1911, Sōseki received a letter from Murdoch. Twenty-three years had passed since Murdoch's first arrival in Japan, and perhaps almost twenty years had passed since Murdoch and Sōseki had last met. After his graduation from the Imperial University, Sōseki went to Matsuyama in Shikoku, and from there he moved to Kumamoto in Kyushu. After four years at the Kumamoto Higher School Sōseki went to study in London. When he came back to Tokyo in 1903, Murdoch was at Kagoshima, teaching English and writing a history of Japan, and cultivating an orchard of orange and lemon trees, an orchard Murdoch had bought in the name of his wife Takeko. Sōseki knew that Murdoch was living in Kagoshima. Yamagata Isoh was Sōseki's friend and told him of his admiration for Murdoch. Two students of Sōseki's got positions at the same Higher School at Kagoshima. Every time they came up to Tokyo, they must have talked about Murdoch to Sōseki, and vice versa: Murdoch must have heard about Sōseki from his young colleagues. But there had been no correspondence between them after Sōseki's graduation. It is not surprising that Sōseki remembered his former teacher Murdoch; but it is surprising that Murdoch remembered his former student Sōseki and that Murdoch sent Sōseki a letter. The exchange began in the following way.

In February 1911, Natsume Sōseki was awarded the title of *bungaku hakushi* by the Ministry of Education. A *bungaku hakushi* in the forty-fourth year of Meiji was not a PhD. It was a distinction which approximately corresponds to today's honour of being selected as a member of the Academy of Arts, *geijutsuin kaiin* or a similar title. Natsume Sōseki, however, declined the honour, and wrote an article in the *Asahi* newspaper, explaining why he preferred to remain Natsume Kinnosuke, an ordinary citizen without any official title whatsoever. Murdoch at that time must have been a subscriber to the *Asahi* newspaper at Kagoshima. He must have felt a strong affinity with Natsume Sōseki's attitudes concerning the worldly honours awarded by officialdom. As for Murdoch's attitudes towards decorations and other distinctions, Yamagata relates the following episode in his *Japan Christian Intelligencer* article:

> Murdoch despised transitory popularity and worldly honours and hated publicity. For his long and meritorious service as teacher, he was twice offered a high class Order of the Rising Sun. He declined to accept the proffered honour. When I asked him why he refused it, he laughed and said: 'A decoration is a toy of grown-ups and an expensive one at that. For, in order to receive it, I shall have to present myself at the (Imperial) Household Department in a formal dress. I have not got one and I cannot afford to order one just for possessing a toy. Besides, I need no decoration. Many of my pupils are now important men in this country. They are my decoration.'[24]

Since Murdoch was a man of this cast of mind, it was quite natural and understandable that he rejoiced over the news that Natsume Sōseki, his pupil, declined the honour of a *bungaku hakushi*. Sōseki needed no decorations. His literary work was his decoration. Murdoch praised highly Sōseki's character and wrote to him that he had a moral backbone. Unfortunately, Murdoch's letter to Sōseki is lost, but in his recollections of Murdoch, Sōseki referred to the contents of the letter. Sōseki tried to translate the word 'moral backbone' into Japanese and coined the new word 'tokugi-teki sekizui', but this neologism sounds rather strange as a Japanese word. In the same letter, Murdoch told Sōseki that he had sent him a copy of Volume I of his *History of Japan* and asked Sōseki to read its introductory chapter and, if possible, to write a comment or a critique of it. Sōseki promised to do so. Sōseki must have heard from Yamagata that Murdoch's first publication, *An History of Japan During the Century of Early Foreign Intercourse,* which was to form the middle volume of his whole *History of Japan,* had been printed at Murdoch's own expense, and only one thousand copies had been printed. Moreover, in Kagoshima, Murdoch had quarrelled with the director of the Higher School and had resigned. Sōseki wrote in the *Asahi* newspaper that Murdoch led the life of 'a British hermit in Japan'. Remembering Murdoch's earlier publication *Don Juan's Grandson in Japan (Nihon ni okeru Don Juan no mago),* he modified the expression into *'Nihon ni okeru Eikoku no inja'.* He must have had a strong desire to recommend Murdoch's history book to the Japanese reading public; Sōseki at that time was the most influential figure in Japanese journalism.

So far as I know at least two Japanese articles recommending Murdoch's first book, *An History of Japan During the Century of Early Foreign Intercourse* have been published. One was by Yamagata Isoh in the monthly *Gakutō,* October, 1903. The other was by the historian Takekoshi Yosaburō.[25] He was known for his voluminous history translated into English under the title *The Economic Aspects of the History of the Civilization of Japan.* Takekoshi was a member of Parliament and it was Ozaki Yukio (Gakudō), another member of Parliament, who strongly recommended Murdoch's *History of Japan.* It is surprising that in the Meiji era, Japan had such scholar-statesmen: Ozaki had read through Murdoch's manuscripts and furnished him with many hints and valuable assistance. Ozaki admired Murdoch so much that he sent his son to the Higher School at Kagoshima, and the son lived under the same roof with the Murdochs. According to the recollection of Ozaki's son, it was a wooden house and the boards had many knot-holes through which the wind blew in.[26] As for his second book, that is, Volume I of *a History of Japan* published in 1910, I do not know if there were any detailed reviews written by Japanese besides the article by Sōseki on 16 March 1911 issue of the *Asahi* newspaper. It is his second article concerning Murdoch. In this article entitled 'Mr. Murdoch's *History of Japan*' (*Mādokku sensei no nihon-rekishi*), Sōseki, however, deals only with the introductory chapter as was requested by the author.

The introductory chapter shows that Murdoch's view of Meiji Japan had considerably changed since the time of his initial stay in Tokyo. As has been stated, Murdoch of the early 1890s agreed with the view that the Westernization of Japan was '*une traduction mal faite*', while Volume I of his *History of Japan* published almost two decades later begins with the following sentence:

> The last half-century has witnessed three great constructive efforts in the field of practical politics. Two of these – the Unification of Italy and the Reconstruction of Germany – have been accomplished among peoples constituting an integral part of the Aryan stock and of the Comity of Modern Christendom.[27]

It is therefore not especially difficult for an American or an Englishman to understand the import of the movements. However, in the case of Japan, its development was not easy to explain, as many people still continued to fancy that anything that was not strictly synonymous with Western or so-called Christian culture could not be regarded as civilization. Incidentally, this kind of view was shared by some Japanese intellectuals, not only in the years following the Meiji Restoration of 1868, but also in the years following the defeat of Japan in WWII. That must be the reason why some once highly-reputed Japanese Christian intellectuals of the left-wing are discredited in Japan today; the historian Ōtsuka Hisao's case is a conspicuous example of this fall in reputation.

Murdoch was an agnostic and found historical works previously compiled by French Catholic writers such as Léon Pagès and Charlevoix not suitable as serious history. The fact that Murdoch was free of any missionary bias in writing a history of a non-Christian country seems to be very important. Moreover, born in a peripheral region, Murdoch could sympathize with, and understood better the aspirations of the small nation that Meiji Japan was.

Sometimes one feels almost an unhealthy religious zeal in some North American historians brought up in missionary families. By way of comparison, I would like to cite Murdoch's and E. H. Norman's views on Saigō Takamori. Murdoch admired the Satsuma hero who played a decisive role in the Restoration and who killed himself in 1877, taking responsibility as the head of the Satsuma

Rebellion. Murdoch had early expressed his sympathy in his *Don Juan's Grandson in Japan:* Murdoch was touched by the final scene when the Imperial Forces commander, Kawamura, also a Satsuma samurai, recognized the corpse of Saigō, his former comrade in arms, washed the head and wept over it. The longer Murdoch stayed in Kagoshima, birthplace of Saigō, the more attracted he became to Saigo's character. All the Japanese books Murdoch had collected for his compilation of *A History of Japan* were unfortunately burnt during an American air raid in 1945. However, according to a report[28] made by Matsumoto Mihoko in 1941, the Japanese book most carefully read with numerous underlines in red and blue, with question marks and various annotations, and many paper slips in it, was a book on Saigō Takamori. Murdoch's admiration, as recorded by his students of the Higher School at Kagoshima, was so identical with the Satsuma people's admiration for their great hero that one might doubt if the Scottish historian was critical enough in his use and interpretation of Japanese materials. Perhaps it was his Scottish blood that made him admire Saigō, who had the character and style of a Scottish hero.

The response to Saigō of E. H. Norman was quite different. The Canadian Marxist historian of Japan denounced the Satsuma leader repeatedly, especially in articles written during WWII. For example, Norman portrays Saigō in a review article 'Militarists in the Japanese State' (*Pacific Affairs*. Vol. XVI, No. 4, Dec. 1943, p.474): 'Behind that placid, fleshy face and the protruding frog-like eyes was the mind of a cool and cunning conspirator.' This is an emotional description, indeed. Norman, of course, had never met Saigō; he had never had a chance to see his photography, as it did not exist. The image of Saigō that the Japanese have, and that Norman must have seen in a book, derives either from the posthumous oil-painting by Edoardo Chiossone said to be based on a photograph or from Saigō's statue standing in the Ueno park by Takamura Kōun. Neither the Italian painter nor the Japanese sculptor had chances to see the Satsuma hero in person. 'The protruding frog-like eyes' were, therefore, their invention. I cannot help smiling at Norman's dead seriousness in reviling Saigō's artistically created physical features. Both the Italian and Japanese artists must have thought the facial traits fit for the Satsuma hero. As for an aesthetical evaluation of Saigō's eyes, as it depends on one's taste, one had better go and look at the statue of Saigō-san in the Ueno Park. One thing is certain: so long as one is incapable of understanding sympathetically why the statue is called by the Japanese people 'Saigō-*san*' – *san* pronounced with reverent affection – , one is far from being a good Japan interpreter. It would be the same with foreign experts on the origins of the modern Italian State; if they saw in Garibaldi, the prototype of Fascist wartime leaders, they would be discredited by Italian scholars.

However, as is often the case with Marxist historians, both in Japan and abroad, they condemn political leaders categorically without examining their individual humanity. They presented Japan as seen through spectacles made in Moscow in 1932 based on the Comintern thesis, which was translated by Kawakami Hajime. Norman, who had read books by the so-called *kōza-ha* Communist historians, whose theoretical base was no other than the Comintern thesis, sees *a priori* in Saigō the prototype of Japanese wartime leaders.

Is it not true that serious persons of deeply religious temperament, although emancipated at the surface level, become sometimes unwittingly ethnocentric in their views and judgements of foreign things, believing that they themselves hold universalistic doctrines? God-centred views sometimes turn out to be self-centred prejudices.

However, Murdoch, too, must have been a prejudiced man. Born of a poor family, in a peripheral region of Scotland, he had deep-rooted anti-establishment sentiments. That must be the reason Murdoch sympathized with the socialist Lane. One of the harshest comments ever written was by George Sansom (1883–1965). In the bibliographical note attached to the first edition of his *Japan; a Short Cultural History* (1931), Sansom criticized his predecessor's *History of Japan,* saying that 'he (Murdoch) presented Japan as seen through spectacles made in Aberdeen about 1880'.

Still, Murdoch was free of that condescending attitude so characteristic of many Western diplomats, teachers and missionaries coming to Japan in the nineteenth century. Sōseki knew that Murdoch was a rare exception in this regard, and very much appreciated it. In a letter to his former student Noma, who had become a young colleague of Murdoch's at the Higher School at Kagoshima,[29] Sōseki said: 'How nice it would be if all the British were just like Mr Murdoch!'

Sōseki had a strong feeling of affection for Murdoch, but still could not agree with him when the historian gave high points to the Tokugawa period. In the introductory chapter to Vol. I, after describing seventeenth- and eighteenth-century Europe, Murdoch says:

> During all this time Japan continued to enjoy the unspeakable blessings of profound and all but unruffled peace. Her government was at once despotic and repressive; but it is tolerably safe to maintain that the average individual of the unprivileged classes, constituting at least ninety per cent of the population, enjoyed a greater measure of happiness than fell to the lot of the average unit in the proletariat of Europe down to 1789 at least.[30]

To some Western Japan experts this proposition of Murdoch is so obvious that they may dismiss it as commonplace. However, this proposition is not so obvious to most Japanese who tend to think that before the Meiji Restoration there was a dark age of feudalism under the Tokugawa regime. In this regard, the title of the great historical novel by Shimazaki Tōson *Yoake mae* is indicative. *Yoake mae* deals with the years preceding the Meiji Restoration. The title means *Before the Dawn;* the sun rises with the collapse of the Tokugawa shogunate. Meiji was the era of enlightenment: by contrast, the preceding Tokugawa period was conceived of in many Japanese minds as the dark age. Ordinary Westerners did not doubt for a moment that the light came to Japan with its forced opening and that Perry's expedition was a civilizing mission. In fact, the Japanese of the midnineteenth century were aware that during those two-and-a-half centuries of national isolation the Western world had made tremendous progress: before the Tokugawa shogunate had cut all communications with Catholic Europe in 1637, the greatest European novelty imported into Japan was the telescope, but in 1854 Commodore Perry was able to present the shogunal officials with a miniature train and a telegraph-line; the very presence of the Black Ships in Edo bay represented a formidable material civilization behind them. The defects of the Tokugawa system were obvious to the Americans of the Perry squadron and even to the Japanese. How could they believe in the latent strength that lay deep in Tokugawa Japan?

Murdoch, however, sketched in the introductory chapter the Japanese intellect and the arena in which it was exercised and disciplined under the Tokugawa regime, and tried to gather why the subsequent seemingly marvellous development had been possible. Murdoch enumerated many positive characteristics of Tokugawa society: the Japanese capacity for organization, the social stability, a strong sense of honour shared by the people, a high degree of literacy as well as of numeracy, and so on. The Scottiish historian posed to sceptical readers the following question: could a nation with no real strength in 1853 ever have achieved the brilliant and gigantic feats of 1904–05? The general impression we get from Murdoch's proposition is that he is fundamentally optimistic. He not only admires the modernization of Meiji Japan but also asserts that the real roots of this strength lay in Tokugawa Japan. Murdoch concludes his introduction by saying that in order to explain the meteor-like rise of the Empire in this comparatively short span of forty years he undertook to write a history of Japan from its origins.

Natsume Sōseki was taken aback by what Murdoch stated in the introductory chapter. Sōseki was born in 1867, one year before the Meiji Restoration. He was a typical Meiji man. To him the history of the Meiji era was almost identical with his own history. Sōseki was surprised and disturbed by Murdoch's propositions, and explained his feeling of malaise in the following way in his 16 March 1911 article: as one does not ask oneself how and why one grows up, so Sōseki had not posed the questions of how and why Meiji Japan had grown into such a country. Sōseki also uses a simile to explain the situation. When certain insects change colour in the course of their growth, the insects themselves do not worry about the changes in colour of their bodies or of their wings. It is up to ento-mologists to take an interest in the phenomenon, and Sōseki continues:

> ... the attitude of Mr Murdoch towards us Japanese is just like that. That a nation should in less than two generations leap from a condition of culture analogous to that of the fourteenth century in the West to one fully in line with that of Europe of the twentieth century can hardly cease to be for him a subject of amazement.[31]

Sōseki agrees that in a sense the history of Meiji Japan was a glo-rious one, and he quotes a passage from Murdoch: 'a country which lay powerless before a small squadron of five American vessels won exactly half a century later the greatest sea-fight since Trafalgar.' 'This country,' continues Sōseki, 'enchants and enthralls Mr Murdoch.'[32]

Up to this point Sōseki simply tells readers what kind of views Murdoch holds on the modernization of Japan. Sōseki could have stopped his *Asahi* newspaper article here. However, Sōseki was a man of intellectual integrity. As he did not share the optimistic views of Murdoch, he expressed in the latter half of the article his own views on the modernization of Meiji Japan. Sōseki's argument could be summarized as follows: the Japanese of the Meiji period have no time to look back. They cannot stay even for a moment at the same spot. They are compelled to go forward. When confronted with peoples of superior wealth, superior intellect, superior physical strength and superior moral power, a nation has no more time to look back at its own past. The only concern that nation has is how to catch up with the superior nations.

Sōseki was not a historian. He was a writer of psychological novels. So when he could not accept the optimistic views of Murdoch, he expressed his own views by explaining the troubled psychological state of the Japanese intelligentsia; and the description of this state of mind is one of the main features of his novels. Sōseki in the year 1911 did not and could not believe that 'Japan would one day become as industrialized as Western nations or Japanese trains could run faster than Western trains or Japan could make investments in foreign countries or Japanese research and inventions could be welcomed one day with respect by Westerners.'[33] Sōseki renounced all such optimistic predictions in his *Asahi* article of March 1911. He further developed an argument of the same nature in a well-known speech delivered at Wakayama in August of the same year. As there are so many parallels and so many elements common to both, we may safely say that his speech *Gendai Nihon no kaika* (the Modernization of Japan) was motivated at least in part by his reading of Murdoch's introductory chapter. Sōseki's main theme in that speech is that the development of modern Japan is not spontaneous and that the Japanese are continuously pressed by external forces to run after the West. I would like to quote some passages which are often anthologized and appear frequently in Japanese high school textbooks:

> We Japanese are obliged to do in ten years what Westerners with their superior intellect and superior physical force have done in one hundred years. It is natural and inevitable that we become neurotic, even though we could boast of the results of our progress. We Japanese are always pushed from behind; we have, so to speak, lost our own initiative. This state will continue for ever and ever. We cannot call the development of modern Japan a spontaneous and internally motivated one. So long as we are pushed and pressed by external forces, we cannot be free.[34]

Sōseki must have felt a strong urge to express these discouraging views to the thousands who crowded the Wakayama Legislature building. It was partly because Sōseki had written in the 1 March article that he himself had different views from Murdoch's and that he felt it his obligation to express them. In the *Asahi* article Sōseki said:

... Professor Murdoch admires the present state of Meiji Japan and he therefore is studying the past of our nation. However, I feel obliged to say here that my views on the future of Japan are pessimistic.[35]

Sōseki must have considered the differences: he first elaborated his general theory of evolution and then detailed his views on the modernization of Japan. Sōseki's somber diagnoses of the future of modern civilization and particularly that of Japan were, however, not new. He had repeatedly discussed these problems in many of his novels. An example is found in his novel *And Then (Sorekara)* written in 1909. The protagonist of the story, Daisuke, an intellectual with a good university education, does not intend to work. When asked the reason, he answers:

'Why not? – well, it's not my fault. That is to say, it's the world's fault. Or, to exaggerate a little, it's because the relationship between Japan and the West is no good that I won't work. First of all, there's no other country with such a bad case of beggar's twitch. When do you think all those debts can be paid off? Oh, the foreign currency bonds might get paid. But they aren't the only debts. The point is, Japan can't get along without borrowing from the West. But it poses as a first-class power. And it's straining to join the ranks of the first-class powers. That's why, in every direction, it puts up the facade of a first-class power and cheats on what's behind. It's like the frog that tried to outdo the cow – look, Japan's belly is bursting. And see, the consequences are reflected in each of us as individuals. A people so oppressed by the West have no mental leisure, they can't do anything worthwhile.'[36]

Probably what Daisuke says in the novel is somewhat exaggerated; nontheless the protagonist's opinion here may be interpreted as the opinion held partly by the author Sōseki himself.

Mori Ōgai was five years older than Natsume Sōseki. Ōgai admired Sōseki greatly and found their concerns identical, but he was not that pessimistic about the future. In a short story entitled 'A Strange Mirror' *(Fushigina kagami)* published in 1912, three years after the serialization in the *Asahi* newspaper of Sōseki's *And Then*, Ōgai describes a conversation between a husband and a wife who apparently stand proxy for Mr and Mrs Mori Ōgai. The wife asks her husband:

'Why do you spend so much money on books? You buy Buddhist canonical texts, old historical documents of Japan, and especially many Western books. Why?'

'Yes ... but I can't help it. I am lacking in wisdom; that is why I borrow it from the West. I know that so long as I borrow I can't compete with those who create by themselves, but without it I can't get along.'

'If you borrow so much from the West, can you pay off the debts one day in the future?'

'I don't think it is possible in my generation; I'm not sure if it will be possible for my children's or grandchildren's generation, but after several generations I hope they'll be able to return the borrowings.'

'How casually you talk about it all!'[37]

The tone of the conversation in the Ōgai story is perhaps flippant, but the author of course knew that the topic was extremely serious. There exists, however, a fundamental difference between Sōseki's view and Ōgai's view. While Sōseki did not believe that Japan could pay off its debts, Ōgai believed that Japan could return the borrowings in several generations' time.

Sōseki's approach to the problems of modernization was essentially psychological, and it had its validity. He compared Japan's strained efforts to aggrandize itself to those of the frog that tried to outdo the cow in Aesop's fable. After the strenuous efforts of the Manchurian Incident, the China Incident and the Greater East Asia War, Japan's belly burst in August 1945. When Japan was defeated, Japanese readers of Sōseki were suddenly reminded of Sōseki's pessimistic prophecy, which had been pronounced some forty years before: Professor Hirota, a character in the novel *Sanshirō* written shortly after the Russo-Japanese War of 1904–05, said coolly: 'Japan is going to perish.' It was when the young Sanshirō began to talk about the new developments of victorious Japan that this unexpected answer was given. Sōseki was very conscious of a late-starting nation's psychological troubles. It is indeed symbolic that all the three nations pointed out by Murdoch as having achieved great constructive efforts in the latter half of the nineteenth century, Italy, Germany and Japan, experienced as frustrated late-coming nations the same frog-psychology competing with the cow, and burst their bellies in World War II.

Now the question that arises is whose view of the modernization of Japan was correct? Sōseki's or Ōgai's? Sōseki's or Murdoch's? To the Japanese of the late 1940s and 1950s, Sōseki's view seemed to be to the point. As Murdoch's *History of Japan* has never been translated into Japanese, by that time his name was all but forgotten. Then in 1960 Reischauer and many other American Japan scholars began to talk about the modernization of Japan in rosy terms. One may understand the reaction of many Japanese intellectuals who could not share Reischauer's interpretation at that time. In the 1980s no Japanese industrialists shared Sōseki's pessimistic view concerning the Japanese industrial progress. With hindsight, and especially looking back from the twenty-first century, Sōseki's prophecy was apparently mistaken: Japan has become the second industrial power of the world; Japanese trains run faster than American trains; Japan makes investments in Western countries and a plant is being built by a Japanese firm in Scotland, not far away from Murdoch's native village. Sōseki's prophecy was mistaken at least in material terms. Many Japanese, especially those in government circles, accept Reischauer's view of the modernization of Japan, and modernization series of volumes edited by Marius Jansen and others and published by the Princeton University Press, too, are appreciated in Japan. At the same time, I hope, we will not forget the fact that the rapid pace of modernization under foreign pressure has taken its toll in human psychological terms.

In the beginning of this chapter, I mentioned the name of the Chinese thinker Lu Xun who was very much interested in Sōseki and Ōgai. Lu Xun's greatest concern was the modernization of China. He was particularly sensitive to the retarded state of his fatherland as he was studying in a modernizing Japan at the beginning of the twentieth century. The situation has not much changed: in the 1980s the common concern among East Asian students coming to Japan was this problem of modernization of late-starting nations. From the 1980s the number of students coming from South Korea, continental China and Taiwan to Japan has increased tremendously. It is said that after English, Japanese is the foreign language most widely studied in that part of Asia. These East Asian students are undoubtedly interested in Kawabata and Tanizaki, but I have observed that they are more interested in Sōseki and Ōgai, especially when these two intellectual writers analyse the psychology of modernization in their novels and essays. For example, in Sōseki's *Sanshirō* there is a description of the streets of Tokyo two or three years after the Russo-Japanese War. The capital of Japan is seen through the eyes of a freshman student recently arrived from a provincial town. Tokyo is full of things that startle Sanshirō. For example:

> What startled him most of all was Tokyo itself, for no matter how far he went, it never ended. Everywhere he walked there were piles of lumber, heaps of rock, new homes set back from the street, old warehouses rotting in front of them. Everything looked as though it were being destroyed, and at the same time everything looked as though it were under construction.[38]

Asian students who came to Tokyo in the 1980s, while reading passages such as this, could not help being reminded of their own capitals under construction, Seoul, Beijing or Taipei. Japan was and still is definitely seen as an economic giant by its Asian neighbours. Tokyo, which Japanese intellectuals found ugly and Western residents of the Meiji period considered a clumsy translation of a European capital, has curiously increased in beauty and charm. To many Asian students that arrived in Japan, the first and most important question that occurred to them was: 'Can my country ever catch up with Japan?'

The psychology of modernization is identical everywhere. To Japanese students of the Meiji-Taishō period (1868–1926) the towering colossus was Great Britain. Sōseki lived in London towards the turn of the century when Great Britain was at the zenith of its power and glory. Sōseki suffered under the high pressure. It must be the same with many thoughtful Asian students studying in Japan in the 1980s. Although it may sound paradoxical, to read Sōseki's pessimistic views on the modernization of Japan pronounced in 1911 is a relief for them. At the beginning of the twentieth century, the most revered Japanese intellectual professed the above gloomy view of the future of his country; but the fact that Japan has become such a prosperous and peaceful country belies Sōseki's pessimistic diagnosis. If it is possible for Japan to achieve such a degree of modernization, other Asian nations that share the same work ethic derived from the same Confucian background may also expect a bright future. This is the logical conclusion and hope East Asian students draw from Sōseki's prophecies, which they consider utterly mistaken. In fact, East Asians are regaining self-confidence because of their 'economic miracles'.

East Asian students, of course, appreciate the Chinese cultural background of Ōgai and Sōseki. The sympathy they feel for them comes in part from that; but it is the Asian students' concern for the betterment of their own country that makes possible their more sympathetic understanding of Ōgai and Sōseki. The reading of Mori Ōgai's short story 'Under Reconstruction'(*Fushin-chū*) by a Chinese scholar and that of an established British scholar shows the point clearly. The late Dr Ivan Morris was a scholar who had an excellent understanding of the Japanese mind. Not a few Japanese scholars were moved, reading the final chapter of his *The Nobility of Failure*.[39] However, even Ivan Morris did not grasp the point of Ōgai's 'Under Reconstruction'. Morris comments in a note added to his English translation of the story that 'Ōgai knew Europe so well himself, that he was able,' as in that story, 'to describe the pseudo-Westernization of his own country with such penetration.'[40] I do not think that Ōgai's intention stopped there. Now, the Chinese student who had spent two years of diligent study in Japan wrote to me of his impressions on returning to the People's Republic of China in the early 1980s. He said: 'In the capital of China everything looks as though it were being destroyed, and at the same time everything looks as though it were under reconstruction.' The first Japanese word the Chinese student was reminded of was *'fushin-chū'*, the title of Ōgai's story, 'Under Reconstruction'. The patriotic Chinese scholar did not want to ridicule the present clumsy state of reconstruction, as Ōgai had not wanted to do so in the capital of Japan in 1910. The Chinese student simply acknowledged the backwardness of China and would like to dedicate himself to the task of modernizing his country. It was the same with Ōgai's story 'Under Reconstruction'. The central figure, a Japanese government official, renounces a German lady's love; he remains calm and externally impassive throughout the encounter. He appears almost inhuman. This renunciation resulted from his strong will: the government official feels that he must remain and work in Japan. The appeal of Ōgai's story lies not only in his description of the pseudo-Westernization of Meiji Japan, but also in the cool and responsible attitude of the Japanese government official. My Chinese student was not a literature student but he grasped correctly the most important implication of Ōgai's story which Ivan Morris had missed.

Finally, I would like to refer briefly to Sōseki's relations with Elisseeff. Sōseki welcomed the young Russian student, and Elisseeff's name appears several times in Sōseki's letters and diaries. Elisseeff adapted himself extremely well to Tokyo life: he came to Japan shortly after his graduation from a high school. Komiya Toyotaka, a student of German literature, became his close friend, as Elisseeff's first foreign language was German. Komiya was Sōseki's disciple, editor of his complete works and his first biographer, a sort of Boswell to Natsume Sōseki. He introduced Elisseeff to Sōseki's salon on Thursday 24 June 1909. The haiku *'Samidare ya momodachi takaku kitaru hito'* is said to have been improvised by Sōseki on that rainy evening. Sōseki wrote the haiku on the frontispiece of a copy of *Sanshirō* which Elisseeff had bought and brought with him. While reading the novel, the Russian student had felt as if his own student life was being depicted. In fact, Elisseeff was called by his Japanese friends *kōmō Sanshirō*, red-haired Sanshirō.

Sōseki, who retained feelings of affection towards his foreign teachers, was kind to Elisseeff. He later gave the young Russian scholar a chance to write about Russian literature in the *Asahi* newspaper. After his return home, Elisseeff lectured on Sōseki's literary works in St Petersburg before and during the Russian Revolution. When taken hostage by the Bolsheviki in May 1919, Elisseeff was allowed to bring into prison four books: two were German books and two were Sōseki's works in condensed pocket editions. After several days Serge Elisseeff expected the worst in his prison cell when he heard firing squads shooting. His brother-in-law had been shot. Elisseeff still continued to read Sōseki's works. I have never heard of a Japanese who in similar circumstances chose to read Sōseki. After having succeeded in getting out of Russia, Elisseeff met his former Japanese friends in Paris; in order to earn his living, he wrote in Japanese his recollections of days passed under the Soviet regime. They were serialized in the *Asahi* newspaper and they are available in pocket-book edition under the title of *Sekiro no hito-jichi nikki* (Diary of a Hostage of Red Russia).[41] These stories and adventures of the Russian Revolution told by an eyewitness must have been very revealing to Japanese readers and especially to Elisseeff's friends. The book is also startling for the stylistic quality of its Japanese. I do not know of any other book written in Japanese by a Westerner that has attained such a level. The most startling thing in the book is the psychological self-analysis of the author. Elisseeff describes his state of mind when he was virtually condemned to death. His description of that crucial moment of his life is quite similar in tone to some descriptions of Sōseki's heroes facing death. The fact that Sōseki had such a strong influence on Elisseeff is impressive.

In 1957, when Elisseeff finally left Harvard to spend the rest of his life in Paris, Reischauer wrote a very good article on Elisseeff in *the Harvard Journal of Asiatic Studies,* 1957. The article is accompanied by a long list of Elisseeff's publications, but as his most memorable work in Japanese, *Sekiro no hitojichi nikki,* is missing, I thought it useful to give here a piece of information about the relationship between Sōseki and Elisseeff. I do not think, though, that Elisseeff was very interested in the problems of modernization while teaching at Harvard University.

I would like to add a few final remarks to round off this chapter. After WWII when Japan was in confusion, opinion leaders were obliged to make a choice between two ways that would seem to enable Japan to achieve a more satisfying degree of modernization: one choice was along the liberal democratic line, and the other was socialism. At that time the word 'socialism' had a tremendous appeal to Japanese youth, as it covered a very wide range of options. Some old liberalists, however, made it clear that they would reject any kind of revolutionary socialism which would have recourse to violence. Those old humanists who took a firm anti-Marxist stand were often ridiculed by a smarter and younger generation of social scientists like Maruyama Masao and Shimizu Ikutarō. Among those old liberalists, who had not collaborated with the military during the war and who did not flirt with communism and the Japan Communist Party after the war, were disciples of Natsume Sōseki: Abe Yoshishige (Nōsei), Watsuji Tetsurō, Komiya Toyotaka and others who later gathered together around the not very popular monthly *Kokoro*. Although labelled as reactionaries by the younger leftist generation, those old liberalists had at least a moral backbone, *mōraru bakkubon,* as it is called now in Japanese. The English word, which was originally used by Murdoch in appreciation of Sōseki's character, has entered the Japanese vocabulary. The encounter between Murdoch and Sōseki left an enduring imprint in Japanese intellectual history. If I were asked who was Sōseki's best friend in his younger days, I would answer that it was the *haiku*-poet Masaoka Shiki; if asked who was Sōseki's best teacher, I would answer that it was James Murdoch.

*Notes*

[1]  This is the English version of my article 'Sōseki no shi Mādokku sensei' (Sōseki's teacher Murdoch) that appeared in May 1981 issue of the literary monthly *Shinchō*. It was later published in book form under the same title (Tokyo: Kōdansha gakujutsu-bunko, 1984).

[2]  Natsume Sōseki's recollections of Murdoch are to be found in his serialized *Asahi* newspaper articles of 6, 7, and 8 March 1911: 'Hakushi mondai to Mādokku sensei to yo' (The question of the doctorate and Mr Murdoch and Myself). Sōseki deals with Murdoch's *History of Japan* in his *Asahi* newspaper articles of 16 and March 1911: 'Mādokku sensei no nihon-rekishi' (Mr Murdoch's *History of Japan*). Both articles are included in *Sōseki zenshū,* vol. 20 shinsho-ban (Tokyo: Iwanami, 1957) pp. 225–231 and pp. 232–236. All English translations of the passages quoted from the two articles are mine.

[3]  The writer of the ten-page biography was Robert Young, editor of the *Japan Chronicle*. Young was one of the few intimate friends Murdoch had.

The identity of the writer was revealed by Yamagata Isoh in his article 'James Murdoch, the historian of Japan', in the English language monthly *The Japan Christian Intelligencer,* vol. 1, No. 8, 5 October 1926, p. 324.

[4] See the ten-page biography 'James Murdoch' in James Murdoch: *An History of Japan* (London: Kegan Paul, Trench, Trubner, 1926) vol. III, p. vii.

[5] See 'Hakushi mondai to Mādokku sensei to yo' *Sōseki zenshū,* vol. 20, p. 228.

[6] James Murdoch: *An History of Japan* vol. III, p. viii.

[7] See Yamagata Isoh: 'Nihon no shika Mādokku' in the monthly *Taiyō,* November, 1926, pp. 173.

[8] Dr D.C.Sissons of Department of International Relations, The Australian National University, gave me this additional information, by his letter dated 18 May 1982. At that time Sissons was writing an article 'Australia's First Professor of Japanese James Murdoch (1856–1921).'

[9] Sasaki Yūtarō is Professor Imai Hiroshi's grandfather. About their travel see Imai's article 'Igirisu to watashi' (Britain and Me) in the *Chikuma,* December 1994 issue, pp. 4–7.

[10] James Murdoch: *An History of Japan* vol. III, p. xv.

[11] 'Hakushi mondai to Mādokku sensei to yo' *Sōseki zenshū,* vol. 20, p. 226.

[12] Ibid. p. 227.

[13] See Natsume Sōseki: 'Watakushi no kojin-shugi' in *Sōseki zenshū,* vol. 21, p. 137. The English translation is mine.

[14] The name of William Lane was known in 1889 when he sent a huge sum from Australia to London in support of the dockyard workers who were on strike. Kawakami Hajime (1879–1946), Japan's most influential popularizer of socialism in the Taishō period, mentions Lane's New Australia movement in some detail in his *Binbō monogatari* (1916).

[15] A photocopy of the translated letter is reproduced in Hirakawa Sukehiro: *Sōseki no shi Mādokku sensei* (Sōseki's Teacher, Mr Murdoch), (Tokyo: Kōdansha 1984), p. 51.

[16] James Murdoch: *An History of Japan* vol. III, pp. xii-xiii.

[17] Sōseki's article, 'Japan and England in the Sixteenth Century' originally printed in the Tokyo educational journal *The Museum,* No. I, May 1890, and No.II June 1890, is included in *Sōseki zenshū.* However, this is only a partial reproduction of Sōseki's essay. His original essay remains still unprinted in the Tōhoku University Library. Masaoka Shiki's essay, 'The Comparison of the English and Japanese Civilization in Sixteenth Century' is included in *Shiki zenshū* (Tokyo: Kōdansha, 1977) vol. 9.

[18] Yamagata Isoh, 'James Murdoch, the historian of Japan' p. 328.

[19] James Murdoch: *An History of Japan* vol. III, p. xv.

[20] Yamagata Isoh, 'James Murdoch, the historian of Japan' p. 343.

[21] Yamagata Isoh, 'James Murdoch, the historian of Japan' p. 343.

[22] George Sansom wrote in the bibliographical note attached to the 1931 edition of his *Japan, a Short Cultural History* (London: Cresset), p. 519:

> ... The leading book in English on Japanese history is 'A History of Japan,' in three imposing volumes, by James Murdoch. (Kegan Paul.) It is an important pioneer work. Its style is unpleasant. It is marred by a dreadful facetiousness and a habit of introducing such maddening analogies as a 'Japanese Jerusalem', 'Japanese Agnes of Dunbar', and even 'Japanese Cornishmen'. These faults bring the writer's judgement under suspicion, while it is clear that his aesthetic sense was but feebly developed. It might be said that he presented Japan as seen through spectacles made in Aberdeen about 1880. But it would be hard to rival his immense knowledge and grasp of primary and secondary authorities and his book will remain the standard work for a long time to come. The middle volume, in which he deals with foreign intercourse, is by far the best. He is at home with European personages and European documents.

Sansom dropped this bibliographical note from later editions, and in the address delivered at the Annual Ceremony of the London School of Oriental and African Studies in 1956 (reproduced in the *Journal of Asian Studies*, 1965) Sansom reviewed the achievements of a few British pioneers in Japanese studies, Aston, Satow and Chamberlain, and added:

> I should like to say a word about Murdoch, the historian. He scarcely comes into the category of spare-time, amateur scholars, since he was a teacher by profession. But he did most of the research for his great 3-volume *History of Japan* while teaching for a livelihood. His work remains a monument of learning and industry. Like other pioneers he shows traces of what today we are pleased to regard as old-fashioned delusions about life and letters. But he and his contemporaries cannot be regarded with condescension, any more than great explorers of the past can be rebuked for crossing mountains and deserts without using internal combustion engines – those obsolete things! If I have criticized Murdoch it was for his manner rather than his matter; and even there I think I should have held my tongue. I apologize to his shade and I hope that he is happily pursuing his studies in the Elysian fields, arguing now and then in his own Doric with Rhadamanthus.

Until the end of his life Sansom kept in mind Murdoch's *History of Japan*. As late as February 15, 1962 Sansom in a letter sent to Japanese scholars who were then translating his *Western World and Japan* explained his (Sansom's) intention of writing three volume *History of Japan*. He said:

> My plan differs from that of Murdoch, since his great work is largely a history of the relations of Western countries with Japan, rather than a study of domestic history.

It is clear which volume of Murdoch's *History of Japan* was most appreciated by Sansom.

[23] Yamagata Isoh, 'James Murdoch, the historian of Japan' p. 342.

[24] Yamagata Isoh, 'James Murdoch, the historian of Japan' pp. 340–341.

[25] Takekoshi Yosaburō (Sansa) wrote his book review of Volumes I and II of Murdoch's *History of Japan* in 9 August 1911 issue of the *Nihon Shinbun*. This article 'Jēmuzu Mādokku shi no Nhon-shi' was later

included in Takekoshi, *Sansa bunson.* Takekoshi finds great merit in Murdoch's use of foreign materials in writing a history of Japan, but he practically says nothing about Volume 1.

[26] Ozaki Yukiteru, son of Ozaki Yukio, was sent to Kagoshima in 1905. His reminiscences are printed in *Shichikō omoide-shū, kōhen,* 1963.

[27] James Murdoch: *A History of Japan* (Tokyo: Asiatic Society of Japan, 1910) vol. I, p. 1.

[28] Matsumoto Mihoko's report, 'Mādokku to *Nihon rekishi*' appeared first in the monthly *Gakuen,* August 1941. The most detailed bibliography concerning J. Murdoch is in *Kindai bungaku kenkyū sōsho,* vol. 20, published by Shōwa Joshi Daigaku. Much of the information in this bibliography is taken from Matsumoto's first report.

[29] Murdoch's name was mentioned twice in Sōseki's letters to Noma Mazuna (14 June 1908 and 24 January 1914).

[30] James Murdoch: *A History of Japan* (Tokyo: Asiatic Society of Japan, 1910) vol. I, Introductory Chapter p. 1.

[31] 'Mādokku sensei no nihon-rekishi' (Mr Murdoch's *History of Japan*) in *Sōseki zenshū,* vol. 20 shinsho-ban (Tokyo: Iwanami, 1957) p. 233.

[32] Ibid.

[33] 'Mādokku sensei no nihon-rekishi' p. 235.

[34] For the original text of the summarized passages, see Natsume Sōseki: 'Gendai Nihon no kaika' in *Sōseki zenshū,* vol. 21. pp. 49–52. I am obliged to summarize the passages, as the original speech, taken down in shorthand, is very desultory.

[35] 'Mādokku sensei no nihon-rekishi' pp. 235–236.

[36] Natsume Sōseki: *And Then,* tr Norma Moore Field (Baton Rouge: Louisiana State University, 1978 and Tokyo: University of Tokyo Press) p. 72.

[37] *Ōgai zenshū* (Tokyo: Iwanami shoten, 1972) vol. 10, p. 125. The English translation is Hirakawa's.

[38] Natsume Sōseki: *Sanshirō,* tr. Jay Rubin (Seattle and London: University of Washington Press, 1977) p. 17.

[39] Ivan Morris: *Nobility of Failure* (London: Secker & Warburg, 1975)

[40] 'Under Reconstruction' in Ivan Morris ed.: *Modern Japanese Stories: Anthology* (Tokyo: Tuttle, 1962) p. 37.

[41] Eriseefu: *Sekiro-no hitojichi nikki* (Tokyo: Chūōkōron-sha, 1976).

# PART IV

# FROM WAR TO PEACE

# SIGNALS OF PEACE NOT RECEIVED: PREMIER SUZUKI KANTARŌ'S EFFORTS TO END THE PACIFIC WAR

———————□———————

'They need to make the effort, and
we need to meet them half way.'
JOSEPH C. GREW

One of the rare American biographical dictionaries which mentions the name of Suzuki Kantarō is *Current Biography – 1945,* in which appears the following article:

SUZUKI, KANTARO, BARON
Japanese statesman
    The Japanese Premier who was in office during the last fateful months of Nippon's defeat is Admiral the Baron Kantaro Suzuki ... he was born December 24, 1867. The Japanese Empire was at that time under the rule of the Tokugawa shogunate, hereditary dictatorship of great feudal lords ... Only ten days after Suzuki's birth came the Meiji Restoration ... Thus Suzuki grew up in an essentially feudal society, strictly disciplined and theocratically based; yet one which was in the process of industrialization and material Westernization. The Japanese, who never questioned their own inherent divinity and superior culture, were shocked to learn that the Occident regarded them as backward and inferior; and Suzuki grew up, also, in a nation seeking to prove its greatness by territorial aggrandizement. Suzuki himself, when his views came to be of importance, was a moderate; but, as the New York *Herald Tribune* wrote editorially, 'a moderate in Japan often is a person just as devoted to the idea of conquering the world as anyone in the Empire. The difference between a moderate and

an extremist frequently has been that the extremist believed the Japanese could enslave the world in a year or two, while the moderate was of the opinion that it might take several decades.'

According to Maurice Crain in *Rulers of the World,* Japanese naval officers are drawn from the Samurai and rich merchant classes. Young Suzuki entered the Imperial Naval College at seventeen and began in 1887 forty years of active service. He was 'an up-and-coming naval officer' during the war with the Chinese Empire in 1894–95, which was fought for the ostensible purpose of freeing Korea ... The second war in which he served, against Czarist Russia (1904–05), ended in a naval victory which not only won Japan 'treaty rights' in southern Manchuria and led to the annexation of Korea five years later, but brought the Empire its first recognition as a power in world affairs.

In September 1917, he left the important shore duty to assume command of the training squadron. On one training cruise which took the squadron to the United States in 1918, Suzuki made a speech at a San Francisco reception; he quotes himself as saying, 'The Pacific Ocean is a peaceful ocean, true to its name, which the gods favor for peaceful trade between Japan and the United States ... If the Pacific Ocean should be used for the transportation of armed forces, both Japan and the United States would never escape Heaven's punishment.'

In 1929, the elderly admiral succeeded the famous admiral Togo as Grand Chamberlain (and Privy Councillor), a post in which he was a member of the Imperial household literally and figuratively close to the 'Son of Heaven,' young Emperor Hirohito. *Time* says he 'walked a few respectful paces behind Hirohito at public functions, helped name the Emperor's first-born son (Tsugu-no-miya Akihito). Most important, he served as the door through which the war lords had access to the throne.' ... Suzuki's 'moderate' counsels enraged the Kwantung Army group of 'young officers' bent on quick conquests in Manchuria in 1931; and on February 26, 1936, he was one of the victims of their 'Showa Restoration' mutiny. As *Time* tells the story, 'the Grand Chamberlain had just come through Tokyo's snowy streets from dinner and movies at the United States Embassy – a "happy evening," Ambassador Joseph Grew noted in his diary. The young officers had just come from their barracks, with swords and submachine guns (they succeeded in killing twenty-four venerable dignitaries and the Premier's brother-in-law, whom they mistook for the Premier) ... The Grand Chamberlain, confronted by a hundred wild-eyed soldiers, argued with them for ten minutes. When words failed, he straightened up, commanded, 'Then shoot me!' They did and he crumpled in a pool of blood. The rebels burned incense over his body, saluted, and hurried off. The incense and the salute were premature.' The rebellion had been called off at the Emperor's order, or, as John Gunther reports in *Inside Asia,* the rebels surrendered bloodlessly because they had no positive program, no place to go from there.

In April 1945, on the resignation of Premier General Kuniaki Koiso, the seventy-seven-year old peer was appointed to succeed him. Adding to the rapidly deteriorating war situation which confronted Suzuki, the Soviet government chose that same day to denounce its neutrality pact with Japan. The Empire's military situation was also critical, with every indication that it was about to become worse; a 'mounting series of disasters' had been topped by the American invasion of Okinawa, only three hundred and sixty miles from the home islands. This island in the Ryukyus chain, nearly seven thousand miles from the United States, was only two hours by bomber from Japan, which was already under bombardment by American Superfortresses based in China and the Marianas. *Time* reports that while making up his Cabinet, Suzuki was forced to take shelter from an hour-long air raid.

Suzuki's Cabinet, which contained fewer military men than his predecessor's, was by no means the 'peace cabinet' which some foreign observers expected, and included several 'violently anti-American' ministers. 'While shunting the more reckless but incompetent militarists into the background,' commented the *New York Times,* 'the new Cabinet is really a Cabinet of national concentration formed for the purpose of an even more vigorous prosecution of the war ... (comprising) the Elder Statesmen, the Manchuria gang, and the Navy, big business, the old political parties, the new and supposedly more dynamic "Sure Victory" party, and above all the Court.' Later that month, on the death of the American President, Franklin D. Roosevelt, Suzuki broadcast his 'profound sympathy' for the 'great loss his passing means to the American people'; but he did not bother to congratulate his ally, Reichsführer Adolf Hitler, on the latter's fifty-sixth birthday. In May, as a result of the German and Italian surrender, Suzuki's Cabinet abrogated all treaties with European countries, and in June it asked for and received dictatorial powers. Within another two months, on August 14, 1945, Nippon's crisis, after repeated bombings by American and British planes, the Russian advance in Manchuria, and the climactic dropping of the two atomic bombs, ended in unconditional surrender ...

Admiral Baron Suzuki is a white-haired, heavy-browed old courtier with a 'soup-strainer' mustache. Photographs show him wearing a number of decorations, although not nearly so many as, for instance, Premier General Tojo... He was said to have much influence with the Emperor. As befits a Japanese official, he is a devout worshipper at the shrines of the state religion, Shinto. As Premier Suzuki had an extraordinary official residence, which John Gunther describes in *Inside Asia,* '... it is built on a kind of floating foundation to resist seismic shocks, and is full of bewildering passageways, interior bridges, and rooms within rooms. It contains, too, various devices to impede assassins, including secret exits and bombproof doors; one legend – the Japanese scoff at it but not very convincingly – is that the Prime Minister, if he is in danger at night, can push a button, where-upon he disappears, bed and all, into a steel vault.' These precautions lose much of their comic quality when it is recalled that the post of

Premier of Japan is beset with occupational hazards; that from 1918 to
1936 more than a quarter of the Premiers were murdered ...
References:
*N.Y. Times* p. 1+Ap 6, 1945 *Time* 45:45 Ap 16 1945
*Who's Who in Japan*, 1937

This article was written more than four months after Japan's surrender. The sentiment with which the writer was animated was a
strong animosity against Japan. He projected his wartime images of
the Japanese in this article on Suzuki Kantarō, who played a vital
role in Japan's decision to end the war.

However, since 1945, American understanding of things
Japanese has made such great progress that this article, written by
an ignorant writer for unknowing readers, must seem in many
points ridiculous to American Japan experts today. The description
of the official residence of the Japanese Premier is of course not
true. Indeed, the passage 'loses much of its comic quality' when it
is recalled that the post of President of the United States since John
F. Kennedy is beset with occupational hazards much greater than
those of the Prime Minister of present-day Japan.

The article is apparently a patchwork: it is rather easy to recognize the sources from which the writer assembled various materials.
Apart from the news sources like the New York *Times* and *Time*
mentioned in the references, the writer used directly or indirectly
books such as Joseph Grew's *Ten Years in Japan*, John Gunther's
*Inside Asia*, newspapers such as the New York *Herald Tribune* and
reports of *The Associated Press*. What is regrettable about this biographical article is that its dubious quality reflects the dubious quality
of many reputable American reports on Japanese matters during
the war. *Newsweek* of 16 April 1945, reports the shift in the Tokyo
Government and predicts that the cabinet change will open the way
for peace feelers; but the picture of Suzuki reproduced on the page
is not of Suzuki Kantarō, but of Suzuki Kisaburō, veteran of the
old political parties. Admiral Suzuki was not a professional politician and was not well known abroad. Joseph Grew, who had served
as United States ambassador to Japan 1932–42, and Eugene
Dooman, his trusted Counsellor in the American Embassy until
1940, were rare American State Department officials who could tell
who Suzuki Kantarō really was. On 6 April 1945, the New York
*Times* made the following comment: 'Suzuki had been considered a
"moderate" in pre-war years ... has been looked upon as an oppo-
nent of the extreme Army clique's program of conquest,' and

added: 'Close students of Japan predicted the succeeding Government would be a "moderate" one that might project peace feelers to the United States and its allies.' The problem was what kind of signals Prime Minister Suzuki would send to the United States, and whether the American side would be sensitive enough to pick up his signs.

Many scholars, both Japanese and American, are very interested in the behind-the-scenes history of Japan's efforts to end the war. ('To end the war', of course, is a euphemism; in reality, it means Japan's surrender.) Among American studies on this subject, Robert J. C. Butow's *Japan's Decision to Surrender*[2] is a standard work. The popular writer John Toland described Japan's efforts to seek peace with some new materials which Butow did not use.[3] Yet in these books, Admiral Suzuki's image is not very clear; the Japanese diplomat Kase, too, wrote in the same vein.[4] The decisive role that Suzuki played in Japan's decision to surrender needs to be clarified, otherwise that misunderstanding concerning not only Suzuki but also Japan's decision to surrender continues to distort and confuse both scholarship and foreign policy-making. I would like, therefore, to explain some euphemisms and indirect means of communication which Japanese leaders like Suzuki Kantarō were obliged to use both to the Japanese and to the Americans.

Suzuki's technique was rather difficult for historians to understand. Butow entitled the third chapter of his *Japan's Decision to Surrender* 'Invisible Technique – The Role of Suzuki and the Concept of *Haragei*.' Actually, the signals with which the Prime Minister tried to convey his intentions of peace to the Americans and to the Japanese were not so invisible. Some understood them immediately, but many did not. It is believed, anyway, that in 1945 the American government did not want to react so long as the Japanese government did not define clearly the basis upon which it was prepared to conclude peace. It remains a question whether it was really wise and sensible for the American government to adopt that attitude. Now, to make clear the points of my argument, I would like first to summarize the one hundred and thirty-three days of the Suzuki Cabinet.

On 5 April 1945, after the resignation of the Koiso Cabinet, the senior statesmen were summoned to recommend a successor to the outgoing Prime Minister. The senior statesmen present were six ex-premiers: Konoye, Hiranuma, Hirota, Wakatsuki, Okada and Tōjō. As the outgoing Prime Minister was generally not present, General

Koiso was not there; and this was the first time that Tojo attended such a meeting as an ex-premier. Also present were Kido, Lord Keeper of the Privy Seal, and Suzuki Kantarō, President of the Privy Council (*sūmitsuin gichō*). At the meeting one senior statesman suggested that the alternatives of fighting on or seeking peace should be discussed first, but others argued that that issue was really outside their authority. Their responsibility was to choose Japan's next wartime Prime Minister. Needless to say, everyone present was very much concerned about the alternatives of fighting on or seeking peace, but as it was General Tōjō who proposed the discussion, and it was obvious to everyone that the Army he represented still wanted to fight to the very end, those senior statesmen who were committed to an early termination of the war purposely avoided the discussion. Nevertheless, the senior statesmen supported almost unanimously the nomination of Suzuki, in spite of Tōjō's repeated insistence on a general on the active service list as the Prime Minister. Tōjō proposed Field Marshal Hata. Suzuki himself was very reluctant to accept the post, referring repeatedly to his old age and to his lack of confidence in his ability to undertake the responsibilities of the premiership. Later in the evening, Suzuki tried again to decline the offer, but the Emperor told him:

> I expected that you, Suzuki, would tell me so. I quite understand your mind. But in this grave crisis of the country, there is no one else. I ask you to accept the post against your will.[5]

Under the circumstances Suzuki felt there was nothing he could do but accept the premiership. According to his reminiscences dictated after the War, Suzuki intuitively understood the Emperor's intention: to seize a chance for peace, to terminate the war, though the Emperor and the Premier-designate could not talk about this vital issue at that time.

Suzuki was inexperienced in politics, and the man who helped shape the cabinet was one of the senior statesmen, Okada Keisuke. Admiral Okada was the Prime Minister at the time of the February 26 Incident, in 1936. He survived the assassination attempt that night because his brother-in-law Matsuo was mistaken for him and killed. Okada and Suzuki were of the same generation. It was clear that neither of them liked military fanatics. Okada's son-in-law, Sakomizu Hisatsune, a shrewd bureaucrat in the Ministry of Finance, became Suzuki's chief cabinet secretary. The first thing Suzuki did the next day was to make a visit to the War Ministry to see the outgoing War Minister, Field Marshal Sugiyama. Suzuki told him very politely that the Premier-designate wanted to replace him with General Anami. Sugiyama, after consulting with the chief of the Army General Staff and the Inspector General of Military Education, recommended Anami provided that Suzuki do his utmost

1) to prosecute the war to the end;

2) to unify the Army and the Navy; and

3) to take every necessary measure without hesitation for the prosecution of the war and for the victory in the coming battle on the Main Island of Japan.

Suzuki accepted the conditions without discussion; otherwise it would not have been possible for him to form a Cabinet. He had known General Anami since the time when Anami was an officer in attendance on His Majesty, and the relationship between Suzuki and Anami was going to be the decisive factor in Suzuki's efforts to end the war. The Army had a virtual veto in pre-war Japanese politics, so if the War Minister disagreed on policy and offered his resignation, the entire Japanese Cabinet was obliged to resign. Under such circumstances it would be extremely difficult for a Japanese government to make a decision to surrender. There had never been a surrender in modern Japanese military history. Challenging the taboo was not an easy task, and the relation between the old admiral – Suzuki was seventy-seven years of age – and the young general – Anami was fifty-seven – was extremely delicate and important. Sakomizu, the chief cabinet secretary, later described the relationship between Premier Suzuki and War Minister Anami 'as one in which each man, at the bottom of his heart, understood the other's mind most sympathetically. Neither spoke his true thoughts more frankly because that form of directness is "not the Oriental way". If the political stage is regarded in terms of the drama, both Suzuki and Anami were "consummate actors."' The interviewer Butow added in parenthesis: 'This is *haragei*'. Sakomizu's comments were recorded on 3 May 1949.

Twenty years after Japan's surrender, a Japanese film was an unheard-of hit in the summer of 1965. Older generations of Japanese filled the cinemas. The film, which dealt with the dramatic process of Japan's surrender, was entitled *Japan's Longest Day*, and the role of War Minister Anami was played by Mifune Toshirō. Anami, who rarely lost his temper, had a different character from the image created by Mifune, but Mifune was a top actor so he assumed the role of Anami, who, after having signed the Imperial Rescript of 14 August, Twentieth Year of Shōwa, took his life by committing the ritual suicide of *seppuku*. About Anami's attitude towards the Suzuki Cabinet, I will discuss more later.

The practical side of Japan's efforts to terminate the war was energetically conducted by Foreign Minister Tōgō Shigenori. Tōgō was born in Kagoshima. He was from a family of Korean Japanese. His ancestors came to Japan at the time of Toyotomi Hideyoshi, in the sixteenth century. He married a German, and knew Nazi Germany well enough to oppose the conclusion of the Tripartite Treaty with Germany and Italy. He was also Foreign Minister in the Tōjō Cabinet at the time of Japan's attack on Pearl Harbor. He died in Sugamo Prison in 1950 as an A-class war criminal.

About the nomination of Tōgō to the important post of Foreign Minister, Suzuki gave the following testimony at the International Military Tribunal for the Far East. Suzuki selected Tōgō because he felt that Tōgō, Foreign Minister at the time of Pearl Harbor, 'had been opposed to the war from the very beginning and ... had resigned from the Tōjō Cabinet as a measure of opposition to Tōjō's dictatorial and high-handed policies'. Suzuki added that he considered it his duty to exert himself to bring hostilities to an end and for that reason chose 'a man who was clearly opposed to the war' to become his Foreign Minister.

Butow has used extensively statements offered in testimony before the International Military Tribunal for the Far East. But as most Japanese consider that the tribunal had a dubious legal basis – ; a sort of victors' show of bad taste – it may be better not to take the statements at their face value.[6] Suzuki made the testimony apparently to give a good impression of Tōgō. In fact Suzuki first asked Hirota Kōki to be his Foreign Minister, but Hirota recommended Tōgō instead. Even so, it was still to the considerable credit of the Foreign Ministry that many veterans of the *Gaimushō* were, in April 1945, not war advocates. They were peace advocates in the sense that they wished to have a quick termination of the war. Shigemitsu was a peace advocate, and so was Hirota. Among the important ministers of the Suzuki Cabinet, Tōgō and Yonai, Navy Minister, were outspoken and made every effort to bring the war to a conclusion. Tōgō had support within the Foreign Ministry. Admiral Yonai Mitsumasa was a very popular figure. As Navy Minister in 1939 and as Prime Minister in 1940 he tried, along with his vice-minister Yamamoto Isoroku, to steer Japan away from the Axis.[7]

Although Butow described Tōgō's and Kido's efforts to make peace in detail, he had a somewhat vague image of Suzuki, whom he calls 'enigmatic'. There are also those who consider him either an opportunist or a man of dual personality.[8] This seems to me far from the truth, and I would like to say something in defence of Suzuki Kantarō, explaining the hints with which he tried to communicate his intentions of peace. Communication through hints is an important technique of *haiku*. People like the Japanese who have a common cultural background depend much on this sort of communication method. Let us try to gauge the hidden part of an iceberg when we catch sight of its tiny upper part.

As Suzuki did not speak openly of ending the war to his Cabinet members, it was not clear even to Tōgō that the Premier-designate had in his mind a quick termination of the war. An often-quoted episode concerns the trouble Suzuki had in convincing Tōgō to join the Cabinet. As Tōgō was interested in Suzuki's opinions on Japan's war capabilities, he asked Suzuki a lot of questions when he saw the new Premier on 7 April. Suzuki, at that time not well informed about the nation's war capabilities, answered that he believed that Japan was still able to continue the war for two or three years. Tōgō was afraid that an effort on his part to end the war would not be supported by a Prime Minister who had such an opinion, and he therefore refused to join the Cabinet. However, ex-premier Okada, whom Tōgō asked for advice the following morning, urged him to enter the cabinet to 'enlighten' Suzuki, if his perspective on the war situation differed from Suzuki's. In the afternoon Sakomizu came to see him. The chief cabinet secretary told Tōgō: under the present circumstances it was not possible for the Prime Minister to openly declare that he was going to end the war. The declaration would certainly provoke reactions. 'But please guess his intention'. Tōgō thought that if indeed Suzuki had a similar intention to his own, and if Suzuki was not frank enough to confide it, then Tōgō could not help him in the present difficult situation. Tōgō found Suzuki too reserved and lacking in intimacy – *mizu-kusai* –. The next day, 9 April, during their second meeting Suzuki told Tōgō that he would be free to act in accordance with the opinions he had expressed on the 7th. Suzuki also accepted Tōgō's position with respect to Japan's prospects (that is, that Japan was incapable of fighting war more than one year). Finally, Tōgō accepted the post of Foreign Minister.[9]

One thing should, however, be remembered: all these details

favourable to Tōgō as a peace-advocate – and he really was – are known today because Tōgō was very eager to defend himself at the International Military Tribunal for the Far East. Among the so-called A-class war criminals Tōgō was surely one of those who were extremely resentful of the 'victor's justice'.[10]

Now let us turn to the central figure, Suzuki Kantarō. One thing is certain: Suzuki was a brave man. As a commander of a small destroyer Suzuki sank two Russian battleships in the battle of Tsushima. He was, it seems, not afraid of being killed. What Joseph Grew said about Admiral Suzuki in *Ten Years in Japan*, and which is partly reproduceed in *Current Biography: 1945* quoted above, is essentially true.[11] According to his autobiography[12] on 26 February 1936, Suzuki, after having argued with the rebelling non-commissioned officers, straightened up and said politely, '*O-uchinasai*' ('Shoot me'). The impression given in the latter account is of a calm and courageous person. However, probably because of the February 26 Incident, both Suzuki and Okada were extremely cautious in 1945, since an open endeavour on Suzuki's part to accept an early termination of the war on the enemy's terms would have caused open revolt in the Army and Navy and even among the common people. Suzuki was obliged to say things which he did not always believe. (*Life*'s reporter Carl Mydans in his interview article 'Jap Admiral Hides,' 1 Oct 1945, makes the criticism that 'on the very day of his first peace feeler Suzuki made a speech to the Diet in which he demanded that the people "fight to the end".') Even though the Prime Minister was going to use diplomatic channels in an attempt to end the war, it was still wise and necessary for him to repeat his and the nation's determination to fight on. Moreover, showing one's weaknesses in the course of negotiations should always be avoided. It must be noted also that Suzuki did not know how bad the war situation really was, the day when he assumed the premiership. It was natural for a warrior like Suzuki to broadcast to the nation the following speech:

> The hour is here, my countrymen! Everyone must steel himself for what is to come. It is my personal wish that we all throw ourselves into the fields of combat, and even over my dead body. I will dedicate myself to our Empire's cause.

The speech was translated into English in various ways, but the original expression '*watakushi no shi-kabane o fumikoete ...*' was impressive even to my ears. I was thirteen years old at that time. The speech was written by Kihara Michio. Sakomizu told the Prime

Minister that it was too high-toned, but Suzuki did not find it necessary to change. In this way Suzuki's image as a loyal warrior was impressed on the Japanese nation at large.

If younger generations of navy officers were technicians and engineers, Suzuki's generation was more cultured and well read. Like his friend Akiyama Saneyuki, Suzuki was interested in traditional war strategies of the Japanese. His favourite subject was the tactics of Tokugawa Ieyasu, who, when he was defeated at Mikata-ga-hara by the Takeda army and obliged to retreat into the castle, threw open the gates and cried to the pursuing army: 'If you want to come, come!' Takeda could not understand the gesture, did not enter the castle, and finally withdrew. Ieyasu and his retainers were thus saved.

Suzuki's younger brother was a retired general and Head Priest of Yasukuni Shrine. He was a sort of early peace advocate and privately recommended seeking Soviet mediation for peace. Even though the Japanese government was at that time already in touch with the Soviet government, the Prime Minister told his brother: 'No, it's no good. We have still strength. We'll fight to the bitter end.'

After peace was restored, General Suzuki Takao recollected:

> Though I am an Army man, I am not a person to repeat to my junior colleagues what I have learned from my older brother. I know what I may and may not say. So I found it rather disagreeable that my older brother was so totally unfrank towards me. But later I changed my mind. If he had not been that prudent, he could not have succeeded in restoring peace. I now respect my older brother the more. Yes, I admire him.[13]

Even his brother was completely fooled by the Mikata-ga-hara tactics of the Prime Minister.

More important and more interesting is, however, the process through which other cabinet members somehow began to understand Suzuki's intentions. Navy Minister Yonai could not really tell if Suzuki wanted to end the war even in early June. Butow quoted the following anecdote as an example of unhappy *haragei*. The American scholar's presentation of the story is perhaps a little exaggerated because of his emphasis on contrasts:

> ... while discussing a plan to negotiate peace through the good offices of the Soviet Union, Navy Minister Yonai expressed his doubts to Marquis Kido concerning Suzuki's intentions. Yonai, who belonged to the end-the-war faction, felt that Suzuki fully intended to continue the war. Kido later took the matter up with the Premier who 'laughingly replied that he had the same idea about Yonai.' Kido reports that it was in this way that he discov-

ered the two men were of the same mind, that is, they both wanted to end the war. Kido considered this a piece of good fortune for the accomplishment of the task which lay ahead and managed to allay the doubts Suzuki and Yonai entertained with respect to each other. (Here is an example of what can result when two men use *haragei*, for this seems to be the most likely explanation of the misunderstanding between the Premier and his Navy Minister.)[14]

Toland's version of the episode reads as follows:

In the meantime Kido talked to Admiral Yonai. He was the only one of the four military chiefs the Privy Seal was sure would not betray the peace plan. He asked the admiral to read the proposal. Yonai reacted with his usual caution. 'Of course, very good idea,' he said with restrained enthusiasm, 'but I wonder how the Prime Minister really feels about the war?'
So did Kido.[15]
...
(Later in Kido's office) Suzuki promised to do everything he could to further its aims (that is, an early termination of the war), but like Yonai, he seemed to have some reservations: 'I wonder what Admiral Yonai thinks about all this?' 'Yonai said the same thing about you,' Kido told him. This struck Suzuki as comical, but Kido was perturbed. How was it that at such a critical point in the war neither the Prime Minister nor his Navy Minister knew what the other 'had in his stomach'?[16]

I have a misgiving about the interpretation. It is true that Suzuki was recorded as saying: *Yonai ga mada nakanaka tsuyoi to omotte orimashita-ga, sō desuka.*[17] (How come; I thought that Yonai was still a strong (war) advocate.) But it was impossible for Suzuki to mistake what Yonai 'had in his stomach'. Yonai had been against the Tripartite Treaty and had openly said that the Japanese Navy was not equipped to fight against both the British and American Navies together. Yonai was outspoken and advocated an early peace at a six-minister meeting, 21 May 1945 (Shimomura Hiroshi, *Shūsenki*; Dr Shimomura was a minister in the Suzuki Cabinet). It is difficult to believe that there were doubts concerning Yonai's intentions at this stage of the war. I guess the misinterpretation arises from a misprint of a *dakuten* in the quotation, that is the sound '*ka*' was misprinted as '*ga*'. What Suzuki really told Kido must be: *Yonai ga mada nakanaka tsuyoi to omotte orimashita-ka, sō desuka.* (How come; did even Yonai think that I am still a strong (war) advocate?)

In this case the subject of *tsuyoi* refers to 'I' (Suzuki).[18] It might be that Kido heard wrongly when Suzuki laughingly replied. My supposition is that Suzuki laughed because he was somewhat amused: a Navy man of the same mind like Yonai could have been fooled by his Mikata-ga-hara tactics. Kido could talk a peace plan with Admiral Yonai; then how could Suzuki entertain doubts with respect to Yonai? Suzuki was just extremely cautious.

The Suzuki Cabinet's tentative peace overture through the Soviet Union, counting on their good offices has often been criticized. Pretending to act as requested by the Japanese government, Russia declared war on Japan, breaking the Japanese-Soviet Neutrality Pact, 8 August 1945. To ask for Russian mediation was a sort of face-saving technique, since it was unacceptable for the Japanese military that the Japanese government deal directly with the United States. Some laugh at Suzuki's political naïveté, for Suzuki said at a cabinet meeting in mid-May that Stalin must be a personality comparable to Saigō Takamori. Stalin and Saigō are quite different in character. However, when the Japanese Prime Minister referred to the name of Saigō at that time, I suppose that many present understood what Suzuki had in his mind or 'stomach'. For the Japanese of Suzuki's generation – he was born in 1867 precisely the year of the collapse of the Tokugawa shogunate – , the precedent of a surrender was that of the Tokugawas. The negotiations were between the Tokugawa representative Katsu Yasuyoshi and the Imperial representative Saigō Takamori, and it was precisely due to their efforts that the city of Tokyo was saved from the ravages of a civil war. The historic event was called *Edojō akewatashi,* transfer of Edo Castle, renowned in Japanese history as a 'bloodless' surrender. For some the name of Saigō means the great leader of the Meiji Restoration, for others Saigō is the chief of the Satsuma rebellion in 1877. But for the Tokyo populace Saigō was a great man who practised the way of humanity. That is why a statue of him with his dog was built in Ueno Park two decades after the Satsuma rebellion, to the great amazement of foreigners residing in Japan. It is as if the statue of Chiang Kai-shek were built in the capital of the People's Republic of China.

It may be difficult for Americans to imagine a historical precedent of surrender. The name of Robert E. Lee must have various overtones, but if some day in the future American Cabinet members were obliged to think about a surrender, and if at that meeting the name of General Lee were pronounced by the President, then some would surely think of Lee as the general who terminated the Civil War by signing the document of the surrender.

The reasons why it was difficult for the Japanese to speak about surrender are 1) Japanese did not recognize the legitimacy of battle-field surrender; 2) the death of so many Japanese civilians in Saipan made a strong impression upon the Japanese, and the idea of death to the last man *ichi-oku gyoku-sai* prevailed in Japan in 1945. Perhaps if Americans and Japanese could have arranged a cease-fire at the battle of Saipan and if Japanese civilians' lives had been spared in the Marianas, the Japanese would not have been so ready to commit national suicide towards the end of the war. As the term 'surrender' became taboo, it would not have been prudent for the Japanese Prime Minister to talk openly about it. Sakomizu's explanation that Suzuki did not speak frankly because that form of directness is not 'the Oriental way' is misleading. (In a sense, Suzuki's autobiography is very interesting because he spoke so frankly of many events and especially failures of his life.)

It is common knowledge that compared with Americans, the British use many more hints and suggestions in their daily life. People with a common historical background can easily communicate through allusions. Saigō's name was an example. It is the more true of the Japanese with their homogeneous background: to try to understand what others do not openly dare to say is a Japanese virtue. The development of a popular art like *haiku* poetry is only possible when people share a common cultural heritage. If they know the code, hints are enough. Those who are sensitive catch what seventeen-syllable poems suggest. Of course, there are Japanese less sensitive who do not understand the poetry of *haiku*. This difference between those who understand and those who do not has something to do with their humanity as well as with their knowledge.

Though it is a universal practice to make allusions to classics, I would still like to show an example of indirect communication, which was so vividly recorded in the *Pillow Book of Sei Shōnagon* of a thousand years ago. A lady-in-waiting wrote:

> One day, when the snow lay thick on the ground and it was so cold that the lattices had all been closed, I and the other ladies were sitting with her Majesty, chatting and poking the embers in the brazier.
>
> 'Tell me, Shōnagon,' said the Empress, 'how is the snow on Hsiang-lu peak?'
>
> I told the maid to raise one of the lattices and then rolled up the blind all the way. Her Majesty smiled ...[19]

It was because Shōnagon, as well as the Empress, had remembered the phrase in Po Chü-i's poem, 'Pushing aside the blind, I gaze upon the snow of Hsiang-lu peak ...' that she instantly took the hint.[20]

This may seem to be an otiose digression from the main subject. However, the point is that this kind of sign was important and might be understood among educated Japanese. If I may use more recent academic jargon, Japanese texts tend to be highly inter-textual, constantly saying things by indirection. Not to know the canon is to be culturally illiterate.

Then the question is: what signals did Suzuki send to the Americans who do not share our Oriental culture? The first visible signal Suzuki sent abroad was one week after the formation of the Cabinet. It was on the occasion of the death of President Franklin D. Roosevelt, 12 April 1945. On Sunday, 15 April 1945, readers of the *New York Times* were surprised when they found on page 3 a headline 'JAPANESE PREMIER VOICES "SYMPATHY".' The editor's surprise was clear from the quotation marks. It is unusual for a prime minister of an enemy nation to extend 'sympathy' on such an occasion.[21] I would like to quote the article at length:

JAPANESE PREMIER VOICES 'SYMPATHY'
Suzuki Says Dead President's Leadership Was Responsible for 'Advantageous Position'

Admiral Baron Kantaro Suzuki has extended his 'profound sympathy' to the American people on the death of President Franklin D. Roosevelt, the Japanese Domei agency declared yesterday.

The new Japanese Premier told a Domei correspondent, the English language wireless dispatch to North America said, that 'I must admit Roosevelt's leadership has been very effective and has been responsible for the Americans' advantageous position today,' and added:

'For that reason I can easily understand the great loss his passing means to the American people and my profound sympathy goes to them.'

But Premier Suzuki 'candidly said', the dispatch continued as recorded by the Federal Communications Commission, that 'he did not expect America's war efforts against Japan to change because of Mr. Roosevelt's death,' He continued:

'On Japan's part, too, there will not be any let-up in her determination to continue fighting for the co-prosperity and co-existence of all nations as against Anglo-American power politics and world domination.'

The Domei dispatch declared that the correspondent was 'almost taken aback' by the 'unexpected reaction' of Premier Suzuki to the 'world-shaking event' of Mr. Roosevelt's death, 'but he quickly realized it as not strange coming from a man of large caliber as the new Premier is.' Then the dispatch went on:

'The Premier's expression of profound sympathy for the Americans in their great loss, the Domei representative immediately perceived, was the explanation why Admiral Suzuki, despite his advanced age, had been given the reins of the Japanese Government in an effort to pull the country through the current crisis.'

'The expression, too, was an explanation why he has accepted the post despite his own avowal that he was inexperienced in politics. In other words, he has assumed the post in an effort to contribute his part to the achievement of Japan's war aims and for the welfare of all nations.'

This news dispatch, mentioned in the *Current Biography 1945* article was unfortunately overlooked by Butow and even by the editor of his biography, *Suzuki Kantarō Den*. It was overlooked, because the news was dispatched to foreign countries in English, but was not printed in Japanese. Suzuki's message was not for Japanese but essentially for Americans. The article is, therefore, worth a close analysis. Suzuki was surprisingly frank when he admitted the great leadership of Roosevelt. The contrast with other Japanese press comments was striking. For example, the *Mainichi* says:

> Roosevelt died. It is Heaven's punishment. As the incarnation of American imperialism, he had a cursed influence on the whole of mankind. He used many religious phrases as camouflage, quoting, for instance, the Sermon on the Mount, and he asked a divine protection for the opening of the Second Front; but probably it would be hard to find a greater cynic than him.[22]

It is true that even the jingoistic *Mainichi* newspaper admonished its readers against rejoicing at the news of Roosevelt's death: 'It would not be in keeping with the greatness of the Yamato race.'

Apart from Suzuki's words, the article contains a very suggestive comment by a Japanese Domei correspondent. He told Americans his surprise: he was 'almost taken aback' by the 'unexpected reactions' of Premier Suzuki to Roosevelt's death. What the correspondent of the Japanese news agency expected from Suzuki was some sort of disparaging comment on the enemy nation's deceased President. However, instead of using abusive language Suzuki praised Roosevelt's leadership. Was this just an expression of politeness on the part of a warrior-statesman of the Bushido spirit? Did his gesture have some political meaning? Or did the concerned correspondent give Premier Suzuki's statement some political interpretations of his own? It seems that Furuno Inosuke, the Domei representative, or someone responsible for overseas affairs, perceived intuitively the Prime Minister's intention.[23] When the correspondent wrote that article in English, he tried hard to make Americans understand that Suzuki's expression of 'profound sympathy' had meanings other than simple condolences. Indeed, the correspondent repeatedly added comments suggesting why Suzuki had been chosen and why he accepted the premiership despite his advanced age. The answer to 'why' must have been Japan's ruling élite's willingness to terminate the war. The writer, of course, could not explain this openly, and was obliged to use euphemisms 'Suzuki has assumed the post in an effort to contribute his part to the achievement of Japan's war aims and for the welfare of all the nations.' By the expression 'the welfare of all the nations' he probably meant peace, though it may sound a little different from 'Japan's war aims'. For those who tried to read between the lines, the article was extremely suggestive.

Yet there could be other interpretations for some Americans. During the war many Americans, like many Japanese, became slaves of their own anti-enemy propaganda: the 'sneaky' and 'treacherous' Japanese could not be trusted. The news dispatch might be seen as a usual move in the conduct of psychological warfare.

Suzuki publicly sent a bolder signal to the Japanese as well as to the Americans. On 9 June 1945, the Prime Minister made a speech in the Diet in which he referred to the speech he had made in San Francisco twenty-seven years earlier when he commanded the training squadron. Suzuki inserted the episode against the negative opinions of some Cabinet members. Suzuki said:

> Once in 1918, I navigated to the western coast of the United States as the Commander of the Training Squadron. When I was invited to a welcome reception at San Francisco, I delivered an address concerning a war between Japan and the United States. To mention an outline of the address, I stated that the Japanese people are no lovers of war, but a people that love peace. I explained by mentioning many historical facts. Then, I said that there was no cause for a war between the two countries, and that if there ever were a war, it would be much prolonged and would invite a very foolish result. I said that the Pacific Ocean is a blessing given by Heaven for the intercourse of Japan and the United States, and if the ocean were ever used for transporting troops, both countries would receive heavenly punishment.

This quotation is taken from the English-language newspaper *The Nippon Times,* 10 June 1945. Suzuki hinted that it was now time to make peace. The Cabinet members who were opposed to the insertion of the anecdote understood the Prime Minister's intentions when he ignored their opposition. The only condition Suzuki wished to impose on the Allies was the retention of the Emperor's position. That must be the reason why he insisted on the peace-loving nature of the Emperor:

For many years I served near the Imperial Throne, and I am very deeply impressed by the great concern His Majesty the Emperor has for the peace of the world and the welfare of humanity. I believe that in the whole world there is none who is more deeply interested in world peace and human welfare than His Imperial Majesty the Emperor of Japan.

In the *New York Times* of 10 June 1945, on page 3, the text of the Japanese Premier's address was reported. However, the episode referring to Suzuki's speech in San Francisco was dropped. I do not know if it was the *New York Times,* the Federal Communications Commission, or the Japanese news agency Domei or some other organization which was responsible for the omission. But in any case the peace signal Suzuki sent to the United States was, purposely or accidentally, overlooked by the American side. Even if the signal was received, I wonder if the American government was in the mood to respond favourably to Suzuki's message. According to *On Active Service* by Stimson and Bundy, 'reports of a weakening will to resist and of "feelers" for peace terms ... merely stimulated the American leaders in their desire to press home on *all* Japanese leaders the hopelessness of their cause; this was the nature of war-making.'

Suzuki's speech seemed to make no impression on the American side on the surface level. However, Joseph Grew, who was a personal acquaintance of Suzuki and who went on to exercise considerable influence in the State Department under the Truman administration, no doubt took up the signal of peace Premier Suzuki sent to the Americans. Grew became director of the Office of Far Eastern Affairs on 1 May 1944. On 20 December, when Edward Stettinius succeeded Cordell Hull, Grew was appointed under-secretary of state; and in that capacity he became acting secretary in the critical months of July and August 1945. If the political stage is regarded in terms of drama, both the first act and the last act were played by the same actors: Suzuki Kantarō was Ambassador Grew's guest on the eve of the February 26 Incident in 1936. They appeared again on the political stage in Spring 1945 to end the war.

The only condition Suzuki set was the retention of the Imperial institution (*kokutai*) and we have evidence that American Japan specialists understood that condition. Grew's memoranda as well as an anonymous letter written by an American Japan specialist appearing in the *Washington Post* on 21 July 1945 clearly show that Suzuki's signal was received: the letter made Japan's conditions for surrender known to American readers. It says:

If, as Admiral Suzuki revealed in the Diet, their chief concern is over Japan's future national structure (*Kokutai*), including the Emperor's status after surrender, the way to find out is to ask.[24]

The British diplomat George Sansom's opinion concerning Japan's conditions for surrender is seen from the top secret telegram sent to Washington on 17 July 1945. He states:

> ... should it not be possible for [the Allies] by exercising the positive power of controlling trade and the negative power of withholding Treaties to induce Japan herself to introduce such reforms in her Constitution and the working thereof, as will justify confidence in her future good behaviour?' Might it not be preferable also for the Allies, instead of suspending the Constitutional Powers of the Emperor, to work through those powers ...?[25]

Suzuki's speech provoked a series of stormy reactions within Japan. Right-wing deputies of the Gokoku Dōshi-kai indignantly attacked the Prime Minister for having said 'both countries would receive heavenly punishment'. Cries of 'Down with the Suzuki Cabinet' echoed in the Diet. Some deputies accused Suzuki of *lèse-majesté*. Navy Minister Yonai, disgusted with the turn of events, insisted that the Diet be dissolved. As his proposal was not accepted by other Cabinet members, Yonai suggested his resignation. What surprised Yonai was War Minister Anami's note which he received the next morning: Anami asked Yonai not to resign: 'If the Navy Minister makes up his mind to tender his resignation, the future will be dark. We will not be able to bring the situation under control. It is absolutely necessary that Admiral Yonai remain in the Suzuki Cabinet.'[26]

This was an unexpected statement from the War Minister who was considered a fight-to-the-end advocate. At the bottom of his heart, General Anami considered that the Suzuki Cabinet should be the last wartime cabinet. So even though he voiced strong views in Cabinet meetings, he never tried to topple the Suzuki Cabinet. The relationship between Suzuki and Anami deserves more careful attention.[27] Anami Korechika should be remembered as an example of nobility in failure.

What Suzuki and Tōgō wanted from the Allies was something only slightly removed from unconditional surrender. If a passage such as:

> The occupying forces of the Allies shall be withdrawn from Japan as soon as there has been established a peacefully inclined, responsible government of a character representative of the Japanese people. *This may include a con-*

*stitutional monarchy under the present dynasty*[28] if the peace-loving nations can be convinced of the genuine determination of such a government to follow policies of peace which will render impossible the future development of aggressive militarism in Japan.

had been included in the Cairo Declaration (1 December 1943) or in the Potsdam Declaration (28 July 1945), how much easier it would have been for the Suzuki Cabinet to make the decision of Japan's surrender. It is true that there were allies that found the Potsdam Declaration lenient. But after all it was the United States that played the decisive role in the war against Japan and it was Supreme Commander MacArthur who let the Emperor system continue. Americans could have responded earlier to Japanese wishes. Then Japan might have been spared two atomic bombs and Korea might have remained united. Nevertheless, in 1945 in Washington many people must have thought that it was not the responsibility of Americans to plead with the Japanese to lay down their arms. American thinking was summarized by Butow: 'It was not their responsibility to cajole the children of the land of the gods into acting sensibly. The important thing was to exert maximum force with maximum speed.'

Wartime Japan was consciously or unconsciously equated with Nazi Germany by Americans. Having little knowledge about Japan, many Americans were obliged to understand 'fascist' Japan by analogies, and some of them were under the influence of policies for Germany. Even after the war, the International Military Tribunal for the Far East was set up as an Asian version of the Nuremberg Trial. Perhaps it was an American mistake not to distinguish between war against Nazi Germany and war against Japan. It was surely a greater mistake for the Japanese to make a pact with Hitler's Reich – a political and also a moral mistake, although the organized atrocities committed in Hitler's concentration camps were scarcely known to the Japanese during the war.[29]

I would like to add one more anecdote at the end: at least one German refugee in the United States could not help noticing the difference in German and Japanese attitudes towards the death of President Roosevelt. Thomas Mann (1875–1955) was a political exile, and was living in California. During World War II the German writer collaborated with the Allies by making almost every month a broadcast in German directed to German people. In all, there was a total of fifty-five broadcasts. In his fifty-fourth broadcast, on 19 April 1945, Mann made the following remarks:

German listeners!

A great man is dead, a hero, a man of great statesmanship, a friend and leader of mankind, who brought his country to a new stage of social education, who made her a mature nation, and who dedicated her power to the service of the society of nations, Franklin Delano Roosevelt ...

Nobody could escape the enchantment of his personality. A greater loss mankind could not have suffered in this fateful time, and so mourning for him spread over the world. It is not surprising that his friends and allies appear deeply affected; Churchill, the old warrior, does not feel ashamed of his tears, Stalin also commemorates him... But what do you Germans have to say about the fact that the Prime Minister of the Japanese Empire called the deceased a great leader and has expressed to the American people the condolences of his country for the loss?

That is amazing, isn't it? It is so even for us; for you it must be beyond your understanding. Japan is in a war of life and death with the United States ... Still, there is in the East a sense of gallantry and tact, still a respect for death and greatness. This is the difference.

Germany's whole misery touches one, if one sees how this once world's most cultivated nation behaves to the death of a man who surely was not Germany's enemy, but the most powerful enemy of her destroyers. Dull insults, that was all that the German press knew to bring forward. Then came the ragged horror of a man Hitler, who declared in an order of the day that fate had removed from earth 'the greatest war criminal of history'.

Shame enough, you stupid perpetrator of genocide! ... Your days are numbered; they were when he became your enemy, and still in death he will be dreadful to you.[30]

Suzuki's overtures of peace were seemingly not received by the Americans in spring 1945. The signals were again overlooked by American historians of the Pacific War. However, at least one of Suzuki's hints had some repercussions in the heart of Thomas Mann. It was an honour for the wrinkled old warrior, who was, as predicted by *Time* (16 April 1945), to be the man on whose 'stooped shoulders might well rest the shameful burden of leading Japan to surrender'.

## Notes

[1] This paper was given at the Washington and Southeast Regional Seminar on Japan at the University of Maryland, 8 April 1978. A more detailed Japanese version appeared in the monthly magazine *Shinchō*, November issue of 1978, under the title 'Heiwa no umi to tatakai no umi'. It was published first in hard-cover book form (Tokyo: Shinchōsha, 1983) and later in paperback (Tokyo: Kōdansha gakujutsu-bunko, 1993). As for a Japanese historian's evaluation of my interpretation, see Hayashi Kentarō: *Shōwashi to watashi* (Tokyo: Bungeishunjū, 1992) p. 116. Kobori Keiichirō's

*Saishō Suzuki Kantarō* (Tokyo: Bungeishunjū, 1982) is a detailed study of
the role played by Suzuki at the time of Japan's decision to surrender.
[2] Robert J. C. Butow: *Japan's Decision to Surrender* (Stanford University
Press, 1954).
[3] John Toland: *The Rising Sun – The Decline and Fall of the Japanese Empire*,
(New York: Random House, 1965).
[4] Toshikazu Kase: *Journey to the Missouri* (Yale University Press, 1950).
[5] The Emperor's words were reported by the only witness to the audience,
the Grand Chamberlain Fujita Shōtoku; see *Suzuki Kantaro den* (Tokyo:
Suzuki Kantarō den henshūkai, 1960), p. 184.
[6] The diplomat Kase, who had offered testimonies in favour of A-class
war criminal Tōgō Shigenori, wrote *Journey to the Missouri* apparently in
defence of his boss. Ex-Foreign Minister Tōgō was imprisoned by the
International Military Tribunal for the Far East. It was in order to save
Tōgō that many Japanese of the time attributed credit for ending the war
to the Foreign Minister in the Suzuki cabinet. That must be a reason why
Suzuki's efforts were put in the shade.
[7] Yonai's conversation with Grew, 19 April 1939, is most revealing. Grew
concludes the entry with the affirmative phrase: 'Yonai can be trusted.' See
J. C. Grew: *Ten Years in Japan* (New York: Simon and Schuster, 1944) p. 281.
[8] See Butow: *Japan's Decision to Surrender*, p. 98.
[9] As for Tōgō's acceptance of the post of Foreign Minister, recollections
of ex-premier Okada Keisuke (Okada Sadahiro ed.: *Okada Keisuke Kaikoroku*, Tokyo: Mainichi shinbun-sha, 1977) are very interesting and
suggestive. They corroborate what Butow wrote in *Japan's Decision to
Surrender* (1954), which I summarized in this paragraph. Admiral Okada
was the *éminence grise* of the Suzuki Cabinet. Okada's son-in-law, Sakomizu
Hisatsune, was Cabinet Secretary. More than nine years before, 26
February 1936, when there was an abortive *coup d'état* by ultra-nationalistic
military officers, both Okada, then Prime Minister, and Suzuki Kantarō,
the Grand Chamberlain, had narrowly escaped assassination. It is understandable that they, therefore, were united against the follies of Japanese
militarists.
[10] As for Tōgō Shigenori, see Ushimura Kei: *Beyond the 'Judgment of
Civilization'* (Tokyo: International House of Japan, 2003), especially chapters 3 and 9. The book includes fascinating portraits of many people
associated with the Tokyo Trial, Justice Röling, defence attorney Ben
Bruce Blakeney, defendant General Imamura Hitoshi and writer
Takeyama Michio.
[11] The American Ambassador writes as follows:

> The story of Admiral Suzuki should live in history; Captain Ando, pointing his
> revolver, discussed the situation with him for ten minutes and when the discussion
> faltered, Suzuki asked: 'Have you anything more to say?' Ando replied: 'No, sir,'
> 'Then shoot,' said Suzuki, and Ando fired the three shots. One grazed his skull but
> failed to penetrate the brain, one went through the chest and lungs, and the third

lodged in the leg. The chest wound was the serious one and the Admiral lost so much blood that only blood transfusions could save his life. It looks now as if he might pull through. (Joseph Grew: *Ten Years in Japan*, p. 176).

[12] The most interesting document which sheds light on Suzuki's character is his autobiography, *Suzuki Kantarō jiden*, posthumously published (Tokyo: Ōgiku-kai, 1949) and reprinted (Tokyo: Jijitsūshin-sha, 1968). It was dictated during World War II (from 1939 to August 1944). The hidden part of the iceberg would be better known if students had a look at books of this kind. I much regret that American scholars had not taken the trouble to read it before publishing books such as Butow's *Japan's Decision to Surrender*.

[13] *Suzuki Kantarō den*, p. 317. The translation is mine.

[14] Butow: *Japan's Decision to Surrender*, p. 72, n.50.

[15] John Toland: *The Rising Sun – The Decline and Fall of the Japanese Empire*, p. 845.

[16] Ibid., p. 846.

[17] *Kido hikokunin sensei kyōjutsu sho*, #292.

[18] Shimomura Kainan took for granted this interpretation. See Shimomura Kainan (Hiroshi): *Shūsen hishi* (Tokyo: Kōdansha, 1950) p. 45.

[19] *The Pillow Book of Sei Shōnagon,* tr. Ivan Morris (Penguin Classics) p. 241.

[20] As to Po Chü-i (Bai Ju-yi, 772–846) and especially his poetical influence in Japan, see the chapter 'Chinese Culture and Japanese Identity'.

[21] A newspaper of a neutral country, the Swiss *Basler Nachrichten,* paid deep respects to Japanese Prime Minister Suzuki for his courteous manner. See its editorial written by Oeri, 15 April 1945.

[22] *Mainichi shinbun*, 14 April 1945, The English translation is mine.

[23] The Domei correspondent remains unidentified.

[24] The anonymous letter was written by Ellis Zacharias. See his *Secret Missions* (G. P. Putnam's Sons, 1946). This book has some credibility problems, but no one can deny the fact that Suzuki's intention was well understood by the American side. The letter is an irrefutable evidence.

[25] Sansom's view was not reflected in the final draft of the Potsdam Declaration, as it omitted explicit guarantees about the Emperor's future. See Ian Nish: 'G.B.Sansom and His Tokyo Friends' (*Transactions of the Asiatic Society of Japan*, vol. 14, 1999, pp. 95–96).

[26] As to Anami's attitude towards Yonai see Shimomura Kainan: *Shūsen hishi*, p. 43.

[27] Anami's farewell call on Suzuki after the last cabinet meeting on 14 August 1945, is the more moving for those who understand that Anami was taking leave of the Prime Minister as well as of this world. Sakomizu recollects in his *Kikan-jū ka no shushō kantei* (Tokyo: Kōbunsha, 1964): 'Every time I go to visit General Anami's tomb in Tama cemetery, I feel grateful to his courage which transcends life or death, and I feel even an impetus to embrace the small tombstone.'

[28] This is the unpublished, deleted phrase of the draft prepared by Grew in late spring 1945. For the draft declaration by the heads of state, see Grew: *Turbulent Era* vol. II, p. 1433.

[29] It was when the *Diary of Anne Frank* was translated and when Takeyama Michio began to write extensively on totalitarianism of all kinds in the 1950s that the atrocities of Nazi gas chambers became widely known in Japan. Takeyama Michio: 'Mōsō to sono gisei' in *Yōroppa no tabi* (Tokyo: Shinchō-sha, 1957) was the first informative book. See also *Tsurugi to jūjika, Takeyama Michio chosakushū* (Tokyo: Fukutake shoten, 1983) vol. 5.

[30] Thomas Mann: *Deutsche Hörer* p. 285 and also Thomas Mann: *Gesammelte Werke XI* (Frankfurt am Main: S.Fischer Verlag, 1960, pp. 1119–1120. Mann talked about Suzuki Kantarō's 'Sinn für Ritterlichkeit und Menschenanstand, noch Ehrfurcht vor dem Tod und der Grösse.' The English translation is mine.

# R.H. BLYTH AND HIROHITO'S DENIAL OF THE 'DIVINE' NATURE OF THE JAPANESE EMPEROR[1]

————□————

The topic I would like to discuss here is certain initiatives taken by the Japanese side, especially by admirals of the older generation, in that decisive year 1945 – initiatives to safeguard the position of the Emperor, which have hitherto been ignored by Western historians as well as by most Japanese writers. I will focus my attention on Hirohito's so-called denial of the 'divine' nature of the Japanese Emperor proclaimed on 1 January 1946; an Englishman, R. H. Blyth, was involved in this historical event, journalistically known as *'Tenno no ningen-sengen'*. In the preceding chapter, I focused on Admiral Suzuki Kantarō's initiative to end the Pacific War: the only condition proposed by the Suzuki Cabinet concerning Japan's surrender was that it would not affect the position of the Imperial House. Let us have a look at how it was possible for the Imperial Dynasty to survive after the defeat of the Japanese Empire. I do not think we should ignore the personal initiatives of some wise men, among whom I count also an Englishman.

Japan has been home to a number of British eccentrics. Lafcadio Hearn was an early example. Reginald Horace Blyth (1898–1964), whom Mrs Elizabeth Vining called 'a kind of modern Lafcadio Hearn'[2] might be counted as another example. Blyth is generally known for his four-volume *haiku* studies and some other books on *Senryū* and *Zen*,[3] but here I would like to shed light on the part Blyth played almost unwittingly in that decisive year 1945: that is, how Blyth was instrumental in bringing about the historical statement made by Emperor Hirohito on 1 January 1946.

In this Imperial Rescript His Majesty Emperor Hirohito is said to have denied the divine nature of the Japanese Emperor. The following is the complete text of the official English translation:

In greeting the New Year, We recall to mind that Emperor Meiji proclaimed, as the basis of our national policy, the Five Clauses of the Charter Oath at the beginning of the Meiji Era. The Charter Oath signified:

1. Deliberative assemblies shall be established and all measures of government decided in accordance with public opinion.

2. All classes, high and low, shall unite in vigorously carrying on the affairs of State.

3. All common people, no less than the civil and military officials, shall be allowed to fulfil their just desires, so that there may not be any discontent among them.

4. All the absurd usages of old shall be broken through, and equity and justice to be found in the workings of nature shall serve as the basis of action.

5. Wisdom and knowledge shall be sought throughout the world for the purpose of promoting the welfare of the Empire.

The proclamation is evident in significance and high in its ideals. We wish to make this oath anew and restore the country to stand on its own feet again. We have to reaffirm the principles embodied in the Charter, and proceed unflinchingly towards elimination of misguided practices of the past, and keeping in close touch with the desires of the people, we will construct a new Japan through thoroughly being pacific, the officials and the people alike, attaining rich culture, and advancing the standard of living of the people.

The devastation of war inflicted upon our cities, the miseries of the destitute, the stagnation of trade, shortage of food, and the great and growing number of the unemployed are indeed heart-rending. But if the nation is firmly united in its resolve to face the present ordeal and to seek civilization consistently in peace, a bright future will undoubtedly be ours, not only for our country, but for the whole humanity.

Love of the family and love of the country are especially strong in this country. With more of this devotion should we now work towards love of mankind.

We feel deeply concerned to note that consequent upon the protracted war ending in our defeat, our people are liable to grow restless and to fall into the Slough of Despond. Radical tendencies in excess are gradually spreading and the sense of morality tends to lose its hold on the people, with the result that there are signs of confusion of thoughts.

We stand by the people and We wish always to share with them in their moments of joys and sorrows. The ties between Us and Our people have always stood upon mutual trust and affection. They do not depend upon mere legends and myths. They are not predicated on the false conception that the Emperor is divine, and that the Japanese people are superior to other races and fated to rule the world.

Our Government should make every effort to alleviate their trials and tribulations. At the same time, We trust that the people will rise to the occasion, and will strive courageously for the solution of their outstanding difficulties, and for the development of industry and culture. Acting upon a consciousness of solidarity and of mutual aid and broad tolerance in their civic life, they will prove themselves worthy of their best tradition. By their supreme endeavours in that direction, they will be able to render their substantial contribution to the welfare and advancement of mankind.

The resolution for the year should be made at the beginning of the year. We expect Our people to join Us in all exertions looking to the accomplishment of this great undertaking with an indomitable spirit.[4]

The question I would like to raise is who the real author of this Imperial Rescript was. Opinions generally shared by writers such as Mark Gayn, John Gunther, Frank Gibney and Leonard Mosley were unanimous that the Imperial Rescript was issued under the pressure of the Supreme Commander for the Allied Powers (SCAP), General Douglas MacArthur. This opinion has equally been shared, almost automatically, by many Japanese historians as well. Sodei Rinjirō's *Makkāsā no Nisen-nichi* (MacArthur's Two Thousand Days) published as late as 1976 still followed uncritically that interpretation. Apart from these popular books, there are two specific studies written in English, which touch upon the question of Hirohito's 'Declaration of Humanity'; one is by Wilhelmus H. M. Creemers: *Shrine Shinto After World War II* (Leiden: E. J. Brill, 1968) and the other by William P. Woodard: *The Allied Occupation of Japan 1945–1952 and Japanese Religions* (Leiden: E. J. Brill, 1972). In both studies, the authors point out the role played by R. H. Blyth, but on the assumption that from November 1945 'Blyth was the agent through whom liaison with the Imperial Household (and the Civil Information and Education Section of SCAP) was maintained' (Creemers, p. 129; a similar view is repeated by Woodard, p. 259). As this assumption gives a misleading impression, I would like to clarify the part of the Japanese initiative taken by Admiral Yamanashi Katsunoshin and the part played by Reginald Horace Blyth.

However, before going into details, let me make a general observation: the tendency among Westerners has been to understand Imperial Japan through analogies. During and immediately after World War II, Japan was often understood as an Oriental version of

Nazi Germany. As there was the Nuremburg Trial for German criminals, so there was the Tokyo Trial for Japanese war criminals. Yet, there were differences between Nazi Germany and Imperial Japan, and it was mainly Germans living outside Germany who perceived these differences.[5] A passage I have quoted from the German writer, Thomas Mann's *Deutsche Hörer* in the previous chapter dealing with Japan's decision to surrender serves as an example.

As is well known, the Japanese Government accepted the Potsdam Declaration 'with the understanding that the said declaration does not comprise any demand which prejudices the prerogatives of His Majesty as a Sovereign Ruler'. In his answer, Secretary of State Byrnes did not give any specific guarantee, so even though the war ended on 14 August 1945, anxiety remained about the future of the Imperial House: the Japanese were not sure if they could retain a constitutional monarchy under the present dynasty. For the Japanese nation at large the war ended in August 1945, but for the Imperial Household it did not end at all. On 2 December 1945, Prince Nashimoto Morimasa was arrested as a war criminal. There was a possibility that Emperor Hirohito himself would be indicted as the Number One war criminal. Under these circumstances, it was natural that some Japanese would take a discreet initiative to defend the Imperial institution by giving it a more appropriate definition – one that would not contradict MacArthur's policy concerning the occupation of Japan.

The greatest difference between Nazi Germany and Imperial Japan in 1945 lies in their manner of surrender. The Japanese Government was able to decide Japan's surrender, in spite of the fanatic opposition of the Army and the fight-to-the-end advocates, whereas Nazi Germany could not. Premier Suzuki, Navy Minister Yonai, Foreign Minister Tōgō and Emperor Hirohito were the leading actors that enabled Japan to stop fighting before Japan itself became a battlefield. The Japanese people were grateful for this, and as it was the broadcast of the Emperor that stopped the war, they were grateful to the Emperor and supported a constitutional monarchy even after Japan's defeat. The Supreme Commander for Allied Powers was, of course, aware of this Japanese sentiment, and that quite a high percentage of the Japanese population supported the constitutional monarchy. MacArthur must have thought that in order to make the occupation of Japan a success, he could not make the majority of the Japanese people hostile towards the occupation forces, and the Supreme Commander did not want Hirohito to be indicted as a war criminal. All the same he must have felt that something had to be done to eliminate any possibility of abuse of Emperor worship by the Japanese. Under these circumstances a Japanese initiative taken towards the middle of December 1945 to redefine correctly the essential nature of the Japanese Emperor must have met with a hearty welcome by MacArthur.

The important point to note is that the initiative was taken by the Japanese side. If the Japanese Emperor's 'Renunciation of Divinity' had been imposed by the Allied Powers, Japanese right-wingers might one day try to restore the position of the Emperor to that of pre-war days. Thus, the question who really wrote the Imperial Rescript has still some relevance today.

The Japanese initiatives have been ignored by most historians for several reasons. In the case of Suzuki Kantarō, his efforts to end the war were ignored mainly because of the International Military Tribunal for the Far East (the so-called Tokyo Trial). Ex-premier Suzuki was not indicted as a war criminal, but Foreign Minister of the Suzuki cabinet, Tōgō Shigenori, was indicted as an A-class war criminal for having been Foreign Minister in the Tōjō cabinet when Japan declared war against the United States and Great Britain on 8 December 1941. In order to defend Tōgō at the Tokyo Trial, Japanese witnesses tried hard to show the former Foreign Minister in a favourable light. Thus, throughout the Tokyo Trial, Tōgō was depicted as the strongest peace advocate in the Suzuki cabinet. This is the main reason why Suzuki Kantarō became such an enigmatic figure. Admiral Suzuki himself did not talk at all about his own initiatives. So the fact that Premier Suzuki voiced sympathy on the death of President Roosevelt was not mentioned even in the Japanese biography of Suzuki Kantarō (*Suzuki Kantarō den, 1960*).[6] American historians who depend so much on the documents compiled through the two-and-a-half-year long Tokyo Trial inevitably ignore many of Suzuki's unexpected initiatives and bold decisions. Moreover, during the seven years of the Occupation there developed a strange alliance between the Americans condemning the militaristic Japan of the 1930s and Japanese left-wing intellectuals condemning the feudalistic nature of pre-war Japan. Together they formed the so-called '*Tokyo saiban shikan*' or historical viewpoints established by the authority of the Tokyo Trial. One of the characteristics of these viewpoints is that all Japanese generals and admirals were bad guys and that they could not have made any pos-

itive contributions to peace.[7] Fortunately, however, Admiral Suzuki
Kantarō's reputation has been restored, at least within Japan.

Now I would like to explain some behind-the-scenes negotiations concerning the so-called 'Declaration of Humanity of the
Emperor'. The Japanese initiative was taken by Admiral Yamanashi
Katsunoshin[8] on behalf of the Imperial Household and R. H. Blyth
played a curious role in it. The first inside report about this Imperial
Rescript of 1 January 1946 was written by the reporter Tōgashi Junji
in the 10 January 1960 issue of the weekly *Sandei Mainichi* (Sunday
Mainichi). In an article entitled 'Tennō kakute ningen to naru' (Thus
the Emperor became a human being), he revealed the names of all
the Japanese involved in that event. According to Tōgashi, who had
had a long career as a reporter specializing in Court affairs, the principal figure was former Admiral Yamanashi Katsunoshin
(1877–1967). Yamanashi was Navy Vice-minister in 1930 when
Great Britain, the United States and Japan concluded the treaty at
the London Naval Disarmament Conference. Yamanashi was energetically in favour of the treaty and because of his assiduous efforts,
he later was obliged to retire from the Navy in 1933. The Emperor,
too, was in favour of the conclusion of that treaty, as well as
Admiral Suzuki Kantarō, his Grand Chamberlain. In 1939, when
the Crown Prince Akihito entered the primary section of the Peers'
School (Gakushūin), Yamanashi was nominated principal of the
School on the recommendation of Matsudaira Tsuneo, Minister of
the Imperial Household, who had known Yamanashi since the time
of the Washington Conference. Appreciated highly for his character and wisdom, Yamanashi, therefore, was now in charge of the
education of the Crown Prince, 'There is a tide in the affairs of
men,' Yamanashi muttered when he moved to the official residence
of the principal of the Peers' School.

In the autumn of 1945, Yamanashi must have thought a great
deal about the future of the Crown Prince and the Imperial House.
He, of course, remembered the abuses of Emperor worship
exploited by right-wing officers and civilians at the time of the
London Conference. Therefore, when Yamanashi hired Blyth as a
teacher of English for the Peers School in November 1945 and
when he heard from Blyth that Blyth had some friends in the CIE
(Civil Information and Education) section of the General
Headquarters, Yamanashi had Blyth ask for the opinions of his
American friends about the desirability of a statement in which the
Japanese Emperor would deny his 'divine' nature. Informed of

Yamanashi's initiative, the Emperor himself was in favour of the idea as he himself had been a victim of the excessive Emperor worship of some of his subjects. In Japan, in the late 1930s and early 1940s many acts had been committed in the name of the Emperor against the will of Emperor Hirohito himself. Towards the end of the year 1945, the *Mainichi* reporter Tōgashi followed almost all the moves of the Japanese officials quite well. However, in one thing the veteran reporter specializing in Court affairs was mistaken. He assumed quite naturally that pressure had come from SCAP and mistook Blyth for an American agent. Hence Tōgashi's mistaken guess that the section chief of CIE, General Dyke, had requested Dr Henderson to secure Blyth's help and so on. Yet Blyth could not have been the agent through whom Americans maintained liaison with the Imperial Household from as early as November 1945.

Reginald Horace Blyth was born in Essex in 1898 and died in Tokyo in 1964.[9] During World War I, Blyth was a conscientious objector. He then became a student of English literature under William Ker at London University. He went to Keijō Imperial University (known since 1945 as Seoul National University) in Korea as a lecturer in 1927. In 1935, he was divorced from his British wife and later married Tomiko, a Japanese woman. In 1940, they moved to Kanazawa, where Blyth taught at the Fourth Higher School. During World War II, while interned near Kobe, Blyth wrote his *haiku* books. In 1942, although Japan was at war with Great Britain, the Hokuseidō Press published Blyth's first book *Zen in English Literature and Oriental Classics*.[10] After Japan's surrender, Blyth moved to Tokyo, and like most Westerners living in Japan at that time tried to find a job at General MacArthur's General Headquarters. In November, Blyth met there Lieutenant Colonel Harold G. Henderson of the U.S. Army, whose small book on *haiku*, *Bamboo Broom* (1933) Blyth had praised as 'a little masterpiece' in his *Zen in English Literature and Oriental Classics*. Henderson, of course, was flattered and he, in fact, found a job for Blyth in the General Headquarters, but Blyth declined it, as he had found employment as an English teacher at the Gakushūin (Peers' School). However, as Henderson and Blyth shared a common interest in Japanese *haiku,* Blyth came to see Henderson quite often at the CIE section of the General Headquarters. In 1958, when Henderson published *An Introduction to Haiku* (Doubleday Anchor Books) he expressed his thanks to Blyth, because he owed so much to Blyth's monumental four-volume work on *haiku,* and added: 'my personal contacts [with Mr Blyth] have been most stimulating even outside the *haiku* world'. At that time Henderson still could not talk openly, but let us examine what kind of contacts Blyth and Henderson had had in the last two months of 1945.

It was in November, 1945 that Blyth, upon the recommendation of Suzuki Daisetz[11] and Saitō Takeshi, an eminent professor in the English Literature Department of Tokyo University, went to meet Yamanashi, principal of the Peers' School, Gakushūin. Blyth was accepted, and it was arranged that Blyth's teaching at Gakushūin should begin on 1 December 1945, with the annual pay of 6000 yen. Yamanashi, who was very good at English, must have conversed with Blyth on many topics. Blyth was to give lessons in English to the Crown Prince, too. It was natural, then, that Yamanashi and Blyth talked about the future of the Imperial House, even though they met for the first time. They got on extremely well. Blyth was of the opinion that there was a misunderstanding concerning the 'divine' nature of the Japanese Emperor.[12] When Yamanashi learned that Blyth had a friend in the CIE section of SCAP, Yamanashi naturally tried to gather information through Blyth. On his own initiative Yamanashi had Blyth ask for Dyke's or Henderson's opinions concerning the desirability of proclaiming a new Imperial Rescript. Yamanashi, after listening to Blyth, got in touch with Prime Minister Shidehara and Imperial Household Minister Ishiwata Sōtarō (1891–1950). Ishiwata did not like the idea of a new Imperial Rescript in which the Emperor would deny his 'divine' nature,[13] but Emperor Hirohito, informed of the idea through another high official of the Court, approved of the idea. Ishiwata, then, began to collaborate with Yamanashi, and they let Blyth go back to CIE. Henderson in a statement drafted late in 1946 recalled his contacts with Blyth as follows:

> ... Next week – early December – Mr Blyth came back with the announcement that the Emperor was not only willing but anxious to renounce his 'divinity' as soon as possible; that he did not believe in it himself; that he knew what evil uses had been made of the idea by the militarists; that he wished to prevent the possibility of this happening again; but that neither he nor his advisors knew how to do it. Could I make a suggestion?
>
> As General Dyke was away at the time, I suggested waiting till the next day before giving an answer, but was told that the time was too short – would I not at least give some personal and wholly unofficial suggestion. I promised to do so, went back to the Dai-ichi hotel, and during the lunch-hour concocted a formula intended to be perfectly clear and yet not impossibly derogatory to the Imperial dignity. At 1:30 I gave it to Mr. Blyth and he departed.

The next day Mr. Blyth arrived with a copy of the essential part of the proposed rescript, which turned out to be my formula (the part beginning: 'The ties which bind Us and Our people...') with the change of only one word. This we took in to General Dyke, who considered it, approved of it, and undertook to get General MacArthur's views.

After, it was out of my hands, except that word of General MacArthur's approval was transmitted through me to Mr. Blyth and so back to the Imperial Household.[14]

That draft was most probably a draft written in English by Blyth[15] after a consultation with Yamanashi. It begins with the phrase:

This is a New Year, a New Year for Japan, a new world with new ideals, with Humanity above nationality as the Great Goal.

and contains the part:

The ties between Us and Our people have always stood upon mutual trust and affection. They do not depend upon mere legends and myths. They are not predicated on the false conception that the Emperor is divine, and that the Japanese people are superior to other races and fated to rule the world.

and ends with the phrase:

His Majesty disavows entirely any deification or mythologizing of his own Person.

According to his detailed account appeared in the March, 1962 issue of the monthly *Bungei shunjū*, the Japanese version of the Imperial Rescript was written by Education Minister, Maeda Tamon,[16] who inserted the part 'The ties between Us and Our people ...' together with some ideas of his own. The reference to the Charter Oath was Hirohito's idea. Maeda already remarked it in his *Bungei shunjū* article, and as late as in 1977 in his interview with journalists Emperor Hirohito insisted that the most important aim of the Rescript was to put in the Five Clauses of the Charter Oath and that the question of his 'divine' character came only second.

The official Japanese version (Maeda's draft) was rendered into English most probably by Premier Shidehara himself, as he was remarkably fluent in English. Yamanashi who arranged the whole matter later recalled: 'It would have been nonsensical if the Americans had dictated our Imperial Rescript, but it would have been equally nonsensical, if the Americans had not agreed with the contents of the Rescript.'[17] Yamanashi had checked American reactions beforehand through the good offices of R. H. Blyth. In Woodard's book an interesting episode is quoted: A year later, in recalling these events, Henderson reflected that it could hardly have been thought at that time that the Emperor was 'prepared to formally renouce his alleged "divinity"'. Henderson had not expected that such a denial would be made, even though he gave a written suggestion to Blyth.

> The next day, something happened that seemed 'very silly', at least as far as Henderson was concerned. Blyth appeared with the yellow sheet of paper on which Henderson had written his suggestions and said that the palace officials wanted it burned in his (Blyth's) presence and this was 'solemnly' done there in the office.[18]

Woodard then describes in a footnote a scene from his interview with the 88-year old admiral that took place some twenty years later in 1965:

> Yamanashi was ordinarily very deaf and the interviewer found it difficult at times to make him understand. At this point, however, he interrupted the author with a sharp, 'Do you have that paper?' 'No,' was the reply. 'You asked them to burn it,' at which Yamanashi seemed very much relieved. It was very evident from Yamanashi's reaction that he knew all about the paper and thus he had unwittingly verified the fact of its existence. [19]

Yamanashi's reaction verified also the depth of responsibility and love he had for the Imperial House and his countrymen. Moreover, Yamanashi knew to see affairs from without as well as from within. He quickly understood the point of view of SCAP. Thus, he won the trust of those who shared his noble concern. The relationship between Emperor Hirohito and Yamanashi should be mentioned in this connection. It is said that His Majesty Emperor Hirohito is a very discreet person. For example, he likes sumō matches very much. He of course has his favorite sumō wrestlers, but he never mentions the names of the wrestlers he likes. He always refrains from mentioning any particular names. However, several years after WWII, when asked by Nagayo Yoshirō and other writers and scholars who later gathered around the monthly *Kokoro*, in whom his Majesty had put the greatest confidence in the turbulent years of the Shōwa era, the Emperor at once answered: 'Yamanashi Katsunoshin'.[20]

Blyth respected Yamanashi very much and often said to his friends and students: 'If Yamanashi were Japan's Prime Minister and if Suzuki Daisetz were Japan's Archbishop, Japan would be a much better country.'

It is indeed a great pleasure for the present writer to give a paper about Blyth, who was my teacher of English at Tokyo University, and about peace-loving admirals. I should add that Suzuki Kantarō (1867–1948) and Yamanashi Katsunoshin (1877–1967) were the finest products of the Japanese Navy when the Japanese Navy was under strong British influence. Yamanashi was twenty-three years old when he came over to England in 1900 to receive the battleship *Mikasa*, built at a shipyard in Barrow.

Before ending I would like to raise one more question about the renunciation of the alleged divinity of the Japanese Emperor. Has Hirohito ever been a God-Emperor to the Japanese? I do not think that he has. At the beginning of this chapter I said: to try to understand Japan through analogy is often misleading. The English expression 'God-Emperor' is itself a Christian analogy. The Shinto notion of *kami* and the Christian notion of God are different.[21] Although there was strong Emperor worship in wartime Japan, the Japanese did not believe that the Emperor was divine in the Judeo-Christian meaning of the word 'God'. In the Imperial Rescript of 1 January 1946 there is a famous passage: 'the false conception that the Emperor is divine'. Who held that false conception? Wartime Japanese? Or wartime Americans? To answer the question, I would like to quote the following passage from Wilhelmus H. M. Creemers's book, *Shrine Shinto After World War II*:

> Blyth, in 1962, confirmed Maeda's assumption that there had been no pressure from SCAP: 'SCAP had almost nothing to do with the matter … Everything came from the Japanese side, if you will count me among the Japanese …' (Blyth's letter to Creemers, dated 14 July 1962). He recalled that someone in SCAP – he thought it was Major H. G. Henderson casually mentioned that it would be a good thing if the Emperor would renounce his divinity, which, according to Blyth, he did not have anyway.[22]

*Notes*

[1] This paper was given at the Tenth Annual Conference of the British Association for Japanese Studies held at the University of Edinburgh, April 1985.

[2] Elizabeth Vining, *Windows for the Crown Prince* (J. B. Lippincott, 1952) p. 28.

[3] As for Blyth's works, *The Genius of Haiku* is available in Britain and EC.. The book, published by the British Haiku Society in 1994, offers a representative selection.

[4] The English translation of the text is found in the *Nippon Times*, 1 January 1946, and is reproduced in Wilhelmus H. M. Creemers: *Shrine*

*Shinto After World War II* (Leiden: E. J. Brill, 1968) William P. Woodard: *The Allied Occupation of Japan 1945–1952 and Japanese Religions* (Leiden: E. J. Brill, 1972). The English translation of the Charter Oath on this occasion was apparently modified from earlier translations either to suit the tenor of the occasion or the translator had no time to check other translations by other translators.

[5] Joseph Roggendorf, S.J.: *Wakon Yōkon* (Kōdansha: 1979, English translation under the title of *Joseph Roggendorf: Between Different Cultures*, Global Oriental, 2004) is an example of observations made by Germans living in wartime Japan.

[6] I have already discussed the case of Suzuki Kantarō in the chapter 'Signals of Peace Not Received'.

[7] As is often the case with terms given to schools of thought in Japanese historiography such as *kōza-ha* or *rōnō-ha* of pre-World War II years, *Tokyo saiban shikan*, too, is a notion not scientifically defined. It is, however, undeniable that the term indicates a certain tendency in Japanese historical thinking that dominated certain academic circles. If I should name a scholar of that tendency, Inoue Kiyoshi (1913–) was the most well known historian of that school. Inoue and his group's Marxist views were welcomed by Communist Chinese ideologues. It is no exaggeration to say that Chinese understanding of the history of Japan was based largely on Inoue's history books that were translated into Chinese and used as history textbooks. Inoue, finally, was a passionate supporter of the Cultural Revolution in China as well as of Japanese students' rebellions in the late 1960s.

[8] About Yamanashi Katsunoshin there is an article written by Fukuda Haruko in Cortazzi ed.: *Britain and Japan 1859–1991* (Routledge, 1990). The article, however, contains many factual mistakes. For example, Saitō Makoto, governor-general of Korea and later Prime Minister, assassinated 26 February 1936, is described as Saitō Minoru, Commander-in-chief in Korea. I depend heavily on Yamanashi's autobiographical writings, *Yamanashi Katsunoshin sensei ihōroku* (Tokyo: suikō-kai, not for sale, 1968) for the description of his early career. Yamanashi was a man of culture. I have never seen a Japanese who was able to quote verses of Shakespeare so aptly. Mrs Elizabeth Vining also wonders at the breadth of his quotations and refers to it in her *Windows for the Crown Prince* (Philadelpuia: Lippincott, 1952, chapter 3).

[9] About Reginald Horace Blyth and his works, see Hirakawa Sukehiro: *Heiwa no umi to tatakai no umi* (Tokyo: Shinchō-sha, 1983) pp. 139–185. There are also a book of personal reminiscences edited by his friends and students, *Kaisō no Buraisu* (not for sale, 1985) and Yoshimura Ikuyo: *R.H. Buraisu no shōgai* (Tokyo: Dōhō-sha, 1996).

[10] Contrary to what many people believe and say, English education continued in Japan during World War II, surely on a smaller scale than before, but on a scale which surpasses the general image of wartime Japan. As late

as April 1944, 28000 copies of Kenkyū-sha's *New English-Japanese Dictionary* were printed and sold. The number of twenty-eight thousand is considerable. It should be noted also that Japanese translations of American books such as *Franklin's Letters* were still published even during the Pacific War. It was unthinkable for a Japanese or even for a Japanese-American interned in the United States to publish a book during World War II.

[11] Blyth was a devoted disciple of Suzuki Daisetz. About Suzuki Daisetz and R. H. Blyth's relationship see Suzuki's words on Blyth in *The Eastern Buddhist* (September issue, 1965)

[12] Edward Seidensticker is of the following opinion: the Shinto notion of *kami* and the Judeo-Christian notion of *kami* (God) are quite different. *Kami* in Shinto tradition is not an absolute being; *kami* is a little higher being than other human beings. *Kami* is of the same nature as other humans. There is, therefore, continuity. The denial of the 'divine' nature of the Japanese Emperor, therefore, had no decisive meaning. (Edward Seidensticker, 'Nihon bunka no hoshusei' in E. Saidenstekka *Nihon tono gojūnen sensō*, Tokyo: Asahi shinbun-sha, 1994, p. 270. English re-translation mine).

[13] Ishiwata Sōtarō denki henshū-kai ed.: *Ishiwata Sōtarō*, (Tokyo: not for sale, 1954) passim. Many details were told by Yamanashi Katsunoshin, who did not, however, say a word about his own role in the process. Exact dates of the process were not recorded.

[14] William P. Woodard: *The Allied Occupation of Japan 1945–1952 and Japanese Religions* (Leiden: E. J. Brill, 1972) p. 318.

[15] Only the first and the last phrases of the draft were reproduced in Tōgashi's article of the *Sandei Mainichi*, 10 January 1960. The draft was said to have been burnt later.

[16] Maeda Tamon gave a detailed account in his article 'Ningen sengen no uchi soto' in the monthly *Bungeishunjū*, March, 1962.

[17] See Hirakawa: *Heiwa no umi to tatakai no umi.* pp. 228–229 and *Yamanashi Katsunoshin sensei ihōroku*, p. 315–317.

[18] Woodard, p. 261.

[19] Woodard, p. 261, n. 2. Woodard wrongly writes Yamanashi Kakunoshin instead of Yamanashi Katsunoshin in this book.

[20] See Nagayo Yoshirō: 'Tennō ron' originally written in 1952 in *Satomi Ton, Nagyo Yoshirō shū: Nijon gendai bungaku zenshū 50* (Tokyo: Kōdansha, 1963) pp. 410–411. In Nagayo's article Yamanashi Katsunoshin is referred to as Admiral Y. K., and also what Inada Shūichi told Fujimura Yoshirō, which is recorded in *Suikō*, 176 (Tokyo: Suikō-kai). Inada was the Chamberlain who attended the gathering of writers and scholars around the Emperor.

[21] Lafcadio Hearn explains the difference between God and *kami* in his essay 'A Living God' in *Gleanings in Buddha-Fields*. Bonner Fellers, aid-de-camp to MacArthur, wrote a famous memorandum dated 2 October 1945

concerning the position of the Japanese Emperor. His memorandum was presented to MacArthur, five days after Hirohito's visit to the Supreme Commander at the American Embassy. Fellers understanding of the difference between the 'divine' attributes of the Japanese Emperor and those of the Christian God derives probably from his reading of Hearn's essays.
[22] Wilhelmus H. M. Creemers: *Shrine Shinto After World War II* (Leiden: E. J. Brill, 1968) p. 128.

# PRISONERS IN BURMA[1]

———————□———————

With the passage of half a century since World War II, we might hope for a convergence of views on the hostilities of the 1940s. Concerning the war fought between the British and the Japanese in Southeast Asia, however, a shared understanding has not been attained. Even among Japanese there are opinions ranging from, on the left, Marxist views holding to Japanese imperialistic aggression and, on the right, nationalistic justifications of the cause of the war. There are also differences in states of knowledge. In English, one finds such books as Christopher Thorne's *Allies of a Kind – The United States, Britain, and the War Against Japan, 1941–1945*.[2] Although his analysis is familiar to Japanese scholars, similar expressions of Japanese views are generally ignored in the West. My aim in what follows lies less in historical details themselves than in the views held and in the knowledge of those views.

There are three works that have fixed images of the Anglo-Japanese hostilities in Japanese minds. The first work is a film, *The Bridge on the River Kwai* (1957), produced by Sam Spiegel and directed by David Lean. The immense popularity of the film has made it widely familiar. It deals with the notorious construction of the Burma-Siam railway by British prisoners of war in 1942–43. The British virtues of perseverance, inventiveness and human dignity are personified by Alec Guinness in his unforgettable role as Colonel Nicholson. The hell of cruelties in the Japanese camps is memorably depicted. This film was based on a novel by Pierre Boulle, *Le pont de la rivière Kwaï*[3] For many years this novel was prescribed as a text for the A-level examination in French in Britain, both reflecting and sustaining the popularity of the novel in that country.

The second work deals not with British but with Japanese

prisoners of war in Burma after Japan's surrender in August 1945. The author, Aida Yūji, records in detail life in a British labour camp. His book, *Āron Shūyōjo* (The Ahlone Concentration Camp), was translated into English under the title *Prisoner of the British*.[4] The original was widely read among Japanese, becoming a best-seller in 1962. It contributed to forming among the Japanese an image of the British that differs greatly, I fear, from that which the British have traditionally held of themselves.

The third work is Takeyama Michio's *Biruma no tategoto* (Harp of Burma).[5] This work remains a classic of post-war juvenile literature and, following a not unfamiliar pattern, has also been taken up by an adult readership. I hope some of my readers have seen the film versions of the story. The work will be the focus of the next chapter and I would like to discuss the first two books above-mentioned in this chapter.

These titles of such varied origins may lead us to a kind of bifocal review of cultural aspects of what some term 'civilization'. Our first concern with this large subject will be the origins of the ideological background of what Japan called the Greater East Asia War while it was going on, and what many Americans and Japanese today call the Pacific War, although the battles between the Japanese and the British took place mostly in Southeast Asia.

The most influential ideologue of Japan's war against the Anglo-Saxon nations was definitely Tokutomi Sohō (1863–1957).[6] What is interesting about this journalist is that his opinions were formed as a reaction of sorts against typical opinions voiced in the West. In the nineteenth and early twentieth centuries Western opinion leaders could ignore the reactions of Asians, while Asian opinion leaders were more or less obliged to pay attention to what was going on in the West. That asymmetry in attention comes of course from the inbalance in power relations of the countries concerned. Throughout the nineteenth century the superiority of Western civilization appeared so evident that the British poet Rudyard Kipling could write a poem like 'The White Man's Burden' without taking into account the reactions of races other than his own. Kipling's poem begins:

> Take up the White Man's burden –
> Send forth the best ye breed –
> Go bind your sons to exile
> To serve your captives' need;
> To wait in heavy harness,

On fluttered folk and wild –
Your new-caught, sullen peoples,
Half-devil and half-child.

Take up the White Man's burden –
In patience to abide,
To veil the threat of terror
And check the show of pride;
By open speech and simple,
An hundred times made plain,
To seek another's profit,
And work another's gain.

Take up the White Man's burden –
The savage wars of peace –
Fill full the mouth of Famine
And bid the sickness cease;
And when your goal is nearest
The end for others sought,
Watch Sloth and heathen Folly
Bring all your hope to nought.

Altogether there are seven stanzas in which the civilizing mission of 'the White Man' is glorified.

The ports ye shall not enter,
The roads ye shall not tread,
Go make them with your living,
And mark them with your dead.

Born in India in 1865, Kipling was two years younger than Tokutomi. The poem was written in 1899, one year after the outbreak of the Spanish-American War. It was the time when the United States was emerging as an imperialistic power in Asia, having occupied the Philippines and made them its colonies in the Pacific.

'The White Man's Burden' was written by the most popular British poet of the time and was addressed to the American people. The poem was actually sent first to Theodore Roosevelt, then vice-president of the United States, before it was printed in Britain, appearing in *The Times* on 4 February 1899. Kipling was so popular as the national poet at that time that his poem was printed not in a literary magazine but in London's leading newspaper, and it appeared in the United States in the Baltimore *Sun* and the Chicago *Tribune* on 5 February. Just one day later, on 6 February, the Senate voted to approve American administration of the Philippines. Roosevelt wrote to Henry Cabot Lodge about Kipling's poem, saying that it 'is rather poor poetry, but good sense from the expansionist standpoint'.[7] Roosevelt recognized that Kipling's poem held a strong political appeal to the public.

All these matters are more or less familiar, and I know that any number of better poems by Kipling make it clear he was not a simplistic racist. What is interesting – and what is still not very much known to Westerners – is the reaction that the poem provoked in Japan. As I have noted, Tokutomi was one of the most influential opinion leaders of Japan, a position he held for more than half a century until Japan's defeat in 1945. At the outset, he was an Anglophile. Then, after Japan's victory over Russia in 1905, he began to talk about the 'Yellow Man's burden'. He advanced this concept in his journalism because he knew that after the breakdown of the myth of the invincibility of the White Man, new political movements were underway in colonies of the British Empire. His arguments, however, were not as self-assertive as Kipling's poem. Kipling urged his fellow countrymen and 'peers', that is, Americans, to take up the burden of races other than their own. Tokutomi urged his fellow countrymen to take up the burden of oppressed peoples of the same 'yellow' race of Asia, who were aspiring to independence. In short, 'Asia for the Asians' was Tokutomi's argument – a sort of Asian version of the Monroe Doctrine.

These were not simple matters. Because Tokutomi's assertion was considered a challenge to the status quo of British supremacy in Asia, the Japanese ruling oligarchy did not like the propagation of this idea. Pan-Asianism, however, began to gain strength, especially after the Russo-Japanese War of 1904–05. Okakura Kakuzō's slogan 'Asia is One' found ears in India and elsewhere in the British colonies.[8] Ironically, the reason Okakura's slogan was able to gain a sympathetic reception in some parts of Asia is that his books were written in English. Linguistically and therefore culturally Asia is *not* one. The common denominator among Asians of the Pan-Asianistic creed was political, namely, that they were against the White Man's rule. It was this anti-colonialist sentiment that was more or less shared by peoples living in various parts of Asia.

In this context some reflections on the racial aspects of the problem are indispensable. We have referred in the chapter dealing with 'the Yellow Peril and the White Peril', Anatole France's view that triggered a series of reactions among Japanese intellectuals at the beginning of the twentieth century. Leading figures among them, like Yanagita Kunio and Watsuji Tetsurō, agreed with the view voiced by Anatole France, who insisted that the yellow peril was created by the white peril. That argument by one of the most prominent French intellectuals of the time had strong repercussions in Japan. It should be noted that these intellectual undercurrents were strong even among pro-Western Japanese, and that must be one reason why the majority of the Japanese wholeheartedly supported Japan's war effort during World War II, once the war broke out.

The Japanese government of the Meiji (1868–1912) and Taishō (1912–1926) eras behaved itself as a 'good boy' within the comity of nations from the opening of the country in the nineteenth century through to the late 1920s. Leading oligarchs like Yamagata Aritomo (1838–1922) were very circumspect about international politics, and they did not venture to challenge Anglo-Saxon supremacy. Japan took part in the international expedition to North China in 1900 to put down the Boxer Rebellion, and the Anglo-Japanese Alliance was concluded shortly thereafter. So long as that alliance was maintained, there was not much conflict between Britain and Japan. However, Pan-Asiatic opinion-leaders like Tokutomi began to win followers among the younger generations. The Anglo-Japanese Alliance was terminated in 1921. Meanwhile, movements against Japanese immigration grew rather violent on the west coast of North America. The Japanese senior statesmen now steered the ship of the Japanese Empire with difficulty; Japan tried hard to play the role of the Britain of the East.

There was still much respect and admiration for Britain among Japanese businessmen, diplomats, and naval officers as Japan made efforts to build its colonial empire, studying the British imperial administration in Egypt and elsewhere as it annexed first Taiwan and then Korea. One conspicuous difference between the British and Japanese histories of colonization is that no member of the British aristocracy ever married a member of a colonial princely family, whereas Japan's Princess Masako, from a branch of the imperial family, married Prince Yi Un, the heir of Korea's former ruling house, in 1920. As the British Royals constantly married Royals of European stock, this politically arranged marriage gave the impression to the Japanese public that the annexation of Korea was conducted on equal terms, but this was certainly not the case. Furthermore, the railways and factories Japanese engineers built in Korea no doubt primarily served Japan's colonial purposes. All the same, it should be borne in mind that the development of heavy industry in a colony was something quite new and was rarely seen in European colonies.

We can identify the problem posed by Japanese Pan-Asianists like Tokutomi. They very much admired the builders of the British Empire. In Hong Kong and in Singapore, Japanese travellers marvelled at the magnificent government buildings, splendid hotels and majestic churches. The Japanese, too, built government buildings in Taipei, in Seoul and later in Changchun, the capital of Manchukuo. They also built Yamato Hotels and Shinto shrines. Nevertheless, even as they strove to make Japan the Britain of the East, the Japanese had mixed feelings towards the British, and some openly resented the White Man's dominance in Asia.

From the 1860s to the outbreak of World War II, the main route from Japan to the Western world was by sea, starting from Yokohama or Kobe and proceeding to Marseilles or London with stops on the way at ports like Hong Kong, Manila, Saigon, Singapore, Penang, Colombo, Aden, Suez and Port Said. The educational value of the Eurasian sea route was so high that a detailed description of the voyage appeared in the elementary-school Japanese language reader. The first mission of the shogunate to Europe took this route in 1862. Among the party was a young interpreter called Fukuzawa Yukichi, who later became the intellectual leader of the 'civilization and enlightenment' movement. Itō Hirobumi who, after distinguishing himself in the Meiji Restoration of 1868, was to become the chief political architect of Meiji Japan, also made this trip, travelling to England first as a stowaway aboard a British ship. Almost all the leading intellectuals of Japan's modernization took that route and, consequently, shared common experiences.

Even those Japanese who had formed an idealized view of Western civilization through their bookish knowledge were obliged to recognize the vast and ruthless expansion of the Western colonial powers. Once the Japanese left their own country, all the intermediate stops on the way to Europe were under Western, mainly British, rule. The reactions of Japanese travellers to the colonizing Europeans and colonized Asians were vividly recorded in many of their diaries. Not only army or navy men of chauvinistic temper but also Japanese of various civilian walks of life bridled at the manifestations of the White Man's dominance in Asia. There was a surprising degree of coincidence in the reactions of Japanese travellers witnessing similar scenes when white passengers threw coins from the sides of ships and native boys dived into the water to catch them. Mori Ōgai's observations in 1884 and Natsume Sōseki's remarks in 1900 were practically identical.[9]

Against the historical background of the age of nationalism, it was quite understandable that slogans like 'Asia for the Asians' became popular among the common people of Japan, whose voices began to grow stronger as education and democratization progressed through the 1910s and 1920s. Japan's expansion into Korea and Manchuria was first justified in terms of Japan's national survival and security. Later, it was declared an expression of Japan's duty towards less advanced peoples of Asia who needed leadership in their struggle against Western imperialism. In this way, Tokutomi's 'Yellow Man's burden' became the political slogan of the Japanese army and right-wing politicians.

There was, however, an apparent contradiction in the Japanese attitude towards Britain. While Japan followed the British model, building an empire and maintaining colonies, self-righteous Japanese journalists began to denounce British colonialism. In the 1930s the Japanese military together with some journalists began to attack the policy of the Japanese government, symbolized by Foreign Minister Shidehara Kijurō, as an Anglophile pacifist diplomacy.

Following the Manchurian Incident in 1931, Japan's policy became what I would like to call anti-imperialistic imperialism. Objectively speaking, the Japan of the 1930s and early 1940s should be labelled an aggressor. Subjectively speaking, however, for many Japanese the war was fought for the liberation of East Asia. That sort of national self-conceit was something similar to the attitude of Saddam Hussein and the Iraqi people on the eve of the Gulf War. Their strongly nationalistic attitude and their 'holy war' rhetoric reminded older Japanese of the atmosphere of Japan on the eve of war in the early 1940s.

The sketch hitherto is a rough historical background of the development of the Japanese attitudes that led to the Anglo-Japanese conflict, and not upon the problems of justice or injustice of the two parties' conduct in Southeast Asia. Speaking of justice or injustice, in the film *The Bridge on the River Kwai* Japanese atrocities were vividly depicted. Yet I imagine that the reality of the British prisoners of war in the hell of a Japanese labour camp was even more gruesome than shown in the film.

However, there are some basically mistaken conceptions perpetuated by the British film of the Japanese. *The Bridge on the River Kwai* deals with the recovery of faith in British virtues of perseverance and inventiveness. In short, it is a glorification of the superiority of Western civilization. The fall of Singapore on 15 February 1942 was a national humiliation for the British, one that was taken to heart by Prime Minister Winston Churchill and his colleagues.[10] The British officers and soldiers taken prisoner there were later mobilized by the Japanese army to finish the nearly 300 miles of the Burma-Siam railway in less than a year over a route that Western engineers had pronounced insuperably difficult. In the film, Colonel Nicholson could successfully defy Japanese orders, because he had a trump card: the British ability to do what the Japanese army could not, namely, build a bridge over the River Kwai. In the book written by Boulle, the bridge built by Japanese engineers was described in these terms:

> On this uncouth superstructure, which sometimes reached an enormous height, thick beams were laid in two parallel rows; and on top of these, the only timber to be more or less properly shaped, went the rails themselves. The bridge was then considered to be finished. It fulfilled the need of the hour. There was no parapet, no footpath. The only way to walk across was to step from on beam to another, balancing above the chasm – a feat at which the Japanese were adept.[11]

The insinuation that the Japanese are ape-like or ant-like continues.

> The first convoy would go jolting across at low speed. The engine sometimes came off the rails at the point where the bank met the bridge, but a gang of soldiers armed with crowbars usually managed to heave it upright again. The train would then move on. If the bridge was damaged at all more bits of timber would be added to the structure. And the next convoy would cross in the same way. The scaffolding would last a few days, a few week sometimes even a few months, after which a flood would sweep it away, or else a series of more than usually violent jolts would make it capsize.[12]

In the novel and film alike, every time the Japanese rebuilt the bridge, it would become unusable after a short time. Colonel Saitō, the Japanese commander, was obliged to ask the help of British engineers among the prisoners. So began the reversal of relations. The British prisoners were now becoming masters of the situation. Boulle can explain the secret of the superiority of the methods of Western civilization (his Captain Reeves was formerly a civil engineer):

> The methods of Western civilization, of course, are not so elementary. Captain Reeves represented an essential element of that civilization – the

mechanical – and would never have dreamed of being guided by such primitive empiricism.

But when it comes to bridge-building, Western mechanical procedure entails a lot of gruelling preliminaries, which swell and multiply the number of operations leading up to the actual construction … These figures in their turn, depend on co-efficients worked out according to 'standard patterns', which in the civilized world are given in the form of mathematical tables. Mechanics, in fact, entail a complete a priori knowledge; and this mental creation, which precedes the material creation, is not the least important of the many achievements of Western genius.[13]

Pierre Boulle, it seems, was under the influence of Paul Valéry and his *conquête méthodique*. His explanation is very Cartesian.

The successful defiance by the British prisoners, with their superior technological ability, makes a highly interesting story. However, as Ian Watt, one of the former British prisoners recollects, it certainly seemed odd that Boulle should base his plot on the illusion that the West still had a monopoly of technological skill.[14] Culturally speaking, one of the lessons to be learned from the Japanese capture of Singapore should have been that the myth of Western superiority in technology had already been dispelled, and needless to say, nothing much like Colonel Nicholson's successful defiance had actually taken place along the Burma-Siam railway. There was a self-complacency both in the film-maker and in the audiences enjoying the film.

There are some sentimental fallacies, too. In the film, Siamese girls are depicted as if they volunteered to help Allied commandos. But during the conflict, the poor villagers of Southeast Asia had no notion whatever of wanting to devote their lives to either the support of Western democracy or to the cause of the Greater East Asia War. Their daily life inevitably imposed on them a much more limited and self-interested horizon.

Local inhabitants of many areas of wartime Southeast Asia disliked the Japanese, although the degree and nature of the hostility differed considerably from one region to another. In the Philippines, for example, where battles were fought bitterly from October 1944 through to the end of August 1945, many civilians were killed and the animosity towards the Japanese grew very strong. However, in the Dutch East Indies and Malaya, where the Japanese army had quickly swept away the Dutch and British forces, the inhabitants were friendly towards the Japanese liberators. In some places, the degree of hostility varied among different races of the local population. In Singapore, for example, there was a sharp

contrast between the inhabitants of Chinese ancestry and those of
Malay or Indian ancestry, since the former suffered during the
Japanese occupation because of their pro-China or pro-communist
attitudes.

It is of course an illusion that Japanese forces were welcomed as
liberators. It is, however, equally an illusion to think that after
Japan's defeat former colonial masters were welcomed back to
Southeast Asia. The power vacuum following the successive defeats
of the two imperialistic powers, Britain and Japan, gave Asians the
chance to become independent earlier than expected.

These are observations occasioned by *The Bridge on the River Kwai*.
The more successful the film was, the wider became the discrepancy
between the myth of Western superiority in technology and British
industrial reality. The belief that the British were the leading bridge
builders of the world was severely shaken in 1985 when a Japanese
company underbid them for the construction of a second bridge
linking Europe and Asia at the Bosporus. Prime Minister Margaret
Thatcher, who suspected at first that the Japanese company had
secretly dealt with the Turkish government by unfair means, seems
finally to have discovered that Japan had made progress during the
preceding century.

Our second work, *Prisoner of the British*, is an account of two years
spent by Professor Aida Yūji, or more exactly, by the then Private
Aida, in Burma after Japan's surrender on 15 August 1945.
Hundreds of popular novels and non-fictional narratives describing
many gruesome atrocities committed by the Japanese in battle or in
prison camps were published in the English-speaking world. The
Japanese themselves were indoctrinated by the repeated propaganda under the American Occupation – which lasted longer than
did the war itself. The American reeducation programme held that
the war had been carried out by the angelic forces of democracy,
fighting the wicked fascists. Japanese leftists, ranging from communists to pacifists, echoed this American view. Immediately after the
war the situation was very curious. The continuing psychological
alliance between Americans and Russians led to a kind of alliance
between Americans and Japanese leftists. Marxist historians, who
dominated Japanese academic circles, held to this revised interpretation of the war. Tokutomi Sohō was described by George Sansom
as a 'celebrated journalist and popular, if tendentious, historian'.[15]
Yet, Tokutomi's later career was never studied by post-war Japanese
historians. The reason is that they were afraid of ostracism. Anyone

daring to write not unfavourably about the leading ideologue of the Greater East Asia War would certainly have been labelled a fascist. A problem with the post-war propaganda is it created taboos among the Japanese, while that with the propaganda employed in the wartime is that the victors continued to believe in it. This was shown, for example, by the drastic curtailment in 1995 of the Smithsonian Institution's exhibit on the atomic bombing of Hiroshima and Nagasaki, which was reduced to a display of the *Enola Gay*, the plane that dropped the first A-bomb, when veterans protested plans to show photographs of the victims.

The black-and-white terms of the victors' rhetoric have naturally a one-sided tendency and it is almost inevitable that many Japanese could not accept them, and the Tokyo Trial (International Military Tribunal for the Far East) provides an example. The victors' justice of this war crimes tribunal was accepted by the Allied nations. In Japan, its assumptions were imposed by the American authorities, who controlled the mass media just as strictly as the Japanese authorities had during the war.[16] That justice was accepted in Japan by leftists. Who, however, could believe that the Soviet army that invaded Manchuria on the eve of Japan's capitulation was part of the angelic force of democracy? That stage of the war, which lasted less than a week, led to several years of Soviet detention in Siberia after the war for over half a million Japanese. A tenth of the Japanese prisoners died in Russian labour camps. A tenth is lower than the percentage of the British prisoners of war who died during the construction of the Burma-Siam railway. It should not be forgotten, however, that the death of more than fifty thousand Japanese in Siberia was not in times of war.

Let us have a look, therefore, from another angle. Two years after Japan's surrender, a history professor was repatriated from Burma. He was amazed to find his sister totally changed by American propaganda. Aida was not at home in that intellectual milieu of Japan then. His account of his post-war experience in a British labour camp, *Āron Shūyōjo*, finally appeared in 1962, becoming a bestseller.[17] The book is full of interesting factual observations.

There was no brutal treatment of the Japanese prisoners of war after Japan's surrender in August 1945 in Burma. (Aida became a prisoner of war only after the war ended.) The Japanese were not mistreated physically, as their British counterparts had been before 1945. However, according to Aida, the British were cruel 'with detachment'. Was this true or not? Was Aida just too touchy? Aida describes his experience and what he disliked most, because it was most humiliating. Certain passages have always caught the attention of my students, both Japanese and foreign. One concerns British women auxiliaries:

> We (Japanese prisoners) entered the women's quarters with bucket, rag, broom and dustpan – *without* knocking. It was not necessary for us to knock when we entered any part of the barracks, including the lavatory. When we were first told this we felt flattered, thinking mistakenly that it showed how much we were trusted. But it was not a question of trust. Ordinarily, you assume that it is necessary to knock before entering a room because somebody may need time to cover himself or herself when they are not dressed or to recover from an embarrassing position. The British did not think this necessary if the person who entered was a Japanese or a Burmese ...
>
> One day as I entered the barracks to begin cleaning I was taken aback. A woman was standing completely naked before the mirror combing her hair. She turned round at the sound of the door opening but when she saw that it was only a Japanese soldier she resumed her position and continued combing her hair with complete indifference. There were a few more women in the room lying on their beds reading *Life* or some English magazines, but none of them took any notice. They remained exactly as they were. I swept the room and scrubbed the floor. The naked woman continued to comb and when she had finished she put on her underclothes, lay on her bed and began to smoke.
>
> If a European had entered the room, the women would probably have shrieked and made a great fuss. The presence of a Japanese did not seem to register on their minds as the presence of a human being.[18]

The last remark is interesting. It is true we do not feel embarrassed being naked in the presence of a cat or of a dog. Aida at first was astonished by the attitude of the British and wondered quite wrongly, why they had to put up a show of looking so lordly and arrogant. Aida was mistaken. They were not pretending to be lordly. Their sense of absolute superiority over Asians, now reconfirmed by their victory over the Japanese, was quite spontaneous and came naturally to them. According to Aida's belated understanding, when the British women gave orders with their chin or feet or threw cigarettes to him on the floor, they were not acting intentionally to spite the Japanese prisoners of war. That kind of behaviour was as natural to them in the late 1940s as breathing. Aida has an interesting comment:

> I felt a great resentment towards this superior attitude on the part of the British, but there were two opposite reactions towards it amongst our men. Some, like me, felt very bitter; others did not seem to mind at all. I gradually became less sensitive about it myself, but the moment that happened,

I realized that I had become part of the world … where the British were somehow accepted a special kind of superior being.[19]

The problem I wish to reconsider is the actual nature of this superiority. It certainly deserves examination. The assumption of Western technological superiority is a myth no more valid than the glorification by Boulle of a methodological conquest. This ends in cultural infatuation. What, then, of the kindred myth of racial superiority?

Within the span of a mere three-and-a-half years, the colonized peoples of Southeast Asia witnessed two historical defeats: first, the British surrender of Singapore; second, the Japanese surrender. The psychological effect of these surrenders upon the peoples of the region was immense, as was recalled so vividly by the founding father of the state of Singapore, Lee Kuan Yew. There was no doubt that the movements towards national independence were much accelerated by the defeat of their former European masters as well as by the defeat of their new conquerors from Japan. When Lieutenant General A. E. Percival surrendered Singapore to the Japanese in February 1942, Ken Harrison, sergeant in the Eighth Australian Division, wrote: 'For the British it would never be the same again.'[20] That is, the lands of Southeast Asia could not be the same colonial entities as before.[21]

Although potentially misleading, there is certain similarity between a colonizing action and a civilizing mission. I do not oppose all applications of the ideas Kipling propounded in his 'White Man's Burden'. The idea of peace-keeping operations, for example, is in a sense similar to the idea of taking up the burden. It would be a worthy mission for United Nations forces to 'fill full the mouth of Famine' and 'bid the sickness cease'. The soldiers in peace-keeping operations should indeed accomplish their duties 'in patience', taking care to 'veil the threat of terror' and 'check the show of pride'. It may happen that we should 'send forth the best [we] breed' to places suffering in today's 'savage wars of peace'.

In *The Western World and Japan*, George Sansom observed that successful colonization is an expression of health and vigour in the colonizing people.[22] I warily agree with the British historian. The indexes of success or failure in colonization are assessment through the outcome and the relationship with the native population. The inhabitants of Gibraltar do not wish that Gibraltar be returned to Spain. This is a clear sign that the British occupation of the peninsula is a success. The majority of the inhabitants of Hong Kong do

not seem to have been very enthusiastic about the return of the territory to China. This may not be a sign of British success, but is a
clear sign of the unpopularity of the People's Republic of China
among the people of Hong Kong. In places like Singapore, where
per capita income is now higher than in Britain, independence is a
blessing, and the economic success of Southeast Asia will contribute to destroying the myth of racial superiority of so-called
Aryans or Anglo-Saxons. Some rich Singaporean families hire nan-
nies from Britain to teach their children English. That kind of new
master-servant relationship has become possible because of the
island-state's economic success. Historically speaking, Chinese
came to Singapore first as coolies, and the complaint that many
British prisoners voiced against their Japanese wardens was: 'The
Japs treat us as if we were Chinese coolies.' Very probably some
Japanese soldiers ordered British soldiers to do the menial jobs that
Chinese coolies had done, cleaning toilets and the like. That must
have been very humiliating.

It is undeniable that the Anglo-Japanese conflict in Southeast
Asia also had an aspect of racial war. Chinese students coming to
Japanese universities are very proud of their national or racial dignity. Some of them grew angry reading *The Bridge on the River Kwai*
when they came on passages where, for example, British officers
and other prisoners complain that they are treated by Japanese and
Korean soldiers as if they were poor Chinese.

Then there is also the third work concerning Japanese prisoners
of war in Burma. I will discuss Takeyama Michio's *Harp of Burma* in
more detail in the next chapter.

Finally, some words about the meaning of the war in Southeast
Asia seen from the British perspective. The British and Indian soldiers who fell in Burma are remembered in an inscription at the
memorial at Kohima, one of the hard-fought battlefields:

> When you go home
> Tell them of us, and say:
> For your tomorrow,
> We gave our today.[23]

In a sense, this memorial is very sad. These soldiers did not give
their today for a tomorrow that was in any sense national or imperial. Soon after the war the British presence in Burma was rendered
impossible. The country became independent and quit the British
Commonwealth of Nations; subsequently the government closed
its borders to most foreigners except those very few Japanese ex-

officers who had helped the Burmese organize their army of independence during the war. Thus, indeed, it was quite an exception for the retired Lieutenant General Fujiwara Iwaichi to visit the cemetery at Kohima at a time when the British were not allowed to visit the graves of their own dead there. The retired general prayed over the graves of the British as well as the Japanese dead. On his return to Tokyo, Fujiwara wrote a letter to Queen Elizabeth to say that he had done so and that the graves were well looked after. To his surprise he received a reply from the queen, thanking him for what he had done.[24] On learning that, I felt hope that there had been a reconciliation between the British and the Japanese.

Such books as Aida's and Takeyama's open for us a perspective different from that given by *The Bridge on the River Kwai*. For Boulle, the superiority of Western technological achievement was self-evident. For that French author, *la civilisation* meant Western civilization, and in the years following World War II, Japan and the Japanese were accused of having breached the law of nations as well as the Law, with a capital L. Precisely in the name of civilization Japanese class A war criminals were indicted by the American chief prosecutor, Joseph Keenan, when the Tokyo Trial was opened in 1946, and some were sentenced to death.[25] A citizen soldier in Takeyama's *Harp of Burma*, although recognizing the responsibility of the Japanese militarists, still murmurs: Was it not modern technological civilization itself that was partly responsible for so much destruction and so many calamities?[26]

When we look back at what happened half a century ago, we are amazed at the rapidity with which the basic myths concerning technological, racial, religious, or cultural superiority, on the premise of which so many judgements were once formed, have come tumbling down. Probably everyone has a personal cultural perspective through which to look back at the history of the Anglo-Japanese conflict in Southeast Asia. One's perspective tends to become one's prejudice, and so my view may be jaundiced as well. Yet, I hope I was successful in revealing a wider perspective of the theme. In future I hope there will be a much fuller study made of it with much broader scope.

*Notes*

[1] This article was published in December 1999 issue of *Japan Echo*, pp. 43–50 under the title: 'Prisoners in Burma: The Anglo-Japanese Hostilities from a Cultural Perspective.'.

[2] Christopher Thorne, *Allies of a Kind – The United States, Britain, and the War Against Japan, 1941–1945* (New York: Oxford University Press, 1978).

[3] Pierre Boulle: *Le pont de la rivière Kwaï* (Paris: Julliard, 1952); *The Bridge on the River Kwai*, tr. Xan Fielding (London: Secker & Warburg, 1954; reprint, London: Fontana Books, 1956).

[4] Aida Yūji: *Āron Shūyōjo* (Tokyo: Chūōkōron-sha, Chūkō Shinsho, 1962); Yūji Aida: *Prisoner of the British*, tr. Louis Allen and Hide Ishiguro (London: Cresset, 1966).

[5] Takeyama Michio: *Biruma no tategoto* (first published in 1948; Tokyo: Shinchōsha, Shinchō Bunko, 1959); Michio Takeyama: *Harp of Burma,* tr. Howard Hibbett (Rutland VT: Tuttle, 1966).

[6] A Vietnamese-Canadian scholar, Vinh Sinh, wrote a study of Tokutomi: *Tokutomi Sohō, The Later Career* (Toronto: Joint Centre for Asia Pacific Studies of the University of Toronto and York University, 1986).

[7] Charles Carrington: *Rudyard Kipling, His Life and Work* (London: Macmillan, 1955), p. 278.

[8] Concerning the psychological awakening of Asians after Japan's victory over Russia, the *Autobiography* of Jawaharlal Nehru is most revealing.

[9] See Ōgai's diary entry for 11 September 1884, and Sōseki's for 25 September 1900.

[10] Churchill's dejection is reported by Lord Moran in *Winston Churchill* (London: Constable, 1966), p. 27.

[11] Pierre Boulle: *The Bridge on the River Kwai,* p. 60.

[12] Ibid. p. 60.

[13] Ibid. pp. 60–61.

[14] Ian Watt, 'Bridges Over the Kwai', *The Listener*, 6 August 1959, pp. 216–18.

[15] George Sansom: *The Western World and Japan* (London: Cresset, 1950), p. 283.

[16] About the impact of censorship upon a Japanese mind, see Etō Jun, 'The American Occupation and Post-War Japanese Literature' in *Hikaku Bungaku Kenkyū,* (Tokyo: Asahi shuppan-sha) No. 38, 1980, pp. 1–18.

[17] In 1978, when I was visiting Princeton University, I referred to it casually, since an English translation had appeared under the title, Yuji Aida: *Prisoner of the British* (London: Cresset, 1966). One after another, most of the faculty members of the Department of East Asian Studies began to read it, and they discussed it animatedly. I think the book is worthy of attention.

[18] Y. Aida: *Prisoner of the British*, pp. 31–32.

[19] Y. Aida: *Prisoner of the British*, p. 34.

[20] Harrison's comment is taken from an exhibit at the Singapore History Museum. The museum originally had pictures only concerning Japan's surrender in August 1945; pictures concerning the British capitulation of February 1942 were added years later.

[21] In the long run, there was a psychological chain reaction in South-East Asia: Independence movement of Malaysia came out of the fall of Singapore (1942). The fall of Dien Bien Phu (1954) came out of the fall of Singapore, and the fall of Saigon (1975) came out of the fall of Dien Bien Phu.

[22] Sansom: *The Western World and Japan*, p. 73.

[23] Louis Allen: *Burma, The Longest War* (London: Dent, 1984), p. 635.

[24] Ibid. p. 636.

[25] Ushimura Kei: *Beyond 'the Judgment of Civilization'* (tr. Steven J. Erickson; Tokyo: International House, 2003) deals with the meaning of civilization and other intercultural issues in the Tokyo Trial. This meticulous study is very revealing.

[26] See Takeyama Michio, 'Haido shi no saiban,' *Takeyama Michio chosakushū* (Tokyo: Fukutake shoten, 1983) vol. 1, pp. 299–316.

# THE IMAGE OF FORMER ENEMIES IN TAKEYAMA MICHIO'S *HARP OF BURMA* (1948)[1]

───────□───────

Takeyama Michio's *Harp of Burma*, which I counted in the former chapter as one of the three books that have fixed images of prisoners in Burma in the Japanese mind, remains a classic of post-war juvenile literature. The nature of the Anglo-Japanese hostilities described in the book, however, differs considerably from that in the two other books: *The Bridge on the River Kwai* by Pierre Boulle and *Prisoner of the British* by Aida Yūji. The author Takeyama's emphasis is on overcoming the hostilities. *Harp of Burma* is a requiem for the fallen.

Before discussing the images of former British enemies and other foreigners in Japanese author Takeyama's *Harp of Burma*, written immediately after World War II, a general historical view of the images of Westerners in literatures of the Far East, and, additionally, images of Orientals in literatures of the Far West is necessary for the further understanding of the significance of Takeyama's novel.

It seems that at the first stage of forced contact with foreign powers, foreigners were first depicted as devils in imaginative literatures of the East Asia. In popular literature of the Middle Kingdom not only Westerners but also Japanese men were often represented as barbarians, as they were called in Chinese either *xiyang guizi* or *dongyang guizi*, that is, devils from the West or devils from the East. It is the same with Japanese popular arts, literary as well as pictorial, of the mid-nineteenth century. Westerners were often represented as devil-like figures in *ukiyo-e* prints, while Chinese were often caricaturized because of their hair-style, which was disdainfully called pig-tail by Westerners. By the way, Dutch men are depicted both by a Korean intellectual, Lee Duk-muo (1741–93) and by a Japanese *Rangakusha* (Dutch scholar), Ōtsuki Gentaku (1757–1827) alike, as having 'the habit of raising one leg while urinating, just like dogs'. Lee's *Byeongjibiyeron* was said to be written around 1780. It seems that Lee had that knowledge from the Japanese who had commercial relations with the Dutch.[2]

This self-centered tendency to denigrate others must be the same with Chinese or Japanese and probably with Koreans of pre-modern times or even of later days. It is true that under strong Confucian influence Korean men of letters were deferential towards Chinese Confucian literati, but not always so towards Western barbarians or Japanese barbarians. So long as a country is physically and mentally closed, popular imagination inevitably tends to become inimical towards 'treacherous' foreigners and 'sneaky' inferiors. Generally speaking, it is in popular literary works that various 'underground' fears and fantasies within a people's psyche find expression. Accusatory tones and exaggerated expressions are the main stylistic characteristics of this kind of literature, and such characteristics seem to be symptoms not only of the first stage of contact with Westerners, but also of war-time propaganda of later stages.

Then follow a series of reactions of various kinds; what is perceived to be foreign and different from the self inspires fear as well as admiration. Any study of the images of foreigners held either by Asiatic or Western people is inevitably a study of that people, as the images created cannot help but mirror the minds of those who create them. In case of Japan, after the opening of the country, there was a Europeanization fever in the 1880s, and beautiful Western women appear on this second stage which shows a reversal in popular imagination: at that time of the early Westernization movement Christian missionaries from the West played an important role in shaping images of Westerners. For example, a beautiful daughter of a Western missionary is idolized in Izumi Kyōka's novel *Chikai no maki* (1896).

As there is idealization on the one hand, there is debasement on the other. To be more exact, as the Western powers became to Japan both a threat and a model to emulate, the images of Westerners became more complex and ambivalent. This mixed feeling of

love-hate towards Westerners has existed more or less in all the
regions of East Asia, where local inhabitants have suffered from
real or imaginary imperialism from the West or from its Japanese
proxy. In continental China, after the Communist take-over, there
was a time of strong anti-Western campaign, and xenophobia was
rampant during the Cultural Revolution. In case of Japan, as Japan
fought a total war against the Americans and the British in World
War II, wartime propaganda used exaggerated expressions. Some
jingoistic journalists of the Japanese empire went so far as to depict
American and British enemies as devils and animals, *kichiku beiei*,
although ordinary readers of Japanese newspapers secretly despised
the over-enthusiastic tone of wartime rhetoric. Putting the 'beast'
radical to the *kanji* (Chinese characters) signifying Americans and
British was too much. It is true that even in the height of the
war the Japanese never went so far as to destroy the cemeteries of
foreigners.

Historically speaking, popular works of anti-Western literature
such as those written by Yamanaka Minetarō, classmate of Tōjō
Hideki, are worth the attention of intellectual historians, as they
exercised considerable influence in shaping nationalistic sentiments
in Japanese youths during the 1930s and 1940s. Artistically
speaking, however, they are of low quality and are generally ignored
in histories of Japanese literature. I am afraid, however, that in
dealing with the problems of images of foreigners, what is interesting is often something fantastic and exaggerated: animal-like
Western men or over-sexed Orientals or women full of angelic
grace or vamps of irresistible sex-appeal of any ethnicities or
nationalities other than one's own appear more often in popular literature, films and comics. In short, studies of stereotypically
distorted images are important, if not from a purely literary viewpoint, but at least in a wider historical context.

Concerning this aspect of Japanese literature, there is a study in
English entitled *The Walls Within: Images of Westerners in Japan* edited
by K. Tsuruta,[3] and an enlarged version in Japanese edited by
myself.[4] The Japanese edition called *Uchinaru kabe* contains also a
number of studies concerning images of the Japanese abroad.
According to the Japanese-Canadian scholar Kinya Tsuruta,
Westerners are portrayed in modern Japanese literature in terms of
two general, and extreme, categories: they are either beautiful god-
desses or ugly monsters, virtually lacking in any realistic 'human'
qualities. Although almost all scholars who participated in that con-

ference entitled, 'The Walls Within' deplore stereotypes used by Japanese writers to represent foreigners and stereotypes used by Westerners to represent the Japanese, I have become, since then, of the opinion that the use of stereotypes is, to a certain degree, inevitable.

On the other side of the world, too, of course, peoples of different nationalities are represented in works of Western literature. The first comedy, in which a British gentleman, a French monsieur, a Spanish señor and a jealous Italian count are depicted for the interest of their national characteristics rather than for their individual characteristics, is Carlo Goldoni's *Vedova Scaltra* (Shrewd Widow) written in 1748. The heroine of the comedy, the shrewd widow called la signora Rosaura, has human qualities, and the Venetian lady is the more attractive and her personality the more conspicuous precisely because others are described in terms of stereotypes, that is, not for their individuality but for their nationality. I very much appreciate the contrast between the individually depicted signora Rosaura and the stereotyped gentlemen, which makes the impression we have from the Venetian protagonist all the more effective. Goldoni's comedy is successful, because it satisfies at the same time two needs of the audience. The audience even today is curious to know something about the national characteristics of the dramatis personae, and the audience is, moreover, pleased with finding the discreetly self-assertive character of the widow, who finally succeeds in choosing a husband who really loves her. The use of stereotypes is necessary in this kind of comedy in which comparisons of national character play an important part. In addition, the use of stereotypes is inevitable in literature as well as in our daily existence, as it has something to do with the limitations of our mental capacities. We are linguistically and, therefore, culturally limited. Intellectual economy necessitates the use of abstracted notions, that is, stereotypes. In order to locate people of various countries in the simplified world-map of our mind, we are obliged to use them.

With the passage of time, the repertory of comparisons became richer. Orientals of the Far East began to appear more often in literatures of Europe and America, from the second half of the nineteenth century, as the round-the-world trip was made easier thanks to steamships. The new genre called geographical novels (*romans géographiques*) appears with Jules Verne (1828–1905), Pierre Loti (1850–1923), Rudyard Kipling (1865–1936) and other less known globe-trotters. It is said that the typical Chinese gentleman was described for the first time with acuity by the French navy officer and writer Claude Farrère in his unforgettable novel *la Bataille* (1909). The Japanese were first caricaturized by Pierre Loti and then more sympathetically described by Lafcadio Hearn around the turn of the century.

Compared with those descriptions of Asiatics by Westerners, descriptions of Westerners by East Asians began much later and more slowly. It was easier for aggressive Westerners to come to the Far East and to become masters of the situation, while challenged Asians never sent their black ships either to the river Thames or to the Potomac. They began to send students to Europe and America only from the 1860s. It is understandable that Westerners were depicted for the first time by those who had been abroad.

In case of modern Japanese literature, various types of Germans were depicted by Mori Ōgai (1862–1922) around the year 1889.[5] Among the three portraits of Westerners[6] by Natsume Sōseki (1867–1916), the portrait of an Irish Shakespeare scholar William James Craig (1909) pleases its readers for its human qualities.[7] Lu Xun (1881–1936), the greatest of modern Chinese writers, translated Sōseki's 'Kureigu sensei' into Chinese as 'Kelaika xiansheng'. Through that experience of translation Lu Xun was inspired to write the portrait of his foreign teacher Tengye xiansheng or Fujino sensei.[8] It was Sōseki's portrayal of Mr Craig that moved Lu Xun, although some critics categorically deny that human quality in Sōseki's reminiscences. According to Ōshima Hitoshi, both Ōgai's and Sōseki's descriptions of Westerners are more bookish than real, and only the literary critic Masamune Hakuchō's Westerners have soul and flesh.[9] In order to emphasize the values of the critic Masamune Hakuchō, Ōshima has given an over-generalized evaluation of other Japanese writers. This seems an overstatement on the part of Ōshima, a hasty, stereotypical judgement at that. It happens that Westerners in works of Japanese literature are borrowed from Western literature of the country in question, and that writers are influenced by what they have been reading. Those Japanese writers may fail to attribute the Western character with real human quality. However, bookish experience is not everything in the case of Ōgai and Sōseki, who spent many years abroad.

Both in the East and in the West stereotyped images of foreigners, and although less in number, images with human qualities exist. Furthermore, in Asian countries where the minimum of freedom of expression has at least been guaranteed, against the overwhelming existence of distorted images of Westerners, some men and women of letters have portrayed Westerners or former enemies more humanely in a manner very different from propagandistic literature, and I may count among them Takeyama Michio, whose *Harp of Burma* (1948) is a literary work of reconciliation with enemies and a requiem for the fallen.

However, it is not intended to provide an analysis within the simplistic dichotomy of classification as humanely or inhumanely written, politically correct or politically incorrect. Too much emphasis on that can lead the reader to a narrow-minded appreciation of literature, missing the overtones and undertones of the works. Here, what I would like to examine are the problems concerning the use of stereotypes in a work otherwise known as a masterpiece for its human qualities.

The author of *Harp of Burma*, Takeyama Michio[10] (1903–84), professor of German at the prestigious Dai-ichi kōtō-gakkō – which now forms an important part of Tokyo University, known as Komaba campus – was a rare Japanese intellectual who dared to criticize the inhumanity of Nazi Germany in April 1940 in the monthly *Shisō* (Tokyo: Iwanami shoten), and who wrote extensively in defence of intellectual freedom after Japan's defeat in 1945. In pre-war years, he was criticized by right-wing nationalists, and in post-war years, he was more violently attacked by left-wing intellectuals for his 'bourgeois democratic liberalism'. Takeyama, however, was adamant in his criticism of the inhumanity of totalitarian regimes, whether Hitlerian, Stalinist or Maoist.[11] Although an intellectual giant and very influential during his lifetime, Takeyama is most widely known in Japan for his imaginative tale *Biruma no tategoto* (Harp of Burma) originally written for children two years after Japan's defeat in World War II. The book has had an immense appeal for Japanese adults as well. *Harp of Burma* is a classic of postwar Japanese literature. The book, *Biruma no tategoto* has been translated into more than eight languages, including Chinese,[12] Thai and Basque.

*Harp of Burma* tells the story of a company of Japanese civilian soldiers in Burma during and after World War II. Amid severe hardship, the men maintain their morale by learning to sing together. Their captain, a young musician fresh from music school, enthusiastically teaches his conscripted soldiers to sing together. In that matter alone is Takeyama's work based on a historical fact. The rest of the story is fictional. Although Takeyama had been to Taiwan and knew the semi-tropical climate rather well, he had never been to Burma before he wrote the book.

The story takes place at the war's end. The unit was completely lost in the mountains on the Burma-Siamese borders. Having no contact with Japanese headquarters, they did not know that the war had already ended on 15 August 1945. One evening, the company was suddenly surrounded by British troops in a Burmese village. Corporal Mizushima, who was a virtuoso on the Burmese harp, played a tune and had the men sing. They pretended that they were not aware of the presence of their enemies. 'We can't let on we know what's coming. We've got to keep singing as if nothing is wrong,' the captain ordered. While furtively preparing to attack, they sang 'Hanyū no Yado'. Their military preparations were more or less completed by the time they reached the end of the song. Now they were ready. Let us quote from Hibbett's translation:

> The captain drew out his saber. Those of us who had brought the cart stopped singing and took up our rifles. During that brief interval of still-ness you could hear, quite distinctly, the river flowing in the valley far below. The birds that had been busily twittering until a few minutes ago were now all fast asleep.
>
> The captain raised his sabre. The soldiers were poised, ready to shout their battle cry and charge. But just then the captain checked his command and stood transfixed. An extraordinary thing was happening. Out of the forest soared a voice a high, clear voice, fervently singing 'Hanyū no Yado.'
>
> The captain grabbed one of our men who had started forward, and blocked others by spreading out his arms.
>
> 'Wait!' he shouted. 'Listen to that!'
>
> The voice in the forest was joined by two or three more, and then by voices from here, there, and everywhere. It was 'Hanyū no Yado' sung in English: 'Home, home sweet home ...'
>
> We looked at each other in astonishment. What could this mean? Weren't the men in the forest the dreaded enemy soldiers who were out to kill us? Were they only the villagers? In that case, we needn't have been so anxious. We gave a sigh of relief and lowered our guns.
>
> Now the forest was full of singing voices. A chorus arose even from the base of the cliff hanging over the river. We joined in and sang too.
>
> The moon was shining. Everything was dyed blue in its cool light. There seemed to be luminous pillars of glass between the trees. One by one, shadowy figures came running out of that forest into the open space.
>
> They were British soldiers.
>
> Gathering into little groups here and there, they sang 'Home Sweet Home' with true feeling. We (Japanese) had always thought 'Hanyū no Yado' was a Japanese song, but it is actually an old English melody.

Englishmen sing it out of nostalgic pride and longing for the joys of their beloved home; whenever they hear it, they think of their childhood, of their mothers, of the places where they grew up. And so they were astonished and moved to hear their enemy – the dangerous enemy they had surrounded high in the mountains of Burma – singing this song.

By this time we were no longer enemies. The battle never began. Before we quite knew what happened, we were all singing together and coming up to one another to shake hands.[13]

This episode of fraternization is skillfully conceived. The Japanese soldiers thought that they were singing a Japanese song, while the British soldiers were impressed by the coming of a melody from the enemy side. The theme reminds me of the Nō play '*Atsumori*' in which samurai of the Minamoto clan were moved by the sound of a flute coming from the enemy camps. However, no such fraternizing actually occurred at the Burmese front. It is pure fantasy. Louis Allen, author of *Burma, the Longest War*,[14] supposes that the Japanese author Takeyama must have used World War I narratives about Christmas in the trenches in 1914. Moreover, in *Harp of Burma* the end of the hostilities is rationalized in this fashion:

That night we learned that the war had ended three days earlier. Having no way to let their ferocious enemy know, the British troops thought they might have to annihilate us in order to mop up resistance. We threw down our guns.[15]

Thus, the Japanese singing unit surrendered. To be held prisoners in a foreign country is a physical shock as well as a cultural shock. The shocks provide, in Takeyama's story, the general background. They are not used on the individual basis of character-building; they offer occasions to examine the nature of the national character of those involved. Aside from Japanese and British, there appear Burmese in *Harp of Burma*. Each of them is to an extent the embodiment of their respective cultures.

Shocks eventually become questions. Among Japanese soldiers in the prison camp the discussions are held upon questions. 'Why did we fight?' 'For what purpose have we made such strenuous efforts to modernize our country?' The novel invites its readers to think over the merits and the demerits of the modernization movement and its aftermath. Having three different cultural values instead of two provide a better means of comparison in their discussion:

The Burmese are so religious that every man spends part of his youth as a monk, devoting himself to ascetic practices ...

What a difference! In Japan all the young men wore soldiers's uniforms, but in Burma they put on priestly robes. We often argued about this. Compulsory military training or compulsory religious training – which was better? Which was more advanced? As a nation, as human beings, which should we choose?

It was a queer kind of argument that always ended in a stalemate. Briefly, the difference between the two ways of life seemed to be that in a country where young men wear military uniforms the youths of today will doubtless become the efficient, hard-working adults of tomorrow. If work is to be done, uniforms are necessary. On the other hand, priestly robes are meant for a life of quiet worship, not for strenuous work, least of all for war. If a man wears such garments during his youth, he will probably develop a gentle soul in harmony with nature and his fellow man, and will not be inclined to fight and overcome obstacles by his own strength.

In former times we Japanese wore clothes that were like clerical robes, but nowadays we usually wear uniform-like Western clothes. And that is only to be expected, since we have become one of the most active and efficient nations in the world and our old peaceful, harmonious life is a thing of past. The basic difference lies in the attitude of a people; whether, like the Burmese, to accept the world as it is, or to try to change it according to one's own designs. Everything hinges on this.[16]

Some readers may find this kind of argument nonsensical. Indeed, some Burmese students are not satisfied with this kind of explanation concerning Burma, because they, too, are eager for modernization of their country.

This argument seems to be a comparison between the Japanese and the Burmese ways of life. The real source of the conversation, however, is most probably the conversation that took place between the Chinese Governor General Li Hongzhang and the Japanese minister Mori Arinori in Beijing in 1876. It is recorded in English as the conversation was conducted through that language, Governor Li using an interpreter and Mori speaking in English:

> Li said: I think very highly of almost everything that has recently been done in your country, but there is one thing I cannot so well appreciate: that is the change of your old national costume into the European fashion.
>
> Mori: the reason is quite simple and needs only a little explanation. You may have ever seen our old-fashioned costume. It is a very loose and comfortable one and excellent for those who pursue a life of ease and idleness, but wholly unsuitable to one of activity ... By discarding the old-fashioned costume for the new, we have gained manyfold advantages.
>
> Li: The costume is one of those that recalls the sacred memory of the ancestors and ought to be kept on with reverence by the posterity for ever.
>
> Mori: If our ancestors were still living they would without doubt do exactly what we have done in regard to this very simple business of

changing costume. Our ancestors about a thousand years ago adopted the Chinese costume as they then found it better than one they had. It is one of our national characteristics to readily take in anything that is both good and beneficial.[17]

The prototype of the discussions that take place in the prisoners' camp is clearly here. Takeyama's choice of Burma as the scene of the story simply derived from the dramatic necessity. It had to be a battlefield where the British and the Japanese fought, so that 'Hanyū no Yado'/'Home, home sweet home' can be sung by each in his own language. The unexpected development of the story is made possible by the fact that 'Hanyū no Yado' which the Japanese soldiers took for a Japanese song is originally an English one. According to Takeyama's own explanation concerning the origin of the story, he first had in mind China as the scene of the story.[18] Such being the case, the discussions about the merits and demerits of adopting a Western costume, the Burmese and the Chinese are, to a certain degree, exchangeable. It goes without saying that it is not always sound to interpret literally what is written in works of literature. Burmese are not always Burmese in the work entitled *Harp of Burma*.

Neither are the cannibals, with whom the wounded Mizushima spent precarious days and nights in the Burma-Siamese borders, real ones. It is easy to condemn Takeyama for his exaggerated use of their habits and customs.[19] In fact, the author Takeyama received towards the late 1970s a letter of protest from a Burmese student, studying in California.[20] The difficulty, here, lies in its semi-fictional setting, Burma – today's Myanmar. The tendency now seems for anybody anywhere who is concerned with the not-based-on-fact negative images of peoples to level condemnations at them. However, it is a literary convention to have a semi-real setting; and the readers are required to read the works in that spirit. The author's intention was to create effective fictional suspense and it is obvious there was no intention of citing the episode as real fact.[21]

As has been stated, Burmese are not always Burmese in *Harp of Burma*. Then, how about the Japanese protagonist of the story? Is Corporal Mizushima a genuine Japanese? If in some parts of *Harp of Burma* the Burmese are the Chinese in disguise, it is possible that the same sort of character borrowing has taken place also with the Japanese hero of the story. In the end, Mizushima makes up his mind to stay in Burma as a priest and to pray for the dead, refusing the repatriation, which all the Japanese prisoners of war had waited for for so long in their concentration camps. Indeed, they were retained there for more than two years after Japan's capitulation. His attitude is beyond the comprehension of his comrades as well as his readers.

It is not too far off to say that the prototype, or at least an element of the idealist Mizushima is the Christian missionary and musician Albert Schweitzer (1875–1965). Although a conjecture, and because in the story the religion is Buddhism and the protagonist a Japanese, it may not be easy to make the link between the two. However, there are the facts that Schweitzer preferred to remain in Gabon in Africa during the wartime and Takeyama had translated Schweitzer's autobiographical writings from German in the early years of World War II.[22] Not only that: Takeyama had even sent money to Schweitzer to help his humanitarian work. Schweitzer's letter of thanks to Takeyama is dated 8 February 1940 at Lambaréné, Gabon.[23] With this information, the surmise is not so unreasonable, rather coherent with the facts.

Quite a few readers of *Harp of Burma* worldwide have been moved by the author's deep feeling of compassion for those who had fallen in the flower of their youth – indeed many of Takeyama's students, the élite of Japan, who had been to the front, had never come back again. The teacher Takeyama's compassion is genuine, and there is no doubt that it is this heart-felt emotion that made Takeyama write *Harp of Burma*. Many members of the bereaved families have read and understood it. I know, therefore, that my conjecture that Takeyama must have been inspired, at least partially, by Schweitzer for the creation of the idealist side of Mizushima will offend some Japanese readers of older generation, who saw in Mizushima their son who had never come back home from the Southern front. However, in a peaceful manner, the metamorphosis from Schweitzer, a virtuoso on the pipe organ into Mizushima, a virtuoso on the Burmese harp has taken place. It is because of Mizushima's missionary-like determination, so unfamiliar and so unexpected to the practical-minded Japanese of the mid-twentieth century, that readers, both adults and children alike, are at first puzzled by Mizushima's so-called desertion from the camp. It is precisely because of this enigmatic attitude of Mizushima that the story has a most effective suspense. There is an element of the detective story in *Harp of Burma*. Readers are obliged to wait for the last chapter of the story to be informed of the protagonist's true motive of 'desertion'. When the captain reads Mizushima's letter to his men and when the enigma is finally solved, they are already on board the repatriation ship. Burma is far away and the land has disappeared behind the horizon. Mizushima is not to be seen again.

In this case of partial borrowing, I would not say that Mizushima and Schweitzer are interchangeable; but still one might recognize the possibility that even when a Japanese author is creating an image of a Japanese idealist, or any author creating any hero out of his or her people, there remains the possibility of incorporating elements of foreign origin and of foreign values.

I know that for many Japanese ex-prisoners of war in Burma Takeyama's *Harp of Burma* is a fairy tale in the negative sense that it is not true to the realities of life in prisoners-of-war camps. To them the realities are described better by Aida Yūji.[24] Some of them think that the real British soldiers were more cold-blooded than those depicted by Aida.[25]

However, works of art should not be judged by the measure of their realistic description only. Instead of discussing images of Westerners per se for their exactitude in description, I have analysed images of various backgrounds in Takeyama's *Harp of Burma*. I have gone so far as to find an image or at least an echo of a Westerner in the Japanese Buddhist monk Mizushima. Works of literature are works of fictional art. They are products of various influences and, to analyse the chemistry of the composite images seems to be the task of us comparatists.

*Notes*

[1] This paper was presented at the forum, 'The Image of Westerners in East Asian literature', which was held in August 1997 during the 15th Congress of the International Comparative Literature in Leiden and was published in Meng Hua and Sukehiro Hirakawa ed.: *Images of Westerners in Chinese and Japanese Literature* (Amsterdam & Atlanta: Editions Rodopi, 2000), pp. 213–225.

[2] The information about Lee Duk-muo and his *Byeongibiyeron* was given by a Korean scholar, Prof. Choi Park Kwang in his paper entitled '*Hongmo*, (Red hair, that is, the Dutch, in Korean Literature') presented at the International Comparative Literature congress held in Leiden in 1997.

[3] K. Tsuruta ed., *Walls Within: Images of Westerners in Japan*, (Vancouver: The Institute of Asian Research, The University of British Columbia, 1989).

[4] Hirakawa S. et al ed., *Uchinaru kabe*, (Tokyo: TBS Britannica publishers, 1990).

[5] Germans who appear in Ōgai's works and who play an important part

are a dancing girl in 'Maihime', an artist's model in 'Utakata no ki', a daughter of noble family in 'Fumitsukai', and a middle aged artist who visits her Japanese old acquaintance in Tokyo in 'Fushinchū'.

[6] Three portraits of Westerners by Sōseki are the following. First, the Shakespeare scholar and Sōseki's tutor in London, William James Craig in 'Kureigu sensei'. The second is a historian of Japan and Sōseki's teacher at Dai-ichi kōtō-gakkō James Murdoch in 'Hakushi mondai to Mādokku sensei to yo' and in 'Mādokku sensei no nihon-rekishi' (See Chapter 'Natsume Sōseki and his Teacher James Murdoch'). The third is a German philosophy professor and Sōseki's colleague at Tokyo University, Raphael von Kœber in 'Kēberu sensei'.

[7] About the relationship between Sōseki and Craig, see the chapter 'Intellectual Loneliness or Intellectual Companionship: Portraits of a Foreign Teacher by Sōseki, E. V. Lucas and Lu Xun.'

[8] For a more detailed study on the relationship between Sōseki's 'Kureigu sensei' and Lu Xun's 'Tengye xiansheng', see Hirakawa: *Natsume Sōseki hiseiyō no kutō* (revised edition, Tokyo: Kōdansha, 1991). Hirakawa's argument is summarized in English in *Tamkang Review*, vol. X, nos. 3&4, 1980, pp. 547–554 as well as in *Zhong-Ri wenhua yu jiaoliu*, no. 2 (Beijing: Zhongguo zhanwang chubanshe, 1985), pp. 72–98.

[9] Hitoshi Ōshima, 'The Image of Westerners in Modern Japanese Literature' in Meng Hua & Sukehiro Hirakawa ed.: *Images of Westerners in Chinese and Japanese Literature*, (Amsterdam & Atlanta: Editions Rodopi, 2000), pp. 187–197.

[10] For those who wish to know more about Takeyama, see the biographical notes attached to the last volume of his selected writings, Takeyama Michio Chosakushū, in 8 vols, (Tokyo: Fukutakeshoten, 1983). *Biruma no tategoto* is available in a Shinchō bunko paperback edition. As for an English version, see Takeyama: *Harp of Burma*, translated by Howard Hibbett (Rutland, Vermont and Tokyo: Tuttle, 1966). It is in the UNESCO Collection of Contemporary Works. The strength of the appeal of Takeyama's story may be suggested by the fact that the film version created by Ichikawa Kon won the San Giorgio prize at the 1956 Venice Film Festival. It is the only Japanese film on the list of 45 films and directors that the Vatican has cited as having special artistic and religious merit. In 1985, Ichikawa remade the film in colour, and it was again an immense success in Japan. (On the Vatican list of films, see Gustav Niebuhr, 'How the Church Chose the Best Films Ever,' *New York Times Review*, 7 April 1996.)

[11] Takeyama Michio's grandfather was Okada Ryōichirō. Ryōichirō's first son was Okada Ryōhei, who served as Minister of Education. Ryōichirō's second son was Ikki Kitokurō, chairman of the Privy Council. Ryōichirō's third son was adopted by Takeyama family as Takeyama Junpei, who was a banker. Takeyama Michio was Junpei's second son. Brought up with such a family background, Takeyama Michio was far more knowledgeable

about Japanese politics than most of his contemporary intellectuals. Moreover, having studied from 1927 through 1930 in Germany and in France, he was also knowledgeable about the rise to power of Nazism. These backgrounds, together with his intellectual integrity, made it possible for him to publish critical writings against totalitarian tendencies of any kind. It should be added also that, compared with countries like Germany, Russia or China, there was a minimum of freedom of expression in Japan even in 1940.

12  The Chinese translation which I have is Zhushan Daoxiong (Takeyama Michio), *Miandian-de Shuqin* (Taipei: Xingguang publishers, 1986).

13  Takeyama: *Harp of Burma*, pp. 29–30.

14  Louis Allen, *Burma, the Longest War, 1941–45* (London: Dent, 1984) pp. 621–622.

15  Takeyama: *Harp of Burma*, p. 31.

16  Takeyama: *Harp of Burma*, p. 46.

17  See Ōkubo T. ed., *Mori Arinori Zenshū* (Tokyo: Senbundō shoten, reprint, 1972) Vol. 1, p. 181. As the conversation between Mori and Li was rather well known, it was highly possible that Takeyama used it in his *Harp of Burma*. Still, this is a conjecture.

18  Takeyama Michio, '*Biruma no tategoto* ga dekirumade', *Shin-joen*, January, 1954.

19  Masaki Tsuneo published a book entitled *Shokuminchi Gensō* (Tokyo: Misuzu, 1995). Masaki discusses the problems of fantasies related with British colonies from a post-colonial viewpoint, and criticizes Takeyama for his use of stereotypes of cannibals.

20  In later editions, Takeyama modified the expression slightly, deleting the name of the Burmese minorities living near the Siamese borders.

21  Who could accuse story-tellers of not having been realistic? No one condemns the poet Li Bai for his use of rhetorical exaggeration. His famous expression 'white hair thirty thousand feet long' (Baifa sanqian zhang) is a classical example very popular even among the Japanese. What one should keep in mind in this case is that it is a literary expression and that three thousand *zhang* or thirty thousand feet means simply much or many in the poetical language of the Chinese. To accuse others on the basis of such numbers is nonsensical.

22  Takeyama's Japanese translation of Schweitzer's *Aus meinem Leben und Denken* was published under the title *Waga seikatsu to shisō yori* (Tokyo: Hakusuisha, 1939).

23  Schweitzer's letter is mentioned in the later editions of *Waga seikatsu to shisō yori* (Tokyo: Hakusuisha, 1952).

24  Aida's bitter recollections in his *Prisoner of the British* (London: Cresset, 1966) are discussed in the previous chapter entitled 'Prisoners in Burma.'

25  See Aida Yūji and four other ex-prisoners, 'Āron shūyōjo dōsōkai,' *Shokun*, (Tokyo: Bungeishunjū, October, 1971) pp. 232–241.

PART V

ATTEMPT AT CROSS-CULTURAL
ELUCIDATION

# AESOP'S *FABLES* AND THEIR JAPANESE TRANSLATIONS: AN ATTEMPT AT COMPARATIVE WORK ETHICS[1]

———————————☐———————————

Isoppu yo
Kike kenmei no
Kirigirisu.[2]

This essay does not represent in itself a study of Aesop's *fables*. What will be attempted here is a study of comparative ethics, using Japanese and other mainly European versions of some of his fables. The aim of the study is to illustrate differences in philosophies of life.

The term 'comparative ethics' may be unfamiliar to some readers. Yet, inasmuch as there is a broad field known as 'comparative culture', comparative ethics can conceivably be one aspect of that larger study. The subject, however, will not be treated in terms of a purely speculative way, but as a theme which involves instances of cultural friction, inevitable in today's ever-shrinking world.

Allow me to make first a macroscopical observation on the West European education of secular wisdom, as this is in contradistinction to the East Asian moral education. In Western societies, where the struggle for existence is strongly felt and the idea of 'survival of the fittest' prevails, people are taught not only wisdom based on Christianity but also secular wisdom and practical philosophy. People are more or less taught what is actually required rather than what is considered as a lofty ideal, in order to survive and get ahead in life. For a long time, the role to cultivate people in such ways has been played in considerable measure by Aesop's *fables* or by their translations or adaptations such as, in the case of the French elementary education, *les Fables de La Fontaine.* .

Needless to say, the Bible is *the book* in the Western world, and teachings centre around Judeo-Christian ethics, but apart from it, one of the most influential books of secular wisdom has been Aesop's *fables*. Ethical standards for ordinary people have been provided by his fables, and they are quite different from Judeo-Christian teachings. This two-tiered structure of their moral education has often been overlooked.

The Jesuit missionaries who came to Japan from Southern Europe towards the end of the sixteenth century started on the job of translating Western theological books, the catechism and language textbooks for use in evangelical work in this 'heathen' country. Among works rendered into Japanese at their hands were such religious works as *Contemptus Mundi*, *Guia do Pecador*, *Doctrina Christião*, the catechism and Aesop's *fables*. Aesop's *fables* were then used in Europe for beginners' textbooks in Latin. A single copy of a Japanese version of Aesop's *fables* in Roman letters, entitled *Esopo No Fabulas* and printed at the *colegio* in Amakusa, on the western coast of Kyushu, in the second year of Bunroku (1593), is extant today at the British Museum. Judging from its high stylistic level, the translation, commonly known as the Amakusa version of *Esopo No Fabulas* (known also as *Isopo monogtari*), was undoubtedly a work of a well-educated native Japanese. As will be seen later, this book ranks among the best in Japan's translated literature.

With this *Esopo No Fabulas*, as a start, I would like to attempt a study of comparative ethics, drawing on examples of how Aesop's *fables* have undergone cultural metamorphosis in various countries. It need not be mentioned that even in one and the same country, ethical standards are liable to change with the passing of time, and that shall be taken into consideration too.

The following is a retranslation into English of one of the *fables* contained in the Amakusa version, which was produced while Japan was under the military domination of the powerful lord Toyotomi Hideyoshi (1536–98).

MOTHER AND CHILD

A boy attending a private school stole a textbook from one of his classmates but his mother did not scold him. Elated, the boy thereafter stole writing brushes, ink sticks and whatever else he could lay his hands on, thinking that nothing was more exciting than stealing.

Thus, he grew to be a notorious robber, and when his crimes were exposed, he was handed over to the local magistrate. Eventually he was brought to the place of his execution.

Hearing his mother cry in grief behind his back, he asked a samurai on guard, 'Please allow my mother to come near so I can give her my last words in secret.' The mother, grief-stricken but gulping down her tears, drew near and placed her ear to his mouth as asked, when the man suddenly sank his teeth into the lobe of her ear and bit it off.

The diabolical look on his face horrified the people around him. 'What a villain he is!' they said. 'We have never seen or heard of such a brute of a man who, on top of all the robbery he has committed, bites his own mother.'

Then the robber railed back: 'The world has never produced such a hard and merciless mother as mine. All that I am I owe to her. In my childhood, I stole books, ink sticks and writing brushes from my friends, but not once would she chastise me for stealing. Thus, unable to break the habit of stealing, I have grown up to be what I am today. It is none other than my mother who is now finishing me off.' So saying, the robber was beheaded.

(Moral) Everyone should know that if petty offences are left unpunished, great evil will prevail in the world.[3]

The story, written in sixteenth-century Japanese, is somewhat old-fashioned. It was a rewrite of the original fable, using such Japanese props as writing brushes, ink sticks and other samurai-related expressions to make it fit smoothly into the mode of life then prevalent in Japan. Indeed, the extent of the story's 'Japanization' becomes all the more impressive when one notes the use of such terms as *shugo no tokoro* (office of the local magistrate) and *keigo no bushi* (samurai on guard). However, as to the ethical content, the Amakusa version is more faithful to the original than some of today's Japanese versions.

Now, for the sake of comparison, let me retranslate into English the last paragraphs from the same story, this time a twentieth-century Japanese rendition by Kōno Yoichi in *Isoppu no ohanashi*, most authoritative Iwanami publishers' Shōnen Bunko (collection for juniors) series:

His mother, deep in grief and beating her breast, went with him. The son said to her: 'Mother, I have a word or two to put into your ear.' The moment the mother drew close to him, the son grabbed the lobe of her ear and slapped her on the face. When the mother reproached him and called him an unfilial son, he snorted back: 'If you had given me a good scolding when I stole that writing tablet, I would not have grown up to be like this, about to be finished off at the hands of the executioner.'

A minor wrongdoing, if unchecked, will develop into a great evil.[4]

In the Amakusa version, the lesson to be learned is labelled *shitagokoro* (moral), and goes: 'Everyone should know that if petty offences are left unpunished, great evil will prevail in the world.' Identical in sense is the English proverb 'Spare the rod and spoil the child'.

Few parents give their children a caning nowadays. Nonetheless, the custom still exists in the West in the form of what is called 'spanking' in English and *fessée* in French. Some readers may hold the view that there are ethical aspects common to both East and West.

Be that as it may, Tominaga Akio, professor of French, wrote an interesting essay in the 17 May 1976 issue of the Tokyo University *Kyōyōgakubuhō* bulletin. The gist of his essay is as follows: A, a six-year-old daughter of Japanese parents, born in Paris and bilingual, and B, a seven-year-old girl of mixed Japanese and French parentage, who also speaks the two languages but prefers French when it becomes necessary to make her points clear, were playing a game in A's room. Tominaga and his wife, as well as their nine-year-old daughter, were visiting and talking with A's mother:

> Suddenly, a quarrel developed between them when, as was learned later, A had played a trick on B. Apparently A was to blame, but instead of admitting her foul play, she became sulky and finally started crying. (Perhaps she was aware that since they were in her room, she was 'secure' anyway.)
>
> A's crying and B's angry voice grew louder, and presently B came up to A's mother to make a direct appeal. Her appeal, in effect, was that since A was in the wrong and she herself was in the right, the mother must give A a *fessée*.
>
> But the mother failed to react to the situation properly. Though she had lived in France for years, the mother was, after all, a typically Japanese woman – born and brought up in Japan. Assuming a typically Japanese attitude, she treated B's complaint only perfunctorily and gave her daughter no more than a mild scolding.
>
> This stiffened B's attitude. 'If you do not punish her, I will give her a *fessée*. Is that all right?' The furious glare of the seven-year-old girl as she filed her protest dumbfounded the adults, all of whom had a typically Japanese mentality.
>
> Perhaps it was due to B's strong character, but all the same, one could hardly imagine a young girl of B's age back in Japan censuring her playmate and asking the other's mother for permission to inflict corporal punishment on her – and in someone else's house, at that.
>
> B would not budge an inch from her demand, and finally the mother gave in. What came next was the scene of a naughty kid with her pants lowered in the standard manner, ready to be spanked. B slapped A's bottom, and the two girls shook hands.[5]

Watching every detail of the 'incident' and awed by B's proud look and determined statement, 'I will not forgive her unless she is given a *fessée*,' Tominaga thought that the kind of attitude taken by B, confident in the name of justice and clear in speech, can never be expected in contemporary Japanese society. 'Indeed, it is French society that has brought up this little one, a Japanese by all appearances, to be what she is.'

Another witness of the scene was Tominaga's daughter, born and brought up in Japan, and she had only this comment: 'I was scared'.

Having learned of this occurrence in France, I am inclined to share Professor Tominaga's concluding remark that, although going to France is no problem today for a Japanese, it still remains a faraway country. Admittedly, the methods of disciplining and bringing up children, that is, educational and ethical standards in child-rearing, vary from country to country and from generation to generation.

Even Aesop's *fables*, usually published as juvenile literature, have frequently been retold in accordance with changes in the trends of thought in a specific country and at a specific time. The story translated by Kōno as 'A Light-fingered Boy and His Mother' has been rewritten to read that the moment the mother drew close to him, the son grabbed the lobe of her ear and slapped her on the face. The original says that the son wanted to whisper into her ear, but that the moment she went up to him, he bit her earlobe. Apparently a cultural metamorphosis has taken place. Obviously working behind such an arbitrary recasting was the 'educational consideration', *kyōikuteki hairyo* peculiar to Japanese publishing circles. Some Japanese educationists must have thought that describing a son as biting his mother would be too cruel and not educational. The change is in a way comical, for the robber, whose hands must have been tied with a rope, to slap his mother on the face is not possible.

In some countries Aesop's *fables* have retained their original form, while in other countries the stories have been recast to increase their appeal to the contemporary juvenile readership. In the process of rewriting, different interpretations of the *fables* were introduced, causing delicate changes in their content according to the cultural background and ways of life in the countries concerned.

Conversely, by tracing back such a process, one may be able to grasp the trend of thought peculiar to the specific country and age in which the rewriting was done. By cultural metamorphosis, I mean a change inevitably wrought in the substance of a story as it reaches a different cultural sphere. Aesop's *fables*, originally in Greek (or Egyptian?), have been variously translated into many languages; and in Asian cases there have been also many adaptations. Thus they have been transfigured in every place and age. In view of this, one may regard Aesop's *fables* as the litmus paper, testing cultural metamorphoses that took place through the process of translations and adaptations.

The following is a review of the actual phases of cultural metamorphosis by drawing on other examples, Aesop's *fables* feature, as is well known, a number of animals that speak with emotions proper to human beings. The following is a literal translation from the Greek version into English by S.A. Handford of a fable commonly known as 'The Lion and the Mouse':

> A mouse ran over the body of a sleeping lion. Waking up, the lion seized it and was minded to eat it. But when the mouse begged to be released, promising to repay him if he would spare it, he laughed and let it go. Not long afterwards its gratitude was the means of saving his life. Being captured by hunters, he was tied by a rope to a tree. The mouse heard his groans, and running to the spot freed him by gnawing through the rope. 'You laughed at me the other day,' it said, 'because you did not expect me to repay your kindness. Now you see that even mice are grateful.'
>
> A change of fortune can make the strongest man need a weaker man's help.[6]

Contained in the Amakusa version is an excellent translation from a Latin version of the story. It reads in part:

> The mouse, frightened under the lion's paw, apologized and said: 'Please listen, your excellency, I had not the slightest intention of being impolite to you.'[7]

As regards the reason for the lion's releasing the mouse, a modern adapter, for example, Ann MacGovern says: 'The King of Beasts was so amused at the thought of a Mouse being able to help him that he let the frightened creature go.' In Japan, the Amakusa version came into being in the sixteenth century, when the samurai valued honour above everything else. Thus, in the Amakusa version the lion thought: 'I would bring dishonour on myself if I killed such a little mouse,'[8] and let it go.

Here, the lion was moved by his sense of honour and magnanimity, as befits the king of beasts, to release the mouse. A similar motivation is found in a French rendition done by Jean de la Fontaine, who served Louis XIV. (In terms of Japanese history, La Fontaine was born in 1621 at the time when the second Tokugawa shogun, Hidetada, ruled over the country. He died in 1695, that is, the 8th year of the Genroku era under the fifth shogun, Tsunayoshi.)

According to La Fontaine, the lion spares the life of the mouse in order to demonstrate his magnanimity, but is later rescued by the faithful mouse, who wants to repay the kindness.

Now, let us examine how this fable was recast in an English textbook in use at elementary schools in the United States in the 1970s. In this adaptation, the characters are a lion and two mice:

THE LION AND THE MOUSE
Have you heard the story of the Lion and the Mouse? It is a very good story.

One day, a big lion was sleeping under a tree. He looked very beautiful there in the sun.

A little mouse began to play near the sleeping lion. Soon another mouse began to play near the lion, too.

'Look at me!' said the first mouse. 'I am not afraid of this big old lion!' And he ran right over the lion's head.

The other mouse wanted to show his friend that he was not afraid of the sleeping lion. 'Just look at what I can do!' he said.

Then, to show that he was not afraid, he ran right up to the lion's head! He stopped near the lion's month.

The lion's sleep was about over. He heard the little mouse and he opened one of his eyes. The mouse was so afraid that he could not run.

Then the lion opened his other eye. 'Well!' he said, 'What are you doing here, little mouse?'

The poor mouse had never been so afraid. He did not know what to say.

'You bad little mouse. I think I will eat you,' said the lion.

'Oh, please do not eat me!' said the mouse. 'If you will let me go, I will help you someday.'

The lion thought this was very funny. 'How could a little mouse help me?' he asked.

But, because he was not hungry, he let the mouse run away. 'Oh, thank you! Thank you very much!' said the mouse. 'And I will help you some time when I can.'

This story is carried in *Storyland Favorites.*[9] In this American adaptation of Aesop's fable the lion refrained from eating the mouse not to maintain his honour as the king of beasts but because he was not hungry at the time, and so he released the mouse although he thought the proposition of the mouse's deal ridiculous. Still thanks to it, the lion was freed when captured by three hunters: the mouse gnawed through the net.

I hope that the above examples are enough for the reader to see the point of my contention that Aesop's *fables* have been liable to change almost imperceptibly according to the specific cultural backgrounds of the countries in which they have been introduced at various times, and that, conversely, by grasping the delicate changes thus wrought in the originals, one is able to gain insight into some of the cultural traits peculiar to these specific countries.

It is also possible to discern the degree of cultural maturity or refinement in the stylistic levels of the translations and adaptations done in various countries. As one example, let me quote a translation into English of the story about the town mouse and the country mouse in the Penguin Classics, which I consider to be almost identical with the original in terms of content:

> A field mouse invited a friend who lived in a town house to dine with him in the country. The other accepted with alacrity; but when he found that the fare consisted only of barley and other corns, he said to his host: 'Let me tell you, my friend, you live like an ant. But I have abundance of good things to eat, and if you will come home with me you shall share them all.' So the two of them went off at once; and when his friend showed him peas and beans, bread, dates, cheese, honey and fruit, the astonished field-mouse congratulated him heartily and cursed his own lot. They were about to begin their meal when the door suddenly opened, and the timid creatures were so scared by the sound that they scuttled into chinks. When they had returned and were just going to take some dried figs, they saw someone else come into the room to fetch something, and once more they jumped to take cover in their holes. At this the field-mouse decided that he did not take care if he had to go hungry, 'Good-bye, my friend,' he said with a groan. 'You may eat your fill and enjoy yourself. But your good cheer costs you dear in danger and fear. I would rather gnaw my poor meals of barley and corn without being afraid or having to watch anyone out of the corner of my eye.
>
> A simple life with peace and quiet is better than faring luxuriously and being tortured by fear.[10]

Let us take a look at the same story in the 1593 Amakusa edition, whose plot is more or less identical with that of the original fable up to the passage describing the mice being scared by the sound of the door opening. The rest is changed considerably. Whereas in many well known other versions there is a parallelism, for example, between the Greek version, Horace's Latin version (*Satires*, ii, 6), and La Fontaine's French version, in that the frightened mice flee together, in the Amakusa version, however, the story ends this way:

> The city mouse had no difficulty in taking cover since the granary was his beloved home and he knew every inch of it. But the country mouse was

unfamiliar with the layout of the building and had to run about before he could find a hiding place and thus barely save his life from the danger.[11]

The Japanese *kyōgen* farce has a tradition of ridiculing the bewilderment of someone who has come up to the capital from the country. A touch of this traditional humour is recognizable in this adaptation of Aesop's fable, making the story all the more vivid and amusing. Because the country mouse's panic is skillfully described, his later complaint appears quite convincing.

In the original, someone comes into the room twice and each time the mice are frightened. According to both the Japanese and the French renditions, however, a man enters the room only once and yet the shock is strong enough for the country mouse to decide to go home. On the other hand, the city mouse is over-sophisticated. Notwithstanding the danger, he affects *sang-froid* and says to the country mouse: 'Please don't allow yourself to be surprised, my dear friend. The virtue of residing in the capital lies in eating such gorgeous fare and always enjoying oneself. So, don't stand on ceremony. Eat anything you want.' Thus, the city mouse is described as being a sophisticated rogue. He dwells triumphantly on the 'virtue of residing in the capital' and prides himself on his evil practice of parasitism.

In his French version of the fable, La Fontaine reverses the order of the visits exchanged between the two mice, making the town mouse invite the country mouse to dinner first. Like the original, this seven-quatrain poem gives a brief account of how they run to take cover when the door suddenly opens while they are at table, but concludes with the country mouse's firm, even vigorous, statement in the last two stanzas.

As soon as the sound dies down, the frivolous town mouse says: 'Let's dispose of the dishes!'

> – C'est assez, dit le rustique;
> Demain vous viendrez chez moi,
> Ce n'est pas que je me pique
> De tous vos festins de roi:
>
> Mais rien ne vient m'interrompre.
> Je mange tout à loisir.
> Adieu donc. Fi du plaisir
> Que la crainte peut corrompre![12]

Between the lines, some may see the spirit of self-confidence of the French peasantry. Others may even feel the author's own emotions in his 'le Rat de ville et le Rat des champs', as La Fontaine was known at the time to be in despair over the life in Court after his patron, Nicolas Fouquet, had been imprisoned for his involvement in a financial scandal.

It is worthy of note in this connection that Robert Dodsley's English translation of this fable, put out in 1764, or about a century after La Fontaine's rendition in 1668, also contains no allusion to the so-called countryman's humility. Despite their whiskers, the mice that appear in the Dodsley version are females, obviously reflecting the trend of English society in the eighteenth century, when women stood in the limelight of social life. The following is the gist of the story:

The country mouse treated her guest to the *best* cheese and bacon available in her cottage, as well as to the *purest* water from the spring. (The country mouse can only afford a scratch meal, but her hospitality is symbolized by the two adjectives in the superlative.)

> The repast was homely indeed, but the welcome hearty; they sat and chatted away the evening together very agreeably, and then retired in peace and quietness each to her little cell.[13]

The above paragraph describes the ideal style of living maintained by country ladies and gentlemen, whom Dodsley calls the 'contented' people who lived in the country in eighteenth-century England.

However, the court mouse, when taking her leave the next morning, 'pressed her country friend to accompany her; setting forth in very pompous terms, the great elegance and plenty in which she lived at Court.'[14] And in one of the rooms at the palace, 'they found the remains of a sumptuous entertainment', such as 'creams and jellies, and sweet-meats, Parmesan, and ... champagne'.[15] This was exactly the kind of food served at dinner in English high society in the eighteenth century.

> But before they had half finished their repast, they were alarmed with the barking and scratching of a lap dog; then the mewing of a cat frightened them almost to death; by and by, a whole train of servants burst into the room and everything was swept away in an instant.[16]

The country mouse said as soon as she had recovered courage enough to speak,

> 'If your fine living is thus interrupted with fears and dangers, let me return to my plain food, and my peaceful cottage; for what is elegance without ease; or plenty, with an aching heart?'[17]

Explicit in this English translation – even more so than in La Fontaine's version – are the sound spirits of self-assertiveness and independence proper to rural life. Recognizing, further, the secret of the Anglo-Saxon mode of social life, with its emphasis more on conversation than on dining, one may indeed call Dodsley's a well 'Anglicized' fable.

In France, education begins with La Fontaine's fables, which children are required to learn by heart. Ever since La Fontaine translated Aesop's *fables* into his smooth, well crafted verse, generation after generation of French children have been immersed in these stories to acquire *le bon sens*. It was a kind of their first bath. Thus, for French children, La Fontaine's *fables* have played the role of a moral textbook as well as a language primer. French people may be unfamiliar with the name of Jean-Paul Sartre, but they cannot remain ignorant of Victor Hugo and Jean de la Fontaine.

There is a substantial difference, in terms of the points emphasized, between the cultivation of moral habits, or education for character building. On the one hand is the Confucian-oriented East Asian cultural sphere, and on the other is the Western sphere of elementary education, drawing on such materials as Aesop's or La Fontaine's *fables*.

The East Asian method of moral cultivation for the molding and remolding of personality by inculcating in people's minds each and every word of the emperor's edicts or the chairman's sayings tends to become idealistic. It demands too much from people and emphasizes 'what should be' or 'what one should do'. Time was when the Japanese were disciplined to 'sacrifice personal interest to the public good', a precept laid down in the Imperial Rescript on Education of 1890.

To be sure, exhortation towards self-sacrifice or self-denial for the good of all is virtuous in itself. Yet paradoxically, because all such moral teachings are impeccable, advocating them is liable to end in nothing more than 'crying for the moon'. In contrast, education by use of Aesop's or La Fontaine's French renditions of his *fables* is characterized by the way it divulges at the outset the truth that egoism and vanity are intrinsic qualities of human beings.

'The Crow and the Fox' is one of the fables first-year pupils in French elementary schools are told to learn by heart.

LE CORBEAU ET LE RENARD

> Maître Corbeau, sur un arbre perché,
>   Tenoit en son bec un fromage.
> Maître Renard, par l'odeur alléché,
>   Lui tint à peu près ce langage:
> «Hé! bonjour, Monsieur du Corbeau.

Que vous êtes joli! que vous me semblez beau!
    Sans mentir, si votre ramage
    Se rapporte à votre plumage,
Vous êtes le phénix des hôtes de ces bois.»
A ces mots le Corbeau ne se sent pas de joie;
    Et pour montrer sa belle voix,
Il ouvre un large bec, laisse tomber sa proie.
Le Renard s'en saisit, et dit: «Mon bon Monsieur,
    Apprenez que tout flatteur
    Vit aux dépens de celui qui l'écoute
Cette leçon vaut bien un fromage, sans doute.»
    Le Corbeau, honteux et confus,
Jura, mais un peu tard, qu'on ne l'y prendroit plus.[18]

### THE CROW AND THE FOX

Master Crow sat in a tree,
    A piece of cheese in his beak.
Master Fox, allured by the smell,
    Spoke to him as follows:
    'Hello! Good day, Mr. Crow.
How beautiful you are! How elegant you look!
    Take my word for it, if your voice is
    As beautiful as your feathers,
You are the phoenix of all the denizens of this forest.'
At these words the crow could not contain his joy;
    And to demonstrate his beautiful voice,
He opened wide his beak, letting fall his prize.
Snatching it up, the fox said: – 'My dear friend,
    Learn that all flatterers
Live at the expense of those who hear them:
No doubt this lesson is well worth a piece of cheese.'
    The crow was ashamed and perplexed,
And, though belatedly, swore that he would be tricked no more.[19]

In many English versions of this fable the lesson to be learned is labelled 'Application', not 'Moral', presumably to suggest that the story can be applied on such and such an occasion. The use of the word *application* is striking for Asians, because it evidences how very different the utilitarian and pragmatic Anglo-Saxon concept of morals is from the Asian concept of virtue.

It seems that in the West even elementary schoolchildren are taught to squarely face the stark realities of the world without glossing over the egoism inherent in human nature. – Of course, children will at first accept the story of the crow and the fox as simply a tale of two animals. However, when they grow older, the story will return to their minds with a new significance as a fable providing analytical insight into the psychology of flattery. That British and French youths often appear far more mature than their Japanese counterparts is probably not unrelated to the kind of education they have received and the educational outlook to which they have been subjected in childhood, in which no attempt has been made to glorify and idealize humanity.

If the crow-and-fox story is the second of Aesop's *fables* that French children learn, first and foremost comes the story about the cicada and the ant. By way of comparing national traits in different cultures, La Fontaine's version as against a Japanese rendition offers a good example of cultural metamorphosis *à la japonaise*.

### LA CIGALE ET LA FOURMI

La Cigale, ayant chanté
　　Tout l'été,
Se trouva fort dépourvue
Quand la bise fut venue:
Pas un seul petit morceau
De mouche ou de vermisseau.
Elle alla crier famine
Chez la Fourmi sa voisine,
La priant de lui prêter
Quelque grain pour subsister
Jusqu'à la saison nouvelle.
«Je vous paierai, lui dit-elle,
Avant l'oût, foi d'animal,
Intérêt et principal.»
La Fourmi n'est pas prêteuse:
C'est là son moindre défaut.
«Que faisiez-vous au temps chaud?
Dit-elle à cette emprunteuse.
—Nuit et jour à tout venant
Je chantois, ne vous déplaise.
—Vous chantiez ? j'en suis fort aise;
Eh bien! dansez maintenant.»[20]

### THE CICADA AND THE ANT

The cicada, having sung all summer,
Became a pauper
When the north wind began to blow;
Without a morsel, not even a fly or a worm.
Complaining of hunger,
The cicada asked the ant next door

To lend her some wheat so she could live
Until the next year.
'I'll repay you in August,
   on my faith as an animal,
Both interest and principal.'
The ant was not a lender;
She had no such defect.
'What were you doing when it was hot?'
The ant asked the borrower.
'Night and day, all day long,
I was only singing.'
'So you were singing? Very well!
Why don't you now dance?'[21]

This story appears at the beginning of the first volume of La Fontaine's *Fables*. Since both *cigale* (cicada) and *fourmi* (ant) are of the feminine gender in French, the two insects are treated here as females.

The story describes the industrious ant as being an exceedingly thrifty character who considers that the proclivity to lend people things is a shortcoming from which she herself is lucky enough to be completely free. Thus the ant, affecting ignorance, sarcastically asks the cicada what she was doing when it was hot, and when the cicada somewhat apologetically replies that she was singing and chirping all day long, the ant pitilessly retorts that that is fine and maybe now she should dance, refusing to give her anything to eat. The ant's cold, hard, merciless attitude does not necessarily reflect either La Fontaine's or Aesop's personality. Be that as it may, the story teaches the chilling lesson that the world is not merciful.

In Japan the new school year begins in spring, whereas in France it starts in autumn. First-year pupils in French elementary schools are probably told to memorize the cicada-and-ant story at about the time that the freezing north winds begin to blow.

'Prepare for winter', the lesson furnished by the cicada-and-ant story, is indeed an important topic in language and moral education in the West. On the contrary, in the tropics, for instance in Java, where nature bestows on human beings an abundance of fruit and permits rice harvesting all the year round, the virtues of industriousness and frugality, as taught by this fable, not only lose their persuasiveness but even become altogether unintelligible to local children. In the tropics, it is impossible to imagine a climate where a gust of north wind makes people paupers. Indeed, the work ethic of a 'winter culture' naturally differs from that of a 'summer culture'.

Even between Japan and Europe, where the year consists of four clearly defined seasons, there are subtle differences in the work ethic as well as in the rules governing interpersonal relationships, and these differences are reflected in the Japanese and European versions of the cicada-and-ant story. First examination is with the retold Japanese version in *Esopo No Fabulas* of the Amakusa version.

> One midwinter day, columns of ants were taking their store of grain out of their nests to dry and air when a cicada came and begged for a morsel. One of the ants asked, 'What did you do to make a living?' and the cicada replied, 'I was so busy singing all during the summer and autumn that I didn't work at all.' The ant said, 'Well, well, just as you were then singing and playing, why don't you now enjoy your esoteric music to your heart's content?'
> After scathingly ridiculing the cicada, the ants nonetheless gave him a bit of food and let him go.[22]

Thus, *Esopo No Fabulas* of sixteenth-century Japan tells of the ants giving the cicada a bit of food. It is substantially different from the French version, which ends with the words 'Eh bien! dansez maintenant'. In the La Fontaine version, the ant sharply rejects the cicada's request. However, not only in the French version but also in the Greek and Latin texts, as well as in many of the British and American versions, we see the ants invariably depicted as exceedingly cold-hearted and without an ounce of sympathy for the cicada, who is only 'reaping the harvest of his own sowing'.

The Japanese have always disliked flatly rejecting others' requests. The statistics show where Westerners will say 'no' ten times, the Japanese will do so only seven times and will either make ambiguous remarks or even choose to keep silent for the rest.[23] Thus, it is often witnessed that Japanese comply with strong requests for their signatures in support of others' campaigns, even though they actually disapprove, so as not to sour the atmosphere. (In such a case, the tacit understanding among the people concerned is that the significance of affixing one's signature to a document is merely that of affirming that one has seen it.)

The traditional Japanese habit of placing harmony among people above all else is fully reflected in *Esopo No Fabulas*, translated and published towards the end of the sixteenth century, in which the ants 'gave the cicada a bit of food and let him go'.[24] Today we often hear of the contemporary equivalent of this attitude when a business firm, succumbing to the unreasonable demands of a *sōkaiya*,[25] 'gives him a small amount of money and lets him go'. In many post-war editions of Aesop's *fables* put out by leading Japanese publishing houses, an extensive emphasis on harmony is performed, praise of altruism and blind belief in social welfare are seen. The ant heartily welcomes the cicada, saying, 'Here you are, Mr Cicada. Please feel free to help yourself.'[26]

To be sure, nowadays we come across many people in the world of politics, as well as in the world of juvenile literature, who cajole children into accepting a sugar-coated make-believe world as real. While there is nothing wrong with advocating welfare and the spirit of mutual assistance, the benefits of welfare should be strictly limited to those at the bottom of society and should not be made available to others.

Aesop's *fables* represent a compilation of practical wisdom, offering a broad spectrum of pragmatic counsel to their readers so that they may make their way through everyday life without committing serious blunders. Some critics have it that, just as Aesop was himself a slave, his *fables* reflect a 'slave morality' and are devoid of idealism. Such a view is shared by the Japanese translator of Aesop whose commentary appears in *Isoppu gūwashū* in the Iwanami Bunko series.

Aesop's *fables* certainly do not include a single story with a 'lofty' theme, such as noble deeds of self-sacrifice. It does not mean that the stories should necessarily be dismissed as unrefined or low-brow. Looking it from another angle, the contemptuous tone of the appraisal given to Aesop's *fables* by Japanese scholars may be cited as evidence of the Japanese intellectual inclination to indulge in idealized, rosy illusions rather than confront grim realities.[27]

*Notes*

[1] This essay was published in the monthly *Shokun* (Tokyo: Bungeishunjū), April and May 1977 as 'Isoppu monogatari: hikaku rinri no kokoromi'; its English translation appeared in *Japan Echo,* vo.4 nos 3 & 4, 1977 under the title of 'The Japanese and Aesop's *Fables*'.

[2] The English translation of the *haiku*: *Isoppu yo/ kike kenmeino/ kirigirisu* by Eileen Kato is as follows:

> Oh! Aesop, listen
> To the earnest grasshopper
> Begging for his life!

This is a *haiku* by Yonezawa Hyakki, who lives in Kōfu-city. The contribution appeared in the *haiku* column of the daily newspaper *Sankei*, November, 17, 1996. The amateur *haiku* poet protests in this short poem the author Aesop's harsh treatment of the grasshopper in the fable. In this *haiku* the seasonal term is *kirigirisu*; grasshopper is associated in the Japanese mind with Autumn. In Japan's case, as Aesop's *fables* were often translated from their English version, *kirigirisu* (grasshopper) appears as often as *semi* (cicada).

[3] Shinmura Izuru ed.: *Kirishitan bungaku shū* (Tokyo: Asahi shinbun-sha, 1960) vol. 2, pp. 288–289. The English translation by *Japan Echo*.

[4] *Isoppu no o-hanashi*, tr.& ed.Kōno Yoichi (Tokyo: Iwanami shoten, 1955) pp. 162–163.

[5] See Hirakawa Sukehiro: *Higashi no tachibana nishi no orenji* (Tokyo: Bungeishunjū, 1981, pp. 283–285.

[6] *Fables of Aesop*, tr. S.A.Handford (London: Penguin Classics, 1988) p. 41.

[7] The original Japanese of *Esopo No Fabulas* in today's romanized transcription is as follows: ikani shishi ō, kikoshi mesarei. Kwantai o zonjitewa tsukamatsuranu.(*Kirishitan bungaku shū*, vol. 2, p. 260).

[8] The original Japanese is as follows: Shishi mo shinjū ni omōwa,'mono no kazu demo nai konezumi domo o, waga te ni kakete korosō koto, kaette waga na o kegasu ni nita' to omōte, tachimachi yuruite yatta. (Ibid. p. 260)

[9] *Storyland Favorites* (Laidlaw Brothers Publishers, 1977).

[10] *Fables of Aesop*, tr. S. A. Handford p. 43.

[11] The original Japanese of the country mouse's panic is as follows: inaka no nezumi wa annai wa shirazu, koko kashiko o nigemawattaga, toaru mono no kage ni kaurete karai inochi o ikite sono nan o nogareta (*Kirishitan bungaku shū*, vol. 2, p. 256).

[12] La Fontaine: *Fables Choisies, Classiques Larousse* (Paris: Larousse, 1934?) vol. 1, p. 26.

[13] 'The Town Mouse and the Country Mouse', tr. Robert Dodsley, in John J. McKendry: *Aesop, Five Centuries of Illustrated Fables* (New York: The Metropolitan Museum of Art, 1964) p. 56.

[14] Ibid.

[15] Ibid.

[16] Ibid.

[17] Ibid.

[18] La Fontaine: *Fables Choisies*, p. 20.

[19] The English translation by *Japan Echo*.

[20] La Fontaine: *Fables Choisies*, p. 19.

[21] The English translation by *Japan Echo*.

[22] The English translation by *Japan Echo*.

[23] Statistics were taken on the basis of Henri Frei: *Deux Mille Phrases de Tokyo* (Tokyo: The Institute of Language Teaching, Waseda University, 1971).

[24] According to Hayashi Chikio (Hayashi: *Nihonjin no shinsō ishiki*, Tokyo: NHK books, 1982, pp. 11–39) the ants became less cold-hearted, espe-

cially towards the aged and the sick, in the Portuguese version by Miguel Do Couto Guerreiro, published in Lisbon in 1788. Some people think that the good translator was a Japanese Jesuit preparing works for Japanese Christians. The ants, therefore, are practicing a Christian virtue of Charity. I have doubts about this interpretation, as *Esopo No Fabulas* in Roman letters was printed as a textbook of Japanese for Iberian Jesuits.

[25] Sōkaiya: A person who holds a few shares of stock in a number of companies and attempts to extort money from them by threatening to cause trouble at the stockholders' general meetings.

[26] *Isoppu e-banashi* (Tokyo: Shōgakkan, kodomo hyakka shirīzu, 1976). Shūeisha's *Shōgakkō ichinensei yō ehon* ends with the ant's kind words: 'Sorewa o-kinodoku ni, kondo kara ki o tsukenasai yo.' (Oh I'm sorry about that. Please take care from this on.) The Japanese ant, of course, gives a morsel to the grasshopper. One of the strong advocates of rewriting of the kind was Mrs Hatano Isoko who often wrote editor's notes to works of Aesop and others.

[27] Among Japanese scholars of French literature, few specialize in La Fontaine; among Japanese scholars of Western classics, virtually no one specializes in Aesop. It appears to me that present-day Japanese, who have chosen to prettify Aesop's *fables* in recasting them, have no true liking for them at all.

# THE *DIVINE COMEDY* AND THE NŌ PLAYS OF JAPAN: AN ATTEMPT AT RECIPROCAL ELUCIDATION[1]

———————□———————

In 1939, William Butler Yeats wrote a drama entitled *Purgatory*. Yeats's title suggests immediately that he might have been influenced by Dante's *Divine Comedy*. Sung Hae-Kyung has shown, however, that Yeats's play was influenced not by the *Divine Comedy* but by Japanese Nō plays, especially the Nō of spirits.[2] We may suppose that there are some similarities between Irish supernatural backgrounds in Yeats's drama and Shinto supernatural backgrounds in ghostly Nō plays. Yeats's interest in such plays goes back at least to the introduction he wrote to a selection of the Fenollosa-Pound translations of Nō plays published by his sister in 1916. Evoking Dante but relying instead on a medieval Japanese dramatic form, Yeats's *Purgatory* poses important questions for comparative study. How was it possible for Yeats to transpose radically separate cultural codes successfully? What common features might the *Divine Comedy* share with the Nō plays? How do those features illuminate the artworks and the traditions sustaining them? In this chapter the analyses are, first, of one play typical of Yeats's dramatic model 'Atsumori' and, second, of the common artistic and cultural features, which will clarify Dante's narrative and the Japanese Nō plays as well.

A main feature of Japanese literature is that it deals with this world and also, conspicuously with the other world of the dead. In modern works, such as Kōda Rohan's *Taidokuro* (Encounter with a Skeleton), Izumi Kyōka's *Kōya-hijiri* (The Kōya Priest), or Tanizaki Junichirō's *Ashikari* (The Reed Cutter), one finds the same structural pattern which one recognizes as specifically Japanese.[3] Roughly speaking, the pattern is structured in the following way: a living traveller meets a person at a spot redolent of historical memories. While talking, the traveller, all of sudden realizes that the person is not of this world. The person reveals his or her identity, and tells the agonizing moments of the person's life. But the traveller's prayers have been answered, and the ghost of the person has broken its bonds and is free to depart. The ghost recedes and disappears.

The same pattern appears, however, in many cantos of the *Divine Comedy*, and this similarity suggests the same sort of background influence exerted on these literary works by the religions that inform them. In addition, there are in both texts more ancient beliefs in ghosts. While reading the Nō plays of Japan, Ezra Pound was reminded of Dante and wrote also that 'the parallels with Western spiritualist doctrines are more than interesting'.[4] I believe that the *Divine Comedy* will shed light on Nō plays of spirits and I believe that the Nō plays will shed light, in turn, on Dante's spirits in *Inferno* and especially *Purgatory*.

The type of Nō play on which Yeats based his *Purgatory* is often translated into English as 'vision play', 'vision Nō', 'ghost play' or 'Nō play of spirits' which are English renderings of the Japanese technical term 'mugen nō.' 'Mu', which is the *on*(Chinese)-pronunciation of *yume,* means dream and 'gen', which is the *on*-pronunciation of *maboroshi*, means vision.

The structure of this form can be clearly seen in Zeami's Nō play, 'Atsumori', translated by Arthur Waley.[5] The first actor who comes on the stage, approaching from the 'bridge' (*hashigakari*), is the *waki* or deuteragonist. Generally speaking, *waki* is a traveller and usually a pilgrim priest. He may have a companion or a fellow traveller called *wakitsure*. The principal actor is called *shite*, protagonist, and may have a companion called *tsure*. In 'Atsumori' the first actor who comes on stage is a Buddhist priest called Rensei, formerly the famous Minamoto warrior Kumagai. Rensei is the *waki*. On entering the stage, he intones a preliminary couplet called *shidai*, which is generally taken from Buddhist teachings. The couplets are mysterious and their meanings often enigmatic. In the case of the play 'Atsumori' the priest chants:

> Life is a lying dream, he only wakes
> Who casts the World aside.

This couplet suggests the whole tenor of the play, but its symbolic meaning becomes clear only after the play is over. What the couplet means is rather ambiguous at the beginning. Then the priest introduces himself:

> I am Kumagai no Naozane, a man of the country of Musashi. I have left my home and call myself the priest Rensei; this I have done because of my grief at the death of Atsumori, who fell in battle by my hand. Hence it comes that I am dressed in priestly guise.
>
> And now I am going down to Ichi-no-Tani to pray for the salvation of Atsumori's soul.

Rensei's self-exposition establishes the historical context of the play. In the twelfth century two powerful clans, the Taira and the Minamoto, contended for supremacy. In 1183 the Taira were forced to flee from Kyoto, the capital. They camped on the shore of Suma, where they were protected by their fleet. Early in 1184, the Minamoto attacked and utterly routed them at the Battle of Ichi-no-Tani, and at this battle the young Taira prince Atsumori fell. When Kumagai, who had slain Atsumori, bent over him to examine the body, he found lying beside him a bamboo flute wrapped in brocade. The episode, first told in the *Tale of the Heike* (Heike monogatari), is so famous that it has been adapted to the Nō stage and also to the Kabuki theatre. Many Nō plays take their themes from old romances such as the *Tale of Genji*, or the *Tale of Ise*. The audience of the Nō play 'Atsumori' is familiar with who Atsumori is and why the former warrior Kumagai has become a Buddhist monk. After the self-introduction there follows a song of travel, *michiyuki*, in verse. As the verse part is full of word-play and very difficult to translate into English, Waley omits it, and gives an explanation in parenthesis: '(He walks slowly across the stage, singing a song descriptive of his journey.)'

Nō plays are not realistic theatre. In three minutes the Nō actor completes a three-hundred-mile journey:

> I have come so fast that here I am already at Ichi-no-Tani, in the country of Tsu.
>
> Truly the past returns to my mind as though it were a thing of today.
>
> But listen! I hear the sound of a flute coming from a knoll of rising ground. I will wait here till the flute-player passes, and ask him to tell me the story of this place.

The song of reapers is heard, somewhat in the tone of Gray's *Elegy*:

> They that were reaping,
> Reaping on that hill,
> Walk now through the fields
> Homeward, for it is dusk.

The young reaper comes on stage accompanied by another reaper. Even though there is only one companion, this *tsure* may represent several reapers. Both the young reaper and his companion carry a stylized bunch of cut grass in their hands. The priest calls to the young reaper, and a dialogue follows between the two. While the conversation continues, the other reaper or reapers all exit, and the young reaper alone remains in the dusk. Sensing a certain strangeness the priest asks abruptly:

PRIEST.
> How strange it is! The other reapers have all gone home, but you alone stay loitering here. How is that?

REAPER.
> How is it, you ask? I am seeking for a prayer in the voice of the evening waves. Perhaps you will pray the Ten Prayers for me?

PRIEST.
> I can easily pray the Ten Prayers for you, if you will tell me who you are.

REAPER.
> To tell you the truth – I am one of the family of Lord Atsumori.

PRIEST.
> One of Atsumori's family? How glad I am!
> Then the priest joined his hands (he kneels down) and prayed:
> Namu Amidabu.

The priest recites a passage from the Buddhist scriptures called *Kanmuryōjukyō*. The words are Buddha's words. 'I' here means Buddha before he is enlightened:

> 'If I attain to Buddhahood,
> In the whole world and its ten spheres
> Of all that dwell here none shall call on my name
> And be rejected or cast aside.'

The chorus sings the reaper's words for him while he retreats from the stage. It picks up the last phrase of the Buddhist scriptures:

CHORUS.
> 'Oh, reject me not!
> One cry suffices for salvation,
> Yet day and night
> Your prayers will rise for me.
> Happy am I, for though you know not my name,
> Yet for my soul's deliverance
> At dawn and dusk henceforward I know that you will pray.'
> So he spoke. Then vanished and was seen no more.

The first part of this two-part Nō play closes here. In the second part the true identity of the young reaper is revealed. Since it is so strange to meet a reaper who says he is one of the family of Lord Atsumori, after his disappearance, Rensei delivers a monologue and performs Buddhist rites and prays.

PRIEST.
> Since this is so, I will perform all night the rites of prayer for the dead, and calling upon Amida's name will pray again for the salvation of Atsumori.

The ghost of Atsumori appears, dressed as a young warrior. It is the same protagonist who is now dressed gorgeously as a Taira prince and who this time wears a mask, which means that the person does not belong to this world. Supporting actors such as *waki* do not wear masks, as they are living persons. Most *shite* or main actors in vision plays are ghosts, and they come on stage masked. Atsumori, the sixteen-year-old-prince, wears a beautiful mask.

ATSUMORI.
> Would you know who I am
> That like the watchman at Suma Pass
> Have wakened at the cry of sea-birds roaming
> Upon Awaji shore?
> Listen, Rensei. I am Atsumori.

The Suma Pass, looking out on the Inland Sea and the island of Awaji, is the site of the decisive battle. Kumagai, who cut off the head of prince Atsumori, returns to the place to perform the rites of prayer for the dead and now sees Atsumori coming back. Kumagai says:

PRIEST.
> How strange! All this while I have never stopped beating my gong and performing the rites of the Law. I cannot for a moment have dozed, yet I thought that Atsumori was standing before me. Surely it was a dream.

ATSUMORI.
> Why need it be a dream? It is to clear the karma of my waking life that I am come here in visible form before you.

The Taira clan lost the battle and prince Atsumori was killed in the confusion on the beach near Suma Pass. Those who die satisfied with what they have accomplished in their lifetime do not haunt the world of the living, but those who die filled with resentment continue to come back to the living world. Atsumori's ghost cannot leave this world without being released from the bonds of karma. His soul cannot be saved so long as he harbours bitterness. To appease Atsumori's resentment and wipe away his sin (resentment itself is conceived of as a sin in Buddhism), someone with priestly powers must pray for his salvation. Rensei explains:

> Is it not written that one prayer will wipe away ten thousand sins? Ceaselessly I have performed the ritual of the Holy Name that clears all sin away. After such prayers, what evil can be left? Though you should be sunk in sin as deep...

ATSUMORI.
As the sea by a rocky shore,
Yet should I be saved by prayer.

PRIEST.
And that my prayer should save you ...

ATSUMORI.
This too must spring
From kindness of a former life.

PRIEST.
Once enemies ...

ATSUMORI.
But now ...

PRIEST.
In truth may we be named ...

ATSUMORI.
Friends in Buddha's Law.

Texts of Nō plays are like the libretti of Western opera. After this dialogue between the two former enemies, who seem to be reconciled as friends in Buddha's Law, singing the same words together, the chorus glorifies the virtues of religion by quoting a popular proverb. The chorus chants Rensei's words for him:

CHORUS.
There is a saying, 'Put away from you a wicked friend; summon to your side a virtuous enemy.' For you it was said, and you have proven it true.
And now come tell with us the tale of your confession, while the night is still dark.

The tale that Atsumori feels compelled to tell is the story of his final hours. The downfall of the Taira clan, their defeat at the battle of Ichi-no-Tani near the Suma beach, and his beheading by the Minamoto warrior Kumagai are all sources of his profound resentment and rancour. Atsumori cannot refrain from telling the circumstances of his hour of agonies. It is only by retelling the story

of his death that his soul feels relieved, just as sinners are cleansed
by confession. After the chorus chants some Buddhist lessons,
Atsumori begins the story of the decline and fall of the Taira clan:

ATSUMORI.
> Now the clan of Taira, building wall to wall,
> Spread over the earth like the leafy branches of a great tree:

CHORUS.
> Yet their prosperity lasted but for a day;
> It was like the flower of the convolvulus.
> There was none to tell them
> That glory flashes like sparks from flint-stone,
> And after, – darkness.
> Oh wretched, the life of men!

ATSUMORI.
> When they were on high they afflicted the humble;
> When they were rich they were reckless in pride.
> And so for twenty years and more
> They ruled this land.
> But truly a generation passes like the space of a dream.
> The leaves of the autumn of Juyei
> Were tossed by the four winds;
> Scattered, scattered (like leaves too) floated their ships.
> And they, asleep on the heaving sea, not even in dreams
> Went back to home.
> Caged birds longing for the clouds, –
> Wild geese were they rather, whose ranks are broken
> As they fly to southward on their doubtful journey.
> So days and months went by; Spring came again
> And for a little while
> Here dwelt they on the shore of Suma
> At the first valley.
> From the mountain behind us the winds blew down
> Till the fields grew wintry again.
> Our ships lay by the shore, where night and day
> The sea-gulls cried and salt waves washed on our sleeves.
> We slept with fishers in their huts
> On pillows of sand.
> We knew none but the people of Suma.
> And when among the pine-trees
> The evening smoke was rising,
> Brushwood, as they call it,
> Brushwood we gathered
> And spread for carpet.
> Sorrowful we lived
> On the wild shore of Suma,

Till the clan Taira and all its princes
Were but villagers of Suma.

ATSUMORI.

But on the night of the sixth day of the second month
My father Tsunemori gathered us together.
'Tomorrow,' he said, 'we shall fight our last fight.
Tonight is all that is left us.'
We sang songs together, and danced.

PRIEST.

Yes, I remember; we in our siege-camp
Heard the sound of music
Echoing from your tents that night;
There was the music of a flute...

ATSUMORI.

The bamboo-flute! I wore it when I died.

PRIEST.

We heard the singing...

ATSUMORI.

Songs and ballads...

PRIEST.

Many voices

ATSUMORI.

Singing to one measure.

(ATSUMORI dances.)

First comes the Royal Boat.

CHORUS.

The whole clan has put its boats to sea.
He will not be left behind;
He runs to the shore.
But the Royal Boat and the soldiers' boats
Have sailed far away.

ATSUMORI.

What can he do?
He spurs his horse into the waves.
He is full of perplexity.
And then

CHORUS.

He looks behind him and sees
That Kumagai pursues him;
He cannot escape.
Then Atsumori turns his horse
Knee-deep in the lashing waves,
And draws his sword.

> Twice, three times he strikes; then, still saddled,
> In close fight they twine; roll headlong together
> Among the surf of the shore.
> So Atsumori fell and was slain, but now the Wheel of Fate
> Has turned and brought him back.

(ATSUMORI rises from the ground and advances towards the PRIEST
with uplifted sword.)

> 'There is my enemy,' he cries, and would strike,
> But the other is grown gentle
> And calling on Buddha's name
> Has obtained salvation for his foe;
> So that they shall be re-born together
> On one lotus-seat.
> 'No, Rensei is not my enemy.
> Pray for me again, oh pray for me again.'

With the final dance by Atsumori, the Nō play comes to the end.
If Atsumori struck his former enemy with his sword, while dancing
and miming his final hours, the play would become a play of
vengeance. If the vengeance had really taken place, the dramatic
effect of the play might be more directly impressive; but the philosophy which lies behind the Nō play is Buddhism, and vendetta,
therefore, is not possible.[6] By virtue of the prayers Atsumori and
Rensei will be reborn together on the same lotus-seat in Buddha's
Paradise. Rensei's very name, which Kumagai adopted in
renouncing the world, means 'born (or reborn) on a lotus-flower'.
In other words, Kumagai wishes to gain Buddhahood, and
Kumagai, now Priest Rensei, prays also for Atsumori to gain
Buddhahood.

In his introduction to the *Nō Plays of Japan*, Waley suggests a
means of transposing the medieval Japanese drama into terms
roughly cognate with Western drama. He particularly admires the
structure of Zeami's Nō plays and illustrates how John Webster's
*Duchess of Malfi* might have been treated by a Nō dramatist.[7] The
five-act structure of Renaissance tragedy would have to be compressed and comic elements excluded. Only two personages are
needed – the Pilgrim, who would correspond to the *waki*, and the
Duchess, who would be the *shite*. The Pilgrim would take the stage
first, telling the story of his travels. When the *shite* appears, he would
ask her if the spot where he now kneels is not the shrine where the
Duchess of Malfi took refuge. She would recite the story of the
Duchess's flight in a way that prompts the Pilgrim to ask, 'Who is it
that is speaking to me?' The first part would close with her reluctant

disclosure of her identity. In the second half, the Duchess would relive the memory of her final hours, experiencing each scene until the chorus takes up the final word 'quiet'. The Pilgrim's prayers are answered, and the ghost of the Duchess recedes slowly from sight, freed at last from its bonds.

Despite its compressions and dramatic liberties, Waley's recasting of Elizabethan revenge tragedy into the form of a Nō play opened up the possibility of pursuing comparisons between two literary genres belonging to culturally different Middle Ages. Let us examine, then, Dante's *Divine Comedy* from a comparative perspective: a work whose characters, spiritual values, and structure will be considered as sharing important features with the Nō theatre.

The dramatis personae of the *Divine Comedy* correspond in interesting ways to the traditional figures of the Nō plays. The pilgrim-narrator of Dante's allegorical journey is a counterpart to the Nō *waki*, the traveller who first comes on stage accompanied by another traveller, the *wakitsure*. In Nō drama, both figures are living persons, and the corresponding figures in the *Divine Comedy* show the complications that Dante introduces. Virgil and later Beatrice are Dante's *wakitsure*, accompanying the pilgrim through a series of encounters with the souls of the dead. Just as Rensei's meeting with the vanquished prince in 'Atsumori' occurs at an imaginative level, Dante's journey through the otherworld is a literal fiction and allegorical reality. Henry Francis Cary gives a plausible interpretation of this situation by entitling his translation *The Vision of Hell, Purgatory, and Paradise of Dante Alighieri*. In a sense, each canto of the *Divine Comedy* stands as a separate vision play. The souls whom Dante meets are famous, notorious and sometimes anonymous – Francesca da Rimini, Count Ugolino, and the sinners we know only by place in a scheme of divine justice. They are like the *shite* of Nō plays, encountering Dante, the living traveller, and engaging him in conversation about their histories.

One of the most notable of these encounters is staged at the beginning of Canto III of the *Purgatory*:

> Then of them one began. 'Whoe'er thou art,
> Who journey'st thus this way, thy visage turn;
> Think if elsewhere thou hast ever seen.'
> I towards him turn'd, and with fix'd eye beheld.
> Comely and fair, and gentle of aspect
> He seem'd, but on one brow a gash was mark'd.
> When humbly I disclaim'd to have beheld
> Him ever: 'Now behold!' he said, and show'd

High on his breast a wound: then smiling spake.
'I am Manfredi, grandson to the Queen
Costanza: whence I pray thee, when return'd
To my fair daughter go, the parent glad
Of Aragonia and Sicilia's pride;
And of the truth inform her, if of me
Aught else be told. When by two mortal blows
My frame was shatter'd, I betook myself
Weeping to Him, who of free will forgives.
My sins were horrible: but so wide arms
Hath goodness infinite, that it receives
All who turn to it. Had this text divine
Been of Cosenza's shepherd better scann'd,
Who then by Clement on my hunt was set,
Yet at the bridge's head my bones had lain,
Near Benevento, by the heavy mole
Protected; but the rain now drenches them,
And the wind drives, out of the kingdom's bounds,
Far as the stream of Verde, where, with lights
Extinguish'd, he removed them from their bed.
Yet by their curse we are not so destroy'd,
But that the eternal Love may turn, while hope
Retains her verdant blossom. True it is,
That such one as in contumacy dies
Against the holy Church, though he repent,
Must wander thirty-fold for all the time
In his presumption past; if such decree
Be not by prayers of good men shorter made.
Look therefore if thou canst advance my bliss;
Revealing to my good Costanza, how
Thou hast beheld me, and beside, the terms
Laid on me of that interdict; for here
By means of those below much profit comes.'[8]

Manfredi was the illegitimate son of Emperor Frederick II, and after his father's death in 1250, he ruled South Italy and Sicily. In 1252, Conrad IV, the legitimate son and successor of Emperor Frederick II, came from Germany and drove Manfredi out. When Conrad IV died in 1254, his son Conradin was expelled by Manfredi. Manfredi then spread false reports of Conradin's death and crowned himself in Palermo in 1258. The Church excommunicated Manfredi. At the battle of Benevento Pope Clement IV and Charles I of Anjou destroyed Manfredi's army. Manfredi was killed on 25 February 1266. Villani says in his *Chronicle* vi.46:

> (King Manfredi was) comely of his body and as dissolute as his father, and more so. He was a musician and singer, and delighted in the company of

jesters, courtiers, and courtesans, and always dressed in green; ... but all his life he was an Epicurean, caring neither for God nor His saints, but only for bodily pleasure. He was an enemy of the Church and the clergy.[9]

Dante does not recognize Manfredi by sight, since he was born in the spring of 1265, only nine months before Manfredi's death. With his golden hair and green attire, Manfredi is the handsome and impressive figure portrayed by the chroniclers.

A common creative motive lies behind the *Divine Comedy* and the Nō plays, and makes them still attractive to us. In both, the spirits are tortured by passions and resentments so strong that they feel compelled to speak and appeal to the travellers coming from the world of the living. It is the raging resentment of the souls caught in Hell that is most remarkable. Dante gives this description of Count Ugolino:

> His jaws uplifting from their fell repast,
> That sinner wip'd them on the hairs o'the head,
> Which he behind had mangled, then began:
> 'Thy will obeying, I call up afresh
> Sorrow past cure; which, but to think of, wrings
> My heart, or ere I tell on't. But if words,
> That I may utter, shall prove seed to bear
> Fruit of eternal infamy to him,
> The traitor whom I gnaw at, thou at once
> Shalt see me speak and weep.'[10]

Manfredi, who is waiting before the Gate of Purgatory to enter, is not so enraged or savage as Count Ugolino, whom we see in the ninth circle of Hell. However, just as Atsumori or the Duchess of Malfi feels compelled to narrate the story of their final hours to the pilgrim, Manfredi as well as Ugolino feels the need to speak to the traveller Dante. Manfredi shows Dante the fatal scars on his eyebrow and breast, and tells him that he was not cast down into Hell, as the Church and the people of the world have thought. Manfredi emphasizes the fact that he is waiting to enter Purgatory.

Manfredi cared 'neither for God nor His saints' and was 'an enemy of the Church' during his lifetime; but 'when by two mortal blows (his) frame was shatter'd, (he) betook himself weeping to Him, who of free will forgives'. Manfredi never lost faith in God or His divine mercy; he was therefore saved and is now waiting his turn to enter Purgatory. Dante believes that anyone who repents his earlier sins may be saved despite excommunication by the Church. Manfredi says, 'My sins were horrible: but so wide arms/Hath goodness infinite, that it receives/All who turn to it.' The Church, however, did not allow Manfredi's body to be buried in papal territory. Although his body was once buried near Benevento at the bridge's head where he had died and where each passing soldier put a stone on the mole, the bishop of Cosenza, who had impeached Manfredi at Pope Clement's command, refused even that burial and had the body moved beyond the confines of the kingdom. The cortege marched without lights, *lume spento*, as in the case of those who were excommunicated, and deposited the corpse on the banks of the river Verde without burying it. Rain now drenched his bones, and the wind battered them. The resulting resentment and pain compel Manfredi to speak to Dante, who is travelling through the other world. Like other spirits, he hopes that Dante may bring back a message to living relatives and friends.

Both in the Nō plays and in the *Divine Comedy* the author becomes a kind of spiritual medium, who is possessed by the characters and speaks on their behalf. The irresistible feelings of the dead thus find expression. A cathartic effect is achieved by telling, and by having someone listen to and pray for them. In this respect, both the Nō plays and the *Divine Comedy* serve the function of a requiem. The Nō theatre, which is conceived for stage performance, includes dance, music and song, and belongs by its ritualistic origin to a different genre from the *Divine Comedy*. As poetic literature, however, it shares with Dante's work the convention of a ghost appearing in order to tell a living person his or her own past story. The *waki* or traveller also prays for the ghost or agrees to deliver his or her message to the family. In the Nō play 'Kagekiyo', the hero, a defeated Taira warrior, says to his daughter:

> Go to your home;
> Pray for my soul departed, child, candle to my darkness,
> Bridge to salvation![11]

In a similar fashion Manfredi asks Dante to visit his daughter Costanza and requests that she pray for her father. In Canto V of the *Purgatory*, Buonconte also begs Dante to ask his wife to pray for the repose of Buonconte's soul, for prayers help souls in Purgatory to climb more quickly the steep mountain path to the Earthly Paradise.

The common motive joining the *Divine Comedy* and the Nō plays also points up some differences in the conceptions of hell in Christianity and Buddhism. In Christianity it is futile to pray for those who are cast down in Inferno, as they cannot be saved ever. In Buddhism it is not so, as there remains the possibility that the prayers of the living may help save souls condemned to Hell. In this regard, the Buddhist Hell resembles rather the Catholic Purgatory. Still, images of hell in the two religions are quite similar. Buddhist images of hell scrolls are very powerful. Uchimura Kanzō (1861–1930), a late-nineteenth-century convert to Christianity, was terrified by the idea of hell throughout his life, as he sincerely believed in the eternity of the soul. Towards the end of his life, he realized that his fear came to him from having heard about and seen a *jigoku zōshi* or Buddhist hell scroll in his early childhood. A traumatic experience of the same kind was shared by another Japanese convert, Masamune Hakuchō, who took a psychoanalytical interest in what Uchimura said in the last days of his life. Uchimura and Masamune wrote about Dante, and the demons of hell they imagined while they were reading the *Divine Comedy* are, pictorially speaking, Buddhist rather than Christian. This was in general true with Japanese, for Japanese translators of the *Divine Comedy* use without hesitation Buddhist terminology to describe the Christian Inferno.

Culturally speaking, Dante's Hell itself cannot be called uniquely Christian, in so far as its images are concerned. Almost all the monsters – Minos, the infernal judge; Cerberus, the three-headed watchdog; the Harpies, who torture with their sharp claws and beaks – are derived from pagan Greek mythology. Tortures of the same kind appear, too, in Nō plays. In 'Motomezuka', the heroine Unai suffers the tortures of the damned in the following way:

> And once more – how horrible!
> The ghosts take flight, and there appears
> Before my eyes a mandarin duck,
> Now changed to a bird of iron!
> Its beak is steel, its claws are daggers,
> It tears at my skull and now it will devour
> The marrow of my bones!
> Is this the punishment for my sins?
> How horrible!
> Priest, I implore you,
> Find a way to free me from this pain![12]

Human passions and pains are universal, and so similar images of hell have repeatedly appeared, although the Japanese did not have images so vivid as the hell scrolls before the introduction of Buddhism to Japan.

Another important feature common to East and West is a concern with salvation: how to avoid damnation and the horrors of hell. One soul who wishes to enter Purgatory tells Dante in Canto V:

> Then said another: 'Ah! so may the wish,
> That takes thee o'er the mountain, be fulfill'd,
> As thou shalt graciously give aid to mine.'[13]

The man speaks to Dante as 'friends in God's Law', if I apply here Atsumori's expression, 'friends in Buddha's Law'. Both the spirit and the traveller Dante share the same aspiration to climb the steep mountain path of Purgatory. As is usual with many souls in Purgatory, the conversation begins with a self-introduction. Here is the literal translation of the line 88, Canto V, *Purgatory*:

> I was of Montefeltro, I am Buonconte.

In the self-introduction the verb 'to be' is first put into the past tense and then into the present. The original Italian reads (italics mine):

> Io *fui* da Montefeltro, io *son* Buonconte.

The distinction of the past tense and the present tense means that his earthly existence as the lord of a territory is already over, but his soul, which is eternal, still lives on after the death of his physical body. We are reminded here of Webster's heroine in Waley's adaptation, when she spoke of herself (italics mine):

> I *am* the soul of Duke Ferdinand's sister, she that *was* once called Duchess of Malfi.[14]

Buonconte relates his story in a form that we have seen before in both Dante and the Nō plays:

> '... Of Montefeltro I; Buonconte I:
> Giovanna nor none else have care for me;
> Sorrowing with these I therefore go.' I thus:
> 'From Campaldino's field what force or chance
> Drew thee, that ne'er thy sepulture was known?'
> 'Oh!' answer'd he, 'at Casentino's foot
> A stream there courseth, named Archiano, sprung
> In Apennine above the hermit's seat.
> E'en where its name is cancel'd, there came I,
> Pierced in the throat, fleeing away on foot,
> And bloodying the plain. Here sight and speech
> Fail'd me; and, finishing with Mary's name,
> I fell, and tenantless my flesh remain'd.

I will report the truth; which thou again
Tell to the living. Me God's Angel took,
Whilst he of Hell exclaim'd: 'O thou from Heaven!
'Say wherefore hast thou robb'd me? Thou of him
'The eternal portion bear'st with thee away,
'For one poor tear that he deprives me of.
'But of the other, other rule I make.'
'Thou know'st how in the atmosphere collects
That vapour dank, returning into water
Soon as it mounts where cold condenses it.
That evil will, which in his intellect
Still follows evil, came; and raised the wind
And smoky mist, by virtue of the power
Given by his nature. Thence the valley, soon
As day was spent, he cover'd o'er with cloud,
From Pratomagno to the mountain range;
And stretch'd the sky above; so that the air
Impregnate changed to water. Fell the rain;
And to the fosses came all that the land
Contain'd not; and, as mightiest streams are wont,
To the great river, with such headlong sweep,
Rush'd, that nought stay'd its course. My stiffen'd frame,
Laid at his mouth, the fell Archiano found,
And dash'd it into Arno; from my breast
Loosening the cross, that of myself I made
When overcome with pain. He hurl'd me on,
Along the banks and bottom of his course;
Then in his muddy spoils encircling wrapt.'[15]

Buonconte da Montefeltro, like his father, was a Ghibelline leader. In 1289, he led the Aretines against the Florentines at Campaldino, where the Aretines were defeated and he was killed, but his body was never identified. Both Manfredi and Buonconte meet violent deaths but escape damnation in Hell, because they call 'the name of Mary'. Expecting to carry away Buonconte's body and soul because of his evil deeds in this world, a devil is waiting for his death. He is convinced that Buonconte would be his, soul and body together. When he finds that he cannot take away Buonconte's soul, he is furious and cries out against the angel coming from Heaven. The devil accuses the angel 'who has robbed me':

'... Thou of him
The eternal portion bear'st with thee away,
For one poor tear that he deprives me of.
But of the other, other rule I make.'

He says that if God's angel takes Buonconte's soul away, he will claim the other part – Buonconte's body – and dispose of it as he likes. Then follows the famous passage (*Purgatory* V.109–129), describing how Buonconte's body was never found. The devil has not only evil will but also intelligence and power, and he has the power to control the physical world.

The idea that demons have the power to control the physical world is found also in Buddhism: the Great King of Hell, who corresponds roughly to Minos in Dante's Hell, is called Yama (or Enma in Japanese).[16] In the Nō play 'Ikuta', which also deals with Atsumori, Yama's messenger comes to fetch Atsumori who has secretly come back from the other world to the forest of Ikuta to meet his dear child:

ATSUMORI.
  Who is that?
  (Pointing in terror at a figure which he sees off the stage.)
  Can it be Yama's messenger? He comes to tell me that I have out-
  stayed my time. The Lord of Hell is angry: he asks why I am late?
CHORUS.
  So he spoke. But behold
  Suddenly black clouds rise,
  Earth and sky resound with the clash of arms;
  War-demons innumerable
  Flash fierce sparks from brandished spears.
ATSUMORI.
  The Shura foes who night and day
  Come thick about me!
CHORUS.
  He waves his sword and rushes among them.
  Hither and thither he runs slashing furiously;
  Fire glints upon the steel.
  But in a little while
  The dark clouds recede;
  The demons have vanished,
  The moon shines unsullied;
  The sky is ready for dawn.[17]

As in the *Divine Comedy*, messengers from Hell control the physical world of dark clouds, storms, and lightning.

In the same way, belief in Mary's intercession, especially the idea of achieving salvation by simply calling on her, is reminiscent of the Japanese belief in Amida Buddha. In 'Atsumori', the soul of the dead warrior mentions to Rensei, 'One cry suffices for salvation'.

This phrase is taken from a poem by the tenth century priest Kūya (903–72):

> Once you recite Namu Amidabu
> You shall not fail to be re-born
> On the lotus-seat in Paradise.[18]

In the twelfth-century collection of popular songs and ballads called *Ryōjinhishō*, there is a similar passage:

> We put our complete trust
> In Amida Buddha's Vow
> That any who invoke his
> Holy Name, if only once,
> Will thereby gain salvation.[19]

The statue of the priest Kūya, the founder of the Jōdo or Pure Land sect of Buddhism in Japan, is another example. The wooden statue shows the emaciated monk fervently reciting the prayer, *Namu Amidabu*, as little Buddhas stream out of the saint's mouth. Despite historical differences, there is a remarkable resemblance between the cult of the Holy Name in medieval Europe and the cult of Amida's name in medieval Japan.

The common features I have been discussing might be summarized as follows:

| Vision Nō plays | *Divine Comedy* |
|---|---|
| 1) dramatis personae: | |
| *shite* (main actor): a ghost | spirit(s) in each canto |
| *waki* (supporting actor):living traveller | Dante (the pilgrim) |
| usually a pilgrim priest at time of play | |
| *tsure* (companion to *shite*) | companion to the principal spirit of the canto: for example, in the case of Francesca Paolo is her *tsure* |
| *wakitsure* (companion to *waki*) | Virgil who accompanies Dante |

2) dramatic construction which links this world with the other world (i.e. reality and vision)

3) *shite*'s or ghost's motive for telling his or her final or decisive hours in life

4) dramatic characteristics of the past as recollected by the main actor

5) concept and psychology behind the prayers offered by the living to ensure the repose and salvation of the dead

6) concepts of Paradise and Hell

7) belief in salvation by calling the name of Amida or Mary

8) the dramatic functions of the two religions, Buddhism and Christianity, which lead to a peaceful ending

9) pre-Christian animistic belief in ghosts, Shamanistic beliefs and pre-Buddhistic Shintoist belief in ghosts, which invigorate the dramatic force in Nō plays as well as in the *Divine Comedy*

It is clear that the dramatic function that both Buddhism and Christianity play in the two cases is quite similar. Dante's poem and Zeami's plays share some common religious features and imagery. The Nō plays emphasize the word 'tie' or 'bond', which means the passion that keeps the soul attached to this world. Both in Buddhism and Catholicism, the foremost desire of the soul is to cast off its bonds and be free to depart. The souls of the *Divine Comedy* who wish to go up to Paradise share the same wish with the main actors of the Nō plays. Souls of both groups ask the living to pray for them and for their release or deliverance.

The comparison of the two literary works that belong different religious backgrounds and different artistic genres might not have taken place, had it not been for Waley and his English translations. I am, therefore, most grateful to Waley, otherwise Nō plays and the *Divine Comedy* would not have been put on the same plane of comparison. So long as I read Nō plays in Japanese and the *Divine Comedy* in Italian, I could not recognize this common pattern of structure and imagery. My thinking was compartmentalized according to the languages. The Buddhist terms such as *shūchaku* which means attachment or *kizuna* which means bonds or ties, or quasi-theological terms such as *tokudatsu* or *gedatsu* which mean salvation achieved by severing such an earthly tie have different cultural and religious connotations and it never occurred to my mind to associate these words with Western equivalents.

I have tried, therefore, to pick up common characteristics of the *Commedia* and Nō plays, by juxtaposing them. Through that process the *Divine Comedy* has illuminated some aspects of the Nō plays, and, in turn, the Nō plays of spirits have shed light on some structural mechanisms in the cantos of Dante's poem, especially in *Purgatory*. The reciprocal explanation surprisingly elucidates the meanings of conversations between ghosts (the main characters) and the living traveller, who is not the mere representative of the audience, as was formerly suggested by some Japanese authorities on Nō such as Nogami Toyoichirō,[20] but is the deuteragonist who takes part in the actual play. Similarly, Dante as a dramatis persona is not a simple observer representing readers of the *Divine Comedy*. He is one of the main characters engaged in the dramatic actions of the *Commedia*. Thanks to their conversations with Dante and thanks especially to the prayers of the living, the souls in Purgatory are often able to become reconciled with themselves and they vanish at the end of the play.

This function played by religion may be seen as a kind of dramatic convention. There is a strong element of theatrical technique in it. In the case of the Nō plays and in the case of Dante's *Purgatory*, the subconscious primitive beliefs in ghosts revive once dead characters. On the surface, Nō plays are tinged with Buddhist terminology and ritual; however, the driving force lies in the underlying animism. In order to placate evil spirits, Buddhist prayers are borrowed and recited, and the ghosts vanish from sight. Religiously speaking, Nō plays are double-structured: although the upper structure is Buddhist, the lower structure is animistic Shinto, as Pound intuited.[21] In Western Europe, some psychological need of the same kind seemed to allow the creation of Purgatory, which did not exist in the Bible itself. According to Jacques Le Goff, the belief in dreams and ghosts (*revenants*) of the people and the monks of the Middle Ages propagated the notion of Purgatory.[22]

It is suggestive that Yeats, who was agnostic, wrote *Purgatory*, basing his play on the pattern of Nō theatre. There he dramatizes the encounter between the natural and supernatural worlds, as a wandering priest meets a ghost at a particular place associated with memories of the past, and an unforgettable tragic event in life is unfolded by the ghost. Yeats was of the opinion that 'the dead suffer remorse and recreate their old lives.'[23] Yeats was strongly interested in the animistic druidic atmosphere of ancient Ireland as well as that of Japan, and by rejecting the immediacy of ordinary life, he could recede into what he calls 'the deeps of the mind'. One dramatization of ghosts in this purgatorial state is precisely the drama in which Yeats puts his 'own conviction about this world and the next'.[24] The state that Yeats calls 'dreaming back'[25] is the one in which the spirits of the Nō plays and the souls of Dante's vision return. Like the *Divine Comedy* and the Nō plays of Japan, some of Yeats's dramas show common features in their inner inspirations as well as in their outer forms.

*Notes*

[1] This essay is an amplified English version of the first chapter of Hirakawa: *Yōkyoku no shi to seiyō no shi* (Tokyo: Asahishimbun-sha, 1975). I thank the Pennsylavania State University for the permission to reproduce

this article which appeared in *Comparative Literature Studies,* vol. 33, no. 1, 1996.

[2] Sung Hae-Kyung, 'Yeats and the Noh', *Hikaku Bungaku Kenkyū,* no.54 (Tokyo: Asahi-shuppan, 1988), pp. 24–47.

[3] Kinya Tsuruta suggests this view in *Nihon kindai bungaku niokeru mukōgawa* (Tokyo: Meiji-shoin, 1986).

[4] Ezra Pound: *The Translations of Ezra Pound* (London: Faber & Faber, 1970), p. 264.

[5] Arthur Waley: *Nō Plays of Japan* (London: Allen & Unwin, 1921) pp. 64–73.

[6] One of the greatest differences between Christianity and Buddhism in terms of expression is that while there exists God's vengeance in Christianity ('vendetta di Dio' in the *Divine Comedy*), there is no corresponding expression in Buddhism which means Buddha's vengeance, although the expression 'butsu-bachi' exists which means 'Buddha's punishment'. Probably 'vendetta di Dio' and 'butsu-bachi' are not so different in concept. For Christians it means generally: human beings must not take revenge; leave it to God to deal with evil!

[7] Arthur Waley: *Nō Plays of Japan,* pp. 53–54.

[8] All quotations of the *Divine Comedy* will use Henry Francis Cary, tr.: *The Vision of Hell, Purgatory, and Paradise of Dante Alighieri* (London: J. M. Dent & Sons, 1948) pp. 158–160.

[9] Dante: *The Divine Comedy, II, Purgatory,* tr. Dorothy Sayers (London: Penguin Classics, 1959) p. 94.

[10] *The Vision of Hell, Purgatory, and Paradise of Dante Alighieri,* p. 139.

[11] Arthur Waley: *Nō Plays of Japan,* p. 133.

[12] 'Motomezuka' is translated by Barry Jackman as 'The Sought-For Grave' in D. Keene, ed.: *20 Plays of Nō Theatre* (New York: Columbia UP, 1970) pp. 47–48.

[13] *The Vision of Hell, Purgatory, and Paradise of Dante Alighieri,* p. 166.

[14] Arthur Waley: *Nō Plays of Japan,* p. 54.

[15] *The Vision of Hell, Purgatory, and Paradise of Dante Alighieri,* pp. 166–168.

[16] The notion of *Yama,* found originally in the Indian mythology of *Veda,* had considerably changed when it arrived in China and Japan, where *Yanwang* and *Emma* are considered Kings of the Nether World.

[17] Arthur Waley: *Nō Plays of Japan,* p. 79.

[18] The original *uta*-poem by Kūya is as follows: Hitotabimo Namuamidabu to yū hito no hachisu no ue ni noboranu wa nashi.

[19] *Ryōjinhishō* (Tokyo: Iwanami shoten, Nihon kotenbungaku taikei, 73) p348. Translation mine.

[20] Nogami Toyoichirō, 'Nō no shuyaku ichinin shugi', *Shisō* (Tokyo: Iwanami shoten, February, 1923). Nogami's view was dominant among Japanese students of Nō theatre for half a century.

[21] Pound remarks on the Nō plays of spirits that 'the plays are, I think, more Shinto than Buddhist.' (*The Translations of Ezra Pound* p. 222).

[22] Jacques Le Goff: *La naissance du purgatoire* (Paris: Gallimard, 1981).

[23] W. B. Yeats: *Interviews and Recollections* (London: Macmillan, 1977) p. 232.

[24] *The Letters of Yeats* (London: Rupert Hart-Davis, 1954) p. 913.

[25] W. B. Yeats: *The Variorum Edition of The Plays of W. B. Yeats* (London: Macmillan, 1966) p. 777.

# DANTE'S *INFERNO* FROM A
# JAPANESE PERSPECTIVE

————————□————————

L et me explain first why I have come to analyse Western literature's masterpiece from a Japanese perspective. I translated
Dante's *Divina Commedia* into Japanese some thirty-five years ago. I
was then 'in the midst of my life' and I was teaching comparative
literature and comparative culture at the Graduate School of Tokyo
University. When I retired at the statutory retirement age of sixty, I
felt I was still intellectually vigorous and I accepted an invitation to
teach at a provincial women's college in Fukuoka, and I taught this
time using for textbook my Japanese translation of Dante. I was
surprised by the difference in the quality of the students: at Tokyo
University, an intelligent student is like any intelligent student at a
European or American university. When a Tokyo University student
reads Dante's *Divine Comedy*, he or she reads not only the text in
Italian, but also reads commentaries attached to the *testo critico* of the
edition Hoepli of the Italian Dante Society. Moreover, some students read reference books – T. S. Eliot's essays on Dante,
Benedetto Croce's book on Dante's poetry, or *Nueve Ensayos
Dantescos* by Jorge Luis Borges. Some even try to apply quite a new
literary theory when they read classical works in Western literature.
In short, the more intelligent a Japanese student is, the more international or the more European he or she tends to become. The
student very often wishes that his or her doctoral work may become
a part of Italian Dante studies.

The situation, however, is quite different in my Fukuoka
Women's College, which remains rather provincial. The students do
not read anything other than my Japanese translation of Dante's
*Divine Comedy*. For examinations they do not prepare anything more

than is absolutely necessary. They do not read other commentaries
or essays at all. In short, the only preparation they do is that they
read Dante at least once again the night before the term examination. Incidentally as my students respond more to Dante's *Inferno*
than to *Paradiso* which they find rather boring, I generally do not go
beyond Canto V of *Purgatorio*. The female students, therefore, prepare rather carefully until that part of Antipurgatorio. One may
smile at their energy-saving attitude, they focus their attention solely
on designated parts of a classic for the examination. I, however,
find them healthier in their appreciation of literature than some
graduate students of Tokyo University who are more interested in
recent literary theories and forget to appreciate the texts themselves
of classical masterpieces of world literature. The questions I put to
Fukuoka female students, too, are very simple. For example: which
is the proverbial expression in the *Divine Comedy* you like best?

There is near unanimity in Japanese female students' answer to
this question. It is the words spoken by Francesca da Rimini in
Canto. V, line 103 of *Hell*. I quote Henry Cary's translation:

> Love, that denial takes from none beloved,

In the Italian original it is simpler:

> Amor, che a nullo amato amar perdona,

which means 'Love, which allows no loved one other love'. You see
Fukuoka girls are still very romantic in their expectation of reciprocal love. This statement is of course not always true. Francesca,
daughter of Guido Vecchio da Polenta, was married to Gianciotto
Malatesta of Rimini. Gianciotto was a brave and able soldier, but
apparently deformed, and Francesca fell in love with his younger
brother Paolo, known as 'il Bello', the beautiful. The two were slain
together by the outraged husband. Incidentally, Ueda Bin's Japanese
translation of the line 103 is as follows:

> Aisarete mata aisazaru mono ya aru.

Then who do you think is the person appearing in Dante's Hell
that impresses most Japanese female students of the province of
Fukuoka? and why? When I put the question, I was expecting that
the person chosen by the students would be either Francesca da
Rimini, Count Ugolino or Ulysses. I was mistaken: the person
selected by my female students was Virgil, or Uerugiriusu, as he is
called in Japanese. Here are the statistical results of the main per-

sons named: Virgil, 35%; Francesca, 16%; Ugolino 14%. A discussion of the meaning of this preference will be the main topic of this chapter, I will return to it later.

I began, therefore, to be gradually interested in these spontaneous reactions of ordinary Japanese female students towards Dante's *Inferno*, as they show average Japanese appreciations of the masterpiece of Western literature. I subsequently found that the reactions are generally not so different from a college in Western Japan to a college in the Eastern part, or from year to year. Though different from intellectually snobbish Tokyo University's graduate students' reactions, the unpretentious responses of these regional Japanese students towards the *Divine Comedy* show something typically Japanese. I became, therefore, less disappointed by the difference in quality of my new students. I confess, however, that I was very much surprised by the difference in quantity of my audience. When I was invited to give a lecture to more than two hundred and fifty students in a great auditorium, I was frankly a little frustrated. However, my opinion changed as soon as I began to be interested in reactions of the so-called ordinary Japanese students: the more numerous my audience are, the more reliable they are for my statistical approach to checking Japanese responses to Dante. Their examination papers and their essays reveal to me, if not anything new or original about Dante studies, at least what the Japanese general reactions are. Our image of Dante is the image perceived through our cultural sensibility, which might be called a cultural bias. However, this prism, be it a bias or not, is a very important thing to check in comparative studies. At any rate, the image of the other is often closely related to our own self-image. Dante is a great mirror, and some interesting reflections can be found from a Japanese perspective. Readers now understand, I hope, what my comparative method is in conducting these Dante studies, which may be called my Japanese studies in disguise.

First, an explanation is given to some ethical reactions of the Japanese towards the Christian poet, and, second, an explanation of a typically Japanese approach to Dante's 'psychology of dependence'. The latter is an attempt at psychoanalytical approach, by using Doi Takeo's theory of '*amae*' or so-called anatomy of dependence, to the relationship between Virgil and Dante in the *Divine Comedy*.

In order to get ethical reactions from students, I put questions like these: what is the most shocking point in the *Divine Comedy*?

Japanese students are generally shocked by Dante's ferocious attitude towards the Islamic religion. In the ninth gulf of the Eighth Circle the schismatics are punished. I quote J. A. Carlyle's translation:

> Even a cask, through loss of middle-piece or cant,
>   yawns not so wide as one I saw, rippled from the
>   chin to the part that utters vilest sound:
> between his legs the entrails hung; the pluck
>   appeared, and the wretched sack that makes
>   excrement of what it swallowed.
> Whilest I stood all occupied in seeing him, he
>   looked at me, and with his hands opened his
>   breast, saying: 'Now see how I dilacerate
>   myself!
> see how Mahomet is mangled! Before me Ali
>   weeping goes, cleft in the face from chin to
>   forelock;
> and all the others, whom thou seest here, were
>   in their lifetime sowers of scandal and of
>   schism; and therefore are they thus cleft.
> A Devil is here behind, who splits us thus
>   cruelly, reapplying each of this class to his
>   sword's edge,
> when we have wandered round the doleful road;
>   for the wounds heal up ere any goes again
>   before him.[1]

Thomas Carlyle, the brother of the translator, explained that Dante regards Mahomet as 'a mere Sectarian who had taken up Christianity and perverted its meaning'. Dante seems to suggest that Ali, Mahomet's son-in-law and fourth successor, completed the schism which Mahomet had begun. Sometimes humans seem not to be satisfied with a single death penalty. It is the same with Buddhist theologians in whose Hell executions are repeated: when those who have been put to death are resurrected like phoenix, they are killed again by a devil. This part of the Buddhist Hell, where everyone is 'equally resurrected' is called *tōkatsu jigoku* in Japanese, and *samjivah narakah* in Sanskrit.

Dante's treatment of Mahometans is harsh. Already in Canto VIII of *Inferno* a scene which has apparently something to do with Mahometanism appears, when Dante and Virgil are approaching the City of Satan. Virgil says to Dante:

> '... Now, Son, the city
> that is named of Dis draws nigh.'[2]

And Dante responds:

> … 'Master, already I discern its mosques,
>   distinctly there within the valley, red as if
>   they had come out of fire.'
> And to me he said: 'The eternal fire, which
>   causes them to glow within, shews them red,
>   as thou seest, in this low Hell.'[3]

This is an impressive scene. As most mosques are originally white, the flames of Hell that fire them from within make them red. This scene, once read, is impossible to forget. Carlyle rightly calls Dante's pen 'pen of fire'. Japanese readers, too, are impressed. They, however, feel somewhat uneasy, as the Christian author Dante chooses Islamic mosques to indicate that the City of Dis is devoted to a perverted and infidel cult.

Japanese students find Dante's Inferno extremely interesting, more interesting in many ways than Buddhistic Hell as described by the Japanese monk Genshin (942–1017) in his *Ōjō yōshū*. At the same time, they generally show a kind of repellent feeling, finding that the Christian religion, as presented in the *Divine Comedy*, is too intolerant to those who belong to other faiths. At the beginning of Canto IV there are passages like the following. Dante and Virgil are now entering the First Circle of Hell:

> Here there was no plaint, that could be heard,
>   except of sighs, which caused the eternal air
>   to tremble;
> and this arose from the sadness, without torment,
>   of the crowds that were many and great, both
>   of children, and of women and men.
> The good Master to me: 'Thou askest not
>   what spirits are these thou seest? I wish thee
>   to know, before thou goest farther,
> that they sinned not; and though they have merit,
>   it suffices not: for they had not Baptism, which
>   is the portal of the faith thou believest;
> and seeing they were before Christianity, they
>   worshipped not God aright; and of these am
>   I myself.
> For such defects, and for no other fault, are we
>   lost; and only in so far afflicted, that without
>   hope we live in desire.'[4]

It is Limbo which contains the spirits of those who lived without Baptism or Christianity. There are no pains in this First Circle of

Hell. The repulsion Japanese students feel here is not physical, as there are no physical punishments. Intellectually, they cannot accept the idea that those who have not received Baptism in a Christian church are obliged to go into Hell. In Japan, too, there is a religious custom of presenting a new-born baby to a nearby shrine, which is called *o-miya-mairi* or *ubusuna-mairi*.[5] This is a religious custom of the Japanese native religion, Shinto. However, it has never been heard that those who die before going to *o-miya-mairi* are condemned to go to the nether world. The idea is too cruel for Japanese students. In the quoted line above, 'of children, and of women and men', is said in the original Italian 'd'infanti e di femmine e di viri'. The writing order, putting children in the first place, has its meaning. The mortality rate of infants was very high towards the year 1300 and many babies died before going to church to be baptized; and that is precisely the reason why there are so many children in the First Circle of Hell. Japanese female students instinctively resist Dante's idea that those innocent children died without baptism in a Christian church are eternally condemned to Hell.

To Western professors already familiar with students coming from other religious backgrounds than Christianity these Japanese reactions to Dante's *Divine Comedy* may be more or less predictable. Dante himself must have been not totally convinced of the justice of the situation. After having heard Virgil's explanation about the conditions of those who could not have chosen Christ during their life, he says:

> Great sadness took me at the heart on hearing
> this; because I knew men of much worth,
> who in that Limbo were suspense.[6]

Though I explain that Dante belonged to his time and place, Japanese students find Dante's attitude intolerant and self-righteous and wonder if this attitude of his has something to do with Dante's personal character, or with his understanding of the Christian religion, or with the intrinsic nature of monotheistic religion.

In many Japanese families there still co-exist a family Buddhist altar called *butsudan* and a small Shinto altar called *kamidana* for ancestor worship. Buddhism is a religion of Indian origin, which was propagated in Japan via China and Korea from the sixth century. The success of Buddhism in Japan was due to its non-exclusive nature as a religion. Buddhism made very few religious wars compared with monotheistic religions. Buddhism recognized Shinto, by letting it exist side by side with Buddhism. Religious roles are shared among them. Thus most Japanese parents present their babies to a local Shinto shrine, while they ask Buddhist monks to pray at their funerals. While Westerners from a monotheistic Christian cultural background are generally puzzled at this eclectic attitude of the Japanese, the Japanese are mostly shocked finding that the Christian God does not allow believers in him to worship other deities than himself. The Christian God is a jealous God, as is so described in the Bible.[7] The word 'jealous', however, sounds so shocking to Japanese ears as an attribute of God that a committee composed of both Protestants and Catholics made a change in the latest Japanese translation of the Bible in 1987. The expression *'netamu kami'* which was the former translation of 'a jealous god' now disappears, and instead there is 'netsujō no kami,' which if we retranslate into English, using standard Japanese-English dictionaries, will be either 'an ardent god', 'a passionate god', or 'a god of strong emotions'. There may be a theological justification in this change in expression; however, the impression left of the change is in Japan the exclusive character of the Christian God has been intentionally toned down by recent translations, which may be called somewhat hypocritical and misleading. The literal translation of a jealous God should be *'shitto suru kami'*. Some Japanese students, even if they have been brought up in Christian surroundings, do not know that such 'accommodations' have been made. They are shocked, finding Dante's relentless attitude towards heretics in the *Divine Comedy*, and some of them go so far as to accuse Dante for his 'unchristian' attitude.

The *Divine Comedy* has, however, interesting remarks towards the pre-Christian religion: they remind me of some Japanese Buddhist attitudes towards pre-existing religion of Japan. As is well known, Dante quotes quite a lot from Graeco-Roman mythologies. In the *Divine Comedy* he refers to historical precedents, by quoting alternately from the Bible and from the pre-Christian mythologies, and by drawing parallels, one often ends up by equating them. In Japan's case, native Shinto gods were often understood as differently incarnated forms of Buddha and Bodhisattvas. The Shinto-Buddhist eclectism was called *honji-suijaku-setsu*. For example, the native divinity of martial art, Hachiman, was interpreted as the Japanese incarnation of Amidabutsu or Amitbha Buddha. This kind of equation is also found in the *Divine Comedy*; this is the case of the so-called double vocabulary. Westerners generally equate Jupiter with Zeus. The poet Dante goes one step farther: he equates Zeus with God. This is the case, when in Canto XIV of Inferno what Capaneus called 'Jove' in line 52 was called 'God' in line 70 by Virgil, the latter in the sense of the Christian God. This kind of identification of Jupiter with the Christian God was possible, in the case of the *Divine Comedy*, probably as all divinities of the pre-Christian religions had practically been discarded by the time of Dante; otherwise it would be blasphemous for a Christian writer to call 'Giove' by the name of 'Dio'.

Nontheless Dante let a Florentine suicide make a very suggestive remark about the co-existence of religions towards the end of his journey through the wood of self-murderers. The city of Florence, as is known by the building of the Baptistery of San Giovanni in the centre of the city, changed its first patron, Mars the pagan god of martial art, for Saint John the Baptist. An anonymous Florentine says:

> I was of the city that changed its first patron for
> the Baptist, on which account he
> with his art will always make it sorrowful; and
> were it not that at the passage of Arno
> there yet remains some semblance of him,
> those citizens, who afterwards rebuilt it on the
> ashes left by Attila, would have laboured in
> vain.[8]

When Florentines were converted to Christianity, they built the Baptistery of St John on the site of the temple of Mars, and the statue of Mars was mutilated. However, after the burning of the city by the Goths, it was set up on the passage of the Arno, that is, on the Ponte Vecchio; but for this, so the folk legend ran, Florence could never have been rebuilt. Dante refers again to 'that mutilated stone which guardeth the bridge' in Canto XVI line 146 of *Paradiso*.

Although these discreet references are not taken very seriously by present-day Western readers of Dante, they are highly interesting to the Japanese, as they suggest a locally deep-rooted thinking that a late-arriving major religion should pay due respect to a pre-existing faith and that religions should not proclaim themselves to be exclusively absolute. The legend of the statue of Mars, which remained on the Ponte Vecchio until the great flood of 1333 carried away the bridge and the statue alike, reminds the Japanese of the existence of a small Shinto altar of Hachiman-sama, the Japanese guardian god of martial art, in some modest corner of a great Buddhist temple.

To find a small Shinto shrine within the precincts of a great Buddhist temple in the ancient capitals like Kyoto or Nara is not at all uncommon.

Japan, therefore, is a multi-religious country, in the sense that its native animistic religion still co-exists together with other imported religions, Christianity excepted. Japanese students' reactions to Dante's masterpiece show consciously or unconsciously, Japanese preference of passive harmony over active self-assertion. That must be a reason why my Japanese students find Dante too self-righteous and ego-centric.

However, what is interesting about the students' reactions is that they find Dante very much dependent. Contrary to what Italians say in eulogistic terms that Dante is the symbol of Italian independence, average Japanese female students have a different perception. In the eyes of the Italians, the greatest of their compatriots is decidedly Dante, *il sommo poeta cristiano*. By his forbearing conduct through the years of exile, by his unswerving character as a political theoretician, and especially by his indomitable will-power which enables him to complete the *magnus opus* of Western literature, Dante stands alone, and much higher than his contemporaries. He seems rightly to be called a man of independence. Even so Japanese female students find this towering poet dependent, they find the king of all Western poets naked just like a mother-seeking baby, and find Virgil most sympathetic.

It must be borne in mind that, as I explained earlier, my Fukuoka students are free from connotations. They know practically nothing other than the text of the *Divine Comedy*. They know very little about Dante's life or his Florentine background. To them, Dante the author is less familiar than the person called Dante who appears in the *Divine Comedy*. It is all the more so with Virgil. Virgil is not a Latin poet for them. Virgil, the author of the *Aeneid* has nothing to do with them. Virgil is the person who appears in the *Divine Comedy* to conduct Dante through the nine Circles of the Inferno. Virgil to them is not an object of philological studies but an object of psychological interest.

In the *Divine Comedy*, as Dante is a living person, he is called to account at many of Hell's check-points. Virgil and Dante come to the river Acheron, where Dante is refused the passage by Charon:

> And lo! an old man, white with ancient hair,
>   comes towards us in a bark, shouting: 'Woe
>   to you, depraved spirits!

> hope not ever to see Heaven: I come to lead
>    you to the other shore; into the eternal dark-
>    ness; into fire and into ice.
> And thou who art there, alive, depart thee from
>    these who are dead.' But when he saw that
>    I departed not,
> he said: 'By other ways, by other ferries, not
>    here, shalt thou pass over: a lighter boat must
>    carry thee.'
> And my guide to him: 'Charon, vex not thy-
>    self: thus it is willed there, where what is
>    willed can be done; and ask no more.'[9]

Charon, the classical ferryman of the dead, refuses to take the living body of Dante till Virgil silences him with a word of power. This is the first of the series of the same pattern. When Dante tries to descend into the Second Circle, he again is refused to enter by Minos, the Infernal Judge:

> 'O thou who comest to the abode of pain!'
>    said Minos to me, when he saw me leaving the
>    act of that great office;
> 'look how thou enterest, and in whom thou
>    trustest; let not the wideness of the entrance
>    deceive thee.' And my guide to him: 'Why
>    criest thou too?
> Hinder not his fated going; thus it is willed
>    there where what is willed can be done: and
>    ask no more.'[10]

Scenes of the same kind are repeated in Inferno, at the entrance of the Fourth Circle by Pluto,[11] on the river Styx by the ferryman Phlegyas,[12] at the gate of the City of Dis by the rebel angels.[13] This patterned scene repeats itself in Boiling Pitch,[14] where Dante is terrified by the demons, and even in Canto I of *Purgatorio*, on the isle of the Southern hemisphere, when Dante is abruptly warned by Cato.

The repetition of the same pattern is easily recognizable like a leitmotiv in a symphony. There are generally three persons involved: a barrier-keeper who refuses the passage of a living person, Dante, who is scared every time, and Virgil who always frees Dante from peril. To define the nature of Japanese students' response, a look into Dante's horror is useful. Dante was helpless before the gate of the City of Dis when he and Virgil were denied admittance by the fallen angels, who mockingly said to Virgil:

> ... 'Come thou alone; and let that one go,
> who has entered so daringly into this kingdom.
> Let him return alone his foolish way; try, if
> he can: for thou shalt stay here, that hast
> escorted him through so dark a country.'[15]

Dante was wholly terrorized; he believed that he never would return alive to the world of the living. He asked Virgil to retrace their steps together rapidly:

> 'O my loved Guide, who more than seven
> times hast restored me to safety, and rescued
> from deep peril that stood before me,
> leave me not so undone,'[16]

'*Non mi lasciar così disfatto*' is the Italian original of the last line: Dante felt himself totally broken down into a state of helplessness. The expression 'seven times', as is often the case in the Bible, does not mean exactly seven but many times. Virgil has, indeed, brought Dante safely through more than ten times by that time (*Inferno*, I 91, II 43, III 19, III 94, IV 13, V 21, VI 25, VII 3, VIII 19, VIII 41). This Virgil-Dante relationship with many similar scenes continues until their separation in Canto XXX of *Purgatorio*. On their way, Virgil rescues Dante from perils that lie in his path. In many of these cases, as there is no intervention of a barrier-keeper and consequently as communications are limited only between Dante and Virgil, the psychological situation may not be so outwardly conspicuous. Even so, when Japanese female students witnessed these scenes, they understood it as what might be called a mother-child relationship. Dante, the child who needs a loving protection, and Virgil, the mother who provides it. Every time Virgil helps the infantile Dante, they saw a mother in him. In the chasm of the pitch, Dante sees the Demons coming with outstretched wings:

> My Guide suddenly took me, as a mother – that
> is awakened by the noise, and near her sees
> the kindled flames –
> who takes her child and flies, and caring more
> for him than for herself, pauses not so long as
> even to cast a shift about her ...[17]

Virgil takes Dante in his arms, and rapidly glides down with him into the next chasm. Virgil is acting like a mother. Another example of the same nature is seen when the monster Geryon conveyed Dante and Virgil down to the Eighth Circle. When Dante sat down on the monster's huge shoulders:

> I wished to say, only the voice came not as I
> thought: 'See that thou embrace me.'
> But he, who at other times assisted me in other
> difficulties, soon as I mounted, clasped me
> with his arms, and held me up;
> then he said: 'Geryon, now move thee!'[18]

At first, when I encountered Japanese female students' preference for Virgil, I thought rather simply that the reason must be the
following: they are looking for a life companion, a man as gentle
and as tactful as Virgil; he is the most trustworthy guide indeed.
However, that was too easy an explanation, they are interested in
Dante's feelings towards Virgil as well as in Virgil's feelings towards
Dante. What the students responded to was in the role Virgil plays
in relation to Dante. Dante and Virgil's relationship is, as stated in
the beginning of the *Divine Comedy* a master-disciple relationship,
and a very good one. What it does not mention and the students
picked this out is that a good master-disciple relationship is a
sort of continuation of an earlier one – a good mother-child
relationship.

A single word that defines the feelings that Dante harbours
towards Virgil in the *Divine Comedy* is *amae*. The term refers, initially,
to the feelings that infants at the breast harbour towards the mother
– dependence, the desire to be passively loved, the unwillingness to
be separated from the warm mother-child circle.

Japanese female students immediately sense that Dante harbours
these feelings of *amae* towards Virgil, whom Dante calls his master,
guide, lord, father and the sweetest father *(dolcissimo patre)*.[19]

The reason why I have used here the Japanese word *amae* is
because there is no corresponding single word either in English or
Italian. The Japanese psychiatrist Doi, having found the conspicuous presence of the word *amae* in Japanese and the absence of it
in English, thought over the psychological meaning of the difference and implications of it, and wrote a book called *Amae no kōzō*
(Tokyo: Kōbundō, 1971), which was translated into English as *The
Anatomy of Dependence*.[20] It is the first book by a Japanese trained in
psychiatry to have an impact on Western psychiatric thinking. The
book has been welcomed as the key analysis of Japanese behaviour
but more than that as a key to a new understanding of all basic
human needs. It created a pathway to th discovery of a new vista in
the *Divine Comedy*. Stimulated by Japanese female students' and also
by Japanese readers' opinions that Dante harbours feelings of *amae*

towards Virgil and that Virgil is very much maternal, taking care of Dante, I have applied Doi's theory to interpret Dante's affective relationship with Virgil.[21]

To conclude, one more thing has now become an explicit illustration of Dante's dependence in the *Divine Comedy* and the affective relationship between master and disciple, which arouses Japanese readers' maternal instinctive sympathy.

According to Dr Doi, one of the characteristics of the mother-child relationship is non-verbal communication. Immediately after Virgil's explanation of the inscription over the Gate of Hell, which was a verbal communication, there follows this scene:

> And placing his hand on mine, with a cheerful
> countenance that comforted me, he led me
> into the secret things.[22]

In the *Divine Comedy* Dante is supposed to be thirty-five years old. Nevertheless, Virgil carried him away upon his breast, not as his companion but as his son,[23] and lovingly took Dante by the hand (*caramente me prese per mano*).[24] The reaction of Dante in the Sixth Chasm[25] is typical of an infantile reaction before his mother. In this Canto, the despair of the poor peasant, who cannot feed his sheep, and thinks he is going to lose them, gives a lively image of Dante's dependence on his Guide: when Dante saw the Master's brow troubled, he too was disheartened, and when Dante saw Virgil's face brighten, he too was cheered up.

Dante is said to be the symbol of Italian independence. It is true that the poet Dante is a man of strong character. However, it is also true that the dramatis persona, Dante in the *Divine Comedy* acts like a child, and sometimes seeks to be babied. That desire is *amae*. The feelings of *amae* colour beautifully Dante's relationship with Virgil in the *Divine Comedy*. To the unlearned eyes of Japanese female students, Dante is very dependent, full of *amae*, and their intuitive understanding is correct. When Virgil finally disappears, Dante 'turned to the left, panting like a baby, who runs to his mother's breast'.

> volsimi alla sinistra col rispitto
> col quale il fantolin corre alla mamma
> quando ha paura o quando egli è afflitto,[26]

These lines may hopefully confirm our Japanese interpretation of Dante's anatomy of dependence.

*Notes*

[1] *The Inferno of Dante*, tr. J. A. Carlyle (London: J. M. Dent, 1962), Canto XXVIII 22–42, p. 313.

[2] *The Inferno of Dante*, Canto VIII 67, p. 83.

[3] *The Inferno of Dante*, Canto VIII 70–75, p. 83.

[4] *The Inferno of Dante*, Canto IV 25–42, p. 39.

[5] In my case, the first photographic picture of mine was taken the day my mother brought me to a nearby Kishibojin-temple for *o-miya-mairi.*.

[6] *The Inferno of Dante*, Canto IV 43–45, p. 39.

[7] Exodus, 20:5, Deuteronomy 5:9.

[8] *The Inferno of Dante*, Canto XIII 143–150, p. 143.

[9] *The Inferno of Dante*, Canto III 82–96, pp. 31–33.

[10] *The Inferno of Dante*, Canto V 16–24, p. 49.

[11] *The Inferno of Dante*, Canto VII 1–12, p. 71.

[12] *The Inferno of Dante*, Canto VIII 15–24, p. 81.

[13] *The Inferno of Dante*, Canto VIII 82–93, pp. 85–87.

[14] *The Inferno of Dante*, Canto XXI, 21–139, pp. 229–235.

[15] *The Inferno of Dante*, Canto VIII 89–93, pp. 85–87.

[16] *The Inferno of Dante*, Canto VIII 97–100, p. 87.

[17] *The Inferno of Dante*, Canto XXII 37–42, p. 253.

[18] *The Inferno of Dante*, Canto XVII 92–97, p. 187.

[19] The expression 'dolcissimo patre' (sweetest father) appears in *The Purgatorio of Dante* (London: J. M. Dent, 1962) Canto XXX, 50, pp. 382, 383.

[20] Takeo Doi: *The Anatomy of Dependence* (Tokyo: Kodansha International, 1973), tr. John Bester.

[21] I wrote an article in Italian about the affective master-disciple relationship in the *Divine Comedy*. See Sukehiro Hirakawa: 'Anatomia della dipendenza di Dante: un'interpretazione giapponese dei rapporti affettivi fra maestro e discepolo nella *Divina Commedia*,' in *Atti del XVII Convegno di Studi, AISTUGIA* (Firenze: M.C.S. Edizioni, 1994) pp. 15–39.

[22] *The Inferno of Dante*, Canto II 19–21, p. 27.

[23] *The Inferno of Dante*, Canto XXIII 51, p. 253.

[24] *The Inferno of Dante*, Canto XXXI 28, p. 349.

[25] *The Inferno of Dante*, Canto XXIV 16–18, p. 263.

[26] *The Purgatorio of Dante*, Canto XXX 43–45, p. 380.

# HOW TO GO INTO *INFERNO* IN THE LITERATURES OF EAST AND WEST: BRECHT'S ADAPTATION OF THE JAPANESE NŌ PLAY *TANIKŌ*[1]

---

How to go to the other side? How to be cast into Hell? Human beings have spent a good deal of time thinking of this world and the other. Literature has abundant traces of ghostly fancies connecting the two spheres. The Japanese Nō plays of spirits have as their main theme and concern the relations between the world of the living and the world of the dead, especially hell. *Tanikō*[2] is one such Nō play, by which Bertolt Brecht (1898–1956) was attracted. Thus, the focus of this chapter is *Tanikō* and Brecht's dramas. In the 1930s the German dramatist had applied *Tanikō* as a vehicle for communicating his politically motivated educational agenda. A close look at *Tanikō* and Brecht's *Lehrstücke* such as *He Who Says Yes* and *He Who Says No*[3] provides an insight into the psychology of those who are spellbound by a cult, religious as well as political.

Arthur Waley's English translation of the Japanese Nō play *Tanikō* begins in a daily conversation between a Teacher and a Young Boy.

> TEACHER: I am a teacher. I keep a school at one of the temples in the City. I have a pupil whose father is dead; he has only his mother to look after him. Now I will go and say good-bye to them, for I am soon starting on a journey to the mountains. *He knocks at the door of the house.* May I come in?
> BOY: Who is it? Why, it is the Master who has come out to see us![4]

This is an ordinary conversation, indeed. A teacher's visit to a pupil's home, and he tells the boy's mother that he is starting on a mountain-climb, in which the boy insists on taking part. As his mother is ill, the boy wishes to pray for her in the mountains.

In the latter part of the play something unexpected happens:

TEACHER: We have climbed so fast that we have already reached the first hut. We will stay here a little while.
LEADER: We obey.
BOY: I have something to say.
TEACHER: What is it?
BOY: I do not feel well.
TEACHER: Stay! Such things may not be said by those who travel on errands like ours. Perhaps you are not used to climbing. Lie there and rest.
LEADER: They are saying that the young boy is ill with climbing. I must ask the Master about it.
PILGRIMS: Do so.
LEADER: I hear that this young boy is ill with climbing. What is the matter with him? Are you anxious about him?
TEACHER: He is not feeling well, but there is nothing wrong with him. He is only tired with climbing.
LEADER: So you are not troubled with him?
*A Pause*
PILGRIM: Listen, you pilgrims. Just now the Master said this boy was only tired with climbing. But now he is looking very strange. Ought we not to follow our Great Custom and hurl him into the valley?[5]

At the beginning of the play the conversation was so everyday that we did not expect such a barbaric thing as the boy's being hurled into the valley would take place. However, as *Tanikō* had been a Great Custom from ancient times, those who failed on such a ritual journey had to be cast down. The more religious the pilgrims are, the more fervently they ask for it. The boy knows the Law and accepts it, only grieving for his mother's sorrow at the news of his death. Waley's translation ends with the following chorus, as he cuts the *deus ex machina* solution of the original play.

CHORUS:
Then the pilgrims sighing
For the sad ways of the world
And the bitter ordinances of it,
Make ready for the hurling.
Foot to foot
They stood together
Heaving blindly,
None guiltier than his neighbour.
And clods of earth after
And flat stones they flung.[6]

This Nō play has two distinctly different spaces: a secular one in the City, and a sacred one in the mountains. The dramatic effect lies precisely in the contrast of the two, and Waley, by adding a daily element such as 'knocking at the door of the house' which was not a Japanese habit in fifteenth-century Kyoto, gives Western readers an impression as if the first scene might take place any time, anywhere. Waley indeed omits all the proper nouns of the original to enhance the universal character of the drama. In the Japanese play we know from the beginning that it is about a ritual mountain-climb of a religious character. However, Waley's modern translation gives an impression of modern rock-climbing. Even if the word 'danger' is mentioned from the beginning, we tend to think of it in terms of hazardous perils relating to any modern sport mountain-climbing. The more ordinary and the more homely the atmosphere of the first scene, the more shocking and the more dreadful the final scene becomes. The logic of the secular space does not hold any more in the sacred space of the mountains, where the Great Custom prevails and the Law dominates the minds of all the climb-party members. The authority of the Law may not be challenged by any party member.

It is well known that Brecht takes up this Japanese Nō play, *Tanikō* as the starting basis for his *Lehrstücke, Jasager* (He Who Says Yes) and *Neinsager* (He Who Says No). These short didactic plays together with *Massnahme* (The Measures Taken), written during 1929 and 1930, the period of Brecht's most sharply Communist works, are highly formalized pieces intended for performance by schoolchildren, on the principle that the lessons contained in them can best be taught by participation in the play. Peter Szondi edited *Der Jasager und Der Neinsager* (Suhrkamp, 1966) with 'Vorlagen, Fassungen und Materialien' and a very interesting 'Nachwort'. In critical judgement of these works, I would like to offer a view that differs from some of Western or Japanese Brechtian studies.

Apart from some additional elements such as the Great Chorus at the beginning, Brecht's first version of *Der Jasager* follows *Tanikō* in almost all points. Some notable slight changes are made as follows: as a man committed to 'scientific socialism', Brecht changes the purpose of the journey; religion being the opium of the people, the original pilgrimage now becomes a journey for research (in his first version; in his second version it becomes a journey to obtain medicine and instruction as a terrible disease has broken out among the city-dwellers. The boy's mother, too, has fallen ill from that). In both versions 'in the city beyond the mountains there are great doctors', doctors whom one may interpret in many ways, from medical doctors to ideological doctors. As a proletarian artist, Brecht adds also the mother's toil for her son. Other than these small modifications, *Der Jasager* follows *Taniko* line by line. The second scene where the boy falls sick in the mountains in German is as follows:

DER LEHRER: Wir sind schnell hinangestiegen. Dort ist die erste Hütte.
Dort wollen wir ein wenig verweilen.
DER KNABE: Ich muss etwas sagen.
DER LEHRER: Was willst du sagen?
DER KNABE: Ich fühle mich nicht wohl.
DER LEHRER: Halt! Solche Dinge dürfen nicht sagen, die auf eine solche Reise gehen. Vielleicht bist du müde, weil du das Steigen nicht gewohnt bist. Bleib ein wenig stehen and ruhe ein wenig.
DIE DREI STUDENTEN: Es scheint, dass der Knabe krank ist vom Steigen. Wir wollen den Lehrer darüber befragen.
DER GROSSE CHOR: Ja. Tut das!
DIE DREI STUDENTEN *zum Lehrer*: Wir hören, dass dieser Knabe krank ist vom Steigen. Was ist mit ihm? Bist du besorgt seinetwegen?
*Lange Pause*
DIE DREI STUDENTEN *untereinander*:
Hört ihr? Der Lehrer hat gesagt
Dass der Knabe nur müde sei vom Steigen.
Aber sieht er nicht jetzt ganz seltsam aus?[7]

Until now Brecht's work follows *Taniko*'s English version[8] most faithfully except for changes in the numbers of persons concerned. For example, the original leader becomes three students and the Great Chorus which is supposed to represent the will of all the group intervenes from time to time. The Chorus is indeed representative of a pressure group called the climbing party. However, as the party goes to the mountains for the sake of scientific researches (first version) or to seek medicine and instruction (second version), the reason given for the valley-hurling of the boy becomes different. A new element is introduced here by Brecht. The mountain ridge is so narrow that only by gripping the sheer rock with both hands can one traverse it. As they cannot carry the boy, the three students propose the valley-hurling.

Sollten wir also dem grossen Brauch folgen und ihn
In das Tal hinabschleudern?[9]

This dreadful sentence is the exact translation of 'Ought we not to follow our Great Custom and hurl him into the valley?' and the

German play *Jasager* in both its first and second version ends in the same way. I quote here Wolfgang Sauerlander's English translation:

> THE BOY:
> I well knew that if I came on this journey
> I might lose my life.
> Only the thought of my mother
> Induced me to join you.
> Take my jar
> Fill it with medicine
> And bring it to my mother
> When you return.[10]

The new element which does not exist either in the Japanese Nō play or its English adaptation by Waley is the jar.[11] Apart from it, the Great Chorus by Brecht ends in just the same phrase as in the chorus by Waley. For the sake of comparison, I quote Sauerlander's English translation of *Jasager*:

> THE GREAT CHORUS:
> The friends took the jar
> And, sighing for the sad ways of the world
> And its bitter law
> Hurled the boy down
> Foot to foot they stood together
> At the edge of the abyss
> And blindly hurled him down
> None guiltier than his neighbour
> And flung clods of earth
> And flat stones
> After him.[12]

It is well known that some young German students participating in the actual production of *Jasager* protested against the blind indoctrination that an individual member should sacrifice himself in the interest of the great cause. In Brecht's first version, the Three Students as well as the Great Chorus insist:

> We will ask him (the boy) whether he wants us
> To turn back on his account.
> But even if he should want us to do so
> We will not turn back
> But will hurl him down into the valley.

The last line is changed in the second version into:

> But let him lie here and go on.[13]

And in both versions Brecht's Teacher says something which the Japanese Teacher has never said:

THE TEACHER:

... But it is right to ask a person who has fallen ill whether the expedition should turn back on his account. And Custom also ordains that he who has fallen ill should answer: You should not turn back.[14]

And the Boy after a pause says he agrees to die:

THE BOY: Yes, I consent.[15] (Ich verstehe.)

However, Brecht, listening to the protests of young German students, writes not only *Jasager* second version, but also *Neinsager*. In the latter version the Boy, after a pause for reflection says: 'No. I do not consent.' (Nein, ich bin nicht einverstanden.) and the expedition, though not at all heroic, turns back, carrying the sick boy. This later development by Brecht is often highly praised, as is the case with Szondi's concluding remarks.[16]

As a drama *Neinsager* is, however, without interest. A boy goes to mountains, falls sick, and the climbing party comes back with him, following common sense. This plot lacks any theatrical tension: although, what is praiseworthy about all the modifications must lie in the simple fact that Brecht comes back to this common sense. It is, indeed, not easy to say that the emperor has no clothes on when all others believe in his Law.

Brecht's *Jasager* has been translated into Japanese under the erroneous but still very suggestive title of *Yes Man*. This mistranslation is interesting as it sheds light on the psychology of party members who are compelled to say 'yes, yes' all the time. They are obliged to consent to their own death sentence, as was the case with the Moscow 'open' trials of the 1930s.

For a Japanese scholar, what is particularly interesting and in many ways revealing is the psychological similarities between Japanese sect members climbing up the holy Katsuragi mountain in the middle ages and German party members of the 1930s. The contents of the Law or the Great Custom of course differ, but that difference does not count, as psychological subjugation to the Law – be it either Buddhist belief or scientific socialism – is almost the same. Their similarity is striking. In order to attest their genuine belief in the Law, party members are psychologically programmed to show a sort of religious fervour in their execution of missions. In the Japanese case, one of the pilgrims shouts: 'Ought we not to follow our Great Custom and hurl him into the valley?' In the German case the three students, some kind of political commissars, shout the same words. They are there to maintain their ideological purity.

The dramatic effect, however, derives from this 'purity'. The fifteenth-century Japanese monk Ikkyū, known also for his *Knabenliebe*, left two poems on the Nō play *Tanikō*. He says the drama is wonderful because of the boy's death in the valley. The same emotion is felt when we hear the boy sing his pathetic part in Kurt Weill's opera *Der Jasager*. It should be noted, moreover, that the theme which really captivated Brecht is expressed in the boy's self-sacrifice in *Jasager* and not in the common-sensical *Neinsager*. In *Die Massnahme*, a play written shortly after, the same theme is eloquently taken up again by Brecht: one should submerge one's private feelings in the interests of The Great Cause.

One of the Chinese students coming from the mainland to Tokyo University frankly told his impressions after having read *Tanikō*, *Ikeniye*, Shirley Jackson's *Lottery* (1949) and Brecht's *Lehrstücke*. He said among other things that through Brecht he understood why his countrymen had committed that great folly called the Great Cultural Revolution: at that time no Chinese could say no, as there were so many students dedicated to the Law of the Party. As you know, the scene of *The Measures Taken* is China and the play ends in this way. An echo from the Japanese Nō play *Tanikō* can be recognized as well:

THE THREE AGITATORS:
Rest your head on our arm.
Close your eyes.
THE YOUNG COMRADE:
... In the interests of Communism
In agreement with the progress of the proletarian masses
Of all lands
Consenting to the revolutionizing of the world.
THE THREE AGITATORS:
Then we shot him and
Cast him down into the lime-pit
And when the lime had swallowed him up
We turned back to our work.[17]

In the twentieth century most people do not believe in Hell. Medieval thinking seems to be something of the past, especially for those who believe in the progress of mankind. However, comparing some twentieth-century German works with a Japanese play of the fifteenth century, we are obliged to acknowledge that there still exist infernal pits – pits of an ideological Hell. If *Tanikō* may be said to deal with 'ruthless exactions of religion' (Waley),[18] Brecht's plays may also be described as dealing with ruthless exactions of ideology, and 'the barbaric quality of the climax' attributed by R. Tyler[19] to the Japanese medieval play seems also attributable to the Brechtian plays of the early 1930s.

*Notes*

[1] This paper was presented at the 12th Congress of the International Comparative Literature held August 1988 in Munich.
[2] Arthur Waley: *The Nō Plays of Japan* (London: George Allen and Unwin, 1965) pp. 230–235.
[3] Bertolt Brecht: *The Measures Taken and other Lehrsücke* (London: Methuen, 1977) tr. C.R. Mueller & Wolfgang Sauerlander.
[4] Arthur Waley: *The Nō Plays of Japan*, p. 230.
[5] Arthur Waley: *The Nō Plays of Japan*, pp. 233–234.
[6] Arthur Waley: *The Nō Plays of Japan*, p. 235.
[7] Bertolt Brecht: *Der Jasager und der Neinsager* (Frankfurt am Main: Suhrkamp, 1966) pp. 23–24.
[8] Or more precisely the German version by Elisabeth Hauptmann, who made a literal translation from Waley's English version. See Bertolt Brecht: *Der Jasager und der Neinsager*, pp. 13–18.
[9] Bertolt Brecht: *Der Jasager und der Neinsager*, p. 24.
[10] Bertolt Brecht: *The Measures Taken and Other Lehrstücke*, p. 69.
[11] Waley's translation reads as follows:

> BOY:
>   I understand: I knew well that if I came on this
> journey I might lose my life.
>   Only at the thought
>   Of my dear mother,
>   *How her tree of sorrow*
>   *For me must blossom*
>   *With flower of weeping, –*
>   I am heavy-hearted.

The above three lines in italics do not exist in the Japanese original of *Tanikō*; Waley borrowed them from another play *Ikeniye* which he was translating at almost the same time. As for a more detailed study of the same topic, see Hirakawa, *Yōkyoku no shi to seiyō no shi* (Tokyo: Asahi Shinbun-sha, 1975).
[12] Bertolt Brecht: *The Measures Taken and Other Lehrstücke*, p. 69.
[13] Bertolt Brecht: *The Measures Taken and Other Lehrstücke*, p. 68.
[14] Bertolt Brecht: *The Measures Taken and Other Lehrstücke*, p. 68.
[15] Translation mine. In *Der Neinsager*, the boy, having changed his attitude, answers, 'No, I do not consent'. ('Nein, ich bin nicht einverstanden.' in Sauerlander English translation). I translate, therefore, for *Jasager* 'Yes, I consent.' instead of 'Yes, I understand.' The latter literal translation of the original 'Ich verstehe.' is by Sauerlander.

[16]  Peter Szondi writes in his *Nachwort*: Selten sind im Text eines Marxisten das ungebrochene Pathos und die Zuversicht des Aufklärung so lebendig geworden wie hier – Brecht an diese Herkunft des Marxismus erinnert zu haben, ist das Verdienst jenes anonymen Kar Marx-Schülers, der fand, das 'das mit dem Brauch nicht richtig ' sei.(Bertolt Brecht: *Der Jasager und der Neinsager*, p. 109).

[17]  Bertolt Brecht: *The Measures Taken and Other Lehrstücke*, p. 34.

[18]  Arthur Waley: *The Nō Plays of Japan*, p. 229.

[19]  See R. Tyler's new complete translation and introduction to *Tanikō* (The Valley Rite) in D. Keene, ed.: *20 Plays of the Nō Theatre* (New York: Columbia University Press, 1970).

# ARTHUR WALEY'S AESTHETICS IN TRANSLATING THE NŌ PLAY *HATSUYUKI*[1]

——————□——————

When Edith Sitwell was presented with the English translation of Wu Ch'eng-en's *Monkey* by Arthur Waley, she wrote in her letter of thanks:

> Really, Arthur, more and more – if such a thing were possible – do I feel what a miraculous art you have. I do not know of any work which so abolishes the horrors of time and wretched material worries, as these works of yours. To me, *Hatsuyuki* is the most wonderful abstract beauty I know. Absolutely incredible. I *can't* dream how you do it. That is only an example.[2]

The reason why she wrote 'the horrors of time and wretched material worries' is that this letter was written in 1942, when the world was plunged into World War II and England was not yet sure of victories. One of the women writers of the Bloomsbury Group, Virginia Woolf, had drowned herself the previous year. In such dark days, Waley's *Monkey* comforted the poetess with its engaging story and limpid English. Furthermore, charmed by the beauty of the English sound in it, Edith Sitwell remembered the Nō play *Hatsuyuki* which Waley had translated more than twenty years before.

Reading her words of praise, some Japanese would feel that they cannot understand why Sitwell picked out *Hatsuyuki* from among many Nō plays. Even those who have seen *Hatsuyuki* on the stage might doubt if it is so praiseworthy. And some would also wonder what she meant by 'abstract beauty', and they might tend to conclude that she said irresponsible things, being a foreigner. Indeed,

Professor Ichikawa Sanki, dean of English studies in Japan for the first two decades of Shōwa (1926–45) and a connoisseur of Nō plays, criticized Waley's choice of little-known pieces like *Hatsuyuki* for his English translation of *Nō Plays of Japan*. Ichikawa felt, moreover, that Waley's selection of pieces like *Taniko* and *Ikeniye* was of a 'perverse' taste, and went so far as to conjecture that the translator must not be well versed in Nō plays or that he or his Japanese adviser must have had some prejudice against them. In any case, *Hatsuyuki*, which is played only by the Komparu school, is by no means a representative Nō play of Japan.[3]

However, the value of a translation does not always depend on that of the original, the act of translation is a display of literary talent in itself. Therefore the reason why Waley's translation of *Hatsuyuki* impressed the English poetess so deeply requires a further analysis. The whole translation is as follows:[4]

HATSUYUKI (EARLY SNOW)
By KOMPARU ZEMBŌ MOTOYASU (1453–1532)

PERSONS
EVENING MIST, a servant girl.
A LADY, the Abbot's daughter.
TWO NOBLE LADIES.
THE SOUL OF THE BIRD HATSUYUKI ('Early Snow').
CHORUS.

SCENE: *The Great Temple at Izumo.*

SERVANT.
I am a servant at the Nyoroku Shrine in the Great Temple of Izumo. My name is Evening Mist. You must know that the Lord Abbot has a daughter, a beautiful lady and gentle as can be. And she keeps a tame bird that was given her a year ago, and because it was a lovely white bird she called it Hatsuyuki, Early Snow; and she loves it dearly.

I have not seen the bird to-day. I think I will go to the bird-cage and have a look at it.

(*She goes to the cage.*)

Mercy on us, the bird is not there! Whatever shall I say to my lady? But I shall have to tell her. I think I'll tell her now. Madam, madam, your dear Snow-bird is not here!

LADY.
What is that you say? Early Snow is not there? It cannot be true.

(*She goes to the cage.*)

It is true. Early Snow has gone! How can that be? How can it be that my pretty one that was so tame should vanish and leave no trace?

Oh bitterness of snows

That melt and disappear!

Now do I understand
The meaning of a midnight dream
That lately broke my rest.
A harbinger it was
Of Hatsuyuki's fate.
(*She bursts into tears.*)
CHORUS.
Though for such tears and sighs
There be no cause,
Yet came her grief so suddenly,
Her heart's fire is ablaze;
And all the while
Never a moment are her long sleeves dry.
They say that written letters first were traced
By feet of birds in sand
Yet Hatsuyuki leaves no testament.
(*They mourn.*)
CHORUS (*'kuse' chant, irregular verse accompanied by dancing*).
How sad to call to mind
When first it left the breeding-cage
So fair of form
And coloured white as snow.
We called it Hatsuyuki, 'Year's First Snow'.
And where our mistress walked
It followed like the shadow at her side.
But now alas! it is a bird of parting[5]
Though not in Love's dark lane.
LADY.
There's no help now. (*She weeps bitterly.*)
CHORUS.
Still there is one way left. Stop weeping, Lady,
And turn your heart to him who vowed to hear.
The Lord Amida, if a prayer be said –
Who knows but he can bring
Even a bird's soul into Paradise
And set it on the Lotus Pedestal?[6]
LADY.
Evening Mist, are you not sad that Hatsuyuki has gone?... But we must
not cry any more. Let us call together the noble ladies of this place and for
seven days sit with them praying behind barred doors. Go now and do my
bidding.
(EVENING MIST *fetches the* NOBLE LADIES *of the place.*)
Two Noble Ladies (*together*).
A solemn Mass we sing
A dirge for the Dead;
At this hour of heart-cleansing
We beat on Buddha's gong.

(*They pray.*)
NAMU AMIDA BUTSU
NAMU NYORAI
Praise to Amida Buddha,
Praise to Mida our Saviour
(*The prayers and gong-beating last for some time and form the central ballet of the play.*)
CHORUS (*the bird's soul appears as a white speck in the sky*).
Look! Look! A cloud in the clear mid-sky!
But it is not a cloud.
With pure white wings beating the air
The Snow-bird comes!
Flying towards our lady
Lovingly he hovers,
Dances before her.
THE BIRD'S SOUL.
Drawn by the merit of your prayers and songs
CHORUS.
Straightway he was reborn in Paradise.
By the pond of Eight Virtues he walks abroad
With the Phoenix and Fugan his playtime passing.
He lodges in the sevenfold summit of the trees of Heaven.
No hurt shall harm him
For ever and ever.
Now like the tasselled doves we loose
From battlements on holy days
A little while he flutters;
Flutters a little while and then is gone
We know not where.

The theme of this Nō play – a beloved bird has flown and left its cage – is universal. There is a popular Italian song by an anonymous poet of the thirteenth century:

Out from the fine cage flies the nightingale.
The little child is crying because he does not find
His little bird in the new cage,
And he says with grief: who opened the door for him?
And he says with grief: who opened the door for him?
And he started walking in a little wood, he heard
The fledgling that so sweetly sang.
O lovely nightingale, come back into my garden:
O lovely nightingale, come back into my garden.[7]

The Italian poet seems to be expressing his love for his sweetheart in the guise of a child lamenting the loss of a bird. Such a manner of expression suggests the *dolce stil novo*, and the poet's sentiment seems to be more sophisticated than a simple child song.

*Hatsuyuki*, too, seems to be, both in the original and in the English translation, more than a story of a bird's flight. According to Sanari Kentarō's comment,[8] the play gives an impression of 'a story of a transitory love, a girl's love' with such expressions as: 'Her heart's fire is ablaze' and 'Never a moment are her long sleeves dry',[9] and near the end of the play, Hatsuyuki is no longer called 'it' but 'he', which suggests the love:

> Flying towards our lady
> Lovingly he hovers
> Dances before her.

In the Italian song, the child meets his bird again in the wood and has a chance to call to it: 'Come back into my garden.' Whereas the lady in *Hatsuyuki* has to give up hope of meeting the bird again: 'There's no help now.' Then she turns her heart to Amida, and while she is praying, 'the bird's soul appears as a white speck in the sky'. The scene in which the white bird comes flying to her is so vivid that it is like something from a modern Western ballet.

This fine evocation of glittering whiteness reminds me of the scene in *the Divine Comedy* in which a gleaming white angel steers the Ship of Souls which swiftly approaches the shore:

> I saw a light come speeding o'er the sea,
> So swift, flight knows no simile therefor.
> ......
> ... then looked again, and lo!
> Bigger and brighter far it seemed to me.
> Then, from each side of it, there seemed to grow
> A white I-knew-not-what; and there appeared
> Another whiteness, bit by bit, below.
> ... Those first two whitenesses
> Were wings;...
> ......
> 'See how he scorns all instruments of earth,
> Needing no oar, no sail but his own wings,
> 'Twixt shores that span so vast an ocean's girth.
> See how each soaring pinion heavenward springs,
> Beating the air with pens imperishable
> That are not mewed like mortal coverings.'[10]

It is presumably because travel between Paradise and the world has similar connotations in Christian and Buddhist concepts that in the last part of *Hatsuyuki*, we see a very similar sight:

CHORUS (the bird's soul appears as a white speck in the sky).
Look! Look! A cloud in the clear mid-sky!

> But it is not a cloud.
> With pure white wings beating the air
> The Snow-bird comes!

Although the stage direction says 'the bird's soul', it seems as if the missing Hatsuyuki had now flown back again. But when the bird says aloud, 'Drawn by the merit of your prayers and songs', and when the reader hears the following chorus, he fully realizes that the bird has died and been reborn in Paradise thanks to prayer:

> CHORUS.
> Straightway he was reborn in Paradise.
> By the pond of Eight Virtues he walks abroad:
> With the Phoenix and Fugan his playtime passing.
> He lodges in the sevenfold summit of the trees of Heaven.
> No hurt shall harm him
> For ever and ever.

The reader is also indirectly told that the bird was attacked and received a deadly wound, as the original phrase '*tanoshimi sara ni tsukisenu mi nari* (his delights will last forever)'[11] is changed into 'no hurt shall harm him for ever and ever' in the translation. Waley's alteration is considerable. The last five English lines especially remind one of a medieval European city surrounded by ramparts:

> Now like the tasselled doves we loose
> From battlements on holy days
> A little while he flutters;
> Flutters a little while and then is gone
> We know not where.

The chorus gives us the same impression as a chorus of angels in Western church music.

*Hatsuyuki*, in Waley's translation, ends with a poem. It leaves a very pure and clear impression. The freshness of Waley's aesthetic sense has a sort of Shinto beauty, probably because the play takes place at the Great Shinto Shrine at Izumo, although the subject deals with the miraculous virtue of Amida Buddha. The white bird is a sacred bird, whose whiteness seems to be a symbol for the soul. Waley perhaps remembered that a white bird is the ancient Cabalistic symbol of the soul, too. In John Webster's poetic drama, *the White Devil*, the protagonist Vittoria says at her last moment:

> My soul, like to a ship in a black storm,
> Is driven, I know not whither.[12]

If the impression of this Jacobean play is the blackness of Hell, that of Zembō's play would be the brightness of Paradise. What

Edith Sitwell called 'abstract beauty' must be some such evocation. Although the play is very short, the beauty of 'Early Snow' is moving in the English translation.

Then, a question to be posed is, does the aftertaste of Waley's English rendition of *Hatsuyuki* have the same quality as that of the original? Or has Waley's master hand transformed and sublimated the original into the beautiful poetic world of the 'white bird'? The translator says at the end of his introduction to *The Nō Plays of Japan*:

> In short, what I have been able to give bears the same relation to the original as the photograph of an oil-painting bears to the painting. One whole element, and this a vital one, is lost. But a clear photograph, which though it omits much, at least adds nothing foreign, is generally preferable to a hand-copy. Sometimes, indeed, physical conditions not unfavourable to the camera may make hand-copying impossible. Analogous, I think, is the case of Nō. I give the reader black-and-whites. He must colour them by the exercise of his own imagination. But I have carried the metaphor too far. For a photograph can never be a work of art. And if I have failed to make these translations in some sense works of art – if they are merely philology, not literature – then I have indeed fallen short of what I hoped and intended.[13]

Although Waley had planned accurate and faithful translations like black-and-white photographs – and, in fact, he made a number of such, including *Kagekiyo* – there are some deliberate alterations in some of his translations, including *Hatsuyuki*. Let us take up this problem and consider the purpose and effect of such alterations.

The play begins with the *nanori* (self-introduction) as follows. Waley says he used as the Japanese texts Ōwada Tateki's *Yōkyoku Hyōshaku* and Haga Yaichi and Sasaki Nobutsuna's *Yōkyoku Sōsho*, but where the two texts differ, he takes the more interesting variant as it suits him, and he sometimes relies on such Japanese texts as *Nōgaku Daijiten*.[14] Here I shall make an English translation from the Iwanami *koten bungaku taikei* edition, keeping, however, Waley's translation as much as possible as its base:

SERVANT.
   I am a servant of the Lord Abbot of the Great Temple at Izumo. My name is Yūgiri (Evening Mist). The Lord Abbot's daughter is beautiful and gentle as can be, and so someone presented a cock to her the other day. As it is a very beautiful white bird, she is especially fond of it. She named it Hatsuyuki (Year's First Snow) and pets it from morning till evening. I have not seen the bird this morning, so I think I will open the coop door and have a look at it.
   (*She makes a gesture of opening the door.*)

Goodness gracious me! Hatsuyuki is dead! I shall tell her quickly.
Madam, I beg to tell you, Hatsuyuki is dead.

What I should like to discuss here is Waley's real motive for the series of deliberate mistranslations in *Hatsuyuki*. The first such alteration was already contained in the passage quoted above. Though almost all the original Japanese texts say: 'Hatsuyuki is dead' (*munashiku nari mōshite sōrō*), Waley lets Evening Mist say, 'Your dear Snowbird is not here!' Therefore, it would be a matter of course for the reader to think simply that the bird has flown. Waley knew that *munashiku naru* meant 'to be dead' when he read Ōwada's text because the editor's note indicates it, but he chose Haga and Sasaki's text for his translation, in which the servant girl says (I translate literally):

'. . . I think I will go and feed the bird. Goodness me,
how strange! Oh dear, oh dear, what has happened?'[15]

On the whole, Waley has changed the image of the bird in this play intentionally and systematically. For example, when we hear Evening Mist say, 'I have not seen the bird to-day. I think I will go to the bird-cage and have a look at it,' we associate the word 'bird-cage' with a small one which a young lady might carry in her hand. The bird in it should be a little pet bird. Nevertheless, the original word is *toya* which should normally be translated into English as a coop, a hen-coop, a hen house, an aviary, or a roost. That is to say, the bird in it is, in fact, a cock. Both the Ōwada and the Haga-Sasaki texts clearly say Hatsuyuki is a cock. There lies Waley's aesthetic reason for such an alteration. The alteration being quite intentional, his aesthetic concept to which he conformed his English translation – or rather recreation – of *Hatsuyuki* is to be sought.

For the Japanese cocks and hens were sacred birds. The Ise Shrine feeds them in its precincts to this day. Presumably the Great Shinto Shrine of Izumo used to do the same thing, which inspired Zembō to write this play. However, a cock is not necessarily appropriate for this 'vision play'. First of all, it is difficult for us to imagine a cock flying and hovering in the sky, as Nogami Toyoichirō remarks: 'The play is slightly unnatural in that such a flightless bird as a cock flies over from Paradise and dances'.[16] Secondly, Waley might have thought that such a domestic fowl was too ordinary and realistic to be visionary. He avoided on purpose such a concrete image as 'since this bird was hatched' (*kaigo wo idete*, more literally, 'leaving the egg-shell') and put 'when first it left the breeding-cage' instead. Perhaps Waley was conscious that a new-hatched bird could not be 'white as snow'.

In the last scene of the play, where Hatsuyuki dances, the original text says:

CHORUS.
The bird, *yūtsuke-dori*, saying
His delights will last for ever,
Flutters and hovers a little while,
Hovers a little while and then is gone
We know not where.[17]

Although Waley knew from the notes that *yūtsuke-dori* (a bird with a tuft of white threads attached to it) is another name for a cock, he replaced it with 'dove.' Waley knew that in ancient Japan people used to perform rites of purification by putting tasselled cocks at the four great gates around the capital, and so he chose 'tasselled doves' as the Western equivalents of the *yūtsuke-dori*. Similarly he changed the original '*en'ō*' (mandarin ducks) into the legendary Phoenix which is more suggestive to Europeans, whereas he merely transliterated the Japanese word *fugan* (wild ducks and wild geese, birds which were thought to disport themselves in Buddhist Paradise).

Waley must have felt the delight of creation in such a free approach to the translation. The original stage direction is in general very practical and specifies Hatsuyuki's costume, hairdress and mask in detail, while Waley's is very poetic and exempt from theatrical technicalities. Here is an example:

The bird's soul appears as a white speck in the sky.

This line is, as it were, an integral part of the play. It was Mori Ogai who said that even the stage directions are poems in Maeterlinck's plays. It is sometimes equally true of Waley's stage directions.

Waley, undoubtedly, was able to produce poetic effects by the series of alterations. As the cock is changed into an ordinary bird, it diminishes in size to become a 'white bird' which can hover freely in the sky. As for colour, the red of the cockscomb is impressive in Zembō's original play, whereas Waley's version gives the reader a purely white impression: the 'white bird' is abstract beauty. Furthermore, since the cock is found dead in the coop in the original, the reader might unpleasantly imagine its dead body, but the 'white bird' in the English translation is not such a realistic creature.

It has left the bird-cage, and so it seems natural for Hatsuyuki to come back 'as a white speck in the sky', for the prayers of the girl and the noble ladies have been heard:

> With pure white wings beating the air
> The Snow-bird comes!
> Flying towards our lady
> Lovingly he hovers,
> Dances before her.

We have the impression that the missing bird is really coming back, for the bird's death has not yet been clearly stated in the English translation: (There have only been some hints,[18] in the Chorus: 'yet Hatsuyuki leaves no *testament*'; in two noble ladies' words: 'A solemn Mass we sing/A *dirge* for the *Dead*'; and in Waley's stage direction: 'the bird's *soul* appears as a white speck in the sky'.) The bird's coming back appears natural because it is a 'white bird', not a farmyard fowl. Waley's 'white bird' freely comes and goes between the other world and this; it is something which transcends 'the horrors of time and wretched material worries'.

Waley, who presumably thought that the '*deus ex machina*' kind of denouement would be hardly accepted by Western readers accustomed to naturalistic modern drama, cut the final scene of resuscitation in plays such as *Tanikō* (The Valley-Hurling) and *Ikeniye* (The Pool-Sacrifice). I imagine this was one of the reasons why Waley decided to leave Hatsuyuki's death vague. The reader will probably infer that Hatsuyuki has not only left the bird-cage but died when the chorus later sing: 'Who knows but he (the Lord Amida) can bring even a bird's soul into Paradise.' And yet there are not such explicit expressions of mourning as 'I think I will pray for the dead bird' (*kono tori no ato wo tomurawabaya to omō*) which are the words of the original.

These devices of the translator and these delicately different touches turned the original to a kind of fairy tale in Waley's translation. *Hatsuyuki*, which is originally a religious story of the soul's gaining Buddhahood – Hatsuyuki was granted salvation and admitted to Paradise – seems to have become something beautifully different. There is actually a scene of the Buddhist rite of praying for the dead, but this would give Western readers an exotic rather than a religious impression. (Conversely, such an English expression as 'a solemn Mass' could remind Japanese readers of a Catholic Mass and import thereby an exotic flavour.)

From the literary point of view, it has the fresh atmosphere of modern lyric drama in its English version. It may sound strange, but to the eyes of a Japanese like the present writer, Waley's version seems closer to Maeterlinck's *Blue Bird* than to medieval Japanese literature. By drawing parallels between Waley's *White Bird* and the Belgian playwright's *Blue Bird*, some features common to both these poetic works will be apparent.

One would look in vain for Maeterlinck's 'blue bird' in a picture-book of ornithology, for the 'blue bird' is not a real creature like a turtledove or a cock. The 'blue bird' is an idea and a symbol like Novalis's 'blue flower'. 'Hatsuyuki' was turned into 'abstract beauty' because the cock lost its concreteness in the process of the English translation until it became the 'white bird' – a symbol, an incarnation of spiritual beauty. In Maeterlinck's play, Tyltyl and Mytyl start on a journey in the other world. Although they are in fact in this world, they go to the other world in their vision; their situation is practically the same as that of *waki* and *wakitsure* in a Nō play of spirits (*mugen nō*), and that of Dante and Virgil in their journey through Hell and Purgatory. Since they come and go between the two worlds in their vision, they forget the distinction, and Tyltyl says to his grandfather in the Land of Memory, 'So you are not really dead?'[19] – to Gaffer Tyl's embarrassment, because there is no word like 'dead' in the Land of Memory, where the dead remain alive as long as the living remember them. Similarly in Waley's translation *Hatsuyuki*, the distinction between life and death is unclear. It is the idea in *the Divine Comedy* that the souls in Purgatory can ascend to Paradise more quickly if the living pray for them, and in *Hatsuyuki*, too, the bird is reborn in Paradise and can fly back to this world on gleaming white wings because people prayed for it. Perhaps Hatsuyuki flew back only this once to give thanks as it was saved. Saved souls, East or West, do not 'haunt' earth any more.

Yet the 'blue bird' or the 'white bird' is not outside the sphere of man. Neither Tyltyl or Mytyl or the lady or Evening Mist could find their dear birds so long as they looked outside themselves. Tyltyl cries out nearly at the end of the play: 'Why, that's the blue bird we were looking for! ... We went so far and he was here all the time!'[20]

What Tyltyl meant by 'here' was in his soul, though he was not clearly aware of it himself. The 'blue bird' is a symbol of the soul's desire, and, in consequence, one cannot keep it caged. It changes its colour as soon as it is caged. The Blue Bird escapes from the Little Girl's hands and flies away just as Tyltyl is going to feed it. When Mytyl cries out in despair, Tyltyl says:

'Never mind ... Don't cry... I will catch him again ... (*Stepping to the front of the stage and addressing the audience*) If any of you should find him, would you be so very kind as to give him back to us? ... We need him for our happiness, later on ...

    CURTAIN[21]

Maeterlinck's play is yet another variant on the theme: 'Out from the fine cage flies the nightingale.' Once it has gone away, even if one finds it again, one may not possess happiness permanently in this world. In the Nō play *Hatsuyuki* the bird which has flown back hovers a little while, but eventually goes away, leaving an infinite nostalgic suggestiveness.

Both *the Blue Bird* and *Hatsuyuki,* follow more or less the same structure pattern: One possessed happiness, but lost it. One goes in search of it and discovers it. When one is about to possess it again, it flies away. The role of the bird in both plays is similar.

That these two fairy tales are so similar is not a mere coincidence. According to Arthur Waley's brother Hubert, the translator was fond of Maeterlinck's poetic drama. When Hubert began learning French:

... As a first reading-book for my studies he chose Maeterlinck's plays, because, as he pointed out, you couldn't conceive works of literature using fewer difficult words or simpler grammatical constructions.[22]

One notes that the above words describe Arthur Waley's own literary style, which is simple and poetic.

Obviously, the language of a translation depends on that of its original text. But it should also be noted that the style of a translation depends much more on the translator's mastery and taste in his mother tongue. Waley loved the theatre, and especially the poetic drama. *L'Oiseau Bleu* (1908) became world famous when Waley was in his twenties. The taste of the times must have somewhat influenced Waley's selection, translation and recreation of the Nō plays. It may have been Waley's own personal taste (probably together with his interest in ballet) that made him include *Hatsuyuki* in his nineteen Nō plays, which has become like a piece of modern poetic drama in his English rendition. An Orientalist of the first generation, Arthur Waley could behave daringly, making his own free decisions and following his own intuitions, when translating East Asian literature. He may not even have imagined that anyone would examine his translations and later compare them with originals. However, even if Western Japanologists or Japanese scholars of comparative literature find fault with Waley's translation as a result of the later development and specialization of Japanese studies, his versions of Nō will long be respected as works of English literature in their own right. One must not regard Edith Sitwell's words of praise as applying directly to the Japanese Nō play *Hatsuyuki*. These words of the modern English poetess are of praise and thanks for Waley's own miraculous art. I shall end this essay by quoting from her letter once more:

> To me, *Hatsuyuki* is the most wonderful abstract beauty I know. Absolutely incredible. I *can't* dream how you do it. That is only an example.

*Notes*

[1] The original Japanese version is the chapter 2 'Uērī no shiroi tori' of Hirakawa Sukehiro: *Yōkyoku no shi to seiyō no shi* (Tokyo: Asahi shinbun-sha, 1975) pp. 71–105.

[2] Letter from Edith Sitwell to Arthur Waley in Ivan Morris ed.: *Madly Singing in the Mountains, An Appreciation and Anthology of Arthur Waley* (London: George Allen & Unwin, 1970) p. 97.

[3] Ichikawa Sanki criticized Waley in the article 'Yōkyoku no honyaku' (translation of Nō plays) which is included in Nogami Toyoichirō ed.: *Nōgaku Zensho* (1942) vol. 3. See especially p. 401 and pp. 430–431. Waley, conversely, criticized Japanese efforts to translate representative Nō plays into English. Waley's opinion is that translation of works of art should always be done into one's mother tongue. See Waley, 'Notes on Translation' (1958) in *Madly Singing in the Mountains*, pp. 152–164. Incidentally, Nihon gakujutsu shinkōkai's collective efforts to translate Nō plays into English were headed by Ichikawa Sanki.

[4] Arthur Waley: *The Nō Plays of Japan* (London: George Allen & Unwin, 1921).

[5] 'Wakare no tori,' the bird which warns lovers of the approach of day.

[6] Turn it into a Buddha.

[7] *The Penguin Book of Italian Verse* (Harmondsworth, Middlesex: Penguin Books, 1958) p. 51.

[8] Sanari Kentarō: *Yōkyoku Taikan* (Tokyo: Meiji shoin, 1930–1931) p. 2573.

[9] As Japanese used the sleeves of kimono to wipe tears, 'Never a moment are her long sleeves dry' means that she is continually weeping. The expression is a conventional description of great grief.

[10] Dante: *The Divine Comedy*, tr. Dorothy Sayers (Penguin Books, 1953) Purgatory, Canto II, 17–36.

[11] For the Japanese text of *Hatsuyuki*, *Nihon koten bungaku taikei*, vol. 41: *Yōkyoku-shū, ge* (Tokyo: Iwanami shoten, 1963) pp. 244–248 is easily available. Waley used various texts, when he translated *Hatsuyuki*. As for Waley's selected short bibliography of Japanese texts used, see *The Nō Plays of Japan*, pp. 304–305.

[12] John Webster, 'The White Devil', in *Plays by Webster & Ford* (London: J. M. Dent, 1949) p. 93. To explain the structure of a Nō Play, Arthur Waley used John Webster's another play, 'The Duchess of Malfi' in his introduction to *The Nō Plays of Japan* (pp. 53–54). An additional reason to quote Webster's verses for the sake of a poetical comparison.

[13] Arthur Waley: *The Nō Plays of Japan* (London: George Allen & Unwin, 1921) p. 55..

[14] For example, Waley apparently used *Nōgaku Daijiten* when he translated the first phrase: 'I am a servant at the Nyoroku Shrine in the Great Temple of Izumo.' It reads as follows in *Nōgaku Daijiten*: 'Kore wa Izumo no kuni no Ōyashiro Onna Roku no Miya ni tsukae tatematsuru Yūgiri to mōsu onna nite sōrō.' Waley made a mistake when he thought that 'Onna Roku no Miya' (or Nyo Roku no Miya) is a shrine. It is a lady.

[15] The original text in Haga and Sasaki ed. *Yōkyoku sōsho* reads as follows: Esa o kai mōsōzuru to omoi sōrō. Toto toto ara fushigiya. Izukata e yukite sōrōyaran. Miemōsazu sōrō.

[16] Nogami Toyoichirō in his comments on *Hatsuyuki* in Nogami Toyoichirō ed.: *Yōkyoku Zenshū* (1935–36) vol. 3, p. 93.

[17] Translation mine. The original text in *Nihon koten bungaku taikei*, vol. 41, reads: tanoshimi sarani, tsukisenu mi narito, yūtsuke-dori no, hakaze o tatete, shibashi ga hodo wa, tobimeguri......(p. 248).

[18] To indicate the hints, I used italics.

[19] Quotations of *The Blue Bird* are from the English translation by A. T. de Mattos (London: Methuen). As for the French original, see 3 tableau, acte II, Maurice Maeterlinck: *l'Oiseau Bleu* (Paris: Charpentier et Fasquelle, 1913).

[20] See 12 tableau, acte VI.

[21] Ibid.

[22] Hubert Waley, 'Recollections of a Younger Brother' in *Madly Singing in the Mountains*, p. 124.

# LOVE IN THE WEST, FRIENDSHIP IN THE EAST: POETICAL PREDILECTIONS AS PERCEIVED BY ARTHUR WALEY AND NATSUME SŌSEKI

————————□————————

Cultural traditions tend to give privileged values to certain poetical topics. Love in Europe and friendship in East Asia are examples of these poetical predilections. Poetical aesthetics that have derived from these poetical priorities tend also to form certain attitudes towards other human beings.

The great Orientalist, Arthur Waley (1889–1966) once made a very generalizing remark about the contrasting difference between East Asian literature and European literature. The eminent translator of *170 Chinese Poems* said in his introduction to the first edition (1918):

> The most conspicuous feature of European poetry is its preoccupation with love. This is apparent not only in actual 'love-poems', but in all poetry where the personality of the writer is in any way obtruded. The poet tends to exhibit himself in a romantic light; in fact, to recommend himself as a lover.
>
> The Chinese poet has a tendency different but analogous. He recommends himself not as a lover, but as a friend. He poses as a person of infinite leisure (which is what we should most like our friends to possess) and free from worldly ambitions (which constitute the greatest bars to friendship)... He would have us think of him as a boon companion, a great drinker of wine, who will not disgrace a social gathering by quitting it sober.

> To the European poet the relation between man and woman is a thing
> of supreme importance and mystery. To the Chinese, it is something com-
> monplace, obvious – a need of the body, not a satisfaction of the
> emotions. These he reserves entirely for friendship.[1]

These two tendencies, European and Chinese, have been noticed
also by Natsume Sōseki (1867–1916), the first Japanese professor of
English Literature at the Imperial University of Tokyo at the beginning of the twentieth century. In his lecture, which was later
published in 1906 under the title of *Bungakuron* (Theory of
Literature), Sōseki confessed his dismay at finding European preoccupation with love in Western literature. Sōseki states that 'ninety
per cent of Western literature deals with love between man and
woman ... which Westerners tend to consider sacred'.[2] That dismay
becomes a curious undercurrent running through literary works that
Sōseki produces later as a Western-style novelist, that is, whose main
topic is the relationship between man and woman. I will talk later
about the characteristics peculiar to Sōseki's heroes, which are often
mistakingly interpreted by Western readers as homosexualistic.

In order to understand the importance given to friendship in
Chinese literature, the most influential book in East Asia, the
*Analects* of Confucius (552–479 BC) needs to be consulted. The classical book begins with a phrase about the joy of meeting an old
friend: 'Is it not delightful to have friends coming from distant quarters?'[3] '*You peng zi yuanfang lai, bu yi le hu*'. The authenticity of the
feeling of this saying is undeniable. Chinese literature is rich in
poems dealing with friendship, as poets have mainly been bureaucrats selected because of their Confucian literary studies. The other
side of this high regard for male friendship, however, is low esteem
towards women and petty men who 'are very hard to deal with. If
you are friendly with them, they get out of hand, and if you keep
your distance, they resent it,' as Confucius confesses in the *Analects*.
It is essentially men who have appreciated friendship in Chinese literature, as those poet scholars, who had passed the examination for
civil service, were in general closely tied by friendship.

Here is a poem by Bai Juyi (Po Chü-i, AD 772–846), whose influence in Japan is comparable to Virgil's influence in European
countries, as I have discussed in the chapter dealing with Chinese
culture and Japanese identity. The translation is by Arthur Waley:[4]

### The Old Age

We are growing old together, you and I;
Let us ask ourselves, what is age like?

The dull eye is closed ere night comes;
The idle head, still uncombed at noon.
Propped on a staff, sometimes a walk abroad;
Or all day sitting with closed doors.
One dares not look in the mirror's polished face;
One cannot read small-letter books.
Deeper and deeper, one's love of old friends;
Fewer and fewer, one's dealings with young men.
One thing only, the pleasure of idle talk,
Is great as ever, when you and I meet.

The poem is addressed by Bai Juyi (Po Chü-i) to Liu Yuxi who was born in the same year as Bai Juyi 772. It is undeniable that Chinese scholar poets excel in poems on friendship, although among popular songs, there are plenty that deal with love between man and woman. In anthologies of Tang poems, there are many of which the topic is friendship. They are familiar not only to Chinese but also to Korean and Japanese men of letters. That traditional preoccupation with friendship is not a thing of the classical past. It continues on to later generations. Here is another example from the Qing poet Yuan Mei (1716–97), also translated by Waley:[5]

Don't laugh at my tower being so high;
Think what pleasure I shall gain from its being so high!
I shall not have to wait till you arrive;
I shall see you clearly ten leagues away!
But when you come, do not come in your coach;
The sound of a coach scares my birds away.
When you come, do not ride your horse;
For it might be hungry and try its teeth on my plants.
When you come, don't come too early;
We country people stay late in bed.
But when you come, don't come too late;
For late in the day the flowers are not at their best.

If you compare this poem with sonnets by Folgore da San Gimignano (ca.1250–1317), you see how the Chinese poet introduces himself as a timid recluse, while Dante's contemporary straightforwardly glorifies his towers and possessions. Let us quote the English translation of Folgore's poem on 'August' by Dante Gabriel Rossetti:[6]

For August, be your dwelling thirty towers
    Within an Alpine valley mountainous,
    Where never the sea-wind may vex your house,
But clear life separate, like a star, be yours.

> There horses shall wait saddled at all hours,
> 　That ye may mount at morning or at eve:
> 　On each hand either ridge ye shall perceive,
> A mile apart, which son a good beast scours.
> So alway, drawing homewards, ye shall tread
> 　Your valley parted by a rivulet
> 　　Which day and night shall flow sedate and smooth.
> There all through noon ye may possess the shade,
> 　And there your open purses shall entreat
> 　The best of Tuscan cheer to feed your youth.

The poem is as gorgeous as a late gothic-style Sienese painting of the Renaissance. The poet says that he will give generously his possessions to his friend. There is no doubt that the poet Folgore exhibits himself as a romantic hero.

The introduction is dropped from Waley's later editions of *170 Chinese Poems*. However, his distinction between European poetry and Chinese poetry is not without foundation and I regret that he dropped it. Waley says among other things:

> It has been the habit of Europe to idealize love at the expense of friendship and so to place too heavy a burden on the relation of man and woman. The Chinese erred in the opposite direction, regarding their wives and concubines simply as instruments of procreation. For sympathy and intellectual companionship they looked only to their friends. But these friends were bound by no such tie as held women to their masters; sooner or later they drifted away to frontier campaigns, remote governorships, or country retirement. It would not be an exaggeration to say that half the poems in the Chinese language are poems of parting or separations.[7]

There are, of course, in any literature poems dealing with friendship. 'Old Familiar Faces' is a common topic of humanity. The two tendencies, which have been picked up, have many exceptions. These tendencies should not be considered as something eternally inherent in cultures, Eastern and Western.

A fact, however, should not be overlooked: even in East Asia, there is a tradition of love poetry. Even if Chinese literature was a male-dominated one, Japanese literature had a double structure: the upper male part had long been under strong Confucian influence until the end of the nineteenth century, as written Chinese played a cultural role analogous to Latin in European countries. However, the lower part has always been vernacular, in which Japanese lady writers have had a free hand since the time of *Genji monogatari* (*Tale of Genji*, ca 1000). *Monogatari* or romances developed in court culture by lady writers, and it seems women everywhere show preference for love over friendship, at least, for their literary topics. The situation is almost similar in Korea, although to a lesser degree, as the use and recognition of the vernacular for literary expression is far more recent and reticent in Korea than in Japan. Korea is geographically and culturally adjacent to China; moreover, it has had a system of recruitment of bureaucrats conceived on the Chinese model. Confucian orthodoxy has inevitably been very strong. Korean men of letters have been more rigoristically Confucianistic than the Chinese.

If friendship is idealized at the expense of love in Confucian cultures of East Asia, then how about family ties? If East Asians do not place too much weight on the relationship between man and woman, do they also neglect the importance of family ties? The answer is of course not, and family ties are as strong as ever in Asian countries where public institutions have not always guaranteed the welfare of the people.

One of strange sensations that East Asians feel, while learning English or any European language, is when they find that they are called 'creatures' in a Western tongue. East Asians generally do not believe in the myth of creation, even if they happen to be Christians in their own way. If they have a vague belief in the origin of mankind, it is in the myth of generation that they tend to believe. Although the Jesuit father Matteo Ricci (1552–1610) tried hard to identify the Christian God (Deus) with Confucian Heaven (Tian) when he entered the Middle Kingdom towards the end of the sixteenth century, it is difficult for East Asians to believe the myth that Tian or Shangdi (Heavenly Emperor) created the world.

So long as one does not believe in a Heavenly Father, the Creator of all creatures, one has to seek someone else for help; or one has to rely on one's own; or more probably on your relations or, in this age of social welfare, on social security systems. In the case of many East Asians, it is natural that instead of a transcendental father, they should traditionally rely more heavily on their blood father. Family ties have therefore been very important: in degree of importance father and mother come before wife and husband in the Confucian ethical order. In the Christian Bible that ethical order is different: it is said that 'a man shall leave his father and mother, and shall be joined unto his wife'. (Ephesians 5. 31).

The difference in traditional ethical orders may be explained this way. One of the strange absences in English or in any European languages that East Asians find strange, while learning them, is the lack of a single term meaning *xiao* in Chinese and *kō* in Japanese, which is the same Chinese character generally translated into English as 'filial piety' or 'filial duty'. Europeans need two words: an adjective and a noun to express this cardinal virtue of humanity.[8]

While this sense of difference between the Western world and East Asian countries exists, family ties, of which the importance has long been placed on its vertical relationship between parents and children rather than on its horizontal relationship between man and woman or husband and wife, has its literary expressions.

Its importance might be understood by quoting one of the passages in Dante's *Divine Comedy* which strikes the filial chord of traditional East Asians. The scene in question is when Count Ugolino through agony bit on either hand in Canto XXXIII of *Inferno*:

> I gnawed at both my hands for misery;
>     And they, who thought it was for hunger plain
>     And simple, rose at once and said to me:
> 'O Father, it will give us much less pain
>     If thou wilt feed on us; thy gift at birth
>     Was this sad flesh, strip thou it off again.'[9]

This cry of the children is an expression of *xiao* and no mistake. Chinese literature is rich in ghastly stories of famine with grotesque variations of filial obedience of this kind, that is, children sacrificing themselves for the sake of their parents. It should be added that there are plenty of literary aberrations both in Korea and Japan that blindly glorify filial duties.

Parental care of course finds its expressions in East Asian literature. The poems of Yamanoue no Okura (660–733) in the *Manyōshū*, thinking of his children, are the first remarkable examples of the kind in Japanese poetry. Bai Juyi wrote of his dead daughter named Golden Bells in the following pathetic way. The feeling expressed in this poem is humane and universal:[10]

Remembering Golden Bells

Ruined and ill, – a man of two score,
Pretty and guileless, – a girl of three.
Not a boy, – but still better than nothing:
To soothe one's feelings, – from time to time a kiss!
There came a day, – they suddenly took her from me;
Her soul's shadow wandered I know not where.
And when I remember how just at the time she died
She lisped strange sounds, beginning to learn to talk,

*Then* I know that the ties of flesh and blood
Only bind us to a load of grief and sorrow.
At last, by thinking of the time before she was born,
By thought and reason I drove the pain away.
Since my heart forgot her, many days passed
And three times winter has changed to spring.
This morning, for a little, the old grief came back,
Because, in the road, I met her foster-nurse.

Some feminists may complain of the male preference of the poet, expressed so frankly in the third line: 'Not a boy, – but still better than nothing.' However, the purpose of this quotation is to show the authenticity of Bai Juyi's feelings revealed in the last line; this kind of parental affection is genuine. It is also universal.

Love in the East seems to take a more subdued form of expression. Some stories of devoted wives, united with their spouses through arranged marriages, also, are very moving. For example, the first modernizer of Japanese literature, Mori Ōgai's (1862–1922) portrait of an old couple (*Jiisan Baasan,* 1915)[11] is as touching as the Greek legendary couple of Baucis and Philemon. Ōgai's ambivalent relationships with his wife and mother as reflected in his naturalistic works as well as in his historical novels such as *Shibue Chūsai* (1916) are worth a closer analysis than stereotyped 'Orientalist' explanations, which tend to justify Westerners' moral practices by denouncing Asiatic family ties as 'feudalistic.' I will discuss the matter, by going through Ōgai's novels written in his thirties, forties and fifties in the following chapter.

More simply, the Japanese ideal of the conjugal tie is shown in folkloristic *dodoitsu* songs, which is often recited at marriage banquets. Let us read Lafcadio Hearn's translation of one of them. Hearn, by the way, 'went native'. He married a Japanese woman and obtained Japanese citizenship.

You, till a hundred years; I, until nine and ninety;
Together we still shall be in the time when the hair turns white.[12]

Even though some Japanese feminists protested against 'the male supremacist idea' that the husband lives longer than the wife, there is poetry precisely in the difference of one year. To understand the psychology of a good traditional couple, you might give thought to the nuanceful conversation of an old man and an old woman. The aged Japanese couple are talking with a crafty smile:

'You and I, who will be the winner?'
'The one who dies first, of course.'

The tacit understanding of the joke is that the one who dies first will not feel the sadness of being left alone. That is why the one who dies first is 'the winner'.

What is surprising in Chinese and Korean literatures is the relative absence of the topic of sons' and daughters' revolt against their parents. The hold of family ties of flesh and blood seems to be still very strong, and we can recognize the continuing effects in many of 'modern' writers.

Chinese modernizers have expressed the strength of family ties also. Zhu Ziqing's (1898–1948) portrait of his father, *Beiying* (Sight of My Father's Back, 1925) is a good example. The story is in a sense banal. His father comes to see him off at Nanjing railway station. The son, already twenty years old, finds the aged father's solicitude ridiculous. However, when he sees the corpulent father walk across railroads to buy some oranges for him, climbing down the platforms and up again, the son cannot help being moved. When the father, on his way back, drops oranges on the tracks and climbs down from the platform again to pick them up, the son dashes from the wagon to fetch him. The father, after putting all the oranges on the son's coat stretched on the seat, clears dust and mud from his blue clothes, and then goes away, saying: 'So-long. When you arrive there, write me.' This is a piece as sentimental as *Mikan* (Mandarin oranges, 1919)[13] by the Japanese author Akutagawa Ryūnosuke (1892–1927) in which a country girl of about thirteen years of age, apparently now going to the city to work, opens the window of a running train. Akutagawa coughs because of the smoke that is coming in. The girl, all of a sudden, throws oranges to her younger brothers who have come to a crossing to see their elder sister off. Both stories may be called sentimental mush. However the emotional intensity of family ties, symbolized by mandarin oranges in both cases, is sincere. The fact that both stories by Zhu Ziqing and Akutagawa give us a similar impression suggests that the feeling of *xiao* is, in its wider sense, a feeling of affection surrounding family ties. In the case of *Mikan* it is almost a parental care that makes the older sister throw mandarin oranges to her younger brothers.

Lao She (1899–1966) portrays his mother in a sketch *Wo de muqin* (My Mother, 1943). He tells the life of his widowed mother and concludes that no teacher has had so much influence on him as his mother and that it was that illiterate person who formed Lao She's character. If one calls this author a man possessed with a mother-fixation, then all East Asian readers who are moved by the sketch should be considered to be suffering from the same psychological problem.[14]

The notion of *xiao* should not be interpreted in a narrow oppressive sense of filial obedience to parental authority. There is something reciprocal in one's affective dealings whether with one's parents or one's children. Family ties, therefore, have been sacred in China, as people have so much depended on it for living. As there are feudalistic aspects in every binding relationship, it is of course easy to criticize traditional family bonds. It is natural that young people revolt against them from time to time. There is, however, a limit that humans should not overstep. For example, those young Red Guards, who in the name of Chairman Mao denounced their own 'bourgeois' parents to the party authorities, committed the most grave of human sins, because they unethically broke that human tie. Confucius said: 'The father conceals the misconduct of the son, and the son conceals the misconduct of the father. Uprightness is to be found in this.'[15] The *Analects* are indeed full of truthful observations of human nature, which attract us by their frankness.

Let me refer to an episode by way of conclusion. Natsume Sōseki was baffled by his discovery of the Western preoccupation with love in European literatures. Sōseki as a young man had been deeply impregnated with Chinese culture before becoming the first Japanese professor of English Literature. Later, as the champion of modern Japanese literature, Sōseki analyses love between man and woman in many of his novels. It is said that towards the end of his life, in order to keep his psychological balance, Sōseki, after having written novels dealing with love affairs in the morning, passed the rest of the day, composing Chinese poems.

One of his last masterpieces dealing with love is *Kokoro* (1914) which is said to deal with the question of how to maintain sincerity in a morally corrupt world[16]. Contrary to the usual supposition which considers Sensei (the master) and his wife's relationship most important, it is the relationship between Sensei and his student (the narrator of the story, 'I') which is the most important.[17] In his actual life, Sōseki's relationship with his students was extremely good. It was something very precious to Sōseki as well as to his disciples. The numerous letters Sōseki wrote to them testify to their good relationship. In Sōseki's case, the teacher-disciple relationship was a variation of friendship, and that tie constitutes the central bonding relationship, probably more vital than any other relationships in the novel. Sōseki, in this sense, is in line with the remark made by Waley.

At the end of the novel Sensei commits suicide, confiding to 'I', his student, the secret that Sensei does not wish to reveal even to his wife. Here is the passage in question of Sensei's testament to the student 'I' in Kondō Ineko's translation:

> I am intending to make my past, good and bad, public property. But please understand that my wife is the only exception. I don't want to tell her anything at all. *My only wish is to keep her memory of the past as pure as possible*, so long as my wife is alive please keep everything I have told you in your mind as a secret confided to you only.[18]

The italicized passage reads as follows in Sōseki's original Japanese:

> 'Sai ga onore no kako ni taishite motsu kioku o, narubeku junpaku ni hozonshite yaritai no ga watakushi no yuiitsu no kibō nanodesu... '[19]

'onore no' refers to 'her' and 'onore no kako' is '(her memory of) her past'. As has been revealed in the preceding part of the testament, in his youth Sensei and his friend K were rivals in a love affair. When Sensei outmanoeuvered K and got the hand of the girl – who is none other than Sensei's wife – K committed suicide. Incapable of enduring his sense of guilt, Sensei, too, after many years, is about to commit suicide. Sensei, however, does not wish to let his wife know the reason for his suicide. It would be too cruel for her to know the secret of the unhappy chain reactions.

Here is, however, the British Japan scholar Edwin McClellan's translation of the same part:

> I want both the good and bad things in my past to serve as an example to others. But my wife is the one exception – I do not want her to know about any of this. My first wish is that her memory of me should be kept as unsullied as possible. So long as my wife is alive, I want you to keep everything I have told you a secret.[20]

As a whole Edwin McClellan's English translation is far better than Kondō's translation. However, as to the interpretation of 'onore no', McClellan makes the typical Western error of putting too much weight on the relationship between man and woman. Generally speaking, it would be impossible for a husband who commits suicide to expect that her memory of him be kept clean. Leaving his wife alone without telling her the reason of his suicide is a kind of betrayal. However, for the very sincere Oriental Sensei, the betrayal of friendship is a sin far greater than the betrayal of

marital love. It is interesting that McClellan's mistranslation has
something to do with his misunderstanding of that cultural background. McClellan imagined wrongly that the Japanese husband
had still at the moment of his suicide a romantic vanity that his
widow would keep a memory of him as 'unsullied as possible'.

Because of the precedence Sōseki's hero accords to friendship
over love, Sensei's wife is, in hindsight, neglected with condescending care by the husband. She is to be left in ignorance of the
two tragic suicides of which she was, without knowing, the cause.
Some readers may find in Sensei's circumspection an ethical beauty.
However, this considerate attitude of the husband, who dies,
leaving his wife in a state of ignorance, is not really acceptable. This
treatment of the other is not beautiful, but can even be seen as
cruel.

With the coming of the age of the computer, our norms, both
material and spiritual, will become more and more uniform in this
global society. Our value systems will become identical everywhere,
at least in financial terms. However, in our field of literature, different cultural characteristics will remain even within the three
major East Asian traditions of China, Korea and Japan. Differences
will still be more numerous and greater between an East Asian
nation and a Western nation. As long as there are cultural differences, comparative scholars will be busy comparing them. Even in
the field of aesthetics, sometimes we shall admire others and sometimes we shall come back to our own old traditions in order to keep
our cultural identity and to maintain our emotional balance.

'Love in the West, Friendship in the East' is an essay that
attempts to interpret poetical priorities in Christian European tradition and Confucian Asian tradition. The psychological pendulum in
judging and criticizing others will continue to swing. Even without
making any value judgement, sometimes people insist on differences, as Waley did in 1918 in his introduction to *170 Chinese Poems*,
and sometimes people stop making that kind of generalization, as
Waley did more than forty years later. Waley replaced that sweeping
judgement in 1960, writing another introduction for the paperback
edition of the same book published by the same Constable & Co
Ltd. The new introduction is very interesting, as it reveals Waley's
personal history as an Orientalist. It does not, however, contain any
specific view concerning comparative aesthetics. Then, it would no
doubt be wise for me, who have been partly inspired by Waley, to
stop here. To give too general a talk about love in West European

literature, as contrasted with friendship in East Asian literature is a perilous undertaking, as there are so many exceptions.

## Notes

[1] The introduction to the first edition of Arthur Waley: *170 Chinese Poems* (London: Constable & Co, 1918) is partially reproduced in Ivan Morris ed.: *Madly Singing in the Mountains* (London: George Allen & Unwin, 1970), pp. 295–296.

[2] Natsume Sōseki: *Bungakuron: Sōseki zenshū* (Tokyo: Iwanami, 1957), vol. 18 (dai 1 pen, dai 2 sho), p. 59, p. 63.

[3] Confucius: *Analects, Great Learning, and Doctrine of the Mean* (New York: Dover, 1971), tr. James Legge, p. 137.

[4] Arthur Waley: *Chinese Poems* (London: George Allen & Unwin, 1961) p. 168.

[5] Arthur Waley: *Yuan Mei* (London: George Allen & Unwin, 1957) p. 48.

[6] D.G.Rossetti: *Poems and Translations* (London: J.M.Dent, 1954) pp. 214–215.

[7] *Madly Singing in the Mountains*, p. 296.

[8] In Japan, the importance of the two notions of *chū* (loyalty) and *kō* (filial piety) was very much stressed in pre-war years, as they were considered cardinal virtues in the Rescript on Education issued in 1890. In 1922, however, Naitō Torajirō (Konan, 1866–1934) contested the idea of the continued existence of the morality based on *chū* and *kō* throughout all periods of Japanese history, by pointing out the absence of a single word of Japanese origin (Yamato-kotoba), representing the notion of *kō*. The Japanese *kun*-pronunciation of the word of Chinese origin *kō* (*xiao* in Chinese) is either *yoshi*, which means 'good' or *taka*, which means 'high'. See Naitō, 'Nihon bunka towa nanzoya' in Naitō Torajirō: *Nihon bunkashi kenkyū* (Tokyo: Heibonsha, 1963) p. 11.

[9] Dante: *The Divine Comedy: Hell* (Harmondsworth, Middlesex: Penguin Classics, 1968) tr. Dorothy Sayers, Canto XXXIII, 58–63, p. 279.

[10] Arthur Waley: *Chinese Poems*, p. 124.

[11] Translated as 'The Old Man and the Old Woman' in David Dilworth and J. Thomas Rimer eds.: *Ōgai: The Historical Fiction of Mori Ōgai* (Honolulu: University of Hawaii Press, 1991) pp. 201–207.

[12] Lacadio Hearn, 'Out of the Street', in *Gleanings in Buddha-Fields: The Writings of Lafcadio Hearn* (Boston and New York: Houghton Mifflin, 1922), vol. 8, p. 32.

[13] 'Mikan', *Akutagawa Ryūnosuke zenshū* (Tokyo: Iwanami shoten, 1996) vol. 4, pp. 231–236.

[14] The presence of a mother figure is said to be especially conspicuous in Korean literature. In Yi Sang (1910–37)'s celebrated novel *Wings* (1936), the protagonist's relationship with his wife is a strange one, as she earns

their living by prostitution. However, that relationship is adroitly interpreted by Sung Hae-Kyung in Hirakawa & Tsuruta ed.: *Amae de bungaku o toku* (Tokyo: Shinyōsha, 1996, pp. 185–220), as a transformed guise of the husband's dependency (*amae*) on a motherly figure. The young man, who has no wings or who does not wish to have wings, remains in a childish state. The young man in his regression is at home, as he is taken care of by a surrogate motherly figure. He clings to an artificial family bond and cannot fly away. He tries to cut the tie almost in vain.

[15] Confucius: *Analects, Great Learning, and Doctrine of the Mean*, tr. James Legge, p. 270.

[16] This tendency to judge a work of literature from an ethical point of view is conspicuous in the critical evaluation of *Kokoro* given by Komiya Toyotaka (1884–1966), Sōseki's disciple and the first editor of Sōseki's complete works. See his *kaisetsu* attached to *Sōseki zenshū* (Tokyo: Iwanami shoten, 1956), vol. 12 in shinsho-ban, pp. 235–244.

[17] I have dealt with this problem in Hirakawa ed.: *Sōseki no 'Kokoro' o yomu* (Tokyo: Shinyōsha, 1992) pp. 32–65, and also in Lin Lien-hsiang ed.: A *Symposium on Natsume Sōseki's 'Kokoro'* (Singapore: Department of Japanese Studies, National University of Singapore, 1996), pp77–87.

[18] Sōseki Natsume: *Kokoro*, tr. I. Kondo (Tokyo: Hokuseido, 1941) pp. 282–3.

[19] Natsume Sōseki: *Kokoro: Sōseki zenshū* (Tokyo: Iwanami, 1956) vol. 12, p. 234.

[20] Sōseki Natsume: *Kokoro*, tr. E.McClellan (Tokyo: Charles E.Tuttle, 1984) p. 248.

# PART VI

# JAPANESE WRITERS BETWEEN
# EAST AND WEST

# MORI ŌGAI'S AMBIVALENT RELATIONSHIP WITH HIS MOTHER AS EVOKED IN HIS LATER HISTORICAL WORKS

———————□———————

M ori Ōgai (1862–1922) was a successful man. As a writer, he was a towering figure in the Meiji-Taishō period (1868–1926). Together with Natsume Sōseki (1867–1916), he is generally considered to be one of the two greats in modern Japanese literature. As an army surgeon, he attained the highest rank of Surgeon General.[2] His only failure is said to be his first marriage with Akamatsu Toshiko. What draws our attention here is that their divorce seems to have something to do, first, with Ōgai 's having experienced a much freer, happier life in the Western world in his mid-twenties. Ōgai indeed spent four years of his youth in Leipzig, Dresden, Munich and Berlin, from 1884 to 1888, studying medical science and devouring Western literature. He apparently enjoyed the many freedoms of German university life, individual freedoms of spirit which he had not known to such a degree before in his own country. Second, their divorce seems to have something to do with his too close ties with his mother Mineko.

On his return home, Ōgai not only advanced in the military medical corps, but also made a brilliant debut as the champion of a new literary movement. He seemed to symbolize all the new changes brought from Europe. However, the young returnee continued to follow strictly the feudal norm in one important point: Ōgai respected the traditional cardinal virtue of filial piety. In fact, when Ōgai got married six months after his return to Japan, he did not choose his spouse by himself, but let his mother Mori Mineko decide the choice of his life companion, and the match turned out a failure: Ōgai divorced Toshiko in 1890 immediately after the birth of his first son.

As literature is something which deals mostly with love affairs in all the countries of the world, the case of the writer Mori Ōgai is very curious, as there seems to exist a discrepancy between his personal obedient attitude as the eldest son and heir of the Mori family and his assertion and aspiration for individual freedoms as the leading writer and ideologue of modernizing Japan. The question which I would like to raise here, therefore, concerns Ōgai's relationship with his mother Mineko, and the way in which that relationship was reflected in his literary works, especially in his later historical novels.

About Ōgai's commitment to filial duty, there is a well-known comment made by Kinoshita Mokutarō (1885–1945). According to this disciple of Ōgai's, Ōgai attributes higher value to the Confucian virtue of filial piety than to the Western notions of individual freedoms, such as the freedom of choosing one's own job as well as that of selecting one's own spouse.[3] This comment made by Mokutarō in 'Mori sensei – the man and the work' (*Mori sensei no hito to waza to*, 1936) is so famous that it is often quoted as the last word on the subject.

However, Mokutarō's comment on the matter is, in any event not the final verdict. It is not that simple. There is evidence enough to suggest that Mokutarō might have projected his own situation onto Ōgai. Like many contemporaries of his generation, Mokutarō himself could not choose the job of his liking: when he was young, Mokutarō wanted to become a painter, and it was because of his respect for the will of his family that he became a medical doctor. Not only that, Mokutarō, too, married a woman whom his family had decided would be his wife. Like Ōgai, Mokutarō must have pondered a great deal over those contradictory issues, issues typical of the transition period from pre-modern to modern times. Since Mokutarō himself was obliged to choose between his familial obligations and his personal preferences, he was most probably in a position to well understand Ōgai's state of mind. It may well have been as justification for his own conduct that Mokutarō defines in such a clear-cut, affirmative manner Ōgai's attitude as an obedient son. It is hard to believe that *kō* (*xiao* in Chinese) or filial piety practised in reality had such a perfected virtue as extolled by Mokutarō.

Ōgai himself was not that simple a mind to believe in this traditional value without suffering from contradictions. It would be difficult to believe that failure to find an ideal wife for himself could be remedied without leaving a lasting wound to a sensitive man like Ōgai. It must have left some profound traces in Ōgai's literary works.

In this chapter I will first biographically examine Ōgai's relationship with his mother, Mori Mineko (1846–1916, née Mori), second, his unhappy experience of divorce reflected in his early literary works, third, his admiration for Western women as his ideal, and fourth, his reconciliation or his identification with the past and the image of his own mother evoked in his historical works.

### 1. Biographical Background

The Mori family is described by Ōgai himself in his unpublished literary work *Head Family, Branch Family* (Honke bunke), written in 1915 (now included in Ōgai's collected works[4]). They had lived for generations in Tsuwano, principal town of the small Iwami fief in the western part of Honshu. All the heads of the Mori family served the lord Kamei as the clan's medical doctors. Ōgai's great-grandfather did not have children. He adopted a son, Mori Hakusen (né Sasada) and chose a bride for him, Kiyoko (née Kijima), daughter of a rich farmer from the province of Nagato, and thus continued the line of the Mori house.

According to *Head Family, Branch Family*, the Mori family had been very much impoverished in the time of his great-grandfather. His grandfather Mori Hakusen was not only a good medical doctor serving the Kamei clan but also a Confucian scholar of considerable learning. It was Hakusen's wife Kiyoko who helped her scholarly husband, by paying back within several years all the family debts and saving gradually a considerable sum of money. A boy was born between the couple but soon died, and then a girl, later known as Mineko, was born in 1846. As they did not have a male heir, they married the heiress Mineko, at the early age of thirteen, to an adopted husband, Mori Shizuo (né Yoshitsugu), a medical doctor of Dutch learning, and soon their first son, Mori Ōgai (Rintarō), was born: a long expected male child, on whose shoulders the future of the Mori family so much depended. When Ōgai was born in the first month of 1862, his father Shizuo was twenty-six years old, his mother Mineko fifteen and his grandmother Kiyoko forty-two, and she was already a widow. It should be noted that his grandfather Mori Hakusen had died suddenly in autumn of 1861 at Tsuchiyama on his way back from the capital of Edo. After that incident the Mori family must have been in a miserable state, when the joyful news of the son's birth was announced.[5] The Mori family is characterized by Ōgai in his *Head Family, Branch Family* as follows:

> In that family there was a kind of dignified tradition originating with the grandfather (Mori Hakusen) and transmitted through the mother (Mori Mineko) that the family members looked down upon the gregarious public at large. They had a firm will to cultivate real abilities in their daily life and to advance in life once an occasion was offered.[6]

It was through the education of the first son that the Mori people sought a higher status in that changing society.

All the reminiscences of the Mori family, such as the memoirs written by Ōgai's sister Koganei Kimiko[7] and Ōgai's first son Mori Oto,[8] concur in this regard: Ōgai as an infant was extremely well taken care of by the Mori family, especially by his mother Mineko and his grandmother Kiyoko. Ōgai began to learn the Confucian classics from the year 1867. From 1869 he attended courses given at the clan academy for three years. His education was supervised at home by his mother, who educated herself in order to be able to teach her son. Either Mineko or Kiyoko always accompanied the child to his personal teacher Yonehara's house or to the clan academy. This discouraged boys of the same age from playing with him, and Ōgai had instead books as his playmates. Ōgai, therefore, was destined to advance and to climb the social ladder. He was the hope of the Mori family, and his mother's will was preponderant. In his first novel *The Dancing Girl* (Maihime, 1890), the hero Ōta is described as a young Japanese boy 'obedient to his mother's teachings'.[9] There are passages such as this: 'My mother, I thought to myself, had tried to make me into a walking dictionary'.[10] Surely there are autobiographical elements in that characterization of the infant prodigy. When Ōgai completed the translation of Andersen's *Improvisator* in 1901, he mentioned in its explanatory notes that he had the book printed in large characters so that his aged mother with feeble eyesight could enjoy reading her son's literary productions.[11] This she continued to do until late in life. In Ōgai's family, women, namely his grandmother and mother, were strong-willed and more forceful than his moderate father.

Ōgai got married again in 1902. When the newly-married couple moved from Kokura to Tokyo, the tension heightened between the mother Mineko and Ōgai's second wife Shigeko. In the Mori family, it was always the mother Mineko, and not the wife Shigeko, who held the purse. Mineko indeed was very competent in financial matters. Ōgai was obliged to keep the peace between the two when they lived together. During the Russo-Japanese War of 1904–05, Shigeko and her daughter Mari lived separately from Kiyoko, Mineko and Oto, Ōgai's first son by Akamatsu Toshiko being taken care of by Mineko. On 12 January 1906, Ōgai returned from Manchuria and went first to his mother's house to greet Mineko and his friends and relatives, and to attend a banquet. However, past midnight he walked a long distance to come to see his wife Shigeko. Shigeko had fond memories of Ōgai and she told her children that she could never forget the approaching sound of her husband's footsteps that winter night.

In March 1909, Ōgai, to the surprise of his readers and to the indignation of his wife, exposed the tense triangular relationship among husband, mother and wife in a novel entitled *Half a Day* (Hannichi), which bears unmistakable similarities to the relationship existing in the Mori family. In it there are the following descriptions:

> His mother is an exceptionally strong-willed woman; when she goes to bed at night she decides when she will get up the next morning, and invariably wakes up at that hour by autosuggestion. His wife, on the contrary, is exceedingly weak-willed.[12]

As his wife was a natural sleepy-head, even after her son's marriage his mother still got up early every morning and took charge of breakfast for the whole family. That is the reason why a sharp voice was heard from the kitchen: 'Do you mean to tell me the water hasn't boiled yet!'[13] The person who railed against the maid in the kitchen was the mother.

> 'Oh, what a terrible voice. She's always waking our daughter with it.' When the daughter hears her mother's shrill, loud voice – not the one from the kitchen – she suddenly thrusts two plump little fists out, stretches her body, and opens those black eyes she inherited from her mother.[14]

Ōgai is extremely good at evoking the antagonistic atmosphere of the Mori family. There is, moreover, a description of the wife. Whenever she has complaints, she repeats the same phrase:

> 'Please don't force me to do something which I don't like.' It is like a refrain. His wife never does anything which she doesn't like. In any case, she never does anything which requires special effort. She doesn't have an ounce of self-discipline. This is a remnant of her girlhood days when she was pampered by her father, Chief Justice of the Court of Cassation. The

slightest hint of some obligation produces three vertical wrinkles between her beautiful long eyebrows. She lacks the will to get out of bed when she is supposed to.[15]

It is understandable that Mori Shigeko, Ōgai's second wife here described as a sleepy-head, did not wish this novel to be included in Ōgai's collected works as long as she lived. Let us have a look at their dining-room:

> It is the custom in this house for his mother to serve him and his daughter, and to eat with them. The cushion behind his wife's place is empty. She eats in another room after everyone else has finished. And this is not just at meals: she does not sit in the same room with his mother. In the early years of their marriage, she would immediately stand up and leave whenever his mother came in, but she eventually arranged it so that his mother could not get near him.[16]

In January 1911, Ōgai published a novel entitled *The Snake* (Hebi). Although there is no concrete description of the mother, this, too, deals with the triangular relationship between husband, mother and wife: the irreconcilable conflict between the modern wife and her traditional mother-in-law. Ōgai gives literary form to personal concerns and this is one of his methods of relief from psychological distress. Caught between them, Ōgai actually helped his wife Shigeko to write novels, which were later collected in a book entitled *Adabana*.[17] Since Shigeko's novels, too, were written as a kind of psychological therapy and as Ōgai helped her so considerably, one cannot be sure to what extent these are her own creation.

In the early morning of 28 March 1916, Ōgai's mother Mineko died at the age of sixty-nine. On that day, Ōgai's second daughter Annu, while appearing on the stage of the kindergarten in a play, was surprised to find her father in the audience. Ōgai later explained, smiling, that as he had discharged his duties towards his mother most faithfully while she was alive, it was not necessary for him to attend at the bedside when she was dead.

These are some biographical anecdotes suggestive of Ōgai's close relationship with his mother. Some of Ōgai's letters sent from Kokura to his sister Koganei Kimiko are also very indicative, as they clearly show his conservative views concerning the relationship between a bride and her mother-in-law. Ōgai advised Kimiko to be as agreeable as possible towards her mother-in-law. The priorities given by Ōgai in the family relationship were apparently traditional. However, he did not forget to admonish the gifted sister to cultivate herself. Kimiko and her mother-in-law unlike Ōgai's wife and his mother had a happier relationship: Kimiko's mother-in-law came to her house to spend her last years and to die.

## 2. *Ōgai's Unhappy Experience of Divorce Reflected in his novel: The Courier*

In his third novel *The Courier* (Fumizukai, 1891), Ōgai makes a critique, through the novel's heroine Princess Ida, of the social custom of arranging marriages through the fathers' wills without taking into consideration the feelings of the persons concerned. The gist of the story is as follows: Fräulein Ida was betrothed to Count Meerheim, whom she could not love, 'though the Count was honest and looked very handsome'.[18] Her father was of the opinion that to those who were born to an aristocratic family, the most important duty is to continue the family line without breaking or degrading it. There was, therefore, no personal freedom of choosing a consort of one's liking. In order to avoid the undesirable marriage without wounding the feelings of her father and the Count, Ida secretly planned to enter the royal palace as a lady-in-waiting through the good offices of her aunt Countess Fabrice. A Japanese military officer was involved to be the liaison as a courier between Ida and the Countess, and Ida could enter the palace forever.

Three months before the publication of the novel, Ōgai left the house at Ueno Hanazono-chō, leaving his first wife Toshiko behind. The circumstances of their marriage and divorce are as follows. Ōgai, on the recommendation of his influential relative Nishi Amane, married Akamatsu Toshiko, daughter of vice-admiral Akamatsu, on 9 March 1889. Nishi and Akamatsu had been two of the first Japanese students sent abroad in the 1860s, and Baron Akamatsu was a new aristocrat. Ōgai's mother was extremely glad of the offer of marriage, and Ōgai, too, accepted the proposal. However, Ōgai, who could endure many things, could not endure Toshiko and made up his mind to dissolve the marriage by leaving the house possessed by the Akamatsu family. Ōgai must have pondered a lot over the Japanese custom of arranged marriages, their social complications, and his own ambivalent attitude towards the matter. Kobori Keiichirō's analysis of how Ōgai's actual experience is reflected in the novel *The Courier* is very revealing.[19] Ōgai himself failed, while the heroine Ida succeeded in avoiding the undesired marriage. It is significant that in the final scene Ida tells the Japanese officer that he rescued her from a life of suffering, and explains:

> Recently, I've been reading a couple of books about Japanese customs in which the European authors note with scorn that in your country mar-

riages are arranged by the parents, and that consequently many couples don't know what real love is. Such scorn is ironical, for the same thing happens in Europe. Long friendships before an engagement are supposed to enable a couple to get to know each other before they decide whether to marry or not, but among the nobility marriages are arranged by one's superiors, and even though the couple may not be suited for each other, there is no getting out of it.[20]

The words put by Ōgai in the mouth of Ida are the sentiments Ōgai himself must have felt at the failure of his own first marriage. Indeed, Ida repeats to the Japanese officer the words pronounced by her father: 'For people born into the nobility...personal rights must be sacrificed to the rights of heredity.'[21]

### 3. *Ōgai's Admiration for Western Women*

When Ōgai published his first novel, *The Dancing Girl* (Maihime) in January 1890, it was already a kind of defiance. By writing of his past love affair with a German girl in Germany, Ōgai apparently expressed his dissatisfaction with his Japanese wife. Toshiko at least interpreted it that way, and was jealous of Ōgai's former German girlfriend. According to *Turmoil* (Haran, 1909), a novel by Ōgai's second wife Mori Shigeko, Toshiko seemed to have caused a domestic fight over the issue, 'scattering burning charcoal on the floor'.[22] It is not known whether this really happened or was a metaphor for her jealousy.

However, that jealousy of Toshiko was misplaced: the type of woman Ōgai admires is different. The German heroine of *The Dancing Girl* is a naïve uncultured girl belonging to the lower class of society. Ōgai, instead, appreciates culture and a certain ethical conduct in women. His straightforward admiration for Western women of quality is reiterated in many of his writings. The impression Ōgai received from L'Arronge's play *Doktor Klaus* is an example. He went to see it on 2 April 1887 in Munich and wrote a detailed, heartfelt impression of it in his diary. Ōgai was impressed with the story of Dr Klaus and especially with the sympathetic understanding shown by his daughter towards the profession of a medical doctor.

However, no example is more revealing than the eloquent preface which Ōgai wrote in 1914 for the Japanese translation of Wilhelm von Kügelgen's *Jugenderinnerungen eines alten Mannes*. Ōgai's long preface is as lyrical as a prose poem, and he lays stress on the importance of the role played by the lady of the house in German families. In it Ōgai depicts the type of mother and wife he most admires. According to Ōgai, Kügelgen's mother 'sought no honour other than to be a good wife and good mother', although she was beautiful in appearance and natural in behaviour; she was correct in her judgement, and was cultivated in many ways thanks to a careful education; moreover, she was socially brilliant and knew how to draw interesting topics from guests coming to her house. She was a good harpist, but it was only before her husband and children that she played the instrument:

> Compared with such a home where parents are discussing even the great-ness of Goethe, our [Japanese] homes seem lacking in culture ... Through this book we are able to catch a glimpse of what German homes were like in the first half of the nineteenth century. This book will be of help to Japanese families where culture will be respected.[23]

In that preface to Kügelgen's autobiography, Ōgai adds a com-ment which seems imbued with a touch of personal reminiscence:

> When we read a lively record written by a man who really led a lively life, we cannot help being moved by a certain sadness in recollecting our own past. The paradise is already lost and remains behind us as a beautiful dream. There are only two ways left to recover what is lost. One is recol-lection and the other is longing. This book is a key to enter that paradise.[24]

To Ōgai, German homes where mothers and wives played an active role were a paradise. That paradise was the more beautiful, as Ōgai himself had failed in his first marriage to build 'a sweet home', and in his second marriage he was still to suffer from the domestic conflicts between his mother and his young wife. He was obliged to compare German homes with Japanese homes.[25] Moreover, describing Western things in rosy terms was a standard kind of lit-erary tactic. In this way Japanese intellectuals have always tried to attract those young Japanese readers who are not satisfied with the present state of affairs in Japan.

It is, however, interesting to note that 1914 was not only the year when Ōgai wrote the preface to the Kügelgen translation; it was also the year when Ōgai began to look back for ideal Japanese wom-anhood to Tokugawa Japan.

## 4. Truth and Fiction in Ōgai's Later Historical Novels

Ōgai was a novelist able to discern and describe the different aspects of an ambivalent psychology. This method of his is con-spicuous in the novels dealing with *seppuku*, or ritual suicide. On 13

September 1912, when General Nogi committed ritual suicide following the late Emperor Meiji on the day of his state funeral, Ōgai,
deeply moved, immediately poured his instinctive emotion into the
historical novel, *The Last Testament of Okitsu Yagoemon* (first version),[26] which deals with the ritual suicide of the samurai Okitsu
Yagoemon. It shows indirectly the author Ōgai's admiration for the
loyal soldier Nogi, who followed the Emperor to the grave.
However, when Ōgai became aware of the pressure of reactionary
opinions which not only expressed admiration for General Nogi for
his ritual suicide, but also put sinister pressures on the late
Emperor's doctors to follow the example of General Nogi, the
same Ōgai wrote another piece entitled *The Abe Family* (Abe
ichizoku, 1913),[27] in which he coolly analyses the psychology of the
samurai of the Abe family who were socially obliged to commit suicide in spite of their own wishes. When there is an ambivalent
feeling in himself, Ōgai knows, as a good novelist, how to use two
contradictory elements in his literary writings.

Ōgai's personal feelings towards his mother are also indirectly
reflected in his novel of manners *The Wild Geese* (Gan), written in
the early 1910s. The novel is set against the background of social
change from the Tokugawa to Meiji eras in downtown Tokyo, ca.
1880.

The proud attitude 'to set the world at naught' is the characteristic of the Mori family, as described by Ōgai in his *Head Family,
Branch Family*.[28] Practically the same expression '*isshu no seken o
bakanishita yōna kishō*'[29] is used in the novel *The Wild Geese* (chapter
twenty) to describe the character of the heroine Otama, the mistress kept by a rich money-lender Suezō, after she had had the
painful experience of the outward contempt shown a mistress and
the inward envy of the people around her. The author Ōgai apparently puts some of his personal feelings into his heroine, and the
son Ōgai's devoted relationship with his mother, too, is somehow
reflected, in a transgendered way, in the daughter Otama's affectionate relationship with her father. This supposition may sound
odd, as readers take the 'I' of the novel for Ōgai himself. However,
a closer look at Otama's awakening of ego (*jiga no mezame*) reveals
something else. In chapter sixteen it is written:

> But one day she was startled by an awareness of something sprouting
> inside her. This embryo within her imagination had been conceived under
> the threshold of consciousness and, suddenly taking definite shape, had
> sprung out.[30]

This has happened to Otama whose aim in life had been her father's happiness, so after the failure of her first marriage she had become the mistress of a rich money-lender. It was the only way to make his father's life a little more comfortable. She knew she had degraded herself, yet she had still sought a kind of spiritual comfort in the unselfishness of her choice. In short, Otama followed the traditional virtue of filial piety.

About the awakening of ego of Ōgai himself, no definite written record exists. However, in his first novel *The Dancing Girl*, there is a well-known passage. The hero Ōta Toyotarō had been studying assiduously at Berlin University, proud to hear himself praised as a prodigy:

> ... But all that time I had been a mere passive, mechanical being with no real awareness of myself. Now, however, at the age of twenty-five, perhaps because I had been exposed to the liberal ways of the university for some time, there grew within me a kind of uneasiness; it seemed as if my real self, which had been lying dormant deep down, was gradually appearing on the surface and threatening my former assumed self.[31]

Toyotarō had been doing what his mother had taught him. Toyotarō, an alter ego of the author Ōgai, followed faithfully the traditional virtue of filial piety. Thus, when he experienced the awakening of self, his first thought was directed to his mother. ('My mother, I thought to myself, had tried to make me into a walking dictionary.') Toyotarō is somehow critical of his mother. However, Otama is so devoted to her good-natured, weak-willed father that she finishes her conversation with him without disclosing her dissatisfaction with her present humiliating state. It is when she makes up her mind not to speak about the matter that Otama feels that she is independent. In both cases there must be elements of Ōgai's own feelings towards his parents, which are, as is generally the case, ambivalent. He uses two contradictory emotional elements to his advantage in his literary creation, probably because Ōgai is extremely good at dissecting his psychological reactions.

It is the same with his mixed feelings towards Japanese women: while introducing Ibsen's problematic 'liberated women' to the Japanese public, Ōgai simultaneously began to discern virtues among the Japanese women of the so-called feudal times. Ōgai's sense of balance works extremely well again. In his day, Ōgai was, on the one hand, the most influential supporter of the new women's movement in Japan, and Japanese Blue Stockings of the 1910s found in Ōgai an understanding sympathizer. Ōgai, indeed, let his second wife write novels which appeared in the Blue Stockings magazine *Seitō*.

However, while admiring and even idealizing some Western women, Ōgai looked back and found ideal Japanese women such as the wife of Yasui Chūhei (*Yasui Fujin*) or Run, the old lady of the novel *Jiisan Baasan*, or Io, the wife of Shibue Chūsai, of whom Edwin McClellan showed an excellent appreciation.[32]

Some of Ōgai's secret preferences regarding women becomes clear by analysing his historical novels. Although essentially based on historical facts, these moving tales are still written in fictional terms in many of their most interesting parts. The latter elements are often the products of the author Ōgai's own imagination.

Ōgai in these historical novels suggests something of the quality of affection that existed between husband and wife in Tokugawa Japan, and the method with which Ogai suggests that quality is quite personal.[33] Some key episodes are based on historical facts, but others are not. For example, Yasui Chūhei's father thought he must find a proper wife for his son, who was ugly, and asked Chūhei's older sister, the wife of Nagakura, to take on the role of go-between for the father. She went to the Kawazoe house carrying some branches of dark pink peach blossom which she had cut as a present. She handed Toyo the branches. The elder daughter of the Kawazoe house took them and started for the kitchen with them:

> Toyo took a wooden pail from a kitchen shelf, carried it out to the well, drew a bucket of water and put the peach branches to soak. Every motion she made was very efficient. Thinking of her reason for coming, Nagakura's wife could not help smiling as she speculated to herself how this efficient Toyo would quickly be a benefit to the Yasui house if she became Chūhei's bride. Toyo, who had slipped out of her wooden clogs and entered the kitchen, was drying her hands on a towel hanging on the wall. Nagakura's wife came over to her side.
>
> 'In the Yasui family it has been decided to arrange a wedding for Chūhei,' she announced directly to Toyo.
>
> 'Oh, from where?' Toyo said.
>
> 'The bride?'
>
> 'Yes, who?'
>
> 'The bride chosen,' she said as she looked straight into Toyo's eyes, 'is yourself.'
>
> Toyo's face registered annoyed astonishment, but she said nothing. After a while she began to smile and said: 'It must be a lie.'[34]

Then Toyo adds calmly, 'I am sure that Chūhei is an excellent person, but I would not want to be his wife.'[35] This is a very beautiful and interesting scene. It is often said that Ōgai's historical novels are based on historical facts. There is, however, no mention whatsoever of peach blossom or the conversation that takes place between the wife of Nagakura and the beautiful elder sister in Wakayama Kōzō's *Yasui Sokken sensei* (1913), the biography of Yasui Chūhei, on which Ōgai relies heavily for historical material. The more impressive the arrival of the wife of Nagakura with the branch of peach blossom is, the more effective become the scenes that follow: the blunt refusal of Toyo and the unexpected accept-ance of her younger sister Sayo, who suddenly inquires if she could be Chūhei's bride in Toyo's place. Examining to what extent Ōgai is faithful to historical facts and to what extent Ōgai is imaginatively creative in his artistic retelling, may lead to the real source of Ōgai's inspiration.

What is interesting about the younger sister Sayo, who will later become Yasui Chūhei's wife, is the fact that her personality is com-pletely created by Ōgai, and that she resembles very much Shibue Io, the heroine of *Shibue Chūsai*, a biography which would be serial-ized two years later in 1916 in the *Tokyo Nichinichi* newspaper. Sayo resembles Io in two important respects: first, both Sayo and Io were discreetly aggressive in their pursuit of their ideal husband. 'Sayo came to me [Kawazoe's wife, that is, Toyo and Sayo's mother] as if she had something on her mind,'[36] and when questioned, Sayo pos-itively said that she wanted to be Chūhei's wife. Io's case is more audacious: 'without a touch of coyness, she persuades a mutual acquaintance to act as her go-between'.[37] Second, both Sayo and Io, upon becoming the new mistress of a scholar's household, assumed the considerable responsibilities so tactfully that 'the guests bowed spontaneously'.[38] It was the same with the Shibue house, since with their rise in the world had come greater social obligations and expense.

## 5. *Ōgai's Reconciliation with Japan's Past*

Critics agree that Ōgai was disposed to like and admire Japanese women like Sayo, Run and Io. Such a disposition is not only a pre-rogative of any biographer but it has something to do with Ōgai's upbringing. Ōgai's discussion of these marriages is quite eloquent, and no one doubts that behind his admiration for these women, there is a sad reminder that such a marriage would have been nearly impossible in Ōgai's own case. Ōgai's feelings towards his mother

and Japan's social mores of his time must have been very ambivalent.

However, what is surprising about the women in Ōgai's historical
novels is that they somehow recall Mori women, at least in some
respects. A remarkable resemblance is seen between the Shibue
house and the Mori house. Shibue Io, the daughter of a merchant
family in nineteenth-century Japan and wife of a distinguished
scholar-doctor of the samurai class, Io's position is practically identical with that of Ōgai's grandmother. Shibue Io was as 'bossy' a
mother as either the grandmother Mori Kiyoko or the mother Mori
Mineko. In order not to lag behind, Io began to learn English in her
sixties. Both houses are rich not only in scholars but also in art-
lovers: Chusai's son Yutaka was a playboy and theatregoer just like
Ōgai's brother Mori Tokujirō. There is no need to say that Ōgai
finds in Shibue Chusai an old acquaintance, quite similar to him in
temperament and tastes, in scholarly interests and profession. Ōgai
seems in this historical biography at last to have found his own
identity as a writer. The relationship between Io's preferred son
Tamotsu and his mother has something to do with Mineko's preferred son Ōgai and his mother. Both mothers in their old age
depend on their filial sons. Born into a house steeped in the
Confucian learning of the medical profession, Tamotsu became a
scholar of Western learning, just like Ōgai, after the opening of
Japan in 1868. The Shibue house produced also an independent,
free, self-supporting woman like Kuga, a master of *nagauta*. She
almost foretells Ōgai's eldest daughter Mori Mari's independent life-
style as an artist in her later years, an independence which Ōgai
himself did not know in his lifetime.

Ōgai's novels like *Half a Day* and *The Snake*, which deal with the
triangular relationship among husband, mother, and wife, leave so
unfavourable an impression about family relations that it is almost
impossible for most readers to imagine that Ōgai secretly appreciates Mori women.

All the resemblances between the two houses, however, suggest
that there is a sort of reconciliation with Japan's past in Ōgai's later
historical novels. There is no doubt that for Ōgai, who was most
instrumental in introducing European literature to Meiji Japan, the
Japanese past had become immensely important by the time he
reached his fifties. He looks to Tokugawa Japan for the traditional
elements which have enabled modernizers like himself to assimilate
Western culture to such a degree. He is searching for the back-

ground that has made him what he is, and among such elements there are not only scholars of various traditions but also Japanese women. That quest must be the driving force which lets Ōgai write historical novels and biographies about men and women of pre-modern Japan. It should be stressed that Ōgai is interested not only in people like Shibue Chūsai and his wife Io but also in their posterity, because by telling the biographies of more than two generations of a single family, Ōgai is able to tell us what made Meiji Japan what it was.

It is of course true that Ōgai's identification with the past is possible because of his devoted love to people like his father Mori Shizuo, his mother Mori Mineko and his grandmother Mori Kiyoko. Among his parents it is Mori Shizuo alone who is openly portrayed in his previous literary works ('Safuran', 'Kazuisuchika'). It is true that the portrayal of his father is exceptionally sympathetic, while Ōgai's reticence concerning his mother and his grandmother is conspicuous by the absence of sympathetic description. This does not mean, however, that Ōgai feels no sympathy towards them. On the contrary, Ōgai is so closely linked with his mother that it is hardly decent for him to write positively about her. (One remarkable exception is the novel *Half a Day*. Although the triangular relationship between husband, mother and wife is described in it with the surprising frankness of a naturalist writer, the mother looks less eccentric to Japanese readers of the time than the hysterical jealous wife. In any event, while the wife is minutely analysed, the mother is more discreetly sketched and remains behind the scenes).

It is significant that the year, 1916, when Ōgai's mother Mineko died, in March, at the age of sixty-nine, was the year when the historical biography *Shibue Chūsai* was serialized. It is true that Shibue Io was more learned than most contemporary women. It should not be forgotten that Ōgai's mother, while an autodidact, still was able to help Ōgai with proofreading. Moreover, the Mori family produced many women with remarkable literary aspirations: Ōgai's sister Koganei Kimiko, his wife Shigeko, his daughters Mari and Annu. The literary fame of Koganei Kimiko or of Mori Mari is of course much greater than the name of Shibue Io, whose existence would have been totally forgotten, if she had not had a sympathetic biographer like Ōgai. Shibue Io, of fierce spirit, was good at choosing sides and surviving the pre-Restoration civil war. In the Mori family it was the young Mori Mineko who gave proper advice to her husband, a man of good taste but without interest in public affairs, when the Tsuwano clan was involved in the civil war. It was through his latent reminiscences of his mother's house that Ōgai was able to create so many attractive women of premodern Japan in his later historical novels. It was through a longing for a lost paradise that Ōgai searched for an ideal Japanese womanhood in his fifties. While they have the power to move, Ōgai's women will live forever in the hearts of readers.

As to the cause of Ōgai's reconciliation with Japan's past, I think it is a natural phenomenon of aging. Ōgai finally was a happy man who was able to evoke the past of his motherland and his mother in an affirmative way. As a child, Ōgai could depend with total trust on his mother and could *amaeru* to his heart's content, so too the quinquagenarian writer could recall the past without acrimonious sentiments. The presence of neither hatred towards his mother nor narcissistic idealization suggests that Ōgai's relationship with his mother was, after all, balanced and sound.[39]

*Notes*

[1] This paper was written for Kinya Tsuruta ed.: *Mothers in Japanese Literature* (Vancouver: Department of Asian Studies, University of British Columbia, 1997) pp. 75–96.

[2] Some recent scholarship, however, is strongly critical of Mori Ōgai's achievement as a medical officer. Among others Mori's medical policy concerning beriberi is being severely criticized. According to Yamashita Seizō's *Meiji-ki ni okeru kakke no rekishi* (Tokyo: Tokyo daigaku shuppankai, 1988) and other medical historians, Mori recommended boiled rice, but should have recommended boiled barley to the Japanese Army during the Sino-Japanese War and Russo-Japanese War.

[3] Kinoshita Mokutarō, 'Mori sensei no hito to waza to', *Kinoshita Mokutarō zenshū* (Tokyo: Iwanami shoten, 1982) vol. 16, p. 65.

[4] Mori Ōgai: *Ōgai zenshū* (Tokyo: Iwanami shoten, 1971–1975) vol. 16, pp. 143–157.

[5] For Mori Ōgai's family background see Seki Ryōichi, 'Ōgai kakei kō'. *Mori Ōgai Nihon bungaku kenkyū shiryō sōsho* (Tokyo: Yūseidō, 1970)

[6] *Ōgai zenshū*, vol. 16, p. 147. Translation mine. Real names in round brackets are added by the translator to clarify the situation.

[7] Koganei Kimiko, *Ōgai no omoide* (Tokyo: Yagi shoten, 1956).

[8] Mori Oto, *Chichioya toshite no Mori Ōgai* (Tokyo: Chikuma shobō, 1969).

[9] *Ōgai zenshū*, vol. 1, p. 428.

[10] Mori Ōgai, 'The Dancing Girl' tr. Richard Bowring, *Monumenta Nipponica* 30 (1975) p. 153.

[11] Ōgai's translation of Andersen's *Improvisator* (Sokkyō shijin) would be a good starting point for the study of psychological aspects along with Doi's *amae* theory. They provide hints to the popularity of the image of Mary and the mother's image in Japan since the 1890s. Japan is not a Christian nation, the number of Christians being less than one per cent of the population. Nevertheless, the image of Mary, *Maria-sama*, is very familiar. It seems that her popularity has something to do, not with Catholicism, but with the sentiment of *amae*, so prevalent among Japanese who wish to depend on something maternal. More than Catholic or Orthodox priests, Ōgai seemed to be instrumental in introducing into Japan those tender feelings which Europeans, especially Catholics, have towards the Virgin Mary. Ōgai's admiration for Raphael's Madonna (National Gallery, Dresden) is vividly recorded in his diary of 13 May 1885. However, it was through his translation of Andersen's *Improvisator* (Sokkyō shijin) that Ōgai made known those feelings to the Japanese reading public. The author Andersen was himself very much impressed with the intensity of Madonna worship in Italy when he came from Denmark to Italy in 1833–34, and he vividly describes it in his semi-autobiographical novel *Improvisator*. Ōgai, too, in his translation of it into Japanese, reveals an admirable intensity of feeling. We may be allowed to recognize, in the heartfelt translation of the tender Madonna worship and of the tender, close relationship between the boy Antonio and his mother, Ōgai's own sentiments towards his mother Mineko. It is understandable, therefore, why Ōgai wished the translation to be printed in large characters.

One further note: the Madonna worship described in *Sokkyō shijin* gave birth to the descriptions of the Buddhistic Maya worship in many of Izumi Kyōka's stories. Maya is the mother of Buddha, who died seven days after the birth of her son. Kyōka was known as a great admirer of *Sokkyō shijin* and also as a fervent believer in Lady Maya. Mother worship has a contagious nature, and seems to transcend the barriers of religions.

[12] *Ōgai zenshū*, vol. 4, p. 461. Translation of 'Hannichi' mine.

[13] *Ōgai zenshū*, vol. 4, p. 459.

[14] *Ōgai zenshū*, vol. 4, p. 462.

[15] *Ōgai zenshū*, vol. 4, p. 462.

[16] *Ōgai zenshū*, vol. 4, p. 464.

[17] Mori Shige: *Adabana* (Tokyo: Kōgakkan shoten, 1910), included as 'sankōhen' in *Ōgai zenshū*, vol. 38, pp. 321–447.

[18] Mori Ōgai, 'Fumizukai', in *Ōgai zenshū*, vol. 2, p. 45 and, Mori Ōgai, 'The Courier' tr. Karen Brazell in *Monumenta Nipponica* 26 (1971) p. 113.

[19] Kobori Keiichirō: *Wakaki hi no Mori Ōgai* (Tokyo: Tokyo daigaku shuppankai, 1969) p. 665.

[20] Mori Ōgai, 'The Courier' p. 113.

[21] Ibid.

[22] *Ōgai zenshū*, vol. 38, p. 388.

[23] Mori Ōgai, '*Oitachi no ki* jo' in *Ōgai zenshū*, vol. 38, p. 275. Translation of the preface mine.

[24] *Ōgai zenshū*, vol. 38, pp. 274–5.

[25] For an analysis of Ōgai's preface to Kügelgen's autobiography, see 'Oitachi no ki jo ni tsuite' in Hirakawa Sukehiro: *Wakon yōsai no keifu* (Tokyo: Kawade, 1971) pp. 318–326 and Hirakawa Sukehiro: *Kaikoku no sahō* (Tokyo: Tokyo daigaku shuppankai, 1987) pp. 166–198.

[26] As for Mori Ōgai, 'The Last Testament of Okitsu Yagoemon', tr. Richard Bowring, see David Dilworth & J. Thomas Rimer eds: *The Historical Fiction of Mori Ōgai* (Honolulu: University of Hawaii Press, 1991) pp. 47–52.

[27] Ibid. pp. 67–99.

[28] Mori Ōgai: *Ōgai zenshū*, vol. 16, p. 147.

[29] Mori Ōgai: 'Gan' in *Ōgai zenshū*, vol. 8, p. 578.

[30] Mori Ōgai: *The Wild Geese*, tr. Ochiai, Kingo, and Sanford Goldstein (Rutland, Vt., and Tokyo: Charles E. Tuttle, 1959) p. 76.

[31] 'The Dancing Girl', tr. Richard Bowring, p. 153.

[32] Edwin McClellan's *Women in the Crested Kimono – The Life of Shibue Io and Her Family Drawn from Mori Ōgai's 'Shibue Chūsai''* (Yale UP, 1985) is a rare work of sympathetic understanding.

[33] For a discussion of truth and fiction in Ōgai's historical novels, see Inagaki Tatsurō's studies collected in *Mori Ōgai, Nihon bungaku kenkyū shiryō sōsho* (Tokyo:.Yūseido, 1970).

[34] David Dilworth & J.Thomas Rimer eds: *The Historical Fiction of Mori Ōgai* p. 262.

[35] Ibid. p. 262.

[36] Ibid. p. 263.

[37] Edwin McClellan: *Women in the Crested Kimono – The Life of Shibue Io and Her Family Drawn from Mori Ōgai's 'Shibue Chūsai'* (Yale UP, 1985) p. 34.

[38] *The Historical Fiction of Mori Ōgai*, p. 264.

[39] For a diametrically opposed view, see Tanaka Miyoko: 'Mori Mari yori mita Ōgai'. Hirakawa Sukehiro, ed.: *Kōza Mori Ōgai* (Tokyo: Shinyōsha, 1997), vol. 1, pp. 254–284. Tanaka insists on Ōgai's hidden motive as a mother-curser. According to Tanaka, that is the reason why Ōgai translated Strindberg's *Pelican* as late as 1919.

# INTELLECTUAL LONELINESS OR INTELLECTUAL COMPANIONSHIP: PORTRAITS OF A FOREIGN TEACHER BY SŌSEKI, E. V. LUCAS AND LU XUN[1]

The problem which will be discussed is that of intellectual companionship between an Asian writer and a Western scholar. This kind of intercultural companionship will be more common in the twenty-first century, but it was an extremely rare thing at the beginning of the twentieth century, when the Japanese scholar-writer Natsume Sōseki (1867–1916) went to England in the year 1900. Although Japan had been open to the Western world since the Meiji Restoration of 1868 and Japan had been sending students abroad for more than three decades, Sōseki was the first Japanese ever sent on a government scholarship to study English literature. As is generally the case with developing nations, the first students sent abroad tend to study practical matters such as engineering, medicine, politics and especially military science.

Born a year before the Meiji Restoration in Edo, the capital of the Tokugawa Shogunate, soon to be renamed Tokyo under the new government, Sōseki was brought up in Japanese and Chinese literary traditions; so much so that, confronted with Western literatures, he was obliged to become a comparativist. Indeed, what Sōseki wrote as an aspiring scholar was comparative literature *avant la lettre*. He often wrote quite frankly that he was not at home in English poetry partly because of his incomprehension but also because of his aesthetic judgement as a *haiku* poet and a *kanbun* writer. During his two-year stay in London, Sōseki formulated a theory of literature, *Bungaku-ron*, about which he lectured at Tokyo University on his return. However, as is often the case with literary theories, Sōseki's analytical approach to literature did not give emotional satisfaction to his Japanese students. It was a disappointment not only for his students, but also for the scholar Sōseki himself and may have been the cause of his resignation from Tokyo University as early as 1907 in order to devote the rest of his life to creative writing. Sōseki had been unhappy while teaching English literature and he did not like to recall the two lonely years he had spent in the capital of the British Empire. In fact, in the preface to *Bungaku-ron* he described himself as having lived a miserable life comparable to that of a lost dog in London, then a city of five million inhabitants.

Nevertheless, once his fame as the leading Japanese writer had been established, the same Sōseki began to recollect his London days in a much warmer light, and in 1909 he wrote a portrait of his private teacher and Shakespeare scholar William James Craig (1843–1906). A portrait of Craig as general editor of the *Arden Shakespeare* has also been sketched by Edward Verrall Lucas (1868–1938), in the essay entitled *A Funeral* (1906).[2] I would like to compare the two literary portraits, one by the Japanese writer Sōseki and the other, slightly shorter, by the English man of letters Lucas.[3] Through this comparative appreciation I hope to measure the degree of sophistication of the two prose pieces, and thereby first, to clarify what sort of human relationship existed between Sōseki and his Irish teacher, and, second, to explain why Sōseki's *Kureigu sensei* (Professor Craig) became the most important source of inspiration for the Chinese author Lu Xun's much celebrated story, *Tengye xiansheng* (Professor Fujino) in the 1920s. The attempt at a comparative literary interpretation will, hopefully, open a new intercultural perspective.

The story begins this way in Sōseki's essay. Let us read its English translation:[4]

> Like a swallow, Professor Craig had perched his nest on the fourth floor, so lofty an aerie no window could be glimpsed from the pavement below. As I laboured up the staircase, I knew when my thighs began to ache that I was nearing his entrance. This 'entrance', though, boasted neither roof nor gateway, it was just a black door not three feet across with a brass knocker. After taking a moment to catch my breath, I would strike the lower part of this hanging contraption against the door, whereupon it would be opened from within.

It was always the same woman with a perpetually startled expression who answered the door. Though he is not yet present, Craig's life-style is already suggested by this opening.

Lucas is more orthodox in composing his essay. After a brief description of a Surrey churchyard where only a few mourners had gathered, the writer recollects his dead mentor and friend William James Craig without naming him. Indeed, it is of little use to quote the name of the little known hermit-like scholar. With less formality Lucas is able to express himself more freely in this eulogy:

> ... He was an old scholar – not so very old, either – whom I had known for some five years, and had many a long walk with: a short and sturdy Irish gentleman, with a large genial grey head stored with odd lore and the best literature, and the heart of a child. I never knew a man of so transparent a character. He showed you all his thoughts: as someone once said, his brain was like a beehive under glass – You could watch all its workings. And the honey in it!

The foreigner Sōseki's description of his teacher is much less deferential. Their handshaking is recorded by Sōseki as by one who is not accustomed to this British habit:

> ... When he saw me come in, he would utter a word of greeting and extend his hand. This indicated a handshake was in order, so I would duly give the proferred member a squeeze, but he never responded in kind. I took no pleasure in shaking his hand, and felt we should abandon the ritual; yet each time he would thrust that hairy, wrinkled, invariably limp paw in my direction. Custom is a strange thing.

Sōseki then explains who 'the owner of this hand' was:

> Professor Craig was an Irishman, which made him exceedingly difficult to understand. Were he the least bit out of sorts, he was as hard to follow as an argument between a native Tokyoite and a denizen of southern Kyushu. Given his disorganized impatient character, this meant that I frequently had to throw up my hands and content myself with just studying his face.
>
> And what an unusual face it was! Although his nose had the fine high bridge common to Europeans, it was hooked and rather flabby, not unlike my own. Such noses, I fear, are hardly constructed to draw admiring glances. Still, there was something agreeably rustic about my mentor's shaggy countenance. His beard was a hopelessly dishevelled riot of white and black hair. When I chanced upon him one day in Baker Street, I mistook him for a cab-driver who had forgotten his whip.

One now has a clear picture of this old bachelor's appearance. Sōseki's reference to Craig's nose comes from his over-consciousness about his own nose scarred by smallpox in his early childhood. What sort of professor the man really was is depicted in Sōseki's

writing. According to what Craig had told Sōseki, he had given up a
Chair in English Literature at a certain university college in Wales,
freeing himself to commute daily to the British Museum. Craig
must have repeated the same thing to others. Sidney Lee, a friend of
Craig's, writes in the *Dictionary of National Biography* that he resigned
from his Chair at Aberystwyth in order to devote himself to philological research in London. Responding to the renewal of Japanese
interest in this Shakespeare scholar, Mr Andrew Watt of the Japan-
British society wrote an article for the monthly *Eigo-Seinen* in
January 1983.[5] He revealed interesting information about Craig's
teaching ability which was 'suspect'. Indeed, Craig was practically
dismissed by the University College of Wales. Several letters written
about Craig at the time discuss him quite critically. One member of
the College Council wrote to the Principal in mid 1878: 'Craig is
considered a failure as a Lecturer, which is important, and felt so by
the students.' However, Sōseki depicts this negative aspect of his
teacher in a contrasting way:

> ... I never had the foggiest notion what he was going to talk about. He
> would ramble on, jumping from one topic to another as his fancy dictated
> without a look backwards. As this fancy of his shifted with the seasons and
> the weather, what he taught today might be polarly opposed to what he had
> asserted in yesterday's lesson. Judged harshly, his lectures were complete
> shambles; seen in a kinder light, at least I was being exposed to a steady
> stream of literary discourse. Looking back, though, I see I was a fool to
> expect my paltry seven shillings to elicit cohesive systematic lectures. My
> mentor gave me what I paid for, and it was perhaps fortunate that I, in my
> disgruntlement, never tried to command more impressive performances by
> raising his fee. For his mind, like his beard, inclined towards chaos.

Should we take all these complaining remarks at their face value?
Or are they put here in order to emphasize other aspects of Craig?
Sōseki continues:

> Poetry was Professor Craig's forte. When he recited a poem, his head and
> shoulders would slowly wave back and forth like heated air[6] (This is no
> exaggeration!) Yet he wasn't reading for me, just for himself and his own
> amusement, so I was the one who lost out in the end.

The same thing must have occurred to Lucas, who was almost of
the same age as Sōseki and who began to frequent Craig presumably at the same year, that is around 1901. Lucas recollects his long
walks with Craig:

> ... To walk with him at any season of the year was to be reminded or newly
> told of the best that the English poets have said on all the phenomena of
> wood and hedgerow and sky. He had the more lyrical passages of

Shakespeare at his tongue's end, all Wordsworth and Keats. These were his favourites; but[7] he had read everything that has the true rapturous note, and had forgotten none of its spirit.

Lucas admires Craig; however, he too does not forget comical aspects of the eccentric scholar. Talking about Craig's projected comprehensive glossary of Shakespearean language, Lucas makes the following tragi-comical remark:

> ... His own *magnum opus* he left unfinished; he had worked at it for years, until to his friends it had come to be a something of a joke. But though still shapeless, it was a great feast, as the world, I hope, will one day know. If, however, this treasure does not reach the world, it will not be because its worth was insufficient, but because no one can be found to decipher the manuscript; for I may say incidentally that our old friend wrote the worst hand in London, and it was not an uncommon experience of his correspondents to carry his missives from one pair of eyes to another, seeking a clue ...

And Lucas remembers on one occasion two such inquirers meeting unexpectedly, and each simultaneously drawing a letter from his pocket and asking the other to solve the enigma of Mr Craig's handwriting.

Sōseki also remarks on this peculiarity of Craig's:

> I occasionally received a letter from Professor Craig in the post. I was never able to make out what it said. Although it would be but a few lines long, and I could read and reread it at my leisure, his handwriting always proved indecipherable. Eventually, I learned to save time and trouble by starting with the assumption that each and every missive said the same thing: unforeseen circumstances had forced him to cancel our lesson. Sometimes his startled old housekeeper would write his letters for him, in which case they were exceedingly easy to read. How convenient, I thought to have someone like that in your employ. He, however, would moan to me about what a trial it was to be cursed with such an illegible hand. Yours, he would lament, is so much better.

Those who had no other sources of information than Sōseki's writings must have thought that there was much exaggeration in Sōseki's humorous descriptions. However, not only Lucas but also Sidney Lee, who wrote Craig's obituary for *The Times* (18 December 1906), admits his 'singularly difficult handwriting'. Sōseki continues:

> I was indeed concerned that his penmanship would hamper the manuscripts he was working on. He was the general editor of the *Arden Shakespeare*. It seemed miraculous that a scrawl like his could be transformed into printed copy, yet he went on unperturbedly writing prefaces and appending commentaries.

The coincidental similarities of the two essays, not only in matters of factual observations and character descriptions but also in their impressions are surprising. It is true that there is a difference between Sōseki's relationship with Craig, which was confined within the limits of bookshelves of the fourth floor, and Lucas' relationship with his mentor, when the young Englishman sometimes ascended to Craig's 'eyrie' and lured him out to Hertforshire or his beloved Epping or even dragged him away to dinner.

Both essays give us a similar impression of a spontaneous feeling of affection. While caricaturing the eccentric scholar working unsystematically at all hours, the two authors very much like this old man. It happened once that the reticent Sōseki suggested moving in as Craig's lodger. Presented with this request, Craig, slapping his knee, said: 'Quite right!'

> 'I'll give you the guided tour!' whereupon I was summarily dragged from the dining room to the maid's room to the kitchen and thus through his entire residence. Being a fourth-story rear-corner flat it was, of course, far from spacious. Two or three minutes was enough to see all there was to see. Yet when we had resumed our seats, he didn't say that, as my own eyes had witnessed, there was no room for me, but rather launched into a story about Whitman … Craig had not liked his poems at first, but they seemed to improve with each rereading, so that in the end he had become one of Whitman's devotees. As a result …
>
> Lost entirely was the issue of whether I might become his live-in student – all I could do now was submit to his flood of words.

After his return home Sōseki had at least three occasions to be reminded of Craig. The first time was when he lectured on *King Lear*[8] at Tokyo University. Craig's comments 'did in fact prove invaluable' to him, and Sōseki was firmly convinced that no commentary was as meticulous and concise as Craig's, and he confesses in his essay: 'Yet at the time (while frequenting Craig) although I was astounded at the quantity of research he had carried out, I must confess that I was quite blind as to its quality.'

The second time was when Sōseki heard about his death, and the third time was when Sōseki wrote this essay six years after his return home. Sōseki's reminiscence ends this way:

> About two years after my return to Japan, I happened across Professor Craig's obituary in a recently-arrived literary magazine. It consisted of a brief death announcement with a few lines that noted merely that he was 'a Shakespeare specialist'.

Sōseki then continues to wonder if Craig's 'dictionary' had remained unfinished to the end and become so much waste paper.

The ending of Lucas' essay has the same melancholy tone, as he intuitively knows that Craig's *magnum opus* will be left unpublished. Several of his literary friends returned from the funeral service 'to the town to drink tea in an ancient hostelry, and exchange memories, quaint, and humorous, and touching, and beautiful, of the dead.'

A reader's preference for one of the two essays is a matter of individual taste. Those who read them in English might prefer Lucas, but I believe those who read them in Japanese would find Sōseki's prose far more sophisticated.

However, when attention is drawn from the literary values of the two essays to the following so-called cultural barrier, one may find it blocking the true appreciation of Sōseki's essay. There exists a tendency among both foreign and Japanese scholars to say that the insular-born Japanese look at foreigners only as stereotypes and some Japanese literature specialists go so far as to say that foreigners are not recognized as individuals in Japanese novels. These vocal scholars should be asked if Sōseki's portrait of the Irish gentleman is stereotyped or if Craig's individuality is not recognized. The distinct impression of affection in this heart-warming essay is obvious, although as late as in 1983 Andrew Watt concludes his article 'Sōseki's Professor Craig' by lamenting that 'these two bookish, eccentric men, one Japanese and one Irish, came into each other's lives for a year in 1901, but passed on without touching each other's feelings'. This kind of assessment derives not from a close reading of the texts, but from a foregone conclusion. When Sir Norman Moore read Lucas' account of Craig's funeral in a magazine called the *Country Gentleman*, the old friend of Craig's could not but write to Lucas to say: 'We miss Craig and always shall, and I feel a kindness for anyone who cared for him.' Sōseki was among those who 'cared for him'.[9]

Lastly in support of the argument that Sōseki has written a moving recollection, I would like to cite a major Chinese writer who was touched by it. This admirer of Sōseki was none other than Lu Xun (1881–1936) who had lived in Japan from 1902 to 1909. Coming from a neighbouring Asian nation, the Chinese author inevitably compared his rather lonely life in Sendai with Sōseki's rather alienated life in London. Lu Xun translated *Kureigu sensei* into Chinese as *Kelaika xiansheng* in 1923. While translating, he began to recollect with a feeling of affection his Japanese teacher who was kind to him, and three years later Lu Xun composed the memories

of his Japanese days in *Tengye xiansheng* (Professor Fujino), which is
now often used as a high-school textbook both in China and Japan,
and is regarded as a token of intellectual friendship between the two
nations. What interests me in 'Professor Fujino', however, is how
Lu Xun utilized Sōseki's 'Professor Craig' in his creative imitation.
Sōseki writes humorously that on Baker Street Craig looked like a
cab-driver who had forgotten his whip. Lu Xun, too, is very un-
Confucian in his humorous description of Fujino sensei:

> This Professor Fujino[10] ... dressed so carelessly that he sometimes even
> forgot to put on a tie. Because he shivered all winter in an old overcoat,
> once when he travelled by train the conductor suspected him of being a
> pickpocket and warned all the passengers to be on their guard.

This is only an example of stimuli Lux Xun received from
Sōseki's 'Kureigu sensei'.[11]

In general, alienating experiences abroad are overwhelmingly
negative. However, in the cases of Sōseki and Lu Xun, it is an open
question whether their study years abroad were really that negative.
In the long run, Sōseki's suffering in London as well as Lu Xun's
loneliness in Sendai were highly beneficial in the sense that their
experiences overseas constituted turning points in their careers. For
these men may be said to have been 'reborn' as writers, while living
abroad.

## Notes

[1] This paper was presented at the 13th Congress of the International
Comparative Literature Association held in August 1991 in Tokyo.

[2] 'A Funeral' by Lucas was selected by W.E. Williams for *A Book of English
Essays* (Pelican paperback, 1942, and later Penguin paperback).

[3] E.V. Lucas' article appeared for the first time, according to his *Reading,
Writing and Remembering* (London: Methuen, 1932), p. 138, in *The Country
Gentleman*. The number and date of the magazine, however, are not indi-
cated.

[4] I thank Theodore Goossen and Kawamoto Kōji for permission to use
this English translation. Natsume Sōseki, *Kureigu sensei* is in *Sōseki zenshū,*
(Tokyo: Iwanami, 1956) shinsho-ban, vol. 16, pp. 113–120.

[5] Andrew Watt, 'Sōseki's Professor Craig', in *Eigo-Seinen* (Tokyo:
Kenkyūsha, January, 1983), pp. 15–16.

[6] The original Japanese expression is full of lyricism: 'shi o yomutoki niwa
kao kara kata no atari ga kagerō no yōni shindō shita.' *Sōseki zenshū,*
shinsho-ban, vol. 16, p. 115.

[7] In the Pelican as well as in the Penguin paperback edition the passage

from 'Wordsworth and Keats. These were his favourites; but' is missing. As the large part of Lucas' essay is quoted in his *Reading, Writing and Remembering*, I have accordingly reinserted this passage in the quotation.

[8] In his *Kureigu sensei* Sōseki writes *Hamlet*; this, however, is a mistake.

[9] E.V. Lucas, *Reading, Writing and Remembering*, p. 138.

[10] As Lu Xun was faithful to the Japanese usage of Chinese characters, one has to be careful about their translation. If written, Lu Xun's 'Tengye xiansheng' corresponds to 'Fujino sensei' in Japanese. It should, therefore, be translated not into 'Mr Fujino', as the Chinese word 'Tengye xiansheng' sounds today, but into 'Professor Fujino' or 'Teacher Fujino', as the Japanese word 'Fujino sensei' sounds to the Japanese and sounded to Lu Xun. I have consequently revised that expression in this quotation which I borrowed from Lu Xun, *Selected Works*, vol. 1, tr. Yang Xianyi and Gladys Yang (Beijing: Foreign Languages Press, 1980) p. 406.

[11] Since I have already analysed the relationship between Sōseki's *Kureigu sensei* (Professor Craig) and Lu Xun's *Tengye xiansheng* (Professor Fujino)in a study which has been translated and presented to the both sides of the Taiwan Strait, I will not dwell on it further. As for a more detailed study on the relationship between Sōseki's *Kureigu sensei* (Professor Craig) and Lu Xun's *Tengye xiansheng* (Professor Fujino), see Hirakawa Sukehiro: *Natsume Sōseki – hi-seiyō no kutō* (rev. ed. Tokyo: Kōdansha, gakujutsubunko, 1991). Hirakawa's argument is summarized in English in *Tamkang Review*, 10 (1980) pp. 547–554 and in Chinese in *Zhong-ri wenhua yu jiaoliu*, No.2 (Beijing: Zhongguo zhanwang chubanshe, 1985) pp. 72–98.

# THE POET-SCULPTOR TAKAMURA KŌTARŌ'S LOVE-HATE RELATIONSHIP WITH THE WEST[1]

———————□———————

Takamura Kōtarō (1883–1956) was undeniably one of the most popular poets of the so-called period of Taishō democracy: his love poems for his wife Chieko still constitute the best known single book of modern Japanese poetry. *Chieko-shō*, translated into English as *Chieko and Other Poems*,[2] is indeed a classic for the Japanese. Later in his career Kōtarō became the most vocal poet of the Greater East Asia War: his patriotic poems are most numerous among his poetical writings,[3] and in a sense he personified the national sentiment of wartime Japan. Nevertheless, after the war ended Kōtarō again was able to become the most respected poet of the peace-loving Japan of the Shōwa twenties (1945–54). His post-war poetical works of self-accusation, such as the poems collected in his *Angu-shōden* (A Brief History of Imbecility), were widely appreciated by those Japanese who 'embraced the defeat'.

The British and Americans must have some misgivings about a representative poet of Japan who could be popular during the Taishō democracy era, popular through the years of war against the United States and Britain and more popular still after the war and even after his death. Kōtarō's contemporary, the poet Murō Saisei, made the acute remark in his *Waga aisuru shijin no denki* (Recollections of Poets I love)[4] that Kōtarō had never fallen back in his career as a poet; he had always surpassed other poets and had remained a poet of his time even with his *Brief History of Imbecility*.

In Murō's opinion, Kōtarō had climbed up to the pinnacle in the history of modern Japanese poetry.

Many questions are raised concerning such a poet with such a history. What was his love-hate relationship with the West, especially with America? Was the admiration of the young artist for the West authentic? What did the West mean to him, especially Western art? By what route did Kōtarō make a return to Japan and Japanism in the late 1930s? In the decades following Japan's defeat, why did the Japanese public continue to admire Kōtarō, who openly confessed that he had been an imbecile, supporting positively Japan's war efforts by writing patriotic poems? I would like to discuss these seemingly contradictory problems in their wider cultural context.

Although Takamura Kōtarō is today best remembered for his poetical works, in his lifetime he did not like to be labelled a poet. Instead, he considered himself a sculptor, and there was good reason for that self-definition. Kōtarō was the eldest son of the sculptor Takamura Kōun (1852–1934), and the eldest son of an artisan was expected to succeed to his father's profession. Kōun was a sculptor in the traditional manner: that is to say, he was said to be not at all interested in Western art.

Kōun's best known work is the equestrian statue of Kusunoki Masashige symbolizing the virtue of loyalty, which stands in the Square in front of Tokyo's Imperial Palace. If the father Kōun represents continuity in Japanese art, his son Kōtarō decidedly represents the forces of change – his sculptures show clearly (probably too clearly) the influence of the French sculptor Auguste Rodin. It would be interesting to make a stylistic comparison of the sculpture of the father and the son, but here I would like to try another approach, focusing my attention on the son Kōtarō's love-hate relationship with his father as well as his love-hate relationship with the West – two relationships which, in my opinion, were closely connected.

The father Takamura Kōun, born Nakajima in 1852, a year before the arrival of the American Black Ships, was a disciple of Takamura Tōun and an artisan of Edo.[5] Kōun was not a samurai nor was he a man of culture. He was a woodcarver, specializing in Buddhist statues. With the coming to power of the Imperial Army, however, Buddhism fell into a period of eclipse, when Edo was renamed Tokyo in 1868, the first year of the reign of Meiji. So for some time Kōun was obliged to carve handles for *yōgasa* or Western-style umbrellas to support his large family. Fortunately, the Tokyo

school of Fine Arts was founded in 1888, and the next year Kōun
was asked to join the faculty. Even though he was given a professorship, which he initially declined, Kōun remained a traditional
artisan. His attitude towards his sons as well as his students was that
of the master of a guild towards his apprentices. To an extent, this
worked well. From the outset, Kōtarō, as his eldest son, was destined to continue in his father's trade; at the age of five, for example,
he was given a set of knives and chisels for woodcarving. Although
there seems to be continuity between Kōun and Kōtarō, change is
inevitable when the son of an artisan wishes to become an artist.
Kōtarō's antagonism towards his father was born when he became
conscious of that difference. An artisan can be a qualified artisan
even if he does not know anything about literature, poetry or even
the fine arts, but it was indispensable for a Meiji artist to know
something of the new literature, the new poetry and of course the
new art coming from the West. It should be noted that even the
concept of the artist itself was something totally new, a notion
imported from the West.

The father Kōun was a typical product of Edo, particularly that
part called the Low City, *shita-machi*, while the son Kōtarō was a
product of Tokyo, in the age of Japan's rapid Westernization.
Kōtarō was born in 1883, the year when the Rokumeikan Pavilion
was opened.[6] He received a modern education and entered the
Tokyo School of Fine Arts in 1897. Unlike his father, Kōtarō read
extensively and began to write poetry, the first evidence of his dissatisfaction with his father's way of living. As a young artist he
wished to be a cultured man, an ambition worthy of a Meiji youth.
Kōtarō studied at the various levels of the School of Fine Arts and
graduated in 1902, but when proceeding to the advanced course he
had chosen the Western painting section instead of sculpture,
because he did not wish to remain too close to his father, a professor of woodcarving in the latter section.

Portraying the antagonism between fathers and sons had been
unheard of, at least openly, in East Asian countries where the tradition of Confucianism was dominant. However, it became one of
the most recurrent themes in Japanese literature after the Russo-
Japanese War. Natsume Sōseki's *Sorekara* (And Then), written in
1909, deals with a young man, Daisuke, apparently a Tokyo
University graduate, who does not wish to do anything positive at
all because of his alienation from his father, who is a very practical-
minded businessman. The same theme of the estrangement

between an authoritarian father and a rebellious son is described by Nagai Kafū, who seems to have personally experienced it. The same kind of bitter experience was shared by Shiga Naoya, who, like Kōtarō, was born in 1883. Shiga's masterpieces are mostly auto-biographical novels in which the hero's antagonistic relationships with his father and other members of his family are depicted. The most famous example is *Wakai* (Reconciliation), written in 1917. The fatherly intellectual leader Mori Ōgai (1862–1922) also took an interest in this theme of the father-son relationship, a hot issue of the younger generation, and dealt with it in his *Kano yōni* (As if), written in 1912. To encourage this literary movement, Ōgai made a translation of the German drama, *Mutter Landstrasse*, by Wilhelm Schmidt-Bonn, a very powerful piece of drama, whose productions in Tokyo had strong repercussions in the history of the new theatre movement in Japan.

It seems that the father-son relationship was problematical in Germany, too. Historically speaking, the antagonism between Frederick II and his father Frederick I of Prussia is well-known. Friedrich Schiller deals with it in many of his dramas. Towards the turn of the century, the topic was especially in vogue, with authors such as Wedekind, Emil Strauss, Hauptmann, Hermann Hesse and Rainer Maria Rilke all dealing with it. To Franz Kafka, who suffered terribly under his authoritarian father, the relationship between Benjamin Franklin and his father seemed so ideal that Kafka asked his father to read Franklin's *Autobiography*, in the hope that under-standing the good relationship between Josiah Franklin and his son would change his attitude towards his own son.

Compared with their German counterparts, Japanese fathers of the Meiji era were probably less dictatorial. To the second genera-tion of the Meiji era, however, the first generation of nation-builders were, generally speaking, terribly oppressive fathers. The first generation had not experienced that kind of oppression. As Restoration heroes who had succeeded in overturning the deca-dent Tokugawa shogunal government, they had become very young masters of the situation. It is, therefore, significant that the problem of the father-son relationship arrives only with the coming of age of the second generation. Moreover, this coincides with the appear-ance of the first group of young West-oriented artists in modern Japan.

These new Meiji artists had somewhat similar family backgrounds. Many of them were typical 'second generation' sons: the painter

Kuroda Seiki was the son of an ex-revolutionary of Satsuma, Viscount Kuroda Kiyotsune; the painter Kume Keiichirō was the son of Kume Kunitake, official scribe to the Iwakura mission and later a leading historian; the art critic and art historian Iwamura Tōru was the son of an ex-revolutionary from Tosa, Baron Iwamura Takatoshi and the dramatist Osanai Kaoru, the writers Nagai Kafū, Arishima Takeo, Shiga Naoya and Mushanokōji Saneatsu were all sons of Meij leaders or subleaders. That so many of the *Shirakaba* group were graduates of the *Gakushūin* (Peers' College) testifies to the predominance of this pattern.

In *Buddenbrooks*, Thomas Mann describes the family cycle of a German family of four generations. First comes a man who makes every effort to become a rich merchant; he is full of vitality and vulgarity. His son tries to be a respected man of society. Then among the third generation appears a man of fine tastes endowed with artistic temperament. The family dies out with the delicate but feeble fourth generation. This kind of family cycle seems to turn round more rapidly in modern Japan. The fathers symbolized by the Elder Statesmen had built the nation-state of Japan; their efforts were crowned by Japan's victory over Russia, but immediately afterwards they found, to their greater grief and disappointment, their sons turning away from the course they had pursued since the Meiji Restoration.

This generation gap was most symbolically represented by General Nogi Maresuke, the victor of Port Arthur, and his disobedient students of *Gakushūin*, where he was principal. The Japanese people by and large admired and liked General Nogi, who became the best known father-figure in the last years of Meiji. However, as Nogi stood for traditional conservative values, a veritable incarnation of feudal virtues, he became a butt of ridicule and a hot target of criticism from the young students, some of whom openly made a laughingstock of their principal. When General Nogi committed ritual suicide on the day of the Emperor Meiji's state funeral, Shiga Naoya cold-bloodedly remarked: 'I am disgusted at the news. It's as if an uneducated maidservant had committed a foolish act.' Akutagawa Ryūnosuke ridiculed the general in a short story entitled *Shōgun* (General).

Takamura Kōtarō, too, was one of the second generation who lived against this background. Kōtarō was first known to the world as the eldest son of the woodcarver Takamura Kōun, then as the son of Professor Takamura. That was a rather uncomfortable, even intolerable, situation for the young Kōtarō. Incidentally, the psychological state of the eldest son of a well-known artisan is described by a friend of Kōtarō's, Shiga Naoya, in his short story *Ransai botsugo* (After the death of Ransai, Master of Metal-Carving). Everywhere he goes, Kanazawa Hiroshi is introduced as the eldest son of Ransai the master, as if that were his only merit: it is practically his only title. The son, however, does not like some of his late father's habits. Ransai had written certificates of authentication, for example, knowing full well that some of the works were not authentic. Kōtarō had similarly accused his father Kōun of having written many such bogus certificates of authentication.[7] One explanation for this seeming coincidence is that this custom was rather common among artisans of the Low City.[8]

Kōtarō's attitude towards his father is recollected in his *Kaisōroku* (Notes of Reminiscences) written in January 1945 and in his article *Chichi tono kankei* (Relationship with My Father) written in 1954. As Takamura Kōun died in 1934, these recollections from Kōtarō's later life are toned down, but they still contain some harsh remarks. According to his son, Kōun was a typical craftsman (*shokunin*), a product of the final stage of the Tokugawa era who sculpted in the traditional manner of woodcarving (*kiborishi*) and specialized in Buddhist statuary (*bushiya*).[9] For those who have seen the statue of Saigō Takamori standing at the entrance to Ueno Park in Tokyo, it is a work of art which surpasses the scope of an ordinary artisan. Yet, according to Kōtarō, Saigō's statue has something of the Buddhist image in its underlying touch. It may be that the popularity of the statue derives from such gentleness, although it is often explained in terms of the figure of the dog beside the big, fat man in a cheap kimono. Kōtarō, of course, recognizes the quality of his father's craftsmanship, but he cannot accept some of his ways peculiar to an artisan.

In 1889, several years before Kōun was commissioned to execute Saigō's statue, he was asked by Okakura Kakuzō (Tenshin) to teach at the Tokyo School of Fine Arts. It is curious how well the six-year-old Kōtarō remembered Okakura's visit to his house. The boy's impression was that he was seeing a history-book figure appear before his eyes; the director Okakura was so impressive, and had something of the hero about him. Okakura, who was already drunk, had been very talkative that evening, and Kōun, although older than Okakura by ten years, had responded using the polite – indeed almost obsequious – expression, '*Gyoi ni gozarimasu, gyoi ni gozarimasu.'* It means 'What you have said is quite true' but the literal translation would be 'I obey your august will.' The child Kōtarō felt that his father was being too servile and subservient, and wished that he would never hear his father use that expression again.[10]

Later, when he was an art student, Kōtarō, dissatisfied with old artisan-type masters like his father and Shirai Uzan, entered the oil painting section where Kuroda Seiki was the most influential figure. As mentioned before, this does not mean that Kōtarō was really drawn to oil painting. In fact, his dissatisfaction with his father's way of living was first evidenced in his passion for poetry. When he was seventeen, he wrote *haiku* using the penname Ōson, apparently a combination of 'Ō' from Ōgai and 'Son' from Tōson, for at that time, around the year 1900, he especially admired the poets Mori Ōgai and Shimazaki Tōson for their new style of poetry. Kōtarō then joined the *Shinshi-sha* (New Poetry Society) led by Yosano Hiroshi and wrote excellent *tanka* in a romantic vein. He also read extensively both in Japanese and English. He regularly read the art magazine *Studio* and found in it a picture of Rodin's *le Penseur*, a decisive influence on his later development. In 1905, he read Camille Mauclair's *Rodin* in an English translation. At that time he did not know French, and called Rodin 'Rojin'. Almost a half century later, Kōtarō would recall this in one of his autobiographical poems. Hiroaki Sato's translation of it is as follows:

SCULPTURE ONLY

The first nibble in Japan's expansion tragedy,
the Russo-Japanese War, was remote to me.
Only the dire story of Port Arthur,
the extra on the Japan Sea battle,
and the sharp contrast between Ambassador Komura and Count Witte
were impressed in my memory.
Passing my twentieth year I stayed on at graduate school,
I was absorbed night and day
in training in sculpture.
Utterly ignorant of the world, heaven and earth inside a jar,
I wanted only to grasp the truth of sculpture.
Both father and the other teachers at school appeared to be no more than
    artisans.
I wanted to know more than an artisan would.
In dark surroundings, groping,
I searched for the sculpture of the world.
I don't remember when,
but Takuboku, who came intending to talk to me,

finding a spoiled child interested only in sculpture, who ignored the
world, gave up and went home.
I wanted to know more about a man called *Rojin*
than the outcome of the Russo-Japanese War.[11]

In the School of Fine Arts, Kōtarō learned aesthetics from Mori
Ōgai, and when Ōgai was transferred to Kokura and was replaced
by Iwamura Tōru, Kōtarō studied the history of Western art with
Iwamura. Iwamura was a sort of agitator. His *Pari no gagakusei* (Art
Students in Paris) published in 1902 is a very lively book, vivacious
in style and full of personal reminiscences well calculated to stimu-
late young minds. The life of young artists in Paris was so vividly
described, in fact, that those who read it developed an irresistible
yearning for the capital of France. As Kinoshita Mokutarō recalled,
that book instilled in the young graduate student an unquenchable
yearning (*Sehnsucht*) for countries beyond the sea.[12]

Iwamura advised Kōtarō that he had better go abroad to study
sculpture. Iwamura then told Kōun that his greatest masterpiece
was his eldest son himself and that Kōtarō should be sent abroad.
Iwamura gave letters of recommendation to four American sculptors, including Daniel Chester French and Hermon Atkins
MacNeil, whom Iwamura had met when he was a member of the
jury of the Chicago Exposition. With a ticket to New York and 250
dollars from his father, Kōtarō left Japan for America in March
1906; he was twenty-three years of age.

In New York, he was attracted by the works of the sculptor
Gutzon Borglum (1867–1941) and became his assistant. Kōtarō
worked hard from May through August of that year for six or seven
dollars a week. Although it might still be possible to find some
records about Takamura Kōtarō on the American side, on the
Japanese side we have practically no documentary records and
studies about Kōtarō's fifteen-month stay in New York, the exception being Katanuma Seiji's study.[13]

The first year is hard for any newcomer in America, and under-
standably more so for Kōtarō, who had always been so well looked
after by his mother and others. There was an immense difference
between being an apprentice in a Japanese workshop and working
as an assistant to an American sculptor: Kōtarō found himself
obliged to do all kinds of menial work which had nothing to do
with sculpture. Saeki Shōichi makes a penetrating remark in his
most stimulating *Nichi-bei kankei no naka no bungaku* (Literature in
Japan-US relations)[14] that the unexpected master-assistant relation-

ship in America traumatized Kōtarō for life. Although interesting, I disagree with Saeki's interpretation, since Kōtarō himself wrote a warm recollection of his relationship with Gutzon Borglum.[15] The article was written ten years after they parted, yet, the sentiment it expresses is genuine and heartwarming. The problem with Kōtarō was that, although he maintained a good relationship with Borglum, he still suffered tremendously in New York.

Twenty years later Kōtarō wrote a poem 'Zō no ginkō,' (Elephant Bank) which is translated into English as 'Central Park Zoo.'[16]

CENTRAL PARK ZOO

In Central Park, the elephant, face blank,
Adroitly nimble with his outsize nose,
Fields cents and nickels which the public throws
And drops them, clinking, in the Elephant Bank.

Now nosing forwards, twitching a sad red eye,
He asks this Jap – that's me, diminutive –
To pitch a coin. The elephant says give.
Glad to be asked, I make my dime reply.

The blank-face made-in-India pachyderm's
At one with the lonely stripling made-in-Japan:
I trust 'they' understand why beast and man
So quickly come to be on such good terms.

When, bathed in sunset, out from that park I came
The Egyptian obelisk stared down at me.
One more indignant thing. Indignity,
Back in his garret, flayed Jap blood to flame.

The setting is well chosen: the Central Park Zoo, New York City. The central theme is the indignation of the poet as a 'Jap', but the poem is objective, dry, and skillfully satirical; there is humour in its description of an elephant saving its cents and nickels for his bank, and we are made to smile, realizing that there exists a curious sympathy between the alienated 'I', the Jap, and the elephant. The curious alliance reminds us of the motto of a book published not long before by Okakura – 'Asia is One' – for here is indeed a sort of Afro-Asian solidarity among the made-in-India elephant, the made-in-Japan youth, and the Egyptian obelisk. However, when that laugh ends in the final line, where the rage is too openly revealed, the poem ceases to be truly witty.

There is another poem of the same nature, 'Shirokuma' (Polar Bears) Satō's translation is as follows:

## POLAR BEARS

In windswept Bronx Park with the remains of snow like coarse sugar,
face mute, a typical Jap,
he stands on a precious Sunday before the cage of the polar bears.

The polar bears too, silent, occasionally look at him.
The polar bear, just when you've decided it's too sluggish,
leaps buoyantly, body trembling smashes the ice, and splashes the water.
Sharp icicles hang at the cave made of rock,
shine prismatically
on his head, play continuously a fury-like livening pirouette rhythm.

After taking care of the rent out of his seven dollars pay,
he has left in his pockets a few coins that are stamped with an eagle and
make a noise.
Hands tucked in his pockets, he keeps his mouth shut.

Two big polar bears come out of the water
and, undulating their backs straight as the Arctic horizon,
noiseless, they walk about on the frozen concrete:

dead-honest flat forehead, pinkish greedy lips,
frost-and-snow limbs and body concealing splendid power,
and small, alien, phosphorescent eyes.

Leaning on the fence, cold wind clouting his ears,
in the bleak ice-field of the spirit,
he burns a heart joyful without cause, and valorous.

The polar bear, finally, doesn't give itself to man,
burdened inside with the cross of ferocious instincts
it breathes Northern seas, alone in a New York suburb.[17]

Kōtarō was apparently obsessed by his pay of seven dollars a week. As cents and nickels fit well in the poem on the Elephant Bank, so silver coins stamped with an American eagle suit this poem on Polar Bears. He stands before their cage, and gradually the polar bears, with their agile movements and small alien eyes, begin to be identified with the 'Jap'. The poet succeeds here in projecting his feelings onto the polar bear, as he did with the elephant in the last poem. Atsumi and Wilson use the word 'diminutive' in their translation of 'Central park Zoo', but if the word suggests physical smallness of the Japanese, they are mistaken, for Kōtarō was a tall, well-built, strong bear of a man.

There is a certain anecdote which may help in understanding these poems. While working for Borglum, Kōtarō quarrelled many times with Americans. When he washed the entrance gate of

Borglum's studio, he was sometimes mocked by passers-by who shouted 'Jap' at him. He reacted by watering them with the hose, and whenever this led to further trouble, Kōtarō, whose body 'concealed splendid power', quickly overpowered the passers-by. This anecdote, which was recorded by Sarashina Genzō,[18] explains the state of mind of the polar bear called Takamura Kōtarō living alone in a 'New York suburb'. His poem ends this way:

> The baseness of cozy refinement fills his surroundings.
> A suffocating gratuitous Christian materialism
> is about to kill a dreamer, a Jap.

> The polar bears too, silent, occasionally look at him.
> Not hearing 'All right' for the first time in a week,
> washed in silence, he stands before the vast polar bears.

Saeki's remark on the poems is worth noting: these poems were written two decades later in the mid 1920s, when Japanese-American relations were tense, and then published for the first time in book form two more decades later in 1944. Saeki's conclusion is that Kōtarō's traumatic experience in New York had something to do with the poet's single-mindedness during World War II.[19] Though extremely interesting, this interpretation is far too simple.

Kōtarō hoped to become radically different from his father by acquiring something new in the West. However, in his first year abroad, Kōtarō was stripped of his warm Japanese garments without being able to reclothe himself in something essentially Western in New York. It is true that, having been trained from childhood in the art of carving, he distinguished himself easily, receiving a special prize at the evening course in sculpture of the Art Students League of New York. He then went to Europe, where, from June 1907, he lived in London for a year as an overseas trainee of the Japanese Government, although contradicting his attitude he was able to receive that scholarship through his father's influence. The twelve months spent in London were probably the happiest time of his study abroad, for it was there that Kōtarō met his life-long friend, the potter Bernard Leach. The following year he moved to Paris where he remained for about nine months. Kōtarō's great joy on arriving in Paris can be felt in his poem 'Ame ni utaruru katedoraru' (The Rain-Beaten Cathedral), which has been translated by T. Ninomiya and D. J. Enright.[20] Since the rhapsodic poem is 103 lines long, I quote only the first part:

## THE RAIN-BEATEN CATHEDRAL

Another squall!
Looking up at you, the collar of the overcoat
Lifted against the slanting rain – It is I,
He who makes it a rule to come at least once each day –
The Japanese.

This morning
A terrible storm, increasing since daybreak,
Now rages in the four corners of Pairs.

I cannot distinguish east from west,
Nor even which way the storm is moving, as it runs amok, here in the Île
de France ...

But here I am again,
Oh Notre-Dame of Paris!
Soaked with rain,
Just to gaze at you, to touch you
To steal a kiss from you, your flesh of stone.

'The Rain-Beaten Cathedral' reminds me of the French poet
Charles Péguy's 'Présentation de la Beauce à Notre-Dame-de-
Chartres', a poem as ardent as this one; whether Kōtarō had ever
read it is unknown.

Kōtarō wrote 'The Rain-Beaten Cathedral' in 1921. Then, in
1947 – two years after Japan's defeat – he wrote the poem 'Pari'
(Paris) in which he sums up his Parisian experience. Here is Satō's
translation:

## PARIS

I became an adult in Paris.
It was in Paris that I first knew the other sex.
It was in Paris that I first had my soul liberated.
Paris accommodated any species of mankind
as a matter of course.
It doesn't refuse any lineage of thinking.
It doesn't wither any heterogeneity of beauty.
Be it good or bad, new or old, high or low,
it lets whatever is in human categories co-habit
and leaves the rest to the inevitable self-cleansing process.
The charms of Paris grasp you.
You can breathe in Paris.
Modernity originates in Paris,
beauty becomes ready and sprouts,
new brain cells are born in Paris.

Living in a corner of this bottomless world capital
where France exists transcending France,
I forgot, at times, my nationality.
My native land was remote, small, petty,
it was like some bothersome village.
I was first enlightened to sculpture in Paris,
had my eyes opened to the truth of poetry,
and recognized the reasons for culture
in each citizen there.
Saddened and helpless,
I was an unmatchable gap.
I felt nostalgic for, yet denied,
everything Japanese, the way the country was.[21]

Both poems make us feel that Kōtarō was truly at home in Paris, breathing freely, and even experiencing a kind of 'rebirth'. We should remember, however, that this is a fictionalized image of Paris and of himself. It is, in short, poetry. The aged Kōtarō probably believed in that image himself, but the actual experiences he recorded during or immediately after his stay in France seem very different. It is not difficult to understand his idealization of his Parisian days: on his return home Kōtarō found Tokyo life oppressive and the city drab and miserable, as he later found defeated Japan drab and miserable. His idealization of the West comes as a result of his depreciation of things Japanese. As Satō writes in his introduction: 'A Japanese going home after spending some time abroad often experiences a certain shock: everything seems so drab, so small ... the intellectual élite who went to Western countries felt ashamed of the gap in cultures and even of differences in physical characteristics ... Probably the true victims of Kōtarō's feelings were his parents. They looked forward to his return as a "rebirth" for the Takamura family. However, the man who stepped off the ship "smelled of butter" and soon made it clear that he had acquired a different notion of art and a different outlook on life.'

When Kōtarō returned from his trip abroad, his father Kōun was approaching the age of sixty. The father wished that his workshop with all its many apprentices to be fed would continue under the new master, Kōtarō, and proposed that the son make a statue of his father as a sort of ritual of succession. Kōtarō performed the task as a filial son before all the apprentices. He did the job well, although he felt as if he were under close scrutiny. Then Kōun proposed they establish a company specializing in the production of bronze statues, for in the years following Japan's victory over

Russia, statues of great men were much in vogue. Kōtarō was disgusted by that proposal: artists, he believed, should not work for mercenary motives. His elderly father, however, did not understand why Kōtarō was so dissatisfied with such a profitable project. Kōtarō's behaviour was beyond his father's understanding: the offer of a professorship at his alma mater was turned down without a second thought. Marriage offers suggested by his mother were all dismissed. Kōtarō then began a dissipated life. Two years later he met Naganuma Chieko, a graduate of Japan Women's College, who was a painter and a member of the *Seitō* or the Blue Stocking group. According to Kōtarō's *Chieko shō*, purified by Chieko, Kōtarō was spiritually reborn.

I would like to conclude by pointing out the close connection between Kōtarō's inferiority complex towards the West and his love-hate relationship with his father. The psychological condition which was shared by the second generation of many developing nations, such as Germany under Kaiser Wilhelm II and Japan in the later years of Meiji and Taishō. First, by examining Kōtarō's famous poem, 'The Country of Netsuke' and then turn to the general attitude of the *Shirakaba* group towards Rodin's favourite model, the diminutive Hanako. The poem written in 1910 is as follows:

THE COUNTRY OF NETSUKE

Cheekbones protruding, lips thick, eyes triangular, with a face like a netsuke carved by the master Sangoro
blank, as if stripped of his soul
not knowing himself, fidgety
life-cheap
vainglorious
small and frigid, incredibly smug
monkey-like, fox-like, flying-squirrel-like, mudskipper-like, minnow-like, gargoyle-like, chip-from-a-cup-like Japanese.[22]

The denigration of himself and of the Japanese in the poem in general is quite excessive. Kōtarō wrote in a poem already quoted that it was there in Paris that he first knew the other sex. The same year Kōtarō wrote of his strong sense of inferiority in an article entitled '*Kohiten yori*' (A Letter from a Coffee-shop).[23] The letter begins with a beautiful description of his Parisian experience – how, brought up in the world of sculpture, he always sized the outside world sculpturally. He saw the naked bodies of passers-by through their clothing, and was often intoxicated by the beauty of their movements. He passed a night with a French girl, a sort of prostitute, whose beauty he had admired. Next morning, awakened by her voice, '*Tu dors?*' he found her eyes incredibly beautiful: they gave him the impression of the blue sky over the Indian Ocean or a fragment of the stained glass of the Notre-Dame Cathedral. When he got up and entered the bathroom, he saw a bizarre black-haired man approaching, which he soon realized was himself reflected in the mirror. He felt a strong wave of self-disgust – voices bore down upon him like an avalanche: 'A Jap! You are a Jap!' He fled from the girl. This vivid sense of inferiority is generally believed to have inspired the poem 'The Country of Netsuke.' It may be so.

A somewhat different and new interpretation is the following. Netsuke are little carvings, typical of works of sculpture of the Edo period, which were particularly appreciated abroad after the opening of Japan. Kōtarō disliked them, for they were a representative art not only of Japan, but of his father as well. In other words, the country of netsuke is none other than that of Takamura Kōun himself, against whom the son Kōtarō rebelled. This might be why the poet's attack is so violent.

As stated in the beginning, the father-son relationship constituted a common theme in late Meiji literature. In Nagai Kafū or Kume Keiichirō's case, their fathers were oppressive because they were great men raised in the traditional way. In the case of the Takamuras, however, although his father was nominally a professor, actually he was no more than an artisan, and it was that which became the source of Kōtarō's irritability. As a reaction, Kōtarō became a bookish person who, during his stay in Paris, probably devoted himself to the study of French and French poetry. He believed that without understanding what the models were thinking and feeling, he could not make a true work of art. Although in his later years he recollected otherwise, at the time he felt as if there were a wire netting around himself which prevented true communication between him and his models. He compared his situation to that of a deep-sea fish that cannot survive in a river or to a freshwater fish in a river that cannot live in the sea.[24]

After returning home, however, Kōtarō wrote: 'looking at the girls of my homeland, I find it hard to regard my homeland as good. How sad I feel!' and 'Should someone say to me "Make one of these girls your wife," I'd weep.'[25] As I read these lines, I inevitably was reminded of the shame that Shiga Naoya and other members of the *Shirakaba* group felt when they heard that Hanako, an unknown 'actress', had become the favourite model for Rodin.

Hanako, a girl raised in a geisha house in a provincial town who joined a theatrical group that went abroad, posed many times for Rodin, who took a keen interest in her.

Mori Ōgai immediately understood why Rodin was attracted to the 'diminutive' actress and wrote a short story entitled *Hanako*.[26] The 'second generation' Japanese, however, reacted differently; as Osanai said, they were ashamed that such a monkey-like, fox-like Japanese had been introduced to the great French sculptor. It is interesting to note that those who were ashamed of Hanako and were not confident of their own Japaneseness were precisely those who suddenly became patriotic, hearing of Japan's brilliant attack on Pearl Harbor.

It is clear that when Kōtarō stood against his father, the West and its values were with him. However, the son Kōtarō's attitudes towards his father and his native country were ambivalent. Here is the poem 'My Father's Face':

MY FATHER'S FACE

When I make my father's face with clay,
below the window in twilight
my father's face is sad and lonely.

Its shadings, having some resemblance to my face,
are eerie, the law terrifying,
and the old age of my soul, nakedly
manifest, unexpectedly startles me.

My heart, eager to see what it fears,
looks at the eyes, the wrinkles on the forehead.
My father's face that I made
remains deeply silent like fish
yet tells, alas, of its painful days of the past.

Is it the dark cry of steel
or the ghost's voice of *Hamlet* I saw in the West?
Its piercing echo, though without rancor,
seeps into my nails and throbs like whitlow.

When I make my father's face with clay,
below the window in twilight
the mysterious lineage of the blood whispers...[27]

Since Kōtarō was especially interested in Sigmund Freud and later made a memorial medal of him, it is significant that he mentioned the name of Hamlet here.

When his father died in 1934, to the disappointment of his

father's former apprentices, Kōtarō did not inherit his father's workshop. Instead he who felt freer in the world of poetry than in the world of sculpture became a father figure among his contemporary poets. It was therefore quite natural for him to become director of the poetry section of the Patriotic Association for Literature when it was formed in 1942. I quote one of his poems from that period as an example of his wartime work:

### TO GENERAL KURIBAYASHI

From his camp in the mainland's last outpost, Iwo Jima,
General Kuribayashi wired his last message.
Its words, cutting, do not allow mere perusal;
I read, chewing each word,
and reach the end, three tanka.
The 31-syllable lines rend my ears.
The Empire's marrow general, pushed to the wall,
bullets exhausted, out of water,
leads his remaining troops in the final charge.
First, he speaks a few words,
and the words spit blood.
Still, they're serene, the sound correct,
the thought respectful and of all ages.
Intent on the road ahead of the Empire,
he's determined to be reborn seven times, to take the spear,
to become a fence for the Sovereign.
General Kuribayashi is still on the island.
Living in tens of thousands of deaths,
we too shall simply, simply, smash up the enemy.[28]

After Japan's capitulation, when Kōtarō was accused of 'war responsibilities' by left-wing critics, rather than defend himself he turned his post-war poems into a self-accusatory kind of 'courtroom confession', Atsumi and Wilson write in their 'Poetry of Takamura Kōtarō': 'These poems have little literary merit but, presumably for the reverse of the reasons for his 1942 award, won the Yomiuri Literary Prize in May 1951.' If poets were to be held responsible for tendentious opinions created by their poems, Kōtarō's post-war responsibilities are much heavier than his wartime responsibilities. Satō Hiroaki is of the opinion that 'their (wartime poems') one saving grace may be that Kōtarō never enunciated what he did not believe.'[29]

To sum up the life and work of Takamura Kōtarō: his conjugal life, the reality of Kōtarō's description of his life with Chieko who died insane, requires further study, although I have strong misgivings about it. His book of poems, *Chieko shō*, however, will remain as a classic propagating the myth of their conjugal love. As for his sculptures, although his admirers value them highly, the relative achievments of the sculptors Takamura Kōun and Kōtarō will still be debated by art historians to come. I for one prefer the father Kōun's statue of Saigō Takamori to the son Kōtarō's statues of girls that stand at the lake-side of Towada-ko.

One thing, however, is certain: when it came to poetry Kōtarō knew how to carve with words. He showed us many unexpected revelations by cutting and modulating. Some poems of his have a sense of composition, some are tri-dimensional, and some symphonic – a rare achievement for a Japanese poet. Moreover, Kōtarō carved out his own life in his series of poems. *Sich bilden*, to carve out one's own life, was his ideal, and he came close to realizing it. If one recognizes in that effort a new departure from the old ways of living, then one can say there is a change, but if one recognize in that relentless toil an image of the honest artisan, then one can say he embodies a continuity with the past.[30]

*Notes*

[1] I thank the Pennsylvania State University for permission to reproduce this article which appeared in *Comparative Literature Studies,* vol. 26, no. 3, 1989.

[2] *Chieko and Other Poems of Takamura Kōtarō,* tr. Hiroaki Satō (Honolulu: Hawaii U.P., 1980).

[3] As for Takamura Kōtarō's writings, see *Takamura Kōtarō zenshū,* 18 vols. (Tokyo: Chikuma shōbō, 1957–1958). His wartime poems, which number more than one hundred, are in vols. 2 and 3.

[4] Murō Saisei: *Waga aisuru shijin no denki* (Tokyo: Chūōkōron-sha, 1974) p. 29.

[5] As for the life of Takamura Kōun (1852–1934), see his extremely interesting autobiography, *Takamura Kōun kaiko-dan,* (rpt. Tokyo: Shinjinbutsuōrai-sha, 1970).

[6] See Chapter 'Rokumeikan: the Europeanization Fever in Comparative Perspective'.

[7] Takamura Kōtarō: 'Kaisōroku' *Takamura Kōtarō zenshū,* vol. 10, p. 18.

[8] 'Ransai botsugo' *Shiga Naoya zenshū* (Tokyo: Iwanami shoten, 1999) vol. 5, pp257–268. Shiga wrote the same episode of the bogus certificates of authentication in another story *Kijin Dassai (Shiga Naoya zenshū,* vol. 8, pp. 73–85) whose model is Kanō Tessai. Shiga sympathized with his son Kazuhiro, who wished to become a literary artist.

[9] Takamura Kōtarō: 'Chichi tono kankei', *Takamura Kōtarō zenshū,* vol. 10, p. 225.

[10]  Takamura Kōtarō: *Takamura Kōtarō zenshū*, vol. 10, pp. 11–12.

[11]  *Chieko and Other Poems of Takamura Kōtarō*, p. 136.

[12]  It was later found that Iwamura Tōru's *Pari no gagakusei: Tōyō bunko 182*, (Tokyo: Heibonsha, 1971) was in fact an adaptation of William Chambers Morrow's *Bohemian Paris of Today* (London: Chatto & Windus, 1899). See Imahashi Eiko: *Ito shōkei nihonjin no Pari* (Tokyo: Kashiwa shobō, 1993), pp. 134–198.

[13]  Katanuma Seiji: *Takamura Kōtarō ni okeru Amerika* (Tokyo: Ōfūsha, 1982).

[14]  Saeki Shōichi: *Nichi-bei kankei no naka no bungaku* (Literature in the Japan-US relations; Tokyo: Bungeishunjū, 1984) pp. 205–231.

[15]  Takamura Kōtarō: 'Chōkokuka Gatsutoson Bōguramu shi', *Takamura Kōtarō zenshū*, vol. 7, pp. 50–56. The article was written in 1917.

[16]  Atsumi Ikuko and Graeme Wilson translated 'Zō no ginkō' in 'The Poetry of Takamura Kōtarō,' *Japan Quarterly 20* (1973) pp. 312–318.

[17]  *Chieko and Other Poems of Takamura Kōtarō*, p. 41.

[18]  Sarashina Genzō, 'Takamura sensei no ichimen', *Takamura Kōtarō zenshū dai 8 kan geppō* p. 10.

[19]  Saeki Shōichi: *Nichi-bei kankei no naka no bungaku*, p. 229.

[20]  The translation is in *The Poetry of Living Japan*, eds. T. Ninomiya and D. J. Enright (London: John Murray, 1957).

[21]  *Chieko and Other Poems of Takamura Kōtarō*, p. 137.

[22]  *Chieko and Other Poems of Takamura Kōtarō*, p. 3.

[23]  Takamura Kōtarō: *Takamura Kōtarō zenshū*, vol. 9, pp. 29–44.

[24]  'Dasazu ni shimatta tegami no hitotaba', *Takamura Kōtarō zenshū*, vol. 9, p. 58.

[25]  *Takamura Kōtarō zenshū*, vol. 1, pp. 123–124

[26]  About Rodin and his model Hanako, see 'Mori Ōgai no Hanako' in Hirakawa Sukehiro: *Wakon yōsai no keifu* (Tokyo: Kawade shobō, 1971), pp. 279–312. Reactions of Osanai Kaoru and Shiga Naoya are mentioned p. 292, p. 304 and pp. 308–310.

[27]  *Chieko and Other Poems of Takamura Kōtarō*, p. 7

[28]  *Chieko and Other Poems of Takamura Kōtarō*, p. 84.

[29]  Atsumi Ikuko and Graeme Wilson, 'The Poetry of Takamura Kōtarō', *Japan Quarterly 20* (1973) pp. 312–318.

[30]  About Takamura Kōtarō and his relationship with the West I wrote more in detail in "Takamura Kōtarō to seiyō" in Hirakawa Sukehiro: *Beikoku daitōryō e no tegami* (Tokyo: Shinchō-sha, 1996) pp. 167–304.

# THOSE WHO UNDERSTAND *MONO NO AWARE* AND THOSE WHO DO NOT: HUMAN CAPACITY TO BE AFFECTED BY THINGS OF NATURE IN KAWABATA'S *THE SOUND OF THE MOUNTAIN* AND HÉMON'S *MARIA CHAPDELAINE*[1]

Dear Mr. Yokomitsu,
Please have no worry about us whom you leave bereaved.
I will continue to live and work, following in your way from now on.
My heart is with Japan's mountains and rivers.[2]

Kawabata Yasunari (1899–1972) addressed these words to his friend, the writer Yokomitsu Riichi, at his funeral. Yokomitsu died in 1947 at the age of forty-nine, a broken man. He was a representative writer of Japanism in the late 1930s and early 40s and after World War II he was severely criticized for that. Kawabata's words were the more striking: at that time, when most Japanese intellectuals and writers had lost confidence in traditional Japanese values, Kawabata, a citizen of the defeated country, clearly declared his attachment to his nation's old traditions. Though Kawabata did not show any hatred against things Western, he clearly had a profound love for things Japanese. It is significant that when he was awarded the Nobel prize in 1968, he entitled his reception speech

'Japan, the Beautiful, and Myself'. His attachment to Japan's mountains and rivers was genuine.

Among Kawabata's novels, *The Sound of the Mountain*, which he began in 1949 and finished some five years later, would seem to be a work in which the author showed – to an exceptionally high degree – his appreciation of Japanese nature, or more precisely his understanding of *mono no aware*, the human capacity to be affected by things of nature that move our hearts.

Compared with his earlier works, for example, *The Master of Go*, with its anthropocentric narrative, Kawabata's perceptive acuity and masterly precision in describing the relationship between things of nature (that move us) and human hearts (that are moved) are most extraordinary in *The Sound of the Mountain*. This aspect must be taken into consideration in any study of Kawabata, who personified an important aspect of traditional Japanese aesthetics. The novel allows many possible readings, however, this aspect of his is of particular interest, as it is one of his most attractive charms, though it might offer some difficulties to readers. The nature-human relationship in Kawabata's works seems to have not always been very well appreciated by Western scholars. Many of them were baffled by Kawabata's speech at the Royal Academy of Sweden. Indeed, many such readers find Kawabata's 'Japan, the Beautiful, and Myself' rather illogical. They talk of leaps or gaps in Kawabata's *haiku*-like prose of *The Sound of the Mountain*, gaps which they have not found in the straightforward storytelling of *The Master of Go*. I would therefore try to elucidate some codes or half hidden secrets shared by the author and Japanese readers of *The Sound of the Mountain*.

To begin with, the title of the book, which is also the title of the first chapter, suggests a sort of relationship between nature and man already. To logical-minded persons, titles such as 'The Sound of Music' are 'right' combinations of words, as sound is an attribute of music. If one talks of 'the sound of the mountain', it means that the mountain is animated and has a voice. It also presupposes that there must be someone who listens to the sound or who has an illusion of hearing it. Grammatically speaking, this relationship between things of nature and the human heart is possible. It is the word *no* in *Yama no oto* (the sound of the mountain) that makes it grammatically correct. Moreover, it should be noted that all sixteen chapter titles contain the particle *no* between two nouns. Indeed, it is no coincidence either, that the Japanese title of Kawabata's speech at Stockholm, *Utsukushii Nihon no watashi*, contains the same particle *no*. The title of the third chapter, 'A Blaze of Clouds', is more modern than traditional in its use of imagery and vocabulary. However, this *kumo no honoo* is not just simply a description of an autumn evening. The faint blaze is in the sky as well as in the heart of Shingo, the old head of the Ogata family, who looks at evening clouds.

A correspondence of this kind is a technique already well known in the West as well as in the East. The fact is that *The Sound of the Mountain* is exceptionally rich in subtleties of this kind, even among the works of Kawabata. Compared with this problem of interactions between things of nature and human hearts, other problems common to any novel – general scheme, plot, character descriptions, theme, and so on – seem to be of secondary importance. The events of the novel are real and immediate, yet throughout they are touched and unified by an almost dreamlike correspondence between nature and man. It is for that reason that the focus of this chapter will be on the problem of *mono no aware* in this novel.

However, before analysing this problem, it will be useful for the readers to be introduced to the general scheme of *The Sound of the Mountain*. The story is, on the surface level, very Buddhistic, as the karmic idea of rebirth is pervasive in it. Shingo secretly loved a girl in his youth and a series of unbelievable facts derived from that: he married the girl's younger sister, Yasuko, after the elder sister's death. He could find the beautiful girl neither in Yasuko nor in their daughter Fusako, nor in Fusako's two daughters, and for that reason Shingo was not very tender towards them. Instead, he saw the beautiful girl of the past in his daughter-in-law, Kikuko. Though this underlying karmic cause and effect relationship may be interpreted in modern psychoanalytic terms, along which line, the author in the novel gives explanation and some logical-minded scholars have made commentaries on it.[3] However, these curiously logical consequences do not seem to fully explain the characters, or even they are unrealistic in explanations. It is true that Fusako cried to her father Shingo by quoting her ex-husband's words: 'You made me what I am by not liking me'. These hysterical overstatements, however, should not be taken too seriously at their face value, nor was it Kawabata's intention to explain fully the structure of her character. If there is any consciously pre-established plan for this serialized novel, it must be this karmic scheme. Partial truth lies in the chain reactions of this kind. However to base every explanation on it seems too farfetched to be true. All these fairy-tale-like stories (*inga banashi*) should be considered as significant only so long as they offer good settings in which Kawabata can give his artistic sensitivity free play. He was a sort of aeolian harp within that scheme; he was given a free hand in those settings. Kawabata was a man of keen perception, and the author lent this ability of his to the aging Shingo, the hero of the story.

There follows the curious and almost contradictory fact: readers know practically nothing about Shingo's ability as a company executive, but see through Shingo's eye minute details and subtle changes in nature as well as in human hearts: the hero's eye is as keen as the author's.[4]

With this brief examination of the general scheme, let us now proceed to the problem of *mono no aware*. As for the term itself of this Japanese aesthetic notion professed by the eighteenth century National Scholar, Motoori Norinaga (1730–1801), some concrete examples from Kawabata's novel would be more useful in comprehending its meaning than would abstract theoretical cogitations. A clear demarcation between those who understand *mono no aware* and those who do not is easy to draw without providing any further specific definition. In the novel, Shingo and his daughter-in-law Kikuko fall into a distinct group as they share this sensibility, while others do not. However, to understand *mono no aware* is not uniquely a Japanese sensibility, and in the latter part of this paper some Canadian examples will be discussed. All human beings are capable of being more or less moved by *mono no aware*; that is why this novel by Kawabata attracts some foreign readers through translation. As the discussion in this chapter will be based mainly on Seidensticker's English translation,[5] before looking into the details of the novel, I would like to make some remarks about the translation at the beginning.

A translation is an interpretation of the original. A good translator makes readers understand a text better by his interpretation. This is frequently the case with Arthur Waley's English translations of Japanese literature. Seidensticker's English translation of *The Sound of the Mountain* is also a fine piece of work, though it is not free of errors. As an example of the translator's painstaking art, let us examine his English equivalents for the expression *ozure*. In Section 1 of the first chapter, Shingo tells his son of a blister on his foot. The maid remarked, '*ozure de gozaimasu ne*'[6] (This is *ozure*, isn't it?). Shingo at that moment took the sound *o* in *ozure* as an honorific. An old-fashioned way of translation of the word would be an 'honourable blister'. Shingo, however, later began to believe that the sound *o* in *ozure* was not the honorific, but the word for 'a clog cord'. If so, *ozure* cannot have any gentle ring to it. The word means flatly a blister caused by a maladjusted cord of *geta*; this is a very matter-of-fact expression, indeed. It is, however, impossible to translate these two Japanese homophones into two English homophones with corresponding meanings. Seidensticker therefore tried to find two equivalent English expressions for them. Here is his translation of the passage:

> '... I think it must have been two or three days before she quit. When I went out for a walk I had a blister on my foot, and I said I thought I had picked up ringworm. "Footsore," she said. I liked that. It had a gentle, old-fashioned ring to it. I liked it very much. But now that I think about it I'm sure she said I had a boot sore. There was something wrong with the way she said it. Say "footsore."'
> 'Footsore.'
> 'And now say "boot sore."'
> 'Boot sore.'
> 'I thought so. Her accent was wrong.'[7]

To use 'footsore' and 'boot sore' as equivalents to express the two meanings of *ozure* is in a sense admirable, and Seidensticker is very good at using these translation techniques. Some people may protest against the use of boot sore as the sore had been caused not by a boot but by a *geta*, sandal. But as most English-speaking readers of Seidensticker's translation do not know the Japanese habit of wearing *geta*, it is far better to use these equivalent words than just to stick clumsily to the original, as often happens in English translations of Kawabata's other works by Japanese translators. The substance of the story is better transmitted to readers through the use of 'footsore' and 'boot sore'. The problem, then, is: what is the substance of this episode? For the aging Shingo it is first of all a question of discernment: his ability to distinguish the proper accents of the two homophones was put to the test. Moreover, Shingo perhaps unconsciously wished to recognize womanly gentleness towards himself, and later acknowledged that it was a mistake in understanding. In that misunderstanding there was an element of the old man's sentimentality.

*The Sound of the Mountain* is a novel in which human affairs, changes of seasons and other happenings are seen through the eyes of this aging, forgetful man. So the first episode of *o zure* or *ozure*, footsore or boot sore is, apart from the secondary question of English translation, very important and suggestive. It foretells the peculiar quality of Kawabata's novel. Not only Shingo but also the reader is requested to catch a difference in accents and to appreciate the delicate nuances attached to it. One of the interests of the book lies precisely in our ability to feel and catch undertones. People generally believe that it is plot that runs through a novel, but in this work by Kawabata it is sensibility, which is in the end the unifying principle. Affective stimuli come from various sources, and the main characters of the novel respond to them intelligently, and other characters less so. These interactions form the interest of the novel. The capacity of readers to be affected and to understand is also put to the test. Those who understand *mono no aware* will follow not the plot or the outline of the story, but the half hidden thread which gives this work an admirable wholeness.

As has often been remarked by critics, the story is not architecturally constructed as Western novels tend to be. However, the sixteen chapters of *The Sound of the Mountain* are superbly well linked together, if not logically, at least impressionistically. If I may use a somewhat curious term, Kawabata's novel is 'psychologically logical'. Linkages of different scenes, combinations of natural phenomena with human affairs, symbolic uses of animals and flowers have their own logic. In short, Kawabata's art of juxtaposing different elements is very precise, and those who read the novel with a critical eye and a perceptive ear will ask: Does Kawabata choose plants which are appropriate to a certain state of mind? Is a kite's cry a proper affective reply to a certain situation? Do Shingo and Kikuko, possessed of heart, respond appropriately to these natural phenomena? If not, why not? The development of the story is related not only to the actions of the characters involved (plot), but also to the passing of the four seasons, as readers witness a series of interplays between things of nature and the characters. As is known, elements of nature are considerable in Kawabata's works generally. Some seasonal elements, with their half-hidden implications, affect so much the main characters in the novel that they should be considered something more than a mere background. It should be remembered that in 'Japan, the Beautiful, and Myself', Kawabata's Stockholm speech, he talks first of all, about the priest Myōe's *uta*-poem in which the winter moon becomes a companion[8]. The heart of the priest is engaged in a delicate interplay and exchange with the moon. In *The Sound of the Mountain*, too, the heart of Shingo or the heart of Kikuko is engaged in an interplay with flowers, birds, winds and the moon.

Novels are not academic expositions, and there is no need for novelists to be strictly logical. However, for readers to follow the story there should be some kind of flow. This flow of story-telling need not always be linear. There can be many fluctuations in time and space, and this meandering thread that follows the life process or psychological process of the main characters is often called a plot or an outline. It seems, however, that there is another sort of thread running through *The Sound of the Mountain*. The difference is that it runs through not only the main characters but also through the natural phenomena of the surrounding world. It leaps from human elements to natural elements, and after an elliptic silence runs again through human affairs. Many critics have already noticed this particular sort of thread, which reminds us of the unifying principle that runs through a *renga* sequence. In order to distinguish this thread from the general outline or the plot, I would like to call the former, by a French term, *fil conducteur*.

The general outline or the plot of the story is as follows. It is conceived within the above-mentioned karmic scheme and is rather simple. It is Shingo who hears 'the sound of the mountain' – the faint rumble in the hills or in his ears, that is a muffled hint of unknown occurrences, and a foreboding of his death. Then the author describes Shingo's feelings for his wife, son, daughter and his affection for his daughter-in-law, Kikuko. His son Shuichi has a liaison with a war widow, and his daughter's marriage with Aihara is a disaster. Kikuko has an abortion in protest, but Shuichi and Kikuko are restored to good terms towards the end. As for the psychological relations between paternalistic Shingo and dependent Kikuko, the story is rich in subtleties.

One of the reasons to make the distinction between the outline and the *fil conducteur* is this: there are some people whose interest seems to be focused exclusively on the developments of human relations in novels, and in the case of *The Sound of the Mountain*, on the development of the sexual relationship of the main characters. Although it is clear that Shingo harbours a sort of erotic sentiment for his beautiful daughter-in-law, this aspect should not be exaggerated. Shingo is meant to be an average old man. He is not an erotomaniac. As the plot is less important than the language in this novel by Kawabata, readers who are interested exclusively in the development of human relations, will surely be disappointed when they finish the book without finding any particular development between Shingo and Kikuko. Moreover, it does not quite appear possible that Shingo, a sexually inactive old man, can be drawn into a forbidden relationship with his daughter-in-law. There is this passage in the chapter 'A Dream of Islands':

> He (Shingo) wondered whether this sequence of strange occurrences – he had embraced a girl in a dream, he had thought Eiko quite captivating in the mask, he had almost kissed the *jido* – meant that something was still freshly agitating within himself.[9]

This 'something' of course refers to his sexual desire, but this reflection indicates that the old man had had doubts about his potency. Women had left his life during the war.[10] Shingo had not had sex with his wife for many years. They slept together but 'only when she snored did he reach out to touch her'.[11] These quotations might be superfluous, if numerous people's attention were not focused on the old man's possible erotic entanglement with a young woman.

The second reason to make the distinction between the plot and the *fil conducteur* is that the plot is not very important in Kawabata's *The Sound of the Mountain*. Some literary genres do not need a plot. Neither diaries nor lyrical poems need it, and it is known that Kawabata much liked these genres, *nikki*, (literature in form of diary) of the Heian period, *uta* and *haiku*. In the case of *The Sound of the Mountain*, sixteen chapters are linked together by a general outline and there is a considerable development in human relations. However, inside any single chapter, various elements are laid side by side or paragraph by paragraph. Of the two dominant categories of these components, one concerns members of the Ogata family and other characters (their descriptions, conversations, feelings, etc.) and the other concerns things of nature (seasons, sky, fields and mountains, fauna and flora). With the first category there is a plot: the story progresses, main characters appear and events take place in chronological order except for some flashbacks. It is not the case with the second category. At first glance, apparitions of things of nature seem to be fortuitous and their descriptions casual. However, after careful reading, many Japanese readers feel that elements of nature are there of necessity: insects and birds, trees and flowers, fish and animals – they appear in Kawabata's story in a very well timed way. Like a good host, Kawabata knows how to serve and how to garnish the main characters with things of nature. Their apparitions are psychologically logical, and the unseen thread which coordinates these two categorically different elements is what I call the *fil conducteur*. The unity of impression we get from the juxtaposition of these seemingly heterogeneous components is very real.

The question, then, is what are the roles and connotations of these apparently fortuitous elements of nature in Kawabata's novel? How does the unifying principle work? Why do we feel harmony between what seem to be unrelated elements?

Before analysing some examples, it is worth paying attention to the chapter titles, since the titles provide external facts for the argument that elements of nature count as much as developments in human relations in this novel. The titles given to each of the sixteen chapters of the book clearly indicate how the four seasons are passing in the story. They tell the season or even the month in which events of a certain chapter take place. Chapter 2, with the title 'The Wings of the Locust', is of course summer (locust being the American name for the cicada; readers should not be misguided by its biblical connotation). Chapter 4, 'The Chestnuts', is autumn, especially as it is '*kuri no mi*' and not '*kuri*' in the Japanese original. Chapter 6, 'The Cherry in Winter', is, needless to say, winter, and so with Chapter 9, 'The Bell in Spring'. Chapter 14, 'The Cluster of Mosquitoes', is summer again, and the novel ends with Chapter 16, 'Fish in Autumn'. Even though readers do not know what happens to Shingo and his family, readers guess from these chapter titles that the story covers six seasons beginning from a summer. The only title which consists uniquely of a human element is 'The Scar', but it should be added that the original title of Chapter 13 is not so direct as this English translation seems to be. It is '*kizu no ato*', or literally translated 'After the Wound.' There is, in this title too, a time element.

Comparing them with chapter titles of Western novels, the conspicuous absence of seasonal words is surprising. Stendhal's *Charterhouse of Parma*, one of the representative French novels of the nineteenth century, is composed of twenty-eight chapters, and no chapter contains a season word. The novel begins with 'Milan in 1796' and tells exclusively of human actions: 'The Guns of Waterloo', 'Fabrizio in Parma', 'Flight to Bologna', 'From a Prison Window', 'Escape from the Citadel', 'Death of a Prince', and the tale ends with 'Retreat from the World'. Readers can almost follow the plot by picking up these chapter titles.

*The Sound of the Mountain* is definitely very Japanese in the sense that the world view is not centred on human action and where it takes place. There are precedents of the kind in the history of Japanese literature, that is, the naming of the chapter titles of *The Sound of the Mountain* reminds one of that of *The Tale of Genji*. Lady

Murasaki was interested in things of nature as well as in human affairs. There are many chapter titles which bear the names of characters involved, such as 'Kiritsubo', 'Yūgao', 'Aoi', 'Asagao' and others. All these female names are derived from plants and flowers. The four seasons are well represented in many chapter titles such as 'The Festival of Red Leaves', 'The Wind in the Pine Trees', 'The Butterflies', 'The Glow-Worm', 'The Typhoon', 'Fern Shoots', 'The Gossamer Fly' and others. Categorically speaking, Kawabata's world of literature is very much akin to that of Lady Murasaki or Sei Shōnagon.

To classify pieces of literature according to the four seasons is a long tradition in Japan. The *Kokin* anthology of *uta*-poems already adopted that classification at the beginning of the tenth century. Seasonal terms became indispensable elements in *haiku*, and it is obvious that Kawabata's aesthetic feelings were formed by that tradition. Kawabata Yasunari was a precocious boy who wrote many *haiku* while still a secondary school student. He was well acquainted with the Japanese classics. He very much liked *The Tale of Genji* and *haiku* poets. His selective reception of Western literature was essentially an act of assimilation through his sharp sensibilities. The eyes of this Neo-Perceptionist seem to have been formed early by the Japanese classics which he read again and again during the war years.

The problem of perception in *The Sound of the Mountain* is a problem which has to do with the traditional notion of *mono no aware*. The first incident of 'footsore' or 'boot sore' gives readers the misleading impression that Shingo is a forgetful old man on the verge of senility. This is practically a trick on the part of the author. Shingo in this novel is, after all, a very perceptive and observant family head. He takes care of his family members extremely well. He is a man aware of small niceties in life. Although it is almost incredible that there could be such a refined businessman, this novel would lose its charm if Shingo were not that sensitive. For example, at the fishmonger's shop outside Kamakura station he heard a prostitute saying: 'I wonder if they'll (lobsters) still be here on Saturday. My boyfriend sort of likes them.' In spite of the asperity and disapproval shown by the fishmonger towards these prostitutes of the new sort, Shingo was gentle towards them and their like: 'But I thought they were behaving rather well.'[12] (*Datte shushō ja naika. Kanshin da yo*). This refers of course to the girl's good character. The prostitute wished to treat her G.I. friend well the next weekend when he would be back from an American Occupation base. Shingo immediately recognized a good nature in the prostitute and approved of it. She had her own dream of a sweet home, her dream of eating together with her beloved. Although the fact that Shingo's son, Shuichi, had a mistress and would not eat with his wife and his parents that evening is not yet clear to readers, there is a kind of premonition in the scene.

The Ogata family are four in number, but Shingo had bought only three whelks. He knew that Shuichi would not be home for dinner. The prodigal son had gone out with a girl after work that evening. The father was aware of that because the father and the son were working in the same company in Tokyo. The still very childlike Kikuko probably did not know yet that her husband was having a liaison with a war widow, and she behaved well towards her parents-in-law. There is a sort of born naïveté and fairy-like ingenuousness in Kikuko. The fact that readers hear her speak more often than see her in the novel suggests that unworldly quality about her. Kawabata lets Kikuko behave in a difficult situation peculiar to an extended family: Shingo handed over three whelks to her. A scene of love's arithmetic ensues. The good Kikuko kept one whelk for her husband, even though he did not let her know when he would be back home. She therefore brought two whelks to the table. So far no problem. Kikuko then put out one for her parents-in-law and one for herself. This distribution seems to be hardly possible as a domestic scene of the late 1940s. Was it not the father Shingo who had bought three whelks? And was he given only a half portion? In my opinion this is one of the rare scenes in *The Sound of the Mountain* that lacks reality. Kawabata, however, dared to set up that situation. Did the author already have in mind that numerical correspondence between the three whelks at the beginning and the three trout at the end of the story? I don't think that Kawabata had such a detailed plan while writing. Shingo's reaction after a moment of puzzlement is as follows:

> 'But there should be another,' said Shingo, a little puzzled.
> 'Oh, dear. But the two of you have such bad teeth, Grandpa – I thought you might want to share one nicely between you.'
> 'I don't see any grandchildren around.'
> Yasuko looked down and snickered.
> 'I'm sorry.' Kikuko got up lightly and went to the kitchen for the third.
> 'We should do as Kikuko says,' said Yasuko. 'Share one nicely between us.'

Shingo thought Kikuko's words beautifully apt. It was as though his own problem, whether to buy three or four, had thus been brushed away.[13]

For a Japanese husband of his age and of his time to drop into a fishmonger's shop on his way home may suggest that Yasuko was not a very good housewife. She was in many ways more insensitive than Shingo. Listen to the conversation between the two after Kikuko had gone to the kitchen for the third whelk. Yasuko asked her husband:

'But were there only three in the store? ... You only brought three, and there are four of us.'
'We didn't need another. Shuichi didn't come home.'[14]

In this family it is always Shingo, the old father, who worries about his son Shuichi, his daughter-in-law Kikuko and his daughter Fusako and her children. It is true that he did not like Fusako very much, but it is Shingo who helps her financially. Altogether Shingo is not at all forgetful about the essentials of life, while his wife Yasuko, although in robust health, is 'not alive to such subtleties.'[15] That is the reason she repeats that insensitive question about there being only three whelks in the store. Kawabata's original reads: '*Yasuko wa Shingo no kokoroguma ni kizukanakute ... manukena mushikaeshi o shita.*' '*Kokoroguma*' means recesses of mind, shades of heart, or nuances of sentiment. In the Ogata family neither his wife nor his son nor his own daughter is alive to such subtleties. Only Kikuko is responsive and catches the shades of his heart. It is natural then that the father and the daughter-in-law feel messages that other members of the family do not understand, and the interesting point in *The Sound of the Mountain* is that many subtle psychological reactions are hinted at through the media of things of nature. This is a characteristic that differentiates this novel by Kawabata from other psychological novels, and this is possible because Shingo and Kikuko share a common responsiveness to natural phenomena. It should be added that this is possible because their capacity to be affected by things of nature is also shared by many Japanese readers.

Here is an example. At the beginning of the chapter, 'The Chestnuts', the gingko was sending out unseasonal shoots, and Shingo was troubled, because Kikuko had not noticed them. It might suggest a certain emptiness in her heart. Here is the conversation between the two:

'... Do you have so much on your mind that you come in looking at the ground?'

'This will never do.' Kikuko gave her shoulders that slight, beautiful shrug. 'I'll be very careful from now on to notice everything you do and imitate it.'

For Shingo, there was a touch of sadness in the remark. 'This won't do either.'

In all his life no woman had so loved him as to want him to notice everything she did.[16]

(As for the last sentence, I would suggest the following translation instead: 'In all his life he had never so loved a woman as to want her to notice everything he did.')[17]

If one notices human or natural phenomena that another person is noticing and if one understands the message emanating from them just the same way as the other person does, then these two can communicate without uttering a word.

However, this happy communication or communion does not occur between many couples. When Shingo got married in Yasuko's family house in Nagano, a chestnut fell as they were exchanging marriage cups. The chestnut struck a large stone in the garden and rebounded a very long way and fell into a brook. The rebound was so extraordinary that Shingo was on the point of calling out in surprise. He looked around the room, but no one else seemed to have noticed. This accident is symbolic of their married life: what the husband notices the wife does not.

There is also an interesting subjective description about three swallowtails. In Section 3 of the chapter, 'The Wings of the Locust', Shingo looked at the garden, and said, 'There are butterflies behind the shrubbery'.[18] Yasuko acknowledged her husband's observation by saying, 'Yes, I see them.' (Though omitted in Seidensticker's translation, this appears in the original.[19]) Then 'as if they disliked being seen by Yasuko, the butterflies flew up over the bush clover'. This scene seen through Shingo's mind's eye is superb, as the description suggests the continuing perceptual gap between the husband and the wife. Even if they notice the same swallowtails, they get different messages.

There are, of course, other signs which everyone understands in practically the same way. Shingo's and Yasuko's daughter Fusako came back to her parents' house after the breakdown of her married life. Fusako's daughter, an obdurate child, played with wingless locusts. Whenever the girl caught a locust, she would come running up to anyone nearby to have the wings clipped. What the distasteful practice means is clear to readers. It suggests that there was something in the poor child's nature that responded to that cruel sport.

The little girl had been brought up in a broken family with a hysterical mother. However, what interests us more is the perceptive Shingo's observation:

> Yasuko had blanched when she found a swarm of red ants dragging off a wingless locust.
> She was not, on the whole, a person to be moved by such matters. Shingo was both amused and disturbed.
> Her recoil, as from a poisonous vapour, was perhaps a sign of evil foreboding. Shingo suspected that locusts were not the problem.[20]

Wingless locusts are here used not only to indicate something in the little girl's nature but also something like self-loathing in Yasuko's nature. Yasuko disliked both her daughter and her granddaughter, because they resembled Yasuko herself. 'Locusts were not the problem' is a very sharp remark by the self-conscious husband and, by reflection, it indicates also the feeling the husband holds towards his wife.

The symbolic use of animals and plants is highly explicit in Kawabata's novel. In the chapter, 'A Dream of Islands', the insensitive Yasuko said to her daughter-in-law:

> 'One lady said something interesting. She said that now that Teru (a female dog) had had puppies here we would be having a baby. She said that Teru was urging us on.'[21]

Shingo was shocked by her remark and made a remark in reply that was not tactful either:

> 'You mean there is someone who puts people and dogs in the same category?'

These things are distasteful if they are talked about too openly, but if they are juxtaposed tactfully, they may have a strong evocative power. Chapter 10 is full of these examples. (In the original, Chapter 10 is titled '*Tori no Ie*' or 'The Birds' House'; in Seidensticker's translation, it appears as 'The Kite's House.') It was after mid-May Shingo heard the cry of a kite, 'So it's here again,' he muttered. After having gotten up, Shingo scanned the sky, but the kite was not to be seen. 'It was as if a fresh young voice had departed and left the sky over the roof serene'[22] – a marvellous description worthy of a *haiku*. Shingo apparently felt the renewal of life in the cry of the kite. The original words for 'a fresh young voice' are '*osanageni amai koe*',[23] that is, 'a childlike sweet voice'. This sense of a rebirth has something to do with Shingo's expectation of a renewal in his family. However, very significantly the unhappy

Kikuko did not hear 'their' kite. Shingo added another remark: 'If our kite is here, then our buntings ought to be here too.'[24] Kikuko's thought didn't flow the same way. She replied, 'Yes. And crows,' and mentioned also fleas, mosquitoes and even the name of an *aodaisho* snake.[25] Procreation is not always a hope for everyone. There was apparently an association between a black crow and a night person. Shingo's reaction is as follows:

> 'Crows?' Shingo laughed. If it was 'our' kite, then it should also be 'our' crows. 'We think of it as a house for human beings, but all sorts of birds live here too.'[26]

A night bird called Shuichi lived in that house too. That fact, however, was not openly mentioned by anyone. Readers do not even know if it reached the consciousness of Shingo or Kikuko. In the novel, the scene has a more direct and overwhelming implication, that is, while Shingo was rejoicing over the return of the kite, and was wondering if a new generation had taken the place of the old, Kikuko did not feel that surge of affection. Her remark that fleas and mosquitoes would be coming out is almost black humor. It reflects her state of mind and body. Actually, immediately after this (in the following section of the same chapter), readers discover with surprise that Kikuko had an abortion in protest.

The day after that event Shingo's eye fell on a newspaper headline. It said, 'Lotus in Bloom, Two Thousand Years Old.'[27] Kawabata is very good at picking up these journalistic topics. His change of pace is like that of masters of *haikai* of olden times. He knows how to mix the temporary with the eternal. Here is the scene in which Shingo takes the paper into Kikuko's room. He says to his daughter-in-law, who is lying on her bed:

> 'Did you see in the paper that a lotus two thousand years old has come into bloom?'
> 'Yes.'
> 'Oh, you did,' he muttered. 'If you had only told us, you wouldn't have had to overdo it. You shouldn't have come back the same day.'
> Kikuko looked up in surprise.[28]

Shingo's first remark seems to be banal. It may be interpreted as a pretext for further conversation, as the main point is Kikuko's abortion. However, the casual remark on the blooming of a lotus after two thousand years of sleep leaves in the mind of the reader that hope that human beings share of the revival of life. Neither Shingo nor Kikuko seemed to be conscious of it at that moment.

Yet the author Kawabata must have been aware of that effect, and this news about the lotus comes back again in Section 3 of Chapter 15. The lotus seeds produced two buds, which had opened into pink flowers – and it was Kikuko who put two newspapers on the table before Shingo this time.[29] It is no coincidence that Shingo asked his daughter-in-law on that Sunday morning if she was going to have a baby that autumn. Individualistic people may wonder why the aging Shingo was so concerned with his possible grandchild and may think that neither Shingo nor his insensitive wife had anything to do with the private matters of Shuichi and Kikuko – but what Shingo told Kikuko on that peaceful October morning contains the gist of a life which moves us. It could not be simply interpreted as the hypocritical statement of an old man:

> 'I hope you'll treat it better next time. I argued with Shuichi over the last one. I asked if he could guarantee that you would have another, and he said he could. As if it were all very simple. I told him he ought to be a little more God-fearing. I asked him whether anyone could guarantee that he would be alive the next day. The baby would be yours and Shuichi's, of course, but it would be our grandchild too. A child you would have would be too good to lose.'[30]

Shingo's strong concern for his descendance has something to do with his instinct as the head of the Ogata family. When Shuichi and Kikuko, in the end, return to good terms, the old man says with a sort of resignation, 'A trout in the autumn, abandons itself to the water'[31] – a lesson which we learn here[32] at salmon hatcheries, towards the end of October. Shingo felt that he had finished his mission in life. An element of self-pity can be felt in Shingo's quoting this *haiku*, yet readers know that something is over.

As for the ending of *The Sound of the Mountain*, there is an opinion that this story remains unfinished, and some of the author's own statements seem to support that argument. Moreover, since Kawabata's sayings are rather equivocal, readers may give their own interpretations. It is true that 'Kawabata just lets his language flow in time.'[33] Certainly, the shape of the novel, in the case of *The Sound of the Mountain* as well as that of *Snow Country*, is not architectural, but 'musical in the sense of a continual movement generated by surprise and juxtaposition, intensification and relaxation'.[34] Nevertheless, just as a musical composition has its finale, so has this work its own ending. Moreover, there is a foreboding about it. To have a happy family reunion in the last section of the last chapter is a possible finale. Some would say that Shingo's family are not that happy, but there is significance in the fact that all seven members of the Ogata family are present at dinner one Sunday evening. Yes, life rallies somehow, and Shingo plans to make an excursion to his native place to see the maples. The prospects for the future are at least clearer than before.

While the first chapter begins with Shingo hearing an unusual sound, the ominous sound of the mountain, the last line of the last chapter ends with the common sound of a very usual domestic scene, the clatter of dishes. It is symbolic that Kikuko did not hear Shingo over the sound of the dishes. Their half-hidden communication was over. She was destined to have a separate common life with Shuichi; they would go and live somewhere else.

Things of nature affect human beings, and that affection might be given a name. The Japanese give it an expression, *mono no aware*, which was once translated as the *ahness of things*. Things of nature move us, and thus affected, we say, 'ah'. If so, let things of nature speak for themselves, and let us remain silent, while feeling and listening to them. In *The Sound of the Mountain* both characters and readers have listened to many sounds and voices emanating from the surrounding nature. It must be the reason that Kawabata could produce a novel which leaves so much unstated and yet is eloquent. For that he is erroneously called an elliptic writer. Nevertheless, the necessity for a writer to describe in detail the state of mind of his characters is a question in literature. If things of nature affect characters and if we readers feel their state of mind through that medium, hints and half-questions are probably enough. They are sometimes more eloquent and poetically more effective than minute explanations. The essence of poetry is present in this technique. Moreover, this *mono no aware* relationship between things of nature and human hearts is not uniquely Japanese. To elaborate on the point, I would like to add a comparison with Louis Hémon's *Maria Chapdelaine*, as this is the only well-known Canadian classic among the Japanese of my generation.[35]

It has often been said that Canadian authors, either Anglophone or Francophone, are more concerned with man's conquest of the natural environment than are Japanese authors. In fact, the word 'conquest' is alien to Kawabata's vocabulary. His attitude toward nature, as well as that of his main characters, is not at all hostile. Shingo seems to seek communion with nature. It happens also that he unconsciously communicates with other people through the medium of nature. It is clear that nature is humanized in Japan and is not Shingo's enemy.

On the contrary, one of the main themes of *Maria Chapdelaine* is man's survival. How to fight against a hostile nature is the main concern of every character depicted in the story. The climate north of the Lake Saint John region is extremely harsh and inclement. Needless to say, the life-style of Canadian farmers at the turn of the century was very different from the civilized urban life style of the Ogata family. In spite of these differences, there are some common characteristics which may be of some use for the understanding of *mono no aware*.

In *Maria Chapdelaine*, the flow of time which defines the shape of *The Sound of the Mountain* is also an important thematic element. The plot is more sharply defined in this novel by Hémon than in Kawabata's novel. The plot is in short the farm life of the Chapdelaine family. Maria's betrothal with François Paradis, François's death in a snow storm. Maria's mother's sickness and death, Maria's resolution to continue to live at the place where her ancestors have lived. Maria's acceptance of Eutrope's proposal. Almost every month of the year is represented in this novel. It is merely a coincidence, but this novel, too, is composed of numerically the same sixteen chapters; and while *The Sound of the Mountain* covers fifteen months beginning with August, *Maria Chapdelaine* covers fourteen months beginning with April. More than ten chapters of the Canadian novel begin with a phrase indicating the passage of time: Chapter 4 begins with 'After a few chilly days, June suddenly brought veritable spring'; Chapter 5 with 'The fine weather continued, and early in July the blueberries were ripe'; Chapter 6 with 'In July the hay was maturing'; Chapter 7 says, 'September arrived'; Chapter 8, 'One October morning Maria's first vision on arising was of countless snowflakes sifting lazily from the skies'; Chapter 9, 'Since the coming of winter they had often talked at the Chapdelaines about the holiday'; Chapter 10, 'New Year's Day, and not a single caller'; Chapter 11, 'One evening in February'; Chapter 12, 'March came'; and Chapter 14, 'There came an evening in April' and so forth.

Along this flow of time, Hémon plans a plot: the love story of the heroine. The whole sequence is well schematized, and the story progresses in chronological order to the end. As a piece of art, this novel is very typical.

A question I would like to raise is: is there something like a *fil con-*

*ducteur* in this novel apart from the plot? This thread may run from people to natural phenomena, from humans to animals, from plants to humans or even from humans to humans. It may leap from any one element to another. These leaps may be short or long, direct or indirect. In *Maria Chapdelaine* exists, too, a kind of connection to plants, insects and animals in relation to the psyches of the main characters.

In Section 2 of the chapter 'The Wings of the Locust' of *The Sound of the Mountain*, there is a beautiful description of sunflowers. They reminded Shingo of a giant symbol of masculinity: 'He did not know how stamens and pistils were in this central disk, but somehow he felt there masculinity.'[36] In *Maria Chapdelaine* there are plenty of descriptions of plants and flowers, but none is charged with a sexual association. They are just descriptions, are self-contained, and not charged with many levels of meaning. In Chapter 5 of *Maria Chapdelaine*, there is a minute description of how people drove away mosquitoes when they began to arrive in their legions. A boy set ablaze dry chips and twings:

> When the flame was leaping up brightly he returned with an armful of herbs and leaves and smothered it; the volume of stinging smoke ... was carried by the wind into the house and drove out the countless horde. At length they were at peace, and with sighs of relief could desist from the warfare.[37]

For the Chapdelaines to live in this region was a form of warfare; but that warfare had its lyrical side: the very last mosquito settled on the face of the youngest of the children, Alma-Rose:

> With great seriousness she pronounced the ritual words: 'Fly fly, get off my face, my nose is not a public place!' Then she made a swift end of the creature with a slap.[38]

This domestic scene invites a smile. In *The Sound of the Mountain*, too, there is a description of mosquitoes. In fact Chapter 14 is entitled 'The Cluster of Mosquitoes', and this mosquito scene also has something to do with a type of warfare. But how different this scene is! It was Shingo's dream, and in it he was a young army officer in uniform. He was walking a mountain path and had a woodcutter with him. When he turned on a flashlight, a dark form loomed up in the darkness. It was cedars:

> But he looked more carefully and saw instead a great cluster of mosquitoes in the shape of a tree trunk. What to do, he wondered. Cut his way through. He took out his sword and hacked away at the mosquitoes.[39]

That day he had been to see Kinu, his son's mistress, and had offered a check to settle the affair. He felt ineptness when he faced the war widow. Have the unpleasant dream of mosquitoes and the quixotic acts of an old man in his dream something to do with that day's experience? Here is the latter half of his dream:

> Shingo was finally at home. It seemed to be his childhood home, in Shinshu. Yasuko's beautiful sister was there. Though exhausted, Shingo felt no itching from the mosquitoes.
> The woodcutter who had fled in such haste also made way to Shingo's old home. He fell unconscious as he stepped through the door.
> From his body they took a bucketful of mosquitoes.[40]

To see the piling up of mosquitoes in the bucket is one of the most unpleasant scenes of the novel. Unable to find any keys, I do not dare to interpret Shingo's dreams; but one thing is certain: if the mosquito scene in *Maria Chapdelaine* represents domestic happiness, this one represents the opposite. Actually, in the following chapter the unhappy Ogata couple have a dispute over the use or non-use of mosquito nets. Shingo finds them heavy and oppressive, while Yasuko complains of the deprivation every night and makes a great ceremony of swatting mosquitoes. The difference between Yasuko's ritual and that of little Alma-Rose is extreme. It is surprising how the same image of a cluster of mosquitoes could be charged with different associations.[41]

In Kawabata's novel words and images are charged with associations on different levels. Some are easy to understand, as they are classical and stereotyped, but others are newly found by Kawabata himself. For example, if Shingo had not felt masculinity in sunflowers, no one in Japan would have associated them with a phallic symbol. But now that we have read *The Sound of the Mountain*, the association would be ineluctable. It is also true that silent intervals of Kawabata's prose are charged with significance. White blanks left unstated are like the invisible part of an iceberg. We know that something is there underwater, as we see its upper part, and those who understand *mono no aware* guess the underwater parts of Kawabata's imagery. These white blanks are sometimes more eloquent than words.

Now, let us take a look at the scene of the marriage proposal in *Maria Chapdelaine*, as it is one of the climactic scenes of the novel. It shows that the words pronounced in Hémon's novel are not just simple and self-contained. They are not one-dimensional in their meaning and that there are even scenes where silence is more eloquent than words. The scene has a certain tension mounting in the atmosphere:

> François Paradis looked about him as though to take his bearings. 'The others cannot be far away,' he said.
> 'No,' replied Maria in a low voice. But neither he nor she called to summon them.
> A squirrel ran down the hole of a dead birch tree and watched the pair with his sharp eyes for some moments before venturing to earth. The strident flight of heavy grasshoppers rose above the intoxicated clamour of the flies; a wandering air brought the fall's dull thunder through the alders.[42]

How beautiful this scene is! All these movements of a squirrel, grasshoppers, all these sounds of insects reflect so well the state of mind of François and Maria. Many critics have pointed out the effect of blending the human movement into the occasions of nature in Kawabata's novel. Degrees may vary, but the technique is not only Kawabata's. Hémon's description of nature has almost the same effect. Here nature makes a sign with her eyes: the eyes of the squirrel tell us of the *état d'âme* of the two young people; it is as if the animal understood their sentiment. If Shingo's family have 'their' kite to make readers understand what they are thinking, François and Maria have 'their' squirrel in this moment.

The words in their halting conversation are also charged with hidden implications. François said almost in a whisper, 'I am going down to Grand'Mère next week to work on the lumber dam. But I will never take a glass, not one, Maria!'[43] This last phrase (*Mais je ne prendrai pas un coup, Maria, pas un coup*)[44] may be interpreted on the surface level as François's resolution to lead a good and normal life. Needless to say, in the context of the story these words should be interpreted as his proposal to Maria: 'Will you marry me? I'll work, I'll get money, but I'll never drink.' That is what François said and that is what Maria understood, as everyone possessed of heart knows. After a moment François said:

> 'Next spring I shall have more than five hundred dollars saved, clear, and I shall come back …'
> Again he hesitated, and the question he was about to put took another form upon his lips. 'You will be here still … next spring?'
> 'Yes.'[45]

Readers know what his simple question and her simpler answer mean. After that 'they fell silent and so long remained wordless and grave, for they had exchanged vows'. This additional remark by the author only confirms the impression readers have already got.

There are leaps and blanks, but the *fil conducteur* runs through François's words to a squirrel, and from the squirrel's eyes back again to the pair. Readers share the same feeling as François and Maria, all listening to the strident flight of grasshoppers and the clamour of the flies.

Similar scenes are familiar to readers of *The Sound of the Mountain*. They have already seen and heard many insects in Kamakura. There is a large area of silence that surrounds them; and this silence – which may also be called gaps and blanks – is sometimes more powerful than many human utterances. Readers of Kawabata and Hémon all listen to the silence, and many of them have put, unknowingly, a similar question after finishing *The Sound of the Mountain*: 'Kikuko, you will be here still... next spring?'

*Notes*

[1] This paper was delivered at the panel: 'An International and Comparative Perspective on Kawabata Yasunari, ' held at the Asian Centre, University of British Columbia, Canada, 23–25 May 1984. The Japanese version together with other related papers is in Hirakawa and Tsuruta ed.: *Kawabata Yasunari 'Yama no oto' kenkyū* (Tokyo: Meiji-shoin, 1985).

[2] *Kawabata Yasunari zenshū* (Tokyo: Shinchō-sha, 1982) vol. 34, p. 50.

[3] See, for example, Tsuruta Kinya, 'Maboroshi kara utsutsu e' in Hirakawa and Tsuruta ed.: *Kawabata Yasunari 'Yama no oto' kenkyū*, pp. 18–21.

[4] Readers would not like the idea of getting married and living under the same roof with someone like Shingo. It is almost unbelievable that the half deaf old man could hear what was going on in the young couple's bedroom so well. He saw through everything.

[5] Yasunari Kawabata: *The Sound of the Mountain* tr. Edward G. Seidensticker (Tokyo: Tuttle, 1971).

[6] Kawabata Yasunari: *Yama no oto* (Tokyo: Shinchōsha, Shinchō bunko, 1983) p. 6.

[7] *The Sound of the Mountain*, p. 4.

[8] Kawabata Yasunari: *Japan, the Beautiful, and Myself*, tr. Edward G. Seidensticker (Tokyo: Kōdansha, gendaishinsho bilingual edition of *Utsukushii Nihon no watashi*, 1969) p. 72.

[9] *The Sound of the Mountain*, p. 89. The last phrase is my translation. ' – meant that something was about to shake the foundations of his house.' is Seidensticker's translation, which is apparently a mistake. The original reads: *uchi ni yurameku mono ga aru no ka to, Shingo wa kangaeta.* (*Yama no oto*, p. 101). In this case '*uchi*' is not 'his house', it is 'within himself'.

[10]   *The Sound of the Mountain*, p. 210.

[11]   *The Sound of the Mountain*, p.  7.

[12]   *The Sound of the Mountain*, p. 12.

[13]   *The Sound of the Mountain*, p. 14.

[14]   *The Sound of the Mountain*, p. 15.

[15]   *The Sound of the Mountain*, p. 15.

[16]   *The Sound of the Mountain*, p. 54.

[17]   The original reads: *jibun no mirumono o nandemo aiteni miteoite hoshii, sonoyōna koibito o, Shingo wa shōgai ni motta koto ga nakatta.* (*Yama no oto*, p. 61)

[18]   *The Sound of the Mountain*, p. 29.

[19]   The original reads as follows: '*Asukono hagi no mukōni, chō ga tonderudarō. Mieruka.*' 'E. Miemasuyo.' (*Yama no oto*, p. 33).

[20]   *The Sound of the Mountain*, p. 35.

[21]   *The Sound of the Mountain*, p. 93.

[22]   *The Sound of the Mountain*, p. 162.

[23]   *Yama no oto*, p. 186.

[24]   *The Sound of the Mountain*, p. 163.

[25]   *The Sound of the Mountain*, p. 163.

[26]   *The Sound of the Mountain*, p. 163.

[27]   *The Sound of the Mountain*, p. 174.

[28]   *The Sound of the Mountain*, p. 175.

[29]   *The Sound of the Mountain*, p. 249.

[30]   *The Sound of the Mountain*, p. 250.

[31]   *The Sound of the Mountain*, p. 274. The original *haiku* is as follows: *Kyō wa mi o mizu ni makasu ya aki no ayu.* (*Yama no oto*, p. 315)

[32]   The conference was held at the Asian Centre, University of British Columbia, Canada,

[33]   Masao Miyoshi: *Accomplices of Silence* (Berkeley: University of California Press, 1974) p. 104.

[34]   Ibid, p. 104.

[35]   As for Louis Hémon: *Maria Chapdelaine*, I have used the W.H. Blake translation (Toronto:The Macmillan Company of Canada, 1979).

[36]   Translation mine. The original is as follows: *kono shin no enban de, oshibe to meshibe to ga, dō natteirunoka shiranai ga, Shingo wa otoko o kanjita.* (*Yama no oto*, p. 30). Seidensticker's translation is as follows: He did not know whether they were male or not, but somehow he thought them so (*The Sound of the Mountain*, p. 26).

[37]   *Maria Chapdelaine*, p. 50.

[38]   *Maria Chapdelaine*, p. 50.

[39]   *The Sound of the Mountain*, pp. 237–238.

[40]   *The Sound of the Mountain*, p. 238.

[41]   In Hofmannsthal's '*Der Tod des Tizian*' (Death of Titian) one of the ecstatic moments of life is represented by a cluster of mosquitoes. Gianino described the scene as follows (Hofmannsthal: *Gedichte und Dramen*, Frankfurt am Main: S. Fischer Verlag, 1957, p. 62):

In weissen, seidig-weissen Mondesstreifen
War liebestoller Mücken dichter Tanz.

[42] *Maria Chapdelaine,* pp. 56–57.
[43] *Maria Chapdelaine,* pp. 57–58.
[44] Louis Hémon: *Maria Chapdelaine* (Paris: Bernard Grasset, 1954) p. 90.
[45] *Maria Chapdelaine,* p. 58.

# CHANGING WESTERN APPRECIATIONS OF JAPANESE LITERATURE: BASIL HALL CHAMBERLAIN VERSUS ARTHUR WALEY [1]

————————□————————

I should like to make some reflections on the changing positions Japanese literature has occupied in the European mind for the last one hundred years.

Westerners knew very little of Japanese literature throughout the nineteenth century. They knew almost nothing because there was practically no translation of artistic value at that time. Though there had been great Japan scholars like Kaempfer (1651–1715), Thunberg (1743–1828) or Siebold (1796–1866), the existence of Japan itself impinged on the European consciousness after Japan's victory over Russia in 1905. The existence of Japanese literature gradually became known from the 1910s and the 1920s. It was largely through the pen of the great Orientalist, Arthur Waley and his English translation of the *Tale of Genji* (1925–33) that for the first time a work of Japanese literature came to be as highly appreciated as any masterpiece of European literature.

The change in the evaluation of Japanese literature was conspicuous in the 1920s, although that kind of appreciation was limited to the few elite people of the London world of letters. I should like to make some reflections on it as an observer, as it was a very curious phenomenon for the Japanese. Japanese literature had not all of sudden changed in quality. Japanese classical literature, at least, had remained the same in the Japanese language. Then, the problem concerning the change in appreciation would have lain not on the side of Japanese literature itself, but rather on the side of Western interpreters of Japan of the time. It was the European perception of Japanese literature or Japanese culture that had changed. That is the reason why I wish to discuss with those scholars, who will lead Japanese studies in the twenty-first century, not Japanese literature itself, but Western responses to Japanese literature.

In this chapter I will deal, however, with only two people, because both of them were towering figures in Japanese studies and their writings affected decisively Western appreciations of Japanese civilization: one is Basil Hall Chamberlain (1850–1935) and the other is Arthur Waley (1889–1966). In the past, what did the low or high appreciations of Japanese literature mean?

In former times, for most Europeans, European civilization was the only civilization. The word 'civilization' was used for a long time in the singular. It was unthinkable for many Westerners that there could be civilizations other than their own. It was very like the Chinese attitude to their civilization. Besides, in the nineteenth century the Japanese Westernizer Fukuzawa Yukichi (1835–1901) himself thought that way: Europeans had reached a far higher level of civilization. It seemed natural for Japanese to read and translate Western literatures into Japanese, while it was not so for Westerners to take an interest in Japanese literature. Geographically speaking, there were areas other than Western Europe. However, other parts of the world were to be commercially, culturally and even religiously connected with Europe on Europe's own initiative and terms, not vice versa. In the mind of the Westerners of the time, it should be Westerners who initiated any great enterprise on a global scale.

The worldwide movements of the past may be called a kind of globalization before the term existed. It is true that there have been various kinds of globalization movements since the time of the great navigations and discoveries. After the so-called discovery of America by Columbus during the reign of Queen Elizabeth I (1558–1603), Sir Francis Drake succeeded in the circumnavigation of the world (1580). Puck, a mischievous fairy in Shakespeare's *A Midsummer Night's Dream*, written towards the end of the sixteenth century, answers Oberon, the king of fairies: 'I'll put a girdle round about the earth in forty minutes.' It means that the fairy will make a flying tour of the globe in forty minutes. Shakespeare, a contemporary of Drake, was in fact conscious that the earth is round, and the theatre, where his plays were performed, was called the Globe

Theatre. That was the time when in China the Ming Emperor still believed that he was at the centre of the universe which was supposed to be flat and square.

The globalization movements so far have been led mainly by hegemonic powers of the West: global enterprises were sometimes called colonization, Christianization, Westernization, civilization, modernization etc. The Spanish Conquistadors were the first Europeans who tried militarily a global conquest. Jesuits, Fransicans and Dominicans tried spiritually a worldwide 'conquest' by sending missionaries to the five continents of the world, following closely in the footsteps of conquistadors, their compatriots. Colonization in America, Africa and Asia was first justified in the name of Christian evangelization. In course of time, with the separation of state and religion, Europeans began to insist more on the civilizing aspects of European overseas activities. The French called the colonizing efforts *oeuvre de chrétienté*; they called it later *mission civilisatrice*. Kipling, the most popular British poet of the time, wrote the poem 'White Man's burden' and addressed it to the American people, at the turn of the century when the United States took over the administration of the Philippines. It was in fact the beginning of American imperialism under the slogan 'manifest destiny.' The Westernization of non-Western parts of the globe, however, was considered a step towards civilization.

What has been sketched so far is a very rough overview of modern history of the world. In earlier times, white European Christians asserted and behaved as if they alone were civilized people, and there were many reasons for them to believe in their highly privileged cultural position.

One of the reasons that, for them, justify their civilizing mission was that others were perceived as uncivilized. Westerners believed that as one sign of their civilization there is great literature in Europe and America, while there is not in other parts of the world. This notion is even today still very deeply rooted. From time to time, we hear some American professors frankly complain about the nuisance for them of being obliged to teach 'third world literature in translation', of which the literary quality is doubted. Again, we see that in general the Great Books series, Everyman's Library or Modern Library and the like, published by reputable publishing companies of London, New York or Boston, contain almost exclusively works of the Western world. In France, the Pléiade series include very few writers other than writers of the West. It is a recent trend in undergraduate instruction that stress is being laid on the integration of non-Western cultures into general education programmes in the United States. It was natural, then, that a century ago literary works of other parts of the world were neglected by the Western general reader.

Then, how about scholars and specialists? What the most authoritative Japan specialist of the West wrote about Japanese literature in 1902 will flatly answer questions such as: Is Japanese literature really worthwhile for you to study? Here is the general appreciation of that Japan specialist at the turn of the century. In *Things Japanese* (fourth edition, 1902), Basil Hall Chamberlain concludes his article on 'Literature' as follows:

> Sum total: what Japanese literature most lacks is genius. It lacks thought, logical grasp, depth, breadth, and many-sidedness. It is too timorous, too narrow to compass great things. Perhaps the Court atmosphere and predominantly feminine influence in which it was nursed for the first few centuries of its existence stifled it, or else the fault may have lain with the Chinese formalism in which it grew up. But we suspect that there was some original sin of weakness as well. Otherwise the clash of India and China with old mythological Japan, of Buddhism with Shinto, of imperialism with feudalism, and of all with Catholicism in the sixteenth century and with Dutch ideas a little later, would have produced more important results. If Japan has given us no music, so also has she given us no immortal verse, neither do her authors atone for lack of substance by any special beauties of form. But Japanese literature has occasional graces, and is full of incidental scientific interest. The intrepid searcher for facts and 'curios' will, therefore, be rewarded if he has the courage to devote to it the study of many years. A certain writer has said that 'it should be left to a few missionaries to plod their way through the wilderness of the Chinese language to the deserts of Chinese literature.' Such a sweeping condemnation is unjust in the case of Chinese. It would be unjust in that of Japanese also, even with all deductions made.[2]

If one accepts the low opinion of Japanese literature as expressed in this small Encyclopedia Japonica, one will be discouraged from continuing the study of Japanese literature. Some people will find Chamberlain's view badly jaundiced, but some will agree with him, finding his view not wholly unjustified.

As to the 'Language' the same author writes as follows:

> Japanese – with its peculiar grammar, its uncertain affinities, its ancient literature – is a language worthy of more attention than it has yet received. We say 'language'; but 'languages' would be more strictly correct, the modern colloquial speech having diverged from the old classical tongue almost to the same extent as Italian has diverged from Latin. The Japanese

still employ in their books, and even in correspondence and advertisements, a style which is partly classical and partly artificial. This is what is termed the 'Written Language'. The student, therefore, finds himself confronted with a double task. Add to this the necessity of committing to memory two syllabaries, one of which has many variant forms, and at least two or three thousand Chinese ideographs in forms standard and cursive, – ideographs, too, most of which are susceptible of three or four different readings according to circtumstances, – add further that all these categories of written symbols are apt to be encountered pell-mell on the same page, and the task of mastering Japanese becomes almost Herculean.[3]

It is these facts that discourage most learners, but the best continue. Basil Hall Chamberlain, by insisting on the difficulty of mastering Japanese, tells us consciously or unconsciously that he himself is a Herculean hero in the field of Japanese studies, as he has mastered the language or the languages. When *Things Japanese* was published for the first time in 1890, the author was, according to the frontispiece, 'Professor of Japanese and Philology in the Imperial University of Japan'. This was something unprecedented for a foreigner to achieve.[4]

What sort of a man was Basil Hall Chamberlain? He wrote as follows in his '*Quelques souvenirs personnels en manière de préface*' to the French translation (1927) of his *Things Japanese*:

Né de parents anglais, je fus élevé en France et, sans parler de brefs séjours en Italie, en Grèce, en Allemagne, je passai toute ma dix-huitième annéee en Espagne, vivant exclusivement dans la société d'Espagnols. Ainsi mon adolescence m'avait fourni un arrière-plan d'expériences cosmopolites, et, lorsqu'en mai 1873, alors dans ma vingt-troisième année, j'abordai au Japon, j'étais assez bien préparé à étudier en toute liberté d'esprit un nouveau pays étranger. Je me mis aussitôt à l'œuvre, profitant de tous mes loisirs et des longs mois de vacances que donne la carrière universitaire qui était devenue la mienne, pour parcourir le Japon dans tous les sens …

Après dix-huit années consécutives de cette vie, je publiai, en 1891, en même temps que le Guide Murray du Japon, l'édition anglaise des *Things Japanese* (Choses japonaises), petite encyclopédie ou mieux, recueil d'essais toujours brefs traduits ici sous le titre de *Mœurs et Coutumes du Japon*. Plusieurs éditions suivirent, chacune d'elles comportant de nombreuses modifications afin de tenir le livre à jour, la transformation du Japon ayant été, comme on le sait kaléidoscopique, – pourtant beaucoup demeurait du passé …[5]

George Sansom (1883–1965), who had begun his career of Japan specialist first as a student interpreter in the English legation in Tokyo, then diplomat and later the authoritative historian of Japan, probably being an Englishman of humbler origin, was very much impressed with Chamberlain's background, his authoritative attitude, his erudition, and his Britishness.[6] However, is Chamberlain's educational background, as is referred to in the preface, really so impressive?

Here is additional biographical notice of Basil Hall Chamberlain gathered from sources such as his letters to his Japanese secretary Sugiura Tōshirō,[7] and reminiscences of those who attended the memorial meeting for Basil Hall Chamberlain.[8]

Basil Hall Chamberlain was born at Southsea on 18 October 1850. His father was an admiral in the British Navy and his grandfather, Sir Henry Orlando Chamberlain, represented Britain at Rio de Janeiro. On his mother's side he was descended from a lowland Scottish family, the Halls of Dunglass. Her father, Captain Basil Hall, R. N. was one of the first Europeans to visit the Luchu Islands and the coast of Korea, of which he published an account. On the death of his mother, Basil Hall Chamberlain with his two brothers went to live with his grandmother, Lady Chamberlain, at Versailles. He was educated there by English tutors and a German governess and at the Lycée de Versailles. Thus early in life he became fluent in two foreign languages, and his knowledge was further widened when he went at the age of seventeen to spend a year in Spain. He came to Japan in 1873 at the age of twenty-three. Chamberlain's prestige as the leading authority on things Japanese lasted for almost half a century after his publication in 1882 of the translation of the *Kojiki*, the oldest Japanese book compiled in 712, even though he retired to Geneva in 1911. It should be noted that the young Chamberlain was rejected by Oxford University on account of his poor health; that may explain why he later put so much importance on his title of Emeritus Professor at the Imperial University of Tokyo. It was a kind of psychological recompense for a frustrated youth. In fact, contrary to the impression one gets from what he says about his '*carrière universitaire*', he taught there only for four years, and the exceptional honour was accorded to the forty-year-old dean of Western Japan specialists residing in Japan. He firmly believed in the superiority of the British. As a descendent of glorious nation-builders, Chamberlain attached great importance to the British Empire. In his last book written in French, *Encore est vive la souris*,[9] Chamberlain humorously and anachronistically made the comment that if the British were so foolish as to throw away India, the Russians or, better, the Japanese could take care of that colony instead. Of a conservative cast of mind, Chamberlain was, of course, against the independence of Ireland.[10]

One of the first Westerners[11] who had serious doubts about Chamberlain's statements concerning Japanese literature and the Japanese language was Arthur Waley. He was thirty-nine years younger than Chamberlain, and he began to study Chinese and Japanese when he entered the British Museum in 1913. Laurence Binyon, his sympathetic chief at the Department of Prints and Drawings, encouraged him to study the languages of East Asia. At that time as there was no school to learn these languages in London, Waley learnt them by himself, exchanging lessons with Japanese residing in London. Among them were the future radar specialist Yagi Hidetsugu and the painter Makino Yoshio. As Waley was able to use books in the British Museum's Department of Printed Books, he must have read through many of Chamberlain's Japanese studies, among them were *The Classical Poetry of the Japanese*,[12] and his translation of the *Kojiki* (Records of Ancient Matters).[13]

Chamberlain's attitude was summarized as follows by Richard Bowring (1991):

> Not that he was afraid to have strong opinions. Indeed, one of the attractions of his writing is that, although reticent in some respects, he is often willing to be open and candid. In common with most Englishmen in Japan, he considered that his role as educator was justified and self-evident. By and large it was obvious that Europeans had reached a far higher level of civilization and that in most things they 'knew better' than the Japanese.[14]

Chamberlain's evaluation of *Kojiki* (712) as a work of art is that

> ... there is no beauty of style, to preserve some trace of which he (the translator) may be tempted to sacrifice a certain amount of accuracy. The Records sound queer and bald in Japanese, as will be noticed further on; and it is therefore right, even from a stylistic point of view, that they should sound bald and queer in English.[15]

Then, he adds a typically Victorian comment: 'The only portions of the text which, from obvious reasons, refuse to lend themselves to translation into English after this fashion (of a rigid and literal conformity with the Japanese text) are the indecent portions.'[16]

His low opinion of Japanese literature continues. In *Things Japanese* Chamberlain shows the same attitude in the article 'Literature', from the first edition of 1890 through the sixth edition of 1939.[17] He is adamant in his critical judgement. The 'Collection of a Myriad Leaves' referred to is the first anthology of *uta*-poems, *Manyōshū* (circa 760):

> And now it may be asked: What is the value of this Japanese literature – so ancient, so voluminous, locked up in so recondite a written character? We

repeat what we have already said of the 'Collection of a Myriad Leaves', – that it is invaluable to the philologist, the archaeologist, the historian, the student of curious manners which have disappeared or are fast disappearing. We may add that there are some clever and many pretty things in it.[18]

At the early stage of his Japanese studies, Waley had the good luck to read the manuscripts of Japanese Nō plays, translated by Fenollosa and Hirata. Ezra Pound who edited the manuscripts asked Waley to peruse them. It was in 1915.[19] Interested by the world of Nō theatre, Waley himself began his own translation of *Nō Plays of Japan* together with a very detailed introduction, which was the result of his analytical study of Zeami's dramaturgy. To conclude his introduction Waley adds two remarks, first:

> And if I have failed to make these translations in some sense works of art
> – if they are merely philology, not literature – then I have indeed fallen
> short of what I hoped and intended.[20]

This credo of the scholar-translator Waley is apparently different from the philologist Chamberlain. The second remark is in a sense more impressive:

> The libretti of Greek tragedy have won for themselves a separate existence
> simply as poetic literature. Yet even of them it has been said that 'the words
> are only part of the poem'. Still less did the words of Nō constitute the
> whole 'poem', yet if some cataclysm were to sweep away the Nō theatre, I
> think the plays (as literature) would live.

These are general remarks, in which Chamberlain's name is not directly mentioned. However, it is already clear that Waley from the very beginning did not have a low opinion of Japanese literature.[21]

Waley, while studying Japanese *uta*-poems, got an impression quite different from Chamberlain's. First against the so-called difficulty of mastering the classical Japanese, Waley writes as follows:

> The translations in this book are chiefly intended to facilitate the study of
> the Japanese text; for Japanese poetry can only be rightly enjoyed in the
> original. And since the classical language has an easy grammar and limited
> vocabulary, a few months should suffice for the mastering of it. The reader
> who wishes to pursue this study further should learn the Japanese syllabary
> and some (perhaps about 600) of the commoner Chinese characters. He
> will then be able to use the native texts.[22]

People say that this is true for a genius like Waley but not for scholars in general, even above average. However, what Waley writes is, in fact, a very common sense view of the classical Japanese as used in the *uta* in terms of statistics. As for the limited vocabulary and the number of Chinese characters,[23] numerical facts show the truth of Waley's comments. If other students do not accept what Waley says here, it is because so much has been said about the difficulty of mastering the Japanese language. Many people take what Waley says here only as a sign of his exceptional linguistic capability. However, it could have been that Waley's comment was a sort of antidote to what Chamberlain and the like had exaggerated. The simple fact is it was not necessary for a young Japanese girl of the Meiji period like Yosano Akiko with her limited education (she had never got a university education) to make any Herculean efforts to appreciate the *uta* or the *Genji monogatari*.

Seidensticker, who re-translated the *Tale of Genji* in 1976, stated six years later that to decipher is not the same as to read, and he insisted on the meaning of pace in narrative literature. Around the year 1890 the precocious Akiko caught that pace as early as in her teens, as had the authoress of the *Sarashina nikki* at the age of thirteen in 1020.

Waley's second point of disagreement with Chamberlain concerns the manner of Chamberlain's translation. In *Japanese Poetry, The 'Uta'* Waley lists chronologically nine European books to be consulted. The ninth is B. H. Chamberlain, *Japanese Poetry*, 1911. Here Waley adds the following comment:

> Very free verse translations from the *Manyō* and *Kokin*, in this style:
> I muse on the old-world story,
>     As the boats glide to and fro,
> Of the fisher-boy Urashima,
>     Who a-fishing lov'd to go.

Waley was not satisfied with this manner of translating, like a Victorian jingle, regular, stressed metres, onomatopoeic noises.[24] In 1929, Waley translated the poem in question in his article 'The Originality of Japanese Civilization.'[25] This monograph was written for the British group attending the Conference of the Institute of Pacific Relations at Kyoto in October, 1929. Probably someone of the group had asked Waley to give them a different view of Japan from the one widespread by Chamberlain that Japanese civilization is purely derivative. According to Chamberlain apart from bathtubs, 'almost all other Japanese institutions have their root in China'.[26]

The eighth-century ballad of the *Manyōshū* begins this way in Waley's article:

> One day in spring
> Watching upon a tall cliff all alone
> I saw the fishing boats rocking and rocking
> Down in the misty bay, and to my mind there came
> This tale of long ago.

This is the English translation of the long poem '*Haru no hi no kasumeru sora ni, Sumi-no-e no …*' which Lafcadio Hearn recited to himself so often in the Japanese original that finally his wife also learnt it by heart.[27] Waley writes:

> Perhaps the most completely unique and original poems which it (the *Manyōshū*) contains are the narrative poems which Europeans, for want of a better term, have usually called ballads, though in their smooth grace they are far indeed removed from the poetry that the West has called by this name. Of these the most celebrated is *The Fisher-Boy of Urashima*, which I here give in a new version, since the rhymed one by Professor Chamberlain seems to me unsatisfactory. It is, however, impossible in English to do justice to the delicate, undulating movement which pervades the original from the first line to the last.[28]

Waley, however, gave the name of Beryl de Zoete as the translator of the ballad in the article. As his lady companion never learnt Japanese, it was impossible for her to translate it. What was the meaning of this act? Had Beryl de Zoete polished a rough translation prepared by Waley or did Waley ask Beryl to lend her name to avoid a direct confrontation with the aged Chamberlain, whose scholarly pride had already been wounded?

It is true, though, that Chamberlain had lost face: no one had shattered so completely the credibility of Chamberlain's scholarship as Waley, the English translator of the *Tale of Genji*. Beginning, first, with what Chamberlain had to say about the *Genji Monogatari* in various editions of his *Things Japanese*, then, second, what was said about the *Tale of Genji* when Waley's translation was published in six volumes from 1925 onwards.

In the first edition (1890) of *Things Japanese* the *Genji Monogatari* is referred to, in the article 'Literature', as 'the most celebrated of all, chiefly on account of its ornate style,'[29] and after praising Jippensha Ikku, 'the Rabelais of Japan', Chamberlain continues:

> On the other hand, much of that which the Japanese themselves prize most highly in their literature seems intolerably flat and insipid to the European taste. The romances – most of them – are every bit as dull as the histories, though in another way. The histories are too brief, the romances too long-winded. If the authoress of the *Genji Monogatari*, though lauded to the skies by her compatriots, has been branded by Georges Bousquet as *cette ennuyeuse Scudéry japonaise*, she surely richly deserves it.[30]

Mademoiselle Scudéry (1607?–1701) the French novelist had one of the chief literary salons of Paris in the time of Louis XIV. She wrote two long pseudo-historical novels, full of fashionable sentiment and preciosity: *Artamène* and *Clélie*. Although once translated into English, they had long been forgotten. Chamberlain, in insinuating that Lady Murasaki is a bore, adroitly avoids his own responsibility as a literary critic, by quoting the French jurist Georges Bousquet's low opinion of the authoress of the *Genji Monogatari*. Bousquet was a French jurist who came to Japan as early as 1872 at the age of twenty-six, as a legal adviser to the new Meiji government. Whether Bousquet had really read *Genji Monogatari* in the Japanese original is most unlikely. There was already a translation available. In 1882 *Genji Monogatari*, of which the first seventeen chapters were translated by Suematsu Kenchō,[31] was published by Trübner, London. It is a kind of Victorian paraphrase of the Japanese classic in which all sexual matters are carefully expurgated. You may call that adaptation really *ennuyeuse*. At any rate, the problem with some of Chamberlain's judgements is: – in righting the Europeans, he seems to continually wrong Japanese literature.

Chamberlain, indeed, was persistent in his low opinion of *Genji Monogatari*. From the fourth edition (1902) of *Things Japanese*, he adds the following footnote in small letters, always relying on opinions of British diplomatists:

Sir Ernest Satow's judgment of the *Genji Monogatari* agrees with ours. 'The plot,' writes he, 'is devoid of interest, and it is only of value as marking a stage in the development of the language.' Fairness, however, requires that the very different estimate of this work formed by Mr. Aston, the accomplished historian of Japanese literature, should be here cited. He writes as follows: 'I do not profess to have read more than a small part of this portentously long romance, but judging from a study of a few books of it, the above condemnations appear to me undeserved. The ornate style to which these adverse critics object consists chiefly in the honorific terminations of the verbs, as natural to a courtly dialect as the gorgeous but cumbrous costumes and the elaborate ceremonial of the palace. There is no superabundance of descriptive adjectives or anything to correspond to our word-painting. The want of interest complained of seems to me to proceed from a misunderstanding of the writer's object. She was not bent on producing a highly wrought plot or sensational story. Her object was to interest and amuse her readers by a picture of real life, and of the sentiments and doings of actual men and women. There is no exaggeration in the *Genji*, no superfine morality, and none of the fine writing that abounds in modern Japanese fiction. What Murasaki-no-Shikibu did for Japanese literature was to add to it a new kind of composition, viz. the novel, or epic, of real life as it has been called. She was the Richardson of Japan, and her genius resembled his in many ways. She delighted specially in delineating types of womanhood. Indeed, the whole work may be regarded as a series of pictures of this kind, drawn with minute care, and from a full knowledge of her subject-matter. She does not deal in broad strokes of the pen. Her method is to produce graphic and realistic effects by numerous touches of detail. This is, however, incompatible with simplicity of style. Her sentences are long and somewhat complicated, and this with the antique language and the difference of manners and customs constitutes a very serious difficulty to the student. The *Genji* is not an easy book either to us or to the author's modern fellowcountrymen. The labour of mastering its meaning is probably one reason why it is not more appreciated. As a picture of a long past state of society, there is nothing in the contemporary European literature which can for a moment be compared with it. It contains a host of personages from Mikados down to the lowest court attendants to elucidate whose genealogy the standard *Kogetsushō* edition has devoted a whole volume. Its scene is laid sometimes in Kyoto, but also changes to Hiyeizan, Suma, and other places in the neighbourhood. A whole calendar of court ceremonies might be compiled from it. If we remember that it was written long before Chaucer, Dante, and Boccaccio shone on the horizon of European literature, it will appear a truly remarkable performance.'[32]

Chamberlain's treatment seems fair on the surface level, as he refers to two Japan specialists of different opinions apart from Bousquet. Yet his 'fairness' has its limits: this self-styled cosmopolitan does not listen to non-European opinions. He believes himself to be alien to patriotism. However, for a European like him who believes a priori in the supremacy of European civilization it is difficult not to be a culturally patriotic European. One should know that there is latently a dangerous cultural nationalism: that nationalism which later on was called Euro-centrism which threatens non-Europeans.

Moreover, as is generally the rule, some Europeans who reside abroad for long years tend to idealize Europe: the so-called complex of superiority peculiar to those who live in a foreign settlement. That condescending tendency must have been exacerbated in the case of Chamberlain, as Japanese adulators lionized him. *Things Japanese* is an interesting book, as it reflects many topics talked about among the Western residents in port-cities such as Yokohama and Kobe. Here is an announcement of 'New Edition of a Famous Book' in the *Japan Weekly Chronicle*. The reprint of the fifth edition, revised with the addition of two appendices, appeared in September 1927:

*Things Japanese* remains as good reading as when it was first issued. The fund of learning and research that go to the making of the book is pleasantly concealed under a lightness of touch and a picturesqueness of presentation which make it not only a storehouse of information on all that concerns Japan but also a piece of literature ...

The wealth of information contained in the book makes it indispensable to all interested in Japan. He who reads the book through, from the first page to the last, and has a memory retentive enough to enable him to remember the contents, will receive a liberal education, not only in things Japanese but also in what may be called comparative sociology.[33]

The reprint must have delighted the 77-year-old Chamberlain. The book, moreover, was going to be translated into French. Nevertheless, because of his too great confidence in his ability to produce balanced judgements, Chamberlain ends up by being fatally flawed.

When Waley's translation of the first volume appeared in May 1925, the *Times Literary Supplement* wholeheartedly welcomed the *Tale of Genji*:

A Japanese masterpiece ... The wonderful beauty of this first fragment ... In it a forgotten civilization comes to life with a completeness which is surpassed only by the greatest of our novelists, and with a beauty of arrangement which it would be very hard to find surpassed anywhere.[34]

With the publication of the *Tale of Genji* in six volumes by George Allen & Unwin Ltd., Japanese literature made its debut on the centre court of world literature. When Part II, *The Sacred Tree*, appeared in February, the next year, the *Observer* said:

We surrender ourselves to equal sensations of astonishment and captivity ... Lady Murasaki practically fashioned the instrument she uses with such unfaltering art. This fact alone is enough to make the book a wonder.

The *Times* said:

Clearly one of the great pieces of fiction. The skill and grace of Mr. Waley's translation are evident enough. The prose of this second volume is a constant delight.

Praises are showered upon both the author and the translator. The *Saturday Review* admired:

The omnipresent sense of beauty is the great delight of Murasaki's novel ... As a novelist she is remarkably well equipped. Her sympathy rarely fails her, nor does the delicacy and sureness of her touch ... Mr. Waley's translation is marvelous for the subtlety, precision and beauty of its language.

About Part III, published in February 1927, the *Daily Express* joined other papers in praise of the translator, although the reviewer had no knowledge of Japanese:

To anyone who has not had the luck to read the previous two volumes, the beauty of this book will come as rather staggering. Mr.Waley has translated it into English that is classic in its beauty ... One of the few translations in our language that have all the stamp of original genius.

About the 'modern voice' of the work, the *Evening Standard* said as follows after the publication of Part IV in may 1928:

It is simply marvellous in beauty and truth, and so modern, both in feeling and in technique, that it might have been written yesterday.

Four years had passed when in June 1932 Part V, *Lady of the Boat*, appeared. In the *Daily Telegraph* the novelist and critic Rebecca West compares the Japanese authoress with European authors:

Knowledge of this book adds the same pleasure to life as knowledge of, say, the works of Shakespeare or Jane Austen or Proust.

When, finally, the last volume of the *Tale of Genji,* that is, Part VI *the Bridge of Dreams*, appeared in May 1933, Waley himself commented:

It certainly contains the finest 150 pages[35] in the whole book, and it has been very exciting to get to grips with this part at last. But the greater emotional intensity of this part makes it far harder to do, and it often takes three or four hours to do a single page.[36]

Chamberlain lived in Geneva for almost twenty-three years after his return from Japan in 1912 until his death at the age of eighty-four in 1935. Long forgotten in London, he was twice called before his death 'the late professor Chamberlain' in newspapers; that news was the reason why Chamberlain gave the ironic title to his last book *Encore est vive la souris* in 1933, quoting a verse from Charles d'Orléans. The octogenarian knew, however, that an exceptional reception was being given to the Waley translation of *Genji* in the London world of letters. Chamberlain was now obliged to say something to save face. In the last posthumous edition of *Things Japanese* (1939) he therefore left the following words: 'Very various have been the judgments passed on this celebrated work by competent European critics,'[37] and adds the following footnote:

Mr. Arthur Waley's beautiful English version in six volumes will henceforth enable the cultivated European reader to form his own opinion on the matter, so far, that is, as literary opinion can be founded on a translation.[38] We ourselves formerly accepted Satow's view. But of late years we have come to doubt whether we thoroughly understood the exceptionally difficult text. A Japanese student of European literature might do wisely by abstaining from any judgment on the merits of Browning, Mallarmé, or Jean Paul.[39]

As a Japanese student of Robert Browning, I cannot help smiling, hearing the proud scholar-imperialist Chamberlain's last *makeoshimi*, his unwillingness to own his life-long mistake. *Genji monogatari* or Browning's *Men and Women* are not that difficult. Although there are many scholars everywhere whose false pride prevents them from acknowledging themselves to be in the wrong, there are also those who recognize more objectively what were the drawbacks of Japanese studies in Chamberlain's generation and what were the eye-opening contributions of Arthur Waley. When the great scholar poet passed away on 27 June 1966, the *Times* wrote as follows:

> Arthur Waley did more by the elegance, the vitality and lucidity of his translations from the Chinese and Japanese to introduce the English-speaking world to the literature and civilization of the Far East than anyone of his generation. He freed oriental studies from the charge of pedantry and distortion of patronage which afflicted them in the later nineteenth century, and brought them into the main stream of intelligent reading.

Indeed, more than anyone else, it was a single individual, Arthur Waley and his masterpiece in English, the *Tale of Genji* that so thoroughly changed the Western appreciation of Japanese literature.

*Notes*

[1] This paper was given as a keynote speech at the first annual conference of the Swedish School of Advanced Asia-Pacific Studies which was held at Göteborg, Sweden, 26 September 2002.
[2] Basil Hall Chamberlain: *Things Japanese* (London: John Murray, 1902), p. 294.
[3] Ibid. p. 276.
[4] In the second edition (1891) he was 'Emeritus Professor of Japanese and Philology in the Imperial University of Japan'. That means Chamberlain had already given up the post of professorship of the only university that existed in Japan at the age of forty. From the third edition (1898) through the sixth edition (1939) of *Things Japanese* Basil Hall Chamberlain was 'Emeritus Professor of Japanese and Philology in the Imperial University of Tokyo'. 'Of Tokyo' was added, as other imperial universities had been created in the meantime.
[5] Basil Hall Chamberlain: *Mœurs et coutumes du Japon* (Paris: Payot, 1931, tr. Marc Logé) préface.
[6] As for Sansom's view of Chamberlain, apart from his well known address delivered at the School of Oriental and African Studies, reproduced in the *Journal of Asian Studies*, 1965, pp. 563–567, see his lecture given

in Japanese on the occasion of the memorial meeting for Chamberlain, entitled 'Nihon kenkyūsha no tenkei to shiteno Chenbaren sensei' in Kokusai bunka shinkōkai ed.: *Baziru Hōru Chenbaren sensei tsuitō kinen roku* (Tokyo: Kokusai bunka shinkōkai, 1935).

[7] Chamberlain's letters to Sugiura Tōshirō, especially the letter dated 12 July 1915, Aichi kyōiku daligaku, Chenbaren bunko.

[8] Kokusai bunka shinkōkai ed.: *Baziru Hōru Chenbaren sensei tsuitō kinen roku* (Tokyo: Kokusai bunka shinkōkai, 1935), see especially lectures delivered by Rear Admiral Kimura Kōichi, G.B.Sansom, Professor Ichikawa Sanki and Sasaki Nobutsuna.

[9] Basil Hall Chamberlain: *Encore est vive la souris :Pensées et réflexions* (Lausanne: Square, 1933). My translation is based on its Japanese translation, *Nezumi wa mada ikiteiru* (Tokyo: Iwanami shoten, 1939), p. 97.

[10] *Nezumi wa mada ikiteiru,* pp. 18–19.

[11] One of the first Westerners who had strong doubts about Chamberlain was Lafcadio Hearn (1850–1904). He could not agree at all with Chamberlain's statements concerning Japanese music and religion. Their disagreements are worth a more serious study. About Chamberlain's highhanded attitude, Fenollosa also was extremely critical. He compared Hearn's attitude towards the Japanese and Chamberlain's as 'sympathy versus ridicule'. See Yamaguchi Seiichi: *Fenorosa,* (Tokyo: Sanseidō, 1985) vol. 2, p. 145. As neither Hearn nor Fenollosa was competent in Japanese, they could not judge Chamberlain's statements concerning Japanese literature and language. Those who wish to know more about Basil Hall Chamberlain and his relationship with Lafcadio Hearn, see Hirakawa Sukehiro: *Yaburareta Yūjō: Hān to Chenbaren no Nihon rikai* (Tokyo: Shinchōsha, 1987). Yuzo Ota: *Basil Hall Chamberlain, Portrait of a Japanologist* (Folkestone, Kent: Japan Library, 1998) is a book written in defense of Chamberlain.

[12] Basil Hall Chamberlain: *The Classical Poetry of the Japanese* (London: Trübner, 1880). Waley read its enlarged edition, entitled *Japanese Poetry* (London: Murray, 1911).

[13] Basil Hall Chamberlain: *A Translation of the 'Kojiki' or 'Records of Ancient Matters'* (Yokohama: Asiatic Society of Japan, 1883).

[14] Richard Bowring, 'Basil Hall Chamberlain' in Hugh Cortazzi and Gordon Daniels ed.: *Britain and Japan 1859–1991* (London: Routledge, 1991), p. 133.

[15] *The Kojiki, Records of Ancient Matters,* tr.B. H. Chamberlain (Tokyo: Charles E. Tuttle Co, 1981), Translator's Introduction, p. iv.

[16] *The Kojiki, Records of Ancient Matters,* p. iv.

[17] Chamberlain's manuscript for the sixth posthumous edition (1939) had been written by 1934. He died on 15th February, 1935.

[18] Basil Hall Chamberlain: *Things Japanese,* sixth edition revised (London: Kegan Paul, Trench, Trubner, 1939) p. 319.

[19] We know from a letter of Pound's that Waley first visited Pound in June

1915 to help him with the editing the texts of the Nō left by Fenollosa. See H. Carpenter: *A Serious Character: The Life of Ezra Pound*, (London: Faber and Faber, 1988), p. 279.

[20] Arthur Waley: *The Nō Plays of Japan* (London: George Allen & Unwin, 1921), p. 55.

[21] However, Waley categorically denies poetical value of pieces included in *Kojiki* and *Nihongi*. Waley says in his introduction to *Japanese Poetry, The 'Uta'* (Clarendon Press, 1919): – 'Of the two hundred and thirty-five poems contained in these two chronicles, not one is of any value as literature.' Considering Waley's open appreciation of Nō plays and folkloric elements in poetry, this negative evaluation of poems in the *Kojiki* and *Nihongi* is perplexing. I personally am of quite a different opinion. For example, the poem of the cup pledge by the Empress Suserihime (Vol. I, Sect. XXV) is reminiscent of the coplas of Southern Spain which Waley quotes in his article on 'The Originality of Japanese Civilization': 'Tu querer es como el toro, / Donde lo llaman, va; / Y el mio como la piedra, / Donde la ponen, s'esta.'

[22] Arthur Waley: *Japanese Poetry, The 'Uta'* (Honolulu: The University Press of Hawaii, 1976) p. 12.

[23] As for the numbers of nouns, verbs and adjectives used in *uta*-anthologies such as *Manyōshū*, *Kokinshū* and *Gosenwakashū*, see Miyajima Tatsuo ed. *Koten taishō goi hyō*, (Tokyo: Kasama-shoin, 1972). Waley's view is valid for *uta*-anthologies such as *Kokinshū* and *Gosenwakashū*, while it is not so for *Manyōshū* that has a vocabulary three times richer than that of *Kokinshū* and *Gosenwakashū*. The latter two *uta*-anthologies have about 1000 nouns and less than 700 verbs each. A limited vocabulary, indeed. As for words of Chinese origin, they are less than 0.3% of the vocabulary used in the three *uta*-anthologies.

[24] Interesting remarks concerning poetical devices used by the older generation of Japanologists are made by Carmen Blacker in her 'Introduction to the new edition' of Arthur Waley: *Japanese Poetry, The 'Uta'* (1919), (Honolulu: An East-West Center Book, the University Press of Hawaii, 1976), rpt., p. vii.

[25] Arthur Waley: *The Originality of Japanese Civilization* (Oxford University Press, 1929). The article was reproduced in Kokusai Bunka Shinkokai ed.: *KBS Bulletin on Japanese Culture*, (Tokyo: Kokusai Bunka Shinkokai), No.78, June-July 1966 issue, pp. 1–5.

[26] Basil Hall Chamberlain insists on the view that the Japanese are 'a nation of imitators' at the beginning of *The Classical Poetry of the Japanese* (London: Trübner, 1880). His remark is amusing, but Chamberlain's preference for central civilizations is misleading. Waley had a more balanced view of various civilizations of the world, which may be related to his non-Christian origin. Although of Jewish descent, Waley himself was an agnostic. His view concerning religions and superstitions is also very interesting. When Ivan Morris makes a valiant attempt to define the difference

between religion and superstition, Waley says: 'I would prefer simply to say that "superstition" is any belief that the speaker thinks silly.' See Arthur Waley, 'Review of Ivan Morris's *The World of the Shining Prince*' in I. Morris ed.: *Madly Singing in the Mountains, an appreciation and anthology of Arthur Waley* (London: George Allen & Unwin, 1970), p. 375.

[27] This episode was recorded in Hearn's wife's reminiscences. See Koizumi Setsuko, 'Omoide no ki' in Tanabe Ryūji: *Koizumi Yakumo* (Tokyo: Hokuseidō, reprint 1980) p. 160.

[28] *The Originality of Japanese Civilization* (KBS ed.) p. 3.

[29] Basil Hall Chamberlain: *Things Japanese* (London: John Murray, 1890) p. 209.

[30] Ibid.

[31] At that time the translator spelled his name as Suyematz Kenchio.

[32] Basil Hall Chamberlain: *Things Japanese* (London: Murray, 1902), pp. 294–295.

[33] 29 September 1927 issue of the *Japan Weekly Chronicle*.

[34] I partially reproduce here the reviews cited on the covers of the six volumes of the *Tale of Genji* of the 1920s and 30s (London: George Allen & Unwin).

[35] For the translation of the last ten chapters Waley used mainly Kaneko Motoomi's edition (Tokyo: Meiji shoin) as is mentioned by Waley himself in Volumes V (preface) and VI (introduction) of the first edition of the *Tale of Genji*. Waley relies also on Yoshizawa Yoshinori's translation in modern Japanese, (Vols. VIII and IX of *Zenyaku Ōchō bungaku sōsho*, 1927), which are now in the Durham University library. From Waley's marginal notes on many pages it is apparent that Waley used also this modern Japanese version by Yoshizawa, while translating 'the finest 150 pages' in question.

[36] For somewhat more detailed information concerning the reviews and their sources, see Ruth Perlmutter's doctoral dissertation, *Arthur Waley and His Place in the Modern Movement between the Two Wars* (UMI, 1971), and Roger Thomas's 'A *Genji* Bibliography: Non-Japanese sources', *Yearbook of Comparative and General Literature*, xxxi, 1982, pp. 68–75.

[37] Basil Hall Chamberlain: *Things Japanese*, sixth edition revised (London: Kegan Paul, Trench, Trubner, 1939) p. 319, note.

[38] Concerning the question of Waley's translation, the remark by George Sansom may be quoted here. The British scholar-diplomat writes in his *Japan, A Short Cultural History* (London: Cresset Press, 1931, p. 235 n.) that Waley's modern English is 'incomparably richer, stronger, more various and supple than Heian Japanese'. The remark shows how Sansom was amazed reading Waley's English translation, that reversed the general low opinion of Lady Murasaki's *Tale of Genji*. It had been held in low esteem until then by leading British Japan specialists, as has already been seen. There is, however, some truth in what Sansom says about the richness of

the modern English used by Waley. Our question should be: Is Waley's translation totally different from the Japanese original? Is not every reading of a work of literature a kind of new translation? There are as many possible readings of a work of literature as there are as many inter-pretive readers. As each reader selects different things for attention, a good translator will be someone who knows how to carry the best of the original over into his or her own tongue. Sansom later adds another note to his *Japan, A Short Cultural History* (New York: D. Appleton, 1943, p. 240 n.), praising Waley's translation as 'masterly, and itself comes very near to being a work of creative genius. Is it ungrateful to add that perhaps it does more than justice to the original?'

[39] Basil Hall Chamberlain: *Things Japanese*, sixth edition revised, p. 320, note.

# POSTSCRIPT

It is a common practice in Japan that authors write personal reflections in a postscript to their books. I permit myself, therefore, to write here about the personal background of the author and the geneses of this book.

Over the last sixty years, most academic historical works on modern Japan written directly in English are by those who have studied in the English-speaking world. They have naturally shared certain common attitudes and values with their Western masters, predecessors and colleagues. In terms of academic background they belong to the same circle, however large and varied it may appear.

I was brought up on the other side of that, in the sense that I have never studied at an English-speaking university. Some twenty years ago when I was taxed with being a man brought up on the other side of the East-West divide, I mistook that expression for Cold War terminology, and naïvely answered that I belonged to the free world. The meaning was that while I appreciated much English literature and the language as a communication medium, I was still an ignorant outsider. The only advantage was that I am freer from English-language-centred ways of thinking and attitudes that derive from that training. Furthermore, it provided me with grounds for a comparative study of the 'East' and the 'West'. It is, however, difficult to define what the East is. In the Cold War period, it was easier to define. The walls that divided the two camps were even visible and tangible. Though situated in the East, Japan belonged to the West politically, economically and ideologically. Then how should we define the East and the West, in the case of the East-West divide? What are the invisible walls that separate the two spheres? Western civilization is easier to define as European civilization, while Eastern civilization seems a non-entity, as East corresponding to West in an opposite sense is in reality non-West. I have often used the expression *hi-seiyō* (non-West) in my Japanese books to designate what others emphatically call the East. I have, instead, often used the term East Asia, as there exists such a sphere with distinctive cultural traditions.

In *Japan's Love-Hate Relationship with the West* I have dealt with problems concerning Japan and the West, trying to take East Asia into consideration. Then, why have I come to publish this collection of history-centred essays, writing it in English? Academically, I have led a double life. At Tokyo University, where I worked for twenty-eight years, I belonged primarily to the Romance Languages Department and I taught French and Italian. In Japan, I was known first as the Japanese translator of Dante's *Divine Comedy* (1966). However, my major interest being in intercultural relations, at the Tokyo University Graduate School, I have always taught in the Comparative Cultural History Programme. The topics I have addressed in this book are those that I discussed with my graduate students in the 1970s, '80s and '90s. If, over the years, I have attracted quite a number of students, both Japanese and foreign, the reason may have been in my interpretations that seem to open unexpected vistas, as I have tried to look at intercultural relations, between China and Japan or between the West and Japan, from both sides. As every one is culturally biased, I am not sure if I have really succeeded in my tentative goal.

One of the reasons I wish to publish this book in a language other than my mother tongue is the feeling that there are in this kind of bi-cultural studies many blind spots that are often overlooked. Let me quote, by way of example, a case of ominous chain reactions often ignored on the Anglo-Saxon side. At the beginning of the twentieth century the notion of the 'White Man's burden' was well known throughout the English-speaking world; it was also known among the French-speaking people as *le fardeau de l'Homme Blanc*, while very few people know that Kipling's idea provokingly gave birth to Tokutomi Sohō's 'Yellow Man's burden'. His idea was little known, probably since it was much more modest in its scope than that of Kipling: after Japan's victory over Russia in 1905, Sohō recommended his fellow-countrymen to bear the burden of other Yellow Asians, as they were now trying to liberate themselves from Western colonial rule. Japanese oligarchs, respecting the West-centred *status quo*, did not like Sohō's idea, but the Japanese people at large liked it, and Sohō later became the most influential of the ideologues who led the Japanese nation into that catastrophic Greater East Asia War. There has been an asymmetry not only in our power balances but also in our knowledge and understanding of intercultural relations between the Western world and Japan.

Some aspects of the modern history of Japan bifocally interpreted in this book may give peculiar impressions to readers who are familiar with the US-promoted images of Japan during World War II. Those readers' images of Japan have been created and stamped on their brain, first of all, by repeated wartime propaganda. Moreover, stereotyped notions have been reproduced throughout the years following World War II. One of the worst examples of recreations of this kind – leaning, in fact, towards propagandistic imagery, is Herbert P. Bix's Pulitzer prize-winning book, *Hirohito and the Making of Modern Japan* (New York: Harper-Collins, 2000). I realize that perception gaps are sometimes inevitable. First of all, when ideology works too strongly, it is almost impossible not to reach conclusions beforehand. Preconceived ideas should be challenged with primary source materials. To maintain a language-mediated, first-hand study of primary texts requires the greatest patience. Second, what I would like to point out is that when scholars rely heavily on secondary materials written or translated into English, there will ensue a kind of vicious circle, reproducing ideas and images which are clichés. This is a kind of academic autointoxication, and a transfusion of new blood seems necessary. What is extremely disappointing is that some American Japan scholars have forgotten to question the accuracy and credibility of translation even in studies of Japanese literature.

Differences of view from some of my Western and Japanese colleagues arise partly from my background and from my academic approach. Let me refer, therefore, to my personal record. I entered the First Higher School in 1948. I was sixteen years old and spent a year in the dormitory of the élitist school known as *Dai ichi kōtō-gakkō*, before it was closed under the Occupation to become the nucleus of the Komaba Campus of Tokyo University a year later. Fuwa Tetsuzō, future Japan Communist Party Chairman, shared my dormitory. It was the time when, at squares around the Shibuya railway station, which was only twenty minutes away from the campus and one of the busiest quarters of the capital, many Japanese prostitutes openly embraced GIs. I pitied the impoverished women, but I could not accept the fact that some of the girls seemed to believe that they were more advanced than their conservative compatriots, because they had GI lovers.

Recently, however, a history book appeared in the United States which highly applauded the psychology of those who gladly embraced the defeat. It was true that there were intellectuals who welcomed the Allied forces as an army of liberation. It was the time when Marxist historians like E. H. Norman and his Japanese counterparts put themselves forward as scholarly champions. One of the late followers of Norman, John Dower, wrote *Embracing Defeat* in 1999.[1] The title, to be honest, reminds me of the shameless prostitutes and their ilk. Here again, the framework of the book was fixed before it was written. Dower skilfully wrote the book in order to prove his foregone conclusions. I am quite concerned that historical presentations of this kind, especially such as his and Bix's, may distort and confuse both scholarship and policy-making on Japan.

During the period of the American occupation, I was not anti-American, knowing that a Russian or Chinese occupation would have been harsher. Just think of the long years in the Siberian gulags where Japanese prisoners had to work and die. They were made prisoners of war after only a week of hostilities in Manchuria. Or think of the cruelties committed by the Chinese in Taiwan: in the first five hundred days of their occupation they killed a far greater number of Taiwanese than those killed during the fifty years of Japanese colonial rule. That sort of awareness was the decisive factor that made the Japanese accept the American occupation. It must have been the same with the West Germans, living under the Allied Occupation. In the Nō play '*Atsumori*', there is a saying: 'Put away from you a wicked friend; summon to your side a virtuous enemy.' After the defeat, the majority of the Japanese resumed the course of the Westernization movement that they had been following at the time of the Meiji Restoration. The Japanese of my generation once again recited the Charter Oath of 1868: 'Knowledge shall be sought throughout the world so as to strengthen the foundations of our country.'

There was also concurrently a vocal anti-Americanism. During the time of the Cold War, it was possible for Japanese intellectuals to criticize the United States openly, there was no risk to their life so long as they were accusing a country which guaranteed their freedom of speech, while it was not easy for them to criticize the other side, because there was a latent fear of physical liquidation if one day Communists should come to power. I did not feel in sym-

pathy with the Soviet Union not only because of the cruelties committed in Manchuria but especially for the lack of intellectual
freedom. Contrary to the majority of my room-mates in the dormitory, who later formed the core of the Communist Party's cell at
Tokyo University, I felt 'the scientific socialism' preached by Fuwa
and his comrades was a kind of new superstition. However, there
was already a curious alliance between Japanese leftists and some
North American leftists under the Occupation. I found it strange
that Japanese left-wing historians, especially those of the so-called
*kōza-ha* scholars, relied so blindly on the authority of the 1932
Comintern interpretation of Japanese history. Japan's so-called
Emperor-system was explained through analogies with the Russian
Czarism. As many of the Marxist historians had suffered during
World War II for their anti-militarist stand, it was natural that they
gained credit among Japanese intellectuals and students. They were
respected in the years following World War II. The problem is that,
from that time on, the Japanese academic world of historical science was politically dominated by left-wing scholars.

It would indeed be difficult for those who were not at the scene
to imagine the intellectual atmosphere of the late 1940s and early
1950s. At that time, I did not dare to apply for the History
Department: I did not like the possibility that I would be pressured
into writing theses, using the 'scientific' jargon of historical materialism. I was all the more relieved, when I found George Sansom's
*The Western World and Japan* in the newly-created library of
Comparative Literature and Culture Department of Tokyo
University. Sansom's approach to history was essentially humanistic.
Though not a university graduate, Sansom got a very good education at the Lycée Malesherbes in Caen. He was very familiar not
only with things Japanese but had a sympathetic understanding of
the Japanese mind. He would not allow himself to use existing
works in English and he went to Japanese sources. As for Sansom's
history books, I admired first of all his style. I, too, was educated
early by French professors and I am still a faithful practitioner of
*explication de texte*. First of all, I appreciate an approach which is
humanistic and linguistic in orientation, if we can understand by the
humanities the study of modern languages and literatures of both
hemispheres as well. I recognize the need for long-term, language-
based textual study, for understanding both past and present
cultures through the written word. I do not believe that any 'ism' or
any theory in historical or literary studies is of great value.

From 1945, it so happened that, quite coincidentally, the places where I pursued my studies were defeated countries. Leaving Japan in 1954, I spent six years of my early twenties in France, Germany and Italy, studying comparative literature, as at that time disciplines such as 'intercultural relations' had not yet gained academic citizenship in Japan or in any European university. Intercultural relations, however, became my life-long concern. When a French colleague of l'Université Paris VII, where I later taught, introduced me to the audience saying that my interest lay in *'entrecroisements de cultures'*, I nodded assent: That was and is my specialty.

By living and studying in the three defeated countries that formerly constituted the Axis Powers, I was made aware of many differences between the three 'rogue' nations of Germany, Italy and Japan. When I read Count Ciano's *Diario*, it was a revelation. The shrewd Italian Foreign Minister, hearing from the Japanese ambassador of Japan's decision to attack the USA, wrote in the entry of 3 December 1941 as follows: 'Cosa significa questo nuovo evento? Intanto che Roosevelt è riuscito nella manovra: non potendo entrare subito e direttamente nella Guerra, vi è entrato per una traversa, facendosi attaccare dal Giappone.' Ciano understood, four days before Pearl Harbor, Roosevelt's manoeuver. He wrote: 'What does this new turn of events mean? As it was not possible for the US to enter the War early and directly, Roosevelt has succeeded in entering it by a sideway, letting Japan attack the United States.' Some people may admire president Roosevelt for his superb political ability. It is understandable that the United States could not tolerate Japan's occupation of French Indochina. But I hope you will remember that Japan was pressured into attacking Pearl Harbor.

Although Japan was equated with Nazi Germany by the Allied nations during the war years and even later, I became gradually dissatisfied with the easy generalizations by which the history of modern Japan was explained. Having little knowledge of Japan, Westerners were obliged to understand 'fascist' Japan by analogies. However, superficial comparisons tend to spawn misleading ideas. Some scholars and journalists have tried to define Japan as the Fascist nation of the Far East. There are those who have gone so far as to compare Emperor Hirohito with Hitler. Such sorts of condemnation are too over-simplistic for a nation which surely had fascists of a kind but which had no leading political party comparable to Italy's *il Partito Fascista* or to China's *Guomindang*. Imperial

Japan committed atrocities, but it did not commit organized atrocities comparable to the Holocaust.

Schematic interpretations of history are often misleading. Those who had doubts about the laws of history expounded by 'scientific' historians were often criticized or even ridiculed in the late 1940s. During the decade following the defeat, the inevitability of a Bolshevik revolution in Japan was asserted vocally. Many of the so-called 'conscientious' left-wing intellectuals became fellow-travellers of the Communist Party. Though it makes no sense in hindsight, the possibility of a violent revolution was intimidating.

I respect *petits faits*, concrete details in history. Among Western Japan scholars I highly appreciate Sir George Sansom precisely for that. In the early 1960s, together with Kanai Madoka, I translated Sansom's *Western World and Japan*. Both Kanai and I were interested in intercultural relations, and that was also the beginning of my contact with American and British Japan scholars. Their friendship lies at the heart of the publication of the present volume: *Japan's Love-Hate Relationship with the West*.

Let me explain how the first contact took place. When I published my doctoral thesis *Wakon-yōsai no keifu* (Japanese spirit, Western learning, Tokyo: Kawade shobō, 1971), Marius B. Jansen of Princeton University wrote a review in the May 1972 issue of the monthly *Jiyū*, saying that 'this volume represents the results of five years' work and two decades of study. Its sub-title, *uchi to soto kara no Meiji Nihon* – Meiji Japan examined from within and from without – suggests the attempt: to study the pattern of impact and response to the West in modern Japan, against the background of an earlier pattern of *Wakon-kansai* (Japanese spirit, Chinese learning).'

In that book the leading subject of my study is Mori Ōgai (1862–1922), who begins as a young student in Germany and whose death concludes the volume. I made use of Ōgai's diary, notes, and especially lectures to consider his response to the intellectual challenges that faced him. The book uses the method of comparative literature to trace influences, but it also goes beyond this to present a personal reflection on the meaning of all this for modern Japanese history and world cultural history.

The central figure of my first book, Mori Ōgai, is the leading writer and the surgeon-general towards the final years of the Meiji period (1868–1912). Ōgai is a man 'with two legs',[2] soundly grounded in his own culture and neither slavishly enamoured of the

West nor anxious to reject its values and importance. Ōgai's pattern of response is woven into the development of Meiji concern about the racism of the 'yellow peril' argument, and it is one of dignity, independence, and consistency. It is also interwoven with an official career in which Ōgai was the associate of the bureaucratic greats of Meiji Japan. This makes Ōgai's student years very different from the experience of Natsume Sōseki, and it may be one reason why Ōgai has not been a congenial object of study for Western and particularly American students of modern Japan. Yet my studies are focused on the broader significance of Ōgai for modern Japanese intellectual life.

Ōgai's problem was one of transition from learning to construction, and from imitation to creation. It became important to him to learn that Europe itself had learned from the Arab tradition, that Northern Europe had gone to school to Renaissance Italy, and that Germany had gone to school to classical France. Under these conditions it became natural for Meiji Japan to go to school to Imperial Germany, just as it had for early Japan to go to school to Imperial China. The consequences of this could be optimism rather than discouragement, since the appropriation of the work of others could allow for speed and selection.

However, while this might suffice for utilization of technology, it would not allow for originality in going beyond example. It is this desire to innovate that distinguishes Ōgai, and that gives his exchanges with Dr Baelz, German medical professor employed by the Meiji Government, such interest. Ōgai placed much of his faith for this innovation in the Taishō generation. Our knowledge that much of this faith was misplaced leads us again to a reconsideration of the Meiji generation and its strengths and achievement. The world of the Taishō generation was never that stable.

In my postscript for *Wakon-yōsai no keifu*, I expressed the hope that the essays would be read by general as well as by specialist readers. This early hope of mine has been amply fulfilled, because the book has sold well in its Kawade paperback edition. I modestly expressed also the hope that they would be read with care by specialists in Japanese studies, for they illustrate the rewards of treating a particular case in a pattern of universal significance. My second hope has not been fulfilled outside Japan, as there has been very little reference to my *Wakon-yōsai no keifu* in the West, probably as it was written in Japanese, except a long article by Professor Jacqueline Pigeot (Paris, *la Critique*. February, 1974, pp. 172–188). That is also one reason why

I have come to think I should collect these papers of mine written in English and publish them in book form.

When I was young, a significant number of North American Japan scholars were missionaries and their children. One of the differences in my having studied in West European Catholic countries was that, for obvious reasons, I had not met any of these children of missionaries called 'miskids' with their peculiarly patronizing attitude towards Japan and the Japanese. I guess that is the one single factor that distinguishes Anglo-American Japanese studies from, say, French Japanese studies. Bernard Frank, late professeur au Collège de France, began his Japanese studies, by reading Lafcadio Hearn, whose Japanese studies were very different from those of missionary scholars. Though very much liked by the Japanese, Hearn has become an ignored figure, if not a figure of contempt, for most American Japan scholars. *Quel contraste!*

The dichotomies between 'Christian' and 'Pagan', 'Civilized' and 'Uncivilized', 'Modern' and 'Feudalistic', 'Guilt culture' and 'Shame culture' have often been used as convenient references in American approaches to the Other. They have provided ample justifications for those who wish to believe in the superiority of their own civilization. However, before passing self-complacent judgements in the names of religion, civilization, modernization or whatever, let us try to see Japan's love-hate relationship with the West from both sides. I am still of the opinion that it is important for Westerners to study not only the life and thought of the Orient but also to study those of the Occident from Oriental points of view. Needless to say it is the reverse that is still more important for us living and studying in Japan. One of the difficulties in overcoming the East-West divide lies in tasks of this kind.

Finally, at the end of this postscript and to conclude the introduction of my standpoint as a scholar and myself as a person, I would like to reproduce an article of mine from the *Yearbook of Comparative and General Literature*.[3] It was the comment I made at a symposium following a lecture by Edwin Reischauer during the Conference on Oriental-Western Literary and Cultural Relations at Indiana University in November, 1978. The comment was practically my debut into the American academic world, and it still explains my standpoint as a scholar. It was entitled 'Japanese Culture: Accommodation to Modern Times':

Today trade problems between Japan and the United States are very serious, because everything made in Japan is of such a good quality that Japanese products have flooded the American market. But yesterday evening while listening to Professor Reischauer's lecture on Japan, I found something of very bad quality but which is made in Japan. I refer to our linguistic ability in English made-in-Japan, and I am precisely a made-in-Japan professor and not an American-educated one. But as I am an admirer of American academic achievements in Japanese studies and Comparative Literature, I have come to this country and now am making my first extended stay. I very much admire the American academic system which is widely open to outsiders, so open that last weekend at the annual meeting of the Mid-Atlantic Region of Association for Asian Studies in Washington DC, I had as my discussant a young man who is working for the CIA. In the world of Japanese academics, especially that of Tokyo University to which I belong, there were said to be two lines with which professors should not associate themselves. One is the CIA connection, the other is, or was, the Reischauer line, *Raishawaa rosen*. But yesterday evening I was fortunately informed of the decline of radical students movements in Japan by Professor Reischauer himself. Still, in order to survive any eventual storms of criticisms against me, in order to avoid any mental or physical attacks from my students or from my left-wing colleagues, I think it expedient to take some precautions and level some very harsh criticisms against American scholarship, against American Japan experts and also against American-educated Japanese professors.

First let me tell you the impression I got from Professor Reischauer's lecture. The image he gives of Japan is too rosy, too bright. According to Reischauer Japan is the best modernizer of the non-Western world. But you should always be careful with the best and the brightest, especially when coming from the direction of Harvard, and I think it better to focus our attention to Japan's weak points, her vulnerability, and to think how we can accommodate ourselves to external and internal challenges of modern times.

As most of us here present are interested in comparative literature, comparative culture and intercultural relations, I would like to propose an enlargement of the concept of Comparative Literature as a means of academic accommodations to modern times. Let me explain this enlarged notion of Comparative Literature by telling you briefly about its development in my university. The creation in 1953 of the Department of Comparative Literature in the graduate school of Tokyo University was itself a new accommodation to modern times. Like so many European universities of the nineteenth century, many disciplines were divided by nationality. Until the end of World War II every department of history, such as Japanese history, Chinese history and German history, had its own autonomy. It was the same with Japanese literature, French literature or English literature. Every department had its own national sovereignty. After Japan's surrender, however, as a reaction against narrow nationalism, internationalism was in vogue, and new departments such as international relations, new programmes such as area studies were created especially at the Komaba campus of Tokyo University.

However, Japanese Comparative Literature scholars were also aware that Comparative Literature, as developed in Europe and America, was very much Western-oriented. It is true that great scholars such as Curtius, Auerbach and Wellek wrote their monumental scholarly works in order to overcome nationalism. But to outsiders like me, Western Comparative Literature scholarship seemed to be an expression of a new form of nationalism – Western nationalism, if I may use such an expression. It seemed to me an exclusive club of Europeans and Americans. It was a sort of Greater West European Co-prosperity Sphere. Japanese Comparative Literature scholars were obliged to be conscious that they belong to a civilization other than that of the West, and they cannot apply automatically the methods of Comparative Literature to Japan's case. That is the reason why our Graduate School Programme is called Comparative Literature and Comparative Culture (*hikaku-bungaku hikaku-bunka*). I am interested not only in Comparative Literature but also in intercultural relations and cross-cultural experiences. I will give an example to explain this point.

Thomas Rimer gave a brilliant talk about Shimazaki Tōson's experience in France. As an 'étranger' in a foreign country, Tōson rediscovered Japan. He read Kurimoto Joun's *Gyōsō-tsuiroku* in Paris. Kurimoto was a samurai sent to Paris by the shogunal government just before the Meiji Restoration of 1868, which is why his book was entitled *Gyōsō-tsuiroku* or *Records of Before Dawn*. Tōson himself began to reflect upon the meaning of Japan's modernization and later wrote his masterpiece *Yoakemae*[4] (Before the Dawn). Tōson much admired those Japanese who went abroad to seek knowledge in the 1860s and 70s. Japanese students of Comparative Literature are, of course, interested in literary figures such as Shimazaki Tōson and his experience abroad, but Japanese students are also very much interested in the cross-cultural experiences of Japanese in other professions. Kurimoto Joun was a samurai, but his records in France are also very revealing as a Japanese reaction to French civilization. As students of intercultural relations we have applied the methods of Comparative Literature not only to writers but to Japanese in various careers.

Fukuzawa Yukichi was not a literary artist, but we studied his experience abroad. Professor Reischauer talked about the new mode of using Western umbrellas after the Meiji Restoration. But some years before the opening of the country, according to the records left by Fukuzawa, it was impossible for him to go out with a Western umbrella. Fukuzawa was sure that he would be killed by some anti-foreign fanatics on his way from the port of Uraga to the castle of Edo if he dared to walk with a Western umbrella. It was no laughing matter, and small matters such as this could also be topics of our study. The Iwakura mission, which comprised the better half of the early Meiji government and which spent almost two years in the United States and Europe to study various aspects of Western civilization could also be a subject of our comparative culture study, although the mission did not comprise any professional writer of distinction. Not only men of letters but also the experience abroad of Japanese Navy officers could be subjects of our study. Akiyama Saneyuki, staff officer, was the brain of the Japanese Combined Fleets that defeated the Russian Baltic Fleet at the battle of Tsushima in 1905. Akiyama's American days, his experiences on board an American warship at the time of the Spanish War, his relations with Mahan, were studied with great skill by Shimada Kinji, the dean of Japanese comparatists. His book[5] *Akiyama Saneyuki's American Days* (in Japanese) is today widely read by Japanese businessmen, diplomats and press people residing in North America. Through their own experiences abroad, present-day Japanese can very well understand the state of mind and the activities of a Meiji naval officer.

This extension of the concept of Comparative Literature may seem to some to be a deviation. But I do not consider this application of our discipline to other new fields as improper: it corresponds to a need sensed by the Japanese. Somehow the Japanese must be more sensitive to international relations, must be more careful about intercultural relations, and must study and analyse with care their cross-cultural experiences. This is an aspect of our academic accommodation to modern times.

Let us consider the meaning of Comparative Literature in Japan from another perspective. Students of this discipline in various countries have tried to elucidate the problems of literary and intellectual influences. A country which has not been under the influence of other civilizations, other cultures and other literatures is, therefore, not a country fit for studies of Comparative Literature. As you know, the Japanese archipelago is situated on the periphery of the Asian mainland. Japan developed her culture and literature under the influence of Chinese civilization, and in modern times Japan has emerged as an industrial nation under the influence of the Western civilization. Still Japan has maintained her distinctive cultural identity. The Japanese think of themselves as an 'island people'. This expression indicates Japanese awareness that they have managed to preserve their own identity, but it also suggests the need to assert the Japanese identity in contradistinction to others. That is, the Japanese are conscious of their relation and their debts to other peoples and cultures. I am convinced that the popularity in Japan of Comparative Literature is based on this consciousness of her cultural and geographical position. The Japanese are, so to speak, historically destined to be interested in intercultural relations and the problem of self-identification.

Now, regretfully I feel I must make some harsh remarks on American Japan experts. First, I will try to explain the origin of anti-Americanism among American allies – and this has something to do, I believe, with the imbalance in cultural trade. Thirty-three years have passed since the defeat of Japan, and the importance of Japanese-American relations has increased immensely. The United States and Japan stand first and third in the world in economic production. Between the two countries there has developed the largest transregional trade that the world has ever known. But how about the problem of another form of trade, an interchange of literatures and cultures between the two nations? There is a sort of imbalance not only in commercial trade but also in cultural relations. The attention the Japanese give to what is going on in the United States is much greater than the attention Americans give to what is going on in Japan. The United States occupies the largest part of foreign news columns in Japanese newspapers, while Japan appears not so often in American newspapers. I imagine that for nearly three months Japan has not been mentioned in the *New York Times*.[6] I have the impression that, looking from the Japanese side of the Pacific, the United States looms large and near, as if the Japanese were looking at the United States through a telescope. But looking from the American side, Japan is small and far away, as if Americans were looking at Japan through the same telescope, but from the other end of it. This kind of imbalance in attention is to a certain degree inevitable. For many countries, European and Asian, the United States is the most important country. But the reverse is not always true. There are many important countries for the United States, but none of them is the most important. Neither a West-European country, nor a Latin American country, nor Japan can exclusively monopolize American attention. Such an imbalance in attention is, it seems to me, the principal cause of the present-day love-hate relationship between the United States and other countries around the world.

In Japanese-American relations, the problems of trades, both commercial and cultural, are serious. There is even an anti-Japanese feeling in some quarters of this country; and American Japan experts are very instrumental in promoting good or bad images of Japan. The United States today has many excellent Japan specialists. I greatly admire the spectacular development of Japanese studies in this country since World War II. This dynamic development is a good example of academic accommodation to modern times, and I enjoy the intellectual companionship of Japan specialists. I have great admiration for American Japanese studies, but I have some criticisms too. It surprises me that Japan experts, though very distinguished, have relatively little influence outside their academic circles. American japanologists very often stick together and read their papers among themselves. Their publications have a limited readership. Oftentimes their books sell more in Japanese translation than in their American original. Some people explain that American Japan experts stick together because they have been influenced by the Japanese groupishness: as Japanese tend to stick together, so American Japan scholars too stick together under the baleful Japanese influence. Even though there may be partial truth in the remark, I think there are other explanations. Whatever the reason, the influence of American japanolologists outside their academic circles seems to be very limited. The grossly distorted image of the Japanese created by a single best-seller *Shogun* by James Clavell (1975) is, to my great regret, far more influential and pervasive than many serious Japanese Studies volumes published by American university presses.

Of course there are exceptions: Reischauer's book *The Japanese* has been a best-seller. But there is still one thing which comes to the mind of every American every time our relations become tense and against which even the charismatic ambassador Reischauer's eloquence and books cannot compete. That is the popular image of the Japanese created by American propaganda immediately after Japan's attack on Pearl Harbor. It depends on your viewpoint. To some of you, the Japanese who attacked Pearl Habor are still sly, sneaky and treacherous. But there can be a different frame of reference, and everything depends so much on the measure of comparison, as we comparatists know well. To me all air-raids – against the United States or against Japan, against Dresden or against Hanoi – should be measured by the ratio of casualties suffered by civilians and casualties suffered by the military. If we apply this measure of comparison to the Japanese attack on Pearl Harbor, you will be surprised by the extremely low ratio. The Japanese Naval Air Force killed very few American civilians. The target was definitely military. If Americans could be reminded of this aspect of the attack, Pearl Harbor would be remembered in a different way. The problem of the image of a country or even that of a war is not alien to Comparative Literature. Arthur Waley, by writing *The Opium War Through Chinese Eyes*, opened a new historical perspective.

I would like to say some words on the method of literary comparison, which Professor Kinya Tsuruta so skilfully applied to the analysis of Kawabata and Hemingway. I have said that we comparatists of the both sides of the Pacific Ocean should enlarge fields of Comparative Literature, and we could indeed apply the method of literary comparison to non-literary texts. I would like to suggest that some of you may try to compare, for example, the message which President Roosevelt sent to the Congress, 8 December 1941, requesting the declaration of war against Japan, with the Imperial Rescript of the Termination of the War, read and broadcast by the Japanese Emperor, 15 August 1945. Which document was the more truthful? By making comparisons of this sort, we may perhaps be able to open some new perspectives to history.

*Notes*

[1] John Dower: *Embracing Defeat: Japan in the Wake of World War II* (New York: Norton & Company, 1999)
[2] Ōgai used 'nihon-ashi no gakusha' (a scholar with two legs) in his commemorative article on (Teiken) Taguchi Ukichi, 'Teiken sensei' (*Ōgai zenshū*, vol. 26, pp. 421–423). These terms suit Ōgai better than anyone else in the Meiji- Taishō period.
[3] *The Yearbook of Comparative and General Literature* (Chapel Hill, N.C.: University of North Carolina, 1979, No. 28, pp. 46–49).
[4] Shimazaki Tōson: *Before the Dawn,* tr. William Naff (Honolulu: University of Hawaii Press, 1987).
[5] Shimada Kinji: *Amerika niokeru Akiyama Saneyuki* (Tokyo: Asahi shinbun-sha, 1969).
[6] This was a joke. In the autumn of 1978, the *New York Times* was on strike for more than three months.

# INDEX